From Persepolis to the Punjab

Exploring ancient Iran,
Afghanistan and Pakistan

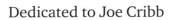

Dedicated to Joe Cribb

Elizabeth Errington and Vesta Sarkhosh Curtis

From Persepolis to the Punjab

Exploring ancient Iran,
Afghanistan and Pakistan

With contributions by
Joe Cribb
Jean-Marie Lafont
St John Simpson
Helen Wang

Edited by
Elizabeth Errington

THE BRITISH MUSEUM PRESS

© 2007 The Trustees of the British Museum

First published in 2007 by The British Museum Press
A division of The British Museum Company Ltd
38 Russell Square, London WC1B 3QQ

A catalogue record for this book is available from the British Library

ISBN-13: 978-0-7141-1165-0

Design by Esterson Associates
Typesetting and layout by Chris Hulin, Oxford Book Projects
Printed and bound in England by Cambridge University Press

Contents

List of tables

List of figures

Acknowledgements

Some readers in pessimistic mood may find it depressing that earlier explorers and scholars working in the field got so much wrong. Optimists will find it amazing – given the paucity of information then available – that they got so much right. We stand forever in their debt. More than a century and a half since men like Masson and Prinsep were making their ground-breaking discoveries, there is as yet some way to go before an agreed understanding is reached. Research on ancient Afghanistan and Pakistan in particular is still in a constant state of flux. Just in the last decade, several fundamental constructs have been demolished or at least redefined by new evidence. Most notable examples of this are the Rabatak inscription, the underpinning of year 1 of Kanishka to *c.* AD 127, the link between the Azes and Yona eras and, most recently, the realisation that the Bactrian era of *c.* AD 233 is actually a Sasanian era of *c.* AD 223/4. Keeping track of all these new developments requires a certain degree of mental agility and flexibility perhaps best summed up by the mantra 'what's a mind if you can't change it?'

This attempt to make sense of the jigsaw of conflicting ideas and information would not have come to fruition without the generous assistance of numerous friends, colleagues and scholars, many of whose contributions are evident throughout the book. First and foremost we owe an immense debt to Joe Cribb, both our mentor and our teacher, without whose support neither of us would have become aspiring numismatists, and whose own research (some of it as yet unpublished) underpins many of the arguments and ideas expressed here. We also would like to thank our other fellow contributors to the volume — Jean-Marie Lafont, St John Simpson and Helen Wang — not least for their forbearance that progress towards publication has been so slow. We hope it will prove worth the wait.

It will soon become apparent to readers of the sections relating to Afghanistan and Gandhara how dependent many of the arguments and conclusions are on research undertaken for the Masson Project. Indeed, the book would never have come into being without the generous funding by the Neil Kreitman Foundation for the Project over the last fifteen years and the continuous support of Gandharan studies in general by Neil Kreitman. We also thank the Townley Group of British Museum Friends for helping to fund the Project.

Several scholars have provided free access to their research prior to publication. As grateful recipients of this untoward generosity, without which this volume would be immeasurably poorer, we thank Gudrun Melzer, Harry Falk, Cristina Scherrer-Schaub, Nasim Khan and Shailendra Bhandare. We are also grateful to Nicholas Sims-Williams for reading the Bactrian coin legends; to Harry Falk and Michael Willis for help with Kharoshthi and Brahmi; to Helen Wang and Wang Tao for standardising the diverse Chinese transliteration systems into Pinyin; and to Paul Luft for his useful comments on nineteenth-century Persia. Their contributions helped to provide new insights that would not have been possible without their specialist knowledge.

We are indebted to David Bivar for undertaking the unenviable task of peer reviewing the volume and for the care he took in correcting any mistakes. Although we beg to differ on a number of points, his constructive criticism forced a re-evaluation and, hopefully, an improved assessment of the available evidence in a number of instances. We are also grateful to Parvis and Shahin Fozooni for their generosity and time.

We greatly appreciate the support we have received throughout the project from our friends and colleagues in the Department of Coins and Medals, in particular Janet Larkin, Kirstin Leighton-Boyce, Paramdip Khera and Elizabeth Pendleton, who have helped with such practical matters as coin selection, photography and scanning. We have to thank Stephen Dodd for photographing all the coins to such a high standard. Photographs of other objects in the British Museum have been kindly supplied by the Departments of Asia, the Middle East and Prints and Drawings. Additional photographs that enrich the diversity and quality of the illustrations have been kindly provided by Georgina Herrmann, Jean-Marie Lafont, Zémaryalaï Tarzi, Francine Tissot, Aman ur Rahman, Kurt Behrendt, John Curtis, David Jongward and Sharokh Razmjou. Photographs have also been supplied by a number of public institutions: the British Library Oriental and India Office Collections; American Institute of Indian Studies, Gurgaon; Bibliothèque Nationale, Cabinet des Médailles, Paris; National Museum of Iran, Tehran and Kyoto University, Japan (the last being provided courtesy of Shoshin Kuwayama). The watercolours and maps from Court's *Mémoires* (figures 127–34, 136) are reproduced courtesy of the Musée Guimet Paris; figures 62 and 193 are reproduced courtesy of Mathura Museum and The Illustrated London News respectively.

Last, but not least, we would like to thank Nina Shandloff and the team at British Museum Press, who have dealt with the practicalities of seeing the book to press: in particular, John Banks for copy-editing, John Hawkins for designing the cover and Chris Hulin for the typesetting and layout of the manuscript.

Preface

Persepolis to the Punjab refers to the vast Iranian empires of the Achaemenids (550–331 BC), the Parthians (238 BC– AD 224) and the Sasanians (AD 224–651), which extended from Mesopotamia and Iran eastwards through Afghanistan to the north-western borderlands of the Indian subcontinent (fig. 2). The history of these regions was unknown to the west and had been largely forgotten, or remembered only as legends by the indigenous peoples. Archaeological remains and artefacts of these dynasties, especially coins, however survived and provided the key to rediscovering their past. From the late eighteenth century onwards western colonial aspirations led to the increased presence of Europeans in these lands and encouraged individuals to embark on fact-finding trails. The period of colonial expansion coincided with the Age of Enlightenment, which 'was not an event, but a way of thinking, a desire to re-examine and question received ideas and values and explore new ideas and new ways' (Sloan 2003, p. 13). This way of thinking encouraged 'enlightened' Europeans to try to uncover the history of the tantalising, often magnificent, material remains of the ancient cultures they found.

Utilising the accounts of Classical authors and other sources, such as the Bible, great strides were made towards revealing the history of ancient Persia, Bactria and Gandhara (modern Iran, Afghanistan and the North-West Frontier region of Pakistan). In the case of Persia and Mesopotamia, inspiration and some knowledge came from earlier travellers, who had recorded the monuments and discussed the history, languages and biblical references. Often these explorers justified their involvement in the archaeology and antiquity of these places with the argument that the locals had no interest in their own heritage (Larsen 1994, p. xii), but in fact there is already evidence in the early nineteenth century that some Persians were equally curious about their history and archaeological sites.

Part 1 of this volume ('Awakening the past') results from an exhibition, *From Persepolis to the Punjab: Coins and the Exploration of the East*, curated by Elizabeth Errington and Vesta Sarkhosh Curtis in the British Museum 16 September – 6 December 1997. It concentrates on the pioneering discoveries of eight men, as primarily revealed by the collections in the Museum: Robert Ker Porter, Claudius James Rich, Henry Creswicke Rawlinson and William Kennett Loftus in Iran; Charles Masson in Afghanistan; Claude-Auguste Court and Alexander Cunningham in the North-West Frontier and Punjab; and James Prinsep at some distance away in Calcutta. Their fascination with the east helped to make the material culture of these regions better known to the west, while the coins, inscriptions and archaeological remains they discovered and studied provided the key to unlocking the ancient history of these lands.

Figure 1 'The plumb-pudding in danger – or – state epicures taking un petit souper' by James Gillray (1757–1815). Hand-coloured etching 26 February 1805, showing prime minister William Pitt and Napoleon carving up the pudding – i.e. the world – with Britain taking the seas and France the land.

In Part 2 ('Constructing the past'), their finds and collections – above all coins – are used as a starting point for a critical appraisal of current views and the sources now available for interpreting the history of these countries. There is a marked difference in the process of reconstructing the past of ancient Iran and the regions further east. The rise and fall of the great Persian empires of the Achaemenids, Parthians and Sasanians was closely linked to the history of Greece, Rome and Byzantium, with the result that historical events in ancient Iran are more fully recorded in classical and later Islamic sources. There is also a strong tradition of monumental art and royal inscriptions in the rock reliefs of the Achaemenid and later kings. In addition, the great Iranian epic *Shahnameh* or Book of Kings of the early eleventh century, which was based on an earlier source, systematically records the dynastic history of the Sasanians and provides important information about Iranian culture and religion. In contrast surviving written records further east in Afghanistan and north-west Pakistan are more fragmented, confused and unreliable. There are fewer inscriptions and coins become the primary, sometimes the only, source of information for reconstructing the past.

Part 3 ('Encountering the past') comprises a collection of papers by Jean-Marie Lafont, St John Simpson, Vesta Sarkhosh Curtis, Joe Cribb, Elizabeth Errington and Helen Wang. These cover specific aspects of the discoveries made by some of the early pioneers and result from a seminar on the subject held in the British Museum on 1 November 1997.

The archaeological discoveries throughout the nineteenth century coincided with a period of intense colonial expansion. From time to time the independent regions from Iran to the Punjab increasingly became the focus of European

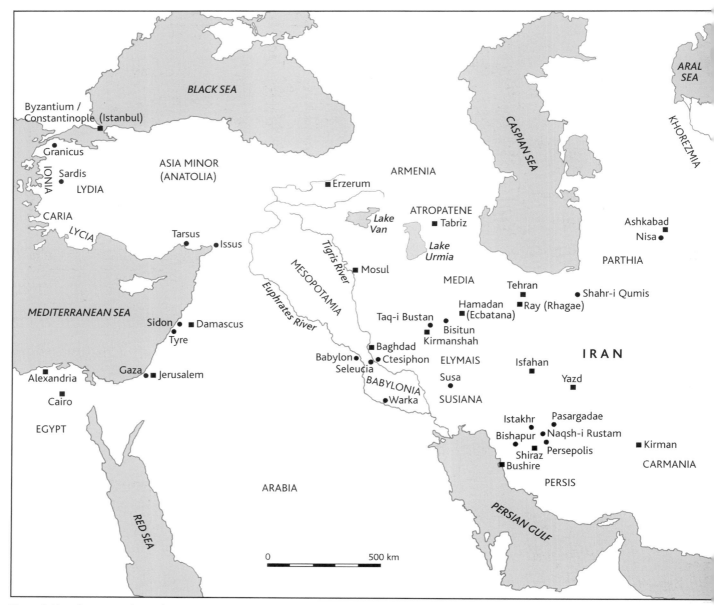

Figure 2 Map of western and central Asia, past and present. Inset map of modern states: **1** Georgia; **2** Armenia; **3** Azerbaijan.

political interest, now encapsulated in the term 'Great Game'. But this 'rivalry did not exist to the extent which has been suggested and which use of the term has fostered, and the consequence of presenting a picture of continuous Anglo-Russian [and earlier French] rivalry in Central Asia from the early nineteenth century has been to distort our understanding . . . of the relation between British and British Indian foreign and defence policy' (Yapp 2001, pp. 186–7). In reality, the problem was not one of Anglo-French, or later Anglo-Russian rivalry in Central Asia, but of rivalry between these powers in Europe (fig. 1; Yapp 2001, pp. 189–90). A more accurate phrase – coined by the Russian foreign minister, Count Nesselrode (1780–1861) – is perhaps 'tournament of shadows' (cf. Meyer and Brysac 2001, p. xviii), which conjures up the ambience of perceived and imagined threats, of bluff and counter-bluff, often fuelled by the personal and political ambitions of men ostensibly on the same side, who time and again attempted to influence policy decisions. In its present sense, moreover, the capitalised phrase 'Great Game' appears to be a later distortion of its original altruistic, humanitarian meaning, used in July 1840

by Arthur Conolly in a letter to Henry Rawlinson, the newly appointed Political Agent at Qandahar and one of the protagonists of this volume (Yapp 2001, p. 181):

> You've a great game, a noble game before you . . . if the British Government would only play the grand game, help Russia cordially to all that she has a right to expect – shake hands with Persia, etc., – we shall play a noble part that the first Christian nations of the world ought to fill.

Certain early European explorers and 'players' – most notably Robert Ker Porter, Claude-Auguste Court and Charles Masson (all of whose discoveries are charted here) – embodied the open-minded spirit advocated by Conolly; but others, including Rawlinson, did not.

The origin of the expression 'Great Game' can be traced back at least to the sixteenth century, when it was used in gaming with either cards or dice (Yapp 2001, pp. 183–4). It developed early connotations of risk taking, although changing associations of the phrase also altered its meaning: cricket, for example, evokes the image of 'a chivalrous, rule bound game', while chess suggests 'a ruthless, impersonal, cerebral contest'. The term, however, has proved so flexible

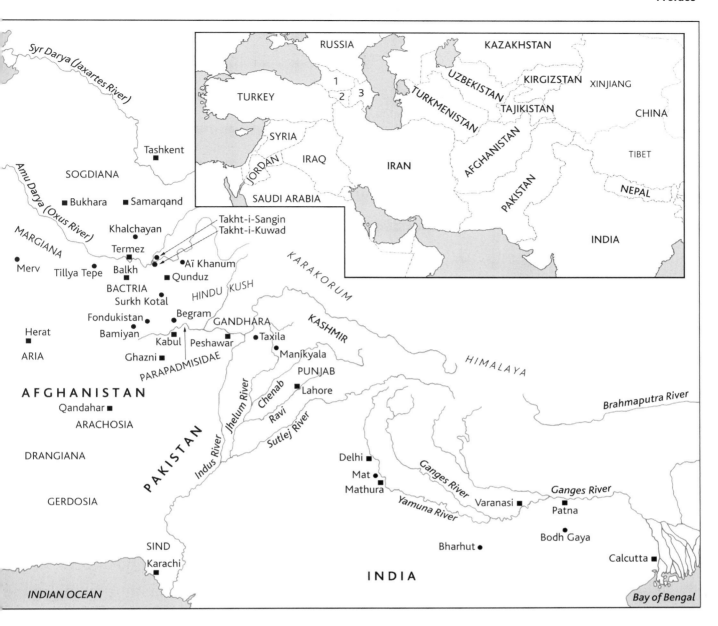

as to be applied, *inter alia*, to such diverse subjects as war, politics, diplomacy, high finance, football, poaching and large quadrupeds (Yapp 2001, p. 186). In its broadest sense it also aptly refers to the process undertaken here, i.e. the great game of trying to piece together the few surviving references of written sources with often conflicting material and inscriptional evidence, in an attempt to create a coherent history of the lands between Persepolis and the Punjab.

What is now familiarly known as the Great Game began with Napoleon Bonaparte (1804–14; 1815), who, at the height of his powers, dreamed of emulating Alexander the Great (336–323 BC) and marching fifty thousand French troops across Iran and Afghanistan to invade India. He proposed to Tsar Alexander I (1801–25), when they met at Tilsit on 25 June 1807, that a Russian force of similar size should join the French in an attempt to wrest India from the British. That Napoleon should even contemplate such an expedition, let alone expect a successful conclusion, is indicative of the lack of European knowledge about these lands at the beginning of the nineteenth century.

Napoleon's interest in Iran seems to have been primarily 'tactical and transitory' in his struggles against the Russians

and the British (Amini 1999, p. 94), although trade and commercial connections also played a role. The Persians, on the other hand, were humiliated by Russia's annexation of Georgia and worried about the threat to other provinces. It was the fear of the Russian advance and disappointment with British indifference that drove them towards Napoleon. In Article 4 of the Treaty of Finkenstein, dated 4 May 1807, Napoleon promised 'to make every effort to force Russia to evacuate Georgia and Persian territory. . . . This evacuation shall constantly be the object of his policy' (Amini 1999, p. 206). Article 8 mentions how, in return for French artillery, engineering and the sending of infantry officers to the Qajar court, 'the Emperor of Persia promises to stop all political and commercial communications with England, immediately to declare war on that country, and to start hostilities without delay . . . the Emperor of Persia will have all English merchandise seized and will forbid England any communications in his States, whether by land or by sea' (Amini 1999, p. 207). The possibility of a French campaign against British India and Iran's role in it is clearly stated in Article 12 (Amini 1999, p. 208):

Should it be the intention of H.M. the Emperor of the French to send an army by land to attack the English possessions in India, H.M. the emperor of Persia, as his good and faithful ally, will grant him passage through his territory. If such be the case, a special agreement will be made in advance between the two governments, stipulating the route to be taken by the troops.

The British government suddenly became alarmed by this potentially proactive Franco-Persian relationship and soon embarked on a series of negotiations with the Qajar court. Meanwhile Franco-Russian relations had also improved, with France turning a blind eye to Russian expansion in the north-west and the siege of Yerivan and Nakhjevan. Although Tsar Alexander could not understand France's interest in Iran, which was 'too far away', he had, at the same time, no intention of relinquishing his own newly acquired territories (Amini 1999, pp. 168, 148):

They threaten me with you, telling me that the Emperor Napoleon has guaranteed the integrity of their territory. It is today as it was when they negotiated with you. Soon they will claim what belonged to the ancient Medes and Persians. . . . The affairs of that country do not concern me, and those that I have with Persia are of no interest to the Emperor.

The Qajar court, realising that they could not rely on France in their struggle against Russia, welcomed the growing British interest in Iran and finally agreed to the alliance proposed by Sir Harford Jones in 1809 (Amini 1999, pp. 170–90).

There is no evidence, particularly after 1815, that the French had any serious designs on reclaiming the Indian territories they had lost to the British in 1763 (Yapp 1980, pp. 13–14). But in India the French (and later Russian) threat was perceived differently. The British East India Company was constrained by Act of Parliament from going to war, unless attacked or under threat. The alleged danger presented by these external enemies (whether believed or not) was a convenient reason for advocating a more active forward policy in British India (Yapp 1980, pp. 158–9). This largely took the form of trying to create a buffer zone along the north-west borders through a series of alliances, primarily with Iran and Afghanistan, but on a few occasions it resulted in direct conflict, as in the Anglo-Afghan wars of 1838–42 and 1878–9.

It is within this political context that the archaeological 'Great Game' took place. The 'enlightened' view gave way to colonial ambitions and archaeology was inevitably affected by politics. In writing this book, we too are playing a 'game':

La vérité historique est souvent une fable convenue.
L'histoire est un mensonge que personne ne conteste.
(attr. Napoleon I Bonaparte)

Courteous historians will generally concede that since no one can describe events with perfect accuracy written history is a branch of fiction. (Golding 1991, p. vii)

Part 1

Awakening the past

1 The explorers and collectors

Sir Robert Ker Porter (1777–1842)

> Indeed I conjure you, in the name of the Holy Antiquity, to mark down nothing but what you actually see; nothing suppose; nothing repair. I only beg you to represent the original ancient remains. (Ker Porter 1821, p. v)

These were the instructions which Robert Ker Porter received in 1817 from A. Olinen, the President of the Russian Academy of Fine Arts, when he was commissioned to record the monuments of Persia, for Olinen was anxious he should not repeat the apparent inconsistencies and inaccuracies made by earlier travellers in recording the same sites.

Ker Porter (fig. 3) was born in Durham in 1777 and trained as an artist in London before being appointed as a 'historical painter' to the court of the Russian Tsar. He quit Russia temporarily during the Napoleonic Wars, but then returned to St Petersburg where he married a Russian princess. On accepting the Russian Academy's commission, he travelled via the Caucasus, reaching Tabriz in north-western Iran in November 1817 (fig. 2). Here he met Abbas Mirza, the heir apparent to the Qajar throne, who invited him to the court of the Qajar ruler, Fath 'Ali Shah (Ker Porter 1821, pp. 220, 249).

On 13 May 1818 he left Tehran, heading southwards for Isfahan. He arrived in the city on 25 May and prepared a comprehensive description of its monuments. By 13 June he had reached the Dasht-i Murghaub, where he identified 'the ruins scattered over the vale of Mourg-aub' correctly as 'those of Pasargadae' (1821, p. 501). He made detailed sketches of the monuments and quoted extensively from such classical sources as Strabo, Arrian and Plutarch, as well as earlier travellers and scholars. He sketched and painted in watercolour the famous winged genie on the stone relief guarding Gate R with the – now lost – trilingual inscription in Old Persian, Elamite and Babylonian (1821, pp. 493, 505, pl. 13; p. 19, fig. 162 below). At Naqsh-i Rustam he recorded the Achaemenid tombs, the Sasanian rock reliefs, the Greek, Parthian and Pahlavi (Middle Persian) inscriptions on the Kaba-i Zardusht, as well as the two so-called fire altars – the *astodans* – on top of the mound (1821, pl. 26). When he saw one of the locals 'scramble up the perpendicular cliff, like a rat hanging by a wall', he followed their example (Ker Porter 1821, p. 521),

> by fastening the rope round my waist, and by their united exertions I was speedily drawn up to the place of rendezvous. The distance was sufficiently high from the ground to give me time for thought; and during my ascent, in a manner so totally dependent on the dexterity of others, I could not but recollect the fate of half-a-dozen kinsmen of Darius Hystaspes, who had all perished at once in the very same expedition.

Ker Porter has been rightly considered phenomenal among British travellers (Wright 1977, p. 152). His drawings are accurate and full of life, leaving those who have seen the original monuments awe-inspired by his artistic talent and eye

Figure 3 Sir Robert Ker Porter. Engraving by W.O. Burgess (1843) from painting by G. Harlowe (1808).

for detail (figs 4–5). His historical interpretations of the rock reliefs are spirited and usually – but not always – correct. His knowledge of Classical history and the religion of ancient Persia was immense. He was a keen collector of coins, proudly describing his collection as 'numerous, though rare' (1821, p. x). He often compared the figures on the Sasanian reliefs with the portraits of the same kings on coins, but sometimes came to the wrong conclusion. He was fascinated with Persian mythology and such legendary kings as Jamshid, 'from whom . . . Cyrus was descended' (1821, p. 527). He also believed in the accuracy of the modern Persian name for Persepolis, Takht-i Jamshid (the Throne of Jamshid), as he associated the site with Jamshid of the Pishdadian dynasty in Iranian mythology (1821, p. 527).

Ker Porter arrived on 21 June 1818 at Persepolis, where he carefully recorded the architecture, reliefs and inscriptions:

> To attempt any guess of the period when the city of Persepolis first rose to from the plain, would be as useless and bewildering as to analyse its various names. . . . The most conspicuous

Figure 4 Ker Porter's drawing of the relief of Shapur I at Naqsh-i Rustam.

Figure 5 Naqsh-i Rustam rock relief of Shapur I's victory over the Roman emperor Valerian (AD 253–60) and Philip the Arab (AD 244–9).

remains in Persepolis, or, as the natives call it Takht-i Jamsheed, . . . are Chehelminar, or the Forty Columns. The immediate impression that struck me in my first walk amidst them, was, that en masse, and in detail, they bore a strong resemblance to the architectural taste of Egypt.

Ker Porter left Shiraz on 30 July 1818, having spent a month and a half recording the ancient Achaemenid and Sasanian sites of the province of Fars (ancient Persis). He made numerous sketches of the reliefs, plans of the monuments and copies of ancient inscriptions, to which watercolours of the monuments and sculptures were added later. He returned to Isfahan and from there continued his journey to Hamadan and Kirmanshah, where he visited and described the ruins of Kangavar (1822, pp. 140–5). On 21 September he sketched the rock sculpture of Darius at Bisitun, which he considered 'of a date far anterior to the Sasanian monarch', comparing it with the sculpture from Persepolis, and correctly regarding it as contemporary 'with the first establishment of the Persian empire' (1822, pp. 150, 159, pl. 60).

After almost three years Ker Porter returned to St Petersburg via Constantinople and Belgrade on 14 March 1820. He was awarded the Order of the Lion and the Sun by Fath 'Ali Shah for recording of the monuments of Persia

In 1824 he diverted his attention to South America, where he embarked on a political career as consul to Venezuela. Together with Simón de Bolívar he played an active role in the formation of Bolivia (Barnett 1972, p. 24). In 1832 he became Knight Commander in the Order of Hanover. He retired to St Petersburg, where he died in 1842. He left behind a vast collection of drawings and watercolours which were acquired by the Department of Oriental Manuscripts of the British Museum (now part of the British Library) and the State Hermitage Museum in St Petersburg.

Claudius James Rich (1786–1821)

Claudius James Rich – the illegitimate son of a Scottish colonel – was born in Dijon in France and grew up with an aunt in Bristol (fig. 6). He became interested in oriental languages in his early childhood and, because of his outstanding linguistic skills, he was encouraged by his teachers to study the subject. Rich joined the British East India Company in 1803 as a cadet officer, but Sir Charles Wilkins, an oriental scholar and librarian of the Company, was so impressed by his knowledge of languages that he persuaded the Directors to transfer the young man to the Company's diplomatic sector (Alexander 1928, pp. 8–9).

In 1804 Rich was sent to Constantinople, where he stayed for only a few weeks. He spent six months in Smyrna (Izmir) improving his linguistic skills and then travelled extensively in Anatolia and northern Syria, where he made himself familiar with the customs and traditions of local people and learnt to speak Turkish fluently. His Arabic was brushed up during a stay in Cairo. He visited Palestine and Damascus and from here even joined a group of Muslim pilgrims to the holy city of Mecca, without being detected as an infidel (Alexander 1928, p. 18). Travelling via Aleppo, Mosul, Baghdad, Basra and the Persian Gulf, Rich arrived in Bombay in September 1807 to accept a new East India Company appointment. It was also here that he met Mary Mackintosh. The young couple – he was twenty-two and she eighteen – married after a brief courtship and in February 1808 set off on their six-week journey via Muscat, Bushire and Basra to Baghdad where Rich took up his new post as Resident at the court of the Pasha (Alexander 1928, pp. 19–25). His appointment was as a replacement to Mr Manesty who, together with his Armenian mistress, was much disliked by Claudius and Mary Rich (Alexander 1928, pp.18, 26–7).

Figure 6 Claudius James Rich by Thomas Philips R.A., donated to the British Museum by his widow Mary in 1825.

Rich stayed in Baghdad until 1820, apart from taking a long break at the end of 1813 to travel to Europe with his wife for health reasons. Although officially he had only three months' leave, the journey to Vienna, Paris, Venice and other Italian cities lasted much longer and he did not return to Baghdad until 1816. His residency was not without political problems, particularly during the first two years, when he and the Pasha often clashed. At one point Rich was refused permission to re-enter Baghdad after having camped outside the city during the hot period (Alexander 1928, p. 57).

During his residency Rich entertained and looked after many European travellers, including Sir Robert Ker Porter (1822, p. 245):

> On arriving at the gate of the British resident's mansion, I was saluted by a Sepoy guard, and then ushered into a spacious saloon overlooking the Tigris. It would be vain to attempt entering into details of my reception. Personally I was a stranger to Mr Rich; yet the most eloquent language cannot describe the friendly warmth with which both himself and his accomplished wife bade me welcome; nor can I express, in any words, my sense of their subsequent kindness.

In October 1818 Ker Porter also met 'Mr Bellino, a German gentlemen, who was Mr Rich's Oriental Secretary', and 'Mr Hyne, the medical professor to the mission' (1822, p. 246). Rich was clearly interested in Ker Porter's drawings of ancient ruins in Persia and shared a common passion for cuneiform scripts (Alexander 1928, p. 258).

Rich travelled extensively in Mesopotamia and, while visiting Kurdistan in 1820, he crossed the mountains to Sanandaj in Iran. In his last letter to Ker Porter that year Rich complained again of ill health, which had improved while travelling to Kurdistan (Ker Porter 1822, p. 810):

> Suppose, then, that my health not being in a remarkably good condition, was finally overturned by the extraordinary hot summer of 1820: from the August of which year I began to decline most alarmingly, both in body and spirits, so much so that I soon became incapable either of sitting on my horse, or attending to the slightest business; my life really was a burden to me. . . . I gradually extended my circles up to Courdistan, where I had resolved to pass this summer, as the only chance of restoring the health both of Mrs. Rich and myself; for Mrs. Rich was nearly as ill as I was. The travelling, change of scene and of air, were quite successful.

But his principal journey to Iran ended in tragedy. In 1821 he left Baghdad to take up an important and highly paid East India Company post as Member of the Council in the Bombay government. While his wife Mary decided to sail to Bombay, Rich and two companions left Bushire on 24 July, riding by night on mules, and arrived in Shiraz on 3 August (Alexander 1928, pp. 303–4). From here he visited Pasargadae, Persepolis and Naqsh-i Rustam, Naqsh-i Rajab and Istakhr.

Back in Shiraz he spent hours at the tomb of Hafiz, enjoying the poetry of this fourteenth-century Persian poet, and also visited the tomb of the thirteenth-century poet Saadi. However, he had no understanding or sympathy for the Persian way of thinking. While taking part in a wedding ceremony in Shiraz he wrote disdainfully (Alexander 1928, p. 317):

> The Persian Paradise is wine, running water and tobacco. To get drunk beside a stream is a delight. They are an unthinking, unreflective people. I have never met a nation so destitute of every kind of feeling, sentiment, or sympathy.

While he was in Shiraz a cholera epidemic broke out, causing more than five thousand deaths. At the beginning of October Rich fell ill, showing symptoms of the infection, and died on 5 October 1821 aged only 35. He was buried at the Armenian Cathedral in Shiraz, but his remains were later exhumed and reburied in the New Julfa cemetery in Isfahan on 17 July 1826 (Alexander 1928, pp. 321–2; Wright 1998, p. 166).

Rich collected much valuable information on the ancient and modern history and geography of Mesopotamia in particular, and produced detailed maps of the areas he visited. He visited and mapped the Assyrian site of Nineveh in northern Mesopotamia, and also discovered other Assyrian sites, including Nimrud near Mosul. He was a keen collector of antiquities, manuscripts, seals and coins, including Sasanian coins. He was also interested in cuneiform scripts and had an excellent library in Baghdad (Alexander 1928, p. 249). Like probably the majority of nineteenth-century travellers, he was passionately concerned about the future of manuscripts in particular and felt that it 'was almost the duty of a traveller to rescue as many as he can from destruction'. Many of his oriental manuscripts, coins and Assyrian sculptures – including his fine collection of Characene coins, mentioned by Loftus (1857, p. 281) in the mid nineteenth century – were purchased by the British Museum for £7000. The manuscripts are now in the British Library, but his finds remain in the Museum. Most of his written work was published after his death.

Henry Creswicke Rawlinson (1810–95)

> Six feet tall, with broad shoulders, strong limbs and excellent muscles and sinews. (Larsen 1994, p. 79)

This is how Rawlinson (figs 7–8) was described by his brother. He was born in Chadlington Park, Oxfordshire, and went to school in Ealing, where he studied Greek and Latin. He joined the British East India Company at the age of 16. Arriving in India in 1827, he studied Arabic, Persian and Urdu, and became interpreter and paymaster to the First Bombay Grenadiers (Budge 1925, p. 31). In 1833 he was recruited by the Intelligence Department and sent to Tabriz in north-western Iran to reorganise the Shah's army. He arrived at Bushire in 1834, marched past the ruins of Persepolis and finally arrived at Kirmanshah almost a year later.

At nearby Bisitun, he saw, for the first time, the monumental and impressive rock relief and trilingual cuneiform inscriptions of Darius I, carved in 519 BC and overlooking the main Baghdad to Kirmanshah highway (figs 22–3). While stationed at Kirmanshah in 1835–7 he took every opportunity to visit the site and study the inscriptions. He also saw the two trilingual inscriptions of Darius and Xerxes at Ganj Nameh (i.e. Mount Alvand) near Hamadan for the first time in 1835 (p. 19 below).

In 1838 he returned to Baghdad but, following the outbreak of the First Anglo-Afghan War later that year and the British occupation of Qandahar in April 1839, he was appointed Political Agent there from 1840 until British withdrawal from the city in May 1842 (Budge 1925, p. 33). In 1843 he succeeded Colonel Taylor as Political Agent in Turkish Arabia, and was based again in Baghdad. In the summer of 1844, with Mr Hester and Captain Felix Jones, he was able to return to Bisitun, where he copied the Elamite inscription and completed his copy of the Old Persian text (Budge 1925, pp. 33–5). In 1846/7 he published the Old

Figure 7 Sir Henry Creswicke Rawlinson. Engraving by S. Cousins.

Figure 8 Royal group at Hatfield House 1888: the Prince of Wales (later Edward VII 1901–10) and Princess Alexandria with Nasir al-Din, the Shah of Persia (1848–96). Rawlinson stands on the far right of the second row.

Persian version of the Bisitun inscription. He visited the site again in 1847 to copy the Babylonian inscription, which he published in 1851 (Wiesehöfer 2001, p. 240). He also produced copies of the two trilingual inscriptions of Darius and Xerxes at Ganj Nameh.

Rawlinson was the first to identify correctly the Bisitun rock relief with Darius the Great (1846/7, pp. xxvii–xxxix):

> the rock of Behistun doubtless preserved its holy character in the age of Darius, and it was on this account chosen by the monarch as a fit spot for the commemoration of his warlike achievements. The name itself is Bhagistan, signifies 'the place of the god'. . . . I certainly do not consider it a great feat in climbing to ascend to the spot where the inscriptions occur. When I was living at Kermanshah fifteen years ago, and was somewhat more active than I am at present, I used frequently to scale the rock three or four times a day without the aid of a proper ladder: without any assistance, in fact, whatever. During my late visits I have found it more convenient to ascend and descend by the help of ropes. . . . The Babylonian transcript at Behistun is still more difficult to reach.

Although desperate to obtain a facsimile of the Babylonian inscription, he felt unable to climb to the spot, but found a Kurdish boy, who volunteered to make the paper squeeze for him (1852, pp. 75–6; see also p. 173 below):

> The boy's first move was to squeeze himself up a cleft. . . . When he had ascended some distance above it, he drove a wooden peg firmly into the cleft, fastened a rope to this, and then endeavored to swing himself across to another cleft at some distance on the other side; but in this he failed, owing to the projection of the rock. It then only remained for him to cross over to the cleft by hanging on with his toes and fingers to the slight inequalities of the bare face of the precipice, and in this he succeeded, passing over a distance of twenty feet of almost smooth perpendicular rock in a manner which to a looker-on appeared quite miraculous. When he reached the second cleft the real difficulties were over. He had brought a rope with him attached to the first

> peg, and now driving in a second, he was enabled to swing himself right over the projecting mass of rock. Here with a short ladder he formed a swinging seat, like a painter's cradle, and, fixed upon this seat, he took under my direction the paper cast of the Babylonian translation of the records of Darius . . . which is almost of equal value for the interpretation of the Assyrian inscriptions as was the Greek translation of the Rosetta Stone for the intelligence of the hieroglyphic texts of Egypt.

Rawlinson also seems to have had a good command of Persian and, when writing 'on the Persian cuneiform alphabet' (1846, pp. 53–186), he tried to give the modern Persian equivalents of Old Persian words. His role in the history of decipherment of Old Persian cuneiform, however, is controversial: some scholars suggest that he was probably aware of the earlier achievements in the field by the German scholar, Georg Friedrich Grotefend, although he claimed not to be (see p. 19). Nevertheless, he was the first to make squeezes of the monumental inscriptions, which no one else had dared to do. He also, with other scholars of the mid nineteenth century, contributed to the successful decipherment of Babylonian cuneiform. Already in 1835, while stationed at Kirmanshah, Rawlinson wrote unequivocally to his sister (Larsen 1994, p. 303):

> I aspire to do for the cuneiform alphabet what Champollion has done for the hieroglyphics . . . my character is one of restless, insatiable ambition – in whatever sphere I am thrown my whole spirit is absorbed in an eager struggle for the first place.

Rawlinson had a valuable collection of antiquities and coins, which he offered to the British Museum in return of a grant to fund excavations in Mesopotamia. During his time in Baghdad 1846–55 he met the young Austen Henry Layard, the excavator of Nimrud and Nineveh, whom he greatly admired. When Layard gave up his archaeological career in 1851, Rawlinson, now a Trustee of the British Museum, ordered William Kennet Loftus to abandon his excavations at Susa in 1852 and follow in the footsteps of Layard at Warka. He himself was appointed by the Trustees to direct Christian Rassam and the excavations at Nimrud and Nineveh (Budge 1925, p. 79).

Rawlinson was appointed Director of the East India Company in 1856 and returned one more time to Persia as minister plenipotentiary for 1859–60. In 1875, when the Qajar ruler Nasir al-Din Shah came to England, Rawlinson took an active part in the royal visit (fig. 8; Budge 1925, p. 32). He was member of the Council of India in 1858–9, rejoined in 1868, and remained on the Council until his death from influenza in London in 1895.

William Kennet Loftus (1820–58)

Loftus's introduction to the Middle East came when he was appointed as a geologist by the Commission set up to draw the border between Persia and the Ottoman Empire (fig. 9). Encouraged by the head of the Commission, Lieutenant-Colonel W. F. Williams, Loftus was able to pursue his archaeological interests, first at Warka in southern Mesopotamia where he excavated for a brief period, and then at Susa in southern Iran (J. Curtis 1993, p. 1).

His archaeological activities at Susa began in May 1850. Here he worked for a month, despite a series of initial problems such as local hostility and the heavy spring rains. During the summer Loftus and other members of the team travelled north to escape the intense heat and it was at this time that they visited Persepolis and Bisitun. During a visit to Taq-i Bustan near Kirmanshah, Loftus carved his name on the seventh-century rock relief of the Sasanian king Khusrau II. Back in Susa in January 1851 permission was finally obtained from the Qajar ruler of Persia, Nasir al-Din Shah (1848–96), to excavate. During this season some column bases were found of the Apadana palace built by the Achaemenid king Darius (522–486 BC) and completed by Artaxerxes II (404–359 BC). The column bases and capitals, as well as other objects found at Susa (figs 33; 167), were carefully drawn by expedition's artist, Henry Churchill (fig. 166). With a grant of £500 from the Treasury secured with the help of Rawlinson, Loftus continued his excavations in 1852, employing up to 350 local workmen at a cost of ½ qaran (about 2 pence) per day (J. Curtis 1993, p. 6).

Rawlinson hoped that Loftus would lay 'the great mound at Susa completely bare' (J. Curtis 1993, p. 6). But despite the discovery of a fair number of objects, coins and architectural remains, some bearing cuneiform inscriptions, the Trustees of the British Museum, particularly Rawlinson, were not satisfied with the results. Rawlinson wrote to Henry Layard, the excavator of the Assyrian sites of Nimrud and Nineveh in Mesopotamia, that Loftus had 'turned the mound of Susa topsy-turvy without finding much' (J. Curtis 1993, p. 15). This was highly exaggerated, as Loftus had achieved a substantial amount under difficult conditions and in hostile surroundings, where work was often interrupted by bad weather, or because the British mission was under attack from the local Luri tribesmen (J. Curtis 1993, pp. 4, 6).

Undoubtedly Layard's successful excavations in northern Mesopotamia were unfairly compared with Loftus's relatively meagre achievements at Susa, which failed to yield the same spectacular results. Nevertheless, Loftus proved that Susa was indeed the biblical Shushan mentioned in the Books of Daniel and Esther. He also reconstructed the plan of the Apadana; found Achaemenid glazed bricks with archers, lions and bulls from this palace, which he claimed were shipped to the British Museum (J. Curtis 1993, pp. 7–10, fig. 2); copied the Old Persian and trilingual cuneiform

Figure 9 William Kennet Loftus.

inscriptions from the time of Artaxerxes II (404–359 BC) on the column bases; and discovered many terracotta figurines – including nude 'goddesses' – of the Middle Elamite period (mid second millennium BC) at the 'Ville Royale' or Great Platform (J. Curtis 1993, p. 12, pls 13–15).

The true splendour and importance of the ancient site of Susa was only revealed once the Délégation scientifique française en Perse began excavating in Iran under Jacques de Morgan in 1897 (fig. 10). Two years earlier the French archaeological mission had bought the monopoly of Susa and all other archaeological sites in Persia for the sum of FF 50,000 and the treaty was renewed in 1900 (Chevalier 1997, pp. 10–15).

Figure 10 Early twentieth-century aerial photograph of Susa with the Acropolis, the Apadana, Ville Royale and the Donjon. The Shaur river is visible on the left.

Figure 11 General Claude-Auguste Court by August Schoefft (1809–88). Detail from *Maharaja Sheer Singh returning from the hunt*, c.1850–5, after drawings made in Lahore, 1841.

General Claude-Auguste Court (1793–1880)

> While climbing up the mountain, we were absolutely unprepared for the rich plain of Pichavor and the Yousufzais which lay before our eyes. So we were struck by the magnificence of the countryside which extended as far as the eye could reach till the Indus. . . . While in contemplation, having no fortune but hopes, I wondered how the necessity to make a livelihood had given me, a mere French officer, the possibility to go so far away and behold the most beautiful scene of Alexander [the Great]'s exploits. (Lafont 1983, p. 86)

This was Claude-Auguste Court's first impression of the region east of Peshawar in early 1827 (fig. 11). It was almost nine years since he had begun his travels eastwards. The son of an army captain from Saint-Cézare in France, Court joined the army in January 1813, but was retired on half-pay following the defeat of Napoleon I in 1815. A military report describes him at that time as physically strong, educated, financially well-off, capable sometimes of 'reprehensible' conduct and also as 'dangerous; to be kept under supervision', presumably because of his Bonapartist sympathies (Lafont 1983, pp. 87–8). Finding little prospect for advancement under the restored French monarchy, Court resigned in 1816 to seek his fortune in the east, ending up by the mid 1820s in the employment of the Persian prince Muhammad Ali Mirza, eldest son of Fath 'Ali Shah, at Kirmanshah (fig. 159; see also pp. 142–3).

Towards the end of 1826 he and Paolo Crescenzo Avitabile (1791–1850), another ex-Bonapartist officer (fig. 125), quit Persia and travelled in disguise as merchants via Kabul, Jalalabad and Peshawar to the Punjab, arriving in Lahore in April 1827 (fig. 176; Lafont 1992, p. 138). There they found employment at the court of Ranjit Singh (1799–1839), training the forces of the Sikh Empire in the art of European warfare (fig. 12). By this time it was quite usual to have European officers in charge of brigades of Indian troops. Following the introduction of this practice in the mid eighteenth century by

Joseph-François Dupleix (1697–1764), of the Compagnie française des Indes, not only the British but many Indian rulers had quickly realised the effectiveness of the European system of a highly disciplined infantry and powerful artillery, and had adopted it for their own armies (Lafont 1982, pp. 32–3).

From notes made during his journey Court compiled an itinerary and a map detailing the geography, archaeology, geology and military aspects of the regions through which he had passed (fig. 134). These documents were bought by the British East India Company for 5000 rupees in 1832 and used in both the Anglo-Afghan wars of 1838–42 and 1878–9 (Grey 1929, appendix II, pp. xxvii–xlviii; Lafont 1992, p. 326). The first archaeological surveys and maps of the Punjab and adjoining areas north-west as far as Kabul were also subsequently produced by Court (1836, 1836a; 1839), and judging from remarks made by Alexander Cunningham were still the best available in 1848 (figs 135–6; Cunningham 1848, p. 130).

Like most Europeans of the period, Court's antiquarian interest was initially inspired by Alexander the Great's conquest of India, but his major archaeological discoveries all postdate the Greek presence in this region. He was one of the first to excavate and record the Buddhist sites of Manikyala, his finds from Mera-ka-Dheri providing the first evidence of the existence of a Kushan era and of chronological links between the Kushans and the Roman Empire in the first to second century AD (pp. 193–4, 212–13, fig. 178). His most spectacular find was undoubtedly the sixth- to seventh-century inscribed bronze shaivite mask dug up at Banamari near Peshawar (figs 122; 137; Errington and Cribb 1992, pp. 237–9).

En route through eastern Afghanistan in early 1827 Court acquired a number of coins (Lafont 1992, pp. 326–8). Once settled in the Punjab he started collecting in earnest and says of the coins (1834, p. 562):

> They were formerly worked up into *lotas* [small, round drinking pots, usually of brass] and cooking vessels and ornaments. It was only in 1829, the period that my researches commenced, that the inhabitants began to appreciate their value. The copper coins are the most numerous; the fear of being supposed to have dug up a treasure leads the inhabitants to melt up those of silver and gold, which makes their preservation comparatively rare.

According to Charles Masson in September 1835, the French officers, especially Court, 'with the advantage that affluence confers, were conducting their operations on a very magnificent scale, and purchasing coins at very extraordinary prices. They had cleared Peshawar of copper medals' (MSS Eur. E 161/VII, section 6, f. 2[47]).

Figure 12 Ranjit Singh in audience facing his European officers, standing (left to right): Court, Allard, Ventura, Avitabile, Foulkes and Argond.

Figure 13 Court's rubbing of a gold aureus of Julia Domna Augusta (AD 170–217) issued c. AD 196–211 in the reign of her husband Septimus Severus (AD 193–211). Rev. busts of her sons Caracalla and Geta.

Court returned to France in 1844. His coin collection was examined and listed in 1873 by Adrien de Longpérier, curator at the Bibliothèque Nationale in Paris: the report lists 797 coins, including 141 Roman silver issues from Syria (Lafont 1994, pp. 26–32, 48–53). After Court's death in January 1880 his collection vanished, seemingly without trace. However, in March 1994, three small albums of coin rubbings entitled 'La collection numismatique du General Court' came to light in an English provincial book sale and were bought by the British Museum (Court MSS). Some idea of the date of the volumes can be gleaned from Court's annotations. For example, beside the rubbing (Court MSS no. 379) of a bronze tetradrachm of Maues (c.75–65 BC), Indo-Scythian king in Gandhara, Court notes in French that this particular coin type was not published in *Ariana Antiqua* (Wilson 1841). This indicates that the volumes were most likely compiled after 1841, probably after Court's return to France in 1844. As the only Roman coin included is one of Julia Augusta, said to have been found on the banks of the Indus (Court MSS, no. 2; fig. 13), it is clear that the 141 Syrian issues were deliberately omitted from the record of a collection made exclusively in the Punjab and North-West Frontier region.

Altogether, there are 627 rubbings, about a third of which illustrate coins acquired by the Museum from Alexander Cunningham between 1888 and 1894. From this it follows that Cunningham must have bought part of Court's collection after the latter's death (Errington 1995, pp. 414–15). Five of Court's coins are in the Bibliothèque Nationale's Cabinet des Médailles and were apparently purchased from Feuardent. It appears likely, therefore, that the rest of his collection was dispersed through this Parisian dealer. It is also probable that Cunningham acquired the volumes of coin rubbings at the same time as the coins, for two rubbings – both silver copies of bronze issues of Azes (bull/lion type) and of Wima Tak[to] (Soter Megas tetradrachms) respectively – are annotated 'false' in English (Court MSS, nos 121, 109).

Court's enthusiasm for collecting seems to have made him a prime target for forgeries: eleven are identifiable from the rubbings, including one of Alexander the Great (Court MSS, no. 108). Three can be dated as early as 1835, for they are clearly copied from a plate of inaccurate drawings published by James Prinsep that year (1835a, pl. XXXVIII.1, 7, 9; Court MSS, nos 13, 22, 26; Errington 1995, p. 415). One coin,

originally dismissed as a fake, is in fact a genuine – and unique – silver tetradrachm imitating coins of the Greco-Bactrian king Eucratides I (c.170–145 BC) and probably issued by the contemporary Yuezhi invaders in Bactria in the first century BC (fig. 52.13; Court MSS no. 40; Errington 1995, fig. 3d). There are several other unique examples, including a silver tetradrachm of the Indo-Scythian satrap Zeionises (c. AD 30–50) (fig. 58.8; Court MSS no. 48; Errington 1995, fig. 2f). The genuine coins range from Greco-Bactrian (i.e. Euthydemus, c.230–200 BC) to the Ghurid period (thirteenth century AD), the greatest quantity (142 coins) being Kushan.

James Prinsep (1799–1840)

> He has in a very short period done more for the restoration of genuine Indian history, than anybody before him; . . . since [he] left India, the historical and antiquarian researches in that country have entirely lost that vigour with which he not only pursued them himself, but which he also knew how to infuse into others. (Lassen 1844)

The seventh son of a prominent English merchant in Calcutta, James Prinsep originally trained as an architect under Augustus Pugin, but changed to assaying after problems with his eyesight (figs 14–15). In 1819 he joined the British East India Company and, on arrival in India, was appointed assistant assay-master to Horace Hayman Wilson (1786–1860) at the Calcutta mint. From 1820 to 1830 he was assay-master at Benares (now Varanasi) mint, but evidently doubled as the architect for a number of projects: a bridge over the Karamnasa River and the construction of a new mint and church. As secretary of the Benares Committee for Public

Figure 14 James Prinsep. Lithograph by Colesworthy Grant.

Figure 15 Silver commemorative medal of James Prinsep, by W. Wyon R.A.

Improvements he was also responsible for designing a tunnel from the Machhodri tank to the Ganges river (which provided a better drainage system for the city) and for the restoration of the Aurangzeb mosque at Madhoray Ghat (fig. 16). Like his brothers William (1794–1874) and Thomas (1800–30), he was an accomplished artist, who produced a series of sketches of Benares because (as he stated in his preface to the resulting published lithographs) he felt the 'The pencil though not entirely idle, has hitherto done little to bring the Holy City to the notice of Europe' (Prinsep 1831–4).

In 1830 he returned to the Calcutta mint as deputy assay-master. He also finished work on a canal linking the Hooghly river to the Sundarbans estuary marshlands, a skilful feat of engineering originally started by his brother Thomas of the Bengal Engineers. He succeeded Wilson in 1832 as assay-master of the mint, where he invented a balance which measured three-hundreths of a grain, reformed weights and measures and, in 1835, introduced the first uniform Company coinage.

His interests were wide-ranging: from chemistry, mineralogy and meteorology to all subjects relating to Indian history and antiquities. He was inventive as well. He adapted a steam engine to power a lathe, a series of ceiling fans and a musical organ, so that he could 'work, keep cool and enjoy music' all at the same time. He also provided the 'gas-making apparatus' for a display in Calcutta by a French balloonist, who ascended a mile 'almost perpendicularly into the sky', before fiddling with the valve let all the gas escape and he plummeted back to earth, the empty balloon fortunately acting as a parachute (Allen 2002, p. 151).

In 1830 Prinsep founded *Gleanings in Science*. This journal provided an outlet for his and other pioneering work in Indian inscriptions, coins and antiquities, for his infectious enthusiasm as editor encouraged men like Masson, Court and Cunningham to send him reports of their finds for publication. When Prinsep became secretary of the Asiatic

Society of Bengal (1832–8), *Gleanings in Science* was renamed *Journal of the Asiatic Society of Bengal*, although it did not replace *Asiatick Researches*[1] as the official publication of the Society until 1842 (Abu Imam 1966, p. 20).

Prinsep's greatest achievements were in epigraphy and numismatics (see pp. 21–4, 186–9, 192–7, 199 below). His work on Indian scripts and coins laid the foundation of studies in these fields. He followed up earlier work by others on the Brahmi script, and in 1837 deciphered the Allahabad Pillar Edict of the Mauryan emperor Ashoka (c.269–232 BC), correctly placing this ruler in the third century BC. He was still working on deciphering the Kharoshthi script, when ill health forced a return to England in 1838. He died of 'softening of the brain' on 22 April 1840 (Prinsep 1858, pp. xiii–xiv).

Three volumes of his manuscripts survive in the Ashmolean Museum, Oxford (Prinsep MSS). These comprise correspondence, rubbings and information on coins and inscriptions sent to him by Charles Masson, Colonel Stacy, Alexander Burnes and others; his own working notes; and a posthumous catalogue of 1066 coins in his collection.

On 1 December 1847 Prinsep's collection of antiquities and 2642 coins were sold to the British Museum by the executors of his estate. The antiquities include the Buddhist relic deposits from the Great Stupa of Manikyala in the Punjab, given to Prinsep by General Ventura (pp. 211–12, fig. 177). The coins comprise one of the most comprehensive collections from the Indian subcontinent in the Museum.

Figure 16 Watercolour of Aurangzeb mosque at Madhoray Ghat, Benares, by James Prinsep.

Charles Masson (1800–53)

> There is a European here by name Masson . . . [who] has lately
> come to Cabul [sic]; . . . he resided some time in Bamian [sic]
> where he amused himself in making excavations, and has
> succeeded in finding several idols. At Cabul he has been engaged
> in the same kind of pursuit, and has been rewarded here also by his
> discovery of several idols quite entire. (Honigberger 1834, p. 117)

This letter, dated 5 June 1833, from Martin Honigberger – a
Transylvanian doctor en route to Europe through Afghanistan
(fig. 179) – was among the earliest scraps of information
received by Claude Wade (1794–1861), the British Political
Agent at Ludhiana, about a man initially thought to be an
American from Kentucky. British East India Company officials
had first become aware of his existence in 1830 when David
Wilson, the British Resident at Bushire in Persia, forwarded
'valuable memoranda on the countries of Central Asia, . . .
obtained from Mr Masson' (Bombay Dispatches 1834, p. 790).
In December 1832 Karamat 'Ali, 'news-writer' (intelligence
agent) for the British in Kabul, reported that an 'Englishman by
name Masson' had arrived in May, who 'understood Persian,
had with him two or three books in a foreign character, a
compass, a map and an astrolabe. He was shabbily dressed and
he had no servant, horse nor mule to carry his baggage'
(Bengal Secret Consultations 1833; Whitteridge 1986, p. 61).
The same year an anonymous source – possibly Karamat 'Ali
again – described him as having 'grey eyes, red beard, with the
hair of his head close cut. He had no stockings or shoes, a
green cap on his head, and a *faqir* or dervish drinking cup
slung over his shoulder' (Grey 1929, p. 188). This seems to be
the only description of his physical appearance. There is no
known portrait.

Whitteridge notes that 'Masson had no need to take any
special precautions during his early travels either as regards
money or costume since he was virtually destitute' (1986,
p. 24). Masson himself remarks that he had found he 'could
do without the first' and had 'purposely abandoned' the
second, to save robbers 'the trouble of taking them' (1842,
vol. I, p. 146). In his account of his travels however, it seems
that both were forcibly taken from him on various occasions
and he only retained his shoes initially because they were the
wrong size or too worn to be worth stealing (Masson 1842,
vol. I, pp. 302, 306–9, 343). But how had he arrived in this
state? He claimed – to the British officers of the East India
Company at Bushire and Tabriz – that he had spent ten years
travelling from the United States through Europe and Russia
to Afghanistan and Persia (Whitteridge 1986, pp. 44–7). Not
only was his story convincing, but he also acquired an
unlikely patron, John Campbell (1799–1870). This 'vain,
untruthful', newly appointed British Envoy to Persia,
'possessed of an ungovernable temper', who 'insulted and
disgusted every Iranian at court and quarrelled with
members of the [British] mission' (Yapp 1980, p. 108),
nevertheless had the foresight to finance Masson's initial
phase of antiquarian research in Afghanistan.

In 1833 Masson submitted a proposal to the East India
Company authorities in Bombay for funding to explore the
ancient sites further. In forwarding his request, Henry
Pottinger (1789–1856), British Resident at Kutch, reported
that Masson was said to be 'well versed in the language of the
East, and of mild and conciliatory manner, so that I should

think his success in the project he has in view would be
certain, were he furnished with the pecuniary means of
carrying on his operations' (Pottinger 1833). But in one
respect these first impressions were deceptive. By 1834 Wade
had gathered enough evidence to reveal Masson's true
identity as James Lewis, an Englishman who had deserted
from the Company's Bengal Artillery regiment while
stationed at Agra in July 1827. From there he had walked
north-westwards across the Bikaner desert of Rajasthan to
the Indus river, turning north-east to follow its course upriver
into independent Sikh territory and ultimately into
Afghanistan, to spend the ensuing years as an itinerant
traveller in lands beyond British control (Wade 1834;
Whitteridge 1986, pp. 101–2). William J. Eastwick (1808–89),
Pottinger's assistant in the 1830s and later a Director of the
East India Company (1846), records that Masson was
educated at Walthamstow and worked as a clerk at Durant &
Co. in London before a quarrel with his father spurred him
into enlisting with the Company in 1821 (Meyer and Brysac
2001, p. 73).

Masson escaped the death penalty – the usual punishment
for desertion – because his observational abilities had already
been recognised, not just in his 'scientific researches' but also
with regard to the political, geographical and other useful
information he had and could continue to supply on
Afghanistan. The fact he had changed his name was seen as
an advantage, for it helped 'remove the embarrassment of
recognising him in his present situation'. In return for a royal
pardon in 1835, he was forced to become a news-writer for
the East India Company in Kabul.

He remained in this post for over two years. In September
1837 a British delegation led by Alexander Burnes (1805–41)
arrived in Kabul. This had originated as a purely commercial
mission, but evolved during the course of 1837 into a political
one, owing to the dispute over Peshawar between the Sikhs
and the ruler of Kabul, Dost Muhammad (1824–39, 1842–63),
and the conflicting political ambitions of Burnes, vain,
boastful, 'sparing of the truth' and 'ready for intrigue' and
Wade, 'a short, fat man fond of eating and sleeping' but also
'acute, knowledgeable and prickly' (Yapp 1980, pp. 207, 227).
When the British authorities rejected Burnes's political
proposals for Afghanistan in early 1838, he retired to Peshawar
(Yapp 1980, pp. 224–40). A disillusioned Masson went with
him, and after some months, when no new appointment was
forthcoming, resigned from government service (Whitteridge
1986, pp. 136–7). He travelled down the Indus, stayed with
Henry Pottinger at Tatta and ended up in Karachi in early
1839, writing his contribution to *Ariana Antiqua* (Wilson 1841)
and an account of his travels (Masson 1842).

At the beginning of 1840 he attempted to return to Kabul,
but unfortunately got only as far as Kalat where a revolt broke
out shortly after his arrival. The city was besieged and taken
and he was imprisoned with the unpopular local British
Political Agent, Lieutenant Loveday. Masson was subsequently
sent by the rebels to represent their demands to Lieutenant
J. D. D. Bean, the Political Agent at Quetta, who immediately
arrested him on suspicion of being a traitor and a spy. Loveday
was killed by the rebels; Masson, embittered but alive, was
finally released by the British authorities in January 1841 and
made his way home via Bombay, Egypt and France, reaching

Figure 17 Charles Masson's sketch of Bamiyan.

London in March 1842 (Masson 1843, pp. 116–269; Whitteridge 1986, pp. 151–7). He received a small pension from the East India Company, but was never compensated for his wrongful imprisonment. He spent the next eleven years working on his archaeological records and his own collection of coins (Masson MSS Eur. E 161, ff. 31, 33, 36, 38; Errington 2002/3, §§ 21–3). He married Mary Anne Kilby on 19 February 1844 and had a son, Charles Lewis Robert, born 13 October 1850, and a daughter, Isabella Adelaide, born 4 March 1853. He died in Edmonton, north London, on 5 November 1853, from an 'uncertain disease of the brain'.[2] After the death of his wife in 1855 the Company paid £100 to the guardian of their children for his papers and coins (IOR/B/233).

Masson was unforgivably proved right in his criticism of the British East India Company's policies that led to the disastrous First Anglo-Afghan War (1838–42). He was also not tactful in voicing that criticism, although he was sometimes sensible enough to remain anonymous, as in his following letter to the press, signed 'a camel driver' (MSS Eur. E 162, letter 4):[3]

> In your paper today I observe that jackasses are employed in place of camels for the transport service of troops employed in Afghanistan. What can be the reason for such a step? Are the camels of the country exhausted? Is it owing to a principal of economy? Seeing that jackasses have been for a long time employed in the Political Department, is it the commencement of a system to introduce them in to the military one, with a view of establishing uniformity in the services?

Masson was dismissed by many of his contemporaries as a deserter, adventurer, spy and writer of bad verse, some of it in a rather fatalistic vein (1848; Possehl 1990, p. 114):

> Although events seem averse, chase sorrow from thy breast,
> If not exactly as 'twas wished, perchance 'tis for the best.
> Against the wish of heaven, forbear unjust reproach;
> If not allowed to land in Scind, why do so in Baloche.

As a result, the value of his archaeological work in Afghanistan was belittled, largely ignored and subsequently forgotten. But his huge collection of coins and Buddhist relic deposits,

together with his manuscript records, are a rich source of information on ancient Afghanistan. These are all now being catalogued and studied in detail, for the first time since their discovery some 170 years ago (see pp. 189–92, 197–8, 200).

Masson's interest in archaeological remains was already apparent in 1831, when, en route through the Punjab from Lahore to Karachi, he discovered and explored the mounds of Harappa on the southern bank of the Ravi river. However, he mistook this ancient Indus Civilisation city site (c.2500–2000 BC) for Sangala, the capital of Porus, who was defeated by Alexander the Great in 326 BC (Masson 1842, vol. I, pp. 452–4; Possehl 1990, p. 111).

His archaeological career began properly only in 1832–3, when funds from John Campbell enabled him to survey the caves of Bamiyan (fig. 17). A scribbled memento of his visit – 'If any fool this high samootch explore, Know Charles Masson has been here before' – was found a century later in one of the caves (Sanctuary XII) above the 55 m Buddha (Hackin and Carl 1933, p. 2). Even in 1976 traces of his signature 'Charles Masson 1833' – probably a separate bit of graffiti – still survived in one of the caves (Possehl 1990, pp. 118–19, fig. 7). A more permanent record of his survey is his folio of drawings and descriptions of the site in the British Library (Masson MSS Eur. G 42).

Between 1833 and 1835, Masson surveyed or excavated more than 50 Buddhist monuments in the Kabul and Jalalabad regions (fig. 176; Wilson 1841, pp. 51–118; pp. 216–21 below). He started with Topdara – one of the best preserved stupas – to the north of Kabul and found a schist relic cell coated with red lead, containing only a bone fragment (Wilson 1841, pp. 116–17). He later thought the lack of finds was perhaps due to his inexperience, for he had more success at Guldara (fig. 109), to the south-east of Kabul, and, above all, at Hadda and in the Darunta district, to the south and west of Jalalabad (figs 18, 183–5). In 1835, when his political appointment curtailed his freedom of movement, he had to resort to deputising a team of workmen to excavate the stupas at

Figure 18 Charles Masson's panoramic view of the Darunta plain, with Passani 'tumulus 6' in the foreground.

Wardak, to the west of Kabul, sneaking clandestinely out of the city to visit the site himself, and being forced to return quickly, before he was missed (Wilson 1841, p. 118).

In July 1833 Masson discovered the remains of an immense ancient city on the plain of Begram, to the north of Kabul (fig. 38). He obtained permission from his friends in the neighbourhood for his work party from Kabul to open the nearby stupa (Wilson 1841, p. 117). He also paid local people to collect 'all coins, seals' and other finds 'indiscriminately' from the urban site, as he instinctively realised 'for the grand object of historical elucidation, the more collected, the better' (Masson 1837; MSS Eur. E 161/VII, f. 5[44]; fig. 19). In this he was ahead of his time. Even as late as 1912 the residue of his vast coin collection was erroneously dismissed as 'mere rubbish' (Thomas 1912). Modern opinion confirms his identification of Begram as Alexandria ad Caucasum, one of the cities founded by Alexander the Great (Bernard 1982). In 1937–40 French excavations of the southern part of the site revealed buildings of the first to second century AD (Hackin 1939; Ghirshman 1946; Hackin *et al.* 1954 and 1959). The rest was never investigated and, according to satellite images, appears to have survived intact. Apparently, this is because the site has been heavily mined. The huge quantity of material amassed by Masson, however, provides evidence for the continuous occupation of the site from about 200 BC to the thirteenth century AD. According to his estimates, he collected more than 68,877 (mostly copper) coins, 30 silver rings, 17 intaglios and 1598 bronze objects (e.g. seals, rings, arrowheads, ornaments and pins) from Begram. To this must be added at least 6753 coins (gold, silver and copper), 19 intaglios and 15 miscellaneous objects bought in Kabul bazaar; 470 coins from Jalalabad, Ghazni and Charikar; and a coin and an intaglio from Peshawar (Masson, MSS Eur. E 161/VII, ff. 3–4, 25–7, 29–31, 33, 36, 38; Uncat. MSS 3). These range in date from the third century BC to the early nineteenth century. The coin collection of the 1835 season alone was said to be 'large enough to supply all the museums in Europe' (Proc. ASB 1838).

In return for funding Masson's antiquarian research, the British East India Company received all his finds, apart from his last collection of about thirty thousand coins (acquired 8 November 1837 – 24 March 1838), which he was allowed to keep. When the 1835 collection finally reached Calcutta in December 1838, the Asiatic Society of Bengal selected an unspecified number of 'duplicates' for their museum (Proc. ASB 1839). The East India Company also made two donations

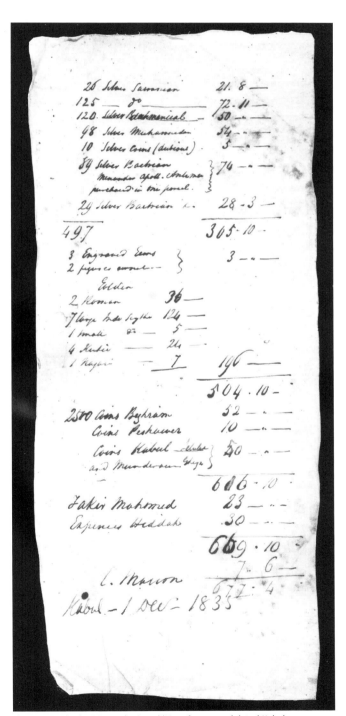

Figure 19 Charles Masson's signed 'List of expenses' dated Kabul, 1 December 1835.

to the British Museum: 116 coins from the 1833–4 collection in 1838 and another in 1845 of 59 Sasanian and Arab-Sasanian coins, possibly from the 1836–7 collection (Acquisitions 1838; British Museum 1845a). The rest of the collections were sent to the Company's India Museum in London, where few records were kept. When this museum closed in 1878, most of the Buddhist relic deposits, the miscellaneous seals and other small finds from Begram and Kabul bazaar, and 2420 coins from miscellaneous sources (including Masson) were transferred, with little or no documentation, to the British Museum (1880–2). Some artefacts inadvertently ended up in the Victoria and Albert Museum, while a number of 'duplicate' coins were donated to the Royal Asiatic Society, the Ashmolean Museum in Oxford and the Fitzwilliam Museum in Cambridge (Desmond 1982, pp. 38–9; Thomas 1912). A large portion of the India Museum's coins were sold at auction for the Government of India in 1887 (Sotheby, Wilkinson & Hodge 1887). A few of these entered the British Museum at a later date from other collectors, most notably Cunningham (p. 15).

By the time the British Museum inherited its part of the Masson collection, the only known resource for identifying any of the material was the illustrated account of the finds in *Ariana Antiqua* (Wilson 1841). By this means, the provenance of some of the small finds, four reliquaries and about a hundred coins was confirmed. Masson's detailed records of his excavations, his original drawings and maps lay forgotten in the India Office archives; two bundles, in fact, were rediscovered only in 1958 (Masson Uncat. MSS). The residue of the India Office's coin collection – including some six thousand Masson coins – was unearthed and transferred from the British Library on permanent loan to the British Museum only in 1995. Masson's manuscript records and all other surviving sources of information on his collections have now been collated together as part of the British Museum's ongoing Masson Project and are being used to identify and document his finds and to reconstruct the archaeological record of the sites he explored. Research has revealed one more link between Masson and the Museum, in the form of the following proposal (Ludlow 1847):

> Having heard accidentally the other day that the employees of the Medal department in the British Museum were just now subjected to unusual trouble in the arrangement of the Bactrian coins, which have been imported into Europe of late years, the thought struck me that the Trustees of the Museum might perhaps have it in their power to confer a real benefit upon the public by the employment of a most deserving and remarkable man, Charles Masson. . . . He is a very modest retiring man, of a very rare character nowadays; one who seeks knowledge for its own sake . . . in the knowledge of the ancient coins of that portion of Aria, & generally of its ancient history, there is no man in England who will be found to surpass him.

The reply came back that 'these coins were already satisfactorily arranged and that Mr Masson's services were not required' (British Museum 1847). But apart from providing evidence of a possible lost opportunity, the letter shows that Masson was not without his champions even in England. The writer of the letter, John Malcolm Forbes Ludlow (1821–1911), was a prominent social reformer, an advocate of reforms in India and of the abolition of slavery. He had met Masson at dinner with Sir Charles Forbes (1774–1849), head of the first mercantile firm in Bombay,

Member of Parliament (1812–32), lord rector of Aberdeen University and also a strong advocate of reforms in India. It reinforces Whitteridge's final assessment (1986, p. 157): 'One thread runs throughout – Charles Masson's remarkable capacity for making friends among all classes of . . . people wherever he went. Without the deep loyalty he inspired . . . he would never have survived'.

Major-General Sir Alexander Cunningham (1814–93)

> I must enter a protest against any Indian sculptures being sent to the British Museum even temporarily as they would no doubt be concealed in the dim vaults of the museum where some years ago I discovered a number of Indian Sculptures as well as seven Indian Inscriptions. (Cunningham 1875a)

> There is a wide spread feeling that Indian sculptures are thrust aside in England – But now that you have got rid of thousands of bottles of preserved entrails and disembowelled peltry, I suppose there may be room for less perishable articles. And as you are now setting up some of the Indian sculptures I will do my best to procure more for you. (Cunningham 1881, para. 5)

It is fortunate that, following the creation of the Natural History Museum (which inherited the maligned 'entrails and disembowelled peltry' in 1880), Alexander Cunningham modified his negative opinion of the British Museum and became, both directly and indirectly, one of its greatest benefactors of antiquities from the Indian subcontinent and Afghanistan (fig. 20). Although now known as the 'father of Indian archaeology', his military titles, C.S.I. (1871), C.I.E. (1878), K.C.I.E (1887), intimate that this was a diversion from his official career. His father was the Scottish stone-mason, author and poet, Allan Cunningham. As secretary to the sculptor Sir Francis Chantrey, Allan Cunningham moved in influential circles and, in 1828, was able to obtain an East India Company military cadetship for his son through the patronage of Sir Walter Scott (Abu Imam 1966, pp. 1–2).

After training at Addiscombe and the Royal Engineer's Estate at Chatham, Alexander Cunningham arrived in India in 1833 as a Second Lieutenant of the Bengal Engineers. Following three years as a Sapper in Calcutta, Delhi and Varanasi, he became an aide-de-camp (1836–40) to the Governor General, Lord Auckland (1784–1849), during which time he was sent on a geographical mission in 1839 to trace the sources of the Punjab rivers (Cunningham 1841). He served as Executive Engineer to the King of Oudh (Awadh, 1840–2) and at Gwalior (1844–5); then as a Political Officer at Kangra (1846). His appointment as a member of the Tibetan boundary commission (1846–8) was combined with a survey of Ladakh and adjacent countries (Cunningham 1848). He also saw action as a field engineer in Bundelkand (1842), at the battle of Punniar (1843) and, during the Sikh Wars, at the battles of Sabraon (1846), Chillianwala and Gujarat (1849). He was sent as Executive Engineer again to Gwalior (1849–53), then Multan (1853–6). His appointment as Chief Engineer, organising the Public Works Department of Burma (1856–7), meant that he escaped the Mutiny, which ended political rule in India by the East India Company. Afterwards he was posted as Chief Engineer to the North Western Provinces (modern Uttar Pradesh, 1858–61). On 30 June 1861 he retired from the army.

His early friendship with James Prinsep encouraged a lifelong interest in Indian numismatics and antiquities, especially the Buddhist remains. The year after his arrival in

Figure 20 Major-General Sir Alexander Cunningham, with sculptures from the site of Jamalgarhi (Peshawar Valley) and miniature stupas from Sonala Pind (Punjab) and eastern India.

India, he launched what ultimately became his second career with a note on the Roman coins excavated by Claude-Auguste Court from the Mera-ka-Dheri Buddhist stupa at Manikyala (Cunningham 1834; pp. 194, 212–13, fig. 178 below). The following year he conducted his first excavations at the Buddhist site of Sarnath near Varanasi (1835–6). His appointment as aide-de-camp in 1836 brought him to Calcutta, where he helped sort and classify the huge numbers of ancient coins sent to Prinsep from all parts of India (Allen 2002, pp. 200–1).

As early as 1838 he began petitioning for the creation of an archaeological survey of India – apparently with the aim of getting himself appointed as surveyor – but, by arguing that Brahmanism 'was of comparatively modern origin', he alienated Horace Wilson, then the most influential man of Indian studies in England.[4] As a result, less competent men such as Markham Kittoe were appointed instead. Cunningham continued his archaeological explorations independently in all the locations he was posted to as an engineer and the antagonism between him and Wilson grew. As his knowledge and archaeological experience increased, so did his 'heavy sarcasm', culminating in several public and, for Wilson, humiliating spats (Allen 2002, pp. 202–17, 229). Cunningham's ultimate assessment, however, is fair, including the comment that Wilson's 'account of Masson's collection of coins [in *Ariana Antiqua*, 1841] makes no advance in Indian numismatics, beyond the point which Prinsep had reached at the time of his death. Indeed, Wilson's archaeological writings have added little, if anything, to his reputation' (1871, p. v).

The converse has to be said of Cunningham. Using the newly translated text of the fifth-century Chinese Buddhist pilgrim Faxian (Rémusat 1836), in 1843 he discovered the site of Sankisa, south-east of Delhi in Uttar Pradesh (Cunningham 1843). At the end of 1847, on his way back from Kashmir, he visited the Gandharan Buddhist sites of Jamalgarhi and Ranigat in the Peshawar Valley (figs 37; 187; Cunningham

1848, pp. 104, 131). From 1849 he worked at Sanchi, initially with his brother, Joseph (1812–51; Political Agent of Bhopal 1846–50) and then with the official archaeological surveyor, Lieutenant F.C. Maisey, in an excavation of this Buddhist site in 1851 (Cunningham 1854; Maisey 1892). He also excavated at Mathura in 1853, 1856 and 1860, discovering from his reading of a Kharoshthi inscription found on site the existence of a monastery called Huvishka's vihara, and correctly identifying this ruler as the Kushan king mentioned in the *Rājataraṅgiṇī* and in the inscription on the bronze Buddhist reliquary excavated by Masson at Wardak in eastern Afghanistan (fig. 114; Abu Imam 1966, p. 33; pp. 131, 133 below).

Wilson's death in 1860 ended opposition to Cunningham in England and in 1861 he was appointed Archaeological Surveyor to the Government of India by the new Viceroy, Lord Charles Canning (1812–62). The post was abolished 'in a cold fit of parsimony' in 1865 (Allen 2002, p. 227). Cunningham retired to England, temporarily, as it turned out, for in 1870, following representations to the Secretary of State, he returned as Director-General of an expanded Archaeological Survey of India, with two assistants (Allen 2002, pp. 230–8). He remained in the post until 1885, during which time he and his assistants explored as many sites as possible, covering vast distances during each tour by any means available. Although of necessity cursory, his surveys and preliminary excavations – with the help of the accounts by the Chinese pilgrims Faxian (Rémusat 1836) and Xuan Zang (Julien 1857) and those of earlier explorers – produced the first understanding of the nature of many ruins, and enabled him to identify correctly such ancient sites as Taxila (p. 224).

Following retirement and his return to London in 1885, Cunningham concentrated on coins, his work providing the first chronological framework for Indian numismatics. He is silent, for the most part however, about the sources and provenance of the coins and sometimes also the artefacts in his collection, as is the case, for example, regarding his acquisition of Court's coin collection. One rare exception occurs in his discussion of 'Ephthalites, or White Huns', where he mentions only that 'Specimens of each kind [of coins with the Hun *tamgha* or monogram] were found together by Masson in No. 10 Hidda [*sic*] Tope' (fig. 83) and, a few pages later, referring to the same group (Cunningham 1895, pp. 106, 111):

> Wilson notes that Masson's coins were found in the great Tope at Hidda [Hadda] . . . I was informed that most of my coins of this and similar classes were found in Stûpas. . . . A few of my coins were purchased at the sale of the remains of the Masson collection in London.

This purchase can be identified in the marked catalogue of the auction held for the Government of India on 6 August 1887 as 43 'Indo-Sassanian dirhems [*sic*] of various types . . . *some broken*', which were sold to Cunningham for 30 shillings (Sotheby, Wilkinson & Hodge 1887, p. 55, lot 753). Eight silver Alchon Hun coins[5] and possibly one Kidarite coin in the British Museum's Cunningham Collection are identifiable as being those found by Masson in the Buddhist relic deposit of Tope Kelan at Hadda, south of Jalalabad in Afghanistan (figs 82.10; 83.2–6; pp. 93–5, 133, 221). Not part of Lot 753, but from the same stupa, is a gold coin of Shailanaviraya, an early king of Kashmir (fig. 82.11; Wilson 1841, Coins pl. XVIII.26), which Cunningham must have acquired at some other time.[6]

Cunningham was Prinsep's successor in many respects, not least in the way in which he encouraged the mutual exchange of information and finds with others working in the field. This gave him access to a wide range of material, from as far away as Central Asia. One of the most important collections that he acquired from this region was part of the Oxus Treasure, which he sold privately to A. W. Franks (1826–97), the British Museum Keeper of Antiquities, after initially offering it for sale to the Museum itself in 1887. This material was subsequently bequeathed to the Museum with Franks's own collection of finds from the same source in 1897 (Curtis 1997, pp. 243, 245–6).[7]

At the same time however, Cunningham fulfilled his promise to Franks to 'procure more' for the Museum by donating over four hundred miscellaneous objects, sculptures and Buddhist relic deposits.[8] In his report of 5 July 1887 Franks notes 'The collections presented by Sir Alexander Cunningham are of great archaeological importance, and they would have been far more numerous had it not been for the disastrous shipwreck by which the donor lost his manuscripts, as well as a number of antiquities' (British Museum 1887). A photograph of Cunningham – as Director-General of the Archaeological Survey of India *c.* 1885 surrounded by artefacts – illustrates one of the objects presented at this time: the miniature stupa-shaped relic casket from Sonala Pind at Manikyala in the Punjab (figs 20–1; 190). The small bearded figure beside it in the photograph and the boxed relief of a seated couple below have not been traced and could be two of the 'antiquities' lost when the *Indus* sank off the coast of Sri Lanka in 1885.

Analysis of the 1887 donation reveals two clear strands in Cunningham's collecting methods, for they are all objects he acquired through his own excavations or in his official capacity as Archaeological Surveyor/Director-General of the ASI. For objects which he had bought himself – such as the Oxus finds, or most notably coins – he recouped his expenses by offering them to the British Museum 'at the prices which they cost him, thus relinquishing the interest on the sum paid and the undoubted profit he would make by a public sale' (Poole 1888, p. 35). So he sold the Museum 118 coins for £83 in 1857 (Acquisitions 1857) and 844 coins for £2539 in 1888 (Poole 1888), and donated only two bronze coins – of the Indo-Greek ruler Strato and the Parthian king Arsaces I respectively – in his lifetime.[9]

From 1888 onwards he corresponded regularly with E. J. Rapson (1861–1931), the Assistant Keeper of the Department of Coins and Medals (1887–1906), who subsequently became Professor of Sanskrit at Cambridge University. Most of the letters concern the publication of Cunningham's book *Coins of Ancient India* (1891), or his coin collection and its acquisition by the Museum (Cunningham 1888–93). One letter, dated 4 February 1889, ends 'I have got a letter from Bodley's Librarian asking about the balance of my coins – But I suspect that the Bodleian authorities have little cash and great expectations of outsiders' liberality!' Instead, he sold another 31 coins to the British Museum for £85 in 1890 and a further 49 coins for £60 in 1993.[10]

In the last year of his life, however, Cunningham's attitude to recouping his costs seems to have mellowed. This must, in part, have been due to his good relationship with Franks and Rapson. In 1892, he donated the residue of his collection of

Figure 21 Relic deposit from Sonala Pind stupa near Manikyala (Punjab): relic casket in the form of a stupa, crystal reliquary and bronze coins of Zeionises and Kujula Kadphises, together with coins of Wima Tak[to] and Sasan found in the surface debris.

seals and other small objects.[11] Records in the Department of Coins and Medals further attest it was always his wish that 'his entire collection should ultimately be preserved intact in the British Museum' (Head 1894). Some months before his death, the residue 4607 coins were 'offered to the Nation' for £500; a few days before he died, he changed his mind again and, accordingly, only 2465 coins were sold for £370, the remaining 2142 coins being bequeathed to the Museum.[12] The Cunningham Collection in its entirety thus comprises 5651 coins and about six hundred miscellaneous sculptures, seals and other objects. A further 177 items from the Oxus Treasure – donated by A. W. Franks – are identifiable as pieces formerly also belonging to Cunningham (Curtis 1997, pp. 243, 245–6).[13]

Notes

1. The first 14 volumes were titled *Asiatick Researches*; the spelling was amended to *Asiatic Researches* for vols 15–20.
2. Information courtesy of Henry Lythe, who has traced the relevant records in the Public Records Office and elsewhere.
3. Reference again courtesy of Henry Lythe.
4. Professor of Sanskrit at Oxford University, Director of the Royal Asiatic Society and Librarian of the East India Company.
5. The term refers to a distinct series of coins bearing variations of the Bactrian legend αλχανο (*alxano*) originally noted by Göbl (1967). For correct readings of the Bactrian legends by Professor Nicholas Sims-Williams see pp. 93–4.
6. Alchon coins: CM 1894.5.6.201, 215, 1164, 1167, 1291, 1293, 1402 (?), OR 0474 (?); Shailanaviraya coin: 1894.5.6.197.
7. Franks was employed by the Museum 1851–96; as Keeper 1866–96.
8. As. 1887.7.17.1–406; 1880.3535; 1880.1213–19.
9. CM 1857.8.13.1–118; 1888.12.7.1–844; 1888.3.2.1 and 1893.10.9.1 respectively.
10. CM 1890.4.4.1–31; 1893.5.6.1–49.
11. As. 1892.11.3.1–196.
12. CM 1894.5.6.1–2465; 1894.5.7.1–2142.
13. ME 1897.12.31.1–177.

2 Deciphering ancient scripts

Hurrah for inscriptions!

(Prinsep to Cunningham 28.3.1838: 1871, p. xv)

Scripts used in ancient Persia

Pahlavi (Middle Persian)

In the eighteenth-century Age of Enlightenment, growing
interest in Bible-related history and Classical sources
produced a desire amongst European scholars to find out
more about the civilisation of ancient Persia. One of the first
was the French writer and linguist A.-H. Anquetil du Perron
(1731–1805). After spending several years in Surat, India,
studying Avestan and Pahlavi with a Parsi priest, he
published a translation of the entire *Avesta* and the Indian
Bundahishn ('Creation') in 1771 (Boyce 1984, p. 131). Carsten
Niebuhr (1733–1815), sole survivor of the 1761–7 Royal Danish
Expedition to Arabia, had visited Naqsh-i Rustam in 1767 and
made the first complete copy of the trilingual inscription in
Pahlavi, Parthian and Greek, which he published in 1778
(Hinz 1975, p. 16).

In 1787–91, working from Niebuhr's copy, the French
orientalist scholar Baron Antoine Sylvestre de Sacy
(1758–1838)[1] first translated the Greek inscription. Reference
to earlier work by fellow Frenchman Joseph Pellerin
(1684–1782) on Parthian and Sasanian coin legends (1767,
pp. 34–40, pls I–II) enabled him to recognise the Aramaic-
based scripts of the Pahlavi and Parthian inscriptions. By
comparing these versions with the Greek text, he successfully
deciphered the names, correctly identifying the author of the
inscription as the Sasanian king Shapur I (AD 241–72)
(Wiesehöfer 2001, p. 234). His systematic comparative
analysis between known and unknown scripts was ground-
breaking for the development of decipherment. Ker Porter,
for example, tried to follow the same methods in his own
attempts to translate Sasanian coin legends. Although he was
no linguist or epigraphist, he had a good knowledge of the
history of the Sasanians, which helped him to identify the
individual kings and to read their legends (fig. 24).

Old Persian cuneiform

The decipherment of Old Persian cuneiform in the first half of
the nineteenth century is associated with the German
philologist Georg Friedrich Grotefend (1775–1853), a teacher
at Göttingen, and the British East India Company officer,
Henry Creswicke Rawlinson (1810–95). However, their
pioneering achievements would not have been possible
without the contributions of earlier scholars.

The rock relief and inscriptions of Bisitun (figs 22–3), near
Kirmanshah and Persepolis in western Iran, date to the time of
the Achaemenid king Darius the Great (522–486 BC). The 413

Figure 22 Inscribed rock relief of Darius I at Bisitun, depicting the triumph of
Darius over the priest Gaumata (the 'false Smerdis') and nine rebel kings
c.520/19 BC.

lines of wedge-shaped letters inscribed on the rock face were
first noted in 1621 by an Italian traveller, Pietro della Valle
(1586–1652), who copied some of the characters and realised,
correctly, that the script was written from left to right. In 1674
Jean Chardin (1643–1713), a French trader, published complete
groups of cuneiforms and noted that the inscriptions appeared
to be in sets of three parallel forms (Güterbock 2005). A
century later, in 1778 (as already mentioned), Carsten Niebuhr
published the first accurate copies of the inscriptions, made
during his 1861–7 expedition, which he correctly identified as
transcripts of the same text in three different scripts (Hinz

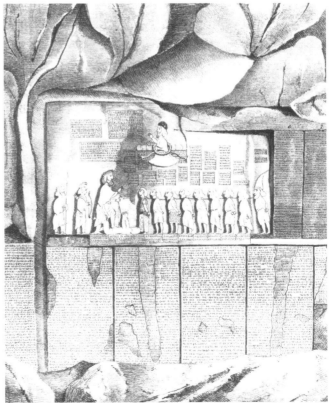

Figure 23 Rawlinson's drawing of the Bisitun relief.

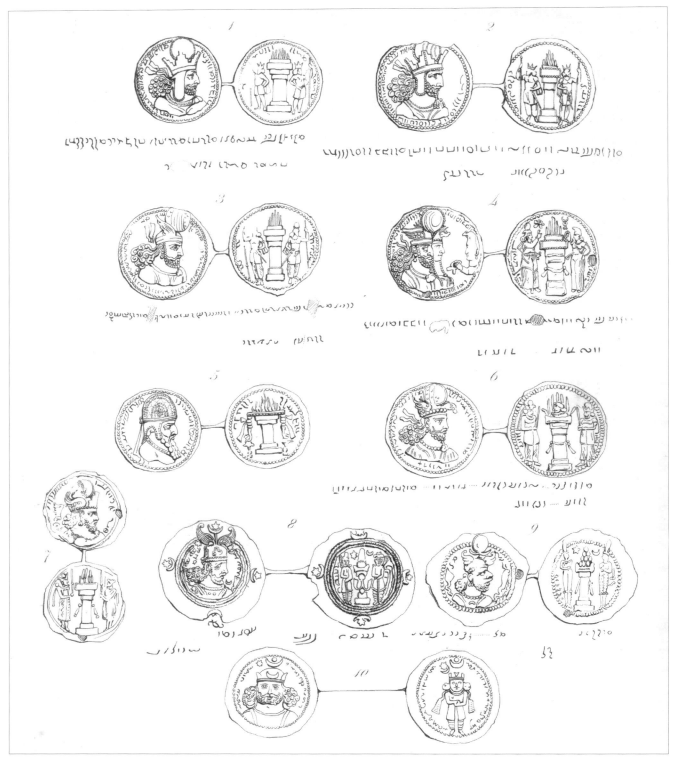

Figure 24 Ker Porter's drawing of his Sasanian coins.

1975, p. 16; Güterbock 2005). These are, in fact, Old Persian, Elamite and Babylonian cuneiforms, the three principal writing systems of the Achaemenid empire.

Old Persian – the youngest and least complex of the three systems – was used only from the beginning of the reign of Darius onwards (522–486 BC) (fig. 30). The inscription in the name of Cyrus (550–530 BC) written in this script at Pasargadae was in fact added later by Darius (Hinz 1973, pp. 19, 21). The last inscription in Old Persian is that of Artaxerxes III (359–338 BC) at Persepolis (A³Pa; see Kent 1953, p. 156). This language, together with other Iranian dialects, such as Parthian and Pahlavi or Middle Persian,

were absorbed into New Persian. This made the task of deciphering easier. Old Persian has a word divider and comprises 36 phonetic characters (Finkel 2005, p. 26).

In 1797 two Danish theologians, who were in correspondence with each other, but working independently, attempted to solve the cuneiform puzzle. These were Oluf Gerhard Tychsen (1734–1815), orientalist and director of the Rostock Museum in Germany, and Friedrich Münter (1761–1830) in Copenhagen, later Bishop of Zeeland (Borger 1975, p. 158). While Tychsen believed that the ruins of Persepolis were Parthian, Münter dated them correctly to the Achaemenid period (Borger 1975, p. 159).

However, the most important first step towards deciphering Old Persian cuneiform was taken by Grotefend in the summer of 1802. While out walking with his friend Rafaello Fiorillo, he made a bet that he would be able to read the inscriptions (Hinz 1975, p. 15). Like della Valle and Niebuhr, Grotefend recognised that the scripts were written from left to right (Finkel 2005, p. 26). In a 'preliminary report about the reading and explanation of the so-called cuneiform inscriptions from Persepolis' on 4 September 1802, he confirmed the existence of three different inscriptions and read the name of Darius (Old Persian *Daryavahuš*) as *Darheush* and Xerxes (Old Persian *Khšarša*) as *Khšerše*. He then correctly identified the ancient Persian title 'king of kings' (*xšayaθiya xšayaθyānām*) by comparing the Old Persian inscription with the already translated trilingual Pahlavi, Parthian and Greek inscription of Shapur I at Kaba-i Zardusht (Hinz 1975, p. 17; Borger 1975, pp. 169, 177). He added another ten characters – *š, t, s, p, t, r, u, kh, f, k* – to the already known Old Persian *a* and *b* (Hinz 1975, pp. 17–18; Finkel 2005, p. 27). Tychsen and the Danish philologist, Rasmus Christian Rask (1787–1832), a founder of comparative linguistics who visited Persia in 1819–20, subsequently each identified several other Old Persian characters.

Some of the Achaemenid cuneiform inscriptions were copied by Ker Porter in 1818 (1821, pp. 505, 527, pl. 13), not only at Bisitun, but, more importantly, also the now lost trilingual inscription in the name of Cyrus at Pasargadae (fig. 162), a copy of which he sent to Grotefend. The contact between the two men was Carl Bellino, the German secretary of Claudius James Rich in Baghdad, who was in regular correspondence with Grotefend and also sent him copies of the Babylonian cuneiform inscriptions to work on. Grotefend erroneously believed these texts were in Persian (Borger 1975, p. 180).

The two trilingual Old Persian, Elamite and Babylonian inscriptions of Darius and Xerxes at Ganj Nameh (i.e. Mount Alvand) near Hamadan were noted and examined by the British officer John Macdonald Kinneir, on an intelligence gathering mission in 1810; by James Morier, First Secretary of Ouseley's Mission, in 1811; and by Ker Porter in 1820, while Carl Bellino had copied them before falling ill in Hamadan (Kinneir 1813; Morier 1818; Budge 1925, p. 32; Ker Porter 1822, p. 120; Barnett 1974, p. 14; see pp. 153–4, 172–3 below). Henry Creswicke Rawlinson also visited Ganj Nameh in 1835, but was better placed to study the inscriptions of Darius at Bisitun, while stationed at nearby Kirmanshah in 1835–7. He spent much of his spare time at the site studying the cuneiform and copying major parts of the Old Persian text. Although he was not able to read the inscriptions, he immediately realised their importance and recognised that they were written in different scripts (Larsen 1996, pp. 79–80). Correspondence with his sister shows that, already in late 1835, with access to an excellent library in Baghdad, he was aware of the progress made by other scholars in deciphering the texts (Larsen 1994, p. 81).

The first announcement of his discoveries was sent from Tehran on 1 January 1838 to the Secretary of the Royal Asiatic Society in London (fig. 23; Larsen 1996, p. 82). In a letter to his sister written around this time he ranked himself only just behind Jean-François Champollion (1790–1832) and Sylvestre de Sacy, the French pioneering giants of the decipherment of

ancient Egyptian scripts (Larsen 1996, p. 82). He also corresponded with Layard on the subject. On his next visit to Bisitun in 1844 he completed copies of the Old Persian and Elamite texts (Larsen 1994, p. 83), while in September 1847 he made two copies and a paper squeeze of the Babylonian inscription (Rawlinson 1852, pp. 73–6; see p. 173 below).

Meanwhile, Edward Hincks, an Irish clergyman and orientalist (1792–1866), gave a lecture in Dublin in June 1846 (published in *The Literary Gazette* in July), in which he proved that the Old Persian script was not alphabetic – as assumed by everyone including Rawlinson – but a mixture of alphabetic and syllabic script (Larsen 1996, p. 179). Around this time Rawlinson sent from Baghdad a revision – remarkably similar to Hincks's version – of his transliterations of the Bisitun Old Persian inscription. Although he insisted that he had arrived at the same conclusion independently, other scholars were not convinced and believed that Rawlinson had claimed success for a discovery which was not his (Larsen 1996, p. 179). Rawlinson was certainly aware of Hincks's work and refers to his achievements in a series of letters dated 1846–7 (Larsen 1994, p. 181).

Elamite cuneiform

Elamite cuneiform is the second script employed in the trilingual inscriptions of the Achaemenid kings (figs 23; 30; 162). It derives from Old Elamite, which is similar to Mesopotamian cuneiform and dates from at least 2200 BC. From 600 BC it adopted new rules. Unlike Old Persian, its application under the Achaemenids was not restricted to inscriptions, but – as the many clay tablets found at Persepolis show – it was also the script used for administrative records (Stolper 2005, p. 20).

The decipherment of Elamite was first attempted in 1844 by the Danish orientalist Neils Ludvig Westergaard (1815–78). Unlike Old Persian, it was not linked to any language then known. The key to unlocking the script therefore lay in the fact that the same text is repeated word for word in each of the trilingual inscriptions. The system contains 96 syllabic signs, 16 logograms and five determinants. The readings of the Elamite characters are in general fairly clear, although some words are still uncertain (Güterbock 2005).

Babylonian cuneiform

Babylonian cuneiform (fig. 25) was in use for more than two thousand years in Mesopotamia at Babylon, Nineveh and other sites between the Euphrates and Tigris rivers. Again, the first clues to its decipherment were provided by the Old Persian inscription at Bisitun, but the similarity of its language to well-known Semitic dialects also helped (Güterbock 2005). It was deciphered through the united efforts of Hincks, Rawlinson,

Figure 25 Babylonian cuneiform tablet from Borsippa, Iraq, dated in the first year of Cambyses, King of Babylon, and Cyrus, King of the Land (538 BC).

Figure 26 Legends on coins:

1   Greco-Bactrian Antimachus I (*c*.180–170 BC): Greek *ΒΑΣΙΛΕΩΣ ΘΕΟΥ* 'divine king'.
2   Kushan Kujula Kadphises (*c*. AD 40–90): corrupt Greek legend of Indo-Greek king Hermaeus; rev. own name in Kharoshthi.
3   Kushan Kanishka I (*c*. AD 127–50): Bactrian.
4   Kushan Vasudeva I (*c*. AD 190–227): Bactrian, with Brahmi control mark.
5   Kushano-Sasanian Peroz 'I' (AD 246–85): cursive Bactrian.
6   Greco-Bactrian Agathocles (*c*.190–180 BC): Greek and Brahmi.
7   Western Satrap Rudrasena I (AD 199–222), son of Rudrasimha: Brahmi.
8   Agathocles: Kharoshthi.
9   Greco-Bactrian Apollodotus I (*c*.180–160 BC): Greek and Kharoshthi.

the French archaeologist Louis-Frédérick-Joseph Caignart de Saulcy (1807–80) and orientalist Jules Oppert (1825–1905) in the mid nineteenth century.

Greek scripts

Greek colonists in the time of Alexander the Great (336–323 BC) and Seleucus I (312–281 BC) introduced Greek as the language and script of administration to Central Asia and Afghanistan. Its pervasive spread was already apparent by the time of the Mauryan emperor Ashoka (*c*.269–232 BC), whose rock edits at Qandahar and Laghman in eastern Afghanistan are in Greek and Aramaic. After Diodotus broke away from the Seleucid empire in *c*.250 BC to form an independent kingdom in Bactria and Sogdiana (p. 50), Greek remained the language of administration for the Bactrian and Indo-Greeks (fig. 26.1), while the tradition of its use on coin legends – albeit in an increasingly modified form – continued among the successor dynasties in these regions down to the Kushans (fig. 26.2).

Bactrian

Over time in Central Asia and Afghanistan, the local dialect known as Bactrian continued to use the Greek script, but with additional letters to denote pronunciations not present in the original language. This was not initially realised by nineteenth-century scholars and collectors. The most notable difference is the Bactrian letter þ (*sh*) which was misread as Greek *ρ* (*rho*) (fig. 26.3; pp. 187–8). So *ΚΑΝΗϷΚΙ* (Kanishka) and *ΚΟϷΑΝΟ* (Koshano, i.e. Kushan), for example, were misread as Kanerkes and Korano, until the distinction was finally comprehended by Cunningham (1890, pp. 6–7; p. 207 below).

Bactrian replaced the use of Greek and Kharoshthi on Kushan coins in the reign of Kanishka I (*c*. AD 127–50). The convention of a monolingual Bactrian legend on Kushan coins continued to the time of Vasudeva I (*c*. AD 190–227), when the addition of a small Brahmi control mark was introduced by one of the mints (fig. 26.4). Brahmi legends gradually became predominant on the coins of successive Kushan rulers, with the Bactrian legend becoming increasingly marginalised around the edge of the flan, before disappearing altogether by the end of the reign of Vasudeva II (*c*. AD 297–310).

In Bactria and the lands ruled by the Kushano-Sasanians and the later Huns, cursive Bactrian script remained the norm for coin legends (fig. 26.5), inscriptions and documents down to the eighth century AD (Sims-Williams 2002, pp. 225–6).

Indian scripts

> In the scarcity of authentic materials for the ancient, and even the modern, history of the *Hindu* race, importance is justly attached to all genuine . . . inscriptions on stone and metal, which are occasionally discovered. . . . If these be carefully preserved and diligently examined; and the facts, ascertained from them, be judiciously employed towards elucidating the scattered information, which can yet be collected from the remains of Indian literature, a satisfactory progress may be finally made in investigating the history of the *Hindus*.
> (Colebrooke 1807, p. 398, cf. Salomon 1998, pp. 202–3)[2]

Brahmi

Indian scripts are syllabic. Brahmi – one of the earliest – appeared in the Mauryan period (third century BC) as an almost fully developed 'pan-Indian national script', used for inscriptions in Prakrit (i.e. Middle Indo-Aryan) languages

(Salomon 1998, pp. 17–31). The script and its derivatives are written left to right. Although Brahmi's own origins are uncertain – and the subject of some nationalistic dispute – all modern Indic scripts evolved from it. Its earliest use in the regions between the Punjab and Afghanistan south of the Hindu Kush occurs on the bilingual bronze coinage of the Greco-Bactrian kings Agathocles (c.190–180 BC) and Pantaleon (c.190–185 BC) which carry a Greek legend *ΒΑΣΙΛΕΩΣ ΑΓΑΘΟΚΛΕΟΥΣ / ΠΑΝΤΑΛΕΟΝΤΟΣ*, 'of king Agathocles'/'Pantaleon' on the reverse and a Prakrit translation of the same legend – *Rajane Agathuklayasa/ Paṃtalevasa* – written in Brahmi on the obverse (fig. 26.6; Bopearachchi 1991, p. 176, pl. 7, ser. 10; p. 182, pl. 9, ser. 6). The use of Kharoshthi in this context was quickly substituted (see below). However, Brahmi re-emerged at the beginning of the third century AD on later Kushan coinage and ultimately replaced the use of both Bactrian and Kharoshthi in the north-western subcontinent.

When Europeans first began to take an interest in Indian epigraphy in the late eighteenth century, all knowledge of archaic scripts had been lost (Salomon 1998, pp. 199–215). The first breakthrough was made by Charles Wilkins (1749–1836), a writer in the service of the East India Company from 1770, who was the first Englishman to acquire a thorough knowledge of Sanskrit.[3] In 1781 he managed to read two inscriptions of the ninth-century Pala period by comparing them with known forms of Devanagari and Bengali scripts (Wilkins 1788, 1788a). By working backwards from this point, he was subsequently able to read the late Brahmi inscription of Anantavarman in the sixth-century cave at Nagarjuni (Wilkins 1788b).

In 1784 the Asiatic Society of Bengal was founded by Sir William Jones (1746–94), a newly appointed judge of the Supreme Court in Calcutta (1783), with Wilkins as a founding member. These two pioneers in Sanskrit learning used the Society and the journal *Asiatick Researches* to create a forum for encouraging the further study of Indian philology and epigraphy, thereby making the subject accessible to Europeans. Jones, the president of the new Society, was an exceptional linguist himself, said to have been fluent in 13 languages, with a working knowledge of 28 others. He was also the first to notice the resemblance of Sanskrit to Latin and Greek.[4] The gradual progress made by the end of the eighteenth century towards understanding Brahmi – with contributions from Jones, the Indian pandits with whom he worked, Wilkins and others – can be traced in the early issues of *Asiatick Researches* 1788–99 (Salomon 1998, p. 202).

Henry Colebrooke (1765–1837)[5] achieved the next big breakthrough in 1801, with his translation of the inscription of Vigrahapala on the Delhi-Topra pillar, in which he correctly read the date as Vikrama 1220 (AD 1164). He produced an accurate transliteration and reliable facsimiles, not just of this text but also of the inscriptions of the Mauryan emperor Ashoka (c.269–232 BC) on the same pillar (1801, pp. 175–82; cf. Salomon 1998, p. 202). There are actually two pillars inscribed with Ashokan edicts in Delhi. They are now generally referred to as the Delhi-Topra and the Delhi-Meerut pillars, both having been brought to Delhi in 1356 by the sultan Firuz Shah Tughluq (AH 752–90/AD 1351–88), from their original sites at Topra and Meerut, north-west of the city, and were recorded by early travellers such as William Finch in 1611 (Cunningham 1871, vol. I, pp. 161–9). Delhi-Topra has the most comprehensive pillar inscriptions, containing edicts I–VII.

Another Ashokan inscription – the rock edict at Dhauli in Orissa – was discovered and copied in 1820 by Colin Mackenzie, then Surveyor-General of India, who recognised it as being 'in the very identical character' as the Delhi pillars (Allen 2002, pp. 122–3). In 1822 a second rock edict was found at Girnar and partially copied by Colonel James Tod, British Resident in Rajasthan, while en route through Gujarat (Allen 2002, pp. 178–9).

Although Colebrooke's accurate facsimiles of the Delhi-Topra edicts made Ashokan Brahmi available to scholars for the first time, actual decipherment of the script did not immediately occur. Instead, over the next 30 years, gradual progress was made in deciphering a variety of later, post-Gupta local scripts which had originally derived from Brahmi. Endeavours to decode earlier forms of the script were given new impetus in 1834, when T. S. Burk obtained facsimiles of the inscriptions, including those of Ashoka and Samudragupta, on the Allahabad pillar.[6] These were sent to James Prinsep as Secretary of the Asiatic Society of Bengal who, although only an amateur with limited knowledge of Sanskrit and other Indian languages, 'displayed a combination of intuition and methodical thought which would do any modern decipherer proud' (Salomon 1998, p. 204).

Prinsep was the first to suspect that the language of the inscriptions was not Sanskrit, primarily because there was only a 'rare occurrence of double letters' (1834f, pp. 116–17). In his initial attempt at the Gupta Brahmi inscription he produced a palaeographic table of the different consonantal characters and correctly identified the phonetic value of most of the vowel signs except ī (Cunningham 1871, p. xi). At the same time efforts by Rev. William Hodge Mill[7] and others concentrated on the same inscription, again with some success, but also some inaccuracies (Thomas 1858, vol. I, pp. 240–6).

Later in the same year, Brian Hodgson (1800–94), the British Resident of Nepal, discovered the Ashokan pillars at Mathiah (Lauriya-Nandangarh) and Radiah (Lauriya-Araraj) in northern Bihar and recognised that the inscriptions were again in the same 'characters' as the Allahabad edicts (1834, pp. 481–3). In the case of Lauriya-Nandangarh, it was actually a rediscovery, for drawings of the inscription, column and capital had already been made by G. N. Rind in 1797 (British Library OIOC BL/WD 3471).

When comparing the two inscriptions with that of Delhi-Topra, Prinsep realised that the texts corresponded, all beginning with a recurrent series of sixteen syllables 'which may be supposed to be some formula of invocation'. He also correctly identified the consonants *ya* and *va* (1834g, pp. 483, 485). The same consonants and ten more were identified by Rev. John Stevenson (1798–1858)[8] by comparing the dedicatory inscriptions in the caves of Karle with the Gupta Brahmi of the Allahabad pillar (Salomon 1998, p. 206). In 1836 another advance was made by the Norwegian scholar Christian Lassen (1800–76), Professor of Sanskrit at Bonn, who correctly read the Brahmi coin legend of Agathocles (fig. 26.6; Prinsep 1836b, pp. 723–4).[9]

At the beginning of 1837, under the auspices of an Asiatic Society of Bengal special committee, it was decided to raise and restore the Allahabad pillar, complete with a reproduction lion capital. But – in the opinion of Cunningham – the attempted replica closely resembled 'a stuffed poodle stuck on an inverted flowerpot' and the pillar was erected without it (Allen 2002, pp. 179–80). However, the exercise, undertaken by the Central Provinces Public Works Department under the direction of Edward Smith, Bengal Engineers, provided the opportunity for more accurate impressions of the inscriptions. These were 'taken off on cotton cloth and on paper' and 'placed at Prinsep's command the full means of checking and correcting the errors of the early copy, while his own more mature experience in the normal forms of these and other Sanskrit [sic] characters rendered his lithographed transcript and transliteration more than usually trustworthy' (Thomas 1858, vol. I, p. 232).

Over the next month the pace of discoveries quickened. In early May Prinsep received engravings of 28 'Saurāshtra' (i.e. Western Satrap) coins, with legible Brahmi inscriptions of the first to early fifth century AD (fig. 26.7; Jha and Rajgor 1994). Beginning on 11 May with an exhortation to Cunningham – 'Oh! but we must decipher them! I'll warrant they have not touched them at home *yet*' – by 7 o'clock the following morning he had realised that each coin gave the names of both the ruler and his father, thereby producing 'a train of some eight or ten names to rival the Guptas!! Hurra! I hope the chaps at home won't seize the prize first. No fear of Wilson at any rate!' (1871, pp. ix–x). Two days later, he reported 'The Sanskrit on these coins is beautiful, being in the genitive case after the Greek fashion . . . [with the] name losing the genitive affix when joined to *putrasya* ['son of']. . . . *Chulao bhai, juldee puhonchoge* [go on brother, we shall soon get there]'.

It was at this point that Edward Smith supplied copies of the dedicatory Brahmi inscriptions on the Buddhist stupas of Sanchi and, in a letter to Cunningham dated 23 May 1837, Prinsep announced that he had finally cracked the code for deciphering the Ashokan edicts (1871, pp. xi–xii):

> I can read the Delhi No. 1 [Delhi-Topra pillar edicts], . . . the Bhilsa [Sanchi] inscriptions have enlightened me. Each line is engraved on a separate pillar or *dhwaja*. Then, thought I, they must be gifts of private individuals, whose names will be recorded. All end in *dānam* – that must mean 'gift', or 'given', *dānam* – genitive must be prefixed. Let's see:
> Isa-pālitasa-cha Sāmanasa-cha dānam
> The gift of Isa-pālita (protected of God) and of Sāmana. . . .
> Eh? will not this do? and the pillar inscription
> Devānam piya piyadasi Raja hevam ahā
> The most particularly-beloved-of-the-gods Raja declareth thus. I think with Ratna Pāla, whom I shall summon, we shall be able to read the whole of these manifestoes.

This is very close to the correct reading of this introductory formula, viz. *devānaṃpiye piyadasi lāja hevaṃāha*: 'the beloved of the gods, king Priyadarshin, speaks thus' (Salomon 1998, pp. 205–6). The same year George Turnour identified the 'beloved of the gods' as the Mauryan emperor Ashoka mentioned in the Buddhist Singhalese Chronicles (1837–8, p. 791). A plea from Prinsep also produced better and complete copies of the Dhauli and Girnar rock edicts, and early in 1838 he discovered in the latter edict the names of the contemporary Greek kings Antiochus, Ptolemy, Antigonus and Magas and suggested a date of *c.* 247 BC for Ashoka (1871, pp. xiv–xv; see p. 38 below).

As Salomon points out (1998, p. 208), it is Prinsep's success as a decipherer which is significant: by 1838 he had produced 'a virtually perfect' reading of the Ashokan Brahmi alphabet (1838a, pp. 271–6); but his translations and interpretations were uneven. Nevertheless, in the words of Charles Allen (2002, p. 190):

> The discoveries . . . did much more than unlock the words on the pillar and rock inscriptions of Delhi and elsewhere. They gave early Indian history a solid foundation it had never had before; they transformed a name into a figure of flesh and blood; and they allowed the world to see into the mind of a monarch of the third century BCE. . . . Only one . . . rock edict, found in Hyderabad in 1915, carries Ashoka's full name, which appears as *Devānaṃ piyasa aśokasa*.

On the success of deciphering Mauryan Brahmi hinged the subsequent decipherment of Kharoshthi.

Kharoshthi

Like Brahmi, Kharoshthi first appears in a more or less fully developed form in the rock edict inscriptions of the Mauryan emperor Ashoka (*c.*269–232 BC) at Shahbazgarhi in the Peshawar Valley and at Mansehra, which lies in the modern district of the same name, in the Hazara Division, east of the Indus river and north of Abbottabad (Salomon 1998, pp. 42–8). The script was used for writing the Middle Indo-Aryan language, 'North-western Prakrit' or Gandhari (Salomon 2002). Unlike all other Indian scripts – but like Aramaic and Pahlavi – it is written right to left. Its grammatical and phonetic structure also differs from other Prakrits; it has a 'high degree of graphic ambiguity' in that there is little distinction between characters such as *da*, *ta* and *ra*; and other aberrant characteristics made decipherment of the script problematic (Salomon 1998, p. 215).

Kharoshthi probably originated in Gandhara or Taxila, but the area of its general use (as evidenced by coin legends and inscriptions) progressively extended under Bactrian and Indo-Greek, Indo-Scythian and Kushan rule (second century BC to third century AD) as far west as Wardak, north of the Oxus, east through the passes of the Karakorum mountains along the trade routes of the Tarim Basin, and south as far as Mathura and the western coastal regions of northern India. The spread of the script was closely linked to the expansion of Buddhism. As Salomon has noted, most of the surviving records are Buddhist, while the dedicatory and memorial inscriptions from such outlying regions as Bactria and China 'are often hardly distinguishable in form from similar inscriptions from India, and presumably reflect the presence of Gāndhārī-speaking Indian monks in the Buddhist monasteries of these places' (1998, p. 46).

The first Greco-Bactrian king to use Kharoshthi on coins was again Agathocles (*c.*190–180 BC). Examples of his (monolingual) Kharoshthi issues are, however, comparatively rare. They combine the Indian designs of a five-arched hill and the name *Akathukreyasa* with a tree in railing and the title (?) *Hiranasame* (fig. 26.8; Bopearachchi 1991, p. 176, pl. 8 ser. 11). The first to introduce bilingual legends in this script and Greek was Apollodotus I

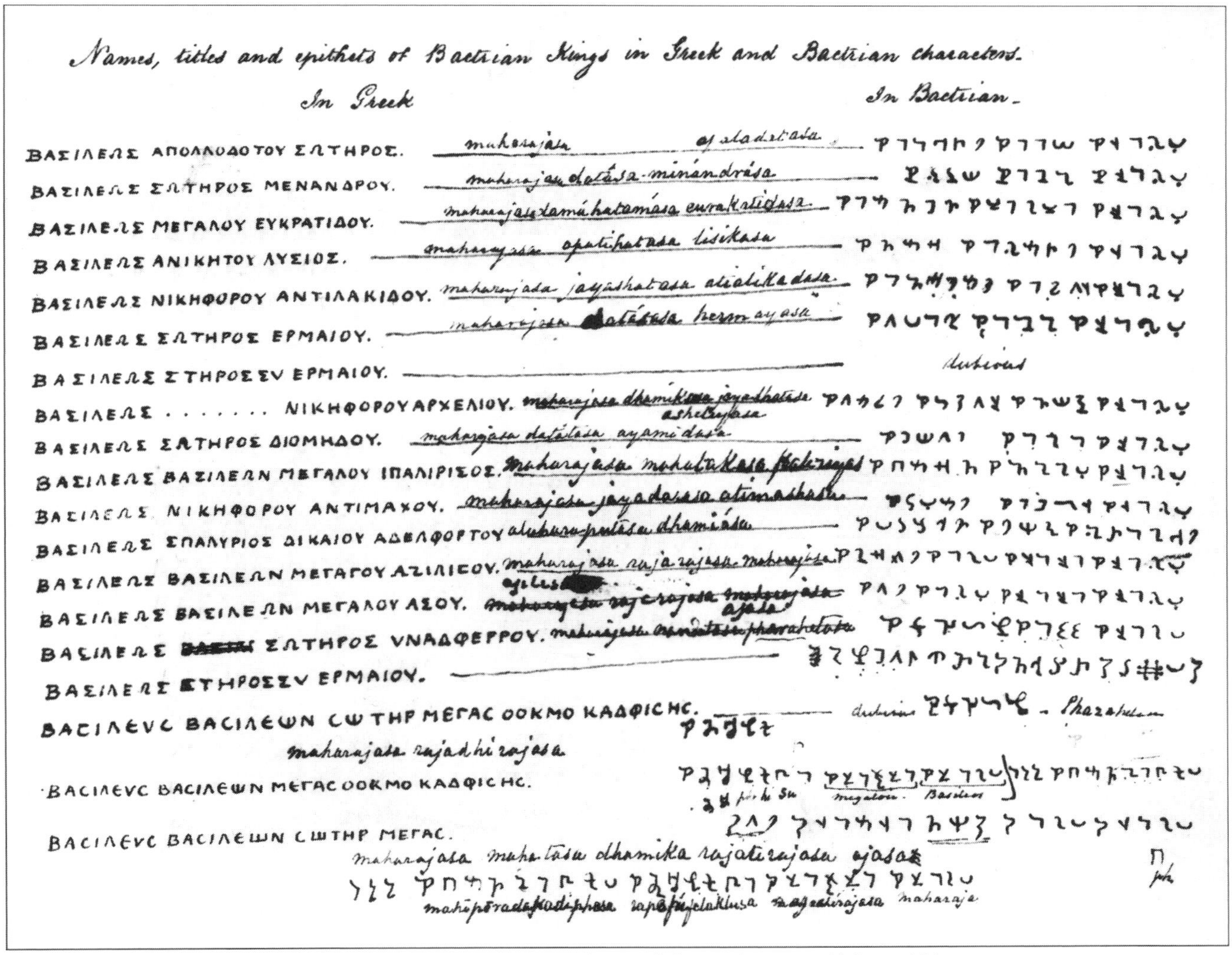

Figure 27 Masson's comparative chart of Greek and Kharoshthi coin legends, compiled December 1835, with later additions.

(c.180–160 BC) (fig. 26.9). The convention was continued by successive rulers and dynasties until the time of Kanishka I (c. AD 127–50), who replaced the (by then debased) Greek and Kharoshthi legends on coins with monolingual legends in Bactrian. The decline in Kushan power in the third to early fourth century saw a parallel demise in the use of Kharoshthi. In Afghanistan south of the Hindu Kush and the Indian subcontinent, it was replaced by Brahmi; in the lands north of the Hindu Kush, Bactrian continued to hold sway.

The earliest nineteenth-century accounts of the script can be initially misleading. When James Prinsep, for example, writes about the 'discovery of the Bactrian alphabet', he is referring to Kharoshthi, not the evolved Greek script now known by that name (1838, p. 636). More usually, however, Kharoshthi was – equally erroneously – referred to initially as 'Pehlvi' (i.e. Pahlavi) and later, as 'Arian' (Cunningham 1872, pp. 181–2). The key to its decipherment was first noticed by Masson, who pointed out in a note to Prinsep (Prinsep 1835, p. 329):

the Pehlvi signs which he had found to stand for the words *MENANDROY, APOLLODOTOY, ERMAIOY, BASILEOS* and *SOTHROS*. When a supply of coins came into my own hands, sufficiently legible to pursue the inquiry, I soon verified the accuracy of his observation; found the same signs, with slight variation, constantly to recur; and extended the words thus authenticated, to the names of twelve kings, and to six titles or epithets. It immediately struck me that if the genuine Greek names were faithfully expressed in the unknown character, a clue would, through them, be formed to unravel the value of a portion of the

alphabet, which might, in its turn, be applied to the translated epithets and titles, and thus lead to knowledge of the language employed. Incompetent as I felt myself to this investigation, it was too seductive not to lead me to a humble attempt at its solution.

The realisation that the reverse legends on the bilingual issues of the Bactrian and Indo-Greeks were direct translations of the Greek on the obverse of the coins was the starting point for deciphering Kharoshthi. The original note from Masson demonstrating his discovery – and annotated by Prinsep – survives in one of the bound volumes of Prinsep's Manuscripts in the Ashmolean Museum (MSS III, f. 16v). In it Masson transcribes the inscription on the steatite casket from Bimaran stupa 2 – excavated in 1834 (fig. 186) – and notes with an asterisk to the right of each line '* the commencement of the inscriptions, if they be Pehlevi, which reads from the right'. He further comments: 'the word Basileos (*BASILEOS*) or its equivalent in Pehlevi, if such be the language on the Greek Bactrian coins, does not occur here'. He goes on to list the identified words on coins – viz. *BASILEOS, SOTHROS, MENANDROY, APOLLODOTOY* and *ERMAIOY* – together with their correct Kharoshthi equivalents (fig. 27).

Prinsep's progress in following up Masson's discovery can also still be traced in his manuscript notes. Several pages show the variants of Kharoshthi letters – some again evidently supplied by Masson (MSS III, f. 18) – or Prinsep's efforts to determine what the actual language was (MSS III, ff. 16v–24).

There is even an attempt to equate Kharoshthi with Hebrew, as well as with all known Indian and Iranian scripts, including the Pahlavi inscriptions on Ker Porter's coin drawings (fig. 24; Prinsep MSS III, f. 17). This was due to the mistaken assumption – shared by Grotefend – that 'the inscriptions were written in, and followed the graphic patterns of, Semitic or Iranian languages' (Salomon 1998, p. 210). The misconception arose largely because it was not yet realised that the ancient Afghanistan regions of Arachosia and the Parapamisadae to the south of the Hindu Kush mountains had often formed part of India in earlier times. Only in 1838 did Prinsep (1838, p. 643; Thomas 1858, vol. II, p. 132)

> throw off the fetters of an interpretation through the Semitic languages, and at once found an easy solution of all the names and the epithets through the pliant, the wonder-working Pālī. . . . The best test of the superiority of a Pālī interpretation will be found in its application to the several royal titles of the Greek kings, which were previously quite unintelligible. The first of these is simply ΒΑΣΙΛΕΩΣ, which is constantly rendered by *maharājasa* ['of the (great) king'].

As with Brahmi, it was again the Prakrit genitive case that provided the key, i.e. Prinsep's recognition that the word-ending character Ρ was *sa* (Salomon 1998, p. 211). Apart from coins, the main source available to Prinsep was the Kharoshthi inscription dated in the year 18 of Kanishka I, which had been unearthed by Claude-Auguste Court in the remains of the Mera-ka-Dheri Buddhist stupa at Manikyala in 1834 (fig. 178; Court 1834; Prinsep 1834e; Konow 1929, pp. 145–50, pl. XXVII.1; see p. 212 below). By 1838 Prinsep 'had so far advanced upon his previous reading, as to define correctly the greater part of the name of the monarch, viz., "Kaneshsm" [*sic*], and to offer a conjectural [incorrect] interpretation of the date' (Thomas 1858, vol. I, p. 143). He was moreover right in thinking that in Kharoshthi the initial vowel signs were 'formed by modification of the alif as in Arabic' and also identified the diacritics for the post-consonantal vowels *i*, *e* and *u* (Prinsep 1838, p. 640; Salomon 1998, p. 212), but fell ill before he could get much further. Working concurrently but independently on the same limited range of material, Lassen also managed to identify a number of characters, realised that the vowel *a* was inherent in all consonants, and that the language was an Indian Prakrit (1838, pp. 18, 26–9, 55). Both 'suspected the absence of long vowels' (Salomon 1998, p. 212).

However, the primary source for deciphering Kharoshthi was an inscription 'almost effaced by time' on a large rock close to the village of Kapurdigarhi (Garhi Kapura), near Shahbazgarhi in the Peshawar Valley (Court 1836a, pp. 394–5; 1836b, p. 481, pl. XXVIII). Court first learned of its existence while stationed at Peshawar in 1836, during Ranjit Singh's bid for control of the North-West Frontier region. Although as an officer of the Sikhs it was unsafe for him to visit the site personally, the local he had employed to search the Peshawar Valley for archaeological remains copied a few of the letters. However, the full import of the Shahbazgarhi rock inscription did not emerge until after Prinsep's death.

In October 1838, while in Peshawar awaiting – in vain – his next East India Company appointment, Masson spent five days at Shahbazgarhi (fig. 28; Masson 1846). He used this time to make the first complete copy of the inscription by coating the rock surface with ink and then taking impressions on cotton cloth. He reports that the work was done to the sounds of battle from local tribesmen 'in mortal conflict', but adds 'we did not on their account remit our labours' (1846, pp. 294, 301, pl. facing p. 298). The impressions covered 50 yards of calico which, together with written copies of the inscription, were presented to the Royal Asiatic Society on Masson's return to London in 1842.

Already by May 1845 it had been realised that 'the subject matter [of the Shahbazgarhi inscription] is intimately connected with that of the Girnar and Dhauli inscriptions' (Proc. ASB 1845), i.e. that the inscription was another edict of the Mauryan emperor Ashoka, with the same text as his edicts in Brahmi already deciphered and translated by Prinsep.[10] Masson's 'labours' made possible a 'nearly perfect' transcription of the Shahbazgarhi inscription by Edwin Norris, Assistant Secretary of the Royal Asiatic Society (1846, pp. 303–14), which was later completed by Horace Wilson, by then Professor of Sanskrit at University College, London (1850).[11]

The manuscript of Masson's article on Begram – dated Kabul, 31 December 1835 and partly published by Prinsep in 1836 – records in a small way this process of decipherment. It includes a page of the 'Names, titles and epithets of Bactrian kings in Greek and Bactrian [i.e. Kharoshthi] characters' (fig. 27; Uncat. MSS 2, f. 35). This was subsequently rearranged and printed without acknowledgement, but with the titles deciphered, as part of Prinsep's 1838 article (Thomas 1858, vol. I, pl. XII). At some point, the manuscript was returned to Masson, with the plates of coin illustrations still retaining Prinsep's pencilled notes selecting specific drawings intended for publication. At a later date – probably after Norris's transcription became available in 1846 – Masson then inserted the correct translations of the script throughout his manuscript. One is the correct reading of *kushana* on a coin legend of Kujula Kadphises (Uncat. MSS 2, f. 32, pl. 3, fig. 30). Yet, even though this identification had been made before Masson's death in 1853, it took a long time before the link between the Kharoshthi *sha* and the Bactrian Þ was made: twenty years later Cunningham still wrote (1872, pp. 181–2):

> This title of *Shao* or *Zao*, was afterwards changed to Rao, PAO, by Kanishka and his successors, in conformity with a peculiar law of the Turki dialect, which changes the initial *sh* or *z* to *r*. The tribal name of KOPANO is represented in the Arian legends of the coins by *Kushān* and *Khusān*, and in the inscriptions by *Gushān*. Here, therefore, we have the same change from *sh* to *r* in the middle of a word.

Figure 28 Masson's sketch of the Shahbazgarhi rock edict of Ashoka.

Already in 1845 Cunningham claimed that he had 'found the Ariano-Pali equivalent for every letter of the Sanskrit alphabet' (1845, p. 430). But how far short this optimistic assertion fell can be partly assessed from his report in January 1848 of his discovery of the Panjtar inscription, which begins (Konow 1929, p. 70, pl. XIII.4):[12]

> Saṁ 1 100 20 1 1 śravaṇasa masasa di praḍhame 1 maharayasa Gushaṇasa raja[mi]
> Anno 122, on the first – 1 – day of the month Śrāvaṇa, in the reign of the Gushaṇa Great King

Cunningham, however, read this as 'Samvat 37, or the first day of the bright half of the month of Sravand, in the reign of Mahadaya, king of the Gushang (tribe)', thus illustrating that he had failed to recognise the title *maharayasa* 'of the Great King' – a slight variation of *maharajasa* already deciphered by Prinsep in 1838 (p. 24 above) – and had completely misinterpreted the date. In fact he appears to have read the date 𝄃3𝄃𝄃 incorrectly from left to right, ignored the three strokes each designating the numeral 'I' and mistaken the Kharoṣṭhī numerals 3 (20) and 𝄁 (100) as '3' and '7', instead of calculating it as 1 x 100 + 20 + 1 + 1 = 122.

As Salomon notes (1998, pp. 213–14), Cunningham subsequently credited himself with identifying the 'true values' of 11 letters and several consonantal conjuncts (1854a, p. 714), and still later complained that 'though all these readings have now been generally adopted, scarcely one of them has been acknowledged as mine' (1888a, p. 204). Salomon's assessment of these statements, however, is just (1998, pp. 214):

> while it is undoubtedly true that Cunningham did discover several of the letters . . . his sketchy presentations and questionable interpretations make it difficult to confirm many of his claims. One cannot help but suspect that his repeated claims to a major role in the decipherment of Kharoṣṭhī are somewhat inflated. Surely he played a significant part . . . but he cannot be said to have equalled the brilliant insights and fundamental contributions of Prinsep and his other predecessors. In balance it may be fairest to say that the decipherment of Kharoṣṭhī was a combined effort in which Prinsep again takes the place of honor [*sic*], with Lassen and Norris making important contributions and Cunningham, Grotefend, and Masson playing significant secondary roles.

A minor quibble is perhaps that greater emphasis should be placed on the importance of Masson's contribution, not in the decipherment of Kharoshthi *per se*, but in supplying all the raw materials – in the form of legends, diligently transcribed from his huge collection of coins, and an accurate copy of the Shahbazgarhi inscription – which made decipherment possible.

Decipherment of all these scripts made a vast wealth of inscriptional and textual material available for the first time, for use in attempting to reconstruct a historical picture of the past. But as Salomon notes (1998, p. 226):

> The main problem is that most inscriptions are not essentially historical documents but rather donative or panegyric records which may incidentally record some amount of historical information. Thus the standards of objectivity, precision, and comprehensiveness that guide modern historical thought are completely absent in these sources, and the modern scholar must exercise cautious critical judgement in evaluating them.

Use of these sources as 'history' – and the chasms between different hypotheses reached by way of different interpretations of the same fragments of written 'evidence' –

is still a hotly disputed academic minefield more than a century and a half after the decipherment of these scripts.

Notes

1 De Sacy was also the first to work on the Rosetta Stone in 1802. Again, by working from the Greek inscription, he discovered the Demotic characters for the names Ptolemy and Alexander.

2 For a detailed account of the history of Indian epigraphic studies see Salomon 1998, pp. 199–225 and Allen 2002, pp. 177–90.

3 Dubbed 'Sanskrit-mad' by Colebrooke (cf. Salomon 1998, p. 200), he established the first printing press for oriental languages in 1778. He published, *inter alia*, two Sanskrit grammars (in 1779 and 1808), deciphered numerous inscriptions and translated the *Bhagavadgītā*, Narayana's *Hitopadeśa* (Fables of Pilpai) and Kalidasa's *Abhijñāna Śākuntala*. He was awarded the 'Princeps Literaturae Sanskriticae' medal by the Royal Society of Literature and was knighted in 1833.

4 He published a Persian grammar (1772), Latin commentaries on Asiatic poetry (1774), and translated a life of Nadir Shah (1770, from Persian into French) and Arabic poems (*Moallakat* 1780), as well as a number of Sanskrit texts, including Kalidasa's *Abhijñāna Śākuntala*, Jayadeva's *Gītagovinda*, Narayana's *Hitopadeśa*, the *Mānavadharmaśāstra* (Laws of Manu) and part of the Vedas (1784–94).

5 The son of Sir George Colebrooke (Chairman, East India Company Court of Directors, 1769), he began his career in India (1782/3–1814) as Assistant Collector in Tirhut and Purnea, later rising to the position of a judge of the *Sadr Diwani Adalat* Court (1801–14). Amongst other things, he was a Member of the Supreme Council (1807–12); unsalaried Professor of Hindu Law and Sanskrit at Fort William College, Calcutta; and President of the Asiatic Society of Bengal (1807–14). In London, he became a founding member and Director of the Royal Asiatic Society (1823). 'At first he disliked Oriental literature, but felt compelled, in the exercise of his duties, to learn law through the Sanskrit language' (Buckland 1906, p. 88). Apart from being a profound Sanskrit scholar, he wrote on such diverse subjects as Hindu and Roman law, Jainism, the Vedas, Indian algebra, astronomy, philosophy and customs, botany, geology, philology and the height of the Himalayas.

6 The Allahabad pillar contains edicts I–VI, the Queen's Edict and the Kaushambi Edict or Schism Edict, as well as later inscriptions of Samudragupta (AD 335–80) and the Mughal emperor Jahangir (1605–28). It was probably originally set up in Kaushambi and was moved to Allahabad fort later, possibly by Jahangir. Before restoration in 1837, the largest section of it 'had been used by an over-zealous public works engineer as a road-roller' (Allen 2002, p. 123).

7 The principal of Bishop's College, Calcutta, and Vice-President of the Asiatic Society.

8 He was sent to India by the Scottish Missionary Society in 1823 and became an East India Company chaplain in Bombay in 1834. Another distinguished Sanskrit scholar, he was a pioneer editor and translator of Vedic literature, a founder of the *Bombay Gazette* and President of the Asiatic Society of Bombay.

9 Prinsep quotes an extract from a letter received from Lassen announcing his discovery.

10 Among James Prinsep's manuscripts there is clearly at least one posthumous insert, for the page is entitled 'Arian alphabet from Asoka's edict on the rock at Kapoordigiri 40 miles NE from Peshawur decyphered [*sic*] by Mr Norris, Royal A. Society, from Masson's cloth and lamp black impressions & manuscript' (MSS III, f. 16v).

11 A second inscription on a smaller rock at Shahbazgarhi was discovered only in 1888 and reported by Harold Deane, Assistant Commissioner of the Mardan District at that time (NWFP 1888).

12 In January 1848, on his first visit to the Peshawar Valley, Cunningham recovered the inscription at Salimpur near Panjtar, in the neighbourhood of Naogram, and another inscription from Ohind, dated year 61. Misreading the dates, he thought them to be 'the oldest dated inscriptions hitherto found in India', so considered 'that the possession of them will be very cheaply purchased at the hire of a single camel for their carriage' (Cunningham 1848, p. 104). Both inscriptions were deposited in the Lahore Residency, but had disappeared by 1853, 'most probably to become the curry-[grinding]stone of one of the Residency servants' (Cunningham 1875, pp. 58, p. 61).

Part 2

Constructing the past

3 Empires and dynasties

There are but few notices of Bactrian history to be found in ancient authors; and some even, of those few, do not agree: so that we are compelled, in the absence of historical aid, to examine the numismatology of Bactria, as Butler's philosophers examined the moon, by its own light. And thus a good cabinet of coins of the Bactrian princes, is to an experienced numismatist
'– A famous history . . . enroll'd,
In everlasting monuments of brass –'
from which he may draw the data for a chronological arrangement of those princes, many of whom are 'of dynasties unknown to history'. (Cunningham 1840, p. 867)

Cunningham speaks here of the ancient province of Bactria – comprising the Amu Darya (Oxus river) region of Uzbekistan, Tajikistan and northern Afghanistan southwards as far as the Hindu Kush mountains – but his words could equally apply to all the terrain east of Iran as far as the Punjab (fig. 2). There are very few precise dates that can be used for reconstructing the history of this region before the advent of Islam. The earliest certain date is the invasion as far as the Punjab in 326–325 BC by Alexander the Great (336–323 BC). So it has been necessary to build a chronology from inscriptions, references in western and Chinese sources and, above all, from the evidence of coins. The history of these lands – and with it, the development of coinage – is linked with a series of great empires, particularly the Achaemenids, Parthians and Sasanians of Iran, the Greek successors of Alexander, the Mauryans and Kushans, whose control over vast areas of territory encouraged not only the use of standardised units of payment but also innovations in coin design.

The ancient history of Iran and the regions to the west is better recorded. Even so, coins – more than any other of the vast array of ancient artefacts – present the most comprehensive visual record of the empires and dynasties that ruled between the Mediterranean Sea and India from the sixth century BC to the seventh century AD. Coins are thus fundamental to the process of reconstructing the history of these regions, since many of the kings and dynasties are not known from other sources. The choice of coin designs and legends also throw light on cultural aspects, such as religion and language. The chronological arrangement here is based on modern scholarship, but attempts at the same time to chart the progress of the nineteenth-century collectors and scholars in their efforts to discover the forgotten history of these lands. What emerges from this process is how quickly the basic historical framework still in use today was established and how little progress has been made since in resolving key problems of chronology and identification arising from contradictory evidence, particularly in the written sources.

Achaemenids (550–330 BC)

For the first time, countries that were hitherto divided among hostile rival kingdoms were gathered into a single, unified state,

Figure 29 Tomb of Cyrus at Pasargadae.

from the Indus to the Aegean Sea. Over the *longue durée*, this is the fundamental contribution of the conquests of Cyrus and Cambyses. (Briant 2002, p. 873)

The dynasty of the Achaemenids came to power in Iran under Cyrus the Great (550–530 BC), a Mede on his mother's side and a Persian on his father's side (Herodotus I.107).[1] When Cyrus successfully rebelled against his maternal grandfather, Astyages, king of Media, the event was recorded in Babylonian sources in the third or sixth year of the reign of Nabonidus (554/3 or 550/49 BC). Cyrus soon turned his attention to Lydia and conquered the capital Sardis in 547/6 BC, followed by Babylonia in 539 BC. He died in 530 BC while fighting the Massagetae tribe on his north-eastern frontier near the Aral Sea and was buried at his capital, Pasargadae (fig. 29). By the time of his death the Achaemenid realm stretched from the Mediterranean to eastern Iran and from the shores of the Black Sea to Arabia (J. Curtis 2000, pp. 39–41).

Under Cyrus' eldest son, Cambyses (530–522 BC), a series of successful campaigns expanded the kingdom into an empire. After his conquest of Egypt in 525 BC, Cambyses adopted the title 'Pharaoh of Upper and Lower Egypt', but during his absence from Iran the Persian aristocracy staged a rebellion under Gaumata, a Median *magus* (priest). Cambyses' brother Bardiya, the younger son of Cyrus, had been appointed satrap of Parthia, Carmania and Khorezmia by his father (Ctesias, *Persica* § 688, f. 13a.10–13).[2] On his way back to Iran to deal with the threat, Cambyses died of a self-inflicted wound, leaving it to Darius I (522–486 BC) to take power, crush the rebellion and install himself as the new king of the Achaemenids (fig. 30). Darius is said to have carried the quiver for Cyrus (Aelian XII.43) and was the lance-bearer for Cambyses in Egypt (Herodotus III.139; Briant 2002, p. 112).

Darius describes the rebellion in his trilingual inscription of 520/19 BC at Bisitun (ancient Bagistana) near Kirmanshah in western Iran (figs 22–3). However, his description of events – such as the murder of Bardiya during Cambyses'

Figure 30 Cylinder seal of Darius with trilingual cuneiform inscription in Old Persian, Elamite and Babylonian: 'I [am] Darius, great king'.

absence and his own encounter with the various rebels – has to be interpreted with caution (DB.I, §§ 10–14; Kent 1953, pp. 119–20):

> When Cambyses had gone off to Egypt, after that the people became evil. After that the Lie waxed great in the country, both in Persia and in Media and in the other provinces. . . .
>
> There was one man, a Magian, Gaumata by name; . . . He lied to the people thus: 'I am Smerdis, the son of Cyrus, brother of Cambyses'. After that all people became rebellious from Cambyses. . . . He seized the kingdom. . . . After that Cambyses died of his own hand. . . .
>
> By the favour of Ahuramazda this I did: I strove until I re-established our royal house on its foundation. . . . So, I strove, by the favour of Ahuramazda, so that Gaumata the Magian did not remove our royal house.

At Bisitun, Darius proclaims himself 'the Great King, King of Kings, King in Persia, King of countries, son of Hystaspes, grandson of Arsames, an Achaemenian' (DB.I, § 1: Kent 1953, p. 119). His great-grandfather is cited as Ariaramnes, whose father was Teispes and grandfather was Achaemenes: 'For this reason we are called Achaemenians. From long ago we have been noble. From long ago our family had been kings' (DB.I, § 3; Kent 1953, p. 119).

Darius clearly tries to link himself with the royal line of Cyrus, who was a descendant of Teispes (Shishpish) on his paternal side, but this lineage may have been constructed in order to win support from the aristocracy. He married Atossa, one of the daughters of Cyrus, and it was Xerxes, the son of this marriage, whom he appointed as his successor, not his eldest son, Ariobarzanes, whose mother was the daughter of Gobryas (Briant 2002, pp. 113, 132).

The fact that, after killing Gaumata, Darius faced rebellion throughout the empire – particularly in Persia, the Achaemenid heartland, as well as in Elam and Media – shows that there must have been opposition to his seizure of power. This is clear in the case of Media, where a Median Phraortes, 'of the family of Cyaxares' (DB.II, § 24; Kent 1953, p. 123), claimed his right to the throne as a relative of Astyages, the king of Media and paternal grandfather of Cyrus. The uprising spread as far as Parthia, Margiana and Arachosia in the east, and Babylonia and Armenia in the west. When Darius lists his ardent supporters who helped suppress the rebellion, he notes that all were Persian: Intaphernes, Otanes, Gobryas, Megabyzus and Ardumanish (DB.IV, § 68; Kent 1953, p. 132). This supports the idea that Persians (fig. 31) played a more important role within the Achaemenid empire than any other group (Wiesehöfer 2001, pp. 58–9). It seems as if the Medes, although culturally and politically related to the Persians, did not enjoy a privileged position, as

Media became a satrapy and had to pay tribute (Briant 2002, pp. 81–2).

Under Darius the empire reached its greatest extent. His supreme achievement was the organisation of his newly acquired territories. This included introducing a system of tribute; the building of new cities, such as Persepolis (figs 32; 144; 154); the conquest of Samos in the west; and the consolidation of Achaemenid dominion over a vast region stretching from Egypt and northern Greece to the Indus river (Briant 2002, p. 137). The extent of the empire is recorded in his inscriptions at Bisitun and Persepolis (DB.I, § 16; DPe, § 2; Kent 1953, pp. 117, 136), where the following tribute-bearing countries are listed:

> By the favour of Ahuramazda these are the countries which I got into my possession along with this Persian folk, which felt fear of me (and) bore me tribute: Elam, Media, Babylonia, Arabia, Assyria, Egypt, Armenia, Cappadocia, Sardis, Ionians who are of the mainland and (those) who are by the sea, and countries which are across the sea; Sagartia, Parthia, Drangiana, Aria, Bactria, Sogdiana, Chorasmia, Sattagydia, Arachosia, Sind, Gandhara, Scythians, Maka.

A similar list is also given by Herodotus (III.90–6). Darius' inscriptions contain tthe earliest reference to Gandhara (Old Persian *Gandāra*; i.e. the modern Peshawar Valley), although the Gandhari people are mentioned in early Indian texts such as the *Rigveda* (I.126.7) as inhabitants of the extreme north-west Indian subcontinent. The country marks the eastern limit of the Achaemenid empire. However, in the Babylonian and Elamite versions of Darius' inscription at Bisitun (King and Thompson 1907, p. lxix), the empire is said instead to extend only as far as the Parapamisadae (Paruparaesanna), a name used in later Classical sources to denote the region south of the Hindu Kush, including Kapisha (Begram) and modern Kabul (Vogelsang 2005).[3]

Darius was keen to make his political achievements known throughout the empire. As he records at Bisitun (DB.IV, § 70; Kent 1953, p.132):

> By the favour of Ahuramazda this is the inscription which I made. Besides, it was in Aryan, and on clay tablets and on parchment it was composed. . . . Afterwards this inscription I sent off everywhere among the provinces.

This statement is generally regarded as evidence for the introduction of the Old Persian cuneiform script at the beginning of the reign of Darius. Fragments of the same

Figure 31 Guards in Persian dress on the northern staircase of the west wing of the Apadana at Persepolis.

Figure 32 Palace of Darius (Tachara) at Persepolis.

inscription, as well as part of a copy of the Bisitun relief, were found at Babylon, while a later Aramaic copy of the inscription dating from the early fifth century BC is known from Elephantine in Egypt (Briant 2002, p. 123).

The Achamenid empire was divided into provinces each with its own governor or satrap (*khshathrapata*). Royal residences had already been maintained at Ecbatana, Sardis, Bactra, Babylon and Susa under Cyrus, while Pasargadae in Persis had become the new capital (Briant 2002, p. 84). Subsequently, Pasagadae became a ceremonial centre for royal initiation ceremonies of the new king, who wore the robe of Cyrus the Elder in the presence of the *magi* (Plutarch, *Artaxerxes*, III.2; Wiesehöfer 2001, p. 32).

Darius established another new ceremonial centre at nearby Persepolis. He also built a palace at Susa (figs 10; 33; 166–7). Texts in form of inscriptions and tablets reveal invaluable primary evidence about numerous aspects of the Achaemenid empire. The foundation inscription from Susa, for example, gives information about the various craftsmen from different parts of the empire who were employed by the court to build the palace, and the diverse types of material used. It mentions (DSf, § 3g-i; Kent 1953, pp. 143–4), amongst other things, that

> *yakā*-timber was brought from Gandhara and from Carmania, . . . the gold was brought from Sardis and from Bactria which was wrought here. The precious stone lapis-lazuli and carnelian which was wrought here, this was brought from Sogdiana. . . . The ivory which was wrought here, was brought from Ethiopia and from Sind and from Arachosia.

'Yakā-timber', i.e. shisham wood (*Dalbergia sissoo*), is still sold at Charsada in the Peshawar Valley and is much used in decorative Indian woodworking.[4] The goldsmiths were Medes and Egyptians, who also decorated the walls, while the bricks were made by the Babylonians (DSf, § 3k; Kent 1953, p. 144).

The centre of the world, according to the countries and peoples listed by Darius and his successors, primarily comprised Persia (Pasargadae and Persepolis), Media (Ecbatana) and Elam (Susa). The Persians and the Medes were related to each other culturally and linguistically as Aryans/Iranians (Briant 2002, pp. 180–1). Although Elam had

Figure 33 Susa column *in situ*.

Figure 34 Doorway to the Hall of a Hundred Columns, Persepolis, built during the reign of Artaxerxes I (465–424 BC).

Throughout his reign until his assassination in 465 BC, Xerxes continued the monumental construction project initiated by Darius at Persepolis and greatly extended the site. More buildings were added under Artaxerxes I (465–424 BC) (fig. 34), but by the time of Artaxerxes III (359–338 BC) only minor additions and alterations were being made (J. Curtis 2000, p. 49). After the murder of Arses (Artaxerxes IV) in 338 BC, Darius III (338–331 BC) came to the throne. During his reign serious conflict erupted in Asia Minor when the invading Macedonian army under Alexander (336–323 BC) crossed the Hellespont in the spring of 334 BC (Briant 2002, p. 818). Despite the supremacy of their fleet, the Persians did not prevent the Macedonians from landing, and there followed a series of Persian military defeats (p. 34), which gave the Macedonians control of the western part of the Achaemenid empire. Darius' mother, wife and children were captured by Alexander's army. Darius himself fled northwards to Ecbatana (modern Hamadan). When his attempt to gather new forces there proved unsuccessful, he moved to the eastern part of the empire, where he was murdered while a hostage of the satrap of Bactria in 330 BC (Briant 2002, p. 866). His assassination was an important factor in the collapse of the Achaemenid empire.

In the west, the earliest coins were first produced in the kingdom of Lydia in western Asia Minor (modern Turkey) in the seventh century BC.[6] These are electrum nugget-like ingots of regulated weight, each with an imprint of one, two or three rough punches on one side and a figural design on the other. The gold and silver issues with the lion and bull motif became known as croesids (Curtis and Tallis 2005, figs 316–17), after the last Lydian king, Croesus (c.560–547/6 BC). Following the Achaemenid conquest of the kingdom in 547/6 BC, Cyrus continued the tradition of minting gold croesids as currency. Early Achaemenid mints were all located in the western provinces of the empire. Sardis (also conquered by Cyrus in 547/6 BC) was the main mint. The practice of minting coins was maintained by his successors, Cambyses and Darius I (Le Rider 2001, p. 123). Darius introduced the gold daric (weighing 8.35g) and the silver siglos (weighing 5.4–5.6g) with a new design depicting the king (fig. 35.1–5; Carradice 1987, pp. 76–7). The siglos circulated only in western Asia Minor. The daric did not serve as general currency, but enjoyed special status as gold – particularly since there was no Greek equivalent – and therefore circulated over a much wider area, well beyond the political boundaries of the empire (Kraay 1976, pp. 33–4; Mildenberg 1993, p. 56). In eastern Anatolia, the Iranian plateau and further east, however, coins were not 'the essential medium of exchange' (Bivar 1982, p. 50) and payments in weighed silver continued.

Both coin types still maintain the roughly circular, weighed, nugget-like form, but with a punched design of the Achaemenid king carrying a bow or spear on the front, and a rectangular impression on the back. The earliest type shows the torso of the king who wears a crenellated crown and holds a bow in his left hand and an arrow in his right. The slightly later type depicts the archer-king in kneeling pose with a quiver on his back and usually holding a spear in his right hand and a bow in his left (Carradice 1987, p. 78). Because of their obverse image, these coins were sometimes

no linguistic links with Persia and Media, it had historical and geographical links (fig. 167). The early Achaemenids saw themselves as heirs to the Elamite kings. The royal title of Cyrus the Great in his famous cylinder seal from Babylon is Kurash, King of Anshan, while his paternal grandfather, Cyrus I, is identified on his seal as 'Kurash of Anshan, son of Teispes' (Briant 2002, pp. 90–2). It has been suggested that Anshan, the highlands of Elam, was at the time of Cyrus 'a more or less independent polity in Fars' (Potts 2005, p. 20). Geographically it covered the same region in south-western Iran as Persis.

Under Darius conflict with Greece resulted in a Persian defeat at Marathon, but also the defeat of the Aegean islands in 490 BC (Briant 2005, p. 13). Under Darius' son and successor, Xerxes (486–465 BC), conflict flared up again. In the sixth year of Xerxes' reign, the Athenians attacked and burned the city and Lydian sanctuaries of Sardis.[5] It was this particular event that made the Persians retaliate in 480 BC. Xerxes attacked Athens and burnt the temple of Athena on the Acropolis (Razmjou 2005, p. 153). He then left the city without causing further destruction, but came face to face with the Greek fleet at Salamis, where the Persians were beaten (J. Curtis 2000, pp. 47–8).

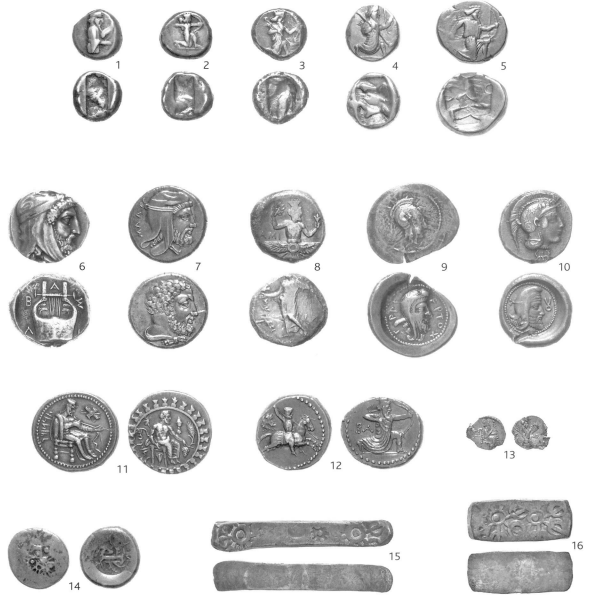

Figure 35

Achaemenid coins:

1–3   Sigloi (*c.* late sixth to early fourth century BC) and
4–5   Darics (*c.* fourth century BC) showing the king as archer.

Satrap issues:

6   Tissaphernes (*c.*420–395 BC). Obv. satrap in floppy hat; rev. *ΒΑΣΙΑ* around lyre;
7   Unknown satrap of Mallus (*c.*400–350 BC). Obv. Heracles; rev. satrap;
8   Tiribazos (*c.*387–380 BC), Issus. Obv. winged figure (*khvarnah* or Ahuramazda?); rev. Baal with eagle, *TRIBZW*;
9   Artumpara (*c.*400–360 BC), Lycia. Obv. head of Athena; rev. satrap, *ARTUMPAR*[*l*];

10   Kherei (*c.*425–400 BC) in Lycia. Obv. Athena; rev. satrap;
11   Tarkamuwa (Datames, *c.*378–372 BC), Tarsus. Obv. Baal; rev. archer with winged symbol above his arm;
12   Royal mint (*c.*340–330 BC). Obv. head of Heracles (?) left, satrap on horseback; rev. royal archer kneeling; *BA*;
13   Mazaios (*c.*361–333 BC), uncertain mint in Samaria. Obv. king with sceptre; rev. winged deity (*khvarenah* or Ahuramazda?) holding a flower and an uncertain object.

Local issues (*c.* fourth century BC):

14   Siglos, Kabul region;
15   Bent bar, Kabul region;
16   Bent bar, Gandhara

called 'archers' (*toxotai*) by the Greeks (Briant 2002, p. 408). An approximate date for the introduction of the image is provided by a seal impression showing the royal archer on a tablet dated to the twenty-second year of Darius (520 BC) from the Fortification at Persepolis (Root 1988, p. 11, pl. 1). However, gold croesids (lion and bull coins) and Greek silver coins – but no archer coins – were found buried beneath the foundation tablets at the north-eastern and south-eastern corners of the Apadana Palace of Darius. This suggests that at the time the building was erected and the inscriptions made, *c.*519–510 BC, the archer coins did not yet exist, or, if they did, the croesids – which were no longer in use – were more suitable archaic symbols of power (Root 1989, pp. 34–5).

However, a small hoard from Smyrna, dating from the very beginning of the fifth century, contains silver sigloi and shows that the archer type must have been in circulation before 500 BC (Kraay 1976, p. 32).

In addition to the archer coins there are also 'satrapal' coins of the fifth and fourth centuries BC, i.e. bronze issues and silver tetradrachms, from mints such as Issus, Solli, Mallus and Tarsus. These were probably issued by satraps authorised by the Great King to mint coins, e.g. Tissaphernes, Tirabazos, the so-called Datames[7] and Mazaios, Artumpara and some unknown satraps (fig. 35.6–13). Artumpara of Lycia has his name around the head of a bearded figure wearing a floppy hat (fig. 35.9) and the name of Tiribazos appears on the reverse (fig. 35.8). Others have a bearded figure on the obverse and an abbreviation of the Greek legend *ΒΑΣ[ΙΛΕΩΣ]* ('of the king') on the reverse (fig. 35.6; Mildenberg 1993, pp. 70–7). Sometimes the mint name appears behind the bearded figure (fig. 35.7), or a dynastic symbol is placed in front of the head (fig. 35.10). Coins of the satrap Datames/ Tarkumuwa show the semi-draped god Bal on the obverse and a male seated figure with 'Median' costume holding a bow and arrow on the reverse (fig. 35.11). Other popular images include a rider carrying a spear (fig. 35.12), a standing royal archer, the king in a chariot, and the winged human figure (fig. 35.8), symbolising Ahuramazda or *khvarenah/ farnah* (Divine Glory). Familiar scenes from the reliefs at Persepolis and Achaemenid seals – of the Persian king seated, or fighting a lion or a bull – occur on 'provincial' coins of the western satrapies of Samaria, Sidon and Byblos (fig. 35.13; Meshorer and Qedar 1999, pls 1–4).

There was no attempt to create a uniform currency for use throughout the empire, for the Chaman Hazuri coin hoard shows that Greek coins from the western provinces of the empire also circulated as far east as Afghanistan in the late fifth century (Curiel and Schlumberger 1953, pp. 32–6, pls I.1–II.33). By the mid fourth century, coins were being produced in Afghanistan by local Achaemenid administrations. The earliest – issued in Bactria – imitated Greek coins, particularly the silver tetradrachms of Athens (*c*.360 BC), with the head of Athena on the front and the owl, the emblem of Athens, on the back (fig. 36.8–9; Curiel and Schlumberger 1953, p. 36, pl. II.31–3, 64; Bopearachchi and Rahman 1995, pp. 80–1, nos 63–9). South of the Hindu Kush, at Kabul, locally produced coins were of two types: silver nuggets resembling the Achaemenid sigloi, but with a small, insignificant symbol on the convex obverse and a larger geometric or animal design on the reverse; and innovative 'bent bars', curved from a geometric design being punched on either end of one side of an elongated, flattened piece of silver (fig. 35.14–15; Curiel and Schlumberger 1953, pp. 37–40, pls III–IV). In Gandhara, the bent bars – or double shekels – were made of wider, flatter pieces of silver (fig. 32.16). Fractions – quarter and eighth shekels – were also produced, on which the same design was punched once.

Alexander the Great (336–323 BC)

> Alexander's great achievement was not invading India but getting there. A military expedition against the Achaemenid empire . . . became more like a geographical exploration as the men from Macedonia triumphantly probed regions hitherto undreamed of. . . . Alexander seems increasingly to have seen his progress in terms of a Grail-like quest for the supposedly unattainable. . . . Through knowledge of this great 'beyond', he aspired to a kind of enlightenment which, although very different from that of the Buddha, would become a cliché of Western exploration. (Keay 2000, p. 71)

After the crossing of the Hellespont in the spring of 334 BC, Alexander and his troops faced the Persian army for the first time at Granicus and were victorious. The Macedonians then captured Dascylium, Sardis, Ephesus and other cities on the coast of Asia Minor. This was soon followed by the rest of the western satrapies. In November 333 BC, at Issus in Cilicia, Darius III personally led the Persians into battle against Alexander, but was also defeated. He fled, leaving behind the royal insignia (robe, shield, bow and chariot) (Briant 1987, p. 827). Alexander refused the Persian king's offer of concessions and pursued his policy of gaining control of all Achaemenid coastal cities. The Phoenician cities of Byblos, Aradus and Sidon surrendered without a fight; Tyre and Gaza (Palestine) resisted and were destroyed. Alexander then went on to annex Egypt. Counter-offensives by the Persians on the mainland of Asia Minor, along the coast and on the islands, failed to halt the Macedonian advance and culminated in the defeat of Darius on 1 October 331 BC at Gaugamela, a small village east of the Tigris river near Arbela.

Alexander then moved westwards to Babylon and Susa, two important centres of Achaemenid administration, which both surrendered without a struggle. In early 330 BC he marched from Susa towards Persis, but en route he encountered opposition from local tribes, first the Uxians (in the modern region of Fahliyan, Fars), then Ariobarzanes, the satrap of Persis. In both cases, the invading forces were superior: after only 24 days the Macedonians reached at Persepolis, 'the ideological center of Persian authority and dynastic grandeur' (Briant 2002, pp. 726, 850–1).

Despite his attempt to win over the Persians by such means as calling himself *philokyros*, 'friend of Cyrus', and promoting the cult of the founder of the Achaemenid empire, Alexander was not hailed as the great conqueror (Briant 2002, p. 852). He gained military victory but not political success, which seems to have affected his behaviour towards the Achaemenid heartland. The burning of Persepolis in 330 BC (Quintus Curtius V.vii.2; Arrian VI.xxx.1) happened after the army had already been there for four months; it was an act of vengeance by a conqueror whose positive later image as liberator was a posthumous piece of propaganda created by his generals and successors (Briant 2002, pp. 852–3). In later Persian literature Alexander is seen not just as a great statesman and philosopher but also as a usurper and destroyer of the holy books of the *Avesta* (V. S. Curtis 2000, pp. 56–8). His fictitious relationship with the ancient Persian kings as the half-brother of Dara (Darius III) in Persian literature stems from an attempt to legitimise the imposition of a non-Iranian regime. According to the religious doctrine of the later Zoroastrian Sasanians, only legitimate kings had the right to rule Iran and to possess the Avestan *khvarenah* or Divine and Kingly Glory (V. S. Curtis 2000, p. 14).

With the defeat and death of Darius, Alexander claimed all the Achaemenid territories. But it took two more years campaigning before he received submission from all the Persian satrapies, especially in the east, where revolts in Bactria, Sogdiana and Paraetacene (modern Tajikistan) were supported by Saka nomadic groups[8] in the Achaemenid borderlands of the Jaxartes river (Syr Darya). As he gained control of each region, he founded new cities, notably in the present context at Begram (Alexandria of the Caucasus) and Aï Khanum (Alexandria of the Oxus) in Afghanistan.

In 327 BC he left Bactria and invaded India in a two-pronged pincer movement, the one force going through the Khyber Pass, while he led the other further north through one of the mountain passes into Swat. He stormed the fortress of Aornus at Pirsar on the Buner border (identified by Aurel Stein 1905, pp. 28–31; 1929, pp. 113–54) and advanced through the Peshawar Valley, across the Indus river to Taxila

Figure 36 Coins of Alexander and his successors.
Alexander (336–323 BC):
1   Mint of Susa. Obv. head of Athena; rev. winged Nike with wreath,
    ΑΛΕΞΑΝΔΡΟΥ ΒΑΣΙΛΕΩΣ;
2   Mint of Babylon probably *c*.324 BC. Obv. Heracles in a lion scalp; rev.
    enthroned Zeus;
3   Posthumous issue, possibly minted at Myriandrus, Asia Minor,
    c.323–317 BC.

Successors:
4   Philip III Arrhidaeus (323–317 BC) in his own name, mint of Babylon;
5   Seleucus I (312–281 BC) in his own name, mint of Seleucia;
6   Lysimachus (306–281 BC), of Thrace and Asia Minor. Obv. Alexander
    wearing the horns of Zeus Ammon; rev. Athena with Nike;
7   Ptolemy I (305–283 BC), of Egypt. Obv. Alexander in elephant scalp; rev.
    Athena with owl.
8   Athens (*c*.322 BC). Obv. head of Athena in Corinthian helmet; rev. owl;
9   Athenian imitation (*c*. fourth century BC), from Begram. Obv. Athena; rev. owl.

and as far as the Jhelum river (ancient Hydaspes) in the Punjab, where he defeated the local ruler Porus. To celebrate his victory, he founded two cities, Alexandria Nicaea and Bucephala (after his horse which had died in the battle). Neither site has yet been identified.[9]

He then proceeded further into the Punjab as far as the Beas river (ancient Hyphases). At this point his troops mutinied and forced a return westwards. He built a fleet of ships and proceeded down the Jhelum and the Indus to the coast, with half the troops on board and the other half marching in two columns on either bank. In September 325 BC, Alexander set out with part of his force from Patala – at the head of the Indus delta – along the coast, intending to set up food depots for his fleet of 100 to 150 ships exploring the coastline to the Persian Gulf. Three battalions, the elephants, baggage and siege train, and the sick and wounded went on ahead via the Mulla Pass, Quetta, Qandahar and the Helmand Valley. But the troops under Alexander were forced inland by the mountainous terrain and, as a result, had to cross the desert of Baluchistan, with a disastrous loss of life. The survivors eventually met up with the rest of the army and the fleet at the Minab river in the Straits of Hormuz at the mouth of the Persian Gulf. By spring 324 BC he was back at the Persian administrative capital of Susa.

During the period of consolidation of his empire (326–324 BC), Alexander replaced all men he had come to distrust, including a third of his satraps. Six others and three

generals were executed. His treasurer, Harpalus, initially escaped with 6000 mercenaries and 5000 talents, but was subsequently murdered. A decree in summer 324 BC requiring all cities of the Greek League to accept back political exiles and their families attempted to reduce the problem of thousands of mercenaries roaming Asia in search of employment. Alexander's active policy of racial integration included his own marriage to Roxana, the daughter of the Bactrian noble, Spitamenes, one of the leaders in the Bactrian and Sogdian revolt against the Macedonians (Briant 1987, p. 829). But further steps – such as the enforced marriage of 80 Macedonian officers and 10,000 soldiers to Persian women, and the employment of Persians on equal terms in the army and administration – were largely unacceptable to the Macedonian elite. Of all the generals, only Seleucus did not divorce his Bactrian wife Apama after Alexander's death.[10]

At Babylon in 323 BC Alexander took ill after an intense bout of feasting and drinking and died on 13 June. He was succeeded by his illegitimate half-brother, Philip Arrhidaeus (fig. 36.4), and his own son, Alexander IV, both of whom were murdered, in 317 and 310/9 BC respectively. The empire fragmented, its provinces or satrapies becoming independent kingdoms under Alexander's former generals.

From *c*.325 BC, Alexander began including the royal title *ΒΑΣΙΛΕΩΣ* on his coinage (fig. 36.1): a practice that continued on posthumous issues in his name (Price 1991, vol. 1, pp. 32–3). However, his most significant innovation was the

Figure 37 Entrance to the Gandharan Buddhist monastery of Ranigat, Peshawar Valley.

earlier introduction throughout the empire of a uniform silver coinage based on the Athenian standard (fig. 36.2; Price 1991, vol. I, pp. 27–9). This, together with the release of vast amounts of bullion from the Achaemenid treasuries, not only boosted trade but also introduced a standardised Greek currency tradition to a vast region (Price 1991, vol. I, pp. 25–9). The foundation of numerous new cities, often combined with the enforced colonisation of Greeks, established an enduring presence of Greek language and Hellenic thought, influence and customs across the whole region from the Mediterranean to the Punjab.

What began initially as Alexander's encouragement of favourable comparisons between his own feats and those of Heracles and Dionysus – and their mythical conquests of the east – developed in the last years of his life into a demand for recognition of his own divine status. The message in his choice of coin designs is implicit: Heracles, the deified hero and son of Zeus, appears on the obverse in a lion-skin head-dress (a reference to his killing of the Nemean lion) and an enthroned Zeus, the supreme god of the Greek pantheon, is depicted on the back as Alexander's patron deity. The images refer back to Alexander's visit in 331 BC to the temple of Zeus-Ammon in Egypt, where he is said to have been acknowledged as a son by the god. Alexander's desire for deification seems to have been considered a self-indulgent whim during his lifetime – the Spartan decree, for example, states 'since Alexander wishes to be a god, let him be a god' (*Encyclopaedia Britannica* 13, p. 227) – but developed into a full-blown cult after his death. Coins of Lysimachus, king of Thrace (306–281 BC), for example, replace Heracles with a portrait of Alexander wearing a diadem and the ram's horn of Zeus-Ammon, while those of Ptolemy I of Egypt (305–283 BC) depict, in addition, an elephant scalp head-dress as a symbol of Alexander's conquest of India (fig. 36.6–7; Errington and Cribb 1992, p. 55).

It is still true today that most westerners' imaginations are stirred by tales of Alexander's legendary conquests as far as the Indus. Certainly in the nineteenth century his exploits

were the starting point for interest in, and the investigation of, the ancient remains in the lands east of Iran. In April 1830 the association of Alexander with the Punjab 'compelled' Ventura to excavate Manikyala, which he identified as the site of Bucephala (figs 124; 175–7; Ventura 1832, pp. 600–3; pp. 211–12). Mohan Lal (1846, p. 32) recounts that, when Alexander Burnes, J. G. Gerard and he assumed Afghan dress and 'pretended to be Duranis' – an 'imposition' that 'would not bear close inspection' – for their journey through Afghanistan to Bukhara in 1832, Burnes adopted the name 'Sikander Khan' (an appropriate enough choice given his Christian name, but one nevertheless that contained overtones of delusions of grandeur).

Court (1836, 1839) and Masson (1837a) both made practical archaeological contributions, for, in their attempts to trace the vestiges of Alexander, they conscientiously surveyed sites in eastern Afghanistan, the Peshawar region and the Punjab, a number of which no longer survive. Most notable was Masson's correct identification of Begram as Alexandria of the Caucasus (1842, p. 140; Bernard 1982). And although Court's surveys did not reveal any remains that can be associated with Alexander, they are also still useful, particularly his records of the sites between the Chenab and Jhelum, which were destroyed by the building of a canal linking the two rivers in the 1890s (fig. 136; 1836a, p. 473; Cunningham 1871, pp. 173–87; Errington and Cribb 1992, p. 168). Most identifications, however, were based on wishful thinking rather than archaeological evidence as, for example, Cunningham's identification of the Buddhist site of Ranigat in the Peshawar Valley as Aornus (fig. 37; Cunningham 1848, p. 131; p. 222 below), or James Abbott's even more erroneous identification of some Gupta sculptures found on the banks of the Jhelum river as Indo-Greek sculptures from Bucephala (Abbott 1847).[11]

Even when a site, like Begram or Aï Khanum, has been correctly identified, few if any traces of Alexander have surfaced. Bernard suggests that the site of Alexandria ad Caucasum was the Burj-i Abdallah citadel on the north side of

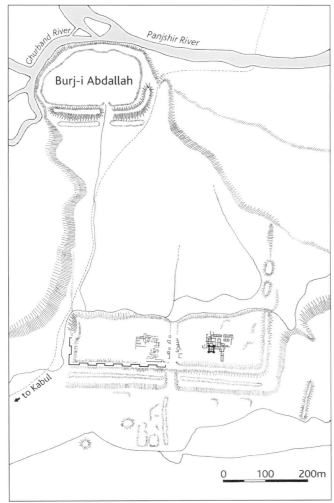

Figure 38 Plan of Begram.

in the rubbings of Court's collection (MSS nos 102, 108): the first actually appears to be a worn half-drachm of Philip of an uncertain eastern mint (Price 1991, vol. 1, pl. CXII, P228), while the second was subsequently annotated by Court as 'fausse'. The recently published gold 'medal', reputedly from Mir Zakah II and said to depict the first lifetime portrait of Alexander (Bopearachchi and Flandin 2005, pp. 49–50), has similarly been dismissed either as a fake (Dahmen 2007; Fischer-Bosser 2006, pp. 62–5, fig. 1) or, at very least, posthumous, for it copies diverse elements from a series of later coin designs, e.g. the *aegis* edging the elephant scalp belongs to the second to third phase of Ptolemy's issues (fig. 36.7); while the elephant trunk imitates the form appearing on coins of the Greco-Bactrian Demetrius I (fig. 52.6; for further discussion see also Bhandare 2007).

The earliest coins in the hoard from Mir Zakah I (near Gardez) are those of Lysimachus and Seleucus (Curiel and Schlumberger 1953, p. 74, pl. VIII). Similarly, Masson found no coins of Alexander among the 68,877 coins that he estimated were collected from Begram; however, the site did produce three, possibly contemporary, locally issued Achaemenid half shekels (BM 1880–3733a–c). In the India Office loan collection of about six thousand coins – the residue of Masson's vast collection – there are also two small, worn, pseudo-Athenian, bronze issues of the fourth century BC, copying the Athenian design of the helmeted head of Athena on the obverse and the owl on the reverse (fig. 36.8), except that the latter image more closely resembles a bull's head (fig. 36.9). The Aï Khanum excavations unearthed a similar series of bronze coins, again with Athena in a Corinthian helmet, but with a clearly executed owl on the reverse, which Bernard identifies as pseudo-Athenian, post-Alexander issues, possibly local to the Oxus region (1985, pp. 32–5, pl. 2.2–7).

Mauryans (c. 321–187 BC)

India . . . following the death of Alexander, had shaken from its shoulders the yoke of servitude and put his governors to death. The man responsible for this liberation was Sandrocottus. . . . He was a man of low birth, but he was called to royal power by divine authority. He had annoyed King Nandrus by his outspokenness; he was sentenced to death by him, and had relied on his swiftness of foot to escape. (Justin XV.iv.12–16)

The man known as Sandrocottus in Classical sources is even said to have met Alexander at Taxila in 326 BC (Plutarch, *Alexander* LXII.1–4). According to Megasthenes (the Seleucid ambassador to India c.300 BC), the heartland of his kingdom was the Gangetic Valley, with his capital at Palibothra (Strabo XV.I.36). The pioneering Indologist Sir William Jones (1746–94), working on ancient texts in Calcutta in the early 1790s (p. 21 above), realised that Sandrocottus equalled Chandragupta (c.321–297 BC) in Indian sources, the founder of the Mauryan empire, who received foreign ambassadors at his capital Pataliputra (modern Patna) (Keay 2000, pp. 78–80).[12]

Opinion differs regarding the sequence of events in Chandragupta Maurya's rise to power from obscure origins in Magadha (modern Bihar), north-east India. According to Buddhist tradition, he was taken by his mentor, the Brahman politician Kautilya,[13] to Taxila, where he was educated. In a reconstruction of events based on Greek sources (e.g. Justin XV.iv.12–22), he campaigned successfully against Alexander's

Begram, overlooking the confluence of the Ghurband and Panjshir rivers (fig. 38; 1985, p. 29, n. 4), but the area has never been excavated. At Aï Khanum (fig. 44), soundings on the citadel to the south-east of the acropolis revealed a stratigraphic layer between that of the Achaemenid period and that of the Bactrian Greeks, which Bernard dates from the time of Alexander (1985, p. 34).

The largest number of coins of Alexander recorded from a single eastern source are 'about one hundred tetradrachms and as many drachms', mostly 'in very poor condition' in the Oxus Treasure (Cunningham 1881a, p. 22). From the evidence at Qunduz (Curiel and Fussman 1965, p. 14, pl.I.1), Aï Khanum (Guillaume 1991, pp. 136–42, 147, pl. XI.57–63) and stray finds allegedly from Afghanistan (Bopearachchi and Rahman 1995, pp. 24–5, 80–1, nos 57–61), the majority of the Oxus coins were probably posthumous issues in the name of Alexander, or his successors such as Philip Arrhidaeus and Seleucus I (fig. 36.3–5) from the period c.320–300 BC, rather than lifetime issues. Two silver tetradrachms – said to be lifetime issues minted in Syria (c.325 BC) – were found in the Bhir Mound at Taxila in 1924 with a coin of Philip III Arrhidaeus, an Achaemenid daric and 1169 punch-marked coins (Walsh 1939, pp. 1–2, pls XL–XLI). Both 'lifetime' issues are, in fact, posthumous coins of the period c.323–317 BC; the one probably minted at Myriandrus in Asia Minor, the other minted by Philip in Babylon (fig. 36.3–4). Two further coins of unknown provenance attributed to Alexander are recorded satraps in Sind and the Punjab from *c*.323 BC, following an uprising after the murder of the local ruler Porus by Eudemus, the commander of the Macedonian garrison in the western Punjab (McCrindle 1901, pp. 43–4; Majumdar 1980, pp. 58–60). The satrap of Sind, Pithon, abandoned his post *c*.321 BC because of Chandragupta's supposed activities, and the withdrawal of Eudemus from the Punjab signalled the final defeat of the Macedonian army of occupation. Chandragupta then went on to conquer the Nanda overlords of Magadha, whose kingdom extended along the Gangetic valley and neighbouring regions (approximately across modern Uttar and Madhya Pradesh, Bihar and Bengal).

Other analyses of the sources propose that, at Kautilya's instigation, Chandragupta overthrew the Nanda dynasty first and established his capital at Pataliputra, before extending Mauryan control over most of north India (Raychaudhuri 1996, pp. 234–9). According to this interpretation, the anti-Macedonian movement led by Chandragupta probably began in Sind after the satrap Pithon withdrew. Both versions appear to accept that Chandragupta's reign should be dated from the assumption of hostilities, rather than from the point of their successful conclusion in *c*.317 BC, which would push his accession down to *c*.316 BC or later, as proposed by Lassen (1874, pp. 53–67).[14] The only secure date for any case is that of the treaty with Seleucus I *c*.303 BC, when the lands south of the Hindu Kush (Arachosia and the Parapamisadae) in Afghanistan were ceded to Chandragupta in exchange for 500 elephants and 'upon terms of intermarriage' (Strabo XV.II.9; Bernard 1985, pp. 85–6).

In Buddhist texts[15] Chandragupta is said to have reigned 168 years after the Buddha's death and for 24 years. His son Bindusara ruled for 25 years according to the *Purāṇas*,[16] or according to Buddhist sources 28 years, followed by an interregnum of four years (Lamotte 1988, pp. 216–17). Called Allitrochades by Strabo (II.i.9), Bindusara received the ambassador Deimachus sent by the Seleucid king Antiochus (probably Antiochus I, 281–261 BC). The reign of the third king, Ashoka (*c*.269–232 BC), is said to have begun 50 years after the accession of Chandragupta and either 218 years or 100 years after the death of the Buddha, in the Singhalese and Sanskrit sources respectively (Lamotte 1988, pp. 13–14, 216–17).

In the Singhalese and Theravada Buddhist tradition, the Parinirvana[17] of the Buddha is fixed at 544/3 BC (Bechert 1995, p. 12). In 1836–7, George Turnour was the first to question the apparent discrepancies in chronology of fifty to sixty years between the Singhalese and Greek sources (1837, vol. I, pp. xlviii–l; Dietz 1995, pp. 54–5). He established what became known as the corrected 'long chronology', whereby the date of the death of the Buddha was amended variously to *c*.486–477 BC to fit the Greek evidence (see also Eggermont 1992, pp. 501–2). A recent re-evaluation of the ages of ordination of the monks recorded in the *Dīpavaṃsa* corrects the chronology further from 218 years to only 136 years between the Parinirvana and Ashoka's inauguration (Gombrich 1992, pp. 237, 244–7). The 'short chronology' follows the Sanskrit sources and dates the death of the Buddha 100 years before the consecration of Ashoka (Eggermont 1992, pp. 502–4).

In 1837, following Prinsep's successful decipherment of the Delhi, Allahabad and Lauriya-Nandangarh pillar inscriptions (1837, p. 469; p. 22 above), the Singhalese Chronicles emerged as another source for determining a date for Ashoka. While translating these texts George Turnour correctly identified *devānaṃpiye piyadasi*, 'the beloved of the gods', as the Mauryan emperor Ashoka of Buddhist tradition (1837–8, p. 791). In all Ashoka set up sixteen major rock edicts, seven pillar edicts and a number of minor rock inscriptions scattered throughout the empire (fig. 28; Thapar 1997, pp. 250–66; Lamotte 1988, pp. 224–5). The text of the edicts is inscribed in the languages or scripts appropriate for each region: Aramaic at Laghman, together with Greek at Qandahar in Afghanistan; Kharoshthi at Shahbazgarhi and Mansehra in north-west Pakistan; and Brahmi throughout India (Allchin and Norman 1985).

Crucially for chronological purposes, the thirteenth major rock edict at Dhanli mentions Ashoka's conquest of Kalinga (Orissa region) in the eighth year after his coronation, together with the names of five contemporary Greek kings: Antiochus, Ptolemy, Antigonus, Magas and Alexander (Thapar 1997, pp. 255–6). There is more than one possible Antiochus or Ptolemy, but the last three kings are identifiable as Antigonus Gonatus (276–239 BC), Magas of Cyrene (*c*.277–250 BC) and Alexander of Epirus (272–255 BC) (Lassen 1874, p. 255; Thapar 1997, pp. 40–1),[18] thereby supplying a possible time frame of 272–255 BC for the inscription and 280–267 BC for the inauguration of Ashoka (Gombrich 1992, p. 244). However, the third rock edict records that Ashoka instigated the creation of the edicts only after he had reigned for twelve years (Thapar 1997, p. 251), which extends the date range for his coronation by at least four years to 284–267 BC (Cribb 1991).

After Ashoka, Mauryan control gradually declined. In *c*.206 BC Antiochus III (223–187 BC) (fig. 43.4) renewed the Seleucid–Mauryan treaty regarding Arachosia and the Parapamisidae (Polybius, *Histories*, II.34; Holt 1995, p. 101), but these regions were conquered by the Greco-Bactrians in the ensuing decades. Elsewhere in India the empire fragmented into a number of smaller kingdoms, tribal states and cities, although the Mauryans held on to their Gangetic heartland until they were overthrown by Pushyamitra (*c*.187–151 BC), the first king of the Shunga dynasty, whose dates are derived from the numbers of years ascribed to Ashoka and his successors in the *Purāṇas* (Bhandare 2006, p. 70).

The Mauryan empire reached its greatest extent under Ashoka. The wide geographical distribution of epigraphic evidence suggests that it spanned most of the Indian subcontinent and part of Afghanistan: from the Hindu Kush in the north to Mysore and Madras (modern Karnataka and Andhra Pradesh) in the south. The Mauryan heartland was under central administration. Royal princes governed as viceroys in four outlying provinces, including Kalinga and Uttarapatha (northern Punjab, with its capital at Taxila), while the frontier regions were ruled by minor feudal kings (Lamotte 1988, p. 226).

Control of such a vast empire encouraged the use of standardised units of payment. The first coinages of India used the same technology as the bent bars of the north-west regions, i.e. pieces of silver of a specific weight, struck with a series of single punches on only one side, but with regional and chronological variations in design and in the number of

Figure 39 Relief from Bharhut stupa (second century BC) depicting punch-marked coins laid out as proof of purchase of the Jetavana Gardens as a refuge for the Buddha.

Figure 40 Cunningham's excavated finds from Bodh Gaya, including the deposit below the *vajrasana* (Enlightenment throne) of the Mahabodhi temple: **1** Gold foil plaque; **2–5** Four worn punch-marked coins.

punches used. As already noted (p. 34), there is a link with earlier Greek coinage in the Achaemenid period through the punch-marked bent bar coinage of the north-west (fig. 35.15–16). This fact has been convincingly used to make a case for a north-west origin for Indian coinage datable to the fifth century BC (Cribb 1985; 2005b, pp. 58–72), but the logical arguments in favour of this premise are not universally accepted, many scholars preferring to claim an Indian origin in the Gangetic valley, *c*.600 BC or earlier (Gupta and Hardaker 1985, p. 1).

The characteristic 'punch-marks' of the later series of coins (fig. 41.1–6) were first noted in 1835 by Prinsep, who described them as 'Buddhist' on account of their symbols, although he acknowledged it was difficult to determine how far the antiquity of the coins 'may have approached the epoch of Buddha (544 BC)' (Thomas 1858, pp. 195–6, 201, 210, 217, pl. XX.25–7). Cunningham went further along the same lines in 1891 (pp. 19–20):

> In the Hindu books they are called *purâna* or 'old', a title which vouches for their antiquity. They are mentioned by Manu ['Noah's equivalent' in Indian tradition[19]] and Pânini [Sanskrit grammarian based at Taxila[20]], both anterior to Alexander, and also in the Buddhist Sutras, which are of about the same age [as Alexander]. The original name of the coin was *kârshâpana*, or *kâhâpana*, from *kârshâ*, a 'weight', and *âpanâ*, 'custom or use', meaning they were pieces of one *kârshâ* weight as established by use or custom. . . . As Buddha's death is placed in the middle of the sixth century BC, the silver *purâņas* of India may be quite as old as any of the coinages of Greece or Asia Minor.

With a few refinements, these arguments are still current. Cunningham was right in refuting the 'general opinion of

classical scholars' that coinage was introduced into India by the Bactrian Greeks, citing the reference in Quintus Curtius (XVIII.13–14) to Alexander receiving a gift of eighty talents of coined silver from the ruler of Taxila (1891, p. 52). But his argument that 'any Indian coins copied from the Greek money would have been in silver' is defective, for the majority of punch-marked coins are of silver. His reason for assigning them – like Prinsep – to the time of the Buddha seems to be inspired by his discovery of the two reliefs from the Buddhist sites of Bodh Gaya (dated 'as old as Aśoka himself, BC 250') and Bharhut ('about BC 150') (fig. 39). Both these *c*. second- to first-century BC reliefs illustrate an area covered with punch-marked coins indicating the price of purchase for the Jetavana Garden as a refuge for the Buddha and his followers (Cunningham 1891, p. 53, pl. A). The punch-mark coins he uncovered at Bodh Gaya are extremely worn examples, which were found with a gold pendant made from two thin impressions taken from a gold coin of the Kushan king Huvishka (*c*. AD 150–90) in a deposit below the *c*. eleventh-century *vajrasana* (Enlightenment throne) in the Mahabodhi temple (fig. 40.1, 3–5; Cunningham 1892b, pp. 20–1, pl. XXII). So he is quoting evidence ranging potentially in date from the fourth millennium BC to the second century AD or later as proof of the antiquity of punch-marked coins. However, his key argument is one that persists down to the present time, i.e. they are mentioned in texts describing the life of the Buddha and his previous lives (also in the *Purāņas* and other sources), ergo, they must have existed by that time or earlier, even though these sources 'were not written down until many centuries later' (Gupta and Hardaker 1985, pp. 1–2).

Figure 41 Mauryan silver punch-marked coins (c. late fourth to second century BC):
1   Series II, GH 253 overstruck by series III, GH305;
2   Series IV, GH 442;
3   Series IV, GH 468;
4   Series V, GH 488;
5   Series VI, GH 566;
6   Series VII, GH 590, from Begram.

Copper cast coins (c. third to second century BC):
7   Obv. tree in railing; rev. hill and crescent flanked by moon and sun;
8   Obv. tree in railing; rev. hollow cross;
9   'Mauryan', from Begram, with auspicious symbols.
Local coins (c. second to first century BC):
10   Taxila, with auspicious symbols;
11   Mathura, issued by Purushadatta;
12   Audambara, issued by Shivadasa (c. second to first century BC). Obv. temple and trident; rev. tree in railing, water and elephant.
13   Bronze punch-marked coin, GH 566 (c. second century BC).

What is now undisputed is that under the Mauryans – but not exclusively – five punch-marks were standard, two being always a sun and a six-armed symbol (figs 41.1–6; 42). This link was not made until the 1930s, by which time the accumulated evidence of 'the great similarity' in late punch-marked coin hoards suggested that 'the issue of these coins' and the 'rough grouping' of their find-spots 'corresponds quite well with the distribution of the Aśoka inscriptions' (Allan 1936, p. lvi). But dating and identifying which coinages are Mauryan is problematic because none are inscribed. In their definitive work on the subject, Gupta and Hardaker have divided the coinages with five punch-marks into seven series and suggest that only series V–VII should be regarded as issues of the Mauryan empire (1985, p. 15, 28, 31–2).

Bivar (1998, pp. 57–65), following Gupta (1963, pp. 151–2), goes one stage further and suggests that coins bearing the three-arched hill and crescent symbol (i.e. Gupta and Hardaker series VI.II: GH 528–539; series VI.IV: GH 542–82; figs 41.5; 42) may be explicitly identified as issues of Ashoka. The quoted evidence for this is that the symbol is found on several 'archaeological objects, which may undoubtedly date to the Mauryan period' (Gupta 1963, p. 151), namely the Sohagaura copper-plate inscription; a polished sandstone pillar and a small matrix, both excavated at Kumarahar (Patna);[21] three terracotta dishes excavated at Bulandibagh (Patna); and the copper bolt which fixed the lion capital to the Ashokan edict column at Rampurwa (Prasad 1937–8, pp. 61–7, pls 7–8). But what Gupta glosses over is that the hill and crescent motif on all these examples – and on

coins – never occurs in isolation, but is always shown together with other symbols, e.g. the tree in railing, temple,[22] standard, taurine and the hollow cross or so-called 'tank' (fig. 41.7–9). While it is true that a similar group of symbols are found on cast coins associated with the Mauryan period (fig. 41.9; Prasad 1937–8, pp. 62–3, pl. 8.3–4), it is equally true that they belong to a store of traditional Indian auspicious and religious symbols that are primarily pre-Mauryan in origin and continued in popular use well into the early centuries AD.[23] They appear not only on bronze coins attributed to Taxila, as Bivar noted (1998, p. 64; fig. 41.10), but also on the post-Mauryan coinages – both struck and cast – of other regions throughout the subcontinent (fig. 41.11–12; Allan 1936, pls XIV–XXIII, XXXII–XXXIX; Maheshwari 1977, pp. 1–8). The third-century BC proposed date of the so-called 'Taxila' issues moreover needs revision, for two different types have been found which are overstruck on Indo-Greek coins of c.160–135 BC (fig. 113.2–3; p. 129 below).

A detailed study of late punch-marked hoards (Errington 2003) shows that they are all remarkably similar in composition, ranging from a few examples of Gupta and Hardaker's series II overstruck by series III down to the end of silver punch-marked production (fig. 41.1–6). Hoards containing series III–VII coins have an extremely wide distribution, corresponding to the Mauryan empire at its greatest extent and beyond, for they have been found at sites from Aï Khanum, Begram[24] and Mir Zakah in Afghanistan to Amaravati in Andhra Pradesh, southern India. This suggests that coins from series III onwards should be associated with the Mauryan period.

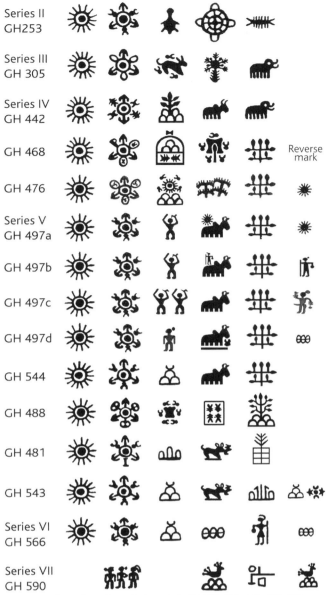

Series II GH253					
Series III GH 305					
Series IV GH 442					
GH 468					Reverse mark
GH 476					
Series V GH 497a					
GH 497b					
GH 497c					
GH 497d					
GH 544					
GH 488					
GH 481					
GH 543					
Series VI GH 566					
Series VII GH 590					

Figure 42 Chart of punch-marked symbols GH 253, 305, 442, 468, 476, 497a–d, 481, 488, 543, 544, 566, 590.

A further point not realised in Gupta and Hardaker's classification – but which is becoming increasingly clear – is that within series V–VI or possibly even series IV–VII (figs 41.2–6; 42), there is a discernible regional concentration and chronological development of certain types that places them later than other issues in the same Gupta and Hardaker series. The classification thus needs some revision. A study of late hoards reveals a regular pattern of rare and common types within each series subgroup (i.e. sharing the same four symbols), plus an apparent regional bias of certain types, suggesting that perhaps each group represents the chronological development of a number of separate, but contemporary, regional mints (Errington 2003, pp. 84, 96–121, figs 2–6). So although specific symbols are not yet identifiable with a particular ruler, some may denote a specific region. For example, the 'candelabra' tree symbol (Gupta and Hardaker 1985, p. 85, no. 5) appears to be closely associated with Mathura (figs 41.3, 11; 42; Gupta 1989, p. 127, fig. 14.2.1). Only one 'extra rare' type, GH 544, carries this symbol in the hill and crescent series VI. In contrast, a number of new types are linked by symbols of the sun, bull

and Balarama to GH 476 (series IV) and GH 497 (series V), thereby placing these groups in the last, post-Mauryan phase of punch-marked coinage.

Similarly, in the hoard excavated at Mahastan in Bangladesh, types GH 481 (series V) and GH 543 (series VI, i.e. with the hill and crescent) predominate (fig. 42). The coins of both types have the five symbols always punched in the same fixed positions. This shared characteristic – together with the addition of a hill and crescent reverse mark on the GH 481 coins when no reverse mark is known elsewhere for this type – suggests they were either concurrent or successive late issues (Boussac and Alam 2001, pp. 237–59). The same phenomenon is even more apparent in GH 566, in which not only the progression of random to fixed positions but also the conversion of silver to bronze and the degradation of the symbols can be clearly traced (fig. 41.5, 13; Errington 2003, pl. 23).

At the one extreme are the hoards with concentrations of a single type, indicative of a very short time span, e.g. Rairh III in Rajasthan (GH 566: 88%), Taxila Bhir mound 2 (GH 575: 91%) and Aï Khanum (GH 575: 77%). The external evidence for dating several of these late hoards comprises a few Seleucid, Bactrian or Indo-Greek coins c.323–95 BC (Errington 2003, p. 86). But, as has been already pointed out, there is, as yet, no way of ascertaining whether the latest Greek coin in each of these hoards is its actual latest coin, since the date of issue of punch-marked coinage is not known, i.e. it shows only 'that the hoards must have been deposited later than the latest datable coin, but how much later cannot be determined' (Cribb 1985, p. 541).

In general, these examples indicate that the decline of the empire in the second century BC signalled a gradual degeneration in coinage design, silver content and weight, but punch-marked coin production appears to have persisted in an evolved – often bronze – form in certain regions after the Mauryan period (fig. 41.13).

Seleucids (312–64 BC)

After the death of Alexander the Great in 323 BC, a prolonged power struggle ensued between his generals for control of the empire. One of the key protagonists was Seleucus I (312–281 BC) who, with the capture of Babylonia in 312 BC, founded the Seleucid kingdom (figs 36.5; 43.1). In c.305 BC he successfully established Greek rule in Bactria and Sogdiana, but had to cede all territories south of the Hindu Kush to Chandragupta Maurya in c.303 BC. By 301 BC he had gained control over Syria, Mesopotamia, Anatolia and Iran. The old Achaemenid administrative centres of Babylon and Susa were maintained. At the time of his assassination in 281 BC his empire extended from Thrace to Central Asia.

However, Seleucid control of such an extensive area did not last long. His son, Antiochus I Soter (281–261 BC) – whose mother was Apama (p. 35) – was almost immediately faced with a revolt in Syria (fig. 43.2–3). He also lost Macedonia and Thrace, being forced to make peace with his father's murderer, Ptolemy Ceraunus of Macedon (281–279 BC), a son of the ruler of Egypt, Ptolemy I Soter (323–283 BC) (http://en.wikipedia.org). By the mid third century BC, the Parthians, Bactrians and Sogdians had all gained independence. Despite an alliance between Antiochus III (223–187 BC) (fig. 43.4) and the Mauryan king Sophagasenus in c.206 BC (Polybius

Figure 43 Seleucid coins:
1 Seleucus I (312–281 BC), mint of Seleucia. Obv. head of king; rev. Athena in elephant quadriga;
2 Antiochus I Soter (281–261 BC), mint of Magnesia on Mt Sipylus. Obv. head of king; rev. Heracles seated on rock covered with lion-skin;
3 Antiochus I. Obv. head of Apollo (three-quarters view); rev. Apollo, from Begram;
4 Antiochus III (223–187 BC), mint of Susa. Obv. head of king; rev. Apollo seated on omphalos;
5 Demetrius II Nicator (145–139/8 BC), mint of Antioch. Obv. head of king; rev. Apollo;
6 Antiochus VII Sidetes (139/8–129 BC), mint of Damascus. Obv. head of king; rev. laurel wreath enclosing Athena with Nike.

XI.43.II–13), south-eastern Afghanistan was lost to the Bactrian Greeks in the early second century BC. In this period the Seleucids also began losing control of large territories in the west, especially after their defeat by the Romans in 191 BC. By 141 BC all lands east of the Euphrates were lost, and what remained (Syria and eastern Cilicia) was conquered by the Romans in 64 BC.

The process of Hellenisation of these regions was more durable, although tangible archaeological evidence proved elusive for the early explorers. Masson's collections at

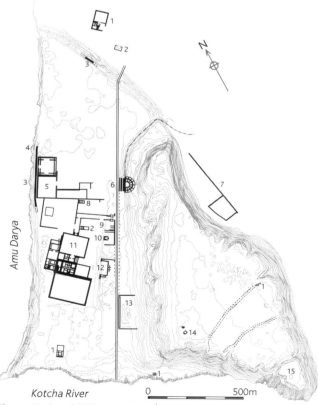

Figure 44 Plan of Aï Khanum: **1** house; **2** temple; **3** ramparts; **4** fountain; **5** gymnasium; **6** theatre; **7** necropolis; **8** mausoleum; **9** propylaeum; **10** sanctuary; **11** palace; **12** agora; **13** arsenal; **14** podium; **15** citadel.

Begram produced a single worn bronze coin of Antiochus I, minted at Seleucia on the Tigris (fig. 43.3).[25] It was only in 1962 that the first substantial remains of a Greek colonial city were discovered at Aï Khanum, in north-east Afghanistan, at the confluence of the Oxus (Amu Darya) and Kotcha rivers (fig. 44) and identified as Alexandria Oxiana, the most easterly of the Greek cities of Asia (Bernard 1973, 1985; Guillaume 1983; Guillaume and Rougeulle 1987; Francfort 1984; Leriche 1986; Rapin 1992; Veuve 1987).

The city was Greek in plan, with an acropolis and necropolis occupying the high citadel area, and a lower town containing temples, an agora, palace and treasury, gymnasium, propylaeum, arsenal, terraced theatre and houses. The grid system of streets and main thoroughfare running from north to south were laid out in a typical Hellenistic way. However, unlike Greek towns, it was built primarily of mud-brick. Stone was used only for important structural elements like columns. Decorative elements, like the Doric, Ionic and Corinthian capitals, similarly combined Greek and local influences. The earliest coin finds from the site are categorised by Bernard (1985, pp. 31–5) as post Alexander/pre-Seleucid, i.e. of the period between the death of Alexander in 323 BC and the suzerainty of Seleucus I being recognised by the satraps north of the Hindu Kush in c.305 BC.

The Seleucids encouraged Greek colonisation of the furthest eastern reaches of their empire, thereby exporting Greek culture and language to these regions. But in certain areas, such as Persis, the heartland of the former Achaemenid empire, indigenous culture remained strong (Wiesehöfer 2001, p. 110). At the same time the Seleucids continued Alexander's innovation of establishing a standardised coinage throughout the empire, i.e. die-struck issues predominantly in silver and bronze, with the royal portrait on the obverse and the patron deity of the ruler on the reverse. These conventions in coin design persisted, with only slight modifications, until the Muslim conquests of the seventh to eighth century AD.

Figure 45 Parthian coins:

1   Andragoras (*c*.246 BC). Obv. head with diadem; rev. chariot with four horned horses, a male figure in armour and Nike;
2   Arsaces I (*c*.238–211 BC), perhaps mint of Mithradatkert (Nisa). Obv. king in soft hat; rev. archer, *ΑΡΣΑΚΟΥ*.

Mithradates I (*c*.171–138 BC):

3   Obv. beardless king in soft hat; rev. seated archer;
4   Obv. bearded king with diadem; rev. *ΒΑΣΙΛΕΩΣ ΜΕΓΑΛΟΥ ΑΡΣΑΚΟΥ*;
5   Rev. Nike in biga, *ΒΑΣΙΛΕΩΣ ΑΡΣΑΚΟΥ*;
6   Rev. seated Zeus with sceptre and eagle;
7   Rev. archer, *ΒΑΣΙΛΕΩΣ ΜΕΓΑΛΟΥ ΑΡΣΑΚΟΥ*;
8   Mint of Seleucia; rev. Heracles-Verethragna, *ΒΑΣΙΛΕΩΣ ΜΕΓΑΛΟΥ ΑΡΣΑΚΟΥ ΦΙΛΕΛΛΗΝΟΥ*, in exergue *ΔΟΡ* (year 174: 139/8 BC).

Phraates II (*c*.138–127 BC):

9   Mint of Seleucia. Rev. enthroned male deity with cornucopia and Nike, *ΒΑΣΙΛΕΩΣ ΜΕΓΑΛΟΥ ΑΡΣΑΚΟΥ ΝΙΚΗΦΟΡΟΥ*;
10 Rev. epithet *ΘΕΟΠΑΤΟΡΟΣ* 'son of god';
11 Mint of Nisa. Obv. *NICAK* behind king's head; rev. *ΘΕΟΠΑΤΟΡΟΣ* .

Artabanus I (*c*.127–124 BC):

12 Mint of Rhagae (Ray). Obv. *PA* behind king's head; rev. *ΒΑΣΙΛΕΩΣ ΜΕΓΑΛΟΥ ΑΡΣΑΚΟΥ ΦΙΛΕΛΛΗΝΟΥ*;
13 Rev. *ΘΕΟΠΑΤΟΡΟΣ*;
14 Mint of Seleucia, 125/4 BC. Rev. seated deity with cornucopia, winged Nike with diadem, *ΒΑΣΙΛΕΩΣ ΑΡΣΑΚΟΥ*.

Parthians (*c*.238 BC–AD 223/4)

[The kingdom of Parthia] took its name from the Parthian Arsaces, a man of low birth; he had been a brigand chief during his younger days, but since his ideals gradually changed for the better, by a series of brilliant exploits he rose to great heights. After many glorious and valiant deeds, and after he had conquered Seleucus [II] Nicator [246–225 BC] . . . and had driven out the Macedonian garrison, he passed his life in quiet peace, and was a mild ruler and judge of his subjects. (Ammianus Marcellinus XXIII.vi.2–3)

The Arsacid Parthians were originally a tribe of Iranian nomads called Parni or Aparni. They were part of the confederacy of the Dahae, a North Iranian nomadic group on the eastern shore of the Caspian Sea,[26] who had a similar nomadic lifestyle to that of the east Iranian Scythians. The Parni gradually moved southwards into the Seleucid province

of Parthia. This may not have been exactly the same as the satrapy of Parthava listed in the Bisitun inscription of Darius, for the Seleucids seem to have amalgamated the two former Achaemenid satrapies of Hyrcania (modern Gurgan) and Parthava (Bivar 1983, p. 24). Under Antiochus I (281–261 BC), the satrap of this province was a Persian called Andragoras,[27] who towards the end of the reign of Antiochus II (261–246 BC) seized power from the Seleucids and minted gold and silver coins in his own name (fig. 45.1).

In 247 BC – which marks the beginning of the Arsacid era – Arsaces (*c*.238–211 BC) was elected leader of the Parni tribe (fig. 45.2). In 238 BC he and his brother Tiridates killed Andragoras and established control over Parthia (Bivar 1983, pp. 28–9). This date marks the independence of Parthia and the beginning of Arsacid rule in this former Seleucid province.

Figure 46 Coins of Characene (*c.* second century AD):
1 Obv. diademed head of ruler; rev. seated nude figure;
2–4 Obverse and rev. head to right.
Coins of Elymais:
5 Kamnaskires I Nikephoros (*c.*150 BC). Obv. Seleucid-style head of king; rev. Apollo on omphalos, holding two arrows, 'King Kamnaskires Nikephoros';

6 Kamnaskires II (?) and Queen Anzaze (*c.*82–1 BC). Obv. anchor symbol, star and crescent behind heads; rev. seated Zeus, names of king and consort;
7 Kamnaskires III (?) (*c.* first century AD?). rev. traces of inscription (?);
8 Orodes II (*c.* late first century AD). Obv. facing head of king in a Parthian tiara/*kolah*; rev. raised pattern of dots;
9 Phraates (*c.* second century AD).

It was after this conquest that the Parni newcomers adopted the language of Parthia – a north-west Iranian language related to Median – and became known as the Arsacid Parthians (Bivar 1983, p. 27).[28] According to Strabo (XV.i.36),

> Such is also the custom among the Parthians; for all are called Arsaces, although personally one king is called Orodes, another Phraates, and another something else.

The tradition that each ruler from now on carried the throne name Arsaces has often complicated the exact identification of many of the kings, particularly in the early period. Strabo (XI.ix.2) also says that

> [The Parthians] grew so strong . . . through successes in warfare, that finally they established themselves as lords of the whole the country inside [east of] the Euphrates. And they also took a part of Bactriana, having forced the Scythians, and still earlier Eucratides and his followers to yield to them.

The growth of kingdom into empire, which took place under Mithradates I (*c.*171–138 BC), is reflected in his expanding coin titles: 'Arsaces' to 'King Arsaces' (fig. 45.3, 5), 'the great king Arsaces' (fig. 45.4, 7–8) , 'philhellene' (fig. 45.8), and 'of divine descent' (fig. 45.3; Sellwood 1980, pp. 29, 35, type 10.i–iv). In June 148 BC Media was still under control of the Seleucids, as indicated by a dated Greek inscription from Bisitun, which mentions a Kleomenes as 'Viceroy of the Upper Satrapies' (Bivar 1983, p. 33). But soon afterwards

Mithradates took Ecbatana (modern Hamadan) and the region was occupied by the Parthians (fig. 45.6).

In 147 BC the Seleucids lost Susa to Kamnaskires, the king of Elymais. Mithradates was also able to capitalise on the internecine struggles of the Seleucids subsequently in 141 BC by invading Babylonia and occupying Seleucia on the Tigris. An attempt in 140–139 BC by the Seleucid ruler Demetrius II (145–139/8 BC) to recover lost territories proved a failure (fig. 43.5). He was taken prisoner by the Parthian army and sent to Mithradates, who by this time had returned to Hyrcania in north-eastern Iran. The capture of Demetrius ended resistance in Babylonia, and Mithradates was able to extend Parthian control over Iran, including Characene on the Persian Gulf, Susa and further east into Elymais (fig. 46; Bivar 1983, pp. 34–5). The Arsacids were now in control of both Iran and Mesopotamia and their empire stretched from the Euphrates river to eastern Iran.

Towards the end of Mithradates' long reign, nomadic movements along the north-eastern and eastern borders created an unsettled situation among the existing tribal groups of the region. In particular, the movement of the Yuezhi confederation westwards pushed the Shaka – a people of east Iranian origin – away from their traditional pastures towards Parthian territory (Bivar 1983, p. 36). Phraates II (*c.*138–127 BC) (fig. 45.9–11) had to deal with both the tribal advance in the east and a Seleucid revival under Antiochus VII Sidetes (139/8–129 BC) in the west (fig. 43.6). After an initial Seleucid victory and their advance into Media, Phraates succeeded in regathering his army and killed Antiochus in battle. Phraates then turned his attention to Syria, but soon had to abandon the western frontier to face nomad invasions in eastern Iran where he died in battle, probably against the Shakas, in 128 BC. Some of his drachms have the epithet 'son of god' (fig. 45.10–11). Phraates was succeeded by Artabanus I (c.127–124/3 BC) (fig. 45.12–14), who is described as a 'philhellene' on both drachms and tetradrachms (fig. 45.12). He also uses the epithet 'son of god' (fig. 45.13), but he is the first Parthian ruler who abandons the Greek costume in favour of a v-necked jacket. Artabanus was also killed on the eastern front while fighting the Tocharis.

A rebellion by Hyspaosines,[29] the ruler of Characene, against Himerus, the Parthian governor of Seleucia on the Tigris, proved initially successful. The father of Hyspaosines was Sagdodonacus, a Persian who has been identified as Saxt.[30] Cuneiform tablets from Warka record his victory in Babylon in 127 BC (Bivar 1983, p. 40). Hyspaosines also minted coins at Spasinou Charax in 124/3 BC, but with the accession of Mithradates II (c.123–91 BC) to the Parthian throne (fig. 48.1–4) his short-lived autonomy came to an end (Assar 2006, pp. 105–8).[31] However, Characene remained a local kingdom under Parthian suzerainty until the advent of the Sasanian dynasty in AD 223/4 (fig. 46.1–4; Bivar 1983, p. 40; Sellwood 1983, pp. 310–11). Mithradates re-established Parthian supremacy over the Shakas, who had invaded Sistan in the south-east. He was also successful in his campaign against Artavasdes of Armenia, whose son – taken as hostage to Parthia at this time – later, with Parthian help, became Tigranes I (c.97–56 BC) of Armenia, in return for 'seventy valleys' of territory. Subsequently, when Tigranes 'had grown in power, he not only took these places back but also devastated their country', extending his control into Parthia, Media and Mesopotamia, and ultimately as far south as Syria and Phoenicia (Strabo XI.xiv.15; Bivar 1983, p. 41).

Parthian administrative centres – such as ancient Mithradatkert, the citadel of Nisa (in modern Turkmenistan) (fig. 47),[32] and ancient Hecatompylos in Comisene (modern Shahr-i Qumis, near Damghan) – seem to have been transferred under Mithradates II from the east to the west. Although early Arsacid rulers resided frequently in Hyrcania, the ultimate aim was to move the centre of power to Ctesiphon in Babylonia. Ecbatana was the favourite summer residence because of its climate. The reasons behind a gradual move to the west may have been the nomad threat in the north-east, as well as the importance of establishing firmer control over Mesopotamia and its trade centres (Bivar 1983, p. 39).

On an eroded relief at Bisitun, Mithradates is shown with a number of satraps who pay homage to the great king. Among the dignitaries identified in the accompanying Greek inscription is Gotarzes, satrap of satraps (Assar 2006, pp. 143–5; V. S. Curtis 2000, pp. 25–6, fig. 7). Towards the end of his reign, a dynastic feud erupted in Parthia between Mithradates II and Sinatruces, who was in control of eastern and central provinces (fig. 48.1–5; Sellwood 1983, pp. 284–5; Assar 2006: pp. 145–6).[33] However, Gotarzes, the elder son of Mithradates (fig. 48.5), appears to have retained control from

c.90 BC of Babylonia, where he remained in power until Orodes I took control in 87 BC (fig. 48.6).[34]

In the middle of the first century BC Parthian internal struggles came momentarily to a halt because of war with Rome. At Carrhae in 53 BC the Roman forces received a fatal blow from the army of Orodes II (c.57–38 BC) (fig. 48.8–10) under the leadership of Surena.[35] The Parthians motivated themselves for battle by beating 'hollow drums of distended hide, covered with bronze bells' which produced 'a low and dismal tone, a blend of wild beast's roar and harsh thunder peal', a sound calculated 'to confound the soul' (Plutarch, *Crassus* XXIII.7; XXIV.3–6):

> When they had sufficiently terrified the Romans with their noise, they dropped the coverings of their armour, and were revealed blazing in breastplates and helmets, their Margianian steel glittering keen and bright, and their horses clad in plates of bronze and steel. . . . At first they proposed to charge the Romans with their lances, and throw their first ranks into confusion; but when they saw the depth of their formation . . . they drew back. . . . Crassus ordered his light-armed troops to charge, but [the Romans] did not advance far before they encountered such a multitude of arrows that they abandoned their undertaking and ran back for shelter among the men-at-arms, among whom they caused the beginning of disorder and fear. . . . The Parthians now stood at long intervals from one another and began to shoot their arrows from all sides at once, not with any accurate aim (for the dense formation of the Romans would not suffer an archer to miss his man even if he wished it). . . . At once, then, the plight of the Romans was a grievous one; for if they kept their ranks, they were wounded in great numbers, and if they tried to come to close quarters with the enemy, they . . . suffered just as much. For the Parthians shot as they fled, . . . and it is a very clever thing to seek safety while still fighting, and to take away the shame of flight.

The Romans suffered the intense humiliation of losing their standards in this battle, but nevertheless continued to campaign vigorously against Parthian expansionist policies in the Near East. Prince Pacorus, a son of Orodes II, crossed the Euphrates and – with the help of a Roman officer, Labienus – invaded Syria in 40 BC, took Apamea on the Orontes river and advanced as far as Jerusalem (Bivar 1983, p. 57). Labienus also invaded Asia Minor and established temporary Parthian supremacy in Caria, Lydia and Ionia, but was soon driven back to Syria and killed by the forces of Mark Antony under the Roman general Publius Ventidius (Schippmann 1980, p. 42). Another attempt by Pacorus to invade Syria in 38 BC also proved disastrous, when he and his forces were trapped and killed by the Roman army.

Rome now planned an invasion of Parthia via Armenia. In the spring of 36 BC Mark Antony advanced through Media and

Figure 47 The Square Hall at Nisa (ancient Mithradatkert), in Turkmenistan, with a quadrilobate column, second to first century BC.

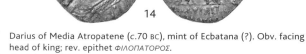

Figure 48 Parthian coins.
Mithradates II (*c*.123–91 BC):
1 Mint of Seleucia. Obv. king in Parthian jacket;
2 Rev. royal archer, *ΒΑΣΙΛΕΩΣ ΒΑΣΙΛΕΩΝ ΜΕΓΑΛΟΥ ΑΡΣΑΚΟΥ ΕΠΙΦΑΝΟΥΣ*;
3 Obv. *MI* behind head; rev. horse's head, *ΒΑΣΙΛΕΩΣ ΜΕΓΑΛΟΥ ΑΡΣΑΚΟΥ ΕΠΙΦΑΝΟΥΣ*;
4 Obv. king wearing Parthian tiara/*kolah* with diadem; rev. *ΒΑΣΙΛΕΩΣ ΒΑΣΙΛΕΩΝ ΜΕΓΑΛΟΥ ΑΡΣΑΚΟΥ ΕΠΙΦΑΝΟΥΣ*.
5 Sinatruces I or Gotarzes I (*c*.91–87 BC), mint of Ecbatana (?). Obv. king in *kolah* decorated with a row of stags; rev. epithet *ΘΕΟΠΑΤΟΡΟΣ* 'son of god';
6 Sinatruces I (?) or Orodes I (*c*.90–80 BC), mint of Seleucia. Rev. epithet *ΦΙΛΟΠΑΤΟΡΟΣ*, 'the lover of his father';

7 Darius of Media Atropatene (*c*.70 BC), mint of Ecbatana (?). Obv. facing head of king; rev. epithet *ΦΙΛΟΠΑΤΟΡΟΣ*.
Orodes II (*c*.57–38 BC):
8 Mint of Seleucia. Rev. king seated with standing Tyche offering a palm frond;
9–10 Mint of Ecbatana (?). Obv. astral signs around king's head.
Phraates IV (*c*.38–2 BC):
11 Mint of Seleucia. Obv. king in v-necked jacket; rev. king with Nike/Tyche;
12 Mint of Seleucia. Rev. king seated, Athena offering a diadem;
13 Mint of Ecbatana (?). Obv. bird (eagle ?) with diadem behind king's head.
14 Tiridates (*c*.29–27 BC), mint of Seleucia, 27 BC, overstruck on coin of Phraates IV. Rev. epithet *ΦΙΛΟΡΩΜΑΙΟΥ*.

Atropatene (Iranian Azarbaijan) to face the Parthian forces under the command of Phraates IV (*c*.38–2 BC) (fig. 48.10–12) in the region around Lake Urmia in north-western Iran. After a long, unsuccessful siege of Praata/Praaspa, the capital of Atropatene,[36] resulting in heavy Roman losses, Mark Antony withdrew, probably eastwards from Maragheh, through the Sahand mountains and the Tabriz plain of north-western Iran (Bivar 1983, p. 64). An attempt by Mark Antony's emissaries to regain the lost Roman standards was rejected by the Parthian king who – in a pose reminiscent of the seated archer image on the reverse of Parthian coins (fig. 48.10) – 'held a conference with them seated upon a golden chair and twanging his bowstring' (Dio Cassius XLIX.27; Sellwood 1980, types 51.44, 59.2).

The Roman standards were formally returned to Rome only in 20 BC, after lengthy negotiations between Augustus (31 BC–AD 14) and Phraates IV, an event which was used to maximum propaganda effect by Augustus (Schneider 2007, pp. 54–5). This so-called victory was commemorated throughout the Roman empire and depictions of the handover appeared on coins (fig. 49), small finds, monuments and even on the cuirass of the Augustus statue from Prima Porta (Schneider 1998, pp. 95–8, pls 1.1–2, 2–3; 2007, p. 55, fig 2–3).

By now the Parthians were fully in control of the ancient Near East, but internal rivalries among the ruling families and aristocracy, as well as external conflicts with Rome predominated. Contenders to the throne often received help

Figure 49 Roman coins of Augustus (31 BC–AD 14), commemorating the return of the Roman standards in 20 BC:
1 Mint of Rome, 18 BC. Obv. Head of Liber; rev. bare-headed kneeling Parthian in tunic, trousers and cloak, holding a standard;
2 Obv. head of Augustus (minted 20 or 19–18 BC); rev. draped Victory kneeling on the back of a bull and cutting its throat, *ARMENIA CAPTA*;
3 Obv. head of Augustus (minted 20 or 19–18 BC); rev. *SIGNIS PARTHICIS RECEPTIS*.

from the Romans, although they were rarely successful. Exceptions in the short term were Tiridates, who twice seized power in the period 29–27 BC and minted coins at Seleucia as ΦΙΛΟΡΩΜΑΙΟΥ 'Friend of the Romans'; and the puppet king Parthamaspates *c.* AD 116 (figs 48.14; 50.10; Bivar 1983, pp. 65–6, 91; Sellwood 1980, type 81).

Despite short periods of peace, Roman–Parthian relations remained tense as the two powers fought for supremacy in Armenia and Mesopotamia. In the first half of the first century AD, when Rome protested about the appointment of a Parthian prince to the throne of Armenia, Artabanus II (*c.* AD 10–38) (fig. 50.4) wrote to the emperor Tiberius that whatever was possessed by Cyrus, and afterwards by Alexander, was undoubtedly his by right, and he was determined to recover it by force (Tacitus VI.31). Parthia's claim to all the territories which in the past had belonged to the Persians and Macedonians was understandably not accepted by Rome, while the latter's interference in Parthian internal affairs and support for rival kings caused instability for the Parthian empire and its nobility.

The second century witnessed a series of Roman campaigns against Parthia, particularly under the emperor Trajan (AD 98–117), who in October AD 113 rejected a request for peace by the Parthian king Osroes (*c.* AD 109–29) (fig. 50.9), and embarked on an expedition to the east (Bivar 1983, p. 87). In AD 114 Armenia was invaded and became a Roman province. In AD 115 Trajan turned his attention to northern Mesopotamia. The following year the city of Dura Europos on the Euphrates – which had been under Parthian control since the early first century BC – fell to the Romans for the first time (Bivar 1983, p. 89).[37] The capital Ctesiphon was also taken by Trajan, who was now awarded the title Parthicus by the Senate. After advancing as far as Babylonia and the Persian Gulf, he returned to northern Mesopotamia and unsuccessfully besieged Hatra. Here a mixed population of Iranians, Arabs and Arameans fully supported the Parthians and forced a complete Roman retreat in the autumn of AD 117 (Bivar 1983, pp. 90–1).[38]

After half a century of peace, hostilities between Parthia and Rome flared up again in the latter half of the second century. Although initially successful, a Parthian offensive under Vologases IV (*c.* AD 147–91) ended with the destruction and burning of Seleucia on the Tigris and Ctesiphon by the Romans under Marcus Aurelius in AD 161.[39] Dura Europos and

the Jabal Sinjar mountains in northern Mesopotamia became the official Roman eastern frontier. At the end of the century confrontation broke out once more between Parthia under Vologases V (*c.* AD 191–208) (fig. 50.12) and Rome. In AD 197 Septimius Severus invaded northern Mesopotamia, captured Seleucia and Babylon, and sacked Ctesiphon. The Roman Senate honoured him with the title of Parthicus Maximus. However, a siege of Hatra proved unsuccessful yet again (Bivar 1983, p. 94). All further Roman military campaigns were halted by Caracalla, when he became emperor in AD 211.

In Parthia central power seems to have been divided between two brothers, Vologases VI (*c.* AD 208–28) and Artabanus IV (*c.* AD 216–23/4).[40] Vologases struck coins at Seleucia on the Tigris and may have controlled Mesopotamia (fig. 50.13; Bivar 1983, p. 94). Artabanus (Ardavan) ruled from Media and also controlled Susa, as recorded on the Artabanus stele of AD 216 from the site (fig. 50.14). During this time a series of successful revolts occurred in south-western Iran. Ardashir, the son of Papak, who had established himself as the local king of Fars, challenged the central authority of Artabanus IV. At the battle of Hormizdgan in western Iran, Ardashir killed Artabanus in AD 223/4 and became the new king of kings of Iran.

The earliest Parthian coins – of Arsaces I, perhaps from Mithradatkert/Nisa – show the head of the ruler on the obverse and a seated archer on the reverse, both turned to the right in the Seleucid fashion (Sellwood 1980, type 1). Soon, however, the direction of the king's head is changed to the left (fig. 45.2; Abgarians and Sellwood 1971, pp. 115–16, pl. 20; Sellwood 1980, types 1–3, 4). The soft cap with the top bent over to one side, worn by the ruler, seems to be derived from the tall, pointed, Scythian hat seen in late sixth-century Achaemenid reliefs like Bisitun and Persepolis. The coin legends are in Greek, but coins from the Bojnurd hoard (dating from the very beginning of the Parthian period) have an Aramaic legend, which could be read as *krny*, i.e. the 'Karen'[41] who – like the Surens – belonged to the top aristocratic families (Abgarians and Sellwood 1971, p. 113). The early coin legends carry the king's name together with the appellation 'Arsaces' and sometimes the additional title 'autocrat' (Abgarians and Sellwood 1971, pp. 111–12; Sellwood 1980, types 1–6).

When Mithradates I captured Seleucia on the Tigris in *c.*141 BC, he immediately struck silver issues (fig. 45.8), in addition to the already existing silver drachms and bronze coins from the highlands of Iran (fig. 45.3–5; Bivar 1983, p. 34; Sellwood 1983, p. 282). The portraits of Mithradates on all these issues look strikingly similar to those of the Seleucid satrap Andragoras (fig. 45.1; Curtis 2007, p. 9). Dates appear for the first time on the tetradrachms of Mithradates minted at Seleucia. The names of the months are in Greek, while Greek letters representing numerical values give the year based on the Seleucid era of 313/12 BC (fig. 45.8). A drachm of Artabanus I has a date which conversely appears to have been calculated according to the Arsacid era of 247 BC (Gardner 1877, p. 27; Wroth 1903, p. 21, n. 3; Sellwood 1980, type 22.2).

Greek legends on early Arsacid coins are short, but from the time of Mithradates I onwards the variety of epithets expanded to include ΦΙΛΕΛΛΗΝΟΣ 'philhellene', ΕΥΕΡΓΕΤΟΥ 'beneficent', ΕΠΙΦΑΝΟΥΣ 'god manifest', ΔΙΚΑΙΟΥ 'the just',

Figure 50 Parthian coins:

1 Phraataces (Phraates V) (c.2 BC–AD 4) and his mother/wife, Musa, mint of Ecbatana (?). Rev. female head, *ΘΕΑΣ ΟΥΡΑΝΙΑΣ ΜΟΥΣΗΣ ΒΑΣΙΛΙΣΣΗΣ*, 'goddess, Urania Musa, queen';

2–3 Vonones I (AD 8/9), mint of Ecbatana (?). Rev. winged Nike/Tyche with wreath;

4 Artabanus II (c. AD 10–38), mint of Seleucia, AD 26/7. Obv. facing king; rev. king on horseback receiving palm frond from Nike;

5 Gotarzes II (c. AD 40–51), mint of Seleucia, AD 45/6. Rev. king's name to left on edge of flan;

6 Vologases I (c. AD 51–78), mint of Ecbatana (?). Obv. Parthian letters *wl* (Vologases) behind king's head;

7 Pacorus II (c. AD 78–105), mint of Seleucia, AD 78;

8 Artabanus III (c. AD 80–90), mint of Seleucia, AD 80/1;

9 Osroes I (c. AD 109–29), mint of Ecbatana (?). Obv. king with tripartite hairstyle;

10 Parthamaspates (c. AD 116), Roman 'puppet king', mint of Ecbatana (?);

11 Mithradates IV (c. AD 140), mint of Ecbatana (?). Obv. name and title in Parthian, *mtrdt MLK'* (Shah Mithradad), in-between Greek legend;

12 Vologases V (c. AD 191–208), mint of Ecbatana (?). Obv. facing king with tripartite hairstyle;

13 Vologases VI (c. AD 208–28), mint of Seleucia, AD 209/10. Obv. B behind king's head;

14 Artabanus IV (c. AD 216–23/4), mint of Ecbatana (?). Obv. abbreviated king's name *al* (AR).

ΝΙΚΑΤΟΡΟΣ 'victorious' and occasionally *ΣΩΤΗΡΟΣ* 'the deliverer' (Sellwood 1983, pp. 279–85). Phraates II, a son of Mithradates I, used the epithet *ΘΕΟΠΑΤΟΡΟΣ*, which refers to his divine descent (fig. 45.10; Sellwood 1980: type 16.4; 1983: p. 282). *ΦΙΛΟΠΑΤΟΡΟΣ*, 'the lover of his father', is the popular ephithet for a number of kings, including Orodes I (when referring to Mithradates II) (fig. 48.6) and also Darius of Media Atropatene (fig. 48.7; Sellwood 1983, p. 286).

Almost all these epithets – apart from *ΘΕΟΠΑΤΟΡΟΣ* – were common amongst the Seleucid kings (Mørkholm 1991, p. 31). The Greco-Bactrians – the eastern neighbours of the early Parthians – also used some of the same titles. Antimachus I (c.180–170 BC), for example, is described as *ΒΑΣΙΛΕΩΣ ΘΕΟΥ* 'divine king' (fig. 26.1); Diodotus I (c.250–230 BC) and

Menander I (c.155–130 BC) preferred *ΒΑΣΙΛΕΩΣ ΣΩΤΗΡΟΣ* 'saviour king' (fig. 52.7, 16); while from the time of Eucratides I (c.174–145 BC), the title *ΒΑΣΙΛΕΩΣ ΜΕΓΑΛΟΥ* 'of the great king' begins to appear (fig. 52.9; Bopearachchi 1991, pp. 183, 187, 178, 225, 207, 211 respectively).

Greek letters, which can be seen either as mint abbreviations or as initials of the mint masters, begin to appear on the obverse behind the head of the king from the time of Phraates II (c.138–127 BC) and Artabanus I (c.127–124 BC). These are *PA* for Rhagae (Ecbatana) and *TAM* for Tambrax (fig. 45.12). At the same time complete place names – such as *NICAK* for Nisa (fig. 45.11) – are written in full (Wroth 1903, pp. lxxvii–lxxxiii; Abgarians and Sellwood 1971, p. 113). On coins from Mithradates II (c.123–91 BC) onwards, the *M* (fig. 48.3) and *MI* behind the king's head could stand for Mithradatkert (Nisa), while *MP* and *MAP* may be abbreviations of ΜΑΡΓΑΝΗ or Margiana (Gardner 1877, p. 33). The Parthians also apparently had a peripatetic court mint, ΚΑΤΑΣΤΡΑΤΕΙΑ (Sellwood 1980, type 30.28–9; 1983, p. 287).[42]

During the reign of Mithradates II the traditional ancient Near Eastern royal title 'king of kings' or 'great king of kings' was revived by the Parthians, as attested by coins and official cuneiform documents from Warka in southern Mesopotamia of *c*.94 BC (Van der Spek 1998, pp. 214–24; V. S. Curtis 2000, p. 25). This title was not common among the Seleucid and Greco-Bactrian rulers, but was adopted by Indo-Scythians such as Maues (*c*.75–65 BC) and appears on coins of Gondophares (*c*. AD 32–60) and other Indo-Parthian kings as well (figs 56.1–3; 59.1; Mit. 681, 683, 686, 1072–5, 1077–9). It was also used by the Kushans (fig. 61).[43]

The 'Iranisation' process is already evident in the adoption of the Parthian trouser-suit (fig. 51) not only for the archer figure on the reverse of coins but also for the obverse portrait of the king from the time of Artabanus I (*c*.127–124 BC) (fig. 45.12–13). Details of the trousers and belted v-necked jacket are clearly visible on the reverse of Parthian tetradrachms of the first century BC to second century AD (fig. 48; Sellwood 1980, types 39.1, 46–8, 50–7, 60–5, 68–70, 72–9, 84). As part of this costume Mithradates II introduced a bejewelled tall hat – the tiara or *kolah* (fig. 48.4) – which remained popular until the end of the Parthian period[44] and was presented by the Parthian king of kings as one of the royal insignia to local kings (Curtis 1998, p. 65).[45] The archer motif was retained on drachms struck in the highlands of Iran, but from the mid first century BC elsewhere it was replaced by images of the king enjoying divine support. Tetradrachms of Orodes II and Phraates IV, struck at Seleucia on the Tigris, show a striking likeness between the royal portrait on the obverse and the image of the enthroned king in the presence of a divinity on the reverse (fig. 48.8, 11–12, 14). Also popular at this time are symbols, such as stars and crescents, which appear mostly on drachms (fig. 48.9–10). In the first century BC there are also divine symbols, such as a goddess or an eagle with a diadem behind the royal head, as known from coins of Phraates IV (fig. 47.13) and Phraataces/ Phraates V (*c*.2 BC–AD 4) and his mother/wife, the Roman slave Musa (fig. 50.1; Sellwood 1980, type 58).

Artabanus II (*c*. AD 10–38) was from Media Atropatene in north-western Iran and an Arsacid through his mother. He continued the process of Iranisation almost immediately by dropping the title 'philhellene' from the reverse legends of his tetradrachms (Sellwood 1980, types 62–3). The king on the reverse is not only shown seated on a throne but also appears on horseback receiving a symbol of kingship from a deity: either Tyche the goddess of Fortune or Nike the goddess of Victory (fig. 50.4; Sellwood 1980, type 63). His tetradrachms show a facing portrait of the king, a pose which is first seen *c*.70 BC on coins of Darius of Media Atropatene (fig. 47.7; Sellwood 1980, type 35; 1983, p. 286).[46]

From the first century BC onwards personal names were often added to coin legends, either in Parthian script on the obverse and reverse of drachms or in Greek as part of the now formalised reverse legend, as reconstructed from tetradrachms of Mithradates III (*c*.57–54 BC) overstruck by his brother

Figure 51 Bronze statue of a Parthian noble from Shami, south-west Iran, second half of the first century BC.

Orodes II (Sellwood 1980, type 41.1; 1983, p. 289). This is particularly noticeable at times of political unrest and instability. For example, Vonones I (*c*. AD 8/9), one of the sons of Phraates V, who grew up in Rome and enjoyed Roman support, appears on his coins with a short western hairstyle (fig. 50.2–3). The legend mentions the personal name of the king on the obverse in the Roman fashion, while the reverse legends of his drachms and bronzes refer to Vonones as the 'conqueror of Artabanus' (Wroth 1903, pp. 144–5; Sellwood 1980, type 60.5; 1983, p. 293). Gotarzes II (*c*. AD 40–51), the son of Artabanus II and rival to his brother Vardanes (*c*. AD 39–45), is also named in the reverse legend of his tetradrachms (Sellwood 1980, type 66.2).

In the first century AD the personal name of the ruler is also sometimes written in Parthian behind the king's head on the obverse of drachms. This is particularly noticeable on the drachms of Vologases I (*c*. AD 51–78) (fig. 50.6). Coins of later kings, such as Mithradates IV (*c*. AD 140), carry the king's full name and royal title *mtrdt MLK*', 'King Mithradates' in Parthian, on the reverse (fig. 50.11; Sellwood 1980, p. 262, types 71.1, 82.1; Schmitt 1998, pp. 167–8). In the same period, however, personal names are often found as part of the reverse Greek legend on tetradrachms issued by such rulers as Pacorus II (*c.* AD 78–105) and Artabanus III (*c.* AD 80–90), and this continues in the second century (fig. 50.7–8; Sellwood 1980, types 74–7, 79).

Greco-Bactrians and Indo-Greeks (c.250 BC–AD 10)

> The Greeks who caused Bactria to revolt grew so powerful on account of the fertility of the country, that they became masters, not only of Ariana, but also of India; . . . and more tribes were subdued by them than by Alexander, by Menander in particular (at least if he actually crossed the Hypanis [Hyphases: Beas river] towards the east and advanced as far as the Imaüs [Himalayas[47]]), for some were subdued by him personally and others by Demetrius, the son of Euthydemus, the king of the Bactrians. (Strabo XI.xi.1)

According to Strabo (XI.xi.2), the Bactrians also held Sogdiana, between the Oxus (Amu Darya) and Jaxartes (Syr Darya) rivers,[48] the latter forming the boundary with the nomadic tribes to the north. The beginnings of independence are evident in the coins of Diodotus (*c.*250–230 BC), 'the governor of a thousand cities of Bactria', whose earliest issues appear to show his own portrait, but bear the name of his Seleucid overlord, Antiochus II (261–246 BC), while subsequent issues bear his own name (fig. 52.1–2; Kovalenko 1995/6, p. 17). According to Justin (XLI.iv.4–9), during the struggle for power between Antiochus' sons Seleucus II (246–226 BC) and Antiochus Hierax, Diodotus 'broke away and took the title of king. All the people of the East followed his example'. He was succeeded by his son, also called Diodotus (Holt 1999, pp. 55–60).

In coinage the two Bactrians are differentiated by their titles 'Soter' (saviour: fig. 52.7) and 'Theos' (divine) on the pedigree coins of the later Bactrian king Agathocles (Kovalenko 1995/6, p. 17): title changes of this kind provide the standard means of distinguishing between rulers of the same name amongst their successors. However, the reconstructed numismatic sequence produces a genealogy of 'rather too many kings'[49] for a single kingdom within the estimated time frame; a problem overcome by the suggestion that the Greco-Bactrian and Indo-Greek territories must have been often divided between rival rulers, with additional 'sub-kings, joint-kings, expectant kings and satraps or governors', all of whom may have minted coins (Keay 2000, p. 107). Justin (XLI.vi.1–2) gives an indication of their quarrelsome inclinations, for he says the Bactrians 'were so harassed by various wars, that they lost their sway and even their liberty. For when they had been broken by the wars they had waged with the Sogdians, the Arachosians, the Drangians, the Arians and the Indians, they finally succumbed to the once weaker power of the Parthians'.[50] This impression is reinforced by the few other surviving references by Classical authors.

In 212–205 BC, while Antiochus III was campaigning to recover Bactria, he defeated Euthydemus I (*c.*230–200 BC) in battle (Polybius X.49).[51] Euthydemus (fig. 52.3) – who is identified as 'a native of Magnesia', the Ionian city in Asia Minor – then claimed that Antiochus 'was not justified in attempting to deprive him of his kingdom, as he himself had never revolted against the king, but after the others had revolted he had possessed himself of the throne of Bactria by

destroying their descendants' (Polybius XI.39). When Euthydemus sent his son Demetrius to ratify the agreement, Antiochus judged the latter to be 'worthy of royal rank' and conceded Sogdiana, Bactria and apparently also part of Margiana to the west (now southern Turkmenistan).

In negotiating the retention of these lands, Euthydemus also pointed out that, if Antiochus did not grant him the kingdom, 'neither of them would be safe; for considerable hordes of nomads were approaching, and this was not only a grave danger to both of them, but if they consented to admit them, the country would certainly relapse into barbarism'. Strabo identifies the nomads by 'the general name of Scythians . . . who originally came from the country on the other side of the Jaxartes river that adjoins that of the Sacae and the Sogdiani and was occupied by the Sacae' (XI.viii.2). Despite Euthydemus' efforts, Sogdiana was lost, presumably to the Sacae and Sogdians, by the end of the third century BC. However, the local Sogdian kings continued to produce coins in the Greek tradition by copying issues of their former Bactrian overlord, a practice which survived in this region well into the first century BC. In fact, among the earliest Greco-Bactrian coins to enter the British Museum collection are silver tetradrachms of Euthydemus and increasingly crude later imitations collected in 1832 at the 'Khoja-o-ban ruins' (i.e. the site of Panjikent), north-west of Bukhara, by Alexander Burnes (1805–41) and Dr J. G. Gerard (1795–1835) during their exploratory expedition to Central Asia (fig. 52.4–5; Prinsep 1833a, pp. 310–18, pl. XI.1–6; Burnes 1834, vol. II, pp. 463–73; Wilson 1841, pp. 223–5, pls I.4–10, XXI.1–2).

At about the time Sogdiana was lost, Demetrius I (*c.*200–190 BC) and subsequent Bactrian rulers began to extend Greek control into the territories south of the Hindu Kush mountains. Coins of Demetrius (fig. 52.6) depict him wearing the elephant-scalp head-dress of Alexander the Great, a reference to both their conquests in India, which in this period – under the declining power of the Mauryans – included the Parapamisidae (eastern Afghanistan from the southern slopes of the Hindu Kush to the Khyber Pass).

Silver tetradrachms of Agathocles (*c.*190–180 BC), one of the next Bactrian kings in the reconstructed sequence, proclaim his legitimate pedigree by linking the portraits of his predecessors Alexander the Great, Antiochus II, Diodotus I and II, Euthydemus I, Demetrius I and Pantaleon (*c.*190–185 BC), with his own name and titles on the reverse (fig. 52.7). The bronze issues of Agathocles and Pantaleon (figs 26.6; 52.8) are the first to imitate Indian designs and to introduce bilingual legends (in Greek and Brahmi). Agathocles also produced a monolingual bronze issue in Kharoshthi for use in the Taxila region (fig. 26.8; Bopearachchi 1991, pp. 57–8, pl. 8, ser. 11). Apollodotus I (*c.*180–160 BC), who is identified by Pompeius Trogus as a king of India (*Prologue* LXIV), introduced bilingual legends in Greek and Kharoshthi (fig. 26.9), a practice which subsequently became standard for all Greek rulers and their successors south of the Hindu Kush.

The Hindu Kush north–south divide is reinforced by coin finds. Aï Khanum, in Bactria itself, produced a continuous sequence – excepting Pantaleon – down to Apollodotus I (2 coins) and Eucratides I (12 coins; Bernard 1985,

Figure 52 Bactrian and Indo-Greek coins.
Diodotus I (*c.*250–230 BC):
1 Issue in the name of his Seleucid overlord, Antiochus II. Rev. Zeus;
2 Issue in his own name.
3 Euthydemus I (*c.*230–200 BC). Rev. Heracles;
4–5 Euthydemus I imitations from Khoja-o ban, Bukhara;
6 Demetrius I (*c.*200–190 BC) wearing the elephant scalp of Alexander. Rev. Heracles.
7 Agathocles (*c.*190–180 BC) pedigree coin struck in the name of Diodotus I as *ΣΩΤΗΡΟΣ* 'saviour' and 'in the reign of the just king' *ΒΑΣΙΛΕΥΟΝΤΟΣ ΔΙΚΑΙΟΥ* Agathocles. Obv. portrait of Diodotus; rev. Zeus;
8 Pantaleon (*c.*190–185 BC) with bilingual legend in Brahmi and Greek. Obv. Indian goddess, Subhadra (Krishna's sister); rev. panther of Dionysus.

Eucratides I (*c.*174–145 BC):
9 Rev. Dioscuri on horseback, *ΒΑΣΙΛΕΩΣ ΜΕΓΑΛΟΥ* 'of the great king';
10 Obv. Heliocles and Laodice; rev. head of king in Macedonian helmet, *ΒΑΣΙΛΕΩΣ ΜΕΓΑΣ*.
11 Plato (*c.*145–140 BC). Rev. dated *MZ* (year 47), Helios in a quadriga;
12 Heliocles I (*c.*120–90 BC). Rev. dated *ΠΓ* (year 83), Zeus.
Eucratides imitations:
13 Rev. dated *NA* (year 51), Dioscuri on horseback;
14 Rev. star caps of the Dioscuri; dated *ΠΓ* (year 83).
15 Antimachus II Nicephorus (*c.*160–155 BC). Obv. Nike; rev. horseman.
Menander I (*c.*155–130 BC):
16 Rev. *ΒΑΣΙΛΕΩΣ ΣΩΤΗΡΟΣ* 'saviour king', Athena hurling thunderbolt;
17 Obv. elephant; rev. club;
18 Obv. Athena; rev. Nike.

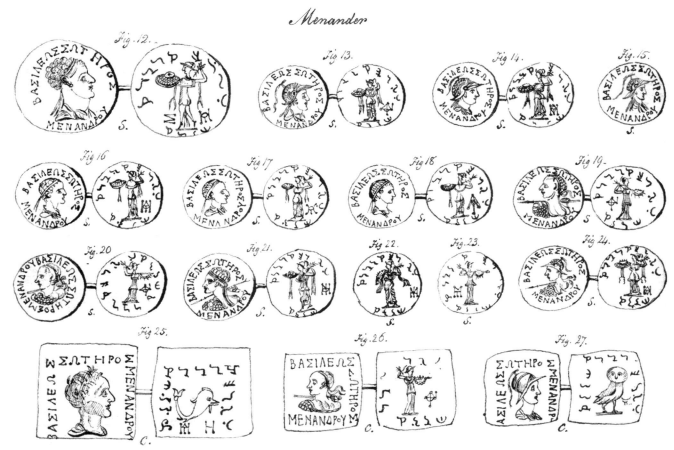

Figure 53 Masson's illustration of coins of Menander I from Begram, 1833–5.

pp. 97–102). This contrasts with Begram, where only a few stray coins of the Bactrian kings Euthydemus I, Demetrius I, Pantaleon and Antimachus I (*c.*180–170 BC) (fig. 26.1) are recorded. Only those of Agathocles, Apollodotus I and Eucratides I (fig. 52.9) occur in any number (IOLC: 28, 37 and 95 coins respectively).[52] The legible monograms on Eucratides' coins (IOLC) are moreover restricted to three, all issued towards the latter part of his reign according to Bopearachchi (1991, p. 212, ser. 19–20, J, L, M; Errington 2001, pp. 361–2).

In the North-West Frontier region, coins from the Greek layers of Shaikhan Dheri (ancient Pushkalavati, north-east of Peshawar) included one Agathocles and five Apollodotus (Dani 1965–6, p. 35). The Taxila excavations produced three coins each of Euthydemus I and Apollodotus I, a single coin of Demetrius I and seven coins of Agathocles (Marshall 1951, pp. 763, 765–6). The Daska hoard (between Gujranwala and Sialkot in the Punjab) contained an unspecified number of coins of Apollodotus I; while the hoard from Wesa (a village on the Chach plain adjacent to the Indus river near Amb, in Haripur District, Hazara) contained 220 tetradrachms and 1000 drachms of Apollodotus I and later kings down to Antialcidas (*c.*115–95 BC) (fig. 54.2), but only a single bilingual drachm of Eucratides I (Bopearachchi and Rahman 1995, p. 14; see also below). Finds from Butkara I in Swat include a single bronze specimen of either Pantaleon or Agathocles (the legend is illegible) and one each of Apollodotus I and Eucratides I (Göbl 1976, p. 13, pl. I.9–11).

One of the Bactrian kings recorded by Classical writers – and perhaps one of the most important for chronological purposes – is Eucratides I. According to Strabo, one of the 'thousand cities of Bactria' was named Eucratidia after him (XI.xi.2). According to Justin (XLI.vi.1–5),

> Almost at the same time that Mithradates [*c.* 171–138 BC] ascended the throne over Parthia, Eucratides began to reign over Bactria. . . . Eucratides engaged in several wars with great spirit, and though much reduced by his losses in them, yet, when he was besieged by Demetrius [II] king of the Indians, he repulsed a force of 60,000 enemies, by continual sallies with a garrison of only 300 soldiers. Having accordingly escaped after a siege of five months, he subjugated India. But as he was returning thence, he was assassinated on his march by his son [Eucratides II], with whom he had shared his throne.

A more or less secure date of *c.*171 BC for Mithradates I provides an approximate date also around the 170s BC for the beginning of the reign of Eucratides I. He seems to have been a usurper, for on his commemorative coinage his parents are identified as Heliocles and Laodice (fig. 52.10; Bopearachchi 1991, p. 209, pl. 19, ser. 13). Not only is his father unknown on coins, but only his mother wears the royal diadem, thereby signifying that he was not in the direct male line of royal descent in Bactria or elsewhere. Unique coins of this ruler found in excavations at Merv in southern Turkmenistan (ancient Margiana) indicate that he minted coins locally (Smirnova 1999, p. 261; Herrmann, Kurbansakhatov *et al.* 1995, p. 41). It is thus possible that he may have first come to power in Margiana, before extending his control into Bactria and the Parapamisidae (Cribb 2004, pp. 65–7, table 4; 2005, pp. 209, 220).

In the destruction levels of the palace treasury at Aï Khanum a fragmentary ceramic olive oil jar was unearthed, dated in an unknown regnal year 24 (Bernard 1985, pp. 99–100). This has been used to suggest the existence of a

Eucratides I era, whereby the year 24 equals *c.* 147 BC (i.e. *c.*171 BC minus 24). A few coins of Eucratides' successors, Plato and Heliocles, carry additional Greek letters which, unlike monograms, are not conjoined but separate and – in line with contemporary Seleucid and Parthian practice[53] – may also be dates (Leschhorn 1993, pp. 35–7; Sellwood 1980, pp. 15–16; Cribb 2005, pp. 214, 221). If this is the case, they appear to be linked to the same era as the Aï Khanum inscription, with *MZ* and *MH* on coins of Plato representing years 47 and 48, and *NZ* and *ΠΓ* on coins of Heliocles I representing years 57 and 83 (fig. 52.11–12). Since the coins of Eucratides are the latest found at Aï Khanum, the year 24 inscription has also been used to propose that the Greeks lost the region to nomadic invaders and the city was abandoned *c.*145 BC (Bernard 1985, pp. 97–102).

The existence of a Bactrian era dating from the Greek period now appears to be confirmed by a new inscription of the Apraca raja Vijayamitra (an early first century AD ruler of the Bajaur region), which identifies year 1 of the 'Yona' era as 128 years earlier than that of the Azes era (Salomon 2005, pp. 359–71; pp. 61–4 below). A modern convention equates the Azes era with the Vikrama era of 58/7 BC still current in India (Bivar 1981). The conversion of a Vikrama era date to a Christian one depends on the broad rule of thumb first proposed by James Prinsep (1858, p. 157):

> To convert Samvat into Christian dates, subtract 57; unless they are less than 58, in which case deduct the amount from 58, and the result is the date BC.

Modern reckonings in the Vikrama era are luni-solar and in elapsed years. The current calendar has a lunar month of 29½ days and a lunar year of 354 days, i.e. 11 days shorter than the solar year of 365 days. In order to correct the difference between the two calendars, an extra month is added in each lunar leap year, which occurs every 30 months. As Prinsep remarked regarding the luni-solar system, the 'year is inconvenient from its varying duration; but as, in the long course of years, the months remain nearly at the same situation, it is less objectionable than the pure lunar year' (1858, p. 133). However, in the north each Vikrama year begins in spring and each month with the full moon, while in Gujarat and some parts of the south the year begins in autumn and the months with the new moon. Such seasonal discrepancies occur naturally over time when the start of the year is based on the cycles of the moon. It suggests that earlier in the history of the era calculations were not standardised. Different computations must have been used at different times in the different areas to maintain the synchronism of each year always beginning in the same season.[54] Bivar's stipulations when proposing the Azes/Vikrama era equation should therefore be borne in mind, specifically, that our knowledge of the early mechanics of the calendars used with dates in the Vikrama era is insufficient and (1981, pp. 269–70)

> When the starting-point was, as often, unknown, it would be unsafe, especially with early dates, to attempt an exact calculation. Furthermore, mediaeval and modern reckonings adjust the solar and lunar years according to the Hindu table, the *Sūrya-Siddhānta*, compiled in the 5th century AD. Before that date, different systems of intercalation will have been in use, less accurate than those of the middle ages. To extrapolate backwards from recent dates would be unlikely to give the same results as the reckonings used by the ancients.

According to legend, the Vikrama era was inaugurated by Vikramaditya of Ujjain to commemorate his victory over the Shakas. But this is a late tradition. The only historical Vikramaditya known to have crushed the Shakas at Ujjain was Chandragupta II in *c.* AD 395, while the earliest reference to the Vikrama era by name is an inscription of Jaikadeva dated 794 (AD 737) from Kathiawar in Gujarat (Sircar 1965, p. 391; 1965a, p. 252). The era is called *kṛta* or *krita* in the earliest records (years 282–481), a name sometimes applied to certain foreign rulers of the north-western subcontinent (Sircar 1966, p.162). In the period *c.* years 461–770, it is also associated with the Malavas (Sircar 1965a, pp. 251–4). Its early use was confined to Rajasthan and Malwa, but Sircar (1965a, p. 254) links the Malavas to the Malloi tribe of the Punjab in the time of Alexander, who from epigraphic and numismatic evidence appear to have migrated to Rajasthan by the early first century AD. So although there is a gap of about 150 years between the last Azes era date (year 136) and the first *kṛta* date (year 282), it is feasible that they refer to the same era. But equally, the Azes–Vikrama conundrum is a reflection of the clear propensity from the first century BC onwards for calendrical calculations to be based on the regnal years of individual rulers. So, in addition to the Azes era, there is evidence for others associated with Maues, Vijayamitra, Gondophares, Kanishka, and possibly even Rajavula; not forgetting the Shaka era of AD 78 which is linked to year 1 of Chastana (table 2 and pp. 54, 59, 62–5, 70).

The modern convention of equating the Azes era with the Vikrama era gives a date of *c.*186/5 BC for the beginning of the Yona era, assuming that it used a solar calendar, like the Seleucid one it probably replaced (Prinsep 1858, pp. 141–2). But any attempt to utilise this construct in playing the game of identifying the king who introduced the Yona era does not produce any cast-iron solution; rather, it potentially raises more problems than it solves (table 1). Inscriptions that appear to be dated in this era – at Dasht-i Nawar and Surkh Kotal (north of the Hindu Kush), various sites in Gandhara and at Mathura – are associated with the Kushan period, more specifically from the reign of Wima Tak[to] (year 270) onwards, the last known possible date being year 384 (table 1).[55] So it seems clear that the era originated in Bactria, was initiated by one of the Greco-Bactrian kings, adopted – and perhaps even adapted – by their Yuezhi successors and remained in use for about four hundred years. But there is, as yet, no way of determining whether it used a solar calendar like the Seleucids, or a luni-solar one, or was exclusively lunar one like the current Hijra calendar.[56] In the period under consideration a purely lunar calendar also appears to have been used by the Chinese and other peoples of north-eastern Asia whence the Yuezhi originated (Prinsep 1858, pp. 145–6).[57]

A stone Brahmi inscription from Maghera, Mathura District, of the year 116 'in the reign of the Yavana kingdom' (*yavanarajyasya*; from Greek 'Ionian') already indicated the possible existence of a Greek era further south in India itself (Mathura Museum no. 88.150; Sharma 1995, pp. 25–6). Assigning the beginning of the Yona era to 186/5 BC – and identifying 'Yona' and 'Yavana' as one and the same era – equates year 116 with 70/69 BC. However, this produces a problematic date, for it has been pointed out that 'Yavana' in

Table 1. Comparative table of eras

Ruler / place of inscription	Linked dates / reign	Regnal year	Yona era	Azes era	Vikrama era 58/7 BC	BC/AD (1)	BC/AD (2)	Shaka era AD 78	Sh: Shuji, HS: Han Shu, HHS: Hou Han Shu
Bactrian Diodotus	independent from Seleucus II 246–226 BC								
Euthydemus I	defeated by Antiochus III 212–205 BC								
Yona era			Yr 1		186/5 BC				
Eucratides I: Yona era	contemporary of Mithradates 171–139/8 BC	[Yr 1]				171 BC	174 BC		HS/Sh: Yuezhi suzereignty over Bactria c.130 BC
Aï Khanum		Yr 24	Yr 24			148 BC	151 BC		
Plato		MZ / ME	Yr 47 / Yr 48		139/8 BC / 138/7 BC	125 BC / 124 BC	128 BC / 127 BC		
Heliocles I		NZ / PG	Yr 57 / Yr 83		129/8 BC / 103/2 BC	115 BC / 89 BC	118 BC / 92 BC		HHS: Yuezhi settled Bactria c.100–75 BC
Indo-Scythian Patika (son of Chukhsa satrap)	a) 'in reign of' Maues b) Maues regnal year 78	Yr 78	Yr 78		108/7 BC	94 BC	97 BC / AD 4		Maues year 1 equals c.75 BC
Yona era: Azes era			Yr 129	Yr 1	58/7 BC	43 BC	46 BC		
Maghera inscription Yavana era	a) Yavana = Yona era b) Yavana = Azes era	Yr 116	Yr 116	Yr 116	70/69 BC / AD 57/6	56 BC / AD 73	59 BC / AD 70		
Sodasa (Great Satrap) Amorhini (Mathura) inscr.		Yr 42 or Yr 72		Yr 42 or Yr 72	16/15 BC or AD 14/15	2 BC or AD 2	5 BC or AD 26		
Vijayamitra (Apraca raja)		[Yr 1]	Yr 175	Yr 47	11/10 BC	AD 4	AD 1		
Indravarma (stratega)				Yr 63	AD 5/6	AD 20	AD 17		
1st yuga (165yrs)		Yr 1				AD 22	– 56 years		
Apracas Vijayamitra		Yr 27	Yr 201	Yr 73	AD 15/16	AD 30	AD 27		
Satruleka (nephew of Vijayamitra)				Yr 77	AD 19/20	AD 35	AD 31		
Vijayamitra		Yr 32		Yr 78	AD 20/21	AD 36	AD 32		
Indo-Parthian Gondophares	St Thomas c. AD 35–40	[Yr 1]	Yr 206	Yr 78	AD 19/20	AD 35	AD 32		
		Yr 26	Yr 231	Yr 103	AD 45/6	AD 60	AD 57		
Shaka era	[Chastana]					AD 78		Yr 1	
Kushan Kujula Kadphises Panjtar inscription	c. AD 40–90			Yr 122	AD 64/5	AD 79	AD 76		HHS: Kushans recorded by Ban Yong from AD 27
↑						AD 84			Chinese envoy to Yuezhi
'Kushan' 'Great King'						AD 86/7			Yuezhi envoy to Chinese
↓						AD 90			Yuezhi defeated by Ban Chao
Taxila scroll				Yr 136	AD 78/9	AD 93	AD 90		
Mathura (1) inscription	'of maharaja'		Yr 270	Yr 143	AD 84/5	AD 99	AD 96		
Wima Tak[to] 'son of Kushan' Dasht-i Nawar & Surkh Kotal	c. AD 90–113		Yr 279	Yr 151	AD 93/4	AD 108	AD 105		Chinese withdrawal from Xinjiang AD 107
Wima Kadphises Khalatse inscription	c. AD 113–27		Yr 284 or Yr 287	Yr 156 or Yr 159	AD 98/9 or AD 101/2	AD 113 or AD 116	AD 110 or AD 113		
Mathura (2) inscription	'of maharaja rajatiraja'		Yr 292 or Yr 299	Yr 164 or Yr 171	AD 107 or AD 114	AD 121 or AD 128	AD118 or AD 125		HHS: Ban Yong returns to Xinjiang AD 123–5
Kanishka I	c. AD 127–50	[Yr 1]	Yr 301			AD 127		Yr 49	
Charsadda stupa inscr. Loriyan Tangai inscription			Yr 303 / Yr 318	Yr 175 / Yr 190	AD 117/18 / AD 132/3	AD 132 / AD 147	AD 129 / AD 144		
Kanishka I	c. AD 127–50	Yr 23				AD 150		Yr 72	
Huvishka	c. AD 150–90	Yr 26 / Yr 60				AD 153 / AD 187			
End of 1st yuga		Yr 165				AD 187		Yr 109	
2nd yuga		Yr 1				AD 188		Yr 110	
Jamalgarhi inscription Hashtnagar inscription	BM 1890.11.16.1		Yr 359 / Yr 384	Yr 231 / Yr 256	AD 173/4 / AD 198/9	AD 188 / AD 213	AD 185 / AD 210		
Vasudeva I	c. AD 190–227	Yr 64 or Yr 67 / Yr 98				AD 191 or AD 194 / AD 225			
Kanishka II	c. AD 227–46	[Yr 1] / Yr [10]5 / Yr [1]17				AD 227 / AD 232 / AD 244		Yr 149	
Sasanian era		Yr 1				AD 233/4			
Vasishka	c. AD 246–67	Yr [1]22 / Yr [1]30				AD 249 / AD 257			
Kanishka III	c. AD 267–80	Yr [1]41				AD 268		Yr 190	
Yavanajātaka date		Yr [1]42				AD 269		Yr 191	
Vasudeva II	AD 280–320								
Gupta era/Chandragupta I	AD 319/20–35	Yr 1				AD 319/20			
Shaka	AD 320–60								

Secure AD dates
Regnal and unknown era dates recorded in inscriptons

Mathura (1): Lüders 1961, § 123, pp. 162-4.
Mathura (2): Lüders 1961, p. 163; Salomon 2004 (Mathura list no. 78)

Indian texts is used indistinguishably to refer to both Greeks and other north-western foreigners and that, in terms of language and content, the year 116 inscription should be assigned to the satrapal period of the late first century BC to first century AD at Mathura (Cribb 1999, pp. 197–8; Fussman 1991, pp. 659–68). Year 116 therefore clearly uses a different, later era (see pp. 59, 63 below and tables 1–2).

Even supposing that the Azes and Vikrama eras do correspond, a Yona era of c.186/5 BC does not fit the proposed chronology (Bopearachchi 1991) for any of the 'great' Bactrian kings mentioned in Classical sources, but falls within the dates suggested for the reign of Agathocles (i.e. c.190–180 BC). The pedigree coins of this king indicate that he had dynastic aspirations (fig. 52.7); as one of the few kings to rule both Bactria and 'India', he was the first to introduce an innovative bilingual coinage, utilising both Greek and Brahmi, as well as being the only Greco-Bactrian king to issue a monolingual coinage in Kharoshthi (fig. 26.6, 8–9); and his coins are found from Aï Khanum to Taxila, especially at the last site, where they occur in some quantity when compared to the coin finds for other Greek kings before Menander (Marshall 1951, p. 766; Bopearachchi 1991, p. 58, n. 1). But his pedigree coins are at pains to emphasise the legitimacy of his rule by direct descent through his immediate predecessors, including Demetrius I and Euthydemus I, to the Seleucids and Alexander. It is thus unlikely he would create a new era, since such an act carries with it implications of a break with the past. The same argument applies for Demetrius I, son of Euthydemus, who is proclaimed in Classical sources and visually on his coins as a conqueror of India, but whose limited coin finds (especially south of the Hindu Kush) indicate that his reign was relatively short. Dismissing these kings as possible originators of the Yona era means either that any exact correlation between the Vikrama and Azes eras has to be abandoned as a working hypothesis or that there is no direct synchronism between the Yona and Vikrama/Azes calendar systems.

An alternative is to assign the Yona era to Eucratides I, the existence of whose era has already been argued by Dobbins, Fussman and others (see Bopearachchi 1999, pp. 103–5). However, equating the Yona era with 186/5 BC and with the proposed Eucratides era of the inscription from Aï Khanum arrives at a date of 162/1 BC for year 24 of his reign. This seems far too early for a king whom coins attest to have been the last Greek ruler of the city. Since the era clearly continued in use for four centuries, fixing its start in 186/5 BC also causes discrepancies with known dates at the other end of the chronological spectrum in the Kushan period (see table 1). Another possibility – that year one of Eucratides equals year one of Mithradates (c.171 BC) equals year one of the Yona era – produces a more convincing result.

A neater symmetry results from identifying Yona year 301 as year 1 of the Kushan king Kanishka I (i.e. AD 127), and working backwards to produce a date of 174 BC for the start of both the Yona and Eucratides eras (Cribb 2005, pp. 221–2). This is possible if Eucratides initially came to power in Margiana while Pantaleon and Agathocles were ruling in Bactria (Cribb 2005, pp. 209–12, 220). The dates of 174 BC and 171 BC are also close enough to fit the evidence from Justin that Eucratides began his reign at 'almost' the same time as

Mithradates, particularly in view of the fact that Justin 'whose interests in the East were never independent of his interests in the West . . . liked to organise historical accounts by pairing events and personalities', thereby creating 'multiple (and contradictory) synchronisms'. In Justin's second- to third-century AD 'condensed and confused Latin epitome of Pompeius Trogus . . . the further habit of linking eastern events to each other by such vague phrases as "at the same time" or "afterward" should alert us again to the inherent vagueness of our chronology' (Holt 1999, pp. 8, 60–1).

In the early second century BC disturbances originating with the rise to power of the Xiongnu, a pastoral, tribal confederacy of the steppes far to the east on the frontier of China, had the knock-on effect of displacing their neighbours, the Da Yuezhi (Han Shu 96A.10b, cf. Zürcher 1968, pp. 362–3). The decisive battle between the two groups seems to have taken place in 177/6 BC, after which the Da Yuezhi – 'Great Yuezhi' – moved westwards, reaching the Jaxartes (Syr Darya) region by about 160 BC. The Da Yuezhi are identified as the nomadic successors of the Bactrians in the Chinese Shiji, Han Shu and Hou Han Shu and are said to comprise five tribes: Xiumi, Shuangmi, Guishuang (Kushan), Xidun and Dumi (Hou Han Shu 118.9a, cf. Zürcher 1968, pp. 367–8).[58] Although there is no immediately apparent etymological link, Strabo may also be referring to the Da Yuezhi when he identifies the 'Asii, Pasiani, Tochari and Sacarauli' as the nomads 'who originally came from the country on the other side of the Jaxartes river that adjoins that of the Sacae [Shakas] and the Sogdiani and was occupied by the Sacae', and who 'took away Bactriana from the Greeks' (XI.viii.2).[59] The coin evidence – not only from Aï Khanum but also from Takht-i-Sangin – dates this event in the time of Eucratides I (Bernard 1985, pp. 97–102; Zeymal 1997, pp. 90–1).

Strabo also says (XI.ix.2) that 'a part of Bactriana' – elsewhere more specifically the satrapies of Turiva and Aspionus (XI.xi.2) – 'was taken away from Eucratides by the Parthians'. These satrapies were probably in the borderlands of Margiana, the buffer zone between Parthia and Bactria, for at the excavated site of Giaour-kala – the capital of the Merv oasis from the Seleucid to the late Sasanian period – Greco-Bactrian coins from Diodotus to Eucratides I (fig. 52.1–10) are superseded by Parthian issues of Phraates II (c.139/8–127 BC) (fig. 45.9–11; Smirnova 1999, pp. 260–1). This evidence extends the potential dates for the end of Eucratides' reign down to c.138 BC (Cribb 2005, p. 212).

The Qunduz region in northern Afghanistan seems to have been initially retained by the Bactrians, for the latest coins of any quantity in the hoard found here are 204 tetradrachms of Heliocles I (Curiel and Fussman 1965, pp. 36–45), who reigned c.145–130 BC, according to Bopearachchi (1991, p. 74). But two Heliocles coins (fig. 52.11) bear the legends NZ and IIΓ which have been interpreted as the numerals '57' and '83' respectively (Cribb 2005, p. 221). If calculated as years in the Eucratides/Yona era (i.e. 174 BC), they produce dates of 118 BC and 92 BC respectively, thereby suggesting that Heliocles was still ruling c.120–90 BC.

The picture, however, is complicated by the fact that the coinages of both Eucratides and Heliocles were extensively copied by the nomadic successors of the Bactrians, and that some of the Eucratides' imitations are similarly dated *NA* ('51') and *ΠΓ* ('83') respectively (fig. 52.13–14). As the 'year 83' Heliocles coins at least appear to be imitations, it is thus feasible that they are also posthumous, rather than lifetime imitations. While the imitations of Eucratides simply reproduce cruder versions of the same coin designs (Bopearachchi 1991, pp. 213–15, pls 21.98–22.119; Smith 2000, figs 8–22, 25), those of Heliocles evolve from silver into bronze, while the standing figure of Zeus on the reverse is replaced by the image of a horse (figs 52.12; 61.12). Several posthumous Heliocles imitations occur in the Qunduz hoard (Curiel and Fussman 1965, nos 582–3; Smith 2001, p. 8), alongside coins of Greek rulers of the Parapamisidae down to Hermaeus (*c*.90–70 BC) (fig. 54.5–6; Bopearachchi 1991, p. 75). The last issuer of Heliocles imitations moreover has recently been identified by the tamgha ⵣ on the rump of the horse as the second Kushan king, Wima Tak[to] (*c*. AD 90–113) (Smith 2001, p. 14, figs 9–10).

Bopearachchi's dating of the end of Heliocles' reign to *c*.130 BC derives from the Chinese envoy Zhang Qian's report of that approximate date that the Da Yuezhi 'had subdued Daxia [Bactria] and dwelt [in that region]' (*Shiji* 123.1a–2a; Bopearachchi 1991, pp. 74–5, n. 2).[60] However, Zürcher (1968, p. 359, n. 4)[61] has shown that this passage was probably miscopied from the *Han Shu* (61.1a–2a), which states that the Da Yuezhi 'had subdued Daxia and were their overlords'. A subsequent statement that the Da Yuezhi 'dwell north of the Guishui [Oxus river]; to the south of them there is Daxia' (*Shiji* 123.3b, cf. Zürcher 1968, p. 360) reinforces the impression that the Yuezhi did not immediately occupy the regions south of the Oxus. The semi-independent status of Bactria in the late second century BC is further confirmed by a later passage in the *Han Shu* (96A.14b, cf. Zürcher 1968, p. 365):

> Daxia originally had no great kings or heads, but everywhere in their walled cities and settlements they had installed small heads. The people are weak and fear war, therefore when the Yuezhi came migrating [to the west] they completely subdued and tamed them. Together they support the envoys of the Han.

The earliest Chinese reference to the actual Yuezhi occupation of Bactria dates from latter part of the first century AD and says: 'The country of the Da Yuezhi has its capital at the city of Lanshi', i.e. Tashkurgan, between Balkh and Qunduz in northern Afghanistan (*Hou Han Shu* 118.9a, cf. Zürcher 1968, p. 367). It dates the Yuezhi settlement of Bactria to 'more than a hundred years' earlier than the unification of the five tribes under the Kushans by Kujula Kadphises in the first half of the first century AD. Since the coin evidence shows Heliocles to have been the last Greek king to rule Bactria, active Yuezhi settlement of the region must have taken place during the latter part of his reign (*c*.100 BC onwards). Given the parallels in the evolution of the posthumous coinages of Heliocles (north of the Hindu Kush) and Hermaeus (the last Greek king south of the Hindu Kush), it is possible they were contemporaries ruling *c*.90 BC (figs 52.12; 54.5; Cribb 2004, pp. 66–8; 2005, pp. 212–13).

South of the Hindu Kush, the initial impression given by Masson's totals for the coins he collected at Begram in 1833–5 (Uncat. MSS 2, f. 1) is that those of Eucratides I (269 coins)

far exceed those of Menander I (153 coins) (Errington 2001, pp. 361–2, 371). But this is potentially misleading, for he includes all Eucratides' lifetime and posthumous issues together. In the IOLC collection, the proportion of Eucratides lifetime to posthumous issues occurs at an approximate ratio of 4:3, i.e. 95 lifetime and 72 posthumous. This ratio should also be applied to the total of 269 coins listed for this ruler in Masson's 1833–5 collections, thereby arriving at an estimated proportional figure of 154 lifetime to 115 posthumous issues. If considered this way, the quantity of Menander coins from the site (1833–5: 153 coins; IOLC: 238 coins) equals or even exceeds those of Eucratides. Apart from a silver tetradrachm fragment (IOLC), all the bronze coins issued in the name of Heliocles I are also later imitations (Uncat. MSS 2, f. 1: 'Dicaio' 33 coins; IOLC: 46 coins).

Pompeius Trogus (*Prologue* LXIV) specifically identifies Menander I (*c*.155–130 BC) (figs 52.16–18; 53) as a king of India. According to Strabo (XV.I.27), the Greeks 'advanced beyond the Hypanis [Beas river], as far as the Ganges and Palibothra' (Pataliputra). Strabo's additional remark (XI.xi.1) that Menander may have campaigned eastwards 'as far as the Imaüs' (Himalayas) has been linked with allusions in several Indian sources to incursions by the 'Yavanas' into India. A text of about the first to third century AD, the *Yugapurāna* (Mankad 1947, §§ 94–5),[62] foretells the invasion of Saketa (near Ayodhya) and the Ganges region east as far as Pataliputra (Patna) by an alliance of Yavanas with forces from Mathura and Pancala.[63] The grammarian Patanjali also apparently refers to the same event in the *Mahābhāshya* when employing the phrase 'the Yavana was besieging' Saketa and Madhyamika, near Chitor in Rajasthan, to illustrate the use of the imperfect tense in describing a recent event (Schwartzberg 1992, p. 140; Kielhorn 1962–5, vol. II, pp. 118–19; Narain 1957, pp. 82–3). The *Yugapurāna* says further that, because of infighting, the Yavanas failed to retain these territories (Narain 1957, p. 83). The hypothesis that Yavanas equals Greeks is based on the tenuous dating of Patanjali as a contemporary of the first Shunga king, Pushyamitra (*c*. 187–151 BC), whose dates in turn are a construct (see p. 38).

In the *Mālavikāgnimitra* (Act V), a play about the Shunga king Agnimitra (son of Pushyamitra), Kalidasa also mentions a Yavana defeat on the banks of the 'Sindhu' (commonly the ancient name for the Indus river, but in this context identified as the Sindh river, an insignificant tributary of the Ganges) (Bhandare 2006, pp. 70–1). Even this late fourth- to early fifth-century reference to Yavana has been interpreted as meaning Greek, rather than its more general connotation of foreigner from the north-west. It has been variously argued that all these allusions refer to a single invasion by Demetrius or Menander, or to two separate incursions by the same two kings in the reign of Pushyamitra (Tarn 1938, pp. 145–7; Narain 1957, pp. 82–8; Majumdar 1980, pp. 96–7, 112–13; Bopearachchi and Rahman 1995, p. 33). However, none of the Indian sources identifies the Yavanas by name. There is also a remarkable concordance noted by Joe Cribb (personal communication) in the inclusion of Saketa and Pataliputra both in the *Yugapurāna* and in the list of conquests by the Kushan king Kanishka recorded in the Rabatak inscription (§§ 2–7, cf. Sims-Williams and Cribb 1995/6, p. 78; see p. 70

Figure 54 Indo-Greek coins:
1 Lysias (*c.*120–110 BC). Obv. Heracles with club; rev. elephant;
2 Antialcidas (*c.*115–95 BC). Rev. Zeus beside elephant; Nike on elephant's head;
3 Philoxenus (*c.*100–95 BC). Rev. horseman;
4 Amyntas (*c.*95–90 BC). Obv. Mithra in Phrygian cap; rev. Athena;
5 Hermaeus (*c.*90–70 BC). Rev. Zeus;
6 Hermaeus imitation;
7 Apollodotus II (*c.*65–50 BC). Obv. Apollo; rev. tripod;
8 Hippostratus (*c.*50–45 BC). Obv. triton; rev. Tyche with cornucopia;
9 Strato II (*c.*25 BC–AD 10). Obv. Apollo; rev. tripod.

below). Given that the *Yugapurāna* and the Rabatak inscription are probably more or less contemporary in date, this can hardly be dismissed as mere coincidence.

In the *Milindapañha*, 'The questions of Menander', Menander is merely given legendary status as a good king and a patron of Buddhism (Rhys-Davids 1890–4; p. 130 below). The same source says he was born in the village of Kalasi-grama in the *dvīpa* or doab[64] of Alasanda (Alexandria) near Kabul (identifiable perhaps as Begram, which lies at the confluence of the Panjshir and Ghurband rivers). His capital Sagala is thought to have been in the North-West Frontier or the Punjab, but the site has not yet been identified. The coin evidence confirms these regions as part of his realm. As already noted, at Begram his coins outnumber those of all the other Greeks (Masson's collections 1833–5: 153 coins; IOLC: 238 coins). The predominant issues are the bronze elephant/ club series (IOLC 146 coins) followed by the Athena/Nike series (IOLC 80 coins), but 13 of his 17 bronze coin designs are present and the four types missing from his collection are moreover rare (figs 52.17–18; 53).[65] After Menander the coins of only three subsequent Greek kings were found in any quantity at Begram: Lysias (*c.* 120–110 BC; 14 coins) (fig. 54.1), Antialcidas (*c.* 115–95 BC; 37 coins) (fig. 54.2) and Hermaeus (*c.* 90–70 BC; *c.* 12 coins) (figs 54.5; 55; Masson Uncat. MSS 2, f. 1; Errington 2001, p. 371).[66]

Within the North-West Frontier region coins from the partial excavation of Shaikhan Dheri (ancient Pushkalavati), at the confluence of the Kabul and Swat rivers near Charsadda, included two of Menander I, one of Lysias, two of Antialcidas, three of Philoxenus (*c.* 100–95 BC) (fig. 54.3), one of Telephus (*c.*60–55 BC) and one 'Heliocles' (probably a posthumous imitation) (Dani 1965–6, p. 35). The Daska hoard (between Gujranwala and Sialkot in the Punjab)

contained coins of Apollodotus I, Antimachus II (*c.*160–155 BC) (fig. 52.15) and Menander I; while the hoard found at Wesa, north of Attock, contained 220 tetradrachms and 1000 drachms of Apollodotus I, Antimachus II, Menander I, Lysias and Antialcidas (Bopearachchi and Rahman 1995, p. 14). Other hoards from Bajaur and Mian Khan Sanghou comprised a similar range of coins; those from Khauzikhelai, Attock and Siranawali are slightly later in composition, with coins of Lysias to Amyntas (*c.*95–90 BC) (fig. 54.4). Indo-Greek coins in the Sarai Saleh hoard from Abbottabad district included most rulers from Menander I (*c.*155–130 BC) to Hippostratus (*c.*50–45 BC) (fig. 54.8; Bopearachchi 1999, pp. 122–5, 145). Finds at Sirkap, Taxila, produced a similar range, although excavation of the Indo-Greek levels was extremely limited: the latest coins occurring in any quantity were those of Apollodotus II (*c.*65–50 BC; 58 coins) (fig. 54.7), with the last four kings down to Strato II (*c.*25 BC–AD 10) (fig. 54.9) being represented by stray coins only (Marshall 1951, pp. 766–7).

The sum of this coin evidence indicates that the Greeks lost control of northern Bactria between 145 and 138 BC to Shaka and Yuezhi nomadic groups from the north-east and were gradually pushed southwards into India. Initially the Greek kingdoms south of the Hindu Kush survived, but in *c.*70 BC the Kabul region was lost to the invaders, followed by Taxila in *c.*55 BC. The coin sequences show that Greek rule at Taxila was temporarily restored by Apollodotus II (*c.*65–50 BC) and Hippostratus (*c.*50–45 BC) (Jenkins 1957). In the eastern Punjab, however, Greek rule lasted until *c.* AD 10. The picture painted by the numismatic evidence of this period is complicated by the fact that the tribal invaders produced coins imitating those of their Greek predecessors, particularly Eucratides I and Heliocles I, the last Greek kings

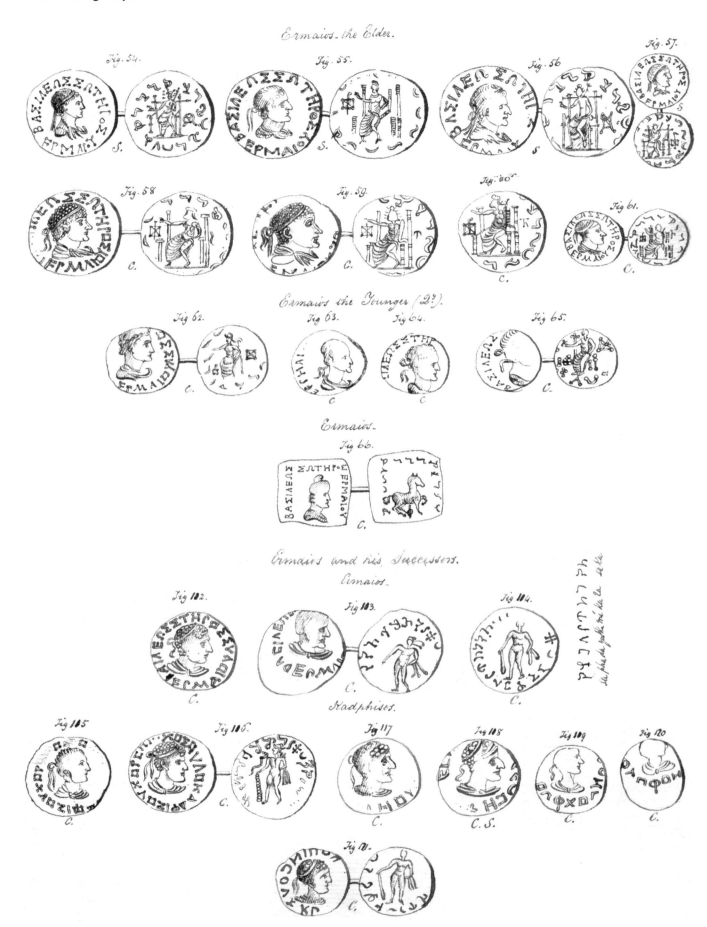

Figure 55 Masson's classification of Hermaeus lifetime and posthumous issues, including imitations in the name of Kujula Kadphises.

in Bactria, and Hermaeus (*c*.90–70 BC), the last Greek ruler in the Kabul region, but with corrupt legends and increasingly crude images (figs 54.6, 55). The silver coinage gradually debased into billon and ultimately bronze; and imitations issued in the names of Heliocles I and Hermaeus became the standard coinages of north and south of the Hindu Kush respectively. This situation continued until the mid first century AD, as evinced by the appearance of the tamgha of Wima Tak[to] (*c*. AD 90–113) on late imitations of Heliocles. Similarly, the design on posthumous issues of Hermaeus evolved from bearing the legends of the king on both sides of the coins, to retaining the name and titles of Hermaeus in Greek on the obverse but citing Kujula Kadphises (*c*. AD 40–90) in Kharoshthi on the reverse, to carrying the bilingual legends of Kujula alone (figs 55; 61.4).[67]

Indo-Scythians (*c*.75 BC–AD 64)

> Formerly, when the Xiongnu had defeated the Da Yuezhi, the Yuezhi went to the West and became the rulers of Daxia [Bactria], whereas the Sai-wang [Shaka king(s)] went southwards and became ruler(s) of Jibin [Kashmir]. (*Han Shu* 96A.10b, cf. Zürcher 1968, p. 363)

During the first century BC the Indo-Greek rulers in Gandhara and Taxila were replaced by nomad invaders – originally from Central Asia – called Sacae or Scythians by the Greeks and Shakas by the Indians. According to Cunningham (1890, pp. 103–4),

> The earliest coins of the Sakas or Sacae-Scythians are certainly those of *Moa*, or *Mauas*, as his name is written in Greek characters. . . . It is certain at least that the coins of Moas are found only in the Panjâb, not a single specimen, to my knowledge, having been found in the Kabul valley. The first coins of this prince were obtained by Ventura in the Panjâb, and the whole of my collection, now numbering over two hundred specimens of more than twenty different types, was gathered in the same country. His silver coins have been found at the old town of Mansera, sixteen miles to the north of Abbottabad, and about eighty miles to the north of Rawul Pindi.

As Cunningam notes, the Indo-Scythians first took control of the Taxila region under Maues (*c*.75–65 BC). Although Masson in fact collected at least two bronze examples from Begram (fig. 56.1–2),[68] it is also generally still true that finds of Maues coins occur principally in the 'Panjâb', which in Cunningham's time included Taxila, the Hazara district to the north-east and the Peshawar Valley to the north-west (fig. 176). Court's collection from this region, for example, contained 12 coins of Maues (MSS nos 235–7, 240, 379–86). Excavations at Sirkap, Taxila, produced 107 coins (Marshall 1951, p. 782). More recently, finds have extended the geographical range of Maues issues to Swat and Kashmir (Senior 2000, vol. I, pp. 29–31). This latest numismatic evidence thus appears to accord with the *Han Shu*'s location of a Scythian base in Kashmir.

How Maues came to power is not known, but he was able to take over the Greek mints without disruption and continued to issue the same denominations. He replaced the traditional Greek portrait bust on the obverse with innovative designs, most notably a rider on horseback, which became the predominant image on the coins of his successors (fig. 56.3). However, the customary Greek deities on the reverse were largely retained, as was the practice of a bilingual legend in Greek and Kharoshthi (Mit. 699–735).

A copper-plate inscription dated 'in the seventy-eighth year of the Great King, the Great Moga' (Konow 1929, p. 29)[69] has been interpreted as referring to an unknown year in his reign, but dated in an earlier unknown era: most recently the newly discovered Yona era, taking year 1 as 186/5 BC, which equates year 78 with *c*.108/7 BC (Salomon 2005, pp. 371–3).[70] But Patika, the donor – son of the Chukhsa satrap, Liaka Kusuluka – is presumably the same person as Patika Kusulu[k]a in the Mathura lion capital inscription of about the late first century BC to early first century AD (fig. 57; Konow 1929, pp. 48–9; see also p. 64 below).[71] While Occam's Razor – i.e. the principle that no more should be presumed to exist beyond what is necessary – needs to be rigorously applied to avoid a complicated proliferation of eras for each problematic date, the interpretation that best fits the inscriptional evidence here is that there was a Maues era (tables 1–2; Cribb 1999, p. 196). An approximate estimate of 75 BC for year 1 of Maues gives a date of AD 4 for Patika before he succeeded his father as satrap. That this is the only known inscription from the north-west citing Maues suggests he had strong (possibly familial?) links with the Chukhsa satraps. Aurel Stein identified Chukhsa with Chach, an alluvial plain near Amb, in Haripur District, Hazara Division (1896, pp. 174–5). This roughly accords with the distribution patterns of the coins of Maues and one of Chukhsa's later satraps, Zeionises (fig. 58.8–9). These are predominantly found in north-eastern Hazara and Kashmir, thereby also suggesting this region as the probable location of the satrapy (Senior 2000, vol. I, p. 96).

The Maghera stone inscription of the year 116 'in the reign of the *yavanarajyasya*' (Yavana kingdom), already mentioned above, could equally refer to a Maues era, if 'Yavana' is understood here in its broader sense as 'north-western foreigner' rather than simply 'Greek'. This would provide a date of *c*. AD 42 for the inscription, which is compatible in language and content with satrapal inscriptions of this period at Mathura (Cribb 1999, pp. 197–8; Fussman 1991, pp. 659–68). But it is hard to justify the use of a Maues era at Mathura when there is no corresponding evidence from the Taxila region or the later Chukhsa satraps that one remained in use beyond year 78. If the Yavana era is that of Azes (where year 1 is equated with 46 BC), year 116 would be AD 70. This solution seems more feasible, particularly in light of the continued use of the Azes era in the time of the Kushan 'Great King', Kujula Kadphises, in years 122 and 136 (*c*. AD 76 and *c*. AD 90 respectively).

The coin sequences show that, after Maues, Greek rule at Taxila was temporarily restored by Apollodotus II (*c*.65–50 BC) and Hippostratus (*c*.50–45 BC) (fig. 54.7–8; Jenkins 1957). Some areas however remained under Indo-Scythian control, as evinced by the coins issued by Vonones (*c*.65–50 BC) as king of kings, together with his brother Spalahores or his nephew Spalagadames, son of Spalahores (fig. 56.4–5; Mit. 681–8). Spalyrises (*c*.50–40 BC), a second brother of the king, also issued coins with Spalagadames, on his own as king, and in coalition with Azes I (fig. 56.6–8; Mit. 689–97). In 1890 the apparent paucity of coins of these rulers from Begram, Kabul and the Punjab led Cunningham to suggest that 'their dominions would have embraced the Kandahar valley, and perhaps also Ghazni', since a 'good

Figure 56 Indo-Scythian coins.
Maues (c.75–65 BC):
1   Obv. Poseidon/Zeus with foot on a river god; rev. goddess holding vine;
2   Obv. elephant; rev. seated king;
3   Obv. king on horseback; rev. helmeted deity with spear, shield and trident.
Vonones (c.65–50 BC):
4   With his brother Spalahores. Rev. Zeus;
5   With Spaladagames, son of Spalahores. Obv. Heracles; rev. Athena.
Spalyrises (c.50–40 BC):
6   Obv. king with battle-axe and bow; rev. Zeus;
7   With nephew Spaladagames. Obv. king on horseback; rev. Heracles;
8   With Azes I. Rev. bow and arrow.

Azes I (c.46–1 BC):
9   Rev. Zeus Nicephorus;
10 Obv. camel rider; rev. bull;
11 With Azilises. Obv. king on horseback; rev. Athena.
Azilises (c.1 BC–AD 16):
12   Rev. elephant, from Kabul bazaar.
Azes II (c. AD 16–30):
13 Rev. Zeus Nicephorus;
14 Obv. bull; rev. lion;
15 Obv. seated king; rev. Hermes;
16 Obv. lion; rev. bull;
17 Obv. king on horseback; rev. Zeus Nicephorus, from Begram;
18 Posthumous imitation from Begram.
Kharahostes (c. early first century AD):
19 Rev. lion.

number of specimens' had been 'obtained by Colonel Stacy and Captain Hutton at Kandahar' (1890, p. 109). But both the Kabul/Jalalabad region and the Punjab produced more examples than Cunningham was aware. Between them, Masson and Wilson illustrated a selection of nine coins from an unspecified number of 'several good' and 'very perfect specimens' of Vonones/Spalahores, Spalyrises/Spalagadames and Spalyrises as sole issuer (Masson Uncat. MSS 2, figs 20–2, 24; 1834, p. 172, pl. XI.43–4; 1836, p. 25, nos 20–2, 24, pl. II.13–15, 17; Wilson 1841, pp. 338, 316, 318, pl. VIII.9, 12–13; Mit. 683, 691, 694 respectively). A few of these came from Begram, most being acquired in Kabul or Jalalabad. Court's rubbings illustrate nine coins from the Punjab and North-West Frontier region, including one of Spalyrises with Azes, but none of Vonones (MSS nos 59, 323, 366–72). Excavations at Sirkap produced 28 Vonones/Spalahores and 4 Spalyrises/ Spalagadames (Marshall 1951, p. 782). Cunningham's statement has been further modified by modern evidence from hoards found in Swat, Kashmir and Sarai Saleh northeast of Taxila, all of which contained coins of these types (Senior 2000, vol. I, p. 39; Bopearachchi and Rahman 1995, pp. 13–14, 47). So, although coins of these rulers are not found anywhere in large numbers, their distribution seems to be quite widespread.

Evidence from coins for a definite regional bias of the North-West Frontier and Taxila is much clearer for Azes I (fig. 56.9–10), whose era – as already remarked (p. 53) – is generally thought to correspond with the Vikrama era of 58/7 BC (Senior 2000, vol. I, pp. 173–87; Errington 1999/2000, pp. 194, 211–13; Mit. 737–62). Although the two eras are clearly close enough in time for this construct to have formed a workable hypothesis, the newly discovered correlation between the Yona and Azes eras demonstrates either the need for the adjustment of the date for year 1 of Azes (e.g. to *c*.46 BC, following the estimates in Cribb 2005, p. 221), or acceptance that the eras are not synchronised because they follow different lunar/solar calendar systems (see table 1). Joint coinage issues of Azes with Azilises (*c*.1 BC–AD 16) (fig. 56.11) confirm the line of succession, the latter subsequently also issuing coins in his own name as king of kings (Mit. 763–812). The largest numbers of Indo-Scythian coins by far, however, are later issues in the name of Azes, usually assigned to Azes II (*c*. AD 16–30; Mit. 814–78).[72] Sirkap produced *c*.1543 coins of Azes II, 1292 coins of Azes I and only 11 coins of Azilises (fig. 56.12; Marshall 1951, pp.130–1, 772), while the Malakand hoard comprised almost 80% coins of Azes II, 12% of Azes I and 8% of Azilises (Bopearachchi and Fröhlich 2001, p. 4). The 53 Indo-Scythian coins from the Shaikhan Dheri excavations comprised 5 Maues, 3 Azilises and 45 Azes II[73] (fig. 56.13–15; Dani 1965–6, pp. 35, 37, pl. LI.8–16).

Masson remarked on the fact that no coins of the 'genuine' Azes kings were found at Begram (Wilson 1841, p. 73). Analysis of his records and surviving collection confirm the absence of coins of Azes I and Azilises,[74] despite Whitehead's contention that Masson failed to recognise some coins as issues of Azes (1950, pp. 206–7). Whitehead claims further that coins from the French excavations at Begram exhibited at the Musée Guimet in 1948 'included eleven large silver Azes, four of the type Zeus Nicephorus, six Pallas to right and

Figure 57 Mathura lion capital.

one Poseidon to right': these are all now identified as issues of Azes II (Mit. 828, 846, 853–5). However, his assertion is not borne out by the cryptic coin data of the Begram excavation report, which does not record any issues of Azes I, only one Azes II coin of unspecified type (Ghirshman 1946, p. 85). It is therefore probable that the coins seen by Whitehead were actually part of the collection acquired by Hackin and Carl from various other places in Afghanistan. Masson's records moreover confirm that he did not find any silver Azes II Zeus or Athena tetradrachms at Begram (fig. 56.13) and that he never saw any Poseidon examples at all (Uncat. MSS 2, figs 153–4; Wilson 1841, pp. 324–5, nos 2, 5, pl. VI.13, 16). He did fail to note two bronze issues which occur in some quantity in his collection, viz. seated Tyche/Hermes (IOLC: 14 coins) and seated king/Hermes (fig. 56.15; IOLC: 78 coins), but these could easily have come – like the bull/lion issues (IOCL: 18 coins) – from Kabul or Jalalabad (Mit. 831, 860–4, 850–2; Wilson 1841, pp. 328–30, nos 16–17, 20, 22, pl. VII.8–9, 12–15; Masson Uncat. MSS 2, fig. 155). On the other hand he noted the existence at Begram of a small, unique lion/bull coin (fig. 56.16), as well as numerous small silver and bronze horseman/Zeus Nicephorus drachms of the 'Azus [*sic*] dynasty', i.e. late posthumous issues in the names of Azes, of which 6 debased silver and 38 bronze examples survive in the India Office Loan Collection (fig. 56.17–18; Masson 1834, pp. 170–1, pls X.31, 33, XI.41).

The exact political situation in the late first century BC and early first century AD is confused. However, a number of inscriptions and coins provide details of the chronological and occasionally also the familial relationship between various Indo-Scythian rulers (tables 2–3). The first of these is the already mentioned copper-plate scroll from Taxila dated in the year 78 of Maues, i.e. *c*. AD 4, which records Patika as the son of Liaka Kusuluka, satrap of Chukhsha. Patika is mentioned again – but as great satrap – on the Mathura lion capital (fig. 57).[75] Rajavula, a contemporary great satrap at Mathura, is identified further in this inscription as the son-in-law of Kharahostes (fig. 56.19) and father of the satrap Sodasa. The last three rulers all issued coins as satraps, Rajavula and Sodasa latterly as great satrap (fig. 58.1–2; Mit. 887–8, 894, 901–10; Senior 2000, vol. II, pp. 125–8). Kharahostes is also recorded as an owner of a silver vessel which was subsequently reused as a reliquary by the Apraca prince, Indravarma, whose dated inscriptions (according to the Azes era, calculated as 46 BC) range *c*. AD 17–27 (table 1;

Figure 58 Indo-Scythian coins.
Mathura:
1   Rajavula (c. first half of first century AD), great satrap. Obv. Greek legend; rev. Athena, Kharoshthi legend;
2   Sodasa (c. mid first century AD), satrap/great satrap. Obv. Lakshmi and tree symbol; rev. Lakshmi lustrated by elephants, Brahmi legend.
Western Satraps:
3   Nahapana (c. AD 54–65). Obv. Greek legend; rev. thunderbolt and arrow, Brahmi legend;
4   Chastana (AD 78–130). Rev. three-arched hill, sun, moon and water, Brahmi legend.

Apracas:
5   Indravasu (c. AD 32–3). Obv. horseman; rev. Athena.
Aspavarma (c. AD 33–64):
6   As Apraca stratega (commander);
7   Under Indo-Parthians. Rev. Zeus Nicephorus with Gondopharid tamgha.
Zeionises (c. AD 30–50):
8   Rev. male figure being crowned by two flanking divinities;
9   Obv. bull; rev. lion; named Jihonika in Kharoshthi.

p. 54; Salomon 1996). This broadly suggests a chronological context of the early first century AD for the Mathura lion inscription and for Patika and Kharahostes.

The situation however is complicated by the Amorhini inscription from Mathura, which is dated in an unknown era in 'the year 42 [or 72] of the Lord, the Mahaksatrapa Sodasa' (Bühler 1894, p. 199; Sharma 1995, p. 25).[76] A calculation in which the Azes era equals 46 BC provides a date of 5 BC or AD 26 for Sodasa as great satrap. But the numismatic evidence from Jammu shows clearly that Rajavula was still ruling when the Indo-Parthian, Gondophares, came to power c. AD 32 (Cribb 1999, p. 195).[77] Various proposed solutions include the date 42/72 being a regnal year of Sodasa, or an era founded by his father or some other ruler (Sharma 1989, pp. 311–12). Since Rajavula's reign clearly overlapped that of Patika at some point and latterly also that of Gondophares, Sodasa's reign as great satrap at Mathura is unlikely to have commenced before c. AD 35. There are good arguments for placing this event even later, not least because Sodasa is succeeded at Mathura by the second Kushan king, Wima Tak[to] (c. AD 90–113).

If the Amorhini inscription is read as year 42 (rather than 72), it fits with a group of dates between year 41 and year 46 inscribed during the reign of the Western Satrap, Nahapana, a contemporary of Sodasa (tables 2–3). Nahapana is identifiable as 'Manbanus', who ruled western India in the time of the *Periplus*, c. AD 54–65 (fig. 58.3; Cribb 2000, p. 46). Overstrikes between Nahapana and Sasan, the Indo-Parthian king (c. AD 64–70) (fig. 59.6), indicate they too were contemporaries (Cribb 2000, p. 42). Nahapana is also the predecessor of Chastana, whose regnal year 1 corresponds to

that of the Shaka era of AD 78 (fig. 58.4; Jha and Rajgor 1994, pp. 3–8). This suggests that the dates ranging from years 41 to 46 should fall within the immediately preceding decade, although the era to which they refer is not certain: from the numismatic evidence Rajavula or Gondophares seem to be the likeliest candidates (Cribb 1999, p. 195).

The Taxila region was lost to the Indo-Parthians by c. AD 32 (if the Azes era equals c. AD 46 BC), but, elsewhere in the north-west, some Indo-Scythians appear to have retained a degree of independence, for they continued issuing coins in their own names and/or in the name of Azes. As already noted, it is not clear whether this indicates that there was an Azes II – i.e. ruling c. AD 16–30 – or whether coins carried on being minted posthumously in the name of Azes I, the actual issuer remaining nameless (as occurs with imitations in the names of Euthydemus I, Heliocles and Hermaeus). Whatever interpretation is correct, the Indo-Scythian Apraca king Itravasu (Indravasu) and his successor, the stratega (Greek *strategos*, commander of forces) Aspavarma, both issued coins giving the name of Azes in Greek on the obverse, with their own and fathers' names and titles in Kharoshthi on the reverse (fig. 58.5–6; Senior 2000, vol. II, pp. 136–43).[78]

An increasing number of Buddhist reliquary inscriptions and the British Library scrolls provide further details of Apraca lineage (Senior 2000, vol. I, pp. 89–90; Salomon 1996, pp. 428–9; 1999, p. 150). Much of this evidence appears to come from the Bajaur region (the still inaccessible borderland between Pakistan and Afghanistan). The clearest genealogy is given in the Indravarman casket inscription of year 63 of Azes (i.e. c. AD 17). It identifies Indravarma as the son of the king of Apraca, and also the son of Vishnuvarma,

Table 2

Dates in uncertain eras

Ruler / Inscription	Date	Yona	Maues	Maues	Azes	Vikrama	Gondophares	Rajavula	Shaka
		186/5 BC	174 BC	75 BC	46 BC	58/7BC	AD 32	AD 27	AD 78
Maues year 1	[Yr 1]	186/5 BC	174 BC	75 BC					
Patika, son of Chukhsa satrap (Maues year 78)	Yr 78	108/7 BC	97 BC	AD 4					
Maghera (Yavana era)	Yr 116	70/69 BC	59 BC	AD 42	AD 70	AD 57/8			
Yona year 129 = Azes year 1	Yr 129	58/7 BC			46 BC	58/7 BC			
Vijayamitra (Apraca raja) year 1	[Yr 1]	11/10 BC			AD 1	AD 1	11/10 BC		
Yona year 201 = Azes year 73 = Vijayamitra year 27	Yr 27	AD 15/16			AD 27	AD 27	AD 15/16		
Gondophares year 1	[Yr 1]				AD 32	AD 19/20	AD 32		
Gondophares year 26 = Azes year 103	Yr 26				AD 57	AD 45/6	AD 57		
Nahapana (contemporary of Chastana)	Yr 41				6 BC	17/16 BC	AD 72	AD 68	
	Yr 46				1 BC	12/11 BC	AD 77	AD 73	
Sodasa 'Great Satrap' (contemporary of Chastana)	Yr 42 or Yr 72				5 BC or AD 26	16/15 BC or AD 14/15	AD 73 or AD 103	AD 69 or AD 100	
Shaka year 1 = Chastana year 1	Yr 1								AD 78

Table 3

Reconstructed chronology for the Indo-Scythians, Indo-Parthians and Kushans in the first century AD if Azes era year 1

AD	Azes era	Apraca rajas	Apraca strategas	Taxila and Gandhara		Chukhsa (Kashmir?)	Mathura	Western satraps	AD
1	47	Vijayamitra 1	Vishnuvarma	Azilises		Liaka Kusuluka			1
4						78 (Maues)			4
5		5							5
10									10
16				Azes II	Karahostes				16
17	63		Indravarma 63						17
20					son of Karahostes	Patika			20
27	73	27	73		Manigula		Rajavula [1]		27
30									30
32	78	32		Gondophares 1	Zeionises/Jihonika				32
33		Indravasu	Aspavarma						33
40							(Jammu)		40
50				(Jammu)				Aubheraka	50
51			Gadana						51
52	98?	98	98						52
57	103		Abdagases	26		Kujula			57
60							Sodasa	Nahapana	60
64									64
68			Sasan					41	68
69							42		69
70	116						116		70
73							(Yavana)	46	73
76	122			122					76
78								Chastana 1	78
80									80
90	136			136					90
91				Wima Tak[to]					91

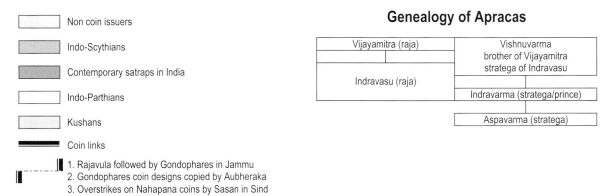

Legend:

- Non coin issuers
- Indo-Scythians
- Contemporary satraps in India
- Indo-Parthians
- Kushans
- Coin links

1. Rajavula followed by Gondophares in Jammu
2. Gondophares coin designs copied by Aubheraka
3. Overstrikes on Nahapana coins by Sasan in Sind

Genealogy of Apracas

- Vijayamitra (raja)
- Indravasu (raja)
- Vishnuvarma, brother of Vijayamitra, stratega of Indravasu
- Indravarma (stratega/prince)
- Aspavarma (stratega)

the brother of Vijayamitra, who in turn is said to be 'the [former] king of Apraca' (Salomon and Schopen 1984, pp. 108–9). But, according to the new Yona inscription, Vijayamitra was still king of Apraca a decade later in Azes year 73 (c. AD 27), the last date attributable to his reign being year 32 on the Prahodia reliquary (Senior 2000, vol. I, p. 90). Vishnuvarma is titled only 'prince' in the undated Dhota reliquary inscription (Salomon 1995, p. 27), and – under the variant spelling 'Vishpavarman' – as stratega (commander) of the Apraca king Indravasu in the undated silver reliquary inscription of Indravarma (Salomon 1996, pp. 424–5). Indravasu – whose name was previously misread on coins as Indravarma[79] – is in turn identified as *Vijayamitraputrasa* (son of Vijayamitra) on his issues (fig. 58.5; Senior 2000, vol. II, p. 136; vol. III, pp. 43–4). This suggests two lines of Apraca descent: two Apraca kings Vijayamitra (c. AD 1–32) and his son Indravasu (c. AD 32–3), and three strategas Vishnuvarma (brother of Vijayamitra), his son Indravarma and grandson Aspavarma (c. AD 33–64). It seems therefore that Indravarma is best identified in the Azes year 63 inscription as the nephew of Vijayamitra and a [grand]son of the previous unnamed Apraca king.

The new inscription equating year 201 of the Yona or Bactrian era (identified here as established by Eucratides c.174 BC) and year 73 of the Azes era (c.46 BC) with Vijayamitra's regnal year 27 (c. AD 27) provides a date of c. AD 1 for year 1 of this Apraca king's reign. Inscriptions in his regnal years show that he reigned for 32 years (Salomon 1996 p. 450). Dated inscriptional dedications of Indravarma – in which he is sometimes referred to as 'prince' as well as stratega – range from c. AD 17 to 27, i.e. during the latter half of the reign of Vijayamitra.

Indravasu is the only Apraca raja to issue coins citing his own name on the reverse (Senior 2000, vol. II, pp. 136–7; Mit. 897),[80] but these are rare, which suggests either that he initially issued coins in the name of Azes only or that his reign was short. In the coin sequence he is succeeded by Aspavarma (*Imtravarmaputrasa*, 'son of Indravarma'), who issued coins of the same type (fig. 58.6; horseman/Athena: Mit. 898), with the same principal monograms and corrupt Azes legend, but with his own name on the reverse as stratega, never as Apraca raja (Senior 2000, vol. II, pp. 138–43). However, his second series of coins (fig. 58.7; horseman/Zeus Nicephorus: Mit. 1136) carries the Indo-Parthian monogram of Gondophares. Directly linked to the latter are coins of the same Zeus type (with horse facing left, corrupt Greek legend and Gondophares monogram) issued by Sasan (c. AD 64–70) in his own name as Indo-Parthian king (fig. 59.6; Senior 2000, vol. II, p. 167; Mit. 1137). A silver drachm issue of Sasan from the Sind/Bannu region further identifies him as *Aspabharataputrasa* 'nephew of Aspa[varma?]' (Mit. 1104; Senior 2000, vol. II, p. 173). So the line of descent suggested by the coin evidence from/for the Bajaur region is Indravasu (as Apraca raja), Aspavarma (as stratega of the Apraca raja and then of the Indo-Parthians) and finally direct Indo-Parthian rule under Sasan.

Another independent Indo-Scythian in the first century AD is identified on his coins as Zeionises in corrupt Greek and as Jihonika, satrap and son of Manigula, in Kharoshthi (fig. 58.8–9; Mit. 879–86; table 3). In an inscription on a silver vase from Sirkap, Taxila,[81] he is further described as satrap of Chukhsa and his father, Manigula, as the great satrap's brother (Konow 1929, pp. 81–2, no. XXX, pl. XVI; Cribb 1999, pp. 196–7). On a few rare coins and in a British Library scroll fragment, Zeionises is also defined as great satrap (Senior 2000, vol. II, p. 122; Mit. 886; Salomon 1999, p. 142). Numismatically his bronze issues copy the Azes II bull and lion design (fig. 58.9; Mit. 850–2, 883–4), one being overstruck on a coin of Gondophares (Mit. 1086c; Alram 1999, p. 24). The obverse monograms and bull design are copied in turn by the first Kushan king, Kujula Kadphises (c. AD 40–90) (fig. 61.4; Mit. 1055–60). The numismatic context thus suggests a date of c. AD 30–50 for Zeionises. The time frame for his coinage suggests that he was the nephew and successor of Patika Kusuluka, described in the Taxila copper-plate inscription of year 78 as son of Liaka Kusuluka, the satrap of Chukhsa, and in the Mathura lion capital inscription as great satrap (Konow 1929, pp. 28–9, 48–9, nos XIII, XV, pls V.1, VI–IX; Cribb 1999, p. 196).

The first recorded coin of Zeionises is a unique silver tetradrachm acquired by Court presumably in the Punjab region (fig. 58.8; Prinsep 1836, pl. XXXV.5). Cunningham found one bronze coin of the ruler (together with a coin of Kujula Kadphises) in the relic deposit of the Sonala Pind stupa at Manikyala (figs 21; 190; Cunningham 1871, pp. 167–8, pl. LXV.b, d) and there are three in Masson's residue collection from Kabul and Begram. Stray coins and one small hoard apart, issues of this ruler generally appear to originate from Kashmir, identifying this region as the probable satrapy of Chukhsa (Cribb 1999, p. 196; Senior 2000, vol. II, p. 119, n. 1). The fact that the coins have been found in some hoards with those of Kujula emphasises the chronological link between the two rulers.

Indo-Parthians (c. AD 32–70)

> At that season all we the apostles were at Jerusalem, . . . and we divided the regions of the world, that every one of us should go unto the region that fell unto him and unto the nation whereunto the Lord sent him.
>
> According to the lot, therefore, India fell unto Judas Thomas [who initially refused to go]. . . . There was there a certain merchant come from India whose name was Abbanes, sent from the king Gundaphorus, and having commandment from him to buy a carpenter and bring him unto him. . . . And the Lord said: 'I have a slave that is a carpenter and I desire to sell him' . . . and wrote a deed of sale, saying: 'I, Jesus, the son of Joseph the carpenter, acknowledge that I have sold my slave, Judas by name, unto thee Abbanes, a merchant of Gundaphorus, king of the Indians'. (*Acts of St Thomas* I.1–2)[82]

According to Strabo (XI.ix.2), the Parthians of Iran 'forced' the Scythians in Bactria 'to yield to them'. In the first century AD they also seem to have extended their sphere of influence south-eastwards into lands controlled by the Indo-Scythians, for a dynasty with apparent Parthian affiliations came to power at Taxila. The principal ruler, Gondophares (c. AD 32–60) (fig. 59.1–3),[83] is mentioned in the apocryphal second- to third-century Christian *Acts of St Thomas* as the king to whom a reluctant St Thomas was sold to convince him that his destiny lay in India (James 1985, pp. 365, 371–5). The text describes the apostle's encounter c. AD 35–40 with the king and his brother Gad and their putative conversion to Christianity.

Figure 59 Indo-Parthian coins.
Gondophares (c. AD 32–60):
1   Obv. king on horseback; rev. Pallas Athena;
2   Obv. bust of king; rev. Nike, from Begram;
3   Obv. king on horseback facing goddess with wreath; rev. Gondopharid tamgha.
4   Orthagnes (c. AD 52–64). Rev. Nike with diadem; named Gadana in Kharoshthi.

5   Abdagases (c. AD 52–64). Obv. horseman; rev. Zeus Nicephorus.
6   Sasan (c. AD 64–70), citing Gondophares as the king of kings.
Imitations of Parthian coins:
7   Phraataces/Phraates V (2 BC–AD 4) imitation. Rev. seated archer;
8–9   Unidentified imitations. Rev. seated archer.
Sanabares (c. AD 135–60):
10   Indo-Parthian ruler in Seistan. Rev. seated archer.

An inscription reputedly from the Buddhist site of Takht-i-Bahi in the Peshawar Valley, dated in year 103 (i.e. AD 57) of the Azes era and in the year 26 of Gondophares, provides a date of AD 32 for the beginning of the Indo-Parthian king's reign (Konow 1929, pp. 57–62). In a numismatic context, coins of Gondophares overstrike posthumous issues in the name of Hermaeus, the last Greek king of the Parapamisidae (fig. 54.6), and are, in turn, overstruck by coins of the first Kushan king, Kujula Kadphises (Mit. 1086a–b).

The Greek philosopher and miracle worker Apollonius of Tyana is said by his biographer Philostratus (c. AD 170–247)[84] to have travelled to India some time after visiting the Parthian court at Babylon in AD 42 (Bivar 2007, p. 26). He was armed with a letter of introduction from the Parthian king Vardanes (AD 39–45) to the satrap of the Indus, who provided a guide for the whole country as far as the Hydraotes (Ravi) river (Philostratus II.17). At Taxila he was told by the king – who is said to be called Phraotes[85] – that (Philostratus II.26)

> the barbarians who live on the border of this country were perpetually quarrelling with us and making raids into my territories, but I keep them quiet and control them with money, so that my country is patrolled by them, and instead of their invading my dominions, they themselves keep off the barbarians that are on the other side of the frontier, and are difficult people to deal with.

The king also recounted a complicated tale of succession following the death of his grandfather (Philostratus II.31–2). As his father was under age, two relatives were appointed regents, but they were killed by conspirators who took control of the state. His father took refuge with a neighbouring king across the Hyphases (Beas) river; subsequently married the king's daughter and was appointed co-heir to the throne with his brother-in-law, but renounced his claim. On the death of one of the usurpers, Phraotes successfully reclaimed his grandfather's throne.

Although doubts have been expressed as to the validity of Apollonius' account (Bivar 2007, p. 26),[86] the coin evidence similarly suggests a complicated rather than a direct line of descent after Gondophares. Abdagases (c. AD 52–64), the next ruler in the Punjab, according to the numismatic sequence, is identified in coin legends as the nephew of Gondophares (ΑΔΕΛΦΙΔΕΩΣ/Gadapharabhrataputrasa). Initially he is titled only king, but later he has the additional appellation 'king of kings' (fig. 59.5). A Buddhist reliquary inscription of doubted authenticity is dated year 98 of Azes, during the reigns of both Aspavarma and Abdagases, which suggests that the latter may have been already ruling, presumably under Gondophares, c. AD 52 (Sadakata 1996, pp. 308–11).

As Senior has pointed out, 'Gondophares' (Old Persian Vindapharna 'Winner of Glory') is in reality a title; one that was adopted in addition to their given names on some issues – notably from Arachosia (Qandahar) or Pathankot – of his successors Sarpedanes, Orthagnes, Ubuzanes and Sasan (Senior 2000, vol. I, pp. 108, 112–14; vol. II, pp. 175–81, types 253, 257, 259–60). However, in other regions such as Sind and Seistan, they also issued coins in their own right as 'king' or 'king of kings'. The numismatic evidence thus suggests a complicated situation in this period of rulers and sub-rulers that echoes the impression left from Philostratus' account of the borderlands being controlled by satraps and 'barbarians' owing varying degrees of allegiance to the Indo-Parthian king.

On the reverse of rare issues of Orthagnes, the Kharoshthi legend identifies him as 'king of kings, the great Gadana'; on others, the reference to Gondophares is included, i.e. *maharajasa rajadirajasa mahatasa Gudapharasa Gadanasa*, but often with the names abbreviated on both obverse and reverse (Senior 2000, vol. I, p. 115; vol. II, p. 179, n. 1). The Seistan coins of Ubuzanes identify him as 'king' and the 'son of king Orthagnes' in Greek, but on his Pathankot issues only his own name is given on the obverse, while the reverse carries a shorter version of his father's Kharoshthi legend: *maharajasa Gadavhara Gadanasa* (Senior 2000, vol. II, p. 181). Senior suggests that, since all Orthagnes' bronze issues carry the name Gadana on the reverse, they represent one and the same personal name (fig. 59.4; 2000, vol. I, pp. 112–13). It is also possible, as Mitchiner suggests (1976, p. 741), that Gad, the brother of Gondophares mentioned in the *Acts of St Thomas*, is identifiable as Orthagnes-Gadana, a contemporary of Abdagases, who claimed allegiance to Gondophares, but who also issued coins in his own right.

Coinage debasement continued under the Indo-Parthians, with ever-increasing amounts of bronze replacing the silver content. Several Indo-Scythian designs were retained, especially the rider on horseback obverse. In particular, following the same tradition as the Apracas Indravasu and Aspavarma, Gondophares issued the horseman/Pallas Athena type (Mit. 1128), while Abdagases issued the Zeus type. Monograms and typology moreover link the horseman/Zeus issues of Abdagases to varieties of the same type issued by the Indo-Parthian king Sasan (*c.* AD 64–70) (fig. 59.6; Senior 2000, vol. II, pp. 159–64, 168–72; Mit. 1126, 1140 and 1125, 1138 respectively). Base silver tetradrachms of Sasan of this type are, in turn, copied by the second Kushan king, Wima Tak[to], one example collected by Court being, in fact, an overstrike by Wima on the earlier issue of Sasan (fig. 61.7; Sims-Williams and Cribb 1995/6, pp. 119–20, fig. 11b).

Given the association of Gondophares with Taxila, finds of his coins at the site are surprisingly few in number. Of the 744 Gondophares coins said to have been excavated at Sirkap, only 107 were issued in his name alone; 636 were issued by Sasan and one by Aspavarma (Marshall 1951, pp. 211, 784). The site also produced 34 Abdagases coins. The Shaikhan Dheri excavations near Charsadda produced only one coin of Gondophares (Dani 1965–6, p. 35).

Masson records collecting 55 coins of Gondophares at Begram in the 1833–5 seasons, all evidently the bust of king/winged Nike type (fig. 59.2; Mit. 1082–5; Uncat. MSS 2, f. 1, figs 92–8). Ten of these are illustrated, some more than once (Masson 1834, p. 170, pl. X.34–6; Wilson 1841, p. 339, no. 1, pl. V.12–14). In addition to two identified pieces in the British Museum (IOC 232/BMC 21, EIC 113), 64 other examples of the same type are preserved in Masson's residue collection (IOLC). Other Gondophares coin types are rare in Masson's collection,[87] as are coins of Abdagases: Masson and Wilson did not record any and there are only two coins of this ruler in the IOLC collection (Mit. 1126, 1140). Coins of Sasan are more plentiful – 25 in the IOLC collection (Mit. 1125, 1138) – but it is uncertain whether any were found at Begram for, of the two illustrated, one is without provenance (IOC 235; Wilson 1841, p.343, no. 5, pl. V.19) and the other was acquired in Kabul bazaar (Masson 1836, p. 27, no. 41, pl. III.30; Uncat. MSS 2, fig. 41; Wilson 1841, p. 343, no. 6, pl. V.20).[88]

There is a pre-existing Iranian tradition in the region, attested by, for example, the name Aspavarma, which is related to the Old Persian Aspačanah (Greek Aspathines) (p. 103, n. 29). Nevertheless, although the precise Indo-Parthian relationship with the Parthians of Iran is not clear, some of the names and coin designs suggest links between the two dynasties. The winged Nike image of Gondophares,

for example, copies the coin design of the Parthian king Vonones I (*c.* AD 8–12) (figs 59.2; 50.3), while that of a king on horseback being greeted by a goddess with a wreath copies coins of Artabanus II (*c.* AD 10–38) (figs 59.4; 50.4; Cribb 2000, p. 41). Distinctive small, thick, bronze coins, found in 'considerable' numbers by Masson at Begram, include an imitation of the Parthian king Phraataces (Phraates V, *c.* 2 BC–AD 4), mixed with Indo-Parthian imitations of similar fabric (fig. 59.7–9; Wilson 1841, pp. 346–7, nos 1–2, pl. XV.6–11; Mit. 1155, 1158–60). Five silver drachms of unknown provenance in the Kabul Museum (Ghirshman 1946, pp. 122, 196, pl. XXII.1–5) provide a clear link between these late imitations and the Pakores and Sanabares silver prototypes of *c.* first century AD from which they derive (fig. 59.10; Mit. 1078, 1150–2).

Kushans (*c.* AD 40–360)

The country of the Da Yuezhi has its capital at the city of Lanshi [Tashkurgan, northern Afghanistan]; to the west it borders on Anxi [Arsak, i.e. Parthia] at a distance of 49 days' travel; to the east it lies . . . 16,370 *li* from Luoyang [the Later Han capital]. Formerly, when the Yuezhi had been routed by the Xiongnu [Huns], they moved to Daxia [Bactria] and divided their country into the five *xihou* [*yabgu*, i.e. tribes] of Xiumi, Shuangmi, Guishuang [Kushan], Xidun and Dumi. More than a hundred years later, the *yabgu* of Guishuang [named] Qiujiuque attacked and destroyed the [other] four *yabgu* and established himself as king; the kingdom was named Guishuang. [This] king invaded Anxi, took the country of Gaofu [Parapamisidae] and, moreover, destroyed Puda [Pushkalavati] and Jibin [Kashmir] and completely possessed their territory. Qiujiuque died at the age of more than 80 years, and his son Yangaozhen succeeded him as king. He in turn destroyed Tianzhu [India] and placed there a general to control it. Since then the Yuezhi have been extremely rich and strong. . . . The country of Gaofu, to the south-west of the Da Yuezhi, is also a large country. Its customs resemble those of Tianzhu and [the people] are weak and easily conquered . . . the three countries of Tianzhu, Jibin and Anxi have possessed it . . . and the Yuezhi obtained Gaofu only after they had defeated Anxi. (*Hou Han Shu* 118.9a, cf. Zürcher 1968, pp. 367–8)[89]

This extract from the 'Account of the Western Region', charting the rise of the Kushans, was based on a report submitted to the Chinese Later Han emperor Andi (AD 107–25) by the general Ban Yong (*Hou Han Shu* 118). In his prologue to the work Fan Ye (AD 398–445) states: 'I have compiled those things from Jianwu onwards' (i.e. from the period AD 25–7 of the Later Han dynasty), and that 'It is all what Ban Yong recorded at the end of the reign of Andi' (*Hou Han Shu* 118.0904.3, cf. Pulleyback 1968, pp. 248–9). As the *Hou Han Shu* purports to include events from *c.* AD 27 onwards, this provides an approximate date after which the amalgamation of the Yuezhi under the leadership of the first Kushan king took place. It also indicates an approximate date for the settlement of the Yuezhi in Bactria 'more than a hundred years' earlier, i.e. *c.*100–75 BC.

The 'Western Region' roughly comprised the province of modern Xinjiang,[90] where Ban Yong was sent to re-establish Chinese relations in AD 123, after a gap of about 16 years, following the Chinese withdrawal from these regions in AD 107 (Pulleyback 1968, p. 249; Zürcher 1968, p. 350; Twitchett and Loewe 1986, p. 421). His report therefore probably contains information only from the earlier period of Chinese presence in the Western Region up to AD 107, especially from the period of direct contact between the two powers. This began in AD 84, when the governor-general, Ban Chao, the father of Ban Yong, 'sent an envoy with many presents of brocade and silk' to the Yuezhi king. In AD 86/7, the Yuezhi sent an envoy with tribute to the Han emperor and 'used this occasion to ask for a Han princess'; and finally in AD 90, the Yuezhi sent troops to attack Ban Chao, who defeated them (*Hou Han Shu* 77.6b–7a, *Hou Han Shu Annals* 3.17a, 4.3b, cf. Zürcher 1968, pp. 369–71; Leslie and Gardiner 1996, pp. 135, 291–3).

The Rabatak inscription, which first came to light in northern Afghanistan in 1993,[91] confirmed the dynastic succession of the first four Kushan kings that had already been largely established by numismatists working on the coin sequences from the early nineteenth century onwards (Sims-Williams and Cribb 1995/6, pp. 77–81; pp. 179–208 below). It states:

> Kanishka the Kushan . . . gave orders to make images of . . . these kings: for King Kujula Kadphises (his) great grandfather, and for King Vima Taktu (his) grandfather, and for King Vima Kadphises (his) father, and also for himself, King Kanishka (Rabatak §§ 1, 11–14).

The first Kushan king, Qiujiuque – who, according to the Chinese, conquered the lands south of the Hindu Kush as far as the North-West Frontier region and Kashmir – is identified on coins and in the Rabatak inscription as Kujula Kadphises (*c.* AD 40–90) (figs 26.2; 61.4–6).[92] Approximate dates for the first two Kushan rulers are indicated by the time frame of the *Hou Han Shu*, i.e. a long reign for Kujula commencing after AD 27, with his successor Yangaozhen – identified in the Rabatak inscription as Wima Tak[to] (*c.* AD 90–113) – coming to power before *c.* AD 107, when the Chinese withdrew from Xinjiang.

The status assigned to the latter king in the *Hou Han Shu* as a conqueror of India is supported by the existence of a large portrait statue, 2.08 m (6 ft 10 in.) high, which is identified in its pedestal inscription as [Ve]*ma Takṣuma*, founder of the Kushan shrine discovered at Tokri Tila near Mat, a village in the vicinity of Mathura in north India (fig. 62; Fussman 1998, p. 607; Lüders 1961, pp. 134–8). His pre-eminence is underlined by the fact that the statue of his now more famous grandson Kanishka I (fig. 63) from the same shrine is a mere 1.71 m (5 ft 7½ in.). His coin legends have been variously read as *vema takto*, *takoma* and *takho* (fig. 61.8–10; Sims-Williams and Cribb 1995/6, p. 102; Falk 2001, p. 134, n. 2). Apart from his usual titles *mahārāja rājātirāja devaputra* 'Great King, king of kings, son of the gods', in the Mat statue inscription Wima Tak[to] is also called *Kuṣāṇaputra*. This has been translated as 'scion of the Kushan' or alternatively – and in the light of other evidence, it seems correctly – as 'son of the Kushan', i.e. of Kujula Kadphises (Lüders 1961, p. 136).

Cunningham first noted the use of the designation 'the Kushan' on 'Heraus' silver tetradrachms, which he linked to Kujula (fig. 61.1). He also identified a Heraus silver obol (fig. 61.2[93] – together with 10 bronze Hermaeus imitations in the name of Kujula (fig. 26.2) – among Masson's finds from the Buddhist relic deposit of Kotpur 2, west of Jalalabad (Cunningham 1888, pp. 49–51, 54). The provenance of similar obols in his own collection is said 'positively' to be the Kabul

region, but the fact that there are none in Masson's Begram collections makes this attribution unlikely. Although stray finds have surfaced as far south as Taxila, their area of issue and use seems, like the tetradrachms, to have been Bactria (Cribb 1993, pp. 119–20). The painted clay sculptures excavated at Khalchayan near the Surkhan river in Uzbekistan also include a royal figure whose facial features and dress are so similar to the coin image as to identify both as portraits of Heraus (fig. 60; Harmatta 1996, p. 343, fig. 13; Nehru 1989, figs 39–40). The excavators consider the site to be a Kushan palace of the early first century AD, with later second- to third-century additions (Pugachenkova 1996).

Evidence for Heraus further south comes in the form of two rare bronze coins in the Cunningham collection (fig. 61.3). Bilingual 'Heraus' legends in Greek and Kharoshthi attest their production south of the Hindu Kush, while their denomination and design are based on the bull and camel coins of Kujula Kadphises (fig. 61.4; Cribb 1993, pp. 118, 121–3, figs 4–5). The persuasive numismatic interconnections equating 'the Kushan' and 'Heraus' with Kujula Kadphises (Cribb 1993) have been disputed, even though the epigraphic evidence has been deemed 'plausible' (Alram 1999, p. 24), i.e. the similar terminology identifying the unnamed 'Great King' as 'the Kushan' occurs in the inscriptions of year 122 from Panjtar (p. 25) and year 136 on the so-called Taxila silver scroll from Dharmarajika chapel G5 (Marshall 1951, pp. 69, 256; Konow 1929, pp. 70, 77). The same symbol ⚕ occurs on the Taxila scroll as on the coins of Zeionises, Sasan and Kujula Kadphises: specifically in the latter instance, the bull and camel coins, with designs derived in part from Zeionises' issues (fig. 58.9; Mit. 1055–60).[94] The unspecified era of both inscriptions is generally thought to be that of Azes, which when equated with 46 BC, provides the respective dates of AD 76 for Kujula in the Peshawar Valley and AD 90 at Taxila. The numismatic evidence places Kujula as the successor of the Indo-Parthians Gondophares and Abdagases in the Kabul–Jalalabad region, the Indo-Scythian satrap Zeionises in Kashmir, and the Indo-Parthian Sasan in Gandhara, Taxila and Sind (Cribb 2000, p. 48). Year 136 is the last date definitely in the Azes era. Subsequent dates appear to be in the Yona era and are possibly,[95] or positively, associated with Kujula's immediate successors, Wima Tak[to] and Wima Kadphises (fig. 61.7–17).

Wima Tak[to] is cited in the year 279 in the Bactrian inscription from Dasht-i Nawar as the 'king of kings, the great salvation, Vima Taktu the Kushan, the righteous, the just' (Sims-Williams and Cribb 1995/6, p. 95). The same date is found on an incomplete inscription from the Kushan dynastic site of Surkh Kotal in Bactria (Bivar 1963, p. 500; Salomon 2005, pp. 375–6). If year 279 is calculated in the Yona era – where Yona equals 174 BC (Cribb 2005, p. 221) – it provides an acceptable date of AD 105. This neatly fits the *Hou Han Shu* record of the existence of a second Kushan king ruling at the time of the Chinese withdrawal from Xinjiang in AD 107.

Another inscription from Khalatse, in Ladakh, is dated in year 284 (or 287) of the same era, i.e. AD 110 (or AD 113), but falls within 'the reign of the Great King Üvima Kavthisa', identified in the Rabatak inscription as Wima Kadphises (Konow 1929, pp. 79–81, no. XXIX, pl. XV.2; Salomon 2005, p. 376). On the basis of the coin evidence for this third

Kushan king, the later date of AD 113 is preferable for the start of his reign, given that the limited number of coins and issues of this ruler argue against him having been in power for a long time.

Coin issues actually in the name of his predecessor Wima Tak[to] are restricted to three (Sims-Williams and Cribb 1995/6, pp. 111–12, 115–18, figs 11b–d, 13b–15f).[96] The first – bronze bilingual tetradrachms from Gandhara and the western Punjab – carry the same horseman and Zeus designs of their base silver Sasan prototype, but have the Kushan king's tamgha with the Greek title 'Soter Megas' (great saviour) on the obverse; and the king's name and titles together with the monogram ⊤⌐ (vi) in Kharoshthi on the reverse (fig. 61.7). The second group – putatively found in Kashmir – are bronze tetradrachms and drachms with a bull and camel design descended via issues of Kujula Kadphises from his predecessor in the region, Zeionises (fig. 61.9). The Greek legend on the obverse is blundered, but Wima's name and titles are again given in Kharoshthi on the reverse. Lastly there is a unique, small bronze coin of uncertain provenance with Wima's name in Greek, depicting the seated king on the obverse and two standing figures on the reverse (fig. 61.10).

The same tendency to derive designs from earlier local types is evident on the coinages issued solely in the 'name' of Soter Megas (Cribb 1993, p. 123; Sims-Williams and Cribb 1995/6, pp. 112–14, 120–2, fig. 12a–c). On a Mathura issue, an imitation of the Heliocles portrait bust/Zeus design is combined with the Wima Tak[to]/Soter Megas tamgha and the usual Soter Megas legend: ΒΑΣΙΛΕΥΣ ΒΑΣΙΛΕΥΩΝ ΣΩΤΗΡ ΜΕΓΑΣ 'king of kings, the great saviour' (fig. 61.11). A further link with the posthumous coinages in the name of Heliocles has recently been demonstrated by the discovery of the Wima Tak[to]/Soter Megas tamgha on the rump of the horse on some examples of the portrait bust/horse type traditionally assigned to the Yuezhi (fig. 61.12; Smith 2001, p. 14, figs 9–10; p. 56 above). The denomination of a Bactrian issue 'seems to relate to the reduced Attic standard used for imitations of Heliocles' tetradrachms', while its obverse design copies the helmeted bust of Eucratides I (fig. 61.13; Sims-Williams and Cribb 1995/6, p. 120). It also carries the Wima Tak[to]/Soter Megas tamgha, together with the Kharoshthi monogram ⊤⌐ (vi). The reverse has a horseman reminiscent of earlier Indo-Scythian and Indo-Parthian designs, except that, in this instance, a Phrygian cap identifies the figure as Mithra.

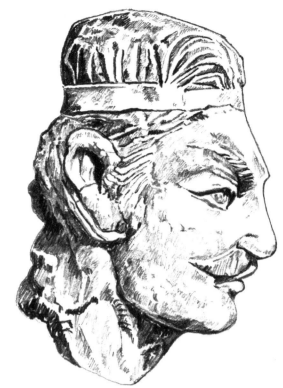

Figure 60 Clay head of a Kushan prince from Khalchayan.

The same reverse image is used with an obverse rayed and diademed bust of Mithra on the principal Soter Megas issues (fig. 61.14–15; Sims-Williams and Cribb 1995/6, pp. 114–15, 121–2, fig. 12d–e). This is a huge coinage, issued over a vast region from Bactria to the Punjab: the India Office residue of Masson's collection from Begram alone numbers 836 coins. There is a correspondingly large number of dies, with subtle variations in such features as the portrait, number of rays (ranging from 15 down to 5) and the use of a square or cursive script, but little variation in weight or quality. There is also a notable transition from a rarer four-pronged to the common three-pronged tamgha, both versions occurring in a few instances on the obverse and reverse respectively of the same coin.[97] Göbl sees the four-pronged tamgha of Soter Megas as being used perhaps 'at one specific mint' and 'perhaps only at the end of his reign', for he considers it 'undoubtedly the next step preceding the four-pronged tamgha of his successor, Vima Kadphises' (1999, p. 152). But if the latter is the case, then what appears to be a logical

Figure 61 Kushan coins.
'Heraus' (c. AD 40–90):
1   Rev. horseman with Nike;
2   Rev. soldier with wreath;
3   Bilingual imitation of issues of Gondophares and Zeionises.
Kujula Kadphises (c. AD 40–90):
4   Obv. bull; rev. camel;
5   Hermaeus imitation. Rev. Heracles;
6   Augustus imitation. Obv. head of Augustus Caesar; rev. seated Zeus.
Wima Tak[to] (c. AD 90–113):
7   Sasan imitation, overstruck on coin of Sasan. Obv. horseman, tamgha and Greek title 'Soter Megas'; rev. Zeus, king's name, titles and monogram (vi) in Kharoshthi;
8   Obv. Heracles; rev. Tyche, (vi) in Kharoshthi;
9   Obv. bull; rev. camel;
10   Obv. seated king; rev. two standing figures, Greek legend;
11   Heliocles imitation. Rev. Zeus, 'Soter Megas' legend in Greek;
12   Posthumous Heliocles imitation. Rev. horse with Wima Tak[to]'s tamgha on rump;
13   Soter Megas issue copying helmeted bust of Eucratides I; rev. Mithra on horseback;

14   Soter Megas issue with four-pronged tamgha. Obv. rayed bust of Mithra; rev. Mithra on horseback;
15   Soter Megas issue with three-pronged tamgha.
Wima Kadphises (c. AD 113–27):
16   Obv. king on mountain-top; rev. Oesho holding trident and lion skin;
17   Obv. king standing at fire altar; rev. Oesho and bull.
Kanishka I (c. AD 127–50):
18   Rev. Greek legend ΗΡΑΚΛΗΣ ('Heracles') overcut by OHРO ('Oesho') in Bactrian;
19   Rev. Oado.
Huvishka (c. AD 150–90):
20   Rev. Nana seated on lion;
21   Obv. king on elephant; rev. Heracles.
Vasudeva I (c. AD 190–227):
22–3   Obv. king standing at fire altar; rev. Oesho with flaming shoulders, trident, noose and bull.
24   Kanishka II (c. AD 227–46). Rev. Ardochsho with diadem and cornucopia.
25   Vasishka (c. AD 246–67).
26   Kanishka III (c. AD 267–80). Rev. Oesho.
27   Vasudeva II (c. AD 280–320). Rev. Ardochsho.
28   Shaka (c. AD 320–60).

Figure 62 Inscribed statue of Wima Tak[to] from Kushan dynastic shrine of Mat.

Figure 63 Inscribed statue of Kanishka I from Kushan dynastic shrine of Mat.

progression from finely executed images with 15 rays to coarser images with only 5 rays has to be stood on its head, for the four-pronged tamghas are all associated with between 14 and 12 rays and the finer portrait. The coins with both four- and three-pronged tamghas have between 12 and 8 rays, a spear with two pennants and square letter forms, as do all the four-pronged examples, but only a small proportion of the three-pronged ones.

Identification of all these coins as issues of Wima Tak[to] is based *inter alia* on his use of the Soter Megas title on coins issued in his own name; the pervasive use of the same tamgha; and the monogram ⫙ (*vi*) on the linked Eucratides bust/Mithra coinage. This equation has not found universal acceptance (Bopearachchi 2001, pp. 417–19), but arguments against it verge on sophistry, especially since it is generally agreed that the Soter Megas issues fit between Kujula and Wima Kadphises in the coinage sequence. While it is true that Wima Kadphises uses the same title 'king of kings, great saviour' on his bronze coinage, there are no discernible characteristics within the Soter Megas coinage to enable a viable division of the issues between more than one ruler. In view of the clear numismatic links to Wima Tak[to], his identification with Soter Megas is the most practical solution until any conclusive evidence to the contrary emerges.

Unification under one political authority brought stability and prosperity to a vast area and international trade flourished. One coin issue introduced by Kujula Kadphises reflects the increasing contact with the west that took place from the first century AD onwards, for it copies, in bronze, the design of silver and gold coins of the Roman emperor

Augustus (31 BC–AD 14: fig. 61.6). Kushan coinage reforms are already apparent during the reign of Kujula, when the prevailing debased silver or billon currency was abandoned in favour of bronze. This was followed by the introduction of the Soter Megas issues as a uniform bronze currency for use throughout most of the empire (fig. 61.14–15). The most radical change however was the introduction by Wima Kadphises of a gold coinage based on the weight standard of the Roman stater (fig. 61.16).

The seventh-century Chinese pilgrim Xuan Zang says that Kushan territories in Central Asia in the time of Kanishka I (figs 26.3; 61.18–19) reached to the east of Cong Ling in eastern Turkestan (Watters 1904, p. 124). This statement receives some support from Kushan coin finds – predominantly of Kanishka, more rarely of the two Wimas – at eastern Central Asian sites such as Khotan and Loulan (Wang 2004, pp. 33–4). According to the Rabatak inscription, the Kushan empire under Kanishka extended along the Gangetic plain eastwards beyond Patna to Campa (modern Bhagalpur) in Bihar (Rabatak §§ 2–7; Sims-Williams and Cribb 1995/6, p. 78):

> In the year one it has been proclaimed unto India, unto the whole realm of the *kshatriyas*, that (as for) them – both the (city of) . . . and the (city of) Saketa [modern Sialkot, Punjab], and the (city of) Kausambi [Kosam, Uttar Pradesh], and the (city of) Pataliputra [Patna], as far as the (city of) Sri-Campa – whatever rulers and other important persons (they might have) he had submitted to (his) will, and he had submitted all India to (his) will.

The Rabatak inscription also says that Kanishka 'inaugurated the year one as the gods pleased' (Sims-Williams and Cribb

1995/6, p. 78). A rereading of the last or seventy-ninth chapter of Sphujiddhvaja's *Yavanajātaka*, the oldest extant Indian text on astronomy, has revealed a viable calculation for the date of year 1 (Falk 2001). It presents an astrological *yuga* of 165 years, which is based on the belief that the repetitive nature of planetary cycles makes it possible to calculate the positions of major constellations at any given time retrospectively or in the future. Written in year 191 (AD 269) of the Shaka era of AD 78, during the second *yuga*, the text states that the first *yuga* began 56 years before the start of the Shaka era (i.e. in AD 22) and lasted 165 years (i.e. until AD 187). It also gives the time difference between the Shaka era and the Kushan era as exactly 149 years, which produces a Kushan date of AD 227 (Falk 2001, pp. 126–7). Taking into account the approximate dates for the first two Kushan kings established by Chinese sources, this is best interpreted as the date for the start of the second Kushan century, which indicates that the first century inaugurated by Kanishka I began in AD 127 (Falk 2001, pp. 130–1). It also confirms the long-advocated hypothesis that a system of dropped hundreds was commonly used in the second Kushan century in inscriptions relating to the later kings from Kanishka II onwards. Inscriptions dated in the era of Kanishka therefore establish the approximate number of years for the reigns of the following Kushan kings (table 1; figs 26.3–4; 61.18–26): Kanishka I, years 1–23 (c. AD 127–50); Huvishka, years 26–64 (c. AD 150–90); Vasudeva I, years 64–98 (c. AD 190–227);[98] Kanishka II, years [1]05-[1]17 (c. AD 227–46); Vasishka, years [1]22-[1]30 (c. AD 246–67); and Kanishka III, year [1]41 (c. AD 267–80).

A series of four inscriptions from Buddhist sites in Gandhara (fig. 175) show that the Yona era continued in parallel use with the Kanishka era. These are year 303 from Charsadda, year 318 from Loriyan Tangai, year 359 from Jamalgarhi (fig. 117) and year 384 from Hashtnagar near Charsadda (fig. 76; Salomon 1997, pp. 368–71; Konow 1929, pp. 106–7, 110–13, 117–19).[99] If Yona year 1 equals 174 BC and AD 127 marks the beginning of the Kanishka era, then year 1 of Kanishka I is also year 301 of the Yona era. In other words, the two Kanishka era centuries are the dropped hundred equivalents of the third and fourth Yona (i.e. Bactrian) centuries (table 1). Such synchronism supplies a logical explanation for the concurrent use of the Yona and Kanishka eras in the North-West Frontier region. If applied to the year 359 inscription from Jamalgarhi, it produces a date of AD 185. This fits neatly with the archaeological evidence from the site, for the room in which the inscription was located belongs to a rebuilding phase of the main stupa complex that coin finds suggest took place from the late reign of Huvishka to the early reign of Vasudeva I (fig. 61.20–3; Errington 1987, pp. 234–5, 274–5).

The Sasanians took control of Bactria c. AD 233, during the reign of Kanishka II (fig. 61.24, table 4). They captured Gandhara from Vasishka (c. AD 246–67) (fig. 61.25) and Taxila from Vasudeva II (c. AD 280–320) (fig. 61.27).[100] From this last king onwards, the Kushan rulers are only known from coins. In the time of Shaka (c. AD 320–60) the southern part of the empire fell to the Guptas (fig. 61.28). The last two kings, Vasudeva III (c. AD 360) (fig. 74.1) and Kipunadha (c. AD 360–80) (fig. 74.2), held the remaining territory until overthrown by the Kidarite Huns c. AD 380.

Sasanians (AD 223/4–652)

> I, the Mazda-worshipping lord, Shapur, King of Kings of Iranians[101] and non-Iranians, who is descended from the gods, son of the Mazda-worshipping lord, Ardashir, King of Kings of Iranians, who is descended from the gods, grandson of the lord Papak, the king, I am master of Iran and possess the countries of Persis, Parthia, . . . Hindustan, the lands of the Kushans up to Peshawar, and as far as Kashgar, Sogdiana and Tashkent. (ŠKZ §§ 1–3)

The history of the Sasanians is well documented by inscriptions and in Roman, Christian and Islamic sources, while a complete list of all the kings is given in the *Shahnameh* (*Book of Kings*), an early eleventh-century Persian epic poem by Firdowsi about ancient Iran. According to Firdowsi, the Sasanians were descended from the Achaemenid kings through Sasan, a shepherd employed by Papak, local governor of the Parthians in Fars, the heartland of the former Achaemenid empire in southern Iran. Although Sasan kept his aristocratic lineage secret, Papak dreamt that Sasan and his sons would one day rule the world, and therefore gave his daughter in marriage to the shepherd. Their son, Ardashir, was then adopted by Papak who had no male heir (*Shahnameh* IV, §§ 2066–113). A similar tale is given in the Pahlavi text the *Karnamak-i Artakhshir-i Papakan* (West 2005, no. 101). This however contradicts the genealogy of the Kaba-i Zardusht inscription of Shapur I at Naqsh-i Rustam, which cites Papak as the father of Ardashir and Sasan as merely an ancestor (fig. 64; Huyse 1999, pp. 22–4). A further variation is given by the ninth- to tenth-century historian Tabari, who identifies Sasan as a local ruler in Fars and the grandfather of Ardashir (Nöldeke 1973, pp. 3–5).[102]

According to the *Karnamak-i Artakhshir-i Papakan* (West 2005, no. 101), Ardashir was summoned to the Parthian court when he was fifteen and, following a quarrel with the king's son, was put to work in the stables. He ran away to Fars with the king's handmaiden and much booty, so was pursued by Ardavan (Artabanus IV), but he was helped to escape by the *khvarenah/khvarrah/farr* (Divine Glory; see p. 115). Several nobles subsequently joined his war against Artabanus, whom he defeated and killed.

A slightly different version again is given by Tabari, who says that Ardashir was brought up by Tir, governor of the district of Darabgird (modern Darab), south of Shiraz. After the death of his foster-father, Ardashir became the *argbed* (governor/lord of the castle) of Darabgird (Nöldeke 1973, pp. 5–6). In a dream an angel prophesied that God would give him the power to rule. Encouraged by this, Ardashir overthrew a series of local rulers and began to challenge the Parthian king of kings (Nöldeke

Figure 64 View of Kaba-i Zardusht at Naqsh-i Rustam, near Persepolis.

Table 4

Relationships between the Sasanians and their contemporaries AD 190–484

AD	IRAN SASANIAN	BACTRIA GANDHARA KUSHANSHAH		PUNJAB KUSHAN	INDIA
190		Vasudeva I (190–227)			
223	Ardashir I (223/4–41)	Sasanian yr 1 (223/4)			
227		Kanishka II (227–46)			
233	captured Bactria from Kanishka II				
241	Shapur I (240–72/3)	Ardashir (233–46) 'I' winged bird crown			
246	captured 'as far as Peshawar' from Vasishka	'II'(?) tripartite crown		Vasishka (246–67)	
260		Peroz 'I' (246–85)			
267		(1) pointed crown		Kanishka III (267–80)	
272	Hormizd I (272/3)	(2) flat crown			
273	Varhran I (273–6)	(3) lion-head crown			
276	Varhran II (276–93)	O/S on Kanishka III			
280				Vasudeva II (280–320) lost Taxila to Sasanians	
285		Hormizd 'I' (285–300) *Kabad*	satrap		
293	Varhran III (293)	lion-head crown	satrap *Meze*	O/S on Peroz 'I'	
	Narseh (293–303)		*Meze* O/S on Vasudeva II	O/S on Hormizd 'I' *Kabad*	
300		Hormizd 'II' (300–9)			
303	Hormizd II (303–9)	winged crown and globe	satrap *Meze*		
305					
309	Shapur II (309–79)	Peroz 'II' (309–35)			**GUPTA**
319		flat crown, crescent and globe			Chandragupta I (319/20–35)
320			satrap *Meze*	Mahi (*c*.320)	
325				Shaka (320–60)	
335		Varhran (335–70)	satrap *Kabad*	vassal of Samudragupta	Samudragupta (335–80)
342	campaign v. Rome (342–6)	flat crown and lotus globe	crown of Shapur		
350		(a) dotted decoration	*Shaboro*		
353	campaign v. Rome (353–6)	(b) zigzag decoration	mural crown	Vasudeva III (*c*.360)	
360	defeat of Constantius (361)		O/S on Hormizd 'II'	Kipunadha (360–79)	
370		'Varhran' (*c*.370–95)			
379		(1) flat crown (a-b) and lotus globe (AU/AE)		Samudra (*c*. 380)	
380	Ardashir II (379–83)	(2) Shapur II foliated mural crown (AR)		Kirada (*c*.380) (AU)	Chandragupta II (380–414)
383	Shapur III (383–88)	(3) Shapur III flat crown (AR)			
388	Varhran IV (388–99)	(4) Varhran IV (facing) winged crown with palmette and flanking diadems (AR)			
395		'Varhran' / 'Peroz' (*c*.395–425)			
399	Yazdagird I (399–420)	(1) horns and lotus globe (AU/AR/AE)			
400		(2) horns with lotus globe flanked by diadems (AU/AR/AE)			
410		(3) Yazdagird I (facing) foliated crown (AR)			
420	Varhran V (420–38)	(4) Varhran V foliated crown (AR)			Kumaragupta I (414–55)
425		Kidara (*c*.425–57)			
439	Yazdagird II (439–57)	(1) flat crown with zigzag decoration, globe flanked by diadems (AU)			
450		(2) facing foliated mural crown flanked by diadems (AR)			
457		(3) Yazdagird II mural crown with crescent and globe (AR)			Skandagupta (*c*. 455–67/8)
484	Peroz (459–84)				

☐ Sasanians

☐ Kushans

☐ Kidarites

1973, pp. 5–6; Alram and Gyselen 2003, p. 21). Concurrently, Papak killed Gochihr, the local king of Stakhr, and wanted his eldest son Shapur appointed as the replacement. But Artabanus refused, accusing Papak and his younger son Ardashir of killing several local rulers in Fars (Nöldeke 1973, pp. 7–8). After the death of Papak, Shapur crowned himself successor and demanded the allegiance of Ardashir, who refused. The two brothers declared war, but, on his way to Darabgird, Shapur was hit by a stone and killed (Nöldeke 1973, p. 8). Following this suspicious incident, Ardashir was crowned in Stakhr.

A variety of dates have been suggested for Papak's reign and the early days of Ardashir's rule in Fars.[103] Tabari dates

Figure 65 Ker Porter's drawing of the investiture of Ardashir I at Naqsh-i Rustam.

Ardashir's uprising to 523 of the Seleucid era, i.e. AD 211/12 (Nöldeke 1973, p. 1). However, calculations based on the figures cited in the bilingual Pahlavi and Parthian inscription from the palace of Shapur I at Bishapur produce an earlier date of AD 205/6, although it is not clear whether the date refers to Papak's or Ardashir's appointment as king of Darabgird (Ghirshman 1971, pp. 10–11).[104] As the new king of Stakhr, Ardashir benefited from the Parthian internecine struggle between Vologases VI and his younger brother Artabanus, following the death of their father Vologases V in AD 208. By AD 212/13, Artabanus IV – based in Media – was widely recognised throughout the empire as the Parthian king of kings, while Vologases VI remained in control of Mesopotamia, where he minted coins until AD 221/2 (Alram and Gyselen 2003, pp. 136–7, n. 141).

Ardashir took advantage of this period of Parthian domestic conflict to overcome his opponents – including some of his brothers, as well as other local kings – first in Darabgird and subsequently, in AD 211/12, in the rest of Fars. He then moved to Gor (Firuzabad), where he founded Ardashir Khvarrah (Glory of Ardashir) and built a palace and fire temple, before going on to defeat Nirrofar, the king of Ahvaz in south-western Iran, and Bandu, the ruler of Maisan on the Persian Gulf. Recent Bactrian documents place the beginning of the Sasanian era founded by Ardashir in AD 223/4 (see p. 100).

But the most decisive victory for Ardashir took place in the plain of Hormizdgan[105] in western Iran, when he killed

Artabanus and was proclaimed *shahanshah*, king of kings, of Iran (Nöldeke 1973, pp.14–15).[106] The date, given by Tabari for the triumph of Ardashir, corresponds to Wednesday 27 Nisan 535 of the Seleucid era (28 April 224), which is cited in the east Syrian *Chronicle of Arbela*[107] as the day Parthian rule ended (Alram and Gyselen 2003, p. 138; Schippmann 1990, p. 14). This historic event is commemorated on Ardashir's jousting relief in Firuzabad (Ghirshman 1962, pls 163- 6).

The earliest Sasanian coins are minted in the names of all three individuals involved in the demise of the Parthian dynasty: Papak and his two sons, Shapur and Ardashir (fig. 66.1–3). Coin legends usually identify the frontal portrait as Ardashir. Both Shapur and his father are shown in profile, facing left in the Parthian tradition (fig. 66.1; Alram and Gyselen 2003, p. 93, pl. I.1–4).[108] Coins of both sons carry a portrait of Papak on the reverse. This was probably for dynastic reasons, to emphasise the role of their father in founding the dynasty (Alram and Gyselen 2003, p. 138). On coins of Shapur, Papak is depicted with a cap and a diadem terminating in a leaf-shaped finial (fig. 66.1). Coins of Ardashir show both his father and himself in the Parthian-style tiara with neckguard and earflaps. This type of royal head-dress appears on Parthian drachms from the time of Mithradates II (123–91 BC) onwards (figs 66.3, 48.4) and was also worn by the kings of Persis prior to the Sasanian takeover of the region. (fig. 97.10)

After his victory over the Parthians, Ardashir is depicted in a variety of head-dresses. On coins, a star and crescent moon –

or in some instances, an eagle – decorate his tiara (fig. 66.3; Alram and Gyselen 2003, pp. 231–2, pl. 16.A47). On the Naqsh-i Rustam rock relief near Persepolis and the relief at Salmas near Lake Urmiah, he wears his top-knot of hair covered by a silk cloth (figs 66.6; 165). Some other coins and the Firuzabad relief portray him simply with an uncovered top-knot and a diadem (fig. 66.7). Some coins show him with a crenellated crown (fig. 66.5), which is associated with Ahuramazda on Ardashir's rock reliefs (figs 65; 164). Yet another coin type carries a double portrait (fig. 66.8), usually identified as Ardashir and his son Shapur I (c. AD 240–72/3). This identification has recently been questioned by Alram (2006), who suggests that the beardless man may be a Zoroastrian priest. According to such sources as the Cologne Mani Codex and Elias of Nisibis, Shapur was appointed co-regent probably just before AD 239/40, with his coronation probably taking place on 12 April 240 (Sundermann 1990; Alram and Gyselen 2003, p. 35; Schippmann 1990, p. 19). Prince Shapur wore a crown terminating in a bird, as seen on coins (fig. 66.9) and Ardashir's jousting reliefs at Naqsh-i Rajab and Firuzabad (Ghirshman 1962, figs 93, 131). On the relief from Salmas, Shapur wears a top-knot and diadem like his father (fig. 165). After his accession to the throne Shapur adopted a crenellated crown, as evinced by his portrait on coins, all his commemorative rock reliefs and a statue of the king from a grotto near Bishapur (fig. 66.10–11; Ghirshman 1971, pls XIII–XIV, XXIX, XXVIa). The crown of Shapur I usually – although not always – has long earflaps (fig. 66.11). The reverse coin motif of a fire altar and throne – introduced by Ardashir – is replaced with a fire altar flanked by two figures, one of whom wears a crenellated crown identifying him as the king, while the other probably represents a divinity.

Carrhae and Nisibis in northern Syria were conquered by the Sasanians probably in c. AD 235/6 (Schippmann 1990, p. 18). In c. AD 240/1 Ardashir took Hatra, a caravan city under Roman influence, with an important role in the trade between the Persian Gulf and Rome (Schippmann 1990, p. 19). He died in the spring of AD 242. In the same year the Romans sent a large army to Syria under the emperor Gordian III (AD 238–44). After an initial victory and the recapture of Nisibis, they were defeated by the Sasanian army near Ctesiphon, the Sasanian capital, in February AD 244 (figs 4–5; Schippmann 1990, p. 20). Gordian's successor, Philippus (AD 244–9), known as Philip the Arab,[109] made peace with Shapur (ŠKZ § 8: Huyse 1999, p. 27):[110]

And emperor Philippus came (to) us pleading
And gave us 500,000 denarii blood (money [?] for their souls)
(and) tribute was imposed on him and therefore we gave Mishik the name Peroz Shapur (Victorious is Shapur).

A few years later peace ended when Shapur attacked Armenia on the pretext that the Roman 'Caesar' had lied and been unjust to the Armenians. In the course of the campaign, 60,000 Romans were killed, 'the land Assyria [Asuristan] and the lands and surroundings above Assyria were set on fire and plundered' (ŠKZ §§ 9–12: Huyse 1999, pp. 28–30). Shapur's son Hormizd was appointed viceroy of the province of Armenia.

The encounter with the Roman emperor Valerian (wly'lnwsy kysly = Waliyaranos Kēsar; AD 253–60) took place during the third campaign, when the Sasanian army advanced into Carrhae (Harran) and Edessa. Here Shapur captured Valerian with 'his own hands' (Pahlavi dastgraw kerd; ŠKZ § 22: Huyse 1999, p. 37). The Roman prisoners (including senators and officers) were taken to Persis, where Valerian probably died in captivity (ŠKZ § 22: Huyse 1999, p. 37).[111] Shapur's victory was commemorated on a number of rock reliefs at Bishapur and Naqsh-i Rustam (figs 4–5; 67) and it was probably after this first defeat of the Romans in AD 244 that Weh Andiyok Shapur, i.e. Bishapur, was founded in southern Fars (Ghirshman 1971, p. 2).

When describing his campaigns in the west against Rome, Shapur uses the phrases 'Iranians and non-Iranians' in the Kaba-i Zardusht inscription, but he does not include the latter term on his coin legends (Alram and Gyselen 2003, pp. 44, 188–9).[112] 'Non-Iranian' (in the Greek version ρωμαίων/αναριανόν; ŠKZ § 30: Huyse 1999, p. 43) includes some of the Roman territories, while 'Eranšahr' refers to Persis, Parthia, Khuzistan, Asuristan (Mesopotamia) and other lands associated with his forebears. Additional listed countries of his empire are Meshan, Nodshiragan (Adiabene), Adurbadigan (Atropatene), Armin (Armenia), Wiruzan (Iberia, i.e. Georgia), Sigan, (Caucasian) Albania, Balasagan, as far as the Caucasus and Elburz mountains, as well as Media, Gurgan (Hyrcania), Merv, Herat, all of Abarshahr (Khurasan), Kirman, Sagestan, Turan, Makran, Paradan, Hindustan, Kushan territory up to Peshawar, Kashgar, Sogdiana, Tashkent and the land of Mazun (Oman) beyond the sea (ŠKZ §§ 2–3: Huyse 1999, pp. 23–4). The much later Middle Persian text shahrestanha-i Eranshahr includes a far larger territory and even parts of Arabia were incorporated in the Sasanian empire. This text dates to the period of Kavad I

Figure 66 Sasanian coins.
Shapur, local king of Fars (early third century AD):
1   Obv. 'King Shapur'; rev. 'King Papak';
2   Obv./rev. 'King Shapur'.
Ardashir, local king of Fars (early third century AD):
3   Obv. facing 'King Ardashir'; rev. 'King Papak'.
Ardashir I (AD 223/4–41):
4–5   Obv. king with tiara/kotah/crown; 'the Mazda-worshipping Lord Ardashir, king of kings of the Iranians'; rev. fire altar and throne, 'fire of Ardashir';
6–7   King with covered top-knot and diadem;
8   Obv. king facing young figure, perhaps Shapur, in plain hat with earflaps.
Shapur I (AD 240–72/3):
9   Obv. king in bird-headed hat with a pearl in its beak, 'the Mazda-worshipping Lord Shapur, king of kings of the Iranians, whose origin is of the gods'; rev. fire altar with two standing figures, 'fire of Shapur';
10–11   Obv. king in crenellated crown with/without earflaps.

Hormizd I (AD 272/3):
12   Obv. king in fluted crown, 'the Mazda-worshipping lord Hormizd, king of kings of the Iranians and non-Iranians, whose origin is of the gods'; rev. king (left of the fire altar) receives diadem from Mithra, 'fire of Hormizd'.
Varhran I (AD 273–6):
13   Obv. king in radiate crown of Mithra; rev. 'fire of Varhran'.
Varhran II (AD 276–93):
14   Obv. king in winged crown; rev. 'fire of Varhran';
15   Obv. king and queen;
16   Obv. king and figure in boar head-dress;
17   Obv. king and queen (?), in boar head-dress, facing small figure in bird head-dress; rev. mint abbreviation LD (= Ray); above, 'fire of Varhran';
18   Obv. king and his queen (?) receiving a diadem from figure in bird head-dress; rev. king (left) receives a diadem from Anahita (?).
Narseh (AD 293–303):
19–20   Obv. king in twig crown/fluted crown; rev. 'fire of Narseh'.
Hormizd II (AD 303–9):
21–2   Obv. king in bird crown with a pearl in its beak; rev. mint abbreviation MLW (= Merv); above, flames with royal bust, 'fire of Hormizd'.

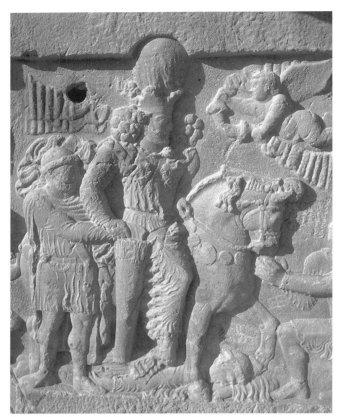

Figure 67 Bishapur relief depicting Shapur I's victory over the Roman emperors Gordian III (AD 238–44), Philip the Arab (AD 244–9) and Valerian (AD 253–60).

and Khusrau II (AD 484–531), when the geographical extent of the Sasanian empire and the Sasanian sphere of influence were much greater (Daryaee 2002, p. 4).

When Shapur died in AD 272 he was succeeded by his youngest son, Hormizd (Ohrmizd) I, the king of Armenia, who ruled for only a year. On coins of Hormizd the royal legend is extended for the first time to describe him as 'king of kings of Iranians and non-Iranians' (fig. 66.12). Varhran (Bahram) I, the king of Gilan, followed his brother to the throne and ruled until AD 276 (fig. 66.13). He was succeeded by his son, Varhran (Bahram) II (AD 276–93) (fig. 66.14–18), who was in turn succeeded by his young son. Varhran III, however, only reigned for a few months, before being removed from the throne by his uncle, Narseh (AD 293–303), king of Armenia and a son of Shapur I (fig. 66.19–20).

By this time the Romans had appointed a Parthian, Tiridates, as king of Armenia. He attacked the north-western Sasanian provinces, initiating war over Armenia c. AD 296–7. Although Tiridates was initially repulsed, the Sasanians were defeated by the Romans under Galerius near Erzerum in eastern Anatolia in AD 297. Narseh's family was taken captive and he was forced to concede the harsh peace terms imposed by Diocletian (AD 284–305) and his Caesar in the East, Galerius (AD 305–11). As a result of the treaty of Nisibis the Romans acquired five Armenian provinces and the river Tigris became the western frontier of the Sasanian empire. The king of Iberia (Georgia) was no longer a Sasanian vassal, but under Roman suzerainty. Roman-controlled Nisibis (modern Nusybin near the Turkish–Syrian border) was established as the sole centre for commercial exchanges between the two empires, with the result that Sasanian merchants trading with the west were directly taxed by Rome

(Schippmann 1990, p. 30). Narseh was succeeded by his son Hormizd II (AD 303–9), who is depicted at Naqsh-i Rustam as a small child on his father's investiture relief (fig. 66.21–2) and as a jousting warrior on another relief at the site (Herrmann 1977, pls 1, 8). When Hormizd II died, his son – also called Hormizd – was thrown into prison, but escaped to the Romans. The Sasanian nobles appointed another son, the infant Shapur II (AD 309–79), as the rightful successor.

Coins from the time of Varhran I to Hormizd II contain many religious symbols, which could be seen both as an indication of internecine rivalry during the second half of the third century and as a sign of the kings' dependence on religious support from the priesthood. Varhran I wears the radiate crown of Mithra, his patron deity (fig. 66.13). The reverse design of Hormizd I depicts the king receiving a diadem from a divine being, who is not named, but again wears a radiate crown identifying him probably as Mithra (fig. 66.12). Investiture scenes occur also on coins of Varhran II, where the divine being offering the diadem is probably Anahita (fig. 66.18). The royal crown of Hormizd II comprises a bird holding a pearl in its beak (fig. 66.21), while Varhran II has a winged crown (figs 66.14–18; 68). Both are probably symbols of the Veregna bird, which is associated in the *Avesta* with the Divine Glory or Splendour (*khvarenah/khvarrah*) and the warrior god Verethragna. The boar, another symbol of Verethragna, is incorporated into the head-dress of Varhran II's companions. All these symbols are closely associated with kings' status as the possessor of the divine right to rule.

As another way of emphasising his legitimacy, Shapur II adopted the crenellated crown of his ancestor, Shapur I. For the reverse of his coins he used three motifs. He continued with the fire altar and two attendants (fig. 69.1), revived Ardashir's design of a fire altar and throne (fig. 69.2) and continued that of the king's bust in the middle of the flames introduced by his father Hormizd (fig. 69.3). The last motif is very much in line with contemporary royal and religious ideology, for it emphasises the importance of the fire lit in the name of the king, as well as the divine association of the king with the holy fire. The motif not only remained popular with later Sasanians such as Varhran V (AD 420–38) (fig. 69.10) but was also imitated by the kings of Bukhara and other local rulers to the east of the empire until the early centuries of Islamic rule.

On a political level Shapur II had to face the ever-increasing attacks by Arab nomads on the Roman–Iranian border in Syria and on the Persian Gulf coast. Constantine I (AD 306–37) moved the Roman capital to Byzantium – renamed Constantinople – and legitimised Christianity within the Roman empire (p. 125 below). In Armenia, where Christianity became the state religion in AD 301, non-converts among the aristocracy encouraged Shapur to invade in AD 338 (Schippmann 1990, pp. 32–3). Following the death of Constantine, Shapur also advanced on Mesopotamia, but was defeated at Singara in AD 344. After a vain attempt to capture Nisibis he was forced to turn his attention to the northern part of the empire, which was under attack from nomads.

Confrontation with Rome resumed in AD 359, after a Sasanian peace offer was rejected (Ammianus Marcellinus XVIII.iv.1):

Figure 68 Ker Porter's drawing of the Naqsh-i Rustam relief depicting Varhran II (AD 276–93), his court and family.

the king of Persia, armed with the help of the savage tribes which he had subdued, and burning with superhuman desire of extending his domain, was preparing arms, forces and supplies, mingling with them counsel from infernal powers and consulting all superstitions about the future; and having assembled enough of these, he planned with the first mildness of spring to overrun everything.

Shapur – with his allies, the Chionites and Albani[113] – invaded Mesopotamia and besieged Amida (modern Diyarbakir in Turkey), which fell after 73 days (Ammianus Marcellinus XVIII.vii.1–XIX.xi.9). The Sasanian capture of Singara followed (Schipmann 1990, p. 34). Julian (AD 360–3) – called the Apostate because he favoured non-Christian religions – undertook the last Roman offensive against the Sasanians with an army of 80,000 to 90,000 soldiers. This force included a brother of Shapur, who had escaped captivity and sought refuge with the Romans. After three months the Roman army reached Ctesiphon, but, faced with superior Sasanian numbers and the prospect of a protracted siege, they retreated along the Diyala river without attacking the city. The retreating Romans were constantly harassed by the Sasanians and during a raid on 26 June 363 Julian got caught up in the fighting and was killed. His successor, Jovian (AD 363–4), was elected emperor by the army (Schippmann 1990, p. 35). A few days later, between Tikrit and Samarra, the Romans made peace with the Sasanians. In the settlement Rome lost all territories gained by Diocletian (AD 284–305), gave up control of Nisibis and Singara and promised not to intervene in Armenia. This Roman defeat gave the Sasanians supremacy in the region.

With the support of some Armenian nobles Shapur next invaded Armenia, punished the king Arshak II and occupied large parts of the country (Schippmann 1990, p. 36). After another dispute with Rome over this region, Armenia was divided between the two superpowers in AD 377. However, the conflict remained unresolved, for it seems to have continued under the next Sasanian king, Ardashir II (AD 379–83), who may have been Shapur's brother (fig. 69.4). Ardashir appears on a relief at Taq-i Bustan flanked by the god Mithra, who stands on a lotus and holds a bundle of twigs or rods, the *barsom* of Zoroastrian ritual. On his other side, a figure

wearing a crenellated crown – probably Shapur II – stands on the defeated Roman emperor Julian (fig. 70).

During the reign of Shapur III (AD 383–8) (fig.69.5), a son of Shapur II, Rome finally recognised the division of Armenia, but actual acceptance of this peace treaty did not happen until the accession of Varhran IV (AD 388–99) (fig. 69.6–7; Schippmann 1990, p. 40). The political situation necessitated a truce at this time. The Roman empire (divided into east and west after the death of Theodosius I in AD 395) was under attack from the Goths, Vandals and other tribes, while Sasanian Iran was similarly threatened by Huns invading Armenia, Cappadocia and Syria, as well as by nomads on the eastern border. Varhran generally enjoys a good reputation in Islamic sources, although he is accused by the tenth-century Persian historian Hamzah Isfahani of being 'arrogant and rude' and of never reading a book or letter, nor seeing to any complaint (*Tārikh-i payāmbarān va shāhān*, p. 52). In contrast his son Yazdagird I (AD 399–420) (fig. 69.8) is condemned by the writer al-Jahiz (AH 160–255/ AD 776–869) as a sinner who 'changed the traditions of the Sasanian dynasty, agitated the earth, oppressed the people and was tyrannical and corrupt', because he allegedly persecuted Zoroastrians and favoured Christians (cf. Frye 1983, p. 143; Shahbazi 2003). But his reputation in Christian sources fares no better (see p. 125), although his good relationship with Marutha, bishop of Maiferqat and ambassador from the Byzantine emperor Arcadius (AD 395–408), resulted in a successful peace treaty between the two powers in AD 409. As part of the agreement, Yazdagird was appointed guardian of the son of Arcadius and ensured his successful ascension – as Theodosius II (AD 408–50) – to the Byzantine throne on the death of his father.

After the mysterious death of Yazdagird, his third son, Varhran V (AD 420–38) assumed power with the support of the king of Hira (a small Arabian kingdom in southern Mesopotamia). Varhran seems to have been controlled by the nobility, yet is hailed in Persian literature and arts as one of the most celebrated Sasanian kings (figs 69.10; 169). There are numerous stories about 'Bahram Gur', the hunter of wild ass,

Figure 69 Sasanian coins.

Shapur II (AD 309–79):

1   Obv. king in crenellated crown; rev. fire altar and two attendants holding barsoms;
2   Rev. fire altar and throne;
3   Rev. royal bust above 'fire of Shapur'.
4   Ardashir II (AD 379–83). Obv. king with diadem and top-knot; rev. royal bust with halo above 'fire of Ardashir'.
5   Shapur III (AD 383–8). Obv. king in crown of arcaded twigs; rev. royal bust above 'fire of Shapur'.

Varhran IV (AD 388–99):

6   Obv. king in crenellated winged crown; rev. fire altar and throne;
7   Rev. fire altar and two attendants, mint abbreviation AS (= Aspahan/ Isfahan?).
8   Yazdagird I (AD 399–420). Obv. king in crown with crescent.
9   Yazdagird II (AD 439–57). Obv. king in crenellated crown with crescent.
10 Varhran V (AD 420–38). Obv. king in crenellated crown with crescent in centre; rev. royal bust below flames of 'fire of Varhran'.

Peroz (AD 459–84):

11 Obv. king in crenellated crown with crescents; rev. mint abbreviation DL (= Darabgird) right, letter M left;
12–13 Obv. king in winged crown; rev. mint abbreviations WH (= Veh Ardashir, south Iraq?) and AS (= Aspahan/Isfahan?) right.
14 Valkash (AD 484–8). Obv. king in crenellated crown, flames on shoulder; rev. royal bust in flames, mint abbreviation DL (= Darabgird) right.
15 Jamasp (AD 497–9). Obv. king in crenellated crown, facing figure with diadem; rev. mint abbreviation ART (= Ardaxshir–Xvarrah, Fars) right.

Kavad I (AD 488–96, 499–531):

16 Obv. king in crenellated crown with crescent.
17 Obv. king in crown with long diadem ties; rev. mint abbreviation AY (= Eran–Xvarrah–Shapur/Susa?) right, year 17 left.

Khusrau I (AD 531–79):

18 Obv. facing bust of king; rev. king holding diadem;
19 Obv. king in crenellated crown with crescent; rev. mint abbreviation AS (= Aspahan/Isfahan?) right, year 10 left.
20 Varhran VI, Bahram Chubin (AD 590–1). Obv. king in a crenellated crown; rev. mint abbreviation AYLAN (= Susa?) right, year 1 left.

Figure 70 Taq-i Bustan relief of Ardashir II flanked by Shapur II (?) right, and Mithra with barsom bundles standing on a lotus, left. Below the feet of Ardashir and Shapur lies the body of the defeated Roman emperor, Julian the Apostate (AD 360–3).

who is glorified in the eleventh- and twelfth-century Persian epics, the *Shahnameh* of Firdowsi and the *Khamseh* of Nizami.

In the early reign of Varhran V conflict flared up once again with Byzantium and subsequently in Armenia. Under pressure from the Armenian nobility, Ardashir – an Armenian prince – was appointed king in AD 422, but in AD 428 the same nobles pressurised Varhran to depose him and a Sasanian governor was appointed instead (Schippmann 1990, p. 42). Various tribal groups along the north-eastern borders of the Sasanian empire – initially defeated by Varhran – increased and continued their attacks during the reigns of Yazdagird II (AD 439–57) and his successors (fig. 69.9; p. 86). Yazdagird's reign began with yet another short war against Byzantium, which ended in AD 442. An attempt by Mihr-Narseh, the Sasanian prime minister, to impose Zoroastrianism as the state religion of Armenia caused civil war, which was crushed by the Sasanians with the help of the Armenian prince Vasag in AD 451 (Schippmann 1990, p. 43).

The death of Yazdagird in AD 457 sparked off yet another Sasanian internecine struggle. His eldest son, Hormizd III (AD 457–9), king of Sistan, was crowned ruler, but his younger son, Peroz, challenged and overthrew his brother in AD 459 with the help of the Hephthalites. The reign of Peroz (AD 457/9–84) was marked with problems, particularly drought and famine (fig. 69.11–13). When he turned against the Hephthalites, his former allies, both he and his son Kavad were taken captive east of the Caspian Sea in c. AD 469 (p. 101). Troubles in the east encouraged Armenia and Georgia to rebel, and a new campaign against the Hephthalites in AD 481/2 ended disastrously in a Sasanian defeat near Bactra (Balkh) and the death of Peroz in AD 484.

After a brief reign of a few months, Kavad was overthrown. Valkash (AD 484–8), another son of Peroz (fig. 69.14) took the throne with the help of vassal kings,[114] who in effect ruled the empire. After suing for peace and the payment of tribute to the Hephthalites, they also made peace with Armenia, allowing the population freedom of religious practice and placing the country under direct Sasanian rule instead of a governor. A threat to the throne by Valkash's brother, Zarer, was successfully eliminated with help from the Armenians. But in AD 488 Kavad seized

power with support from the Hephthalites and Zarmihr, the king of Sakastan.

Kavad I's interrupted reign (AD 488–96, 499–531) (fig. 69.16–17) was marked by internal religious and social revolt led by Mazdak.[115] The emperor seems to have been attracted to the socialist Mazdakite teachings advocating equality of wealth and was therefore deposed by the priests and aristocracy, thrown into prison and replaced by his brother Jamasp (AD 497–9) (fig. 69.15). Kavad escaped and again sought refuge with the Hephthalites who, for a large sum, helped him regain power in AD 499. When Kavad's plea to Byzantium for financial aid was rejected, he marched with Hephthalite troops via Armenia to northern Mesopotamia, where he captured Amida (Diyarbakir) after a long siege. Attacks by nomads along the northern Sasanian frontier forced a halt to the campaign. In the peace treaty, which lasted seven years, the Sasanians agreed to renounce their claim to the conquered regions and Amida in return for a huge sum of gold.

Towards the end of his reign – and possible influenced by his son and successor, Khusrau – Kavad's views towards the Mazdakites changed. In c. AD 528/9, Mazdak and his supporters, including Kavad's influential minister Siyavush, were executed. After Kavad's death in AD 531 the nobility chose his younger son, Khusrau Anushirvan ('of immortal soul') as his successor. Khusrau I (AD 531–79) introduced many reforms in the army, class and tax systems (fig. 69.18–19; Frye 1983, pp. 153–4). Despite his open antagonism towards Mazdak, the Mazdakite revolt seems to have made an impact on the king, for his reforms included family and inheritance laws. (Schippmann 1990, pp. 51–2). He created a new military class of impoverished nobles dependent on his financial support in the form of weapons and salaries, thus ensuring their complete allegiance in return. This greatly reduced the power of the large landowners, who had previously maintained private armies of their own. Families with a duty to protect the frontiers were given land in a buffer zone along the borders. Militarily, the empire was divided into four parts, with a *spāhbad* (general) responsible for each quarter.

Various border conflicts with Byzantium, first in southern Mesopotamia, then in Syria and further north around the Black Sea, produced rich plunder from these wealthy regions. Usually the Sasanian army retreated after collecting a ransom in gold. A Byzantine agreement to pay 2000 gold coins was the price for a five-year armistice. In AD 561, a fifty-year peace treaty was signed between Khusrau and Justinian (AD 527–65). At the same time Sasanian attention was again focused on the threat of a Hephthalite invasion in the east. But the Sasanians had the support of a new ally, Istämi, a Turkic ruler who controlled the region north of the Oxus river as far as the Caspian Sea. Following the defeat of the Hephthalites in AD 560, the victors divided the territory: the lands south of the Oxus falling to the Sasanians and those north of the river to the Turks (Schippmann 1990, p. 58). The alliance soon ended, however, when the Turks began negotiations with Byzantium in AD 568, proposing to Justin II (AD 565–78) joint control of the Silk Route to the exclusion of the Sasanians. But when Justin launched an unsuccessful offensive against the Sasanians in AD 572, it failed owing to

Figure 71 Sasanian coins:
Khusrau II (AD 591–628):
1 Obv. 'Khusrau, king of kings' 'may his glory increase', in crenellated crown with wings; rev. Anahita (?) with halo of flames, 'may the glory of Iran increase' right, year 21 left;
2 Obv. facing bust of king; rev. Anahita (?), year 36 left;
3 Rev. fire altar and two attendants, mint abbreviation BBA (the Court) right, year 39 left.

4 Kavad II (AD 628). Obv. king in crenellated crown, 'Kavad' right, 'victorious' left; rev. mint abbreviation ART (= Ardaxshir–Xvarrah, Fars) right, year 2 left.
5 Ardashir III (AD 628–30). Obv. king in crenellated crown with wings; rev. mint abbreviation AY (= Eran–Xvarrah–Shapur/Susa?) right, year 3 left.
6 Boran (AD 630–1). Obv. queen in winged crown; rev. mint abbreviation WLC (= unknown) right, year 1 left.
7–8 Yazdagird III (AD 632–51). Obv. king in crenellated crown with wings; rev. mint abbreviations NAL (= Nahr Tir, Khuzistan?) right, year 4 left/BBA (= the Court) right, year 20 left.

the lack of hoped-for support from the Turks. In the same period Armenia revolted against its Sasanian governor, while in AD 570 in southern Arabia an Ethiopian revolt was crushed and Yemen became a vassal kingdom of the Sasanians until the arrival of Islam in the seventh century. Khusrau died in AD 579 after ruling 48 years.

Under Hormizd IV (AD 579–90), war with Byzantium continued. In AD 588 the Turks invaded as far as Balkh and Herat, but were successfully driven out by the Sasanians under the leadership of a Parthian general, Bahram Chubin, of the House of Mihran (Schippmann 1990, p. 61). After suffering a small defeat against Byzantium in Armenia, Bahram Chubin was dismissed, which caused not only the

Sasanian army to revolt but also the priests and nobles to rebel against the unpopular Hormizd. While Bahram Chubin advanced on Ctesiphon, Hormizd was deposed and imprisoned in the spring of AD 590. His son Khusrau II Parviz (the 'victorious') was crowned emperor and shortly afterwards had his father murdered. But Bahram Chubin, the victorious and popular general, arrived at the capital, with every intention of becoming king, and was crowned – as Varhran VI (AD 590–1) – in Ctesiphon in AD 590 (fig. 69.20).

Khusrau sought refuge with the Byzantine emperor Maurice (AD 582–602). Varhran offered to cede Nisibis and parts of Mesoptamia as far as the Tigris river to Byzantium, in return for their neutrality in the dispute. But Byzantium

Figure 72 Taq-i Bustan reliefs of Khusrau II.

Figure 73 Detail on left side of the arch at Taq-i Bustan of hunting scene with Khusrau II.

decided to provide Khusrau with the necessary military support to defeat Varhran in AD 591 at the battle of Ganzak in Iranian Azarbaijan. Varhran escaped to the Turks, but was soon murdered. Khusrau II (AD 591–628) was immediately challenged by his uncles, even though they had helped him to power over his father. One in particular, Vistaham, fought his nephew from his base in the Daylam region in the Elburz mountains for almost ten years, until he was murdered c. AD 600. For seven years during this period Vistaham struck coins with the mint of Ray (Göbl 1971, pl. 13.205).

Coins of Khusrau show him on the obverse wearing a crenellated crown with a pair of wings at the top. The reverse motif consists usually of a fire altar and two attendants, but special issues, e.g. years 21, 26 and 36, depict the frontal bust of a beardless deity, perhaps Anahita, with a halo (fig. 71.1–3). At Taq-i Bustan, Khusrau is flanked by Ahuramazda and Anahita on his investiture relief (fig. 72), and shown during a royal hunt (fig. 73).

In the south-west Khusrau turned his attention to the Lakhmid Arab kingdom in southern Mesopotamia on the periphery of Arabia. The reasons for his quarrel with Numan III (c. AD 580–602), the Nestorian king, are not certain, although some sources suggest Numan was imprisoned and killed in AD 602 in retaliation for his earlier lack of support during the crisis with Bahram Chubin (Frye 1983, pp. 166–7). Khusrau abolished the privileges previously enjoyed by the Lakhmid Arabs in return for defending the desert frontier, and appointed a chief of the Tayy tribe in their stead, with a Persian governor as co-ruler. As a result, Bedouin Arabs along the Euphrates raided settlements; the border with Arabia was left unguarded; and a tribal alliance, including *inter alia* the Shayban and the Bakr (one of the largest tribes), defeated the Sasanians in c. AD 604 at the battle of Dhu Qar.

Relations with Byzantium also deteriorated when Maurice was deposed by the army and replaced by Phocas (AD 602–10). In the ensuing war the Sasanians captured a number of northern Mesopotamian cities – including Edessa, Mardin, Amida, Beroia (modern Aleppo), Hierapolis (now partly occupied by Manbij, c.50 miles/80 km north-east of Aleppo) – and reconquered Armenia. Just as the political strength of Byzantium reached its lowest ebb, Heraclius (AD 610–41), the governor of Carthage, revolted; was crowned emperor in

October AD 610; and had Phocas executed. However, he proved unsuccessful against the Sasanians, who captured Antiochia, Damascus and Tarsus in the period AD 611–13. In AD 614 the Sasanian general Shahrbaraz, with support from a Jewish revolt against the Christians, also besieged Jerusalem. The city capitulated after three weeks and the Holy Cross was seized as booty and taken to Ctesiphon (Schippmann 1990, p. 66). By AD 615 the Sasanians had reached Chalcedon, on the opposite bank of the Bosphorus to Constantinople. After attempts to negotiate peace failed, they continued their conquest of towns in Anatolia. In AD 619 they successfully besieged Alexandria and occupied Egypt, the granary of Byzantium, as well as Nubia (Schippmann 1990, pp. 66–7). For a brief period, 'Khusrau had in effect re-established the Achaemenid empire' (Frye 1983, p.169).

This soon changed. In April AD 622 Heraclius began to mount a huge offensive – a virtual crusade – and sailed with his superior navy across the Black Sea to Armenia, outflanking the Persians and then defeating them in Cappadocia. After dealing with an Avar threat in the west, Heraclius invaded Armenia again in February AD 623 and reached Azarbaijan, where he took and plundered the Sasanian fire temple and sanctuary of Ganzak (Schippmann 1990, p. 69). A subsequent series of skirmishes re-established Byzantine control of Anatolia. In retaliation the Sasanian general Shahrbaraz, allied with the Avars, besieged Constantinople in AD 626. But Byzantine naval supremacy rendered the siege ineffectual and Constantinople, under the leadership of Sergios, patriarch of the city, withstood the Sasanian assault. In Mesopotamia the Persians under the general Shahin also suffered a heavy defeat at the hands of Theodosius, a brother of Heraclius.

Allied with the Khazars of the Caucasus region, the Byzantine emperor marched southwards in the autumn of AD 627 through Armenia and Azarbaijan, meeting with little opposition. Heraclius continued on alone to Nineveh, where he defeated the Sasanian army before moving on to occupy and plunder Khusrau's palace at Dastagird. He stopped short of Ctesiphon, as all the bridges over the Nahravan canal had been destroyed, and withdrew. Khusrau tried to blame the defeat on his generals, but a revolt broke out and he was imprisoned and executed with the agreement of his son Shiruy, one of the rebels, who ascended the throne as Kavad II in AD 628 (fig. 71.4).

In return for peace Kavad had to give up all claim to lands in Asia Minor, Egypt, Syria, Palestine and Byzantine Mesopotamia. But in less than a year he was dead, leaving a small son, Ardashir III (AD 628–30), as his successor (fig. 71.5), the empire being run by Mah-Adur-Gushnasp, a priest. The general Shahrbaraz, probably with the support of Heraclius, marched on Ctesiphon, killed Ardashir and seized the throne. After he too was murdered, the crown passed to Boran (AD 630–1), a daughter of Khusrau (fig. 71.6). As part of the ensuing peace treaty with Byzantium, the Holy Cross was returned, and Heraclius personally took it back to Jerusalem in AD 630. A series of rulers followed in quick succession – Azarmidukht (another daughter of Khusrau), Peroz II, Hormizd V and Khusrau IV – none lasting more than a few months. Finally, a grandson of Khusrau II, Yazdagird III (AD 632–51), who had grown up in Istakhr in Fars, was crowned king of kings (fig. 71.7–8). His coins show him both as a young beardless ruler and as an adult. He wears the winged crown of his grandfather.

Meanwhile, in AD 622, the Prophet Muhammad had fled from Mecca to Medina. From their base in Medina his Arab followers – through a combination of conversion and conquest – gradually gained control of neighbouring local kingdoms and buffer states. This was facilitated by the fact that the Sasanian policy of concentrating troops on the frontiers left the interior defenceless once the border had been breached (Frye 1983, p. 154). The decades of strife between the Byzantines and Sasanians had also left both empires exhausted and open to conquest. In AD 636 the Arabs reached Babylonia and the Sasanian army under Rustam was heavily defeated at Qadisiya in the Syrian desert. The Iranian banner fell into the hands of the enemy, Rustam was killed and Babylonia was lost. In AD 637/8 Ctesiphon was captured, and by AD 640 all of northern Mesopotamia as far as Mosul was under Arab control (Schippmann 1990, pp. 75–6). In AD 642 a decisive battle at Nihavand in western Iran ended in the defeat for the Persian army. Hamadan was taken in AD 643 and in AD 650/1 the Arabs advanced into Khurasan in eastern Iran. With the murder of Yazdagird in AD 651 near Merv, the Sasanian empire collapsed. It was replaced by an Arab empire which introduced a new religion, Islam.

Kushano-Sasanians (c. AD 233–370)

> The individual Kushano-Sasanian rulers are recognisable on their coins not only from the inscriptions in Pahlavi or Bactrian which they frequently bear, but also because, just like the Sasanian emperors, each may be recognised by his characteristic personal crown. (Bivar 1979, p. 319)

Two bilingual inscriptions from the Tochi valley in Pakistan – one in Arabic and Sanskrit, the other in Sanskrit and Bactrian – contain dates expressed in three different eras, identified by Humbach (1994) as the Hijra calendar beginning AD 622, the Laukika calendar of c. 3076 BC[116] and an unknown era apparently of Bactrian origin. A computation utilising the

known dates of the first two eras produced a date of c. AD 233 for the beginning of the third, which was thought to be a Kushano-Sasanian era marking the conquest of Kushan territories in Bactria by the Sasanians (Sims-Williams 1999, pp. 245–6).[117] Recently – through the work of Geoffrey Khan, Nicholas Sims-Williams and François de Blois[118] – a closer correlation has been found between dated Arabic and Bactrian manuscripts. This dismisses Humbach's tenuous link with the Laukika calendar and convincingly shows that the so-called Bactrian era is in fact a Sasanian era dating from the beginning of the reign of Ardashir, the first Sasanian king, in AD 223/4.

That the conquest of Bactria was undertaken by Ardashir I (AD 223/4–41), during the reign of the Kushan king Kanishka II (c. AD 227–46), is corroborated by numismatic evidence (p. 72, table 4). The Kushano-Sasanian Bactrian issues are distinctive (fig. 74). Large gold scyphates and small thin bronze coins with Bactrian inscriptions are the norm, apart from a few Sasanian-style gold and silver issues with Pahlavi legends, and two rare gold standard Kushan-style coins (Cribb 1990, pls VI.58–9, 61; III.14; IV.30 respectively). The earliest gold scyphates are posthumous issues in the name of Vasudeva I (c. AD 190–227) and imitations in the name of Kanishka II, but with corrupt legends and latterly with such additions as a swastika and the Brahmi letter er (fig. 74.3–4; Cribb 1990, pp. 154–5, 163, 173). The next coins in the sequence are inscribed in Bactrian *Ardasharo Koshano Shao* (fig. 74.5–6).

According to the Kaba-i Zardusht trilingual inscription[119] at Naqsh-i Rustam (ŠKZ §§ 1–3: Huyse 1999, pp. 22–4),

> I, the Mazda-worshipping lord, Shapur, King of Kings of Iranians and non-Iranians, . . . possess . . . Hindustan, Kushanshahr [the lands of the Kushans] up to Peshawar, and as far as Kashgar, Sogdiana and Tashkent.

The *terminus post quem* for the inscription is Shapur I's defeat of Valerian c. AD 260 – mentioned in the text – which marked the conclusion of his wars with Rome. This was the last of three campaigns, the first taking place in AD 242–4 against Gordian III and Philip the Arab, the second in AD 253–6. 'Hindustan', i.e. 'India', can here be understood in conjunction with 'Kushanshahr up to Peshawar' to mean the region extending from the southern foothills of the Hindu Kush to Peshawar. Since the conquest of these territories is unlikely to have taken place while Shapur was preoccupied with the Romans, the most probable dates for his campaigns to the east are c. AD 246–52 or c. AD 261–7.

In the inscription Shapur I (c. AD 240–72/3) mentions conferring titles on two cities (ŠKZ § 4: Huyse 1999, p. 25): Misiche (modern Fallujah, Iraq) was renamed Peroz-Shapur ('Victorious [is] Shapur') and Ahvaz in Khuzistan was renamed Hormizd-Ardashir, after the heir to the throne (Bivar, personal communication). Sasanian princes appear to have often served as governors of major provinces, including perhaps the Kushan one. Five names common to Sasanian emperors also appear as Kushano-Sasanian coin issuers: Ardashir, Peroz, Hormizd, Shapur and Varhran (fig. 74). However, it does not automatically mean that any of the Kushanshahs can be identified with particular Sasanian emperors, even though they might bear the same names. In fact, only one – Shapur – can be recognised specifically as the

Figure 74 Kushan coins:

1   Vasudeva III (c. AD 360). Obv. king before fire altar; rev. Ardochsho;
2   Kipunadha (c. AD 360–80).

Kushano-Sasanian coins:

3   Posthumous issue in name of Vasudeva I (c. AD 190–227). Rev. Oesho;
4   In name of Vasudeva with corrupt legend, swastika and Brahmi letter *er*.
5–6   Ardashir 'I' (AD 223–46). Obv. ruler with tripartite crown, inscribed in Bactrian *Ardasharo Koshano Shao*; rev. seated deity, *Bago Miiro*.

Peroz 'I' (AD 246–85):

7–9   Obv. ruler with pointed crown (a); with flat crown (b); with lion-head crown (c); rev. Oesho with bull/Ardochsho;
10   Bronze Bactrian issue;
11   Gandharan issue. Rev. fire altar.

Hormizd 'I' (c. AD 285–300):

12   Obv. ruler with lion-head crown; rev. king worshipping Oesho;
13–14   Gandharan issues of satraps *Kabad* and *Meze* with crown of Hormizd 'I'.

Hormizd 'II' (c. AD 300–9):

15   Obv. ruler with winged crown and globe; rev. ruler worshipping Anahita;
16   Gandharan issue of satrap *Meze* with crown of Hormizd 'II'.

Peroz 'II' (c. AD 309–35):

17   Obv. ruler with flat crown, crescent and globe;
18   Bactrian issue. Obv. ruler with flat crown; rev. bust above fire altar;
19   Gandharan issue of satrap *Meze* with crown of Peroz 'II'.

Varhran Kushanshah (c. AD 335–70):

20   Obv. ruler in flat crown with dotted decoration and lotus globe; rev. Oesho and bull labelled βορζοανδο βαγο or οορζοανδο ιαζαδο (*borzoando bago/oorzoando iazado*), 'exalted deity' or 'supreme lord';
21   Bactrian issue.

Shapur II (AD 309–79):

22   Gandharan issue of satrap *Kabad* with crown of Shapur II;
23   Gandharan issue of Shapur II, inscribed *Shaboro*;
24   Gandharan 'reform' issue, inscribed *Shaboro*.

Figure 75 Detail of Naqsh-i Rustam investiture relief of Varhran II (AD 276–93) showing Kerdir and a figure in lion-head crown.

Figure 76 Pedestal of a Buddha statue from Hashtnagar, Peshawar Valley, dated year 384.

Sasanian Shapur II (Cribb 1990, pp. 170, 178). As Bivar has pointed out, 'the familiar Sasanian dynastic names were very widely used, and were borne by many relatives, in addition to well-known rulers. Thus mere identity of name is not in itself an indication of historical identity in this period' (1979, pp. 319–20). Moreover, where figures thought to be crown princes appear on the mainstream Sasanian issues of Ardashir I (AD 223/4–41) and Varhran II (AD 276–93), and in the investiture reliefs of Ardashir and Narseh (AD 293–303) at Naqsh-i Rustam, they are shown with different crowns to those of the Kushano-Sasanians (figs 65–6; 104; Göbl 1971, figs 19–20, 54–71; *Splendeur des Sassanides*, pp. 75–6, figs 59–60). But there is one exception. The relief scene of Varhran II at Naqsh-i Rustam does include a subsidiary figure – probably a Sasanian prince – wearing the lion-head crown of the Kushano-Sasanians (fig. 75; *Splendeur des Sassanides*, p. 80, fig. 65; Trümpelmann 1971, p. 176). Bivar suggests he may be identified as Hormizd 'I' Kushanshah, the brother of Varhran II (1983, pp. 209–10).

It is also not simply a matter of assigning each different crown to a separate ruler, for like some of the Sasanian emperors – Ardashir I and Shapur I in particular – some Kushano-Sasanians appear to have used more than one crown (Cribb 1990, p. 153, n. 2). For example, two different crowns appear on the earliest bronze issues inscribed *Ardasharo Koshano Shao*, and it is not clear if these were issued by one or two Kushanshahs named Ardashir: the first crown comprises a bird's head and wings; the second the crenellated or mural type commonly used by Shapur I and – more rarely – Ardashir I (fig. 74.5–6; Göbl 1971, figs 1a.IV, 2.I–III). Three crowns can be assigned to the next Kushano-Sasanian, Peroz 'I' (fig. 74.7–11), of which one is the same lion-head crown used exclusively by his successor, Hormizd 'I' (fig. 74.12; Cribb 1990, pls I.1–3, III.19–24, IV.30–3).

The Sasanian conquest of the lands south of the Hindu Kush to Peshawar are marked by the issue – in the name of Peroz 'I' – of larger, thicker, bronze coins than their contemporary Bactrian counterparts, denoting the existence of a separate currency system (fig. 74.10–11). These are the earliest Kushano-Sasanian coins found in any quantity in hoards from Gandhara (Cribb 1985a, pp. 308–11, hoards 447, 450–1). An overstrike of Peroz 'I' on Kanishka II (c. AD 227–46) suggests they were contemporaries (Cribb

1985a, p. 314), while a hoard from Andan Dheri in Swat included Kushano-Sasanian issues with coins of Vasudeva I and Kanishka II, but no later Kushans. This suggests they were the last Kushan rulers in this region (Cribb 1981, p. 84, hoard 295). The numismatic evidence therefore implies that Shapur I's conquest probably occurred during the reign of the Kushan king Vasishka (c. AD 246–67). It is noteworthy that the end of the use in Gandhara of the Yona and Kushan eras roughly coincides with the rise of Sasanian supremacy in the region. The last known Yona inscription is the Hashtnagar pedestal of year 384 (c. AD 210 if year 1 equals 174 BC) (fig. 76); that of the Kanishka era is the inscription from Ara near Attock, dated year (1)41 (i.e. c. AD 268) in the reign of Kanishka III (Konow 1929, pp. 117–19, 162–5).

Further east at Hund and Taxila, the hoards contain coins from Hormizd 'I' onwards, who shares overstrikes (in both directions) with Vasudeva II (c. AD 280–320) (Cribb 1981, pp. 85, 88, hoards 299, 304; 1985a, p. 314). As far as can be deduced from the cryptic numismatic records of the Sirkap excavations, the latest Kushan coin finds – from the upper strata and surface – all seem to be those of Vasudeva II, apart from three stray 'Late Kushan' examples (Marshall 1951, p. 793). As already mentioned (pp. 71, 105, n. 100), coins of Vasudeva II also appear to be the last Kushan issues found in any quantity at Taxila as a whole, which suggests that the city was lost to the Sasanians during his reign.

The hoard evidence, overstrikes and an analysis of the stylistic and design links with Kushan and Sasanian coins, together with the progressive stylisation and deterioration in weight standard of the coin sequences, result in a chronology for the Kushano-Sasanians of Ardashir 'I' and possibly 'II' (c. AD 233–46), Peroz 'I' (c. AD 246–85), Hormizd 'I' (c. AD 285–300) and 'II' (c. AD 300–9), Peroz 'II' (c. AD 309–35) and Varhran (c. AD 335–70) (table 4; fig. 74.6–12, 15, 20).[120] Varhran appears to have ruled only in Bactria (fig. 74.17–20), while further south Peroz 'II' was followed by a period of direct Sasanian rule under Shapur II (AD 309–79) (Cribb 1990, p. 171). In addition, from the time of Hormizd 'I' to that of Shapur II, coins bearing the portraits/crowns of successive Kushanshahs were issued in Gandhara in the names of *Kabad* and *Meze*, who are thought to have been satraps (fig. 74.13–14, 16, 19, 22). Initially Shapur II issued degenerate, badly struck, roughly square, lightweight coins in the name of *Kabad* and, subsequently, in his own name (fig. 74.23–4). A second series, with the name *Shaboro* in Bactrian or Pahlavi script, appears to represent a coinage reform, with broadly circular flans and a higher weight standard (fig. 74.24; Marshall 1951, p. 823, nos 279–82, pl. 244; Cribb 1990, p. 178, pl. IV.41).

There is no distinct numismatic break between the Kushano-Sasanians and their successors. They continued to issue imitations of the *Shaboro* bronze coinage, but of smaller size and crude design; and scyphates in the names of 'Varhran' and 'Peroz', still with the title 'Kushanshah'.

Huns (*c*. AD 350–657)

> [In AD 350] the king of Persia [Shapur II], involved in war with his neighbours, was driving back from his frontiers a number of very wild tribes which, with inconsistent policy, often make hostile raids upon his territories and sometimes aid him when he makes war upon [the Romans]. (Ammianus Marcellinus XVI.iii.1)

> Shapur [II], on the remotest frontiers of his realm, was with difficulty and with great bloodshed of his troops driving back hostile tribesmen. . . . Constantius, being [also] involved in very serious wars [on the Danube frontier *c*. AD 353–9], entreated and begged for peace. But while these communications were being sent to the Chionitae [Chionites] and Euseni [Kushans], in whose territories Shapur was passing the winter, a long time had elapsed. (Ammianus Marcellinus XVI.ix.3–4)

While he was 'still encamped in the confines of the frontier tribes', Shapur 'made a treaty of alliance with the Chionitae and Gelani, the fiercest warriors of all' (Ammianus Marcellinus XVII.v.1). These events took place in the period preceding the war in AD 359–61 between the Roman emperor Constantius II (AD 337–61) and the Persians, whose allies included the Chionites and the Gelani.[121] Again in AD 371–6 Shapur was forced to deal with an invasion on his eastern frontier (Lenski 1997), this time by the 'Kushans', according to Faustus of Byzantium (P'awstos V.vii.210–11):

> Now when the war broke out between the king of the K'ušan and the king of Persia, the K'ušan army pressed the Persian forces exceedingly. It killed many of them, took many prisoners, and drove part of them to flight. . . . [In the battle] the K'ušan routed Šapuh.

Frye (1983, p. 146) has pointed out that in Armenian sources use of the anachronistic terms 'Kushan' or 'Huns called Kushans' for subsequent kingdoms in the east 'was analogous to the [earlier] Greek usage of "Scythian" for all nomads in south Russia and Central Asia' (e.g. Elišē, p. 11; Lazar of P'arp, p. 86). But Zeimal notes that it is specifically the Kidarites who are called 'Kushans' in Armenian sources, an observation which receives support from the numismatic evidence (Zeimal 1996, p. 122).

The fragmentation of the eastern part of the Sasanian empire during the latter part of Shapur II's reign, which the sources suggest, is mirrored in coins (fig. 77). From this time onwards there are a series of imitations of Sasanian silver issues, which bear the portrait of successive Sasanian kings from Shapur II to Yazdagird II (AD 309–457), but carry disparate or corrupt legends. There are, for example, two seemingly isolated issues copying the crown of Shapur III (AD 383–8), one with a corrupt Bactrian legend possibly reading 'Kushanoshao', the other with a Brahmi legend *pra sīthati* (fig. 77.1–2; Göbl 1967, I, p. 48, pl. 13.20).[122] Another issue – found at Butkara I in Swat – bears the Brahmi legend '*Buddhaṭala*' and has a central palmette flanked by wings derived from the crown of Varhran IV (AD 388–99) (fig. 77.3; Göbl 1967, type 18; 1971, pl. 8.144; 1976, pp. 34–5, nos 259–61,

pl. XIV). There is also a series of coins imitating issues of Varhran V (AD 420–38) – of the type attributed to Merv mint – with an increasingly corrupt Pahlavi legend in which the name *wrhr'n* (Varhran) and title *mlk* (*malka*/king) are barely discernible (fig. 77.4; Schindel 2004, p. 242, pls 67.87–68.100). The AD 383–435 time-frame exhibited by the crowns on these disparate coins indicates they were issued concurrently with the predominant coinages in this period of the so-called Kidarites and Alchon (from the Bactrian coin legend αλχανο).[123] Apart from the title 'Kushanoshao' in the one instance (fig. 77.2), there is nothing specific, however, to link the other examples to either group.

The group known from later written sources and the name of their most prominent coin issuer as Kidarites are generally thought to have been Huns, but how they rose to power is uncertain (table 4; fig. 77.6–25). Like the Chionites, they perhaps numbered among the 'hostile tribesmen' cited by Ammianus Marcellinus, and may have initially been used as mercenaries by the Sasanians. Since their coinage represents an uninterrupted transition from the gold and bronze Kushan and Kushano-Sasanian issues, and imitates sequentially the silver coin designs of successive Sasanian emperors from *c*. AD 360 to 457, they could have initially been appointed by Shapur II as the successors to the Kushano-Sasanian governors in the eastern part of the empire (Göbl 1967, vol. II, p. 55). As they retained the title Kushanshah, they could even be the 'Euseni' or 'Kushans' (cf. Marshall 1951, p. 791), mentioned by Ammianus Marcellinus *c*. AD 353–9 and Faustus *c*. AD 371–6. Equally, they may have simply adopted the title along with the coin types they imitated (Cribb 1990, p. 181).

Direct references to them in literary sources occur only in the fifth century. Kidara is first mentioned in the Chinese *Wei Shu* (History of the Northern Wei dynasty, VI.2275) *c*. AD 437, the year of Dong Wan's embassy to the west (Enoki 1969, pp. 8–9). His son is said to be king of the Xiao Yuezhi (Lesser Yuezhi), with his capital at Peshawar (Enoki 1969, pp. 14–16, 18; Kuwayama 2002, p. 128). The dynasty is called Jiduoluo (Kidarites) or Guishuang (Kushans)[124] in the *Bei Shi* (History of the Northern and Southern Dynasties, AD 386–589), compiled by Li Yanshou in the seventh century (cf. Grenet 2002, p. 205).

In the *Wei Shu* (VI.2275) Jiduoluo (Kidara) is identified as king of the Da Yuezhi (Great Yuezhi), who – in an action strongly reminiscent of the *Hou Han Shu*'s account of the Da Yuezhi/Kushans – is said at some unspecified time in the past to been forced westwards by the Xiongnu, and subsequently crossed the Da Shan (great mountains), invaded the Bei Tianzhu and 'completely subjugated five countries' to the north of Gandhara. Enoki (1969, p. 8) identifies the Da Shan as the Hindu Kush, in which case the Bei Tianzhu ('northern territory' i.e. northern India) refers to the Kabul–Jalalabad or Parapamisidae region of Afghanistan. Kuwayama, however, interprets the same passage as referring to the Pamir region further east. He thus considers the migration route of the Kidarites – and later, the Hephthalites – to have been 'from Tokharistan [i.e. northern Afghanistan and southern Uzbekistan and Tajikistan] via the valleys between the Hindukush and the Karakorum' (2002, pp. 123–4). But this ignores the numismatic evidence, which places the Kidarites further west, in the former Kushan and Kushano-Sasanian territories north and south of the Hindu Kush.

The Armenian writer Elišē records that the Sasanian emperor Yazdagird II (AD 439–57), in the twelfth year of his reign (i.e. AD 451), 'invaded the land of Italakan where the king of the Kushans lived' (Elišē, p. 18; cf. Frye 1983, p. 146). In this instance, 'Kushan' definitely appears to mean Kidarite, for the contemporary Byzantine historian Priscus of Panium records that in AD 456 Yazdagird requested Roman help to maintain the fortress at the Caspian Gates from the inroads of the neighbouring tribes and also assistance in the Persian war against the Huns known as the Kidarites (fr. 33, *Exc. de Leg. Rom.* 8; Blockley 1983, p. 337; Enoki 1969, p. 19). In *c.* AD 465 Peroz (AD 459–84) is still said to have been occupied 'for some time' on the north-eastern borders of the Sasanian empire with a war against the Kidarites, whom he eventually defeated *c.* AD 468 (Priscus, fr. 41, *Exc. de Leg. Gent.* 15, *Exc. de Leg. Rom.* 12; Blockley 1983, pp. 347, 349; Grenet 2002, p. 209). Earlier translations of this text (e.g. Enoki 1969, p. 20) have the Kidarites paying tribute to the Sasanians, but Blockley shows clearly that the opposite was true (1983, p. 396, n.163):

> The cause of [the war] was that the Huns were not receiving the tribute monies which the former rulers of the Persians and the Parthians had paid. The father of the monarch [Yazdagird] had refused the payment of the tribute and had undertaken the war, which his son [Peroz] had inherited together with the kingdom.

On the basis of the literary evidence some scholars identify the Kidarites as the mid-fifth-century successors of the Chionites (see Grenet 2002, pp. 203–9, 220–1; Sims-Williams 2002, p. 232). But the Chinese sources clearly identify them as descendants of the Da Yuezhi, even to the extent of echoing the earlier *Hou Han Shu*'s account of their migration westwards and their subsequent conquest (under the Kushans) of the lands 'to the north of Gandhara'.

The numismatic evidence moreover exhibits two parallel, but distinct, predominant strands of coinage evolution dating from the latter part of the reign of Shapur II (AD 309–79), the one identified by its tamgha 𐬬 and/or legends with the Kidarites, the other by its αλχανο legend and/or tamgha 𐬀 with Huns who call themselves 'Alchon' (figs 77–8; 80–1; 83; see pp. 90–7). The inclusion of a tamgha follows a tradition established by the Kushans and Kushano-Sasanians, and perpetuated on small silver issues attributed to Shapur II from Kabul mint and to subsequent Sasanians down to Yazdagird II (fig. 80.2; Schindel 2004, pls 16.232–46, 28.29–30, 44.81–2, 57.92, 67.71–86, 72.A31 and *passim*). The coins indicate that from *c.* AD 370 onwards the Kidarites supplanted the Kushano-Sasanians in Bactria, Kabul and Gandhara and replaced Kipunadha (*c.* AD 360–79), the last Kushan and vassal of Samudragupta (AD 335–80) in the Punjab (fig. 74.2). They variously issued Kushano-Sasanian-style gold scyphates in the names of 'Varhran' and 'Kidara', small Bactrian-style coppers in the name of 'Varhran' (figs 77.6–7; 78.1–4), and silver Sasanian-style dinars primarily in the names of 'Varhran', 'Peroz' and 'Kidara' (fig. 77.8–19, 23–5; Cribb 1990, figs 8–13, 28–9, 77–81 respectively).

The penchant for 'Varhran' (i.e Verethragna, the victorious warrior god; p. 116 below) and 'Peroz' ('victorious') should be understood not merely as the use of apparently

Sasanians

Shapur II (AD 309–79)

Shapur III (AD 383–8)

Varhran IV (AD 388–99)

Yazdagird I (AD 399–420)

Varhran V (AD 420–38)

Yazdagird II (AD 439–57)

Figure 77 Coins illustrating crowns of Sasanian kings from Shapur II to Yazdagird II.
Imitations:
1   Crown of Shapur III, inscribed 'Kushanoshao';
2   Inscribed *pra sīthati*.
3   Crown of Varhran IV, inscribed *Buddhaṭala*.
4   Imitation of Varhran V (Merv mint) with corrupt Pahlavi inscription.
5   Details of two crowns of Kushano-Sasanian Varhran (AD 335–70).
Kidarite coins: in name of 'Varhran' (*c.* AD 370–95):
6   Details of three crowns;
8   Imitation of Shapur II crown;

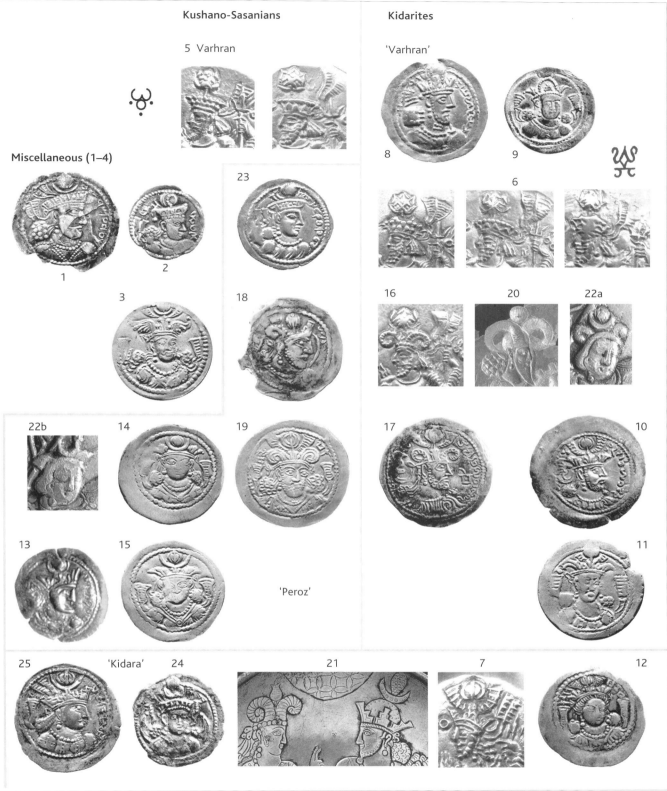

Kushano-Sasanians

5 Varhran

Kidarites

'Varhran'

8   9

6

Miscellaneous (1–4)

1   2

23

3   18

16   20   22a

22b   14   19

17   10

13   15

'Peroz'

11

25   'Kidara'   24   21   7   12

9–10 With palmettes replacing crenellations of Sasanian mural crowns;
11 With foliate imitation crown of Varhran V;
16 With horned crown;
17 With horned crown and Brahmi *pī*.
'Peroz' (*c.* AD 395–425):
13 With Bactrian legend and imitation crown of Varhran V;
14 With Pahlavi legend and imitation crown of Yazdagird I;
15 With Pahlavi legend and imitation crown of Varhran V;
18 With horned crown;
19 With facing bust and horned crown;

23 With Bactrian *piorozo shao* and crown of Shapur III.
'Kidara Kushanshah' (*c.* AD 425–57):
7 Detail of crown;
12 With foliate crown;
25 With crown of Yazdagird II;
24 With legend *Kida Bhāsa/Ravoša* and crown of Shapur III.
20 Detail of royal hunter on silver gilded plate (Hermitage Museum);
21 Detail of royal couple on silver plate (Walters Art Gallery, Baltimore);
22 Details of royal hunters on silver dish (fig. 79), with (a) horned crown,
     (b) foliate imitation crown of Yazdagird I (AD 399–420).

popular personal names but as a reflection of two separate aspects of both Kidarite and Alchon coinage. The first simply follows the well-established tradition of copying the coinages of their predecessors in the regions they controlled or conquered; the second is a pervasive use of titles, epithets or dynastic clan names, the ruler who actually struck the coins remaining anonymous (Alram 1986, p. 330).

Masson's residue collection from Begram includes only 17 Kidarite examples: all small, Bactrian-style 'Varhran' coins with a variety of crowns. However, recent finds from the Kashmir Smast cave site, in the mountainous divide between the eastern Peshawar Valley and Buner, have greatly expanded the range of bronze coin types, which complement many of the designs already known in silver or gold (Nasim Khan 2007). In the Punjab the stylistic progression of the gold series from Kushan to Kidarite is clear: imitation staters were issued first in the name of Samudragupta,[125] then by Kirada, 'Peroz' and finally Kidara (fig. 78.8–11; Cribb 1990, p. 193, figs 82–5). A short-lived Kidarite presence in Sogdiana is also indicated by the existence of seven rare silver coins minted in Samarkand, which continue the portrait/standing archer design of earlier coins from this region, but carry the name Kidara (*kyδr*) in Sogdian on the reverse (Zeimal 1996, pp. 120, 128–9, fig. 1; Grenet 2002, p. 207).[126]

Design links and hoards provide some idea of the relationship between the Kidarites and the Sasanians (fig. 77). In Bactria the first Kidarite gold scyphates were issued in the name of the last Kushano-Sasanian, Varhran, and closely resemble his coinage, except that a new tamgha ⚏ replaces the so-called 'nandipada' symbol ⚐ (figs 74.20; 78.1; Cribb 1990, pp. 185–6, figs 8–13). This tamgha is standard on all subsequent scyphates up to and including issues of Kidara (fig. 78.4). The two Kushano-Sasanian crown variations of Varhran are also copied: both are flat (like the crowns of Shapur III) and surmounted by a lotus globe, but one is decorated with a double row of dots while the other has a zigzag motif surmounted by a row of dots (fig. 77.5–6b). There is also a third Kidarite foliated variation, which is not clearly defined in the earliest 'Varhran' examples but is plainly visible on later 'Kidara' issues (fig. 77.6c–7).

The evolution of crown designs from Sasanian prototypes can be more easily traced in the silver issues. The principal Kidarite series develops from imitating issues of Shapur II, but the stepped crenellations of Sasanian mural crowns are replaced by palmettes (fig. 77.8–10; Göbl 1967, vol. III, pls 9–13, types 5–13, 15–17, 24). These diagnostic foliated elements have a long currency and development down to the end of the period and are found on coins in the names of 'Varhran', 'Kidara Kushanshah' and, in bronze, 'Kujānasya' (fig. 77.8–15; Göbl 1967, vol. I, pp. 41–4; vol. III, pls 9–12, types 5–12, 16–17; Cribb 1990, p. 193, figs 78, 80; Nasim Khan 2006, nos 234–44). Mitchiner interprets the tentative reading *kwš* on the earliest Shapur II imitations of this type as 'Kushanshah' (1975, pp. 157–8), a speculation not pursued by Göbl although it derives from his reading of the corrupt Pahlavi (1967, vol. I, p. 52, type 28A).

Some issues of 'Varhran' bear an additional Brahmi *pī* linking them to 'Peroz' (fig. 77.17; Göbl 1967, vol. III, pl. 9.6). However, there are only three issues of 'Peroz' with foliated crowns: one in profile with a Bactrian legend, and two with a facing bust and Pahlavi legends, which have crowns derived from those of Yazdagird I (AD 399–420) and Varhran V (AD 420–35) respectively (fig. 77.13–15; Göbl 1967, vol. III, pls 12.15, 13.24).

A second innovative Kidarite crown element has certain stylistic affiliations with the winged crown of Varhran IV, but replaces the wings with a pair of ram horns. It is found on gold scyphates of 'Varhran' and on silver Sasanian-style dinars, again issued by 'Varhran' (but with the additional Brahmi *pī*) and also 'Peroz' (fig. 77.16–19; Cribb 1990, pp. 156–8, figs 10, 77, 79). There are no 'Kidara' issues with this crown, but it is depicted on three silver plates. The first shows a royal hunter killing a boar (fig. 77.20; *Splendeur des Sassanides*, p. 198, no. 55). In the second, it is worn by a queen who is being presented a diadem by her consort (in a crown closely resembling that of Yazdagird II) (fig. 77.21; *Splendeur des Sassanides*, p. 211, no. 65). The third (found in Swat) illustrates four riders, one with a horned crown, another with the Yazdagird I-style crown of 'Peroz' (fig. 77.22a–b), the remaining two respectively with a hairstyle and the cranial distortion associated with the Alchon Huns (fig. 79; Göbl 1967, vol. III, pls 93–5).

The last group of coins that can definitely be assigned to the Kidarites imitate the crown design of Shapur III. The earliest is a 'Peroz' silver issue with a profile bust and the Bactrian legend *piorozo shao* (fig. 77.23; Göbl 1967, vol. III, pl. 13.19). Later bronze issues with this crown carry on the reverse the Kidarite tamgha, or the Brahmi legend 'Mahanade', or a fire altar and the name 'Kidara' (Nasim Khan 2007, nos 145–8, 338–56, 169–72). There is also a facing bust silver issue with an uncertain legend, read by Göbl as *Kida Bhāsa* or *Ravoša* (fig. 77.24; 1967, vol. I, p. 49; vol. III, pl. 13.21). A final silver issue directly copies the crenellated crown of Yazdagird II (AD 438–57) and has the Brahmi legend 'Kidara Kushanshah' (fig. 77.25; Göbl 1967, pl. 11.14). With the exception of this last example, on all later Kidarite coins the globe is flanked on either side by diadems, a feature first seen on Sasanian coins of Varhran IV (AD 388–99) and on rare issues of Yazdagird I (AD 399–420) (Göbl 1971, figs 139, 144, 146; Mochiri 1996, pl. XXIII.28). Since the crown of Yazdagird II is the last to be imitated, the sum of all these numismatic analogies suggests a broad time frame of *c.* AD 370–457 for the Kidarites. This can be extended to AD 468, when – according to Priscus – they were defeated by the Sasanians under Peroz (fr. 41, *Exc. de Leg. Gent.* 15; see p. 86). A new gold scyphate seems to mark this event. It depicts a ruler wearing the crown of the Sasanian king Peroz in the second phase of his coinage (a crescent at the front, with a larger crescent above, and crenellations at the side and back. It also bears the Bactrian legend πιρωξο þαυανο þαο (*pirōzo šauano-šao*), i.e. 'Peroz Shahanshah' (fig. 78.5), suggesting that it was issued by the Sasanian king himself.[127]

The Kidarites, however, appear to have survived another decade – probably in Gandhara – for the *Bei Shi* records that the country of Jiduoluo (Kidara), along with other countries of north India and south Afghanistan, sent an embassy and tribute to the Wei in AD 477 (*Bei Shi* VIIa, cf. Enoki 1969, p. 23).

Recent finds from the religious cave site of Kashmir Smast, in the mountains dividing the Peshawar Valley from Buner, have revealed the previously unnoticed existence of

Figure 78 Kidarite Kushanshahs:
1   'Varhran' (*c.* AD 370–95), with crown of Kushano-Sasanian Varhran;
2–3 With horned crown.
4   Kidara (*c.* AD 425–57), with foliate crown.
Sasanian Peroz (AD 457/9–84):
5   With legend πιρωξο ραυανο ραο (*pirōzo ṣauano-ṣao*).

Alchon (*c.* AD 450–500):
6   With Alchon tamgha;
7   With tamgha and legend αδομα . . μορο (*adoma . . moro*).
Kushan-style staters:
8   Samudragupta (*c.* AD 380);
9   Kirada (*c.* AD 380), from Hadda stupa 10;
10 'Peroz' (*c.* AD 395–425), inscribed *piroyasa*;
11 Kidara (*c.* AD 425–57).

an extensive Kidarite bronze coinage (Nasim Khan 2007, nos 118–550). These are all fairly small, unremarkable coins, which have been found in such quantities in the vicinity of the cave as to suggest they were the common currency of this district. Yet they have not been recorded elsewhere in the region, even where Kidarite silver issues have been found (see p. 133). This apparent lack must be due to their insignificant size and design, which resulted in their being either missed or ignored by earlier excavators.

What of the contemporaries of the Kidarites, the Chionites? According to Ammianus Marcellinus (XVIII.vi.22; XIX.i.7–ii.6), in AD 359–60, under their king Grumbates –

'a man of moderate strength, it is true, and with shrivelled limbs, but of a certain greatness of mind and distinguished by the glory of many victories' – they fought for the Persians against the Romans at the siege of Amida (modern Diyarbakir in Turkey). A Bactrian document of *c.* AD 420 records another Gurambad as a member of the royal family of the Rob region (Sims-Williams 1997, p. 13, doc. 4). If, as seems probable, the two men were related, it suggests that the Chionites had settled in this area of northern Afghanistan by the early fifth century AD (Grenet 2005, p. 206, n. 3).

According to the apocalyptic Zoroastrian *Bahman Yasht* (II.49, cf. Bailey 1932, pp. 945–7),[128]

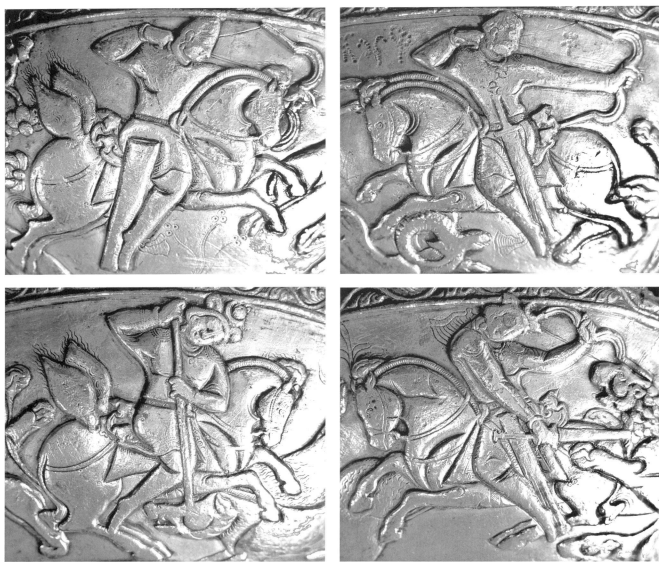

Figure 79 Silver dish from Swat depicting four Huns (two Kidarite, one Alchon and one other) hunting on horseback.

Kingdom and Sovereignty will pass to slaves who are not Iranians, such as the Khyōn [*Xyōn*], Turk, Heftal [Hephthalites], and Tibetans, who are among the mountain-dwellers, and the Chinese and Kābulis and Sogdians and Byzantines and Red Khyōn and White Khyōn. They will become Kings in my countries of Eran.

Bailey equates Pahlavi *Xyōn* (alternative spelling *Hyōn*, i.e. 'Hun') with *Chionitae* (Latin, borrowed from Greek). In Sogdian the word is *Khūn* (Grenet 2002, p. 206, n. 3). It is interesting to note that the *Yasht* divides the group into mountain-dwelling Huns and Red and White Huns, who are listed as a separate people to the Hephthalites.[129] The Chionites have also been identified with the Xiongnu of Chinese sources (Grenet 2002, p. 206; Sims-Williams 2002, pp. 231–2):[130] specifically the Southern Xiongnu who, according to a contemporary Sogdian merchant's account, sacked the Chinese capital Luoyang in AD 311 (Henning 1948; Sinor 1990, pp. 178–9). If *Chionitae* therefore equals *Xyōn/Hyōn/Khūn*/Xiongnu, it seems that it should be understood as a generic term for a number of associated Hun tribes, which were, however, distinct from the Hephthalites. Moreover, according to Wang Tao (personal communication), Xiongnu is always used by the Chinese in this generalised sense of a large confederation of different Hun tribes. If this is indeed the case,

it parallels the all-encompassing and non-specific usage of 'Huna' in India. Further evidence that this practice was perhaps more pervasive than previously realised comes from three clay seal impressions, reputedly found at Sakra in the Kashmir Smast range (Aman ur Rahman, Grenet and Sims-Williams 2006, pp. 125–31). The impressions carry the same portrait and variations of the same Bactrian inscription identifying the owner of the seals as *υονανο βαο οαζαρκο (κ)οϸανοβαο σαμαρκ(αν)ο* (*uonano šao oazarko košanošao samark(an)do*) 'king of the Huns, the great Kushan-shah, the Samarkandian'. He also calls himself *βαγο ολαργο* or *ογλαργο* (*bago olargo/oglargo*), which may either be his personal name – 'lord Ularg' – or a qualification of his Hun tribe or clan, as in the subdivisions *Walkhon* and *Alkhon* attested in the seventh-century *Armenian Geography* (Marquart 1901, pp. 141, 157, n. 2, cf. Aman ur Rahman, Grenet and Sims-Williams 2006, pp. 125–6, 128).

In connection specifically with the 'Red Huns', Grenet draws attention to the fact that *āl* means 'red' in Turkish (2002, p. 207, n. 5). Numismatically and chronologically moreover, it appears that this group of Huns might be identified with the coin series of bearing the tamgha ⚹ and/ or the Bactrian legend *αλχανο* (Alchon) (figs 78.6–7;

Table 5
Interrelationships with the Huns

AD	IRAN — SASANIAN	AFGHANISTAN — KUSHANSHAH / ALCHON / HEPHTHALITES / TURKS	AFGHANISTAN — KIDARITE / NEZAK / Shri Shahi	PUNJAB — KUSHAN	INDIA — GUPTA
309	Shapur II (309–79)	Peroz 'II' (309–35) / satrap Meze		Mahi (c.320) / Shaka (320–60) vassal of Samudragupta	Chandragupta I (319/20–35)
335		Varhran 'I' satrap Kabad (335–70) Shaboro			Samudragupta (335-80)
342	campaign v. Rome 342–6				
353	campaign v. Rome 353–6			Vasudeva III (c.360)	
360	defeat of Constantius 361	ALCHON	KIDARITE	Kipunadha (360–79)	
370			'Varhran' (c.370-95)		
379				Samudra (c.380)	
380	Ardashir II (379–83)	use of Shapur II & Shapur III dies		Kirada (c.380)	Chandragupta II (380–414)
383	Shapur III (383–88)		'Varhran' /	'Peroz' (c.395–425)	
388	Varhran IV (388–99)	αλχον βογο			
399	Yazdagird I (399–420)	ζοοβο			
420	Varhran V (420–38)	χιπιλο αλχοηο			Kumaragupta I (414–55)
425				Kidara (c.425–57)	
438	Yazdagird II (438–57)				
440		Khingila (440-90)			
455					Skandagupta (c.455-67/8)
457	Hormizd III (457–9)	HEPHTHALITES		son of Kidara (c.457–77)	
459	Peroz (459–84)	helped Peroz to gain throne			
460	7 years drought & famine		NEZAK Napki Malka (c.460–560)		
468	defeated Kidarites 468	countermarked Sasanian coins			Narasimhagupta (c.468–73)
473					Kumaragupta II (c.473–6)
476	defeated by Hephthalites	Peroz paid ransom		paid tribute to China until 477	Budhagupta (c.476–90)
477	second campaign v. Heph-				
483	thalites; killed in battle 484				
484	Kavad I (484)	gave refuge to Kavad 486-8		Toramana (c.485–515)	
	Valkas (484-8)				
488	Kavad I (488–97)				
490		tax in Bactria 492			Vainyagupta (c.490–507/8)
497	Jamasp (497–9)				
499	Kavad I (499–531)	aided Kavad v. Romans 502–6			
506					
507		paid tribute to			
510		China 507–58		battle of Bhanugupta v. Huns 510/11	
514				defeat in Malwa by Prakashadharman c.514	
515				Mihirakula (c.515–40)	
531	Khusrau I (531–79)				
535				defeat in Malwa by Yashodharman c.535 retreat to Kashmir	
537		tax in Bactria 537			
540				Narana / Narendra (c.540–80)	
550		defeated by Turks & Sasanians c. 560			
560			Shri Shahi (c.560–620)	reconquers Kabul region/alliance with Nezak	
579	Hormizd IV (579–90)	TURKS			
580					
591	Khusrau II (591–628)	conquered Kapisha c.612–30, but local minting continued			
620					
628	Kavad II (628)				
630	Ardashir III (628–30)				
631	Boran (630–1)				
632	Hormizd V (631–2)				
	Khusrau V (631–3)?	Arabs v.'Hephthalitea' of Herat 651	Nezak tarkhans under the Turks		
651	Yazdagird III (632–51)				

80.1, 3, 5–7; 83.3–6; table 5).[131] As Grenet has already remarked (2002, pp. 206–7, n. 5):

The identity, assumed since Humbach 1966: 28–31, of αλχανο with the Brāhmī legend rājā lakhāna (which coexists with it on one emission) is not self evident, as other names and titles also occur with αλχανο (βαυο ζαοβλ, Khingila). There are still, I think, good reasons to take αλχαννο as originally designating a people or a confederation, just as later on the Hephthalites put their abridged ηβ on Bactrian coins imitating those of Peroz.

Figure 80 Sasanian coins:
1 Shapur II (AD 309–79), with re-engraved Bactrian αλχανο (alxano);
2 Drachms of Shapur II (Kabul mint).
Alchon coins:
3 Shapur II dinar re-engraved αλχοννο (alxonno), with Alxan tamgha;
4 Bactrian αλδα- (written upside-down and back to front), type found at Shah-ji-ki-Dheri;
5 Bactrian þ[auo?] (written backwards) αλχανο (šauo alxáno);
6 Bactrian -λχονο ([a]lxono);
7 Bactrian αλχα (alxa[no]); Brahmi khigi;
8 Brahmi [ṣāhi] mapama (written backwards);
9 Brahmi devaṣāhi khingila;
10 Brahmi jaükha, type found at Taxila;
11 Brahmi ṣāhi javukha;
12 Brahmi jayatu ṣāhi javuvlah;
13 Brahmi raja lakhana udayaditya;
14 Horse-rider with tamgha, inscribed ṣāhi javukha; rev.fire altar;
15 Horse-rider with tamgha, inscribed ζ(a)βοχο–μ(o)–ρο(σανο)–þ(αο) (zaboxo moro [or miro]sano šao); rev. floral chakra;
16 Bust with conch and chakra, inscribed ζαβοχο–[ ]ρο–σανο–þαο (zaboxo [mo]ro [or miro]sano šao);
17 Standing king, inscribed αδομο μ(?)ο[ ]ν(?)ο þαο (adomono m[?]o[ ]n(?)o šao).

As Alram points out, the first phase of Alchon coinage is closely related to the Shapur II dinars of the Tepe Maranjan hoard from Kabul, which also contained coins of Ardashir II and Shapur III, but no later Sasanians (1999/2000, p. 131; Göbl 1984, pp. 55–6, 145–56). Unlike their apparent contemporaries, the Kidarites (who merely imitate Sasanian issues), the earliest phases of Alchon coinage use the original dies of silver dinars of Shapur II (fig. 80.1) and – more rarely – Shapur III, but with the re-engraved Bactrian legend αλχοννο (alxonno) replacing the original Pahlavi one. Using

Figure 81 Alchon coins (cont.).
Toramana (*c*. AD 485–515):
1   Obv. Brahmi *bra-tu*; rev. *tora*;
2   Rev. Brahmi *tora*;
3   Obv. Bactrian αλχανο; rev.traces of illegible inscription;
4   Malwa region, rev. *vijitāva nirvani pati śrī toramāṇa ḍeva jayati*.
5   Budhagupta (*c*. AD 476–90), Malwa region.
Alchon:
6   Bust with flower, inscribed *jayatu baysāra*.

Mihirakula (*c*. AD 515–40):
7   Obv. Brahmi *jayatu mihirakula*;
8   Obv. Brahmi *śrī mihirakula*; rev. *jayatu vṛṣa*;
9   Obv. Brahmi *jayatu vṛṣadhvaja*;
10–11 Kashmir issues, inscribed *Shahi Mihiragula/Shahi -ghola*.
Narana/Narendra (*c*. AD 540-80):
12 Obv. Brahmi *jayatu naraṇa*;
13 Obv. Brahmi *śrī jayatu narendra*; rev. *jayatu śrī narendra*.
Unidentified kings:
14 Obv. Brahmi *purvvaditya*.
15 Uninscribed uniface coin of two plants type.

as an apparent prototype the small Shapur II issues from Kabul mint (fig. 80.2), their tamgha is then added in front of the king's head. Next a crescent appears behind the head (figs 80.3, 83.2; Göbl 1967, vol. III, pls 14.33–15.39; Alram 1999/2000, p. 131, pl. 5.91–3). In this phase, however, the legend is incomprehensible and does not appear to contain even a corrupted form of the Alchon name.[132]

The Alchon do not imitate the crowned portraits of Sasanian kings after Shapur III. Instead their issues depict the distinctive elongated heads of their rulers without a diadem or crown, only diadem ties. The tamgha, together with variations of the Alchon legend and the fire-altar reverse, are retained (figs 80.4–6, 83.3–6; Göbl 1967, types 40–5, 59–61). They also seem to have imitated Kidarite gold scyphates for a time, the derivative design and legend becoming increasingly crude before being replaced by the standing image of a Hun king and the ⵌ tamgha (fig. 78.6–7; Göbl 1967, types 84–5).

The relic deposit of Tope Kelan, the principal Buddhist stupa at Hadda near Jalalabad excavated by Masson, provides a mid or late fifth-century chronological context for the Kidarites and Alchon (figs 82–3). It contained over two hundred coins, said to be mostly Sasanian issues, the earliest apparently being one of Shapur I (AD 240–72/3) (fig. 82.4); the majority being those of Varhran IV (AD 388–99) (fig. 82.5), Yazdagird II (AD 439–57) (fig. 82.6) and Peroz (AD 459–84) (fig. 82.7), together with five imitations of

Roman gold solidi of Theodosius II (AD 409–50), Marcianus (AD 450–7) and Leo (AD 457–74) (fig. 82.1–3), a silver dinar of Kidara 'Kushanshah' (fig. 82.10), gold Kushan-style staters of Kirada and Shailanaviraya (a king of Kashmir) (fig. 82.9, 11), a silver imitation dinar of Shapur III (fig. 83.1) and two of Shapur II with the Alchon tamgha (fig. 83.2).

These were deposited with fourteen Alchon silver dinars of six different types all bearing the diagnostic cranially deformed portraits of these rulers (fig. 83.3–8; Masson Uncat. MSS 2, pls 14–15, figs 1–27; Wilson 1841, Coins pls XVI, XVIII.25–6; Errington 1999, pp. 221, 234–6, pls 13.7–15.27). Most of the latter coins carry variations of the Bactrian legend αλχανο (*alxano*). The legends are usually incomplete, often corrupted, written backwards, or even upside-down, and fall into two categories. The first group has shoulder diadem ties in place of a crown or diadem and the legend 'king Alchon', either in the form ραυο (written backwards) αλχα (*šauo alxa*[*no*]) and no tamgha, or αλχα (written backwards) ραυο with the added name ζαοβ[(*alxa*[*no*] *šauo zaob*[ ) plus a trident (fig. 83.3–4; Göbl 1967, respectively type 60: 3 examples; type 59: 2 examples). While the intended 'Alchon king' is reasonably clear, Sims-Williams is not sure that *šauo zaob*[can be taken to mean 'king of Zabul as is sometimes assumed' since 'the word order is wrong and the spelling with -ao- for ā would be odd' (personal communication). It could perhaps even be an incomplete

Figure 82 Coins from Tope Kelan (Hadda 10) stupa deposit.
Roman imitations:
1 Theodosius II (AD 408–50);
2 Marcianus (AD 450–7);
3 Leo (AD 457–74).
Sasanian coins:
4 Shapur I (?) (AD 240–72/3);
5 Varhran IV (AD 388–99);

6 Yazdagird II (AD 438–57);
7 Peroz (AD 459–84).
Miscellaneous:
8 Shapur II imitation;
9 Kidarite: Kirada (c. AD 380);
10 Kidarite: Kidara 'Kushanshah' (c. AD 425–57);
11 Kashmir king Shailanaviraya (c. late fifth century).

misspelling of the Bactrian ζαβοχο (zaboxo), which equates
with the Brahmi *javukha*, now confirmed as a personal name
(p. 96 below).

The second group of Tope Kelan Alchon coins has the ⊼
tamgha and a diadem surmounted by a crescent, the largest
number all bearing the legend χιγγιλο αλχανο (xiggilo alxano

'Khingila Alchon'), albeit with the -λ- of Alchon omitted on
most examples (fig. 83.5; Göbl 1967, type 61).[133] The latest in
this tamgha plus diadem and crescent series is again
inscribed þαυο (šauo) written backwards, to the left of the
head and carries traces, probably of a form of the Alchon
name, to the right (fig. 83.6; Göbl 1967, type 68). The

Figure 83 Coins from Tope Kelan (Hadda 10) (cont.):
1 Shapur III imitation, in name of Peroz.
Alchon:
2 Shapur II imitations with Alchon legend, tamgha and crescent; inscribed respectively χσοιαδβο avovo (*xsoiadbo anono*) and χμοιαδβο avovo (*xmoiadbo anono*)?

3 Inscribed ραυο (written backwards) αλχα (*šauo alxa*[*no*]);
4 Inscribed αλχα (written backwards) ραυο ζαοβ[(*alxa*[*no*] *šauo zaob*[ );
5 Inscribed χιγγιλο αλχavo (*xiggilo alxano* 'Khingila Alchon');
6 Inscribed ραυο (*šauo*) written backwards; traces, probably of Alchon name;
7 Inscribed ṣā-*hi* in Brahmi;
8 Inscribed *khigi* in Brahmi.

remaining two Alchon examples have the Brahmi legends ṣā-*hi* ('king') and *khiga* respectively, the latter being identifiable with Khingila (fig. 83.7–8; Göbl 1967, respectively type 69: 2 examples; type 57: 1 example).

Further east a survey of the coin finds from the Buddhist sites of Swat, the Peshawar Valley and Taxila reveals a distinctly limited distribution spread for Alchon coins, largely restricted to Taxila and the Shah-ji-ki-Dheri hoard at Peshawar (fig. 80.4, 10; Errington 1999/2000, pp. 211–13; p. 133 below). They are almost completely absent in the regions lying north of the Kabul river and west of the Indus, where issues of Kidara are common. Only a stray 'Jaükha' issue of the same Alchon type as the Taxila examples was found at Ranigat, the monastery closest to the main

Peshawar Valley crossing point over the Indus river at Ohind (figs 80.10, 176; Errington 1999/2000, p. 200, fig. 65). This site lies near the route leading to the important Hindu shrine of Kashmir Smast, where large numbers of Kidarite and a smaller number of Alchon silver and bronze coins have been found (Nasim Khan 2007, nos 118–550 and 551–572 respectively). The distinct pattern of coin distribution re-enforces the impression gained from the Tope Kelan deposit that the Kidarites and Alchon evolved some degree of practical co-existence in the region, the Kidarites apparently remaining in the Peshawar Valley and Swat, and the Alchon south of the Kabul and Indus rivers, in Peshawar and Taxila, and along the principal route to the subcontinent.

The estimated date of c. AD 440–90 for Khingila (Alram 1999/2000, p. 131) fits within the framework supplied by the Hadda deposit. It has been suggested that an inscribed garnet portrait seal identifying its owner as 'lord' Khingila (εϱκιγγιλο ϱωκανο χοηο[134] may belong to this king or to a namesake of his (Callieri 2002; Sims-Williams 2002a). Since the tamgha and crown depicted on the intaglio differ from those on Alchon coins issued by Khingila, the second option seems more likely, for there appear to be several later rulers similarly named. Chinese sources writing about events in the year AD 658 record that the founder of the local dynasty then ruling Kapishi (Begram region) was called Xingnie, i.e Khingal, after whom the line of succession passed from father to son for twelve generations (*Tong shu* XX.6241, *Jiu Tang shu* XVI.5309, *Tang hui yao* 99,[135] cf. Palmer *et al.* 1986; Rahman 2002, pp. 37–8; Kuwayama 2002, pp. 211, 254). Kuwayama identifies Xingnie as a king named 'Khingal' ruling from c. AD 550, but the earlier Khingila of Alchon coins could equally be a candidate, given the stated time-span of twelve generations (see also Grenet 2002, pp. 217–18). However, the marble Ganesha image from Gardez, with its c. sixth- to seventh-century proto-Sharada inscription dated in year 8 of the 'great king of kings', Khingala (Khiṃgāla, cf. Sircar 1963, p. 43),[136] clearly refers to a later ruler. The *Rājataraṅgiṇī* (III.102–3) also lists a king called Khinkhila-Narendraditya as the eighth ruler of Kashmir after Mihirakula, suggestive of a similar, c. seventh-century date (Stein 1892, vol. I, pp. 140–1).[137] Finally, Khinjil/Khinkhil is named by Ya'qubi (*Tarikh* II.479) as the Kabul-shah in the time of the 'Abbasid Caliph al-Mahdi (AD 775–85).

Göbl in fact assigned almost all early Alchon coinage with the ⚇ tamgha to Khingila, but admitted the possibility that 'his coins actually belong to several rulers', for he considered that the typology was frozen for a long period, thereby making differentiation difficult (1967, vol. II, p. 59, types 40–89, 91–107, 112, 117–18). The alternative – i.e. a confederation with several contemporary rulers – is, however, increasingly gaining credence. Only a few issues actually carry the name Khingila (usually in Brahmi, coupled with the title *devaṣāhi*), sometimes in combination with 'Alchon' in Bactrian (figs 80.7, 9; 83.5, 8; Göbl 1967, types 44, 54, 66, 81). A far greater number bear a variety of different names and/or epithets. Apart from the Bactrian examples already cited, there are a number in Brahmi, most notably *mapama*, *lakhana udayaditya* and the variations *jaūkha*, *javukha* and *javuvlah* (fig. 80.8, 10–14; Göbl 1967, types 49–51, 71, 79–80, 82).

A new stupa consecration inscription – putatively from northern Afghanistan – enumerates four Hun kings, all apparently reigning at the same time: Khingila and Mehama both ruling as *mahāṣāhi*; Javukha as *mahārāja*; and Toramana as *devarāja* (Melzer, forthcoming).[138] It is noteworthy that Lakhana is omitted from the list. As Melzer points out:

> The different titles . . . suggest a differentiation in the rank of the princes or rulers. It is possible that the differentiation between *-rāja* and *-ṣāhi* might also have something to do with the geographical regions over which the kings ruled, one being closer to India and the other referring to countries further to the north of India (Pakistan, Afghanistan).

Assuming that Mehama is the *mapama* on coins (fig. 80.8), the substantiation by the inscription of concurrent rule fits the numismatic evidence at least for the first three, who all appear to have issued similar silver coinage which could quite feasibly be contemporary (fig. 80.7–9, 11; Göbl 1967, types 49–53, 71–7, 81–2). Toramana's issues do not belong to this series, but his bronze coinage shares certain links, such as the Alchon portrait and Brahmi letter on the obverse (fig. 81.1–3; Göbl 1967, type 120). So although – following Göbl – he is generally viewed as Khingila's successor, their reigns could have overlapped.

In the Bhitari pillar inscription, datable to c. AD 456/7, Skandagupta (c. AD 455–67/8) claims that when he came 'in contact with the Hunas, with (his) two arms in battle, the earth quaked' (Bhandarkar 1981, pp. 81, 317). The Gupta inscription does not name the defeated Hun king. However, this appears to have been only a temporary setback, for in the time of Toramana (c. AD 485–515) the Huns had control of most of northern India, as attested, for example, by the 'Hunaraja' and 'Toramana' seals found in excavations at Kaushambi (Willis 2005, p. 146). The *Kuvalayamālā* (composed AD 778) says that Toramana enjoyed 'the sovereignty of the world' from his headquarters in the town of Pavvaiya on the banks of the Chenab river (§§ 2–3; Mehta 1928, pp. 32, 34).[139]

On the Varaha inscription from Eran he is recorded as controlling the Malwa region of central India, in 'year 1', either of his occupation or of his reign (Sircar 1965, p. 421). This claim is backed up by coins of the bust/peacock type issued in Malwa by Toramana, which follow on from issues of the same type belonging to the Gupta king, Budhagupta (c. AD 476–90) (fig. 81.4–5).[140] The Sanjeli copper-plate inscription of year 3 also documents Toramana's presence in northern Gujarat (Willis 2005, p. 146). But any territorial gains he made in this vicinity were short-lived. The Eran pillar inscription of Bhanugupta[141] records a huge battle, presumably against the Huns, in Gupta year 191, i.e. AD 510–11 (Fleet 1888, pp. 92–3; Willis 2005, p. 146); and in the Rishtal inscription of Vikrama year 572 (AD 514/15), Prakashadharman, the Aulikara king of the same region, claims to have 'established himself in the kingdom of the Huna ruler through his footstool being flooded with the brightness of the gems of the royal crown of king Toramana' (Raychaudhuri 1996, pp. 787–9).

An extension of the multilingual legends in Bactrian, Pahlavi and Brahmi on individual coins is a discernible tradition of shared titles and epithets (see also Alram 1986,

p. 330). The Brahmi variations *jayatu* ('let him be victorious') and *jaya* ('victory'), for example, have clear affiliations with the Pahlavi 'Varhran' (the victorious warrior god) and 'Peroz' ('victorious') more commonly found on Kidarite coins.[142] An Alchon issue with the legend *jayatu baysāra* seems to fit the gap in silver coinage between Khingila and Toramana, for the royal portrait has the single crescent diadem and hairstyle of Toramana, and is coupled with a chakra-like flower reminiscent of the chakra motif found on the coins of both rulers (fig. 81.6). Subsequent rulers, Mihirakula and Narendra, are similarly called *jayatu* on coins (fig. 81.7–8, 12–13; Göbl 1967, types 135–8, 152, 171–6). There is a further link between Mihirakula's legend on his copper issues – *jayatu vṛṣa*, 'let the *vṛṣa* (bull) be victorious' – and silver anonymous issues of *jayatu vṛṣadhvaja*, 'let he whose banner is the *vṛṣa* be victorious' (fig. 81.8–9). Other linked Brahmi titles found on coins in this series are *udaya[a]ditya*, 'he who is the sun that rises', and *purva[a]ditya*, 'he who is the sun in the east' (figs 80.13; 81.14).

An inscription from Kura in the Punjab refers to the 'king of kings, the great king Toramana *ṣāhi jaû-*' (Bühler 1892, pp. 238–9; Sircar 1965, p. 422). Raychaudhuri suggests that the last damaged word is a title corresponding to *ṣāhi javukha*, *javuvlah* and *jaükha* on coins (1996, p. 788). However, the new stupa inscription translated by Melzer (p. 96) shows clearly that Javukha was a ruler contemporary with Toramana and, therefore, that the variants are merely different spellings of the same personal name and not a title (fig. 80.10–12). Davary (1982, p. 296) suggests – and Sims-Williams agrees – that the Brahmi *javukha* equates with the Bactrian word ζαβοχο (*zaboxo*) (fig. 80.15–16). The complete Bactrian legend on coins is *morosano šao* ζαβοχο or *adomono* (figs 78.7; 80.15–17). Sims-Williams points out that, as the inscriptions are circular, it is not obvious where to start the reading, but it is 'most logical to assume that the title *morosano šao* "king of Morosano", which is common to all, always stands at the end and that the other word (*adomono/ zaboxo*) is his personal name'. There seems to be little doubt that the correct reading of the place name (?) is *morosano*, although it is worth noting a peculiarity in the writing on some coins (fig. 80.17) that the *o* in the sequences *mo* and *no* is apparently left open at the top (Davary 1982, p. 302; Sims-Williams, personal communication). Nevertheless, it is tempting to suggest that *morosano* may be a variant of *mirosano* 'sunrise', or 'east',[143] so that the title *morosano šao* would mean 'king of the east', i.e. the Bactrian equivalent of *udaya-aditya* and *purva-aditya*.

The Gwalior inscription, dated regnal year 15 of Mihirakula (*c.* AD 515–40), identifies him as the son of Toramana[144] and shows that he controlled north-west Madhya Pradesh by *c.* AD 530 (Fleet 1888, p. 162; Sircar 1965, pp. 424–6). But, like Toramana, his progress appears to have been halted further to the south-west, for the Mandasor pillar inscription from Sondani claims that by *c.* AD 535, 'respect was paid' to Yashodharman, the Aulikara ruler in the Malwa region, 'by even that famous king Mihirakula whose head had never previously been brought to the humility of obeisance to any other save Sthāṇu [Shiva]' (Sircar 1965, pp. 418–20; Willis 2005, p. 147). In the same context Yashodharman's reference to the Hun king 'by whose arms the mountain of

snow [Himalayas] falsely prides itself on being styled an inaccessible fortress' has been taken to mean that Mihirakula controlled Kashmir and the adjoining regions (Majumdar 1988a, p. 37); an interpretation reinforced by Kalhana's inclusion of him in the *Rājataraṅgiṇī* as a ruler of Kashmir (1892, vol. I, pp. 43, 140), whom he describes in legendary terms as (I.289, 291, 293)

> a man of violent acts and resembling Kāla (Death). . . . The people knew of his approach by noticing the vultures, crows, and other [birds] which were flying ahead eager to feed on those who were being slain within his armies' [reach]. . . . This terrible enemy of mankind had no pity for children, no compassion for women, no respect for the aged.

Xuan Zang, writing almost a century later, says that Mihirakula 'had his seat of government' at Sakala (modern Sialkot, in the Punjab) and was 'a man of talent and intelligence with a bold and furious nature, and all the neighbouring countries were his vassal states' (IV.888b). He also says that, when Mihirakula invaded the territory of Baladitya, the Buddhist king of Magadha, he was defeated and took refuge in Kashmir (IV.888c–9a; Watters 1904, vol. I, pp. 288–9). Traditionally Baladitya has been identified with the coin issuer Nara Baladitya, and thence with the Gupta Vaishnava ruler, Narasimhagupta Baladitya. However, a convincing reassessment of late Gupta chronology places the latter *c.* AD 468–73, between Skandagupta (*c.* AD 455–67/8) and Kumaragupta II (*c.* AD 473–6), and suggests that Xuan Zang's Baladitya was the son of Vikramaditya, king of Ayodhya, and a pupil of the Buddhist philosopher Vasubandhu, with whose work the Chinese pilgrim was familiar (Willis 2005, pp. 140–1; table 5).

As reported in the later Aphsad inscription of Adityasena, from Gaya district, Bihar, dated year 66 of the Harsha era (AD 672), Hun progress – at an unspecified date and not necessarily under Mihirakula – was also barred further to the east in Uttar Pradesh by the Maukharis, whose 'mighty elephants . . . had thrown aloft in battle the troops of the Hunas' (Fleet 1888, p. 206; Thaplyal 1985, pp. 160–5). According to Xuan Zang, Mihirakula became king of Kashmir only in the last years of his life, after killing the incumbent ruler who had given him sanctuary (VI.889a):

> he then attacked the country of Gandhâra in the west, and by having his troops lie in ambush, he killed the king. The members of the royal clan and all the ministers were slaughtered, and . . . three *koṭis* [i.e. 30,000,000] per class were taken to the bank of the Indus River and put to death, three *koṭis* of people of the middle class were drowned in the river, and three *koṭis* of people of the lower class were granted to the soldiers [as slaves]. After that, he carried the booty he had taken from the conquered country and marched home in triumph.

One last reference to be considered that apparently concerns Mihirakula is the account of the 'Indian navigator', Cosmas Indicopleustes, a merchant from Alexandria, writing *c.* AD 550. He travelled to south India and Sri Lanka some time between AD 525 and AD 547. On his return to Egypt he became a monk (probably a Nestorian) and a proponent of the idea that the world is flat, and that the heavens form the shape of a box with a curved lid. He placed India 'in the east near sunrise' (*Christian Topography* II.148). Pearse notes that 'away from his daft theory, Cosmas proves to be an interesting and reliable guide' (2003, preface), but, while this

Figure 84 Nezak coins:
1 'Napki Malka' (c. AD 460–560) inscribed in Bactrian.
5 Inscribed σηρο (*sēro*) in Bactrian; double struck reverse.
Shri Shahi (c. AD 560–620):
2 Obv. Pahlavi *pk' mlk*; rev. Brahmi *ki-la ha-ki*;
3 Rev. Alchon tamgha;
4 Countermarked in Brahmi *tī-gī*.
Hephthalite imitations of Peroz:
6 Obv. inscribed ηβ (*ēb*) in Bactrian; rev. left: Pahlavi monogram of Peroz M-P (MLK'); right: Bactrian βαχλο (Balkh);

7 Inscribed δηβ (*dēb*); Bactrian countermark ασβ. . . (*asb. . .*) on rim;
8 Obv. rim: illegible Bactrian inscription; countermark of head.
Arab-Sasanian coins:
9 In the name of Khusrau II (AD 590, 591–628). Obv. rim: Arabic *bismillāh*, Hephthalite (?) countermark; rev. Pahlavi mintmark *zw* Zozan or *yz* Yazd;
10 'Abdallah b. Khazim (?). Obv. Bactrian *zolado gōzogano* 'Zhulād Gōzogan'; Pahlavi (behind head and rim) [AH] 69 (AD 688), '*pzwt* GDH 'increased fortune'; Arabic (rim) *bismillāh*. Rev. Bactrian (left rim written backwards) *garigo šauo* 'king of Gar'; (right rim) *ambē*(?)*ro* i.e. Sar-i pul; Pahlavi '*pzwn* 'increase'.

might be true for the places he actually visited, his concept of the topography further north is decidedly muddled. He says that, at the time he was in south India, 'the Phison [Indus river], which discharges into the Persian Gulf', formed 'the boundary between Persia and India' (XI.337; McCrindle 1897, p. 366). Apart from his evident confusion about the juxtaposition of the Indus and the Persian Gulf, he subsequently contradicts himself by saying 'The River Phison separates all the countries of India [lying along its course] from the country of the Huns' (XI.339–40, McCrindle 1897, pp. 372–3). Specifically, he locates the 'White Huns' in north India and says (XI.338–9: McCrindle 1897, pp. 370–1)

> The one called Gollas when going to war takes with him, it is said, no fewer than two thousand elephants, and a great force of cavalry. He is the lord of India, and oppressing the people forces them to pay tribute.

Given the date of Cosmas's account, it is generally assumed that Gollas can be equated with Mihirakula, whose inscriptions on some Kashmiri coins give a similar ending of Mihiragula or -ghola to his name (fig. 81.10–11). Following the identification by Procopius of Caesarea (I.iii.1–6), it is

also generally assumed that the 'White Huns' equal the 'Ephthalitae' or Hephthalites. In order to accommodate the fact that the coins of Mihirakula and his predecessors are inextricably linked with the Alchon, there has been a strong tendency to use 'Hephthalite' as a blanket term for both groups of Huns. But the *Bahman Yasht* (II.49) makes a clear distinction between the Huns – both 'Red' and 'White' – and the Hephthalites, a distinction which is perpetuate by the Bactrian coin legends αλχανο and ηβ, the latter being an abbreviation of ηβοδαλο (*ēvdal*), the Ἐφθαλῖται of Greek and *Hayṭal* of Arabic sources (Sims-Williams 1997, pp. 14–16; 2000, p. 193).

Most influential in this respect has been Marshall's sweeping attribution of the destruction of Taxila to the Hephthalites, on the basis of 32 silver coins found in total at the Buddhist sites in this vicinity (1951, p. 791). On inspection, however, these coins are all Alchon issues. All except two appear to be variations of the same type (fig. 80.10–11; Marshall 1951, pp. 293, 824–5, pl. 245.301, 303–13; Göbl 1967, types 49–51). The one unique example for Taxila – with the Bactrian αλχανο legend – was a stray find at

Bhamala (fig. 80.5; Marshall 1951, p. 824, no. 300, pl. 245.300: misread as 'Balkh'; Göbl 1967, type 67). The other – a coin of Khingila (fig. 83.8; Marshall 1951, p. 824, pl. 245.305; Göbl 1967, type 57) – was found in a doorway of the Bhamala monastery with 19 other Alchon issues of Javukha, of the type with a club in front of the portrait (fig. 80.10–11; Marshall 1951, p. 824, pl. 245.301–13; Göbl 1967, types 56, 49–51). The circumstances of the find suggest it was a hoard, i.e. not necessarily associated with the destruction layer of the site (p. 133 below). A further seven coins of the same type were uncovered in the courtyard of the Lalchak monastery, and three more in the Dharmarajika monastery.

The small hoard of 16 so-called 'Ephthalite or White Hun' slightly debased silver coins, found during excavation of the 'Kanishka' monastery at Shah-ji-ki-Dheri in 1911, in reality also comprises all Alchon issues, but of the earlier type with a crescent behind the head (fig. 80.4; Göbl 1967, types 40–3; Whitehead 1913, pp. 481–2, pl. XI). The earliest bilingual issue with the word *śī* in Brahmi is most common (7 examples: Göbl 1967, type 43).

Masson's Begram collection shows a similar complete lack of any Hephthalite issues. Instead, there are 34 small early Alchon coins from the time of Khingila onwards, including possibly a few of Toramana; three larger coins of Mihirakula of the Kashmiri standing king/Ardochsho type (fig. 81.2–3, 10–11; Nasim Khan 2007, nos 571–2); and eight uniface bronze issues, probably all of the same diagnostic two plants type as the Kabul hoard (fig. 81.15; Alram 1999/2000, pp. 137–43, nos 15–90). This hoard was found in the late 1970s 10 km north of Kabul, i.e. not far from Begram. It comprised 447 copper coins, all of the same uniface type and with the (optimal) Brahmi legend *śrī ṣāhī na*, probably attributable to Narana/Narendra (*c*. AD 540–80), a successor to Mihirakula (Alram 1999/2000, pp. 129–43). A chronological context is provided by two coins in the hoard, which are overstrikes on the Nezak coins of 'Napki Malka' (fig. 84.1), so-called from a misreading of the Pahlavi *nycky mlk'* (Alram 1999/2000, pp. 132–3, pl. 8, nos 44, 50). A second link is a separate billon issue from Gandhara, which is inscribed *nara* and has the same portrait and crown as the uniface Narana/Narendra issues, but with the addition of the Napki Malka diagnostic bull's head above the crown (Alram 1999/2000, p. 134, pl. 6.108A). On the basis of their 'careless fabric and metrology' symptomatic of hasty production, perhaps for a military expedition, Alram interprets the hoard as evidence for a short period of conflict in the Kabul–Kapishi/Begram region between the Alchon (returning westwards from Gandhara) and the resident Nezak. He further points out that 'the overstrikes demonstrate that the debasement of the Nezak coinage in Afghanistan ran more or less parallel to the debasement of the Indian Alchon coinage' (Alram 1999/2000, p. 133).

So how and where do the Nezak fit in? They appear to have been related to the Alchon, at least in the early phases of their coinage (fig. 84; Göbl 1967, vol. II, pp. 72–3). Göbl places them initially in Zabulistan (the Ghazni–Kabul region) on the basis of a hoard of Napki Malka coins reputedly found near Gardez, which he bought in Kabul bazaar in 1962 (1967, vol. II, pp. 36–8). The coinage was clearly issued by several rulers over a long period, as demonstrated not only by the

degeneration of certain stylistic features but also by the debasement of the metal content, which ranges from good silver to pure copper (Alram 1999/2000, pp. 132–3).

In his manuscript record of his 1833–5 collections, Masson illustrates one bronze and three silver Napki Malka coins; as well as one silver and four bronzes of the successor coinage bearing the legend Shri Shahi (Uncat. MSS 2, ff. 26, 46, pl. 11.20; f. 48, pl. 13.44–51), but says only that the bronze coins of these rulers occur 'plentifully' at Begram. Wilson, in fact, assigns the silver Napki Malka coins from Masson to Kabul (1841, p. 397, nos 10–11, pls XVII.5, 7, XXI.21). This seems correct, for in Masson's Begram residue collection there are 61 coins of Shri Shahi alone, none of Napki Malka. A very tentative date for the Napki Malka coin issuers around Ghazni is *c*. AD 460–560; with the inclusion of Kabul *c*. AD 515 following the death of Toramana, although Göbl admits that expansion in this direction 'is sketchy in detail as well as in time' (1967, vol. II, p. 62).[145] From *c*. AD 560 to 600 the Ghazni region fell under Sasanian control as a result of the campaigns of Khusrau I, but Kabul–Begram remained independent, as evinced by the uninterrupted coinage sequences (Göbl 1967, vol. II, pp. 74–5). According to Xuan Zang in AD 632, Gandhara and its capital Purushapura (Peshawar) and the Jalalabad region were subject to Kapishi, with its capital at Begram (II.878b–c, 879b; Watters 1904, vol. I, pp. 183, 198–9). Taxila, on the other hand, had formerly been subject to Kapishi, but was now a dependency of Kashmir, while its chiefs 'were in a state of open feud' (III.844b–c; Watters 1904, vol. I, p. 24).

The coin designs of Shri Shahi follow and maintain the high-quality Nezak portraiture tradition of the Napki Malka coinage, but with the addition of a small Alchon ⹂ tamgha behind the head and a crown resembling that of certain Alchon Narana/Narendra issues (fig. 84.2, 4; Alram 1999/2000, pp. 146–9, pls 6.108, 7.121–2). Other examples have the tamgha on the reverse in place of the usual fire altar design (fig. 84.3; Göbl 1967, type 231). Like the Napki Malka coinage, the issues exhibit a gradual debasement of the silver content, as well as a stylistic degeneration, suggestive of a long period of production *c*. AD 560–620 or even much later. They appear to have had a fairly wide dispersal range south of the Hindu Kush, with coins being found as far afield as Fondukistan near Bamiyan in the west, eastwards to Peshawar, Kashmir Smast and Butkara I in Swat (Hackin, Carl and Meunié 1959, p. 57, fig. 206; Göbl 1967, type 238; Nasim Khan 2007, nos 575–607 *passim*; Göbl 1976, p. 35, no. 262).

According to Kuwayama, Kapishi is called the Cao kingdom in Chinese sources of the Sui period (AD 518–618) and he notes that the kingdom (centred at Begram) sent tributary missions to the Tang court from AD 619 onwards (2002, pp. 195–7, 213–14). Citing Xuan Zang (Watters 1904, p. 123), who visited Kapishi in AD 630 and described the ruler as belonging to the 'kshatriya caste', Kuwayama interprets this to mean that the dynasty had descended from an indigenous warrior caste and was not Hephthalite in origin (2002, pp. 213–14). Li Rongxi's translation of the same passage gives a different gloss: 'the king, who belongs to the Sui tribe . . . has more than ten countries under his dominion' (Xuan Zang I.873c), but the conclusion is the same, viz. the king was not Hephthalite. This point is verified by the coin finds from Begram, although not by Napki Malka issues as thought by Kuwayama, but by the subsequent Alchon–Nezak Shri Shahi issues.

Göbl dates the conquest of Kapishi by the Turks to c. AD 612–30, but notes that it left no imprint on the coinage 'for continued minting permitted the local economy to bear the burden of tribute better'; nor was there a demonstrable break during AD 657/8–705 when Kapishi was incorporated into the Chinese protectorate (1967, vol. II, p. 74). The fusion between Alchon and Nezak are identifiable as the predecessors of the later 'Nēzak *tarhans*' mentioned by the Arabic chronicles. According to the Persian historian Hamzah al-Isfahani, writing in AD 961 (*Tārikh-i payāmbarān va shāhān*, p. 60),[146]

> The king of the Hayatala rose up against Yazdagird III and together with Mahuya took part in the killing of Yazdagird and the children of Mahuya were then known as the king killers.

Grenet – discussing Esin (1977) – identifies this 'king of the Hephthalites' who took part in the assassination of Yazdagird III in Merv in AD 651 as a later Nezak *tarkhan*, as was another who revolted against the Arab conqueror Qutaiba c. AD 703 in the Herat region, but also notes that other Islamic sources refer to Qutaiba's protagonist as a Turk (Grenet 2002, p. 216). If this is the case, some of the Nezak at least had clearly moved from their earlier Kabul–Begram base to regions north of the Hindu Kush by this time. It is moreover possible that the confusion arises in this later period because – as happened earlier with Alchon–Nezak unification – the surviving Huns joined forces or had even merged with their Turkish overlords to a degree that their ethnic origins were obscured. This is implied in Xuan Zang's description of the inhabitants of Himatala, 'an old territory of the country of Tokhara', west of Badakhshan and south of the Oxus: 'They are short and ugly in their features, and their ways and manners, as well as their garments . . . are quite the same as those of the Turks' (XII.940b).

A comparatively rare silver issue with the Bactrian legend σηρο (*sēro*) is stylistically linked to the Nezak group and has the same crescent and lotus crown as the Alchon gold scyphate issues, but it is flanked by wings in place of diadems (fig. 84.5; Göbl 1967, types 241–2 and type 85 respectively). The reverse copies the fire altar and attendants design of the last Sasanian kings, including Yazdagird III (AD 632–51) (fig. 71.7–8). Although relatively few examples now survive, the coinage seems to have reasonably long currency. Seventeen later coins of the same type[147] were unearthed with an inscription dated in year 492 of the Bactrian era, from a Buddhist stupa at Tang-i Safedak, west of Bamiyan in Afghanistan (Lee and Sims-Williams 2003, pp. 164–5, 171–3). Since the era appears to have begun c. AD 223/4,[148] the inscription provides a date of c. AD 714 for the deposit, which appears to have been the restoration or re-establishment of an earlier foundation. According to Sims-Williams, *sēro* appears to be a title rather than a personal name, which is found in several Bactrian documents of the eighth century. It seems always to be associated with the Turks, occurring specifically as σηροτορκο 'ser of the Turks' in a document of AD 692 (Lee and Sims-Williams 2003, p. 172).[149]

Analysis of the Chinese sources led Kuwayama to propose that the 'Hephthalites' – with whom he included Mihirakula,

but not Khingila – reached Gandhara through the Karakorums, not by the western route (Kuwayama 2002, p. 124). But, as already noted, the Hun coins from the Tope Kelan deposit, the hoards from Tepe Maranjan, Kabul and Gardez, as well as the finds from Begram, Kashmir Smast, Butkara I and indeed Taxila are all Kidarite, Alchon or Nezak, not Hephthalite. The numismatic evidence thus 'clearly demonstrates that the Alchon Huns [i.e. Mihirakula's predecessors] reached India via the Kāpiśa–Kabul area' (Alram 1999/2000, p. 131), while those who actually call themselves Hephthalites have not left any evidence of ever having reached India at all. Göbl's remark – made in 1967 – unfortunately still remains true, namely that 'the Hephthalite concept appears as an unwarranted generalisation until further evidence is uncovered' (1967, vol. II, p. 8).

References to the actual Hephthalites in western sources find accord with the numismatic evidence. According to Procopius of Caesarea (I.iii.1–6),

> the Ephthalitae Huns, who are called White Huns, . . . are of the stock of the Huns in fact as well as in name; . . . their territory lies immediately to the north of Persia; indeed their city, called Gorgo, is located over against the Persian frontier, and is consequently the centre of frequent contests concerning boundary lines between the two peoples. For they are not nomads like the other Hunnic peoples, but for a long period have been established in a goodly land. . . . They are the only ones among the Huns who have white bodies and countenances which are not ugly . . . nor do they live a savage life . . . but they are ruled by one king, and since they possess a lawful constitution, they observe right and justice in their dealings both with one another and with their neighbours, in no degree less than the Romans and the Persians.

In the time of Peroz and Kavad I (AD 484, 488–531), according to Hamzah al-Isfahani, the Hephthalites or Hayāṭilah inhabited the borderlands of Khurasan, which in that period included modern Turkmenistan (*Tārikh-i payāmbarān va shāhān*, p. 108). Tabari identifies the Hephthalites more specifically at this time as the conquerors of 'the whole of Khurasan' and also Tokharistan, i.e. Bactria north of the Oxus (I.873, cf. Bosworth 1999, p. 110). In a subsequent expedition against the Hephthalites Khusrau I (AD 531–79) 'penetrated to Balkh and what lies beyond it and quartered his troops in Farghanah', i.e. eastern Uzbekistan (I.899, cf. Bosworth 1999, p. 160). These locations are roughly synonymous with that given for the 'country of Himatala' by Xuan Zang in AD 629–30 as 'an old territory of the country of Tokhara' (above; I.872b–873c, III.887a, XII.940b). More details are provided in the *Wei Shu*, which says that the Hephthalites subjugated Samarkand, Khotan, Kashgar, Margiana and thirty other smaller countries in the Western Region (VI.2279, cf. Kuwayama 2002, pp. 208–9). As Kuwayama notes in citing this passage, all contemporary or near-contemporary documents locate the Hephthalites firmly north of the Hindu Kush. During the reign of Kavad I, the account of the Chinese pilgrim Song Yun in AD 519–20, for example, defines the kingdom of the Yanda (i.e. Hephthalites) as receiving tribute from diverse vassal or neighbouring states: Chile or Chiqin in the north, Bosi (Persia) in the west, Yutian (Khotan) in the east and as far south as the unidentified Dieluo region, probably bordering the Hindu Kush (Chavannes 1903, p. 404). Kuwayama identifies 'chiqin' (*tegin*) simply as 'Turk' (2002, pp. 208–9).

But, while *tegin* undeniably appears as a title on the coins of a ruler of the late seventh century thought by some perhaps to be a Turk,[150] Sims-Williams points out (2002, p. 234):

> The title *tegin* 'prince' is certainly common in Turkish, but its irregular pl. *tegit* has suggested that it may have been borrowed from 'a Mongolian type of language' (Pulleyback 1962: 258). Since we know from Chinese sources [e.g. Song Yun] that the title *tegin* was already used by the Hephthalites, it is tempting to regard this as evidence of the Altaic affinities of the Hephthalites (as Pulleyback does in fact suggest); but in Bactrian, names which appear to derive from *tegin* occur in texts which probably predate the Hephthalite period.

Song Yun on entering Gandhara moreover also says 'After this country was conquered by the Yanda, a *chiqin* (*tegin*) was appointed as ruler; [this dynasty] has governed the kingdom for two generations' (Chavannes 1903, pp. 416–17).[151] So he identifies the Hun rulers or conquerors both of Gandhara and north of the Hindu Kush as the Yanda/Hephthalites and uses the same term 'chiqin' both for the Yanda's northern neighbours and – more clearly in the sense of vassal status – for the dynasty ruling Gandhara. As it is evident from other contexts that Mihirakula must be the king with '700 elephants' who was at war with Kashmir, and who gave Song Yun an audience (Chavannes 1903, p 417), it follows that his predecessor credited with conquering the country must be Khingila. However, from the numismatic evidence, neither king can be identified as Hephthalite, nor is Mihirakula identified as such by Song Yun. The apparent absence of the Hephthalites in Gandhara in this period suggests that if they did ever invade the territory – either alone or as head of a Hun confederacy – they soon withdrew, leaving the Alchon and Kidarites in control, possibly as vassals.

In contrast, the fate of the Sasanian emperor Peroz (AD 459–84) is inextricably linked with the Hephthalites (table 5), who 'had taken over' Tokharistan and who aided him in his ultimately successful struggle against his brother Hormizd III (AD 457–9) for the Sasanian throne (Tabari I.872–3, cf. Bosworth 1999, pp. 109–10). According to Tabari, the early part of his reign was blighted by a severe drought and famine lasting seven years, i.e. at least until *c.* AD 464–5 or later (I.874–6, cf. Bosworth 1999, pp. 113–15). When it was finally over and prosperity was restored, he went to war against the Hephthalites in Khurasan. Joshua the Stylite, writing in AD 507, says that Peroz was captured by the Hephthalites and had to agree to an onerous peace, promising that he would not go to war against them again (Joshua the Stylite § 10):

> Boastfully promising to pay for his own life a ransom of thirty mule-loads of *drachmas*, he sent the order for it back to his own realm but could hardly muster twenty loads, for by the previous wars he had completely emptied the royal treasury (inherited from) his predecessor.

He was forced to leave his son Kavad as hostage until he had paid – with the help of the Byzantine emperor[152] – the remaining ten loads of silver (Frye 1983, pp. 147–8). These events have to be fitted around Peroz's victory over the Kidarites in AD 468, as recorded by Priscus (fr. 41, *Exc. de Leg. Gent.* 15, cf. Enoki 1969, pp. 20–2), and it seems reasonable to assume they took place afterwards: *c.* AD 469, as suggested by Frye (1983, p. 147), or even *c.* AD 476/7, as suggested by Alram (2002, p. 151). Bivar (2006) suggests that Priscus'

mention of the Kidarites in this specific context 'is probably anachronistic, since Procopius (*Persian Wars* I.3.1–7), in his classic account of these Huns, attributes the same role to the (H)Ephthalite Huns'. But this seems unlikely as Priscus was recording contemporary events, while Procopius (*c.* AD 500–65) was writing up to a century later. The new gold scyphate of Peroz (p. 88, fig. 78.5), moreover, fits neatly at the end of the Kidarite issues of this series, suggesting they lost control of northern Afghanistan to the Sasanian king as Priscus records. Coins of the Hephthalites show even closer links with Peroz (see below), so it seems preferable to accept that the Sasanians were at war with both the Kidarites and the Hephthalites at this time.

Procopius says that Peroz, towards the end of his reign, again 'became involved in a war concerning boundaries with the nation of the Ephthalitae Huns, . . . gathered an imposing army and marched against them' (I.iii.1, 8–22; iv.1–13). The Sasanians were defeated, their army destroyed and Peroz killed in battle. After this the Hephthalites 'conquered the whole of Khurāsān' (Tabari I.873, cf. Bosworth 1999, p. 110), and Peroz's successor Kavad I (AD 484, 488–97, 499–531) became their 'subject and tributary' (Procopius I.iv.32–5). Kavad was deposed and imprisoned by Valkash (AD 484–8), but escaped *c.* AD 486 and sought refuge with the Hephthalites, who provided an army to help him regain his throne (Procopius I.v.1–4; vi.1–12). Again in AD 502–6, the Hephthalites appear to have supplied Kavad with troops for his war against the Romans (Procopius I.vii.1–2, 8; viii.13). Kavad then 'retired homeward with his whole army, since hostile Huns [apparently not Hephthalites] had made an invasion into his land, and with this people he waged a long war in the northern part of his realm' (Procopius I.viii.19–20; Schippmann 1990, pp. 49–51).

Bactrian documents confirm Hephthalite dominion of the region to the south and east of Balkh in the late fifth and first half of the sixth century, for they refer to a 'Hephthalite tax' (ηβοδαλαγγο τωγο) in years 260 (AD 483) and 295 (AD 518) respectively of the era of AD 223/4 (Sims-Williams 1999, pp. 247, 254–5; 2000, pp. 52–5; 2002, p. 225). The documents further indicate that the indigenous local rulers such as the 'khars of Rob' remained in place, on payment of tribute to their Hephthalite overlords. The Hephthalites in turn are recorded as regularly paying tribute to the Chinese in the period AD 507–58 (Kuwayama 2002, pp. 128–9, table 2).

Göbl identified the earliest currency of the 'genuine Hephthalites' (fig. 84.6–8) as the large quantities of countermarked dirhams of Peroz – and to a lesser extent, Kavad I – found in Khurasan (1967, vol. II, pp. 89–90, types 283–6).[153] This fits very neatly with the literary evidence of the huge ransom paid in silver to the Hephthalites after their defeat of Peroz in this region, and the subsequent status of Kavad I. The third coin type of Peroz – with a winged crown (fig. 69.13) – was struck in huge quantities and seems to postdate his first unsuccessful campaign against the Hephthalites (Curtis 1999, p. 305). Alram suggests that, in addition to financing his second disastrous war against the Hephthalites, it was also used to pay the subsidies and tribute due to them (2002, p. 151).

The second phase in Hephthalite coinage, as charted by Göbl, is the production of Peroz imitations, copying the winged crown type of this king, but with the Bactrian legend ηβ (for ēb[odalo] 'Hephthalite') and, on the reverse, the mint name βαχλο, i.e. Balkh (fig. 84.6; Göbl 1967, vol. I, pp. 197–9, types 287–9; Alram 2002, p. 151, fig. 4). More debased variations of the same type include two examples in the British Museum (fig. 84.7) bearing the legends δηβ (dēb), which, if intentional, Sims-Williams suggests could be the Indian title deva, 'elsewhere written ddēbo in Bactrian', while the Bactrian countermark ασβ... (asb...) on the rim may be a corrupt ambēro, the old name for Sar-i pul (personal communication). Other coins in this series have monograms and the image of a head in profile countermarked on the rim (fig. 84.8).

Alram points out that the numerous countermarked Peroz coins indicate that the process of making imitations of this type did not start until after Peroz's death, i.e. in the late fifth or early sixth century (2002, pp. 151–2). Also fitting within this time-frame is a more innovative silver issue bearing an imitation bust of Peroz on the reverse and the bust of a Hun prince holding a drinking cup on the obverse, with the Bactrian legend ηβ[οδαλ]αγγο, i.e. 'Hephthalite' (Alram 2002, pp. 149–53, fig. 1).

Significant numbers of Peroz coins also reached China, where they have been found in hoards, tombs and stupa deposits dating from the late fourth to mid eighth century (Alram 2002, p. 151; Thierry 1993, pp. 91–6, 99, 102–5). Sasanian coins found in China range from c. AD 438 to 633, but there is a concentration of Peroz issues (Thierry 1993, p. 107). The finds moreover indicate the use of two different trade routes. Those of the fifth to sixth century correspond with the southern route from Hephthalite-controlled Tokharistan eastwards through the Pamirs to Khotan – which they also controlled from AD 498 – then via Dunhuang or the Koko Nor lake to Lanzhou and into China (Wang 2005, pp. 35–6; Thierry 1993, pp. 110, 113–14, maps 3–4). But in the seventh century Sasanian coins appear to have been a major currency along the northern route through Qiuci and Gaochang, especially in the Turfan area (Skaff 1998, p. 84). This later development was a consequence of a fresh wave of migrants into the region, the Turks, although the establishment AD 657/8–705 by the Tang dynasty of a Chinese protectorate over the 'western provinces' (including parts of Afghanistan) must have also played a part.

In the middle of the sixth century the Hephthalites were defeated by an alliance between the Sasanians under Khusrau I and the western Turks, and their territories divided between the victors (Sinor 1990, p. 301; Sims-Williams 2002, p. 234). But the custom of allowing indigenous local rulers to remain in place appears to have continued: the Turks are attested in Bactrian documents in year 407 (AD 630),[154] again in connection with the khar of Rob (Sims-Williams 1999, p. 255), while in AD 651/2 the Arabs fought against the Hephthalites 'inhabiting Herat' (Tabari I.2885–6, cf. Grenet 2002, p. 214). The practice of minting coins in the name of the Sasanian king also continued even after the arrival of the Arabs in the region (fig. 84.9–10).[155]

From this broad survey of the principal 'Hun' coinages in conjunction with the textual and epigraphic evidence, several trends become apparent. The first is the tendency of coins with Bactrian legends in the regions both north and south of the Hindu Kush to use only titles or generic appellations. As can be seen in the coins of Khingila, Toramana and Mihirakula as they moved further into India, it appears to be only when the issuers begin using Brahmi as well as – or instead of – Bactrian, that the names of individual rulers start to emerge. This habitual use of titles in the coinage of Afghanistan – which continues down into the Hindu Shahi period – is one of the main causes of confusion in identifying the different Hun groups mentioned in the written sources. But the numismatic evidence – based on the patterns of coin circulation and evolution – shows an unmistakable correlation with the texts in identifying four principal groups, i.e. Kidarites, Alchon, Nezak and Hephthalites, and provides a general concurrence of their context in time and place. From the references in later Islamic and Chinese sources it is clear that, following Turkish suzerainty over the regions north of the Hindu Kush, remnants of the Nezak–Alchon and Hephthalites survived, retaining some military power and political autonomy (Grenet 2002, pp. 213–16).

Notes

1 This is Cyrus II. His paternal grandfather Cyrus I – also known as 'the Elder' – was Kurash of Anshan: see p. 32. For an Elamite name of Cyrus and his possible Anshanite identity see Potts 2005, pp. 7–10, 16–18.

2 Briant 2002, pp. 98–106 suggests that Bardiya may have rebelled against his brother while Cambyses was campaigning in Egypt and successfully seized the throne in 522 BC. Ctesias gives the names Tanyoxarces, Tanoxares, Mergis and Mardos for Cyrus' son. Reference kindly supplied by Elizabeth Pendleton and Andrew Meadows.

3 The spelling Parapamisidae – rather than the variant Paropamisidae – follows Arrian VI.xv.3.

4 Personal communication, Professor A. D. H. Bivar, who also supplied the following reference for shisham wood at Susa: see Gershevitch 1957, pp. 317–20, and 1958, p. 174.

5 For complaints by the Jews of Elephantine to Persian satraps regarding the destruction of their temple by Egyptian priests and their expectations of religious protection see Razmjou 2005, p. 153.

6 Traditionally payment in the ancient Near East was by weighed silver, a practice which continued in the Achaemenid and even the Seleucid period. The Nush-i Jan hoard from western Iran had precisely such a weighed value and seems to have been used as currency (Curtis 1984, pp. 19–20).

7 For the new reading of the name as Tarkumuwa on the Cilician issues see Lemaire 1989, pp. 141–56.

8 The Saka (Old Persian) or Sacae (Greek), i.e. Scythians, are called Śaka (Shaka) in Indian sources.

9 Professor A. D. H. Bivar (personal communication) suggests Bucephala may be located at Jalalpur on the Jhelum river, where the ziyarat (built on an earlier Hindu shrine) has foundations of ashlar masonry, but the site has not yet been the subject of a detailed survey or excavation.

10 According to Shahbazi 1987, p. 150, the Seleucids created a fictitious genealogy in which Apama was purported to be Roxana's daughter.

11 After a disastrous start as a British agent in Khiva (Yapp 1980, pp. 392–4, 397–8, 564), Abbott (1807–96) had a successful political career in the Punjab, even to the extent of having a town – Abbottabad – named after him. But his reputation as an antiquarian is hard to understand, for his other forays into the subject (e.g. 1852, 1854) are equally unedifying.

12 The conventional dates for the Mauryans are given here, but these are only approximate and are still the subject of dispute more than two centuries after William Jones's discovery.

13 Kautilya, the politician and kingmaker, is credited with being the author of the Arthaśāstra, the classic text on Mauryan statecraft, now shown to date in its present form to the second century AD and to be a compilation of the work of several authors (Keay 2000, pp. 80–2).

14 Joe Cribb (1991) in an unpublished assessment of the Classical sources comes to the same conclusion. We are extremely grateful to him for generously allowing us to use his manuscript.

15 The 'Singhalese Chronicles', the *Dīpavaṃsa* and the *Mahāvaṃsa*, composed in Sri Lanka fourth to early sixth century AD, cf. Bechert 1995, p. 12.

16 Semi-mythical Hindu texts relating to the early historic period, the compilation of which is thought to have been completed not much earlier than the fourth century AD, see Bhandare 2003, pp. 3–4, 6.

17 The end of existence, of desire, suffering and the cycle of rebirth. See p. 126.

18 The alternative suggestion proposed by Thapar 1997 and others is Alexander of Corinth (252–247 BC), but Cribb (1991, citing Will 1979–80, vol. I, p. 266) makes the pertinent comment that 'this Alexander is surely too obscure to be featured in the rock edict along with the other kings'.

19 Manu is also the law-giver and progenitor of the human race. The earliest account of Manu and the flood is in the *Śatapatha Brāhmaṇa*. The traditional date assigned to this event is 3102 BC (cf. Keay 2000, pp. 1–5; Majumdar 1988, pp. 273–6), although, like most early Indian dates, this is a modern construct.

20 Thapar 2000, pp. 200–1. Panini's date is equally controversial, the most generally accepted being the fourth century BC. The arguments rest on unknown factors, i.e. whether the original text was written in Aramaic or Kharoshthi, and the date of the emergence of the latter script, which some scholars place in the time of Ashoka, cf. Salomon 1998, pp. 11–12, 46.

21 The Kumarahar pillar also has a series of circles with dots which have been identified as masons' marks.

22 The comb-like pictogram has been identified as a temple by Joe Cribb, its early form being still recognisable in the evolved later version appearing on *c*. second- to first-century BC Audumbara coins (fig. 41.12; Allan 1936, pl. XV.1–10).

23 See Hardaker 1992, pp. 14, 16, 19, types 7.1–2, 22.4, 38.4; Gupta and Hardaker 1985, pp. 88, 93–4, 96, nos 96, 98, 167, 246, 248, 323, 325, 335.

24 In 1836 Masson recorded only 11 punch-marked coins from Begram and noted that 'These coins are found more frequently in the bazars [sic] of towns, as Kabul, Ghuzni [sic] &c than at the site of Beghram, where being of only very casual occurrence, we would not venture to affirm that they have been current there . . . the silver coins are more frequent than the copper ones, and both of them are rare' (Uncat. MSS 2, 'symbol coins', ff. 1, 4[9], figs 86–91). However, in later inventories of his own 1837–8 collection, he lists another 85 (List A, 'Type chataiya [sic] with emblems of sun &c': 62; List B, 'Early Buddhist': 23. Uncat. MSS 4; Errington 2001, pp. 391, 394). The IOLC contains 30 silver and 6 bronze punch-marked coins. Most were so encrusted with deposits that it was impossible to determine the metal, or indeed what they were, prior to cleaning and conservation.

25 Houghton and Lorber 2002, p. 278, type 781: two coins of this type have also been excavated at Susa.

26 In Islamic times this area was still called Dahistan.

27 It has been suggested that the name may have derived from Old Persian Narisanka (cf. Narseh), Avestan 'nairya-sanha' but this equation is not generally accepted. See Ghirshman 1974, p. 7; Frye 1987, p. 26; Curtis 2007, p. 1.

28 Schmitt (1998, p. 164) regards the language of the Parni as being related to such east Iranian languages as Sogdian, Khwarezmian and Saka. Evidence for this is found in surviving loan words.

29 The name Hyspaosines appears in cuneiform tablets from Warka as As-pa-a-ši-ni-. Schmitt (1990, pp. 246–7) sees the earliest evidence of the name in Bactrian and equates it with the Iranian Vispa-čanah. It seems to be related to the Old Persian Aspačanah (Greek Aspathines), who is identified as the bow-bearer of Darius in the Naqsh-i Rustam inscription (see Kent 1953, p. 140). We are grateful to Rahim Shayegan for drawing attention to this.

30 See Shayegan (forthcoming).

31 The Persian satrap appointed in charge of Characene under Mithradates was a certain Indupanē (Shayegan, forthcoming).

32 For the monogram of Mithradatkert on coins before Mithradates I see Sellwood (1980, p. 20).

33 Bivar (1983, p. 42) disagrees with Sellwood's interpretation (1983, pp. 285–9) and regards Gotarzes as the opponent of Mithradates II. For the period from the end of Mithradates II to

Orodes II there is no unanimously agreed chronology. Assar bases his chronology on Babylonian texts, especially astronomical diaries, and sees no opposition between Mithradates II and Gotarzes. He identifies Mithradates III as an opponent of Orodes I, whom he ousted in 75 BC (Assar 2006, p. 148).

34 Bivar 1983, p. 44 attributes only a short period, *c*.80 BC, to Orodes I, whose rule is attested by cuneiform tablets from Babylon.

35 Surena fell victim to the king's jealousy and was murdered by Orodes.

36 The exact location of Phraata/Praaspa is unknown. Henry Rawlinson suggested the site of Takht-i Sulaiman near Takab (1840, pp. 65–158). Another possibility is the city of Maragheh (ancient Afrah-Rodh), cf. Bivar 1983, pp. 63–4.

37 To the Parthians and Sasanians this region was known as Arabistan, while the province of Babylonia was Asuristan (i.e. Assyria). The lands to the east of the Tigris between the Greater and Lesser Zab were known by western historians as Adiabene and by Parthians as Norshirakan (Bivar 1983, p. 89).

38 Evidence of a strong Parthian presence at Hatra in the second and early third centuries AD is clearly seen in the iconography of the dedicatory sculpture from the various temples (Safar and Mustafa 1974).

39 It seems that the spread of a smallpox epidemic from the east may have caused the Parthian defeat. This epidemic also affected the Roman army and thence the Roman empire (Bivar 1983, p. 93).

40 Traditionally known as Artabanus V.

41 For the reading of *krny* and its interpretation as the family name Karen, or the Greek word for 'autocrat', as well as indications of anti-Seleucid sentiments in this early period, see Abgarians and Sellwood 1971, p. 113; Sellwood 1983, p. 280.

42 This seems to be attested on early first-century BC coins: see Sellwood 1983, p. 288, pl. 3.10.

43 For Indo-Scythian, Indo-Parthian and Kushan chronology see pp. 59–71.

44 The tiara is not shown on Parthian coins for a hundred years from the middle of the first century BC until the reign of Vonones II (*c*. AD 51). The diadem seems to have been more popular at this time (Curtis 1998, p. 63).

45 The Parthian tiara is similar to the *tiara orthe* of the Achaemenid period, which derived from the tall rounded hat of the Medes (Delegation I) on the early fifth-century BC reliefs at Persepolis (Curtis 1998, p. 61).

46 Other frontal portraits occur on coins of Vonones II (*c*. AD 51), Vologases III (*c*. AD 105–47), Osroes I (*c*. AD 109–29), Vologases IV (*c*. AD 147–91) and Vologases V (*c*. AD 191–208): see Sellwood 1980, types 63.4, 67, 79.50, 80.27, 84.136–43, 86.3–8.

47 Strabo XI.xi.1: after the Loeb translation (p. 280, n. 1) which conjectures Ἴμάον (Imaus), i.e. Himalayas, for Ἰσάμου (Isamus). The Himalayas are variously also referred to in Classical sources as Haemus, Himaus or Imaus-Emodus (Schwartzberg 1992, pp. 17c, 24a, e). This interpretation makes sense as a general indication of direction. Alternative conjectures equate the unknown Isamus with the Iomanes (Yamuna) or the Soamus (Son) rivers (Bopearachchi and Rahman 1995, p. 33; Tarn 1938, p. 144).

48 Roughly the area of modern Uzbekistan and Tajikistan.

49 A total of 45 kings according to Bopearachchi 1991, 14 of whom are assigned to the period *c*.250–145 BC (with the reign of Menander I extending to *c*.130 BC) and the remaining 31 kings to the period *c*.145 BC–AD 10.

50 The Ghazni (i.e. Arachosia), Qandahar (Drangiana) and Herat (Aria) regions of Afghanistan. 'India' in this context includes the Kabul and Jalalabad regions and eastwards to the Khyber Pass.

51 The dates given for the Greco-Bactrians and Indo-Greeks generally follow Bopearachchi 1991, the standard reference work for these kings.

52 For the 1833–5 collections Masson records 43 Agathocles and 73 Apollodotus I (Masson, Uncat. MSS 2, f. 1). For the breakdown of his figures for Eucratides I coins, see below.

53 Tetradrachms of Demetrius I (162–150 BC) from the Seleucid mint of Antioch are dated, for example, ΗΝΡ (year 158, i.e 155/4 BC: Newell 1918, pp. 39–43); those of Mithradates I (171–138 BC) from Seleucia on the Tigris bear the letters ΓΟΡ and ΔΟΡ (years 173 and 174, i.e.140 BC and 139 BC: Sellwood 1980, pp. 42–3).

54 The Laukika era of *c*.3076 BC, still in use in the Punjab and Kashmir, has similar regional variations.

55 The problematic inscription on the Hariti statue from Skarah Dheri has been omitted from the equation, since in the opinion of Harry Falk (personal communication) and others, it is definitely not dated year 399, as read by Konow (1929, pp. 124–7). Alternative readings of the date range from year 179 to 291 (e.g. Boyer 1904; Bivar 1970).

56 The unadjusted, purely lunar calculations of the Hijra calendar produce a year of 354 days and a ratio of 97 solar years to 100 lunar years.

57 The Chinese lunar calendar is the longest chronological record in history, dating from 2600 BC. However it does now contain a luni-solar element, so that the beginning of each year falls consistently between late January and mid February. A complete cycle takes 60 years and is made up of 5 cycles of 12 years each.

58 The *Shiji* (Historical Records) was begun by Sima Tan (*c*.190–110 BC) and completed *c*.100 BC by his son Sima Qian (b. 145 BC), with additions down to *c*.90 BC (for the questioned authenticity of some chapters see Zürcher 1968, p. 358). The [*Qian*] *Han Shu* (History of the [former] Han) covers the period 206 BC–AD 25 and was compiled – partly from work by Ban Biao (*c*. AD 3–54) – in about AD 80 by his son Ban Gu (AD 32–92), and completed by his daughter Ban Zhao (*c*. AD 48–116). The *Hou Han Shu* (History of the Later Han) was compiled by Fan Ye (AD 398–445), from a report (*c*. AD 123–5) by Ban Yong, covering the period *c*. AD 27–125 (see pp. 66–7).

59 According to Pompeius Trogus, 'The Scythian tribes of the Saraucae [Strabo's Sacarauli] and the Asiani [Asii] seized Bactra and Sogdiana' and subsequently the 'Asiani became kings of the Tochari and the Saraucae were destroyed' (*Prologue* XLI–XLII). Bivar (1983, pp. 192–3) remarks that the Da Yuezhi have generally been identified as the Tochari, but this appears to deny the confederacy status accorded the Da Yuezhi by the Chinese sources, for in western sources the Tochari appear to be just another tribe, on equal footing with the Asii/Asiani. Bivar also points out that 'the role played by the Asiani is precisely that of the people who later came to be known as the Kushans'.

60 Zhang Qian was sent as the first Han envoy to the west in 138 BC to seek a military alliance with the Yuezhi against the Xiongnu, then the dominant power in the Western Region. He was captured and detained by the Xiongnu for 10 years before finally reaching Yuezhi territory and returned to China in AD 126 (Twitchett and Loewe 1986, p. 407).

61 For convenience all words given in Wade Giles in Zürcher 1968 have been converted to Pinyin. For a complete list of Chinese names and their conversion from diverse transliteration systems to Pinyin by Wang Tao, see pp. 252-3.

62 In origin perhaps an account of actual events, it is presented as a series of predictions in the astrological handbook, the *Gārgī-saṃhitā*, a work of uncertain date, possibly *c*. first to third century AD (Jayaswal 1928, p. 410; Tarn 1938, pp. 452–6; Bopearachchi and Rahman 1995, pp. 32–3).

63 Pancala is the ancient territorial name, known from the earliest Indian literary traditions, for the region around Ahichchhattra (modern Ramnagar, Bareilly District). Its usage continued at least down into the first century AD, as evinced by its mention in an inscription approximately of this date, thought to have been found at Ramnagar (Banerji 1909–10, pp. 106–8). Proposed dates for Pancala coinage range from *c*.200 BC to AD 350 (Shrimali 1983, vol. I, pp. 55–61).

64 *Dvīpa* is the Sanskrit word for island; doab means 'two waters', i.e. the tract between two confluent waters (Yule and Burnell 1903, p. 321).

65 Masson Uncat. MSS 2, pls 1.25–2.32 and IOLC include Bopearachchi 1991, ser. 17–21, 25, 27–9, 31–2, 36–7. The four missing types are helmeted head of Athena/horse, elephant/lance, camel/bull's head, head of Heracles/lionskin: Bopearachchi 1991, ser. 24/39, 26/38, 30, 35.

66 Masson (Uncat. MSS 2, f. 1, pl. 3.54–7) identifies 92 silver and bronze tetradrachms and drachms in the name of Hermaeus – with seated Zeus on the reverse – as 'Ermaios the Elder'. Of the 8 coins illustrated, only a silver tetradrachm (fig. 54), together with a square bronze 'Ermaios' coin (head of Mithras/horse type: Uncat. MSS 2, pl. 3.66), are lifetime issues of Hermaeus, the rest

being posthumous issues (Bopearachchi 1991, pp. 113–25, pls 52–60). Proportionally, the ratio of 1:8 suggests that – at most – only *c*.11 of the 92 'Elder' coins are lifetime issues (plus the Mithras issue equals *c*.12 coins).

67 In the 1833–5 Begram collections, Masson recorded a total of 714 coins in the name of Hermaeus (Uncat. MSS 2, f. 1, pls 3.54–66, 5.112–14), of which the vast majority (593 coins) were of the type with the image of Heracles replacing that of Zeus on the reverse. Examples on which the name Kujula Kadphises was legible only numbered 99, according to Masson's calculations (Uncat. MSS 2, f. 1, pl. 5.115–21; Errington 2001, pp. 371–2).

68 There is one extremely worn Poseidon/Yakshi example in the India Office Loan Collection (Mit. 721) and a drawing of an elephant/seated king coin found at Begram in 1834 (Uncat. MSS 2, fig. 139; Mit. 734).

69 The inscription was probably excavated from the ruined stupa no. 41 at Taxila in 1859 (Cunningham 1871, pp.132–4; Errington 1987, pp. 174–8, 432, 515, map 8). It was given by Nur, the finder, to A. A. Roberts, Commissioner and Superintendent of the Rawalpindi Division, who in turn donated it to the Royal Asiatic Society. It is now on permanent loan to the British Museum (As. 1967.10.18.5).

70 The alternative suggestion that Yona/Eucratides year 1 equals 174 BC provides a date of 97 BC.

71 The connection with Maues was thought to be further emphasised by the reference to him on the Mathura lion capital as 'the illustrious king Muki', but a close examination of the inscription by Harry Falk (personal communication) shows what was read as *mu* is actually a *sha* damaged by a later scratch.

72 It is not yet resolved if there were two kings named Azes or whether coins in the name of Azes continued to be issued posthumously. In either event, the designation 'I' and 'II' remains a useful tool to distinguish between the two categories.

73 The Azes II coins included two Zeus Nicephorus silver drachms, the rest apparently being all bull/lion bronze tetradrachms.

74 One bronze coin (camel rider/bull type) of Azes I and one of Azilises (horseman/elephant) were purchased in Kabul bazaar and are now in the British Museum: IOC 197/BMC 179 and IOC 215/BMC 26 (Wilson 1841, p. 327, no. 14, pl. VII.6 and p. 320, no. 4, pl. VIII.7 respectively).

75 A red sandstone capital comprising two addorsed lions covered with inscriptions which identify its original site as a Buddhist monastery. It was found 'embedded in the steps of an altar devoted to Sitala, on a site belonging to some low-caste Hindus at Mathura', by Pandit Bhagwanlal Indraji in 1869 and bequeathed to the British Museum on his death in 1888 (Konow 1929, p. 30).

76 Lucknow Museum no. J1. The inscription was found during excavations at the site of Kankali (1888–91) by Alois Führer, Archaeological Surveyor of the Western Provinces and Oude (Sharma 1989, p. 309). Subsequently in 1897, in an attempt to 'prove' he had discovered the Buddhist site of Kapilavastu, Führer was caught inserting clay tokens inscribed with fake 'pre-Ashokan' characters in the small stupas he had excavated at Sagarhawa and was forced to resign (Allen 2002, pp. 276–8).

77 The calculation of *c*. AD 32 equalling year 1 of Gondophares is derived from the Takht-i-Bahi inscription which equates Gondophares year 26 with year 103 of the Azes era (i.e. 46 BC); see Indo-Parthians below.

78 Inscriptions refer to 'Apraca', 'Apaca' or 'Avaca' kings, sometimes using more than one version in the same text (Senior 2000, vol. I, pp. 89–90). These are usually considered as simply variant spellings, since the names all seem to refer to the same group of individuals.

79 His correct reading Ⱶ Ⱶ⅂ Ⱬꟼ *Itravasusa* is confirmed on a clearly legible specimen in the British Museum.

80 Mit. 1135 claims to illustrate one with a Gondophares monogram on the obverse, but the specimen is particularly worn and the photograph is not clear.

81 The figure 191, misread as a date by Konow, has been identified as a weight (i.e. 191 *karshapana*) by Cribb 1999, pp. 196–7.

82 *Acts of Thomas* II.17–24: 'Now when the apostle was come into the cities of India with Abbanes the merchant, Abbanes went to salute the king Gundaphorus, and reported to him of the carpenter whom he had brought with him. And the king was glad, and commanded him to come in to him. . . . And the king said: "Canst thou build me a

palace?" And he answered: "Yea, I can both build it and furnish it; for to this end I have come, to build and to do the work of a carpenter". . . . Now when the king came to the city he inquired of his friends concerning the palace which Judas that is called Thomas was building for him. And they told him: "Neither hath he built a palace nor done aught else of that he promised to perform, but he goeth about the cities and countries, and whatsoever he hath he giveth unto the poor, and teacheth of a new god, and healeth the sick".' Following Thomas's imprisonment, the king's brother Gad became mortally ill and had a vision of the metaphorical palace Thomas had built in heaven by virtue of his good deeds. Gad then miraculously revived and convinced Gondophares to release Thomas and pray 'that I might become a worthy inhabiter of that dwelling for the which I took no pains, but thou hast builded it for me, labouring alone, the grace of thy God working with thee, and that I also may become a servant and serve this God'.

83 These regnal dates derive from the assumption that the Azes era equals *c*.46 BC.

84 Philostratus was a Greek sophist and orator who accompanied Caracalla (AD 211–17) to the east in AD 213–17, when the Roman emperor attempted to benefit from the Parthian internecine struggle between Vologases VI (*c.* AD 208–28) and Artabanus IV (*c.* AD 216–24). He was commissioned by Julia Domna Augusta (fig. 13), the emperor's mother, to write the biography of Apollonius.

85 Bivar (2007, p. 26) suggests that Phraotes equals Phraates, which is reasonable. However, he then equates the name with the coin legend Prahata (?), which is not feasible, for the issue in question belongs to a 'sub-Parthian' king of Arachosia of the second century AD (Alram 1986, p. 268, no. 1215).

86 Philostratus claims as a source notes by Damis, a disciple of Apollonius, who is said to have accompanied the philosopher to India, but who is dismissed by some scholars as a literary fiction.

87 Masson Uncat. MSS 2, fig. 159; Wilson 1841, pp. 342–3, nos 1–3, 7–8, pls V.16–18, VI.2, XXI.16). King on horseback crowned by winged Nike/Gondopharan symbol: three from Begram (Mit. 1114–15: Ashmolean Museum Shortt Collection; British Museum (IOC 233/BMC 22, IOLC); one horseman/Poseidon (Mit. 1116: IOC 231); two horseman/Pallas Athena (Mit. 1128, 1134: IOLC); one horseman/Zeus (Mit. 1129: IOC 228); three crude head/Pallas Athena drachms (Mit. 1142: IOLC).

88 It is also worth noting that, although Masson records 278 'Parthian and Sasanian' coins from the 1833–5 Begram collections, his illustrations identify these as Kushano-Sasanian and Shri Shahi bronze coins (Uncat. MSS 2, f. 1, pls 11.1–16, 13.44–51).

89 As noted above (n. 61), all Chinese names given in Wade Giles in Pulleyblank 1968 and Zürcher 1968 have been converted to Pinyin. For a full list see pp. 252–3 below.

90 For a map of the region see Twitchett and Loewe 1986, p. 406, map 16.

91 Rabatak village lies a short distance to the north-east of the Kushan dynastic site of Surkh Kotal: see Sims-Williams 1999, p. 247, map 1.

92 Dates cited here for the Kushans from Kanishka I onwards follow Cribb 2005, pp. 221–3. The revised dates for Kujula and Wima Tak[to] are based on his calculation that the Azes era began 46 BC.

93 This specific coin has recently been found among the material from the relic deposits excavated by Masson now in the British Museum. It is coated on the reverse with gold leaf.

94 The symbol ⚇ is also found with the tamgha of Soter Megas on the untitled, small denomination Heracles/Tyche issues (fig. 61.8); and on all the bronze and gold issues of Wima Kadphises (again with the latter's own tamgha: fig. 61.16–17). It re-emerges in Bactria on the gold coins of Vasudeva I (AD 190–227) and the Kushano-Sasanians *c.* AD 233–370 (figs 61.22; 74).

95 Two inscriptions from Mathura can be assigned to this group, even though they do not name a specific ruler (Lüders 1961, pp. 162–4, § 123; Salomon 2005, pp. 376–7). The first (from Giridharpur Tila) is dated in year 270 of the 'maharaja'; the second in year 292 (or 299) of the 'maharaja ratiraja', i.e. respectively AD 96 and AD 118 (or AD 125), if Yona year 1 equals 174 BC.

96 Two gold coins appeared on the art market in late 2006 purporting to be issues with the name of Wima Kadphises on the obverse and Wima Tak[to] on the reverse. However, they can be

identified as fakes for a number of reasons, e.g. the inscriptions and designs of both obverses have been executed by the same die engraver, but do not fit into the production sequence of die engravers working at the Kushan mints under Wima Kadphises; the arrangement of the reverse legend on the one example imitates early Greco-Bactrian coins; the design of the reverse of the other is too small for its flan; the head of Oesho on one is a misunderstood copy of Wima Kadphises' bronze issues.

97 *Four prongs:* IOLC 7 tetradrachms, 19 didrachms; CM 12 tetradrachms, 8 didrachms. *Four-pronged obverse/three-pronged reverse:* IOCL 9 tetradrachms, 13 didrachms; CM 1 tetradrachm. *Three prongs:* IOLC 295 tetradrachms, 493 didrachms; CM 37 tetradrachms, 13 didrachms.

98 The Kushan era date on an image of a *nāga rāja* from Mathura was previously read as year 170. It was therefore considered as the sole example where the rule of the dropped hundred for the second Kushan century has not been applied and the inscription was assigned to Vasudeva II (*c.* AD 280–320) (Cribb 1999, p. 188). A new reading (Falk 2002/3, pp. 41–5) corrects the date to year 80 of Vasudeva, i.e. in the reign of Vasudeva I (*c.* AD 190–227).

99 The Hariti image from Skarah Dheri is omitted here, as Konow's reading (1929, pp. 124–7) of its date as year 399 is no longer accepted: see n. 55 above.

100 At Taxila, according to Marshall (1951, p. 788), 'Vasudeva's [bronze] coins are far more numerous than those of any Kushan king from Kanishka onwards. They number 1,904 in all, viz. 1,584 of the "Śiva and bull" type [a] (including 615 of the rude later type [b]) and 320 of the "seated goddess" type [c]'. None of the coins is illustrated, but on the basis of this description they can be broadly subdivided into issues of (*a*) Vasudeva I and (*b–c*) the later Kushans, Kanishka II and III, Vasishka and Vasudeva II. He lists a further 30 'later Kushan period' coins of no 'known rulers'. The only one illustrated is a coin of Vasudeva II (1951, pl. 243, no. 269).

101 The title 'Ērān ud Anērān' is now generally read as 'Iranians and non Iranians' rather than 'Iran and non-Iran' (see Alram and Gyselen 2003, pp. 108, 187–9). See also pp. 108–9 for the occurrence of this title on coins of Hormizd II and later Sasanian kings.

102 He is also reported to have been in charge of the Anahita Temple at Stakhr, i.e. Istakhr (see Nöldeke 1973, p. 4, n. 2).

103 For a detailed discussion of the various dates and bibliographical references see Alram and Gyselen 2003, pp. 135–8.

104 The date given in the inscription is year 58 of an unknown era, which is equated with the fortieth year of the Ardashir fire and twenty-fourth year of the Shapur fire. According to Altheim and Stiehl, this corresponds to AD 223/4 for the Ardashir fire and AD 239/40 for the Shapur fire (cf. Alram and Gyselen 2003, pp. 135–6). The date of the monument at Bishapur is thus AD 262/3 and the beginning of the era is AD 205/6.

105 The exact location of Hormizdgan is not clear. It is generally thought to have been near Nehavand, but a location near Isfahan, en route to Hamadan, has also been suggested (Bivar 1983, p. 97).

106 According to Tabari (Nöldeke 1973, p. 14), Ardashir's son Shapur took part in this battle and killed the Parthian scribe Dadhbundadh.

107 An anonymous work – of disputed reliability – recording the history (*c.* AD 104–544) of Christianity in Arbela (modern Erbil in Kurdistan, eastern Iraq), see Mathews 2003.

108 The direction changes with Ardashir's ascension to the throne of Iran.

109 The name refers to his birthplace, Shattra (modern Shahba), between Damascus and Amman in the Roman province of Arabia (Schippmann 1990, p. 20).

110 English translation by V. S. Curtis from Huyse's German translation. Both the Pahlavi and Parthian versions use the word Kēsar (Caesar) as the title of the Roman emperors: ŠKZ §§ 6, 8–9, 18: Huyse 1999, pp. 27–8, 35.

111 A gold coin showing a royal rider holding a Roman prisoner by his hand has recently appeared on the art market. The legend apparently identifies the figures as Shapur I and Philip (Michael Alram, personal communication).

112 Mosig-Walburg 1990, pp. 125–6, however, does read this particular title on coins of Shapur.

113 The territory of the Albani extended from Iberia (Georgia) to the Caspian Sea. For the Chionites see pp. 89–90.

114 These vassals seem to have been the descendants of famous Parthian families, e.g. Zar-Mihr or Zohra, of the House of Karen, was ruler of Sakastan (Sistan); Shapur, of the House of Mihran, was king of Ray.

115 The particulars of Mazdak and his teacher Zardusht are not certain. It is thought that Mazdak introduced a religious reform based on the teachings of the prophet Mani (Schippmann 1990, p. 47).

116 An era with several slight regional variants, which is used by Brahmans in Kashmir and the Punjab.

117 Bactrian documents and inscriptions dated in this era range from year 35 to year 636 (Sims-Williams 1999, pp. 249, 254), i.e. according to the amended date, from AD 257 to AD 858.

118 F. de Blois, 'Bactrian chronology and Sasanian chronology: new evidence from ancient Afghanistan': lecture at the Ancient India and Iran Trust, Cambridge, 7 June 2006.

119 In Pahlavi, Parthian and Greek.

120 The later dates are slightly modified from those proposed in Cribb 1981, pp. 84–96; 1985a, pp. 308–18.

121 Enoki (1970, pp. 30–1) identifies the 'Euseni' and 'Gelani' both as Kushans, presumably because both are linked together with the Chionites by Ammianus Marcellinus (see also Enoki 1969, p. 4). This is feasible, but it is odd that Ammianus Marcellinus differentiates between the two. It is thus equally possible that the Gelani were a completely separate tribe, albeit not known from other sources.

122 Readings courtesy of Joe Cribb from examples in the British Museum: type (a) CM 1985.7.50.1; type (b) 1894.5.6.1295–6 (Cunningham collection) and 1894.7.11.73.

123 First identified by Göbl (1967) as the name used by a Hun tribe, Alchon remains a convenient term for numismatists working on the group of interrelated coins that appear to have been issued concurrently but independently in the same period as the Kidarite coinage (see below, pp. 90–6). Bivar (2005, p. 321) – following Humbach (1966, pp. 28–31) – disputes the identification of Alchon as the name of a people, preferring to associate the legend specifically with 'the ruler Lakhana or Alkhana', whom he places chronologically after Mihirakula.

124 Transliterated as *Juduolo* and *Juchang* by Grenet 2002, p. 205; and *Juduoluo* and *Jichang* by Kuwayama 2002, p. 128. For Pinyin transliterations, see pp. 252–3 below.

125 The obverse design of the 'Samudra' coins is stylistically intrusive, but the seated Ardochsho reverse fits within the Kushan–Kidarite sequence.

126 Zeimal 1996, p. 120, notes that the portrait/archer coins were minted from the first to fifth century, but that 'out of some 2000 such coins, only 7 bear the name of Kidara'.

127 Reading courtesy of Nicholas Sims-Williams in correspondence with Joe Cribb 30 October 2005.

128 Bahman or Vohu Manah (Vahman), the Amesha Spenta 'Good Purpose', is the guide for all Zoroastrian believers, who led Zoroaster into the presence of Ahuramazda and five other radiant beings from whom he received his revelation (Boyce 2001, pp. 19, 22).

129 Grenet (2002, p. 207, n. 5), referring to Humbach (1966, pp. 28–31), points out that they are also listed separately in the *Armenian Geography*.

130 Zeimal (1996, p. 120), equates the Chionites with the Kidarites, but this ignores the numismatic evidence of two parallel, but separate coinages, both beginning during the latter part of Shapur II's reign.

131 For variations of this reading see Alram 1999/2000, p. 131.

132 We are indebted to Nicholas Sims-Williams for reading the Bactrian legends on most of the British Museum coins discussed and illustrated here, viz. figs 80.4–7, 15–17; 83.2–6; 84.5, 7, 10. He suggests perhaps *xsoiadbo anono* for a coin of this type from Tope Kelan, Hadda (fig. 83.2a); while Nikitin suggests *xmaio abdagazo* for another example (Alram 1999/2000, pp. 144–5, issue 39, fig. 93). A second British Museum coin not seen by Sims-Williams also appears to start *xm-* (fig. 83.2b).

133 The Fitzwilliam Museum example of this type (not seen by Göbl) provides the clearest reading of the legend. Readings again courtesy of Sims-Williams.

134 According to Sims-Williams 2002a, p. 143, 'a well-attested abbreviation for χοαδηο', i.e. 'lord'.

135 *Jiu Tang shu* of Liu Xu (AD 887–946); *Tang hui yao* of Wang Pu (AD 922–82).

136 We are indebted to Nasim Khan for checking the inscription.

137 The name/title Narendraditya occurs also on a proto-Sharada temple inscription on white marble from Hund, which was found with a head of Vishnu, again of marble: see Nasim Khan 1998–9.

138 Our grateful thanks to Gudrun Melzer, who generously provided a pre-publication copy of her important article to read and refer to.

139 Kalhana's *Rājataraṅgiṇī* (III.102–3) – written c. AD 1148–50 – lists Toramana, but as one of the later kings of Kashmir. According to Kalhana's genealogy, he was the nineteenth ruler after Mihirakula (Stein 1892, vol. I, pp. 140–1). He is however credited by Kalhana with minting coins in his own name: silver and bronze coins in the name of Toramana found in Kashmir, which seem to be identifiable with this later king, imitate late Kushan designs of the standing king/seated Ardochsho.

140 Secure dates supplied by inscriptions for Gupta chronology of this period are Gupta years 157 (AD 476) and 165 (AD 484) for Budhagupta, and year 188 (AD 507–8) for his successor Vainyagupta: see Willis 2005, pp. 11–12, 15.

141 According to Michael Willis's revised genealogy (2005, pp. 16–17), Bhanugupta was probably not one of the imperial Guptas but a Later Gupta ruler.

142 We are indebted to Michael Willis and above all Harry Falk for the following translations: *Jayatu* = let him be victorious; *Jaya* = victory (if not a defective *jayatu*); *Jayatu vṛṣa* = let the *vṛṣa* (bull) be victorious; *Jayatu vṛṣadhvaja* = let he whose banner is the *vṛṣa* be victorious; *Udayaditya* = *udaya-aditya* = he who is the sun that rises; *Purvvaditya* = *purva-aditya* = he who is the sun in the east, i.e. the sun that rises, in other words, *udaya-aditya*.

143 According to Sims-Williams *mirosano* is attested in Bactrian documents and is equivalent to Persian Khurasan.

144 According to the twelfth-century *Rājataraṅgiṇī* (I.288–9, Stein 1892, vol. I, p. 140), his father's name was Vasukula.

145 Alram suggests c. AD 460–560 for their rule around Ghazni; with a second phase c. AD 515–650 marked by a move to Kabul following the death of Toramana (1999/2000, p. 148). But given the apparent paucity of coin finds of this type generally and at Begram specifically, it seems preferable to allow more time for the more prolific Shri Shahi coinage than the c. AD 600–20 he proposes.

146 Translated by V. S. Curtis.

147 Reported to have been of gold, but – as this is unlikely – they possibly may have been gilded (Lee and Sims-Williams 2003, pp. 171–2).

148 Previously calculated by Sims-Williams as c. AD 233; recent collaborative research between him and François de Blois has shown that the Bactrian era is synonymous with a Sasanian era instituted at the beginning of the reign of Ardashir I, i.e. AD 223/4 (Ancient India and Iran Trust lecture 7 June 2006).

149 The AD 702 date cited in the article has been corrected to AD 692, in line with the new dating of the Sasanian era to AD 223/4.

150 Inscribed in Brahmi *srī hitivara kharalāva pārameśvara śrī vahi tigina devakāri ṭaṃ*; Bactrian σπι βαυο; Pahlavi *hptwhpt't tgyn'hwr's'n mlk* (cf. Göbl 1967, type 208). Göbl 1967, vol. II, pp. 256–8, cites Ghirshman as the originator of this idea, which he contests, viewing the issue as a continuation of existing Hun coinage traditions.

151 'Ye-ta' according to Chavannes: actually Yenta > Yanda; *tch'e-k'in* > chiqin. Conversion into Pinyin courtesy of Wang Tao, see pp. 252–3.

152 This was either Leo I (AD 457–74) or Zeno (AD 474–91).

153 Small numbers of countermarked coins of Varhran V (AD 420–38) are also found (Göbl 1967, type 282).

154 Calculated in the era of AD 223/4.

155 Readings of Figure 84 coin legends courtesy of Nicholas Sims-Williams.

4 Religion

There are no facts, only interpretations.

(Nietzsche 1885–7, p. 315, f. 7[60])

The assimilation of Greek iconography

On the basis of the coinage, one would have expected to find Greek-style temples in Bactria. It therefore came as a great surprise that the architecture of the temples discovered at Ay Khanum owed nothing to Greek tradition. One of the most important, if not the principal, sanctuary . . . contained a massive temple 20 m × 20 m raised up on a high, three-stepped base with its outer walls decorated with indented niches . . . the burial of votive vases at the foot of the edifice indicates a ritual unparalleled in Hellenistic religion. . . . Inside . . . a large vestibule led into a smaller chapel flanked by two sacristies [Staviskij 1986, fig. 18]. Opposite the entrance stood the cult image. Outside the city walls . . . stood another temple with a closely related plan; . . . another sanctuary [was] built around a monumental stepped platform in the open which was clearly used as an altar. This last place of worship recalls directly Iranian religious sites, where, according to the descriptions of classical authors, the Iranians worshipped the forces of nature in high open places, without erecting any statues to personify them. (Bernard 1994, p. 115)

The plan of the sacred building at Jandial in Taxila illustrates, however, that Greek-style temples did exist, at least further south, for it comprises a typical peristyle, *pronaos* with Ionian columns at the entrance, *naos* and another, separate porch or *opisthodomos* at the rear (fig. 85; Marshall 1951, pp. 222–7, pl. 44). But even here there is a clear structural divergence, for between the *naos* and the *opisthodomos* is a solid mass of masonry with deep foundations to support a heavy superstructure, probably a tower. This evidence, together with the absence of any sculptural remains, led Marshall to propose that the flight of steps on one side led to a fire altar on top of the tower. Marshall also suggested that Jandial is identifiable as the Greek-style temple recorded by Philostratus (*c.* AD 171–247) at Taxila, but, if this was the case, the decorative panels are at odds with the identification of the temple as Zoroastrian (*Life of Apollonius* XI.20):

> They saw a temple in front of the wall, about 100 feet in length and built of shell-like stone. And in it was a shrine which, considering that the temple was so large and provided with a peristyle, was disproportionately small but nevertheless worthy of admiration; for nailed to each of its walls were bronze panels on which were portrayed the deeds of Porus and Alexander; the elephants, horses, helmets and shields are depicted in brass, silver, gold and copper, the lances, javelins and swords all in iron.

Although the Aï Khanum temples are not Greek in plan, the surviving fragment of the cult statue – a foot in a Greek sandal decorated with winged thunderbolts – found in the principal sanctuary, suggests that the deity either was Greek (possibly Zeus) or was, at least, portrayed in Greek form (Bernard 1994, p. 115). Possible confirmation that divinities of Greek origin

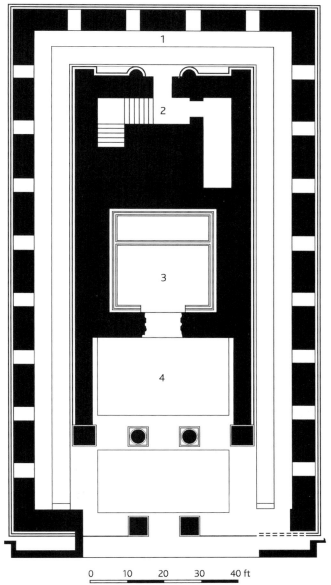

Figure 85 Plan of Jandial temple, Taxila. **1** peristyle; **2** *opisthodomos*; **3** *naos*; **4** *pronaos*.

were worshipped in Bactria comes from the second-century BC temple at Dal'verzin Tepe, which had painted images of the Dioscuri at the entrance to the shrine (Kruglikova 2004).

A number of contemporary objects – particularly toilet trays, coins and seals – survive as material evidence of the Greeks in Afghanistan and Gandhara, while the continued use of Greek iconography long after the Greeks had ceased to be a political power in these regions indicates that its influence was pervasive. The classical scenes of the stone palettes or toilet trays – Aphrodite chastising Eros, or Artemis and Acteon, for example – show moreover that the subject

Figure 86 Yellow soapstone toilet tray depicting Aphrodite chastising Eros (*c.* first century BC).

Figure 87 Gilded silver patera depicting the Triumph of Dionysus (*c.* first century AD).

matter was well known and understood (fig. 86; Errington and Cribb 1992, pp. 152–4).

Some of the surviving artefacts were clearly imported from the west, such as a third-century BC gilded silver medallion found at Aï Khanum, which is thought to be from northern Syria. It shows Cybele (earth goddess of fertility; protector of cities in war) and a winged Nike (Victory) in a chariot pulled by two lions facing a figure on a stepped altar, with Helios (the sun), a crescent moon and star above (Francfort 1984, pp. 93–104, pl. XLI). A series of bronze balsamaria or unguent vases in the form of busts of Athena, Hermes and Ares, and statuettes of Harpocrates, the Egyptian divinity of silence, excavated at Begram and Taxila, are considered later imports of *c.* first century BC to first century AD (Ghirshman 1946, pl. XII; Hackin and Hackin 1939, figs 47–59; Hackin *et al.* 1954, figs 322–5; Marshall 1951, no. 417, p. 605, pl. 186e; Errington and Cribb 1992, pp. 112–14).

There are also a number of small, mostly bronze, figurines and relief images of Greek divinities with a putative Afghanistan or North-West Frontier provenance, some of which may have been imported, while others appear to have been made locally (Errington and Cribb 1992, pp. 99–109, 115–16, 136–7). Typically, those suggestive of a non-western, possibly local, workshop may be iconographically correct, but disproportionate, like the thickset, wreathed Heracles statuette from Ai Khanum (Bernard 1974, p. 302, fig. 13). Or they may exhibit certain misunderstood iconographic details, like the silver patera of *c.* first century AD in the British Museum, which is decorated with embossed and gilded figures depicting the Triumph of Dionysus (fig. 87; Dalton 1964, no. 196 pp. 49–50, pl. XXVII).[1] A third group shows that indigenous divinities were syncretised with Greek gods and represented in Greek iconographic forms. At Takht-i-Sangin on the Amu Darya (Oxus river), for example, the inscription on a second-century BC votive pedestal supporting a statue of Silenus Marsyas playing a double flute[2] shows it was dedicated by the Iranian priest Atrosokes ('fire-brand') to the deity of the Oxus (Litvinsky and Pichikyan 1981, pp. 202–4).

But it is principally coins that exhibit an uninterrupted tradition of Greek religious iconography harnessed to underpin the authority of the rulers. The original Greek tradition – which continued, particularly on copper coins – was to use a divine image on both sides of the coin: issues of Alexander, for example, had the bust of Heracles on the obverse and the seated figure of Zeus on the reverse (fig. 36.2). The innovation of his successors was to replace the divine bust with Alexander's portrait, but in the guise of a god, with divine attributes such as the ram's horn of Zeus–Ammon or wearing an elephant-scalp head-dress and the *aegis* of Zeus around his neck (fig. 36.6–7; Errington and Cribb 1992, pp. 49–51, 55). They next introduced their own portraits, also often with divine attributes, but retained the image of the chosen beneficent deity on the reverse (fig. 43).

The Greco-Bactrians continued these conventions. It is the image of Zeus – the *aegis* over his left arm, the right raised to hurl a thunderbolt – that was adopted by the first king, Diodotus (*c.*250–230 BC), on his coins (fig. 52.1–2). According to Homer the *aegis*, a goatskin shield or cloak, 'girt with shabby fringe, awful, gleaming bright, . . . against which not even the lightning of Zeus can prevail', was given by the smith Hephaestus to Zeus 'to bear for the putting to rout of warriors', but was also used by Apollo and Athena (*Illiad* XV.222–30; XXI.400–2). It is depicted covered in scales and fringed with snakes, with a gorgoneion in the centre (Smith 1988, pp. 41–2). It had the power not only to terrify and put enemies to flight but also to protect friends.

Menander uses the same *aegis* and thunderbolt, but for the image of Athena on his principal coinage, and shows himself on the obverse of one issue hurling a javelin, with the *aegis* over his shoulder; and on another with his helmet seemingly covered by the *aegis* (figs 52.16; 53; Bopearachchi 1991, pls 26–7, 29–31, ser. 3–10, 15–16, 21–2). He also uses the helmeted head of Athena on the obverse with the reverse image of an owl, the *aegis* or Nike on other issues (Bopearachchi 1991, pls 26, 31, 33, ser. 1–2, 17–19, 31–3).

According to Smith (1988, pp. 41–2), the Hellenistic kings in the west 'effectively revived a Zeus association for the [*aegis*] attribute which had been appropriated by Athena [and gave] it a new royal form which associates the king of men with Zeus, king of the gods'. But this does not appear to have been the case in the east, where its strong association with Athena and its sense of evoking her protection appears to have been retained by Menander, copied by various successors and replaced by Zeus only on the coinage of Archebius (*c*.90–80 BC) (Bopearachchi 1991, pl. 51, ser. 9–10).

On Bactrian and Indo-Greek coinage, the Greek pantheon is generally limited to six key divinities or their attributes (Jones 1986, *passim*). These are, roughly in order of popularity:

1   Zeus, supreme god of the heavens; attributes: sceptre, shield/*aegis*, thunderbolt, eagle (figs 52.1–2, 7, 12; 54.5–6; 88.4), and, in one instance, elephant (fig. 54.2; for Alexander the Great and posthumous examples, see fig. 36.3–5)
2   Athena, *inter alia* goddess of war and wisdom; attributes: helmet, shield/*aegis*, owl (figs 52.16; 53; 54.4; 88.2; posthumous Alexander and Seleucid: figs 36.6–7; 43.1, 6)
3   Heracles, immortal son of Zeus and Alcmena, the epic hero of the Twelve Labours; attributes: lion skin, club (figs 52.3–6; 54.1; 88.8; Alexander and Seleucid: figs 36.2–5; 43.2).
4   Apollo, son of Zeus, god of prophecy, medicine and music; attributes: tripod – a symbol of prophetic power – bow and arrow, laurel branch (fig. 54.7, 9; 88.7; 114.1; Seleucid: fig. 43.3–4)
5   Nike, the personification of Victory, represented as a winged female figure, holding a wreath and a palm branch (fig. 52.15, 18; 54.2; Alexander and Seleucid: figs 36.1; 43.5)
6   A horseman, probably representing the deified Alexander (Cribb 2005), or a horse either representing his mount Bucephalus, or perhaps symbolising Poseidon (fig. 52.15; 54.3)

Other divinities appear far less frequently:

1   Poseidon, supreme god of the sea and land; attributes: trident, palm branch, dolphin, horse (figs 26.1; 53.25). The triton (fig. 54.8) can be taken as an allusion to Poseidon, but on coins of Telephus (*c*.60–55 BC) also refers to the ruler's namesake, a son of Heracles, who was set adrift with his mother in a chest on the sea, eventually reaching Mysia where he later became king and founded the city of Pergamum (Bopearachchi 1991, pl. 60, ser. 1)
2   Castor and Pollux/Dioscuri – the immortal twin sons of Zeus – associated with the constellation Gemini, and shown with spears, often mounted on horseback; attributes: twin caps each surmounted by a star, palm branches (fig. 52.9, 13–14)
3   Dionysus, god of wine and fertility; attributes: *thyrsus/ivy-entwined magic staff*, panther (figs 26.6; 52.8; 88.1)
4   Hermes, son and messenger of Zeus, originally a phallic god, patron of wayfarers and guide of the dead to Hades; attributes: winged *petasys*/traveller's hat and sandals, *caduceus*/herald's staff (fig. 88.2–3)
5   Tyche, goddess of fortune, chance and cities; attributes: cornucopia, *polos*/cylindrical head-dress, frond (fig. 54.8)
6   Helios, the sun – often identified with Apollo – is shown radiate and riding a quadriga only on coins of Plato (*c*.145–140 BC). Later Indo-Greeks of the first century BC appear to prefer depicting the equivalent Iranian god Mithra, radiate and wearing a Phrygian cap (fig. 52.11; 54.4)
7   Artemis, sister of Apollo, goddess of the hunt, cities, birth and fertility (attributes: bow, quiver). Although one of the most widely worshipped deities in the Greek world (Jones 1986, pp. 25–8), she is depicted by only three rulers: Diodotus, Demetrius I and Artemidorus (*c*.85 BC), the latter in evident allusion to the name of the king (fig. 88.4–5; Bopearachchi 1991, pl. 1, ser. 8–10; pl. 5, ser. 4; pl. 49)

Strabo exhibits a healthy scepticism regarding the myths about Dionysus and Heracles in India and suggests that in origin they were sycophant inventions to please Alexander (XV.i.7, 9):

> As for the stories of Heracles and Dionysus, Megathenes and a few others consider them trustworthy, . . . but most other writers . . . consider them untrustworthy and mythical. . . . But that these stories are fabrications of the flatterers of Alexander is obvious . . . from the fact that not even the intervening peoples, through whose countries Dionysus and their followers would have had to pass in order to reach India, can show any evidence that these made a journey through their country.

In Euripides' *Bacchae*, Dionysus is rescued from the dead body of his mother by Zeus; brought up by nymphs; and taught by Silenus and the satyrs the use of the vine and ivy (a mild intoxicant and symbol of everlasting life). He is then said to have led his followers – the maenads or bacchants – from Bactria to Greece (Euripides 13–19, 275–300, 555). But according to Arrian (V.i.1–2), when Alexander invaded 'the country between the rivers Cophen [Kabul] and Indus', i.e. the Peshawar Valley, he discovered Nysa, a city said to have been founded by Dionysus 'in the time when he subdued the Indians'.

Dionysus is also said to have named the nearby mountain 'Merus' (Arrian, V.i.6–8) – a direct reference to the metaphysical mount Meru, the axis of the universe in Indian cosmology – where Apollonius of Tyana putatively visited a shrine to the god in the first century AD (Philostratus II.8). But, as Brunt points out: 'ancient Greeks and Romans were always ready to identify foreign gods with their own on the basis of the most slender similarities of myth, cult or function, and it was surely such similarities in what they saw and heard of Indian practices and legends that suggested to them that Dionysus and Heracles had been active in India' (Arrian, *Indica*, appendix XVI.3, p. 437).

Given Dionysus' legendary connection with the east, it is perhaps surprising that there are few overt references to the deity on Greco-Bactrian coins. Only Pantaleon (*c*.190–185 BC) and Agathocles (*c*.190–180 BC) feature him and/or a panther (figs 26.6; 52.8; 88.1). Another, more cryptic reference – bull's horns – came into visual prominence as part of Dionysus' iconography in the Hellenistic period, when they were used to suggest unspecified Dionysus-like divine and royal powers of the king (Smith 1988, pp. 40–1). From the time of Seleucus I they appear – always with bull's ears – on the helmets of the kings (fig. 88.6). Their origin as a royal/divine attribute of the Seleucids is later linked to the physical prowess once shown by Seleucus in preventing a bull that Alexander was sacrificing from escaping. This feature was

Figure 88 Greek deities on coins:
1 Pantaleon (c.190–185 BC). Obv. head of Dionysus; rev. panther.
2 Diodotus (c.250–230 BC). Obv. head of Hermes; rev. Athena.
3 Demetrius I (c.200–190 BC). Obv. elephant's head; rev. caduceus.
4 Diodotus. Obv. head of Zeus; rev. Artemis.
5 Artemidorus (c.85 BC). Rev. Artemis with bow.
6 Seleucus I Nicator (312–281 BC) mint of Susa, excavated at Pasargadae. Obv. helmeted head of king; rev. Nike with trophy.
7 Menander I (c.155–130 BC). Obv. head of bull; rev. tripod.

8 Euthydemus II (c.190–185 BC). Rev. Heracles.
Iranian gods on Kushan coins:
9 Kanishka I (c. AD 127–50). Rev. Selene;
10 Rev. Mao;
11 Rev. Helios;
12 Rev. Miiro;
13 Rev. Hephaistos;
14 Rev. Athsho.
15 Huvishka (c. AD 150–90). Rev. Pharro.

adopted by Eucratides I and the later Indo-Greeks (fig. 52.10–11, 13).

There may be other implicit references, since the most common animal manifestation of Dionysus was the bull, and the Indian zebu (*bos indicus*), in particular, is one of the most popular images – together with elephants – on Bactrian and Indo-Greek coinage (fig. 26.9). On one issue of Menander I just the bull's facing head – a commonplace image on Greek mainland and island coins from the fourth to first century BC – is used in conjunction with a tripod and camel respectively

(fig. 88.7; Bopearachchi 1991, pl. 32, ser. 29–30). But it is impossible in these instances to determine the intended meaning: the bull as a representation of Dionysus; or as a reference to Heracles' seventh Labour (viz. the destruction of the Cretan Bull); or as a symbol of natural potency; or as Nandi, the mount of the Hindu god Shiva;[3] or as an intentionally multi-layered image, open to all or any of these interpretations.

Dionysiac themes are a far more common subject on drinking cups, bowls and reliefs (Errington and Cribb 1992,

Figure 89 Section of a schist panel depicting vine-scroll medallions enclosing an amorino holding a bunch of grapes. Gandhara (*c.* second to third century AD).

Figure 90 Schist relief of the tutelary couple, showing Panchika drinking from a kantharos and Hariti with a cornucopia, from Takht-i-Bahi, Gandhara (*c.* second to third century AD).

pp. 91–5, 97–8, 105, 115–16; Carter 1968, pp. 121–46). An actual bacchanalia scene on a frieze from one of the Gandharan Buddhist sites shows overhanging vines framing a fat, nude Silenus riding on a lion, maenads and two putti trying to persuade a panther to drink from a krater (Ingholt and Lyons 1957, fig. 397). However, although many of the scenes may be incorporated into an undulating vine- or leaf-scroll, they usually contain more generalised figures of drinkers, amorous couples, dancers and musicians, which owe as much to Indian as to Greek traditions (fig. 89; Zwalf 1996, pp. 248–51, 276–80, nos 334–9, 414–27).

In the Kushan period at Mathura a bacchanalian element is particularly associated with the cult of Kubera, the god of wealth, chief of the four yaksha kings (guardian spirits of earth's treasures) and lord of the northern quadrant (Rosenfield 1967, pp. 247–8, fig. 47). In Gandhara, Kubera is often fused with Panchika, general of the yaksha army, who is commonly shown with his consort, Hariti, goddess of fertility and smallpox. Depictions of Kubera–Panchika can also contain Dionysiac references: on the pedestal of the tutelary couple from Sahri Bahlol, there is a figure riding an ass, which could allude to Silenus; while an example from Takht-i-Bahi represents Panchika drinking from a kantharos (fig. 90; Errington and Cribb 1992, pp. 134–5).

The cult of Heracles appears to have been more potent and, from Strabo's account, seems to have been closely associated with Alexander (Strabo XV.i.6, 8):

> Megasthenes . . . says neither was an army ever sent outside the country of the Indians nor did any outside army ever invade their country and master them, except that with Heracles and Dionysus and that in our times with the Macedonians. . . . When Alexander, at one assault, took Aornus, a rock at the foot of which . . . the Indus River flows, his exalters said that Heracles thrice attacked the rock and thrice was repulsed; and that the [local] Sibae were the descendants of those who shared with Heracles in the expedition, and that they retained the badges of their descent, in that they wore skins like Heracles, carried clubs, and branded their cattle and mules with the mark of a club. And they further confirm this myth by the stories of the Caucasus and Prometheus, for they have transferred all this thither on a slight pretext, I mean because they saw a sacred cave in the country of the Paropamisadae; for they set forth that this cave was the prison of Prometheus and that this was the place whither Heracles came to release [him].

For the obverse of his coinage Alexander chose a portrait of Heracles wearing the lion scalp (fig. 36.2). This image was used by a few of the Seleucids – Seleucus I (312–281 BC) and Alexander II (128–123 BC) – but not by the Bactrian and Indo-Greeks, except on the pedigree coins of Agathocles, where the reference to Alexander is explicit (figs 36.5; Bopearachchi 1991, pl. 8, ser. 12). One of the most spectacular images in this genre is a marble head, which is thought to be a portrait of Mithradates VI (*c.*112–63 BC) of the independent kingdom of Pontus (Louvre MA 2321; Smith 1988, p. 171, no. 83, pl. 52.1–2). According to Smith (1988, p. 40):

> In Alexander's image, the lion scalp expressed a relationship and a comparison with Heracles, who was both his forebear and the model for the man-hero become god through earthly battles and virtues. For the few later kings who wear the lion scalp, it has a double or ambiguous evocation of Heracles and/or Alexander; but the latter was clearly the more important.

The elephant scalp head-dress – modelled on the lion scalp – is another Hellenistic innovation, first seen on posthumous coin portraits of Alexander (fig. 36.7; see p. 36). Smith notes that its use was 'open-ended' and non-specific. It could refer to 'eastern conquest in general and conquest of India in particular', and either to Heracles' or Dionysus' legendary conquests of these regions or to Alexander's, or to the later kings' own victories (fig. 52.6; Smith 1988, p. 41).

Many of the animals depicted on coins appear to be equally non-specific, as has already been noted with regard to bulls. Similarly, the boar's head on an issue of Menander copies a common enough image of mainland Greek coinage (Bopearachchi 1991, pl. 33, ser. 35–6). It could be interpreted as a reference to the fourth Labour of Heracles – the capture of the gigantic Boar of Mount Erymanthus – with the palm branch on the reverse signifying victory,[4] but in a Hindu context the boar is an *avatāra* (incarnation) of the Hindu god Vishnu, so any symbolism could be intentionally multi-faceted.

The Near Eastern sites of Arsameia on the Nymphaios, Nimrud Dagh, Dura Europos, Hatra and Palmyra have all produced evidence of Heraclean cults, usually – but not always – in association with other Oriental deities: with Nergal (Sumero-Babylonian god of the netherworld) at Palmyra and Hatra; and merged with Artagnes (Verethragna) and Ares at

Figure 91 Limestone relief depicting Mithradates I Kallinikos (c.100-70 BC) of Commagene with Artagnes-Heracles-Ares, from Socle III, Arsameia on the Nymphaios.

Figure 92 Detail of Naqsh-i Rajab relief of Ardashir I (AD 223/4-41) showing the future Varhran I with Heracles-Verethragna.

Arsameia on the Nymphaios and Nimrud Dagh (fig. 91; p. 118; Flood 1989, pp. 21–2). A bilingual inscription of the year 462 (AD 151) on the thighs of a bronze statue from Seleucia on the Tigris says that it was set up in the temple of Apollo (Parthian: *Tīr*) and identifies the figure in Greek as Heracles and in Parthian as Verethragna, the victorious warrior god of Zoroastrianism and Mithraism (Wiesehöfer 2001, p. 122, pl. XVIb). On the Sasanian relief of Ardashir I at Naqsh-i Rajab, Ardashir's grandson, the future Varhran I, appears in the presence of a nude Heracles–Verethragna (figs 92, 164; p. 116). The name Varhran (Bahram) is the same as Verethragna.

In Buddhism Heracles was assimilated with Vajrapani, attendant of the Buddha (figs 93–4); in Hinduism with Shiva (fig. 95), as well as with Krishna (a pastoral deity, synonymous with Vishnu) and his brother Balarama (Boyce and Grenet 1991, pp. 163–73; Errington and Cribb 1992, pp. 82, 132, 176). However, unlike that of other gods in the Greek pantheon, the depiction of the immortal hero remained consistent, despite his integration with the divinities of other religions. There is little difference, for example, between the representation of Heracles with a club, wreath and lion skin on silver tetradrachms of the Greco-Bactrian king Demetrius I (c.200–190 BC) (fig. 52.6) and that of Heracles as Verethragna on tetradrachms of the Parthian king Mithradates I (c.171–138 BC) (fig. 45.8), or the image labelled *HPAKIΛO* on bronze issues of the Kushan king Huvishka (c. AD 150–90) (fig. 61.21; Bopearachchi 1991, pl. 5, ser. 1; Wroth 1903, pl. III.7; Göbl 1984, types 889–91).

Only in the Buddhist art of Gandhara is there a change in attribute in representations of Vajrapani, with the club being replaced by the thunderbolt of Zeus and Indra (the Vedic war and weather god). When wielded by Vajrapani, the *vajra* or thunderbolt symbolises the 'victorious power of permanent Buddhist knowledge over the impermanence of illusion and evil . . . the truth of the Buddhist *dharma*, ready to crush every enemy', i.e. he features 'when force is necessitated' (Flood 1989, p. 24). Given the legendary Herculean prowess of Heracles, it is not surprising that not only is the influence of his iconography evident in representations of Vajrapani but in some cases the borrowing is explicit. In the *c.* third-century AD clay relief from Tapa Shotor, Hadda, for example, the bearded Vajrapani has the lion skin draped over his shoulder (fig. 93), while, in a British Museum relief, he wears a lion-skin head-dress, with the front paws knotted around his neck (fig. 94; Zwalf 1996, no, 293, pp. 44, 230–1; Flood 1989).

Perhaps the earliest image of Heracles harnessed as an acolyte of the Buddha is a gold medallion from Burial 4 at Tillya Tepe, dated *c.* first century BC to first century AD (Sarianidi 1985, pp. 188–9, 250, no. 25.III.131). It shows a nude, bearded figure, with the head of a lion draped over his right arm, its tail hanging down between his legs, pushing a large wheel. The Kharoshthi inscription *dharmacakrapravatako* ('he who sets in motion the Wheel of the Law') identifies the iconography specifically with Buddhism (Fussman 1987, pp. 71–2). The reverse is inscribed *siho vigatabhayo* ('the lion who chased away fear') and shows a lion standing with one paw raised, facing the 𝍊 motif. This symbol was long thought to represent the *triratna* ('three jewels' representing Buddha, the Law and the Buddhist community), but has been convincingly shown to

Figure 93 Clay relief depicting Vajrapani with a thunderbolt and lion skin from Tapa Shotor, Hadda (c. third century AD).

be nothing more than a *maṅgala*, i.e. an auspicious sign bringing good luck (Bénisti 2003, pp. 193–9). The Buddha is nevertheless evoked through the image of the lion – an intrinsically royal emblem, but also referring to the Buddha's title *Śākyasimha* ('lion of the Shakyas') – while Heracles, the man-hero become god through earthly battles and virtues, is perhaps representative of the trials all mortal disciples of the faith have to undergo to achieve salvation.

The Greek tradition of portraying gods on coins was adopted by their successors in the east, who also appropriated the iconography of Greek deities for their own gods. The images and attributes of Greek gods were adopted and adapted for representations of non Greek deities, not just on coins but also in sculpture, particularly in the Buddhist art of Gandhara. According to Herodotus (IV.59),

> The only gods [the Scythians] propitiate by worship are these: Hestia [goddess of the hearth and home] in especial, and secondly Zeus and Earth [Demeter, a sister of Zeus], whom they deem to be the wife of Zeus; after these, Apollo, and the Heavenly Aphrodite [goddess of love, sometimes war], and Heracles, and Ares [god of war]. All Scythians worship these as gods; and the Scythians called Royal sacrifice also to Poseidon. In the Scythian tongue Hestia is called Tabiti; Zeus (in my judgement rightly so called) Papaeus ['All-Father']; Earth is Api, Apollo Goetosyrus, the Heavenly Aphrodite Argimpasa, and Poseidon Thagimasadas. It is their practice to make images and altars and shrines for Ares, but for no other god.

Although Herodotus is speaking of Scythians in general, the evolutionary process of creating composite images of deities is evident on the coins of the Indo-Scythians. Maues (c.75–65 BC) uses the combined attributes of Zeus (a thunderbolt) and Poseidon (a trident) to represent a Shiva-

Figure 94 Schist relief fragment depicting Vajrapani in lion skin and holding a thunderbolt and a sword (c. second to third century AD).

like deity, with – on one issue – his foot resting on the shoulder of a river god (fig. 56.1). Similarly, although Azes I (c.46–1 BC) directly copies Indo-Greek depictions of Zeus, the god again holds the trident of Poseidon and Shiva (fig. 56.9; Errington and Cribb 1992, pp. 75, 85). These attributes are shared with later representations of Oesho, which suggests that this god may have already existed in the pre-Kushan period in the Hindu Kush region and was not therefore exclusive to the Kushans (Cribb 1997, p. 40).

The Kushans also appropriated the iconography of other Greek and Indian gods for their own Iranian deities. The process of assimilation is perhaps most apparent in the development of Oesho. In the Indian pantheon the deity was equated with Shiva and, as already noted, the same attributes of equivalent Greek gods, particularly Zeus, Poseidon and Heracles, were freely adopted for both (fig. 95; Cribb 1997,

Figure 95 Bronze Kushan seal (with its cast), from Begram, depicting Oesho/Shiva, Oesho and Umma (?)/Parvati, a Kushan worshipping at a fire-altar and Heracles (c. third century AD).

pp. 35–40). On issues of Wima Kadphises (c. AD 110–27) Oesho holds the lion skin of Heracles and a trident – the attribute of Poseidon, Mazdooano and Shiva (fig. 61.16; Cribb 1997, p. 54, A1) – while others of Wima Kadphises and those of Vasudeva I (c. AD 190–227) show him not only with the trident but also the diadem and bull of Shiva (fig. 61.17, 22–3), although the design appears to derive from that of Zeus standing beside an elephant on coins of the Indo-Greek king Antialcidas (c.115–95 BC) (fig. 54.2; Errington and Cribb 1992, pp. 74, 85–8).

A corresponding process – at least initially – was to assign Greek names to their equivalents in the Kushan pantheon. This is best seen on early issues of Kanishka I (c. AD 127–50), where identical depictions of the Kushan moon god in Iranian dress are first identified as the Greek Selene and later designated 'Mao' (Middle Persian *māh*); the sun god Mithra is first 'Helios', then 'Mioro'; and 'Hephaistos' (fire) becomes 'Athsho' (Middle Persian *ādur*; New Persian *ātash*; fig. 88.9–14). The traces – on a former Court collection coin of Kanishka – of the Greek legend ΗΡΑΚΛΗΣ ('Heracles') overcut by ΟΗΡΟ ('Oesho') in Bactrian (fig. 61.18) similarly link this deity to the more traditional – but unnamed – Heracles image on the coinage of the first Kushan king, Kujula Kadphises (figs 55.115–21; 61.5; Cribb 1997, pp. 35–6, 57, fig. G1). Although these gods are initially labelled as their Greek equivalents, they all fit within Herodotus' (I.130) and Strabo's (XV.iii.13) general descriptions of the Iranian practice of sacrificing to the sun, moon, fire, earth, winds and water (see below).

The Iranian tradition

> It is not [the Persians'] custom to make and set up statues and altars, . . . because they never believed the gods . . . to be in the likeness of men; but they call the whole circle of heaven Zeus, and to him they offer sacrifice on the highest peaks of the mountains; they sacrifice also to the sun and moon and earth and fire and water and winds. These are the only gods to whom they have ever sacrificed from the beginning; they have learnt later, to sacrifice to the 'heavenly' Aphrodite, from the Assyrians and Arabians. She is called by the Assyrians Mylitta, by the Arabians Alilat, by the Persians Mitra. . . . Rivers they chiefly reverence; they will neither make water nor spit nor wash their hands therein, nor suffer anyone so to do.
> (Herodotus I.130, 138)

Zoroastrianism is an ancient Iranian religion formulated by the prophet Zarathushtra (Zoroaster in Greek), who lived c.1200–1000 BC.[5] It preaches the ethical value of right conduct in achieving the final triumph of Good (Ahuramazda) over Evil (Angra Mainyu; Ahriman). Fire – a pure element – is the son of Ahuramazda and the symbol of the religion.

The doctrines of the religion are known through Zoroastrian texts under the collective name of the *Avesta*.[6] This originally consisted of 21 *nasks* or holy books written in an archaic east Iranian language which is called 'Avestan', since it is known only from this source. Only a very small proportion of the *nasks* has survived. A summary of them is preserved in the *Denkart*, a Pahlavi book of the ninth century. The *Gathas* – a collection of hymns or songs – are believed to have been composed by the prophet himself. They are placed within the *Yasna*, the liturgical part of the *Avesta*.[7] The 24 *Yashts* – which belong to an ancient pagan tradition – are hymns dedicated to deities or *yazatas*. The *Vispered* is a shorter liturgy, which more or less repeats what is already in the *Yasna*. The *Videvdad* ('Law against the Demons')[8] deals with ritual purity. The *Khordeh Avesta* ('Little *Avesta*') consists of prayers, blessings and invocations.

In the Sasanian period the *Avesta* was written in its original language, but with Pahlavi characters. The editing of the *Khordeh Avesta* is generally attributed to the time of Shapur II (AD 309–79), while a ninth-century source refers to the compilation of the entire *Avesta* under the high priest Veh-Shabur during the reign of Khusrau I (AD 531–79) (Boyce 2001, p. 135). The *Zand* – a Pahlavi commentary – was also produced at this time.

Actual Pahlavi texts – written in the sixth to ninth centuries – include the *Bundahishn*[9] ('Creation'), *Dādestān-i Mēnog-i Khrad* ('Judgement of the Spirit of Wisdom'), *Ardā Virāz Nāmag* (the spiritual journey of Viraz from 'the land of the living to the land of the dead'), *Zādspram* (which includes legends about Zarathushtra), *Dādestān-i Dīnīg* (92 questions about religious matters), 'Epistles of Manuchihr' and the *Dēnkard* ('Acts of the Religion'). In addition there are such sources as the *Tansar Namag*, which is the correspondence between Tansar, the high priest of Ardashir I (AD 223/4–41), and Gushnasp, a priest from Tabaristan in northern Iran. The *Shahnameh* ('Book of Kings'), completed in AD 1010 by the poet Firdowsi of Tus, in north-eastern Iran, is an epic poem written in New Persian, but based on the official Sasanian history, the *Khwaday Namag*. The Persian *Rivayats* consist of fifteenth- to seventeenth-century official letters and treatises by Persian priests in answer to questions raised by Parsee priests in India. Although the *Gathas* are attributed to Zarathushtra and the language of this section of the *Avesta* is supposed to be that of the prophet himself, most of the information about him and his family comes from Pahlavi sources, particularly the *Zādspram*.

In the *Gathas*, Zarathushtra talks about himself as a '*zaotar*', a fully qualified priest (fig. 96), and a '*manthran*', someone who has the power of utterance (Boyce 2001, p. 18). When revelation came to him at the age of thirty – according to later Pahlavi texts – he declared that, as a worshipper of Ahuramazda, the Creator of All, he would 'teach men to seek the right (*asha*)' (*Yasna* 28.4, cf. Boyce 2001, pp. 19–20). It is

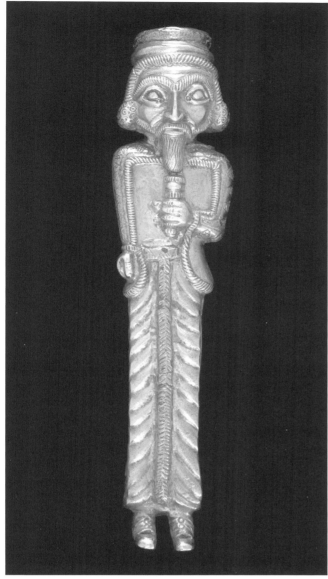

Figure 96 Gilded silver Achaemenid statue of a figure holding the *barsom*, from the Oxus Treasure.

Ahuramazda, but they were demoted to the status of lesser *ahuras* and as creations of the Wise and Supreme Lord (Boyce 2001, p. 23). Ahuramazda is therefore the creator of all things, both in the spiritual (Avestan *mēnog*; New Persian *mīnū*) and material (Avestan *gētig*; New Persian *gītī*) sense. Through the Holy Spirit (Spenta Mainyu), which is inseparable from him, Ahuramazda gives existence to his creations and is helped by six divine and immortal beings, the Amesha Spentas, who together with the Wise Lord and the Holy Spirit form a *heptad* (unit of seven). They are Khshathra Vairya, Spenta Armaiti, Haurvatat, Ameretat, Vohu Manah and Asha Vahishta, who together are (*Yasht* 19.16–18; Boyce 2001, p. 23)

> of one mind, one voice, one act. . . . Of them one beholds the soul of the other, thinking upon good thoughts, good words, good deeds . . . they who are the creators and fashioners and makers and observers and guardians of the creations of Ahuramazda.

The six holy immortals and Ahuramazda are linked with seven holy creations (Boyce 2001, pp. 23–4):

1   Khshathra Vairya ('Desirable Kingdom'; New Persian: Shahrivar) looks after the sky, which is made of hard stone
2   Spenta Armaiti ('Holy Devotion'; New Persian: Esfand) protects the Earth
3   Haurvatat ('Good Health'; New Persian: Khordad) looks after water
4   Ameretat ('Long Life', 'Immortality'; New Persian: Mordad) tends the plants
5   Vohu Manah ('Good Purpose'; New Persian: Bahman) cares for the cow
6   Asha Vahishta ('Best Righteousness', *asha*, the truth; New Persian: Ordibehesht) protects fire, the holiest of all elements. Fire is also the son of Ahuramazda and the symbol of the religion
7   Ahuramazda himself (figs 65; 164) watches over human beings

After the act of Creation (Pahlavi *Bundahishn*), when existence was both immaterial (*menog*) and material (*getig*), Angra Mainyu (Ahriman), the Evil Spirit and falsehood, began to attack the Holy Spirit, Spenta Mainyu, and righteousness (*asha*).

Goodness and righteousness, as well as falsehood and lies (*drug*), exist within each human being and it is up to the individual to choose between good or evil. In their quest for truth and opposition to falsehood, they are assisted by divine beings, *yazata* (New Persian *izad*), who in pagan times played a more prominent role. Prayers to the *yazatas* appear in the *Yasht* (Darmesteter 1975), where each divine being is vividly described. The help of the *yazatas* in the human moral struggle against evil is fundamental to Zarathushtra's doctrines (Boyce 2001, p. 26).

Khvarenah (Old Persian *farnah*; Middle Persian *khvarrah*, New Persian *farr*) is the Divine Glory (fig. 97.3–7), which appears in the shape of the Veregna bird and is bestowed upon the righteous rulers of Iran (*Yasht* 19; Boyce 2001, p. 40). The *khvarenah* is protected by the most important *yazatas*, Verethragna (*Yasht* 14), Anahita (*Yasht* 5) and Mithra (*Yasht* 10), as well as by Atar, the *yazata* of fire and Ashi (also known as Ashi Vanguhi, the 'good' Ashi), the *yazata* of fortune (*Yasht* 17; Boyce 2001, p. 10).

not clear where Zarathushtra came from exactly, but he seems to have preached in northern Central Asia, perhaps Choresmia. The *Avesta* mentions, in this connection, a place called Rhaga, which is traditionally associated with ancient Rhages, south of Tehran, but recent research suggests it was probably in northern Pakistan (Grenet 2005, pp. 36–8). According to the *Yasna*, the prophet was persecuted in his homeland, where his unpopularity was probably a result of his attempts to reduce the power of the 'evil' pagan gods, and his proclamation of Ahuramazda, the Wise Lord, as the sole creator (Zaehner 1961, p. 33).

In the ancient, pagan religion the gods gave protection, support and prosperity only to those who provided offerings, not to the poor. Accordingly, in this pre-Zoroastrian religion, only the powerful and wealthy who could afford to sacrifice to the gods were promised salvation at the end of time. The reform brought about by Zarathushtra was to declare Ahuramazda as the creator of all, and to preach that humankind should follow righteousness (*asha*), the path of truth. All other *ahuras* (Avestan *ahura*; Vedic *asura*: 'Lord') – i.e. the benevolent pagan gods Mithra, Apam Napat, Sraosha, Ashi and Geush Urvan – were still worshipped together with

Figure 97 Coins with Iranian imagery. Fratarakas and kings of Persis:
1 Bagadad (Bagadates) (early third century BC). Rev. enthroned king holding a staff; and
2 Rev. king worshipping before a building.
3 Vadfradad I (Autophradates, early third century BC). Rev. figure with diadem crowns king worshipping before building, winged figure (*khvarnah*) above.
4–5 Vadfradad II (Autophradates, *c.* third to second century BC). Obv. king in soft hat with eagle on top; rev. king before building, *khvarnah* above, eagle standard right.
6–7 Vadfradad III (Autophradates, *c.* second century BC). Obv. diademed head of king, crescent above; rev. king before building, *khvarnah*, eagle standard.
8 Darev II (Darius, *c.* second century BC), in Parthian *kolah*/tiara. Rev. figure worshipping at fire altar.

9 Ardashir (*c.* second century AD), in crenellated crown. Rev. figure at fire altar.
10 Manchihr (*c.* late second to early third century AD). Obv. king in *kolah*; rev. king's father, Manchihr II (?) in bird hat.
Indo-Scythian coins:
11 Maues (*c.* 75–65 BC). Obv. Helios and charioteer in chariot; rev. Zeus seated; and
12 Obv. Artemis; rev. bull.
Kushan coins:
13 Kanishka I (*c.* AD 127–50). Rev. Mozdooano riding a double-headed horse.
Huvishka (*c.* AD 150–90):
14 Rev. Nana and Oesho;
15 Rev. Nanashao;
16 Rev. Nana as Artemis;
17 Rev. Ardochsho.

Verethragna or Varhran (Bahram) is the warrior god (figs 45.8; 92), the victorious force against Evil. In *Yasht* 14 Verethragna assumes ten different forms, including a wild boar, a white horse, a camel, a swift bird and a man holding a sword with a golden blade (V. S. Curtis 1993, p. 13). The prayers to Ardvi Sura (Anahita, goddess of fertility and water) are in *Yasht* 5, where she is described as coming down from the

stars, wearing a gold-embroidered mantle and a crown with stars and fillets (figs 66.17–18; 71.1–2; 74.15; V. S. Curtis 1993, pp. 12–13).

Classical authors like Strabo – who evidently used Herodotus as one of his sources (see p. 114) – clearly associated the Medes and the Persians with Zoroastrianism (Strabo XV.iii.13–15):

But the Persian customs are the same as those of . . . [the peoples of] the countries of Persis and Susis [Susa] . . . and the Medes and several other peoples. . . . Now the Persians do not erect statues or altars, but offer sacrifice on a high place, regarding the heavens as Zeus; and they also worship Helios, whom they call Mithras, and Selenê and Aphroditê, and fire and earth and winds and water; and with earnest prayers they offer sacrifice in a purified place. . . . But it is especially to fire and water that they offer sacrifice.

It is, however, disputable whether the Achaemenids were Zoroastrians or not. While some associate the ideology of the Achaemenid kings with the religion (Zaehner 1961, pp. 154–61; Boyce 2001, pp. 51–3; Shahbazi 1994, pp. 89–90, 2004, pp.103–17; Skjaervø 2005, pp. 52–9, 80–1), others argue that Zoroastrianism was one of the religions of the Achaemenid period; that the Achaemenid kings worshipped Ahuramazda, but other gods also played a prominent role (Razmjou 2004, pp. 103–17; 2005, pp. 150–1). This theory is derived from information about the various Babylonian, Elamite and Iranian gods on the Elamite Fortification and Treasury tablets found at Persepolis, which date to the reign of Darius. These neo-Elamite tablets, which date from the thirteenth to twenty-eighth year of the reign of Darius, for example, frequently mention Mithra/Elamite Mishebaka (Razmjou 2004, p. 109).

As there is no evidence of any state religions in the ancient Near East at this time – just as none existed earlier under the Babylonians or Assyrians – it is unlikely that Zoroastrianism was the state religion of Achaemenid Iran. Nevertheless, the many similarities between the ideology of Achaemenid royal inscriptions and that of the religious texts are difficult to dismiss (Skjaervø 2005, pp. 53–81). Moreover, the absence of any reference to Zarathushtra in Achaemenid inscriptions cannot be considered an indication that the kings were not Zoroastrian, since prophets are not usually mentioned in such contexts (Zaehner 1961, p. 155; Boyce 2001, pp. 56–7).

The only inscription definitely known to have been written by Cyrus himself (550–530 BC) is the Cyrus Cylinder, but it is written in Babylonian cuneiform and follows the tradition of Babylonian official documents, so sheds little light on his religious affiliations (Wiesehöfer 2001, pp. 49–50).[10] His policies in the lands he occupied and his treatment of the conquered peoples of Mesopotamia indicate that he was a tolerant ruler who did not impose his religion on others. He is hailed as a just and liberal ruler in the Old Testament, called the 'Lord's anointed . . . the messiah', and is said to have followed 'the path of truth' (Isaiah 45.1; Ezra 1.13). The phraseology in Isaiah (42.3–4; 45.8, 12), regarding the concept of truth and justice, and the creation of light, darkness, earth and humankind, for example, is moreover thought by some scholars to reflect Zoroastrian influence on the Old Testament in the time of the post-Exilic period and the liberation of Jews under Cyrus (Boyce 2001, p. 52).

The Zoroastrian affiliations of his successors are more explicit. The Old Persian inscriptions of Darius and his son Xerxes refer to Ahuramazda as the sole Creator of all, who bestowed kingship, who protected the kingdom from famine and untruth. Darius, the king of kings, is a friend of truth and an enemy of falsehood, while Xerxes, his son, 'destroyed that sanctuary of the *daivā* [false gods]' and proclaimed that only Ahuramazda and Arta (Truth) should be worshipped (XPh, § 4b.36; Kent 1953, p. 151).

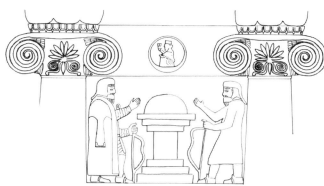

Figure 98 Relief above a rock-cut tomb at Qizqapan, showing figures worshipping at a fire altar.

The tombs of the Achaemenid kings at Pasargadae, Naqsh-i Rustam and Persepolis are built in the Zoroastrian tradition of not contaminating the holy elements with the impure dead body. The tombs at Naqsh-i Rustam and Persepolis depict, *inter alia*, paying homage to the sacred fire, above which is shown the winged disk, probably a symbol of the God-given Glory (fig. 163). In the relief above the entrance to the tomb of Darius at Naqsh-i Rustam, the king is seen standing before a fire altar. The scene is framed by narrow panels, in which six figures are set one above the other, three to each side (Schmidt 1970, pl. 60). According to Mary Boyce (2001, p. 58), these figures

represent the six noble Persians who helped Darius to gain the throne, who thus stand on either side of the Great King as the six Amesha Spentas stand, according to the Pahlavi books, on either side of Ahuramazda. Darius thus declared visually, it is suggested, his conviction that he ruled as Ahuramazda's representative on earth.

When the Persian calendar was reformed around 441 BC under Artaxerxes I (465–424 BC), the months were named after Zoroastrian deities (Zaehner 1961, p. 155). Royal inscriptions from the time of Artaxerxes II (404–359 BC) show, on the other hand, a revival of the pagan tradition of worshipping a variety of gods, for the king prays not just to Ahuramazda but also to Anahita and Mithra (A²Sd, §§ 2–4; Kent 1953, p. 155). At Hamadan, for example, Artaxerxes II invokes Mithra's protection (A²Hb; Kent 1953, p. 155); while his inscription at Susa states (A²Sa § 2.2–4; Kent 1953, p. 154):

This place Darius my great-great-grandfather built, under Artaxerxes my grandfather it was burned; by the favour of Ahuramazda, Anaitis, and Mithras, this palace I built. May Ahuramazda, Anaitis and Mithras protect me from all evil.

Like his father, Artaxerxes III also venerated Mithra, as proclaimed in his inscription at Persepolis: 'Me may Ahuramazda and the god Mithra protect, and this country, and what was built by me' (A³Pa; Kent 1953, p. 156).

Despite the conquest of Alexander and the collapse of the Achaemenid empire in 330 BC, the imagery found on various monuments and objects illustrates a continuity in Persian religious practices. At Qizqapan, for example, a relief above a rock-cut tomb shows figures worshipping on either side of a fire altar, one of whom has a long-sleeved coat slung over his shoulders and holds a bow in his right hand (fig. 98). The scene recalls Achaemenid prototypes (fig. 164).

The iconography on coins of the local kings of Persis, who used the title *frataraka*/governor and ruled Fars in southern Iran under the Seleucids in the early third century BC, displays strong associations both with Persepolis and Zoroastrian imagery (De Jong 2003, pp. 191–202). On one issue Bagadates is shown seated and holding a sceptre in the Achaemenid tradition (fig. 97.1). On others the king is depicted standing in front of a building, with the *khvarrah*[11] – the symbol of Divine and Kingly Glory – appearing above the turrets (fig. 97.3–4). On another coin the king's crown is decorated with a bird (fig. 97.5), probably the Veregna bird, which according to the *Avesta*, was the protector of the Divine and Kingly Glory (*Yasht* 19.vii.34–6).

The local kingdom of Commagene in south-eastern Anatolia had been a province of the Achaemenids and Seleucids, but gained independence *c*.163 BC. Here a distinctive form of religious dualism had evolved by the mid first century BC with Mithradates I Kallinikos (*c*.100–70 BC) and his son Antiochus I Theos (*c*.70–36 BC) claiming divinity and descent from a combined Persian and Greek ancestry and worshipping a syncretic mixture of Iranian and Greek gods. At Arsameia on the Nymphaios and at Nimrud Dagh, images of the king in Iranian dress are shown in the presence of Zeus–Ormasdes (Greek Zeus and Iranian Ahuramazda), Apollo–Mithra–Helios–Hermes (Greek gods of light, the sun and wayfarers, with Iranian Mithra) and Artagnes–Heracles–Ares (Iranian Verethragna, with the Greek immortal hero and god of war) (Curtis 1988, pp. 355–9). Long Greek inscriptions at Nimrud Dagh, the dynastic shrine of Antiochus, refer to his Persian and Macedonian ancestors (Dörner and Goell 1963, pp. 70–1; Waldmann 1973, p. 145). A relief from his mausoleum depicts his Iranian ancestors, Darius and Xerxes (fig. 99; Humann and Puchstein 1890, pls XXX.3, XXXVI.1), while an inscription from Arsameia on the Nymphaios orders the priests to wear Persian dress on his and his father's birthdays (Dörner and Goell 1963, p. 47).

Mithradates Kallinikos is shown clasping the right hand of Heracles–Ares–Verethragna at Arsameia on the Nymphaios (fig. 91) and Antiochus also apparently appears in the same way with Apollo–Mithra at Nimrud Dagh, but the relief is damaged (Rosenfield 1967, figs 151, 154). This gesture, the *dexiosis*, is known from both the Roman and the Iranian worlds and symbolises the ratification of an oath (Boyce and Grenet 1991, p. 317). In Zoroastrianism the act of *hamazor* (New Persian *ham-zur*, 'one strength') is usual amongst priests. It is possible that the handshake between the king and a deity shown on Parthian coins – particularly those of Phraates IV (*c*.38–2 BC) – refers to the Zoroastrian *hamazor* (fig. 48.11; Curtis 2004).

The Arsacid Parthians also introduced a Hellenistic-inspired anthropomorphic iconography, following their conquest of the former Achaemenid empire from the Seleucids in the mid second to early first century AD. But instead of understanding this iconography in a purely Greek context, it is possible to interpret the scenes and motifs from an Iranian religious perspective (Boyce 2001, p. 82). The nude Heracles on the reverse of tetradrachms of Mithradates I (*c*.171–138 BC) should probably be seen as Verethragna, the victorious god of *Yasht* 10 (fig. 45.8). The goddess resembling the Hellenistic Tyche (goddess of fortune), who offers Orodes II (57–38 BC) a palm frond (fig. 48.8), may be the Iranian Anahita (*yazata* of All Waters), or Ashi (*yazata* of Fortune), while on coins of

Figure 99 Relief from the mausoleum of Antiochus I Theos (*c*.70–36 BC) at Nimrud Dagh, depicting his Iranian ancestors, Darius and Xerxes.

Phraates IV the bird behind the king's head, sometimes with a diadem in its beak, is perhaps the Avestan Veregna bird (fig. 48.13; Curtis 2004).

References to fire temples in the Parthian period come from Greek writers such as Strabo (XV.iii.15):

> They also have Pyraetheia [fire temples], noteworthy enclosures; and in the midst of these there is an altar, on which there is a large quantity of ashes and where the Magi keep the fire ever burning. And there, entering daily, they make incantations for about an hour, holding before the fire a bundle of rods and wearing round their heads high turbans of felt, which reach down over their cheeks far enough to cover their lips.

Isidore of Charax, writing in the first century BC, mentions in his *Parthian Stations* that the town of Asaak – which is associated with the first Parthian king Arsaces – had an eternal fire burning (Boyce 2001, p. 87). Some of the ostraca from Nisa, the early Parthian capital now in Turkmenistan, contain references to *ayazan* (holy places or shrines) which 'may have held a fire consecrated for the soul of a dead ruler' (Boyce 2001, p. 90). The months' and days' names on the first-century BC ostraca from Nisa are also Zoroastrian (Duchesne-Guillemin 1983, p. 868). The fire temple at Kuh-i Khwaja in south-eastern Iran is also associated with the Parthian period (Boyce 2001, p. 86). The nearby Lake Hamun has been identified as Lake Kasaoya where – according to Zoroastrian texts – the Saoshyant (Saviour) is expected to appear.

According to the Middle Persian *Denkard*, it was the Parthian king Vologases I (*c*. AD 51–78) (fig. 50.6) who had the various Avestan traditions gathered together (Boyce 2001, p. 94):

> Valaksh, the Arsacid, commanded that a memorandum be sent to the provinces [instructing them] to preserve, in the state in which it had come down in [each] province, whatever had survived in purity of the Avesta and [its] Zand, and also every teaching deriving from it which, scattered by the havoc and disruption of Alexander, and by the pillage and looting of the Macedonians, had survived, whether written or in authoritative oral transmission.

Vologases appointed his younger brother Tiridates, a practising Zoroastrian, as king of Armenia in AD 62. It was only much later in the Sasanian period that Christianity replaced Zoroastrianism as the principal religion in this region (see p. 76).

In the east evidence for the religious affiliations of the early Kushans (first to second century AD) comes from the ceremonial building of mud-brick excavated at Khalchayan in Uzbekistan. In plan it resembles the principal temple at Aï Khanum (p. 107, fig. 44), while the sculptural clay friezes depict the enthroned ruler and his family with busts of their protector divinities above, as well as armed horsemen with bows and spears and other subsidiary figures (Staviskij 1986, pp. 226, 243, figs 18, 30–1, pls XIX–XX). The divinities appear in the Greek form of Heracles (the immortal hero), Nike (Victory) and a helmeted Athena (goddess of war and wisdom). One other divine image included in the reliefs is a radiate, crowned goddess in a horse-drawn chariot. The crown emitting rays of light identifies her with Artemis, twin sister of Apollo, as depicted on coins of several Greco-Bactrian/Indo-Greek kings and the Indo-Scythian Maues, who is here assimilated with the Iranian Anahita in her guise as goddess of war, riding in a chariot (p. 109, figs 88.4–5; 97.11–12; Bopearachchi 1991, pl. 1, ser. 8–10; pl. 5, ser. 4; pl. 49; Mit. 708, 712; Rosenfield 1967, p. 87). The image is also affiliated with that of Cybele riding a chariot pulled by lions on a silver medallion from Aï Khanum (p. 108).

Khalchayan is best interpreted as a small dynastic temple serving a similar function as the principal Kushan dynastic shrines of Surkh Kotal and Mat. Its identification as Kushan derives from the striking resemblance between the portrait of the Khalchayan ruler and that on the 'Heraus' issues – predominantly found north of the Oxus – of the Kushan king identified as Kujula Kadphises (c. AD 40–90) (figs 60; 61.1–3; Cribb 1993, pp. 119, 130–1; p. 67 above). It is perhaps noteworthy in this respect that Heracles also appears as the divine protector of Kujula on the reverse of his main coinage, which imitates issues of the Indo-Greek king Hermaeus (figs 26.2; 61.5). Evidence of the syncretic merging of Heracles with the Kushan god Oesho comes from coin of Kanishka, where the image of the god originally bore the apellation ΗΡΑΚΛΗΣ, but was later recut to read ΟΗϷΟ (fig. 61.18; pp. 113–14).

Like Khalchayan, Surkh Kotal faces towards the rising sun. It is located on a high hill c.15 km north-west of Pul-i Khumri in Baglan Province, Afghanistan, and has a monumental staircase leading up a series of four terraces to a peripteral-style temple at the top (Staviskij 1986, pp. 221–4, fig. 29, pls XIV, XVb, XVIIb). The Bactrian inscription from the site identifies the shrine as the 'the abode of the gods' (βαγολαγγο 'bagolango') of the 'victorious' (or 'victory of')

Kanishka, probably founded by Kanishka I (c. AD 127–50) and repaired by Nukunzuk in year 31 (c. AD 158) during the early reign of Huvishka (c. AD 150–90) (Fussman 1989, p. 196; Staviskij 1986, pp. 236–7; Sims-Williams and Cribb 1995/6, p. 109). The principal monument – set on a podium – comprises a cella containing a central platform and surrounded on three sides by a corridor. The building was identified as a fire temple by Schlumberger, but there is no evidence for this, or for the supposition that it was a Shaivite temple (Rosenfield 1967, pp. 154–63; Fussman 1989, pp. 197–8). It was subsequently abandoned and, later, two smaller shrines – identified as fire temples – were built, one against the southern courtyard wall, the other adjoining it but outside the enclosure (Fussman 1989, p. 197; Staviskij 1986, p. 223). The location of the sites accords with Strabo's description (XV.iii.13; p. 117 above) of the Iranian religious custom of offering 'sacrifice on a high place'; a practice which is visually represented on coins of Wima Kadphises and Huvishka by placing the bust of the Kushan king or his seated figure on a rocky mountain top (figs 61.16, 20; 88.15).

The Rabatak inscription – which also mentions Kanishka and Nukunzuk – was found on a hill in Baghlan, not far from Surkh Kotal, 40 km north of Pul-i Khumri (Sims-Williams and Cribb 1995/6, p. 75). But here the references to Kanishka founding a bagolango and Nukunzuk leading the worship are explicit (Rabatak §§ 7–11; Sims-Williams and Cribb 1995/6, pp. 78–9):

> Then King Kanishka gave orders . . . to make a sanctuary [βαγολαγγο] for these gods, . . . the lady Nana and the lady Umma, Aurmuzd, the Gracious one [μοζδοοανο], Sroshard, Narasa [and] Mihr. And he likewise gave orders to make images of these gods.

The Iranian religious affiliations of the Kushans are clearly stated by the traditional image on the coins of this dynasty – from Wima Kadphises (c. AD 113–27) onwards – of the standing king making an offering at a fire altar (figs 61.17–28; 74.1–2). The Rabatak inscription 'makes it clear that the gods worshipped by the Kushans and seen as the source of their power are of Iranian origin. They represent what could be described as a quasi-Zoroastrian pantheon, resembling, but not precisely matching, the divine figures of the Zoroastrian religion later practised by the Sasanians' (Cribb 1998, p. 89). However, since there was no existing Iranian tradition of cult imagery, the Kushans – like the Parthians and other contemporaries – appropriated the anthropomorphic forms of the nearest equivalents, not just in Hellenistic iconography but also in Near Eastern and other traditions. As Rosenfield has pointed out (1967, p. 72):

> Deities from the Iranian culture sphere predominate. . . . The deities themselves are, however, strangely mixed, for they seem to have come from different levels of religious experience. Some of them – especially the highly abstract Ameša Spentas – were based on the ethical doctrines of Zoroastrianism. . . . Others seem to reflect a more popular form of Mazdaism, rooted in such nature deities as Nana and Mao.

The divinities immediately recognisable as Iranian in the Rabatak inscription are Ahuramazda, Sraosha (*yazata* of Obedience, guardian of prayer and – with Mithra – one of the judges of the soul after death), Nairyosanha/Narseh (the messenger *yazata*) and Mithra (Boyce 2001, pp. 116, 250). The identifications are not without problems however. An insert in smaller writing on the inscription seems to identify two of the last three inappropriately with the Hindu gods Mahasena and Vishakha (both variant forms of the warrior god Skanda/Karttikeya).

'Muzhduwan' (μοζδοοανο, i.e. Mozdooano) – a name thought probably to derive from 'Mazdah vano' ('Mazdah the triumphant') – is usually a Bactrian epithet for Ahuramazda (Rosenfield 1967, p. 83), but here may refer to the supreme Kushan god Oesho, usually depicted on coins in the guise of Shiva (Sims-Williams and Cribb 1995/6, pp. 85, 108–9). Some support for this interpretation comes from later Kushano-Sasanian coins which label the image of Oesho and bull as βορζοανδο βαγο or οορζοανδο ιαζαδο (borzoando bago/oorzoando iazado), variously translated as 'exalted deity' or 'supreme lord' (fig. 74.12, 20), a terminology with certain affiliations to Mozdooano (Errington and Cribb 1992, pp. 86–7, no. 93; Cribb 1997, pp. 29–30). On a rare issue of Kanishka, Mozdooano rides a double-headed horse, carries a trident and appears bearded, diademed and probably wearing a Phrygian cap (fig. 97.13). The combination of horseman and possible Phrygian cap recall the attributes of the chosen divine image – usually identified as Mithra – on the Soter Megas issues of Wima Tak[to] (fig. 61.14–15).

'Umma' (ομμο) appears as the consort of Oesho on coins of Huvishka, as does Nana (figs 97.15; 113.12). Her inclusion in the Rabatak inscription may serve as an epithet of the latter deity, rather than an appearance in her own right as the better known Hindu Uma, the consort of Shiva (Sims-Williams and Cribb 1995/6, p. 84). Nana – labelled Nanaia on Kanishka's earliest issues – appears in the inscription as the foremost deity of the Kushan pantheon, which corresponds to her alternative title Nanashao ('Royal Nana') (fig. 97.14) and the image of the Kushan king kneeling before her on a rare coin of Huvishka (Sims-Williams and Cribb 1995/6, p. 108). The cult of this nature goddess of abundance and prosperity can be traced back to the ancient Mesopotamian Innana–Ishtar, the Lady of Heaven, from which association also derives the image of her seated on a lion (fig. 61.20). At third-second-century BC Dura Europos, second-century BC Susa and on a coin of Huvishka she is assimilated – like the Iranian Anahita – with the huntress Artemis (fig. 97.16; Rosenfield 1967, pp. 85–6, pl. VI.141). Initially she appears on Kushan coinage concurrently with, but is later replaced by, Ardochsho – another goddess of good fortune and abundance, except in a more political and dynastic sense – who becomes, with Oesho, the dominant deity of the later Kushans, and is shown holding a diadem and the cornucopia of Tyche (figs 61.24–8; 97.17; Rosenfield 1967, p. 75).

In the Iranian tradition Ardochsho is the daughter of Ahuramazda and sister of Sraosha, Rashnu and Mithra, whose adherents 'are kings of kingdoms that are rich in horses . . . [victory and] all sorts of desirable things' (Yasht 17, cf. Rosenfield 1967, p. 74). She is more closely equated with Anahita than is Nana, but it is quite possible all three were syncretised to a greater or lesser extent at various times. Given Anahita's importance in the Iranian world, it is unlikely she was so completely absent from the Kushan pantheon as the nomenclature implies (Rosenfield 1967, p. 89).

Like Nana, several other deities of the Kushan pantheon depicted on coins of Kanishka and Huvishka primarily

Figure 100 Schist roundel showing the seated Buddha with flaming shoulders (c. third century AD), excavated by J. G. Gerard from Takht-i Shah near Kabul in 1834.

represent nature and the elements (figs 61.19; 88.9–15): Oado (wind), Mao (moon), Mioro (sun), Athsho (fire) and Pharro (personification of the Iranian khvarenah/khvarrah, as well as messenger of the gods, and god of good fortune, fire and wealth). The supreme Kushan god, Oesho, also seems to be the anthropomorphic manifestation of another Iranian wind god, the Avestan Vayu or Vaiiush Uparo Kairiio, the wind that blows in the upper regions (figs 61.16–18, 22–3; 95; Humbach 1975; Errington and Cribb 1992, p. 87; Cribb 1997, p. 29). Use of the same iconography has led to Oesho being simply labelled as Shiva, but the interchangeability of attributes obscures the differences in origin, function and religious affiliation between the two deities. As far as Oesho is concerned (Cribb 1997, p. 37):

> The clearest confirmation of the Iranian nature of this god is his continued depiction by the Sasanian princes who conquered Kushan territory and adopted the title Kushanshah. . . . The name given to the god by these princes [i.e. the 'high god' or 'god who occupies the high place'; p. 119] . . . show a close linkage between their perception of his identity and that of Vayu.

The Kushano-Sasanians also depicted him as an enthroned, Zeus-like, diademed figure holding a spear, with flames issuing around his head and shoulders (fig. 74.12; Cribb 1997, pp. 38, 62–3).[12] The bust with a flaming head emerging from a fire altar, again holding a spear, may also represent Oesho perhaps integrated with Atar, the yazata of fire (fig. 74.18). A linked motif appears to be the flaming shoulders on coin images of the Kushan and Kushano-Sasanian kings from the time of Wima Kadphises onwards, which in this context is perhaps best interpreted as a divine sign of the right to rule (figs 61.16; 74.3–4, 7, 9, 15, 17). The device was adopted for depictions of the Buddha in the Kabul region, but is rarely found in Gandhara (fig. 100; Tsuchiya 1999/2000, p. 103). It is also found on certain images of Oesho on coins of Vasudeva I and his successors, including on Kushano-Sasanian imitation issues of this king and Kanishka II (figs 61.22, 74.3–4; Cribb 1997, pp. 48–9, D6–8, D12). On early

Figure 101 Detail of Naqsh-i Rustam investiture relief showing Varhran II (AD 276-93).

Figure 102 Detail of Naqsh-i Rustam investiture relief of Varhran II showing the high priest Kerdir.

Alchon coins also from eastern Afghanistan it appears in a more devolved form as plumes attached to the Hun king's shoulders (fig. 83.4–6).

Zoroastrianism was clearly the religion of the Sasanian kings who, from the time of Ardashir I (AD 223/4–41), describe themselves as Mazda-worshipping lords on their coins and inscriptions (fig. 66.3–4). Just like the local kings of Persis, Ardashir continued to depict the fire altar on the reverse of his coins. At the same time he copied the Achaemenid royal throne with its typical lion paws, as seen on the reliefs of Persepolis, and placed it above a fire altar (fig. 66.3–8). The connection with Achaemenid iconography is striking, but, whereas Achaemenid thrones are supported by various peoples of the Achaemenid empire, the Sasanian throne rests on two supports, which are usually interpreted as either incense burners (Göbl 1971, p. 17; Curtis 1996, p. 239) or 'pilzförmige Zierelemente', i.e. mushroom-shaped decorative elements (Alram and Gyselen 2003, p. 107). In fact, the so-called supports seem to derive from Achaemenid fire altars, as seen on the tomb reliefs of the Persian kings at Persepolis and Naqsh-i Rustam (fig. 163). While the Achaemenids were keen to stress the multicultural aspect of their empire, Ardashir I chose a religious motif to indicate that religion was the backbone of the Sasanian state and therefore inseparable from it.[13]

Detailed references to the religion and its practices are also found in early Sasanian inscriptions and other written documents. Some of these, like the 'Letter of Tansar', date to the early Sasanian period, but were later revised in the time of Khusrau I (AD 531–79) (Boyce 2001, p. 103):[14]

> His Majesty, the King of Kings, Ardashir, son of Papak, following Tansar as his religious authority, commanded all those scattered teachings to be brought to court. Tansar set about his business and selected one tradition and left the rest out of the canon. And he issued this decree: The interpretation of all the teachings of the Mazda-worshipping religion is our responsibility, for now there is no lack of certain knowledge concerning them.

Tansar (Tōsar), high priest (*herbad*) to Ardashir, in his letter to Gushnasp, a former vassal of the Sasanians ruling Tabaristan in northern Iran, emphasises that the 'Church and State were born of the one womb, joined together and never to be sundered' (Boyce 1984, p. 109). Tansar's words also suggest that Ardashir was accused of destroying many fire temples in his efforts to bring the religion under centralised direct control. This the high priest passionately denies and he explains how the situation had improved since Parthian times (Boyce 1984, p. 110):

> Next for what you said, that the King of Kings has taken away fires from the temples, extinguished them and blotted them out, and that no one has ever before presumed so far against religion; know that the case is not so grievous but has been wrongly reported to you. The truth is that after Darius each of the 'kings of the people' [i.e. the Parthians' vassal kings] built his own [dynastic] fire temple. This was pure innovation, introduced by them without the authority of kings of old. The King of Kings has razed the temples, and confiscated the endowments, and had the fires carried back to their places of origin.

Tansar (Tōsar) also refers to 'the kingship of God . . . according to the religion of Zardusht' as having been 'restored by Ardashir, the son of Papak' (Boyce 1984, pp. 110–11). He was ordered by Ardashir to collect the scattered teachings, select one tradition and omit other divergent beliefs from the canon. According to another passage in the *Denkard*, peace will come only when 'they give acceptance to him, Tansar the herbad, the spiritual leader, eloquent, truthful, just. Once they have given acceptance, 'those lands, if they wish, will find healing, instead of divergence from Zarathushtra's faith' (*Denkard* 652.9–17; Boyce 2001, p. 103).

Under Shapur I (AD 240–72/3), Ardashir's son and successor, the leading priest was Kerdir, who accompanied the king on his campaigns against the Romans. By the time of Varhran II (AD 276–93) Kerdir was so powerful that he had his inscriptions carved beside the rock reliefs of the Sasanian kings at Naqsh-i Rustam, Naqsh-i Rajab and Sar-Mashad in southern Iran (figs 68; 75; 101–2).[15] He is depicted in the royal reliefs as beardless, wearing the high priestly hat, his right hand raised with the fingers in a pose of reverence.

In his inscription at Naqsh-i Rustam, which dates to the reign of Varhran II, Kerdir describes himself first as a *mobed* (Old Persian *magupati*, *magbad*),[16] in the time of Ardashir and Shapur I (MacKenzie 1989, p. 57, §§ 1–3):

> [He] was absolute and authoritative in (the matter) of the gods [*yazadan*]. . . . And at the command of Shapur, King of Kings, and with the support of the gods and the King of Kings, from province to province, place to place, the rites of the gods were much increased, and many Warahran fires were established and many magians were (made) content and prosperous.

Figure 103 Investiture relief at Naqsh-i Rajab showing Shapur I (c. AD 240–72/3) receiving a diadem from Ahuramazda.

Figure 104 Naqsh-i Rustam investiture relief of Narseh (AD 293–303) showing the king standing with his wife and the smaller figure of the crown prince (?).

When Hormizd I succeeded his father to the throne in AD 272, Kerdir received a 'cap and belt' and became 'the Mobed of Ohrmezd', in the name of 'Ohrmezd [Ahuramazda] the Lord' (MacKenzie 1989, p. 57, § 5; Boyce 1984, p. 110; 2001, p. 109). He retained his prominent position under Varhran I (AD 273–6), but it was under Varhran II that he was elevated to the position of high priest (MacKenzie 1989, p. 58, §§ 7, 10):

> And he made me Mobed and judge of the whole empire. And he made me director and authority over the fire of Anahid-Ardashir and Anahid the Lady (in) Stakhr. And he named me 'Kerdir the soul-saver of Bahram, Mobed of Ohrmezd'.

Kerdir also mentions fires that were established elsewhere in the Iranian empire: Persis, Parthia, Khuzistan (Susiana), Asuristan (Mesopotamia), Meshan (Mesene), Nodshiragan (Adiabene), Adurbadigan (Atropatene), Spahan (Ray), Kirman (Carmania), Sagestan (Sakastene), Gurgan (Hyrcania), Merv, Herat, Abarshahr (Khurasan), Turan, Makran and the Kushan territory up to Peshawar (MacKenzie 1989, §§ 14–15):

> [He also] made arrangements . . . [at] the command of the king of kings, . . .for the magians and the fires in the lands of An-Eran, [i.e.] the city of Antioch and the land of Syria, . . . the city of Tarsos and the land of Cilicia, . . . the city of Caesaria and the land of Cappadocia . . . up to the land of Graecia [Pontus?] and the land of Armenia and Iberia [Georgia] and Albania and Balasagan up to the Gate of the Alans.

Kerdir also claims that he made (MacKenzie 1989, pp. 58–9, § 16)

> the Mazdayasnian religion and the good magians noble and honoured in the empire, and the heretics and the destructive men, who in the magian land did not adhere to the doctrine regarding the Mazdayasnian religion and the rites of the gods . . . were punished and . . . tormented.

It has been suggested that the title 'soul-saver of Varhran' given to Kerdir by Varhran II may have been in connection with his role in the removal of Mani, the heretic, who was killed at the time of Varhran I. His power and authority certainly appears to have reached its apogee during the reign of these two rulers, for although he apparently lived until AD 293, he is mentioned by Narseh in his Paikuli inscription simply as 'Kerdir, the Mobed of Ohrmezd' (MacKenzie 1989, pp. 63, 71, § 10).

The three most important fires of Zoroastrianism – created by Ahuramazda for the protection of the world – were Adur Burzin Mihr, Adur Farnbag and Adur Gushnasp. They may have already existed in the Achaemenid period, but had certainly come into being by the early Parthian period (Boyce 2001, p. 87). Kerdir's references to specific fires and Tansar's explanation of extinguishing fires and establishing royal authoritative fires under Ardashir indicates that the early Sasanian kings and the priesthood were keen to strengthen their hold over religion and create a centralised Zoroastrian church, which was under the control of the king of kings. Zorastrianism became the state religion under Shapur II in the fourth century AD.

From the beginning of the Sasanian period onwards, each king had an official fire bearing his own name, which appeared labelled as such on the reverse of his coins (fig. 66.4–8). Shapur's Kaba-i Zardusht inscription mentions the endowment of sacred fires or named fires, the *pad-nam adur*, for members of the royal family (ŠKZ §§ 33–5). This practice seems to go back to the first Arsacids who founded such fires at Nisa (Boyce 2001, p. 108; Alram and Gyselen 2003, pp. 106–7, n. 101). Shapur mentions by name some of the newly founded fires: 'Famed is Shapur' for his soul; 'Famed is Adur-Anahid' for the souls of his daughter and his queen; and 'Famed is Hormizd-Ardashir' for the soul of his son, the king of Armenia (ŠKZ §§ 33–5; Boyce 1984, p. 110). Ardashir and his sons moreover established many holy Atakhsh-i Varhran (fires named after Verethragna, the god/*yazata* of Victory) in each conquered region (see also Boyce 2001, p. 108). Then there were also local ordinary fires or 'Little Fires', such as *Adurog ipad dadgah*, i.e. 'Little Fire in an appointed place' (Boyce 2001, p. 110).

The Sasanian kings are shown in the presence of divine beings, both on their rock reliefs and on coins (figs 65; 66.12–18; 71.2; 103; 164), but nevertheless fought against the setting up and worship of statues. Their 'campaign of active iconoclasm' against such tendencies amongst the population of their empire is contradictory to their own royal propagandistic art (Boyce 2001, p. 107). In fact, at times it is almost impossible to distinguish between king and deity. It is not clear, for example, whether Ardashir depicts the image of Ahuramazda on some coins, or if the king himself is shown, simply wearing the mural crown of the divine being (fig. 66.5). In the same way on Shapur I's relief at Naqsh-i Rajab the king and god wear identical crowns and look strikingly similar. On the relief of Narseh at Naqsh-i Rustam, the female figure standing beside the king is likewise sometimes identified as Anahita (fig. 104). However, she has a covered hand – the mark of a subservient being or a devotee – and therefore cannot be the goddess, but is probably the king's wife (Shahbazi 1983, pp. 262–6). However, the goddess is shown being worshipped on a rare silver issue of the contemporary Kushano-Sasanian Hormizd 'II' (c. AD 300–9) (fig. 74.15).

One of the most important heresies in Zoroastrianism was Zurvanism. Although accounts of this dualistic form of Zoroastrianism survive only from the Sasanian period and later, it seems to have developed in the late Achaemenid period and continued until the rise of Islam in Iran in the seventh century AD. The heresy arose from the argument that if there were primal twin forces – or 'brothers' – of good (Ahuramazda) and evil (Ahriman), then there must also have been a creator 'father' and the only possible father was Zurvan (Infinite Time). This is totally at odds with Zoroastrianism, where according to the *Gathas*, Ahuramazda is the Father of the Holy Spirit and probably also of the Destructive Spirits (Zaehner 1961, p. 181). Zurvan however remained a remote being, entrusting power in the world to Ahuramazda (Zaehner 2005). The cult therefore appears to have had few rituals and did not influence existing Zoroastrian worship. But it undermined the fundamental Zoroastrian concept of the origin of good and evil as completely separate entities, and the existence of free will that gave each individual faith the power to choose their own destiny. Boyce maintains that it survived only because it gained early influential adherents, including the Sasanian royal family (2001, p. 69).

Mithraism

> Oromazes may be best compared to light, and Areimanius, conversely to darkness and ignorance, and midway between the two is Mithras. (Plutarch, cf. Wiesehöfer 2001, p. 98)

In the pre-Zoroastrian pagan tradition the ancient Iranians had different words for their divine beings (Boyce 2001, pp. 22–4). In common with the Indian tradition, these included the Avestan *daēva* (Vedic *deva*, 'shine', 'be bright'), *baga* ('one who distributes', 'a giver of good things') and *ahura* (Vedic *asura*, 'lord'). One of the most important *ahuras* was Mithra (Vedic Mitra; Greek Mithras). Like the Vedic Mitra, the Avestan Mithra was associated with the sun (figs 54.4; 61.14–15; 70; 88.11–12). He is described in *Yasht* 10 as moving across the sky in a chariot pulled by white horses (figs 45.21a; 53.7–8; 58; 72.11–12), an iconography he shares with Helios (see p. 109 above, fig. 52.11). He carries a silver spear, wears a golden cuirass, and is also armed with golden-shafted arrows, axes, maces and daggers (V. S. Curtis 2003, p. 14). He was furthermore the god who controlled the cosmic order, i.e. night and day and the changes of season.

Mithra, the Lord of Contract, is linked in addition with *rta/asha*, the Iranian principle of order, and the quest for being a rtavan/ashavan ('just and upright'), to the extent that the word 'mithra' – when referring to an agreement between men – means 'contract', 'pact', or 'covenant' (Boyce 2001, p. 27). In the longest *Yasht* of the *Avesta*, which is dedicated to Mithra, his correlation with truth, alertness and knowledge are emphasised (*Yasht* X.7):

> Mithra, the lord of wide pastures, who is truth-speaking, a chief in assemblies, with a thousand ears, well-shapen, with ten thousand eyes, high, with full knowledge, strong, sleepless, and ever awake.

Boyce sees the ancient Iranian Mithra as 'the Judge' who rewarded those following the path of truth, but punished the accused (2001, p. 35). The innocence or guilt of a living being could be tested by Mithra who poured melted metal over the accused. The Iranian Mithra had his own helpers or friends, the Airyaman (Sanskrit Aryaman). These included Arshtat (Justice), Ham-vareti (Courage), Sraosha (Obedience), and Khvarenah, the personification of 'divine' grace the God-given Glory/Fortune (Boyce 2001, p. 10). Mithra was also closely linked with Verethragna, the warrior god, Ashi, the goddess of Fortune, and Atar (Fire), the son of Ahuramazda, as together they protected the *khvarrah*.

Zarathushtra's reforms, which made Ahuramazda the sole and supreme creator, resulted in the demotion of Mithra, who became one of many *yazatas*. He is presented as a creation of Ahuramazda (*Yasht* X.1) and not as an equal.

> Ahuramazda spake unto Spitama Zarathushtra, saying: 'Verily. When I created Mithra, the lord of wide pastures, O Spitama! I created him as worthy of sacrifice, as worthy of prayer as myself, Ahuramazda'.

Mithra's pivotal role becomes obvious in Zarathushtra's vision of the Last Judgement (Boyce 2001, p. 35). Death forces individual souls to leave the world of material existence (*getig*) and to return for a time to the spiritual state (*menog*). The departed spirits face moral judgement at the 'Bridge of Separator' (Cinvat Bridge). Here a tribunal of three *yazatas* – Mithra, Sraosha and Rashnu – watch over the souls of the departed. Rashnu holds the scales of justice and the soul is weighed according to good and bad thoughts, words and deeds. If good is heavier the soul is sent to Paradise, but, if bad prevails, the soul is plunged into hell (Boyce 2001, p. 27). Here Mithra's original status as supreme judge and friend of goodness and truth is evident and he continued to function as such in Zoroastrianism.

To this day Zoroastrian priests receive Mithra's mace to empower them in combat against the Evil Spirit (V. S. Curtis 1993, p. 14), while Zoroastrian temples are called *dar-i* (i.e. *darb-i*) *mihr*, *mihr* ('friendship', 'sun') being the New Persian word for Mithra (Bivar 1999, p. 3).

The secretive Roman cult of Mithraism – with its beliefs known only to initiates – rose in the Near East in the first century BC. Its relationship with the Iranian Mithra is complex, but reference to the cult as the 'mysteries of the Persians' suggests that the Iranian Mithra was known to the Romans. The remains of Mithraic temples show the central icon of each mithraeum was the tauroctony, i.e. Mithras, accompanied by a dog, snake, raven and scorpion, slaying a bull (fig. 105). It is now thought that iconography of the cult

Figure 105 Marble statue of Mithras slaying the bull, from Lazio, Rome (second century AD).

is astronomical in origin, and that the animals all represent a group of constellations located in a continuous band across the sky: the bull equals Taurus, the dog Canis Minor, the snake Hydra, the raven Corvus and the scorpion Scorpio (Ulansey 2005).

Other more explicit astronomical motifs, such as the zodiac, planets, sun, moon and stars, are also often portrayed. The cosmology is tied in with the discovery by Hipparchus in c.128 BC, of the precession of the equinoxes – caused by wobble in the earth's rotation on its axis – which then was understood as a movement of the entire cosmic sphere. This moved the spring equinox – previously in the constellation of Taurus – into the constellation of Aries. The force capable of moving the entire universe was identified as a powerful god, Mithras, the cosmic destroyer of Taurus the bull.[17]

Roman Mithraism became increasingly popular during the first three centuries AD, especially among soldiers of the empire. However, its influence waned as that of Christianity grew. By the fifth century Mithraism had been suppressed by force.

Manichaeism

> The basic teaching of Mani takes the form of a cosmic drama involving a primordial invasion of the Kingdom of Light by elements of the Kingdom of Darkness. The chief deity of the Kingdom of Light is the Father of Greatness and he has four attributes: divinity, light, strength and wisdom. . . . Opposed to the Father of Greatness was the Prince of Darkness . . . [who] is depicted by Manichaeans as a monster consisting of the distinctive parts of five types of animals. (Lieu 1997, pp. 269–70)

The prophet Mani was a Parthian of noble blood who grew up in Babylonia, where his father was a member of an ascetic community. Since he thought that Zoroastrianism, Christianity and Buddhism were 'all in origin the one true faith, distorted by human misunderstandings, which he had been sent to restore', his religion was an eclectic mix of the fundamental tenets of these religions, influenced by the familiar Judaeo-Christian and Gnostic traditions of his youth: that is, a basic belief in God and the Devil, Heaven and Hell, individual judgement at death and the Last Judgement, signifying the final defeat of evil and life everlasting for the blessed. According to Mani's pessimistic view, the world was

evil and the individual should renounce it and 'lead a gentle ascetic life, dying celibate, so that his own soul might go to heaven, and he would have no part in perpetuating the misery of human existence on earth' (Boyce 2001, pp. 111–12).

Mani's mission began in AD 242 during the reign of Shapur I (AD 241–72). He spent many years in the Sasanian court protected by the king, who was sympathetic to his new religion and whom he hoped to convert. His teachings, the *Shahpuhragan*, were translated into Middle Persian for the king (Zaehner 1961, p. 183). Fragments of this book and other texts relating to the faith have been recovered from Manichaean monastic sites in Xinjiang. But after Shapur's death and during the reign of Varhran I, the mood changed at the court. With the growing influence of Zoroastrian priests – Kerdir in particular (figs 68; 75; 101–2) – Mani was inprisoned in Gondeshapur in south-western Iran. He died in captivity in AD 276.

In its guise as a reformed form of Zoroastrianism, Mani gave his religion an Iranian veneer, using the names of the *yazatas* for many of the divinities in the Manichaean pantheon. Thus, in Iranian versions of the Manichaean scriptures, the Father of Greatness was called Zurvan, his 'son' – the First Man – was Ohrmazd and the Prince of Darkness was Ahriman (Boyce 2001, p. 112; Boyce and Grenet 1991, p. 474). Matter – which included fire, water, earth and wind – was a creation of Ohrmazd and therefore holy. Manichaeans considered fire and water the true Bounteous Immortals of this earth and paid homage to the natural world as a reflection of the supernatural and God's creation (Zaehner 1961, p. 183).

In the battle between the kingdoms of Light and Darkness (Lieu 1997, p. 271),

> part of the Kingdom of Light was entrapped by the demonic forces and had to be redeemed by a deity known as the Living Spirit. Among the many Heath Robinson contraptions he devised were the Light Vessels (the Sun and the Moon) which would ferry the rescued Light-Particles back to their land of origin along the Milky Way. The lunar vessel was also the residence of an important deity, the Luminous Jesus. . . . The process of redemption is never complete, as sexual regeneration perpetuates the captivity of the Light-Particles in the physical universe. This suffering is personified by Jesus *patibilis*, the sum total of Light-Particles crucified in matter, whose symbol is the Cross of Light. As this Cross of Light is present in all matter, it could be injured by physical activity.

The belief went beyond vegetarianism in that even harvesting a crop or picking a leaf was thought to hurt the Light-Particles in a plant. In order to avoid hurting any living matter, the Electi were forbidden to collect food. This was gathered and produced by the Hearers (believers of the second rank), who in turn were dependent on the intercession of the Electi to shorten the birth–death cycle they were locked into as lesser beings (Lieu 1997, pp. 271–2).

Christianity

> there is one only God, but under the following dispensation, or *oikonomia*, as it is called, that this one only God has also a Son, His Word, who proceeded from Himself, by whom all things were made, and without whom nothing was made. Him we believe to have been sent by the Father into the Virgin, and to have been born of her – being both Man and God, the Son of Man and the Son of God, and to have been called by the name of Jesus Christ. (Tertullian, *Against Praxeas* 2, cf. Kirby 2001)

The first edict promoting tolerance towards Christians in the Roman empire was issued in Nicomedia during the reign of Gallienus (AD 218–68). By its provisions, the Christians, who had 'followed such a caprice and had fallen into such a folly that they would not obey the institutes of antiquity' were granted an indulgence. By the Edict of Milan in AD 313, Constantine I (AD 306–37) declared that the Roman empire would tolerate all forms of religious worship, officially ending all government-sanctioned persecution, especially of Christianity. In addition to legalising Christianity, it returned confiscated church property and established Sunday as a day of worship. It gave all religions equal status alongside paganism, the official religion of the empire (www.biography.ms).

Traditionally, acceptance of Christianity as the state religion of Armenia is said to have occurred in AD 306, when Tiridates III (AD 238–314) converted from Zoroastrianism, following miracles performed by St Gregory the Illuminator, son of a Parthian nobleman. This claim predates Constantine's edict, but the actual date may have been as late as AD 314.

In AD 325 Constantine convened the ecumenical Council of Nicaea. This condemned the heresy of Arianism – the refusal by Arius of Alexandria to recognise the divinity of Christ and his equality with God the Father – and established the Nicene Creed, i.e. that Father and Son are of 'One Substance' (Frye 1983, pp. 143–4). In AD 381 the Council of Constantinople declared the patriarchies of Rome and Constantinople equal, giving the latter precedence over Alexandria and Antioch.

The theological question that split the early Christian church was how divinity and humanity joined together and related to each other in Jesus Christ. The western church, centred on Rome, maintained the principle asserted by Tertullian of Carthage (c. AD 160–225) that both human and divine natures were united as one in Christ. The eastern church followed two schools of thought: that in Alexandria was also Monophysite, insisting on one nature, simultaneously both human and divine; while in Antioch, the Dyophisites (Greek *duo physis*, 'two natures') considered that Christ's divinity did not eclipse his humanity, but miraculously co-existed in one person (*prosopon*) (www.nestorian.org). Alexandria however interpreted this doctrine of two natures as dyhypostatism, i.e. two persons: the man Jesus, and the divine Christ.

The acceptance of Christians by Rome provoked suspicion of their perfidy in the Sasanian court, as illustrated by the order of Shapur II (AD 309–79) to his generals (cf. Stark 1966, p. 375):

> You will arrest Simon, chief of the Christians. You will keep him till he signs this document and consents to collect for us a double tax and double tribute from the Christians . . . for we Gods have all the trials of war and they have nothing but repose and pleasure. They inhabit our territory and agree with Caesar, our enemy.

The 'Great Persecution' of Iranian Christians, according to Armenian and Nestorian traditions, however, occurred in AD 340–63, after Constantine's death, during the period of renewed Sasanian–Byzantine wars, and included the martyrdom of the Catholicos (principal bishop)[18] of Seleucia–Ctesiphon, Shimun bar Sabbae, with five other bishops and 100 priests in AD 344.

The relationship between the later Sasanians and their Christian subjects was also, at times, uneasy. Yazdagird I (AD 399–420), for example, initially adopted a conciliatory attitude towards both Christians and Jews. Under his patronage a council of the Christians of the empire was held in Seleucia in AD 410. This formally accepted the doctrinal creed of the Council of Nicaea and gave Christians the freedom to follow their faith (Frye 1983, pp. 143–4). Internal church affairs were also regulated in a series of 21 canons. However, in the last year of Yazdagird's reign, a wave of retaliation against the Christian population began after a priest – with the consent of a bishop of Seleucia – destroyed a fire temple in the city of Hormizd Ardashir (probably near modern Ahvaz in Khuzistan), and then refused to rebuild it (Shahbazi 2003). Persecution continued initially under Varhran V, causing Christians to flee to Byzantium and resulting in war when Theodosius II (AD 408–50) refused to extradite them. In the peace treaty of AD 422 Christians were given the freedom to worship within the Sasanian domains. Shortly afterwards a Christian synod held at Seleucia under Dadjesus in AD 424 proclaimed a certain degree of autonomy and separation of the Persian church from its 'western' counterpart under the Patriarch of Antioch (Frye 1983, p. 145).

Nestorius (c. AD 383–450), a Syrian monk from Antioch, was appointed Patriarch of Constantinople in AD 428. He maintained the Dyophysite teachings of Christ as one person (*prosopon*) in two natures (*physis*), human and divine, as opposed to Monophysite doctrine of Christ as one person (*hypostasis*) and one nature (*physis*), both God and man (www.nestorian.org). The controversy came to a head in synods at Rome and Alexandria in AD 430 and at the Council of Ephesus, convened by Theodosius II in AD 431, the chief protagonists, including Nestorius, were excommunicated. In AD 433 a compromise was reached between Antioch and Alexandria, the price being confirmation of Nestorius' excommunication. This lasted until the deaths of their respective patriarchs in AD 442 and AD 444. In AD 451 the Council of Chalcedon confirmed the Dyophysite definition of Christ as one person in two natures, human and divine, thus alienating the Syrian, Coptic, Ethiopian and Armenian Monophysite churches.

In AD 484, at the end of the reign of Peroz (AD 459–84), the Edict of Gondeshapur declared the Nestorian church the official Persian Christian church (Schippmann 1990, p. 45). A permanent break finally took place c. AD 497–9, when a synod held under the Nestorian Mar Babai renewed the decree of independence from Antioch. The Nestorian church in Sasanian Iran now became independent, separate from Byzantium, with its centre at Seleucia.

Despite this doctrinal split with Constantinople and the independence of the Persian church, the status of Christians within the Sasanian empire continued to fluctuate (Garsoïan 1983, p. 585):

> the steady chronological synchronization between Christian persecution and the renewals of the Byzantine war make all too patent the purely political aspects of royal tolerance in Iran. Christians for the King of Kings were either useful or potentially disloyal subjects, their beliefs were of no real interest to him, and the conversion of Persians, as against Syrians and other minority groups, remained rare and severely repressed.

Buddhism

> There is no information on the dates of the historical Buddha, the founder of the Buddhist religion, which has been unanimously handed down by all major Buddhist traditions and universally accepted by scholars, nor have scholars been in a position to arrive at a general agreement concerning this question. While most sources and scholars agree that the Buddha passed away at the age of eighty years, traditional dates of the Parinivāṇa, i.e. the decease of the Buddha, range from 2420 BC to 290 BC, if converted into the Christian Era. (Bechert 1995, p. 11)

The historical founder of Buddhism was Siddhartha Gautama, a prince of the Shakya tribe from Nepal. He is usually known by the titles Shakyamuni (Sage of the Shakyas) and Buddha (Enlightened). Key events in his life are the Great Renunciation of worldly existence and Departure from the palace to become an ascetic; his eventual Enlightenment after meditating under the Bodhi tree at Bodh Gaya; preaching the First Sermon at the Deer Park in Sarnath when he set the Wheel of the Law (Dharma) in motion (fig. 106); and finally his death.

In common with other Indian religions, Buddhism holds the fundamental belief in rebirth or transmigration: an eternal process of cause and effect, in which the actions of each life directly influence one's fate in the next. The ultimate aim is to achieve Nirvana, a state of holiness in which desire, hatred, delusion and suffering – the causes of rebirth – have been eliminated. When the Buddha attained Enlightenment, he attained Nirvana; with his death he attained Parinirvana, the end of existence (fig. 107; Lamotte 1988, pp. 40–1; Zwalf 1985, pp. 9–12).

Tradition also recognises the existence of previous Buddhas (recounted in numerous *jātaka* stories: fig. 108) and a Buddha of the future, Maitreya. The jatakas provided the means whereby specific places in north-west regions between the Punjab and Jalalabad in Afghanistan acquired sanctity through legendary association with events in the former lives of the Buddha: 'each town, each locality soon had its own legend, and its own stûpa to commemorate it'. An extension of this process was the alleged – but fictitious – journey made by the historical Buddha with the yaksha Vajrapani through the region, 'to confer an adequate guarantee of authenticity on the new holy land' (Lamotte 1988, pp. 334–6).

Figure 107 Gandharan schist relief of the Paranirvana, from Takht-i-Bahi (*c.* second to third century AD).

The primary focus of ritual and veneration for Buddhists is the stupa (figs 21; 109–10). It is 'both a monumental reliquary and a commemorative monument' (Lamotte 1988, p. 311). The form derives originally from the ancient Indian custom of erecting a funeral mound or tumulus over the relics of a great ruler. The remains of numerous Buddhist structures were investigated by Masson, Court and others in Afghanistan and the Punjab in the 1830s (pp. 211–21 below). Their discoveries led to a basic understanding of the nature of the stupa. Masson and Court, 'adopting the notions that prevail amongst the people of the country', regarded them as royal burial mounds, while others thought they were shrines enclosing sacred relics attributed to the Buddha. Prinsep realised, correctly, that the stupa embodies both ideas, while also serving as a symbol of the Buddha (Wilson 1841, p. 45).

'Tope', the popular nineteenth-century term for these monuments, derives from the Sanskrit *stūpa*. In Buddhist terms it symbolises the entry into Parinirvana and ultimate achievement of Buddhahood. The first eight stupas were erected over the bodily relics (ashes, bones, teeth, hair, nail clippings) of the Buddha Shakyamuni; the ninth contained the funeral urn; the tenth the ashes of the pyre (Lamotte 1988, p. 23). Known as *śarīrika-stūpas*, this category was subsequently extended to include the remains of the disciples and later Buddhist saints, usually interred in a reliquary.

Figure 106 Gandharan schist relief of the First Sermon of the Buddha (*c.* second to third century AD), from Jamalgarhi.

Figure 108 Gandharan schist relief of the Dipankara jataka (*c.* second to third century AD).

Figure 109 Buddhist stupa of Guldara, south-east of Kabul, Afghanistan, from the north-east.

Pāribhogika-stūpas, the second group, contained relics of use or wear (alms-bowl, staff, clothing). The third, *uddeśika-stūpas*, commemorated sites where events sacred in the Buddhist legend had taken place (Bénisti 1960, p. 50; Zwalf 1996, pp. 36–7, 64). Although not founded on fact, Buddhist establishments in the Gandhara region and eastern Afghanistan (fig. 175) laid claim to their share of the Buddha's relics, commemorated fictitious visits and prophecies of future miracles by him in the region, and located various events in his previous lives at specific sites (Zwalf 1996, p. 20).

The structure of a stupa comprises a solid, hemispherical dome surmounted by a square housing (*harmikā*) from which rises a pole (*chattrāvalī*) supporting a series of umbrellas, an ancient Indian symbol of royalty. The dome stands on a circular or square platform which serves as circumambulatory path (*pradakṣiṇāpatha*) for the faithful and is reached by one or four flights of stairs (fig. 110). At sites in Gandhara and further west, the principal stupa is

Figure 111 Gandharan monastic site of Takht-i-Bahi, Peshawar Valley.

often encircled by numerous subsidiary votive stupas and usually positioned in the centre of a courtyard enclosed by a series of shrines (figs 110–11). There is also ordinarily an adjoining monastery, or caves in the vicinity – when available – are often used instead.

As already noted (p. 38), the Singhalese and Theravada Buddhist traditions date the Parinirvana of the Buddha – and with it, the start of the Buddhist Era – to 544/3 BC, 218 years before Ashoka (Bechert 1995, p. 12). Taking into account the discrepancies with Mauryan dates recorded in Greek sources, this so-called 'long chronology' has been corrected by *c.*58 years to *c.*486 BC for the Parinirvana of the Buddha. This is the conventional date usually cited by the majority of scholars. But Gombrich's (1992) detailed recalculations of the ages given for the pupillary succession in the *Dīpavaṃsa* correct the chronology further from 218 years to only 136 years before Ashoka's inauguration *c.*284–267 BC. These calculations bring the death of the Buddha very closely in line with the 'short chronology' of the Sanskrit sources which date the event only a hundred years before the consecration of Ashoka, i.e. in the late fifth to early fourth century BC.

Ashoka is known in Buddhist tradition as one of the greatest Indian rulers and a convert to the faith. As proclaimed in his thirteenth rock edict (Thapar 1997, pp. 255–7), in the eighth year of his reign he instituted the Dharma (*dhamma*) or 'Law', i.e. general rules pertaining to the practice of moral and proper conduct, including religious tolerance (twelfth edict), non-violence and the sanctity of life in all its forms: 'All men are my children and just as I desire for my children that they should obtain welfare and happiness both in this world and the next, the same do I desire for all men' (second separate edict, cf. Thapar 1997, p. 258). As Lamotte has noted (1988, p. 228), Ashoka's Dharma is only an expression, in its most universal form, of the great principles of a chakravartin or world ruler, of a benevolent, paternalistic king preoccupied with the well-being of his subjects. It is not a proclamation of Buddhist faith,

Figure 110 Reconstruction of a Gandharan stupa and chapels.

but 'carefully formulated so that essential [royal] interests should not be prejudiced while sectarian concerns were being accommodated' (Keay 2000, p. 99). So his apparent patronage of Buddhism can be seen as merely an extension of his impartial support of all religions, just as the inscriptional evidence cited for him as a convert to Buddhism can equally be interpreted as unprejudiced – but not exclusive – interest. In the minor rock edict at Brahmagiri, for example, he claims to have been a Buddhist layman for over two and a half years – 'but for a year I did not make much progress' – while the Bhabra inscription (addressed specifically to Buddhists) attests his deep 'respect for and faith in' the Buddha, the Buddhist creed and the fraternity of monks (Thapar 1997, pp. 36–7, 261). However, the climate of religious tolerance he fostered appears to have aided a great expansion of Buddhism during his reign. So it is hardly surprising that he achieved legendary status in the traditions of this faith.

All sources agree that the first Buddhist Council was held by the Buddha's disciples at Rajagriha, in year one of the Parinirvana, to discuss matters of doctrine and begin compiling the canonical texts. A century or 110 years later (i.e. *c*.386 BC in the long chronology), a Second Council was held at Vaishali. Sanskrit sources using the short chronology place the Second Council in the reign of Ashoka (Lamotte 1988, p. 124). According only to the Singhalese Chronicles, however, there was an additional Third Council at Pataliputra *c*.250 BC, which was convened under Ashoka's patronage (Lamotte 1988, pp. 272–4). Afterwards missionaries were sent to various parts of India, Sri Lanka,[19] Burma and the west, Majjhantika going to Kashmir and Gandhara, and Maharakshita to the Yavana (Greek) country (i.e. Afghanistan; Majumdar 1980, p. 84). The *Dīpavaṃsa* (VI.99) and *Mahāvaṃsa* (V.79, 173; Lamotte 1988, p. 250) also credit Ashoka with founding Buddhist monuments in 84,000 towns throughout the empire. Even in AD 629–45, when the Chinese monk Xuan Zang (AD 596–664) visited northern India, numerous Buddhist stupas were still said to have been founded by Ashoka (Lamotte 1988, p. 333).

By the time of the Second/Third Council, there were numerous Buddhist schools, including the three which appear to have gained prominence in the north-west, namely the Dharmaguptakas, Sarvastivadins and Mahasanghikas. This Council appears to have coincided with a schism between the various sects, from which the Mahayana school of thought began to emerge. The original Buddhist ideal – retained by some sects – was that the holiness of an arhat (spiritual adept) led to his personal Nirvana.[20] Mahayana upholds the bodhisattva path of spiritual adepts – laymen as well as monks – who, on the brink of attaining Nirvana, divert their energies into working for the salvation of others (Lamotte 1988, pp. 81–2, 172–6). The bodhisattva thus progresses successfully towards his own Nirvana by virtue of his compassion towards others.

The first translations of the records of the Chinese pilgrim monks Faxian (Rémusat 1836) and Xuan Zang (Julien 1857) revolutionised nineteenth-century Buddhist studies in India, Cunningham in particular using these sources to identify numerous archaeological sites, including those associated with Ashoka (p. 224 below). Following Cunningham's example, John Marshall, in the early decades of the twentieth

Figure 112 Butkara I main stupa, Swat, showing the original stupa within four subsequent enlargements.

century, identified the Dharmarajika and Kunala stupas at Taxila, and nearby sites at Hasan Abdal and Baoti Pind, as foundations of Ashoka (1951, pp. 233–5, 348–9). By extension and citing the Sanchi stupa in Madhya Pradesh as a prototype, he also included in this group the Great Stupa at Manikyala and Jamalgarhi in the Peshawar Valley (figs 175, 177; 187; Marshall 1951, p. 233):

> The earliest form of stūpa . . . was circular in plan, with a squat, slightly curvilinear dome set on a low plinth or terrace. This was the form of the Dharmarājikā Stūpa . . . Manikiāla [*sic*], and . . . the stūpa at Jamālgaṛhī, which is one of the earliest in Gandhāra, and in all probability copied from the Dharmarājikā.

A fourth site – unknown to Marshall – which shares similarities in plan is Butkara I in Swat (fig. 112; Faccenna 1980). But of all these sites, only the dome of Manikyala survives intact, so presumably it was the origin of Marshall's hypothetical reconstruction for Dharmarajika and Jamalgarhi. Numismatic evidence, however, for dating any stupas in the Punjab and Gandhara to the time of Ashoka is extremely flimsy. At Taxila, both Kunala and Mohra Moradu each produced a single worn silver punch-marked coin of the Mauryan period in the unstratified site debris, while a later bronze example was found at Pippala. Another equally worn silver example was sealed below a structure of the first building phase at Butkara I (type GH 305: fig. 41.1; Errington 1999/2000, pp. 191–2, 211–12; Marshall 1951, pp. 352, 363, 367; Faccenna 1980, part I, p. 193).

Similarly, few Indo-Greek coins before Menander I (*c*.155–130 BC) are recorded at any of the Buddhist sites. Coins of this ruler are the earliest found at Dharmarajika. At Butkara I only three bronze coins of the preceding rulers Pantaleon (*c*.190–185 BC), Apollodotus I (*c*.180–160 BC) and

Figure 113 Coins found at Buddhist sites:
1   Apollodotus I (*c*.180–160 BC); Obv. Apollo; rev. tripod.
Local issues:
2–3 With 'lion and elephant'; with taurine, tree in railing, hill and crescent.
Menander I (*c*.155–130 BC):
4   Obv. chakra; rev. palm branch;
5   Obv. boar's head; rev. palm branch;
6   Obv. elephant; rev. elephant goad.
Kanishka I (*c*. AD 127–50):
7   Rev. Buddha, from Ahinposh stupa;

8   Rev. Buddha;
9   Rev. Maitreya.
Hindu gods on coins:
10 Maues (*c*.75–65 BC). Obv. Balarama with club and plough; rev. unidentified goddess.
11 Azilises (*c*.1 BC–AD 16): goddess Lakshmi being lustrated by elephants.
Huvishka (*c*. AD 150–90):
12 Rev. Oesho and Ommo;
13 Rev. Skanda-Kumara and Bizago (Vishakha);
14 Rev. Skanda-Kumara, Bizago (Vishakha) and Maasena (Mahasena).

Eucratides I (*c*.174–145 BC) respectively were uncovered (figs 52.8–9; 113.1). A stray coin of Menander was associated with the first enlargement of the Butkara Great Stupa (GSt2: fig. 52.17; Errington 1999/2000, pp. 192, 211).

The bulk of coin finds from Butkara I and the Taxila sites comprise so-called 'local' issues, particularly of the 'Taxila lion and elephant' type, i.e. mostly square, bronze, uninscribed coins, some uniface, with a combination of traditional Indian designs, such as taurine, hill and crescent, tree in railing and swastika (fig. 113.2–3; Errington 1999/2000, pp. 191, 211–12, figs 5–7, 9). These coins have been

previously thought to date *c*.200 BC or earlier. However, a uniface example with the combined symbols of hill, tree, taurine and swastika has recently been found overstruck on a coin of Apollodotus I, while one bearing the lion and elephant design is overstruck on a coin of Menander.[21] Crucially, this information shifts the issue of the coins and thus the evidence for the foundation of Butkara I and the Taxila sites to around the mid second century BC, or later.

So the numismatic evidence suggests that, while Ashoka's policies may have provided the impetus for the expansion of Buddhism in the north-west, the actual construction of monasteries and stupas began only at the earliest *c*.50–70 years after his death, possibly from the time of Menander I, who is also said to have become a Buddhist in the *Milindapañha*, 'The questions of Menander' (Rhys Davids 1890–4). This source claims that after a discussion between the king and the Buddhist sage Nagasena on the nature of the soul and Buddhist beliefs, Menander renounced his throne and converted to the faith. This is contradicted by the Greek historian Plutarch, who says only that the king 'died in camp', phraseology suggestive of a military campaign, not Buddhist practice. However, following Menander's cremation, it was 'agreed to divide up his ashes into equal shares and to set up monuments of the man beside all the cities' (*Moralia*, 821D; Lamotte 1988, p. 421). This is an identifiable Buddhist ritual accorded to great benefactors, revered men and saints. It perhaps implies that – like Ashoka – Menander was considered a benevolent supporter of the faith.

His legendary status as a putative Buddhist is not supported by coin evidence, even though the chakra (disk or wheel) depicted on one side of a rare small square bronze issue – found by Masson at Begram – has sometimes been identified as the Buddhist Wheel of the Law (fig. 113.4; Bopearachchi 1991, pl. 33, ser. 37). However, the palm branch on the reverse is a Greek motif: an attribute of Nike and also of Poseidon, the god of earthquakes and the sea. It occurs also on another issue of Menander together with the image of a boar's head (fig. 113.5; Bopearachchi 1991, pl. 33, ser. 35–6). The chakra is a weapon and the boar an incarnation of Vishnu, so the intended symbolism of these two issues, if seen in an Indian religious context, is Vaishnavite, rather than Buddhist. But since the chakra – an ancient Indian emblem of a warrior or world ruler – is coupled with an attribute of victory, it is far more likely that the image should be considered as another example of the overwhelmingly royal imagery, Greek subject matter and oblique references to Menander's conquest of India inherent in the rest of his coinage. Comparable imagery is found on another rare issue of Menander, this time the combination of an elephant (symbolising India) and an elephant goad (*aṅkuśa*), another royal symbol, specifically one of the eight ancient Indian *aṣṭamaṅgala* (auspicious symbols) denoting the importance of a person or event (fig. 113.6).

'Maharaja Minedra' (Menander) is cited in an inscription on the lid of a relic casket from Bajaur (Majumdar 1937–8, p. 7; Lamotte 1988, p. 422), but it has recently been convincingly shown that this part of the inscription is a later forgery (Falk 2005, pp. 349–53). Two other inscriptions superficially appear to provide epigraphic evidence for the possible establishment of stupas in the north-west during the Greek period (*c*. mid second to mid first century BC). The first – on an undated reliquary from Swat[22] purporting to contain the 'relics of the Lord Shakyamuni' – names the donor as a Greek meridarkh (district officer)[23] called Theodorus (Konow 1929, pp. 1–4, no. I, pl. I.1). The second is a copper-plate inscription found in the 1850s in the ruins of a small stupa to the west of Dharmarajika at Taxila, which records the foundation of the stupa by an unnamed meridarkh (Cunningham 1871, pp. 124–5, pls LVII, no. 14, LIX.3; Konow 1929, pp. 4–5, no. 2, pl. I.2; Errington 1987, pp. 166, 169, 430, 515, map 8, no. 14). However, the use of the title meridarkh

Figure 114 Bronze reliquary from Wardak stupa, inscribed in year 51 of Kanishka in the reign of Huvishka (AD 278), with Kushan bronze coins of Wima Kadphises, Kanishka I and Huvishka.

does not necessarily indicate a Greek period date, for it is clear that another title, stratega (Greek *strategos* 'commander of forces'), remained in use under the Indo-Scythian Apraca rajas of the late first century BC to mid first century AD (Salomon 1999, p. 150; 2005; pp. 62–4 above). The Indo-Parthians, moreover, introduced new Greek words and grammatical constructions on their coinage, which shows that Greek was still a living language of the region in the first century AD: e.g. Abdagases is identified as *adelphideos* 'nephew', while other coins replace the title *basileos* 'king' with a present participle, genitive *basileuontos* 'one who is ruling' (Errington and Cribb 1992, pp. 9–10, n. 8).

It is furthermore remarkable that none of the Buddhist sites of the Peshawar Valley – lying between Taxila and Swat – provides any numismatic evidence from the Greek period, apart from a single coin of Apollodotus found in the subterranean chambers at Takht-i-Bahi (Hargreaves 1914, pp. 33–4). The next earliest recorded coin from the region is one of the Indo-Scythian ruler Azes I (*c*.46–1 BC) (fig. 56.9), from the neighbouring site of Sahri Bahlol Mound C (Stein 1915, p. 101). This suggests that the Takht-i-Bahi coin is likely to be one of Azes' immediate Indo-Greek predecessor, Apollodotus II (*c*.65–50 BC) (fig. 54.7), rather than one of Apollodotus I, who ruled a century earlier (fig. 113.1). Generally, the coin finds indicate that Buddhism became established at Taxila from the time of Maues (*c*.75–65 BC) onwards, but elsewhere, especially in the Peshawar Valley and Manikyala, the foundation of stupas can be dated with any certainty only towards the end of Indo-Scythian period in the first century AD (Errington 1999/2000, pp. 194, 211–13). Jamalgarhi – the site of Marshall's so-called 'earliest' stupa in Gandhara – produced only coins from the time of Kanishka I (*c*. AD 127–50) onwards (Hargreaves 1921, p. 21, no. 33).

Going westwards, increasing evidence is emerging from the Bajaur area (between north-west Pakistan and eastern Afghanistan) for Buddhism in the first century AD under the patronage of relatives of the Indo-Scythian Apraca kings (Majumdar 1937–8; Salomon 1999, pp. 150–3, 180; 2005). Still further west near Jalalabad, the coin evidence from Masson and Honigberger's excavations in the Darunta district and at Chahar Bagh and Hadda dates the foundation of the earliest stupas in this region again to the first century AD, from the reign of the first Kushan king Kujula Kadphises (c. AD 40–90) and his successor Wima Tak[to] (c. AD 90–113) onwards (fig. 61.5, 14–15; p. 221).

In the Punjab and north-eastwards into Afghanistan, from the first century AD onwards, coins were also often included in the relic deposits. In Buddhist terms Cunningham suggested that coins could represent one of the 'seven precious things which usually accompanied the relic deposits of the old Bhuddhists [sic], and which are still placed in the *Chortens* of the Buddhists of Thibet [sic]' (1871, p. 167), an idea which is still current (Zwalf 1996, pp. 64–5). The argument, however, that the included coins were considered precious because they were no longer in circulation is refuted by the evidence from the Mera-ka-Dheri stupa at Manikyala excavated by Court, and the Wardak reliquary excavated by Masson, both of which had inscriptions contemporary with the latest Kushan coins in the deposits (figs 114; 178).

There are, moreover, a number of stupas which appear not to have contained any coins at all: of the 48 excavated by Masson, Honigberger and Simpson in the Kabul–Jalalabad region, for example, 20 belong to this category (pp. 216–21). This may reflect the different functions implicit in *śarīrika-*, *pāribhogika-* and *uddeśika-stūpas*, or equally perhaps is indicative of divergent beliefs and customs among the different sects. As Scherrer-Schaub points out (forthcoming, introduction § 3), the material constituting sacred, relic or precious deposits – whether monetary or other items – has in each instance its own particular rationale: 'though theoretically (and textually) the ritual appears as invariable, in fact it changes constantly (its protagonists, the implements, and so on)'. The ideological data transmitted in the *Mahāyānasūtra*, together with Song Yun's account of the Kanishka stupa at Peshawar in AD 519–20 (Chavannes 1903, pp. 425–6), confirm the existence by the sixth century – if not earlier – of the idea that sacred and precious deposits were intended for the restoration of the monument in the event of any future decay. Scherrer-Schaub notes further the association in liturgical and narrative texts between the myth of the end of time (*apocatastasis*), the cult of relics and the subsidiary practice of precious deposits: at the end of time, the smallest donation (e.g. a Buddha relic as tiny as a mustard seed) or most insignificant religious practice (e.g. the recitation of a unique stanza) will bear great fruits. But in the last epoch of famine, wars and calamities, the religion will disappear; the images and stupa will sink deep into the earth to the gold and diamond disks. At the propitious time these relics – particularly the relics of *dharma* – will re-emerge; the gods will remember and return to earth to preach the *dharma*; and a new cycle will begin.

The numismatic evidence from the monastic sites of Gandhara and eastern Afghanistan suggests that the greatest expansion of Buddhism took place in the reign of the Kushan king Huvishka (c. AD 150–90) (p. 221), but it is his father, Kanishka I, who is revered in Buddhist tradition and, according to Xuan Zang (III.886b–887a), organised the Third – or according to the Singalese Chronicles, the Fourth – Buddhist Council in Kashmir (p. 128; Watters 1904, vol. I, pp. 270–1; Zürcher 1968, p. 380; Lamotte 1988, pp. 585–6):

In his spare moments [Kanishka] studied the Buddhist *sûtras*, and daily invited a monk to enter the palace and to expound the doctrine. But because different explanations [of the doctrine] were held by various sects the king was filled with doubt and he had no way to remove his uncertainty. . . . [He expressed] his desire to restore Buddhism to eminence, and to have the Tripiṭaka explained according to the tenets of the various schools . . . [and] issued an edict to assemble saintly and wise men from far and near.

[The Council convened by Kanishka in Kashmir compiled] 300,000 stanzas, 9,600,000 words, . . . in order to explain the Tripiṭaka in full. . . . The general meaning was again clarified, the smallest words explained. This publication was universally known and successors referred to it. King Kanishka ordered the texts of the śāstras to be engraved on copper plates; he enclosed and sealed them in stone caskets, built a stūpa and hid the caskets in the middle of it. He ordered Yakṣas to protect the site and not allow heretics to remove the śāstras from it; but those who wished to study them could do so on the spot.

The convenor of the Council, Parshva, and its president, Vasumitra, compiled the *Mahāvibhāṣa*, an important commentary on the canonical texts, while another leading participant was Ashvaghosha, author of the *Buddhacarita*, an account of the life of the Buddha, and – according to various sources – a spiritual adviser to Kanishka who played a part in the development away from the aniconic tradition to iconic representations of the Buddha (Bivar 1983, pp. 204–5; Bailey 1942, pp. 20–1).

Kanishka is also credited with building a stupa at Peshawar by the Chinese pilgrims of the fifth to seventh centuries, who repeat variations of the same legend (Kuwayama 1997, pp. 62–6; Zürcher 1968, pp. 374–6). According to Faxian (AD 334–420), who visited the site in c. AD 400 (*Taisho* 2085, p. 858.2.11):

Long ago, when the Buddha and his disciples roamed through this country, he told Ananda: 'after my *Parinivāṇa* there will be a king named Jinijia [Kanishka] who will raise a *stūpa* on this spot'. Later king Jinijia appeared in the world. He once went on a tour of inspection, and at that time, Śakra, the king of the gods, wishing to open the king's mind to Buddhism, changed himself into a cowherd who was raising a *stūpa* at the side of the road. The king asked him: 'What are you making?' He answered: 'I am making a Buddhist *stūpa*'. The king said: 'Very good!' and thereupon raised a *stūpa* over the one of the boy, more than forty *zhang* (400 feet) high and adorned with precious materials. Of all the *stūpas* and *vihāras* ever seen by Faxian in his travels, none could be compared with this one for beauty and majesty.

The early eighth-century translation by Yijing (AD 635–713) of the *Bhaṣajyavastu* of the *Mūlasarvāstivādavinaya* gives a slightly different version, in which the Buddha sees a boy making a stupa of earth and tells his disciples that four hundred years after his *nirvāṇa* the boy will be reborn as king Kanishka (*Taisho* 1448, cf. Zürcher 1968, p. 384). The monastic site near Peshawar and its associations with Kanishka survived into the eleventh century, for al-Biruni, when discussing the Kushan king, refers to him as 'Kanik . . . the same who is said to have built the vihāra of Purushavar. It is called after him *Kanik-caitya*' (*Taḥqīq ma li-l-Hind*, cf. Sachau 1888, vol. II, ch. XLIX.11). In 1908, following up Cunningham's earlier identification (1874, pp. 420–1) of the Shah-ji-ki-Dheri mounds south-east of Peshawar as the legendary monastery in question, the site was excavated by Spooner and a gilded bronze reliquary bearing an image of a Kushan king and an inscription citing Kanishka was found in

Figure 115 Gilded bronze 'Kanishka' reliquary from Shah-ji-ki-Dheri stupa.

the ruins of the stupa (fig. 115; 1912, pp. 38–59). In the intense excitement following this discovery, a crucial piece of evidence was ignored: namely that the so-called 'clay seal' depicting an elephant rider in the relic deposit appears from the surviving photograph to be an actual coin of Huvishka coated in clay (Errington 2002). The inscription, moreover, mentions only that (Falk 2002):

> In the town Kaniṣkapura this perfume box . . . is the pious donation of the architects of the fire-hall, namely of Mahāsena [and] Saṃgharakṣita, in the monastery [founded by] the [Mahārā]ja Kaniṣka.

So while the inscription indicates that the monastic establishment was founded by – or in the time of – Kanishka, the contents of the relic deposit and its position off-centre suggests that it was associated with a period of rebuilding or enlargement of the stupa in the reign of Huvishka (c. AD 150–90) or later.

In his account of the country of Kapishi, located between Kabul and the southern slopes of the Hindu Kush (with its capital at Begram), the Chinese pilgrim Xuan Zang (I.873c–874a) credits Kanishka with providing 'different residences according to the seasons' each with its own monastery, for a hostage prince – the son of the ruler 'of a Chinese vassal state west of the Yellow river' – sent to him through fear of his might. 'In the winter he lodged in various states in India; in the summer he returned to Kāpiśī, while in the spring and autumn he stayed in Gandhāra.' A monastery was built in each of these places and, after the hostage returned home, he continued to send offerings to all of them.

The Kapishi monastery was located 'about three or four *li* east of the great city'. The Buddhist site is probably identifiable as Shotorak on the Kuh-i Pahlawan, 4 km to the north-east of Begram (Masson MSS Eur. F 63, f. 23; Foucher 1942/7, pl. XXX.c; Mizuno 1970, p. 126, pl. 50; Ball and Gardin 1982, no. 1088, p. 254, maps 52.1, 111).[24]

Fifth-century Chinese translations of Indian texts represent Kanishka in a more pragmatic light (Zürcher 1968, pp. 384–7). They mention the king's close friendship with his prime minister, physician and Ashvaghosha, each of whom promised him rewards for following their advice: the minister great conquests, the doctor lasting health, and Ashvaghosha everything that was good; an eternal end to all misfortune; and freedom from evil for ever. The king was guided by the minister and conquered all the western northern and southern countries, killing in the process more than 300,000 people. Realising then that he would receive retribution for his sins, he tried to redress the balance by meritorious works and virtuous acts, building lodgings for monks and bestowing 'offerings of all the four requisites' on the *saṇgha* (monastic communities). Although he should have gone to hell, thanks to Ashvaghosha's beneficial influence he was reborn as a monstrous fish with a thousand heads. Clearly this was considered better than his original fate.

Buddhist tales of Kanishka seeking absolution towards the end of his life coincide with his issue of coins depicting the Buddha towards the end of his reign (fig. 113.7–9; Cribb 1999/2000). But otherwise, the rest of his coin issues, together with the evidence from the dynastic shrine at Surkh Kotal and his proclamation on the Rabatak inscription, all indicate that – like those of other Kushans – his religious beliefs were linked to the Iranian cult of fire worship. Nevertheless, he seems to have encouraged religious tolerance. Buddhism in particular flourished, spreading rapidly along from India to Afghanistan and the trade routes into Central Asia and China (Bivar 1983, p. 109):

> It may be concluded that the far-reaching political sovereignty of Kanishka helped to secure a right-of-way for Buddhist travellers along the route to China. Not only did they introduce their characteristic Gandhara art at Miran, they also brought with them their Kharoṣṭhī script, which occurs in the Tarim basin in the documents from Niya, near Khotan, and others from Endere and Lou-Lan. It was also used for writing works of Buddhist scripture, of which an example survives in the *Gāndhārī Dharmapada*.

That the apparent tolerance of Kanishka towards other religions gave impetus to the expansion of Buddhism is evident from the coins and inscriptions associated with this ruler and his successor Huvishka at monastic sites stretching from Sui Vihar and Manikyala in the Punjab westwards into Afghanistan. It is in the period of these two rulers – especially Huvishka – that gold coins begin regularly to appear in the stupa relic deposits at sites such as Manikyala Great Stupa and Mera-ka Pind, Ahinposh and Guldara, thereby attesting to the economic affluence of the donors or the actual monasteries (figs 116; 177–8; Errington 1999/2000, pp. 212–15).[25]

The Chinese pilgrims Xuan Zang and Yijing – who visited India in AD 629–45 and AD 671–85 respectively – record the existence of five Buddhist sects in Udyana: the Mahasanghikas, Sarvastivadins, Mahishasakas, Kashyapiyas and Dharmaguptakas (Watters 1904, vol. I, p. 226; Takakusu

Figure 116 Reliquary from Ahinposh, Afghanistan, containing gold staters of Sabina (c. AD 128–36), Wima Kadphises (c. AD 113–27), Kanishka I (c. AD 127–50) and Huvishka (c. AD 150–90). Rev. Oesho, Buddha, Miiro, Athso, Selene.

Figure 117 Inscription dated Yona year 359 (c. AD 185), from Jamalgarhi main stupa complex, room no. 16.

1998, p. 20).[26] Inscriptions provide evidence for all these schools in the north-west subcontinent and Afghanistan in the time of the Kushans (Salomon 1999, pp. 168–9, 175–8).

The bronze vase excavated by Masson from stupa 1 at Wardak (fig. 114) – dated the year 51 of Kanishka (i.e. AD 178) and citing Huvishka – states that the monastery was established by the Mahasanghikas. This was one of the earliest sects, which greatly influenced the development of Buddhist doctrine and appears to have been active at Mathura in the first century AD, judging from its inclusion on the lion capital inscription (fig. 57; Konow 1929, pp. 48–9, 170). The presence of the school further north in Central Asia is also now attested on twelve potsherd inscriptions from the Kushan-period Buddhist sites of Kara Tepe and Fayaz Tepe near Termez (Salomon 1999, p. 191, n. 10).

Evidence for the Sarvastivardins also comes from the Mathura lion capital; and, in the Peshawar region, from the Shah-ji-ki-Dheri 'Kanishka' casket (fig. 115), the Zeda inscription of year 11 (c. AD 138) and the Kurram stupa reliquary of year 20 (c. AD 147) (Konow 1929, pp. 48–9, 137, 145, 155). They are mentioned on a pot inscription from Tapa Shotor, Hadda, and on two of the five inscribed pots in the British Library collection, dated c. first to second century AD and thought to be possibly from the Jalalabad/Hadda region (Tarzi 1976, p. 409; Salomon 1999, pp. 175, 188). There is only one reference to the Mahishasakas in this period, again on one of the British Library potsherds (Salomon 1999, p. 176), but there is a later sixth-century record of the existence of the sect at Kura in the Punjab (p. 97). Inscriptions alluding to the Kashyapiyas – also relatively rare – have been found at Mahal near Sirkap (Taxila), Bedadi (north-west of Mansehra) and Palatu Dheri in the Peshawar Valley (Konow 1929, pp. 88–9, 121–2; Lamotte 1988, p. 524).

The Yona year 359 inscription records the presence of the Dharmaguptakas at Jamalgarhi in the time of Huvishka c. AD 185 (fig. 117, p. 71; Lüders 1940, pp. 17–20; Salomon 1999, p. 214). This and the other known inscription of the sect – the Qunduz vase from northern Afghanistan – have been recently supplemented by the British Library pot and potsherd inscriptions, all of which lend credence to the

premise that the Dharmaguptakas played a prominent role in the spread of Buddhism into Central Asia and China (Fussman 1974, pp. 58–61; Salomon 1999, pp. 167–71).

The numismatic evidence from Swat, the Peshawar Valley and Taxila indicates that the Buddhist sites continued to flourish in these regions throughout the Late Kushan, Kushano-Sasanian and Kidarite periods, the latest coins in Swat and the Peshawar Valley being, with a few exceptions, silver issues of Kidara Kushanshah (c. AD 425–57) (figs 77.12; 82.10; Errington 1999/2000, p. 213).

A point of interest regarding the distribution of Kidarite coins in the North-West Frontier (pp. 95–6) is that they are apparently confined to the regions north of the Kabul river and west of the Indus, whereas Alchon coins are found south and east of these rivers, at the major centres of Peshawar (Shah-ji-ki-Dheri) and Taxila. Whether this indicates that the Kidarites remained in control of the Peshawar hinterland while the Alchon took charge of the principal urban centres of the region, or that the latter ransacked the Buddhist monasteries of the Peshawar Valley, is not yet clear. Certainly the evidence excavated by Masson from the relic deposit of Tope Kelan, Hadda (figs 82–3; 184), suggests that the Kidarites and Alchon were near contemporaries of the mid or late fifth century and that the foundation of new stupas continued in the Jalalabad region, during the Alchon period (pp. 93–5).

According to Marshall's dramatic reconstruction, the 32 Hun silver coins found at Taxila (1951, p. 791)

> leave no room for doubt that it was the White Huns who were responsible for the wholesale destruction of the Buddhist *sanghārāmas* of Taxila. All but one of their coins were found on the floors of the burnt-out monasteries, where some of the invaders evidently perished along with the defenders. Twenty of the coins were in the doorway of cell 13, and one in front of cell 8 at the Bhāmala monastery, seven in the courtyard of the Lālchak monastery, and three in room 6 of Court J at the Dharmarājikā, where several skeletons of those who fell in a fight, including one of a White Hun, were lying.

The skull in question apparently exhibited the same cranial distortion evident on coins (Marshall 1951, p. 290). But, as has already been shown, Marshall's block allocation of all these coins to the Hephthalites or White Huns is wrong, for they are all Alchon issues of Khingila (c. AD 440–90) and his contemporary Javukha (p. 96; fig. 80.9–12).

The other key piece of evidence on which Marshall based his assumption is Song Yun's identification in AD 519–20 of Gandhara as the country which – 'two generations' previously – had been 'conquered by the Yanda' (Hephthalites) who appointed a *chiqin* (*tegin*, i.e. prince) as ruler (Chavannes 1903, pp. 416–17). Since the Hun king who gave the Chinese pilgrim an audience is identifiable as Mihirakula (p. 101), it follows that his predecessor by two generations, who 'did not believe in Buddhism', must be Khingila or one of his

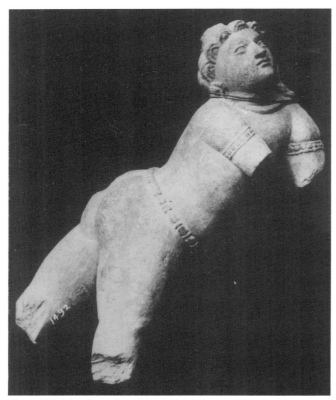

Figure 118 Schist figure from Sahri Bahlol monastery D.

(Errington 1999/2000, pp. 201–3). Although they – or more fleetingly, the Hephthalites – might have played a part, the end seems to have been less dramatic: in fact a slow process over several centuries and due to a number of different factors. Many of the monasteries in the Peshawar Valley do appear to have been abandoned between the time of Song Yun's visit in AD 520 and that of Xuan Zang's in AD 632, but equally, some remained occupied, not necessarily by their original communities. At several of the Sahri Bahlol monasteries, for example, broken sculptures were set up again for worship (p. 222, fig. 188). Some figures also appear to be stylistically later than the main body of sculptures from these sites (fig. 118; Tissot 1990, p. 746, fig. 6).

Xuan Zang says that Mihirakula (*c.* AD 515–40), the successor to Toramana, initially wished 'to apply his leisure to the study of Buddhism [and] ordered the clergy [of Sakala, i.e. Sialkot in the Punjab] to recommend a Brother of eminent merit to be his teacher'. When an elderly monk – one of his servants – was selected, the king was insulted, and 'forthwith ordered the utter extermination of the Buddhist church throughout all his dominions . . . and with this view he caused the demolition of 1600 topes and monasteries, and put to death nine *koṭis* [270,000,000] of lay adherents of Buddhism' (Watters 1904, vol. I, pp. 288–9). If this is the case, the event must postdate Song Yun's audience with the king *c.* AD 520. On the basis of this evidence, moreover, the destruction of the monasteries should, at least in part, be attributed to Mihirakula, whose explicit use of the bull/bull standard on his coins, coupled with the legends *jayatu vṛṣa* ('let the bull be victorious') and – on an anonymous issue attributable to him – *jayatu vṛṣadhvaja* ('let he whose banner is the *vṛṣa* be victorious'), appears to proclaim that he was a devotee of Shiva (see p. 97, fig. 81.8–9).

According to Xuan Zang in AD 632, the situation in the Peshawar Valley was extreme, the towns and villages being severely depopulated and the inhabitants mostly belonging to other religions (Watters 1904, vol. I, pp. 198–9, 202, 214–18). Only five monasteries of the original thousand are said to be still Buddhist: one Hinayanist and two Mahayanist monasteries, each with fifty monks in residence; one at Pushkalavati and the Kanishka monastery at Peshawar, both in ruins, with only a few monks remaining. However, the latter stupa, having been destroyed for the fourth time, was in the process of being rebuilt.

Whether the situation was due to war, persecution or some natural catastrophe – such as an earthquake – or a combination of all three, is not clear. In the Jalalabad region, Swat and Taxila, the population was still Buddhist, but the monasteries had mostly been abandoned, the stupas lay in ruins and only a few monks remained (Watters 1904, vol. I, pp. 183, 226, 240). There is, however, a lack of archaeological evidence of any deliberate destruction. At Jamalgarhi, Takht-i-Bahi, Taxila and elsewhere, the stucco figural reliefs, when first excavated, were in pristine condition, having been protected for centuries by fallen debris from the collapse of the upper sections of the buildings (fig. 119; Errington 1987, pp. 152–3, 305–7). Even though the terminal occupation dates of sites such as Jamalgarhi, Takht-i-Bahi and Butkara I differ, the pattern of debris spread in each case is similar, i.e. a single stratigraphic layer, which uniformly reached high

contemporaries. A second chronological parameter for this event is the Bhitari pillar inscription from the Varanasi region of Uttar Pradesh, which dates the halt of the first Hun advance into India – presumably again under Khingila – to *c.* AD 456/7, during the reign of Skandagupta (p. 96). But although Alchon migration or expansion from eastern Afghanistan into the North-West Frontier region appears to begun *c.* AD 450–6 in the time of Khingila, it is also apparent from the testimony of Song Yun some 70 years later that a number of Buddhist sites remained in cult, not only at Hadda, Shah-ji-ki-Dheri and Swat but also in the Peshawar Valley (Chavannes 1903, pp. 414–30; Errington 1993, p. 56).

In the Kura inscription – recording the construction of a Buddhist monastery for the teachers of the Mahishasaka school in the Punjab – the donor wishes to make over a share of the merit gained by his pious gift to the great king of kings, Toramana (Bühler 1892, pp. 238–9; Lamotte 1988, p. 524; p. 97 above). Again, it indicates the continued existence of Buddhist communities for some time after the arrival of the Alchon in this region. It also hardly seems a likely act if Toramana was a scourge of Buddhism. The late eighth-century *Kuvalayamālā* in fact infers that the king's personal guru Harigupta – 'a scion of the Gupta family' – was a Jaina, thereby implying the somewhat implausible situation of Toramana paying 'homage to a Jaina preceptor and descendant of the Guptas he had defeated' (§ 4; Mehta 1928, pp. 32, 34–5).

The numismatic evidence shows clearly that the Alchon migrated eastwards from the Kabul region in the latter half of the fifth century. Since there is no evidence of Alchon aversion to Buddhism in the region from which they originated, there seems little reason to believe in their sole responsibility for the total destruction of Buddhism in Gandhara and the north-west proposed by Marshall

Figure 120 Rock-cut 55 m and 38.5 m Buddhas at Bamiyan (*c.* fifth and third century AD respectively).

Figure 119 Stucco relief, *in situ*, of a seated Buddha flanked by two standing Buddhas in a niche at the entrance to Mora Moradu monastery, Taxila.

levels within enclosed areas, but was confined to a thin layer in open areas, suggesting it resulted from some natural phenomenon (Faccenna 1980, vol. I, pp. 134–5; Errington 1999/2000, pp. 201–2). At Damkot in Swat the last Buddhist phase of the sixth to seventh century was clearly separated by an intervening layer of debris from the next *c.* ninth-century reoccupation level, but there is nothing to associate the earlier abandonment of the site with a Hun invasion (Rahman 1968/9, pp. 109–10, 117, pls 88a, 90b).

Nevertheless, the evidence of two later pilgrims, the Korean monk Hui Chao, who visited Bamiyan in Afghanistan in AD 727, and the Chinese Buddhist Wu Kong, who saw the ushnisa relic of the Buddha in the 'city of Gandhara' (i.e. Peshawar) *c.* AD 735, suggests that in fact several Buddhist cult centres survived into the eighth century (Tarzi 1977, Appendix IV, p. 183; Watters 1904, vol. I, p. 195; Kuwayama 1997, p. 73). From the sixth century Bamiyan was ruled by a dynasty who, in the first quarter of the eighth century, apparently still professed Buddhism (Chavannes 1903a, pp. 291–2). It has even been argued that the site existed only from the seventh century onwards: the earliest extant painting (above the 35 m Buddha) and both colossal statues being possibly no earlier than *c.* AD 600 (fig. 120; Klimburg-Salter 1989, pp. 12–16, 90). Certainly the Hindu Kush sites of Bamiyan, Foladi, Kakrak, Nigar and Fondukistan all appear to have flourished from the end of the sixth century onwards (Klimburg-Salter 1989, pp. 10, 54, *passim*). Further south, at the site of Shahr-i Kohna (Old Qandahar), the lowest levels of a clay stupa contained a hoard of 68 'mostly Hunnish' coins and at least one Umayyad coin (Blurton 1981, p. 439; Helms

1997, p. 98). The latest coin evidence from the Great Stupa at Manikyala in the Punjab is similarly associated with an enlargement of the structure in the late seventh or early eighth century (fig. 177; p. 212). Coin evidence also implies that Butkara I in Swat was still in cult at this time (Göbl 1976, pp. 35–7, pl. IX.262–6; Errington 1999/2000, p. 211).

The archaeological evidence suggests that Tapa Sardar at Ghazni and Fondukistan, west of Begram, continued in cult throughout the eighth century (Taddei 1968, pp. 119–20; Taddei and Verardi 1978, pp. 134–5; Carl 1940; Hackin *et al.* 1959, p. 57, fig. 206). Arab sources place the destruction of the latter site more precisely in the last decade of the eighth century. According to Ya'qubi – writing in AH 281: AD 891 – Fadl b. Yahya b. Khalid b. Barmak, the governor of Khurasan, sent a force against the Kabulshah in AH 176: AD 792/3, campaigning as far as Chahbahar at the end of the Panjshir Valley, and taking possession *inter alia* of Bandukistan (i.e. Fondukistan) 'where one finds the idol worshipped by the local people. This idol was destroyed and burnt' (Ya'qubi 1937, p. 106).[27]

Although Buddhism had to contend with the ever-increasing pressure of Islam, following Arab conquests in Afghanistan from the seventh century onwards, it is not clear how permanent or effective each Arab 'conquest' was in the beginning. Incursions into Gandhara evidently started in the reign of Mu'awiyah (AH 41–60: AD 661–80), for Baladhuri records a raid in this period by 'Abbad b. Ziyad, who crossed the desert from Sijistan and led an attack on Ohind by boat across the Indus river (Murgotten 1924, vol. II, pp. 212–13). But, initially at least, there seems to have been little iconoclasm, for the seventh-century Buddhists in Sind even sought Muslim support against the local Brahmanic regime (Verardi 1996, pp. 244–5).

No living Buddhist traditions are preserved in the earliest Islamic records of the ninth century. Yet an essentially accurate description of Buddhist ritual at the 'Nawbahar' of Balkh (Skt *nava-vihāra*, 'new monastery') survives in the accounts of several later writers, which shows that their source probably had first hand experience of these events (Melikian-Chirvani 1974, pp. 10–20). According to the *Kitāb al-buldān* of Ibn al-Faqih (1885, p. 322), for example, written *c.* AH 289/90: AD 902/3,

The Barāmika were prominent people at Balkh before the *Mulūk al-Tawā'if* and their religion was the worship of idols. They founded a place of worship which they call in Balkh the Nawbahār – that is to say, 'the new' [vihara]. The Iranians revere this sanctuary and they go there on pilgrimage, they take offerings to it, they dress it in silk and place banners on the dome, which they call 'ustup' [stupa]. The cupola is 100 cubits in diameter, with a circular gallery around it. Around the sanctuary there are 360 cells where the monks and their novices live. The kings of China and the Kabulshah worshipped here and when they made pilgrimage to it, they used to prostrate themselves before the largest of the idols.

The later writer Yaqut al-Rumi (AH 575–626: AD 1179–1229) says that the Barmakid ruler of Balkh became Muslim following the Arab conquest of Khurasan in the time of 'Uthman b. 'Affan (AH 23–35: AD 644–56) and that Nawbahar was destroyed by the Arabs *c.* AH 42: AD 663/4, during the rebellion of Balkh in the reign of Mu'awiyah (Melikian-Chirvani 1974, pp. 21–2). Despite these claims, the native princes still prayed there in AH 90: AD 708/9 according to Tabari (AD 839–923) (*Ta'rīkh al-rusul wa'l-mulūk*, vol. II, p. 1205, cf. Frye 1960, p. 1000). Following the destruction of Balkh some time after this last date, Khalid b. Barmak (*c.* AH 86–165: AD 706/7–81/2), son of the last Barmak, fled with his mother to Kashmir, where he grew up following 'the religion of his fathers' (Yaqut, *Mu'jam al-buldān*, cf. Melikian-Chirvani 1974, p. 21). His father is reported to have rebuilt Balkh in AH 107: AD 725/6, by order of the governor, Asad b. 'Abd Allah al-Kasri (Tabari, vol. II, p. 1490, cf. Barthold and Sourdel 1960, p. 1033). Khalid moved from Khurasan to Iraq and, although he subsequently converted to Islam, he nevertheless is said by Ibn al-Nadim (AH 377: AD 987/8) to have maintained links with India (*Kitāb al-Fihrist* 1970, pp. 826–7).[28]

According to Ya'qubi, Islam was first adopted by the rulers of Bamiyan in the reign of the 'Abbasid caliph Mansur (AH 136–58: AD 754–75). However, the anonymous *c.* ninth-century text copied by al-Kindi and quoted by Ibn al-Nadim says that there were resident ascetics and devotees at Bamiyan, and that the 'people of India go there on pilgrimages by land and sea from the furthest town [regions] of their country' (Ya'qubi 1937, p. 103; Tarzi 1977, vol. I, Appendix VI, pp. 185–7; Ibn al-Nadim 1970, pp. 828–9). This suggests that although the rulers of Bamiyan may have made a token or genuine conversion to Islam in the eighth century, the site continued in cult until – according to the *Tarikh-e Sistān*, another anonymous eleventh-century text – it was captured in AH 258: AD 871 by Ya'qub b. Layth, who sent 50 idols of gold and silver as booty to the caliph in Baghdad (Anon. 1976, p. 171). Iconoclasm seems to have become the official ideology of the Muslim states increasingly from this point, with the active implementation of the destruction of 'idols' being enshrined in the Afghan place-name Butkhak, the 'dust of idols', a halting point on the road east from Kabul.

Hinduism

Nineteenth- and twentieth-century archaeological explorations in Gandhara concentrated on Buddhism, with the result that information on Hinduism in the region is largely gleaned from later evidence of Brahmanical cults at a number of Buddhist sites from the fourth century AD onwards. The inclusion of Vedic gods such as Indra, Brahma

Figure 121 Shiva images from Gandhara and Akhun Dheri near Charsadda.

and Surya in the art of Gandhara, however, illustrates a shared ancient Indian heritage between the two religions. The depiction, for example, of Subhadra (sister of the pastoral deity Krishna) on the bilingual bronze coins of Pantaleon and Agathocles (*c.*190–180 BC), or Balarama (brother of Krishna) on the square, silver drachms of the last king (figs 26.6; 52.8; Mitchiner 1975, type 149), moreover suggests that Hinduism – or at least its earlier Brahmanical form – co-existed with Buddhism in the region from an early period. The phenomenon can be traced through the Indo-Scythian period, with images of Balarama holding a club and plough on a bronze issue of Maues; and Lakshmi (goddess of good fortune) lustrated by elephants on silver tetradrachms of Azilises (fig. 113.10–11). The process gains momentum in the Kushan period. The most prominent evidence of this is Oesho, who is represented in the guise of Shiva on Kushan coins and seals (figs 61.16–18, 22, 26; 95; Cribb 1997, p. 66, figs 15–17), but his consort Umma (Bactrian ομμο; Hindu Uma) is also named on a coin of Huvishka (fig. 113.12) and in the Rabatak inscription (§§ 9–10; Sims-Williams and Cribb 1995/6, pp. 79, 108; p. 119 above).

The increased popularity of other religions, particularly Brahmanism, was evidently accompanied by the decline of Buddhism. Xuan Zang speaks of a number of 'Deva temples' in Swat and the Jalalabad region, and in Gandhara mentions about a hundred heretical temples belonging to various sects who mingled indiscriminately together (Watters 1904, vol. I, p. 202). Statues of Hindu divinities, found at Buddhist sites in Gandhara and Swat from the Kushan period onwards, support his implication of a religious syncretism embracing Buddhism and Brahmanism, as well as more localised minor cults (fig. 121). Excavated examples include a fourth- to fifth-century image of Shiva from Akhun Dheri near Charsadda in the Peshawar Valley, a fifth-century Shiva Mahadeva from Shnaisha in Swat, a fifth- to sixth-century Vasudeva–Krishna from Dharmarajika, Taxila, and a bronze sixth to seventh-century syncretic naga raja/Shiva mask found by Court at Banamari, Peshawar (figs 121–2; 137; Cribb 1997, p. 65, figs 10–12; 14–18; Rahman 1993, pp. 21–2, 46, 81, pl. XXVIIb; Srinivasan 1997/8, figs 1, 3; Errington and Cribb 1992, pp. 237–9). At Tapa Sardar, Ghazni, an eighth-century image of Mahisasuramardini (a form of Durga) was found placed in

Figure 122 Bronze naga raja/Shiva mask (*c.* sixth to seventh century AD) excavated by Court at Banamari village, Peshawar.

Figure 123 Stucco fragment of a female torso (*c.* ninth century), from Sahri Bahlol mound E.

an otherwise purely Buddhist context (Taddei 1973, pp. 203–13, pl. 15.5).

Xuan Zang also mentions the 'great mountain' in the north-east Peshawar Valley, with its image of Bhima-devi (Durga) and, in its foothills, the temple of her consort Maheshvara-deva (Shiva) (Watters 1904, vol. I, p. 221). Despite the usual discrepancies in the pilgrim's estimated distance, from its general location the site must have been linked to Kashmir Smast, which recent discoveries of lingas, Hindu images, inscriptions, Lajja Gauri seals and coins attest was an important shaivite shrine of the second to tenth centuries, particularly from the Kidarite period onwards (Nasim Khan 2001, pp. 1–8; 2001a, pp. 219–309).

The cult of Skanda/Karttikeya appears to have also been popular. Different versions of this single warrior god, the son of Shiva, appear together as separate divinities identified respectively as Skanda-Kumara, Bizago (Vishakha) and Maasena (Mahasena) on issues of Huvishka (fig. 113.13–14; Rosenfield 1967, p. 99). Sculptural images of Karttikeya from the Kushan period have also been found at Kafirkot in Swat and Tahkal Bala near Peshawar; one dating from the sixth century was excavated at Dharmarajika; and another of

the eighth century at Tahkal Bala (Srinivasan 1997/8, figs 6, 15; Errington 1999/2000, pp. 202–3, figs 76–7).

Finally, there is clear evidence from Sahri Bahlol Mound E that some former Buddhist sites were subsequently converted into Hindu shrines. Stein's excavations here unearthed a number of later sculptures (fig. 123), including a marble lingam and Hindu Shahi coins, which indicate that the location was a shaivite temple in the eighth to tenth century (Stein 1915, pp. 115–16, pl. XL.12; Errington 1999/2000, p. 203).

Notes

1 The dish – an heirloom of the Mirs of Badakshan (northern Afghanistan) – was bought from them in 1838 by Dr P. B. Lord (1808–40). He was an ambitious British political officer based at Bamiyan, from where he conducted – partly by bluff – a vigorous forward policy towards Balkh and the north. Yapp remarks that while Lord 'did not lack intelligence, there was an errant impulsiveness which was to cost Britain dear' (1980, p. 353). It also cost him his life. The dish and a Greco-Bactrian silver pedigree coin of Eucratides I (CM IOC 45/BMC 1) – also acquired by Lord – were inherited by the East India Company and transferred by the India Office to the British Museum in 1882 and 1900 respectively.

2 This combines the Phrygian satyr Marsyas, playing the double flute discarded by Athena, with Silenus, son of a nymph and Hermes or Pan, and elderly companion of Dionysus, who is shown balding and pot-bellied, with a horse's ears and tail.

3 The god of the opposing forces of good and evil, fertility, asceticism and destruction. He is part of the triad of supreme Hindu gods, together with Brahma and Vishnu.

4 The palm branch is more explicitly used – together with a wreath and lion skin – on an issue of Antimachus II (Bopearachchi 1991, pl. 15, ser. 2).

5   For a discussion of the date of Zarathrushtra see Shahbazi 2002, pp. 7–45. There is no general agreement amongst scholars. Mary Boyce suggests an early date (2001, p. xiii). Zaehner prefers 628–551 BC (1961, p. 33), which is based on Plutarch's date of 258 years before Alexander, while al-Biruni places Zarathrushtra only 250 years before Alexander (*al-Āthār al-bāqiyah*, p. 176).

6   According to Mary Boyce (2001, p. 3), the word means 'authoritative utterance' in Avestan.

7   Another ancient section within the *Yasna* is the *Yasna Haphtanhaiti* ('Worship of the Seven Chapters'), a short liturgy which on linguistic grounds is very similar to the *Gathas* and is therefore attributed to Zarathushtra (Boyce 2001, p. xiv).

8   The *Vendidad* is an incorrect term often used for the *Videvdad*.

9   The *Bundahishn* is also called *Zand Agahih* ('Knowledge from the Zand'): see Boyce 2001, p. 136.

10 The inscriptions from Pasargadae in the name of Cyrus were probably added later under Darius: Hinz 1973, pp. 1, 19, 21, pls III–V.

11 Cf. Avestan *khvarenah*, Old Persian *farnah*, Sogdian *farn*, Bactrian *far(o)*. See Gnoli 1999, pp. 312–19.

12 For a discussion of the identification of the god as the Sogdian Weshparkar see Cribb 1997, pp. 29–30.

13 There were no state religions in the Achaemenid period and various religions and cults co-existed. In the third century AD Zoroastrianism was competing with Judaism, Christianity, Buddhism and Hinduism.

14 This letter was translated into Arabic in the ninth century, then retranslated into Persian by Ibn Isfandiyar, author of *Tarikh-i Tabaristan* (The History of Tabaristan), in the thirteenth century: see Boyce 1984, p. 109.

15 At Sar-Mashad, Kerdir describes his journey to the world beyond and how he saw heaven and hell.

16 A high ecclesiastic in Sasanian times, with 'virtually indistinguishable functions' from the *herbad*, see Boyce 2001, pp. 97–8.

17 For details and illustrations see Ulansey 2005.

18 Now the ecclesiastical title of the Nestorian and Armenian patriarchs.

19 In Sri Lankan Buddhist tradition, Mahinda, one of Ashoka's sons, is credited with bringing Buddhism to the island.

20 Dubbed 'Hinayana' by the Mahayanists, a derogatory term which usually is politely translated as 'Little' or 'Lesser Vehicle', as opposed to 'Mahayana' meaning 'Great Vehicle'.

21 Information courtesy of Shailendra Bhandare and Joe Cribb who examined the two coins and identified the overstrikes.

22 Discovered by C. G. M. Hastings in the early 1900s being used as a money-box by a village trader.

23 An official title from the Greek *meridarkhes*: Sircar 1966, p. 202.

24 There is a discrepancy in distance as 1 *li* equals *c*.352 yards or 322 metres, so 3–4 *li* is only *c*.1–1.3 km, but this is generally the case with the estimates given by the Chinese pilgrims and should be taken as only approximate.

25 The only earlier example of this phenomenon is a gold coin of Wima Kadphises (*c*. AD 113–27) from Shevaki stupa 1 west of Guldara, near Kabul (fig. 181).

26 Watters follows Cunningham's identification of Udyana as comprising Swat, Chitral, Bajaur and Buner (1871, p. 81; Deane 1896, p. 655).

27 An alternative reading of 'Yandil-Istān' is proposed by Wiet, the translator of this text. The reading 'Bandukistān' is given by David Bivar (personal communication).

28 Al-Nadīm quotes a (probably ninth-century) anonymous manuscript copied by Ya'qub b. Ishaq al-Kindi (AH 283–350: AD 897–961).

Part 3

Encountering
the past

5 From Taq-i Bustan to Lahore: French and Italian officers in Persia and the Punjab 1816–46

Jean-Marie Lafont

The question whether Napoleon considered following in the steps of Alexander the Great and invading India is problematical; and one that is more often than not dismissed on the grounds that no concrete evidence of any such intention exists in French archives and military records. Plans for the invasion of India in the late eighteenth century do exist, but they appear to be merely the routine exercises of *officiers d'état-major* (staff officers), or projects drawn by officers returned from India attempting to rouse the French military establishment to the prospect of an Indian expedition.[1] True, when the French fleet sailed out from Toulon in May 1798, not many people knew what the ultimate aim of the expedition was. Some letters sent by General Bonaparte to Tipu Sultan, seized at Srirangapatnam in 1799, and the appointment of Piveron de Morlat in Bonaparte's Etat-major,[2] do show that the opportunity for a strike in India was not deemed impossible by the twenty-nine year-old general. But this did not materialise and the Indian Native regiments, who sailed from Bombay to fight the French in Egypt, arrived there after the surrender of General Menou to Hutchinson in 1801.[3] Bonaparte was already back in France, and the ultimate cultural achievement of the French expedition was the *Description de l'Egypte* (Jomard 1809–28), which paved the way to the decipherment of hieroglyphics by Champollion in 1822.[4]

British intelligence still suspected Bonaparte, at that time Premier Consul, of sinister intentions regarding India. The fact that Bonaparte had purchased the Malmaison estate, whose extensive lands adjoined General de Boigne's property of Beauregard at Saint-Cloud, seemed to British intelligence yet another indication of French designs on British India,[5] especially since de Boigne was suspected in Calcutta of having been offered the chance to lead a Franco-Russian expedition to India as early as 1803.[6] The same year, when – according to the Peace of Amiens – Pondicherry was to be returned to the French, Lord Wellesley instructed his commanding officer there to delay the retrocession and not to give the city back to General Decaen. This was shortly followed by the launch of full-scale military operations in the Doab and the conquest of northern India by the East India Company, the capture of Delhi by Lord Lake and the extension of British India as far as the Punjab, with a vaguely defined border meandering somewhere between the Jamuna and the Sutlej rivers.

The next threat was in May 1807, when Napoleon and the Persian Ambassador Mirza Reza Khan signed the treaty of Finkenstein. It was followed in July 1807 by the Treaty of Tilsit between Napoleon and Tsar Alexander I, in which it was agreed to organise a joint expedition to attack British India. British intelligence quickly came to know of the plot.[7]

Figure 124 General Jean-Baptiste Ventura (1794-1858).

Hence the three missions sent from Calcutta to Persia, 'Caubul' (in fact Peshawar) and Lahore, to try to build a bulwark against such aggression (Lafont 1992, pp. 107–8, with reference to Yapp 1980). It is during his mission to 'Caubul' that Mountstuart Elphinstone saw and described the stupa of Manikyala for the first time (fig. 175, pp. 159, 211 below; Elphinstone 1815, I, pp. 106–8 and note, pl. 1).

The Gardanne mission in Persia did not last long (1807–8). Yapp correctly states that there was nothing against India in the original purpose of the mission (1980, pp. 39–41), although Jean Tulard no less correctly asserts that the main purpose of Napoleon's oriental policy was the destruction of British power in India and the dismembering of the Ottoman empire (1988, p. 201). Nevertheless, in 1809 the *Voyage dans la Turquie et la Perse 1807–1808* by Ange Gardanne was published in Paris and Marseilles, and kept alive the 'rêve oriental' of Napoleon. Another literary event, the première of *Tipoo Saëb*, a play by Etienne de Jouy staged in Paris in 1813 in presence of the Emperor, is more proof of the continuing interest in France as regards India and past connections between its great historical figures and the French.[8]

We do not yet know of any specific influence which might have given Ventura and Avitabile (figs 12; 124–5) the idea of going to Persia after the defeat of Waterloo and, more

Figure 125 General Paolo Crescenzo Avitabile (1791–1850).

Figure 126 General Jean-François Allard (1785–1839).

pertinently, after the restoration of various monarchies in continental Europe made life miserable for former officers attached to the ideals of the French Revolution. In the case of Jean-François Allard (fig. 126), born at Saint-Tropez in 1785, the living memory of the Bailli de Suffren[9] in that city was the best introduction to the dreams of India for a boy who, at eighteen, had first enrolled in the 23rd Dragoons. His father was a sea-captain who, according to family tradition, sailed several times to the Levant, while one of his relatives was a 'drogman' (translator) at the French legation in Constantinople in the last years of the eighteenth century.[10] Allard, shaken by the political situation in France, where severe royalist reaction and discrimination prevailed in 1815–18,[11] made a successful application for four months' leave from the army to go to Civita-Vecchia in Italy to settle some family business. He did go to Civita-Vecchia, but his passport, which still survives in private archives in France, shows all the stamps collected during his subsequent journey to Aleppo, then Constantinople. On 15 April 1820, while residing in Tabriz, he penned a letter to the French Ministre de la Guerre informing him of his travels and asking permission to enter the service of Shahzada (Prince) Abbas Mirza (fig. 158), who had been particularly impressed by his Légion d'Honneur.[12]

Claude-Auguste Court's father had served in the Indian ocean in 1781–3 in the squadron of Bailli de Suffren, and then in Egypt under Bonaparte.[13] This was more than enough to give his son the idea of quitting Restoration France in quest of his freedom and livelihood in the east. Court (figs 11–12) was a former cadet of the Ecole spéciale militaire de Saint-Cyr (class of 1813),[14] and he was one of the many educated French officers who travelled to the east because of political discrimination in France during the Restoration. In his, as yet unpublished, *Mémoires* (MSS 1, vol. IV, p. 197), Court says he

left France in June 1816 as mathematics tutor to the children of Mr Rousseau, the French consul appointed to Baghdad. Once in Aleppo, he was successful in persuading the consul that his children would get a better education in France (MSS 1, vol. I, p. 45) and he was planning to return with them when Mr Guis, the French consul at Aleppo, advised him to go to Persia where some of his 'frères d'armes' were raising and training the armies of local rulers. When he arrived in Kirmanshah, he met Mr Vigouroux, another French consul general, and Mr Hubert, his old friend and former colleague from the Saint Cyr military academy. Through them he was introduced to the small contingent of European officers in the service of Muhammad Ali Mirza, eldest son and heir of the Shah. He lists the officers he found in Kirmanshah as follows (MSS 1, vol. I, p. 92):

Hubert, from Caen, former Lieutenant of Infantry under Napoleon
Barachin, from Paris, formerly aide-major
Avitabile, from Naples, Lieutenant of Artillery in the Armée d'Italie
Oms, from Spain [for more on Oms, see below]
Ventura, from Finale, Italian officer
Ciatis [elsewhere Ciattis], from Pisa, from the Italian Vélites
Deveaux, from Calais, Captain in the 2nd Regiment of the Imperial Guard
Aubrelique [elsewhere Ambrélique], from Noyon, Captain in the 2nd Regiment of the Imperial Guard
Pietragua, from Milan, Lieutenant in the 1st Italian Regiment
Raymond, from Cambrai, ex-Consul of France in Basra
Demura [sic, correctly spelt 'de Murat' elsewhere], from Baghdad, Interpreter to His Royal Highness

Court did not join this contingent initially. He says he returned to Baghdad with Hubert and Darmandy,[15] with the idea of going to Kabulistan and, if they did not find employment there, to continue on to Lahore. On 10 January 1821 they sailed from Bassora (Basra) to Bushire, where they were informed that the kingdoms of Kabul and Lahore were trying to modernise their armed forces in anticipation of having to defend themselves against the British (MSS 1, vol. I, p. 99). The trio moved from Bushire to Shiraz (MSS 1, vol. I, p. 117), then to Isfahan where they visited Jalfa (MSS 1, vol. I, p. 133) and on to Qom and Tehran (MSS 1, vol. I, p. 156). Court records that (MSS 1, vol. I, p. 161)

> In Tehran, I had the nice surprise of meeting my compatriot Mr Allard, formerly ADC to Maréchal Brune. My fellow travellers also had the pleasure of seeing Mr Ventura again, with whom they had served at the Kirmanshah court. These two gentlemen, recently arrived from Tabriz, were waiting for Dr Lafosse,[16] before implementing their project of going to India.

Court then describes the choice he had to make when offered employment by the Shah through the Vizir Haji Muhammad Husain Khan. This he decided to accept, even though Allard and Ventura invited him to join them in going to Lahore. Although he does not explicitly mention any British pressure to expel the French officers from Persia (Lafont 1992, pp. 117–20; Yapp 1980, pp. 72–3, 98–9), Court makes a long digression on British apprehensions during and after the Gardanne mission to Tehran.[17] He also says that most of the small band of Europeans dispersed: Pietragua and Ciatis left for Tabriz, Allard and Ventura for India, and Court for Kirmanshah, while 'the others remained in Tehran'. We shall come back to Allard and Ventura's journey from Tehran to Lahore later. Let us now follow the story of Court and Avitabile in Persia, until they also departed for Lahore in 1826.

Court returned to Kirmanshah to take up his command under Muhammad Ali Mirza. The only Europeans he found there were Deveaux, Avitabile, Raymond and Oms. Court was given the battalion of 'Korremabad', neglected since the departure of Hubert, while Avitabile was in command of the 'Songour' battalion (MSS 1, vol. I, pp. 219–20). Both of them fought at the battle of 'Chérézour' between the Persians and the Turks, where all the European officers were decorated by the Prince on the battlefield.[18] The first volume of Court's *Mémoires* ends with the Prince's demise at an unspecified date (MSS 1, vol. I, p. 235).

Volume II covers the period from 1821 to 1825, when Court continued to serve in Persia. After the death of the Prince, his youngest brother Abbas Mirza (fig. 158) became the heir apparent and stripped Muhammad Hussain Mirza (the eldest son of his deceased brother) of several provinces. This forced the young man to dismiss all his European officers except Oms, Deveaux and Court, who helped him capture the city of Mendeli.[19] Court then traces the process of modernising the Kirmanshah forces,[20] stating that the drive towards modernisation in Persia was implemented by Abbas Mirza, who was fascinated by Napoleon and initially employed English officers who had come with the Malcolm mission (in 1808). When these officers went back to England or India, he persisted by recruiting whoever he could to continue this policy.[21] This influenced his eldest brother at Kirmanshah who first employed Hubert (a former cadet of the Military Academy of Saint-Cyr) and Barrachin, followed by Oms, Avitabile, Ventura and Ciattis. Court informs us that Oms, together with an Armenian assistant, was originally in charge of the gun foundry and then in charge of the arsenal which he had established. Kirmanshah assumed a rather martial

aspect, especially after the arrival of Deveaux, Ambrélique, Bacheville and Court. When the Prince died, his son wanted to keep up this military establishment, but he was obliged to reduce it considerably. He kept Deveaux in charge of the infantry and Court for the artillery. Court then gives an account of this artillery unit (2 companies, each 120 strong), which had been formed in 1818 by Avitabile, a former lieutenant of artillery in the Neapolitan army, who had left Naples after the fall of Murat. When Avitabile was given the command of the Soungour battalion, he relinquished the artillery to Oms. After Oms was dismissed by the Prince in 1824, Court was given charge of the units. This is the only detailed reference in Court's *Mémoires* to Oms, whom the French officers were to meet again in Lahore in 1826. During this period in Kirmanshah there were five battalions of regular infantry, providing a force 3400 strong.[22]

By this time, but at an unspecified date, Deveaux and Court had received an invitation from the Pasha of Baghdad to join him in modernising his own troops. Although the salary offered was high, they refused because they remembered the difficulties that had been encountered in Constantinople by Baron de Boneval, when trying to introduce European discipline among the Turks. They remained at Kirmanshah till 1824, trying unsuccessfully to raise a force of regular cavalry.[23] Their failure was due to the hostility of the local nobility, who were amused, but not tempted, by these '*Bazi Farengi*'.[24] Court then writes at length about the decorations he received from Muhammad Ali Mirza (MSS 1, vol. II, pp. 53–5), and includes some richly illuminated miniature paintings pasted on a page of his *Mémoires* (figs 127–33), together with translations (dated Kirmanshah, 15 July 1822) of the diplomas by 'J. de Murat, interprète de SAR le prince de Kermansha [*sic*]'. Other interesting illustrations in this volume are five drawings of the 'Takht-e-Boustan' with the signature 'A. Court Delivit' (MSS 1, vol. II, pp. 74–5).

In 1824, as the general feeling was that Muhammad Hussain Mirza would soon lose Kirmanshah owing to the jealousy of Abbas Mirza, Court planned to go to Russia where, at that time, 'French officers were most welcome'.[25] However, he was refused permission to leave the Prince's service and had to remain in Kirmanshah. Then Avitabile (who had returned from Italy to Persia) and Court both received letters from Allard and Ventura inviting them to Lahore. This time the Prince granted them leave and, on 28 May 1826, they both left Kirmanshah for Kabul and Lahore (MSS 1, vol. II, p. 129). In early June they were in Hamadan, where Court called on 'the local Armenian wife of Mr Oms'. Oms had already left for the Punjab and his wife was inconsolable: 'In order to comfort her, I beguiled her with the hope that her husband would return to her some day'. But Oms, as we know, never returned to Persia, for he died in Lahore in 1828. In Hamadan, Court and Avitabile were met by Abet (Habid?), who had been sent by Allard and Ventura to escort them to Lahore; and it seems he did not conceal the fact that the two officers were going to the Punjab, for four of their servants refused to accompany them (MSS 1, vol. II, p. 132). At Djulfa (a suburb of Isfahan), Court met George Clerk of the British East India Company, whom he says in his *Mémoires* he met again later as Political Agent at Lahore.[26] He

Figure 127 'Koulam Pish-Kedmat, Garde du corps', 165 × 237 mm. Watercolour on paper; watermark: crown + 1818.

Figure 129 'Kalioumtchis' (hubble bubble/narghile seller), 124 × 179 mm. Watercolour on paper; watermark: 180[last number under glue].

Figure 128 'Ecuyer persan tenant en laisse un cheval de parade', 147 × 182 mm. Watercolour on paper.

Figure 130 'Cavalier afghan', 144 × 190 mm. Watercolour on paper; watermark: crown.

adds that after serving as Governor of Agra, then Bombay, Clerk had just been appointed Secretary General of the East India Company.[27] This precise information allows us to date the final draft of Court's *Mémoires* to 1856–8.

The third volume of the *Mémoires* is entitled 'Voyage à travers la Perse centrale et l'Afghanistan' (fig. 134). It survives, at least in part, as two separate manuscripts: the revised account of the voyage written or copied in 1856–8; and also a much earlier version which Court had produced when first in Lahore. As acknowledged by Alexander Burnes (1834, vol. III, pp. 157–8), the East India Company knew

Figure 131 'Prêtre arménien', 136 × 204 mm. Watercolour on paper.

Figure 133 'Koulam' (servant), 163 × 214 mm. Watercolour on paper.

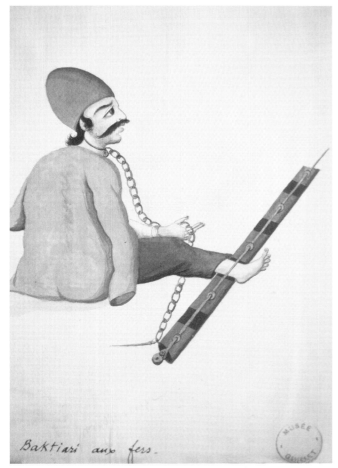

Figure 132 Bakhtiari aux fers', 170 × 208 mm. Watercolour on paper; watermark: crown with fleur de lis.

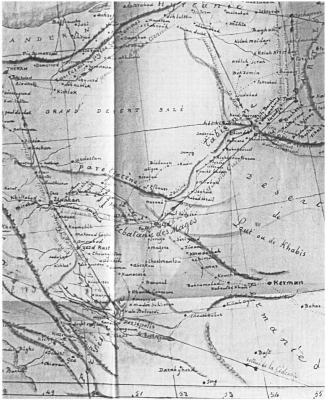

Figure 134 Detail of Court's map of Persia: from Rasht and Zanjan to Herat, from Shatt el-Arab to the desert of Bunpur.

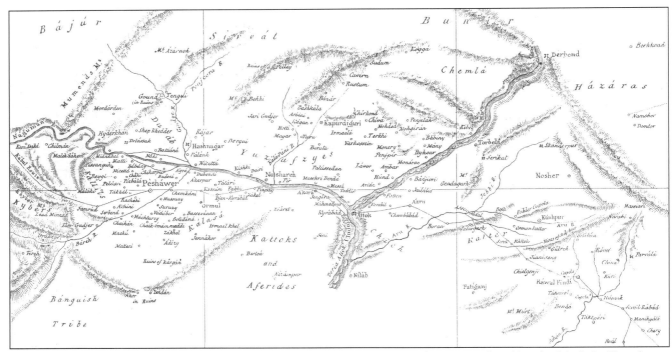

Figure 135 Detail of Court's map of the Peshawar Valley: 'Route map of the provinces comprising the ancient Taxila and Peucelaotis in the Panjáb made . . . in 1826-1835'.

almost nothing at that time of the regions between Yezd and Herat. When Court became aware in 1833 of the Company's interest in such information, he generously offered them – through Wade, the Political Agent in charge of 'Sikh' affairs at Ludhiana – a copy of his manuscript on this part of his journey.[28] This document still survives in the Imperial archives in India.[29] It gives the best available account of the road between Yezd and Peshawar as it was in 1826, including a description of the monuments and surroundings of Herat, and a reference to the city in the time of Alexander the Great. It also illustrates coins from Begram.

Court then describes the vicissitudes of his journey from Herat to Peshawar. The constant turmoil and danger included a murderous assault on Avitabile and their imprisonment at Ghazni (from where they were saved by Nawab Jabbar Khan, half-brother of Dost Muhammad Khan and a close friend of Allard and Ventura). He also gives details of each area they visited: the crops, manufactures, villages, markets and wells and, of course, the armed forces and defensive situation of the country. From Kabul en route to the Khyber Pass, they travelled with Nawab Jabbar Khan, who was visiting his estates in the Laghman Valley. However, on approaching Jalalabad, they were caught up the rush and frenzy of the *ghazis* (the equivalent of the present-day *mujahidin*), who were flocking to Peshawar to join the *jihad* of Syed Ahmed Barelvi 'against the Sikhs'.[30] For their own safety they accompanied Jabbar Khan to the Laghman Valley, where Court busied himself in exploring the archaeological remains of the region. Jabbar Khan then provided an escort for their passage to Peshawar, which they reached unscathed by pretending that they were Persian merchants also joining the *jihad*. It was at Peshawar that Court first had time to begin putting his notes in order, before he and Avitabile were able to slip away from the city and proceed to the Indus river at Attock (fig. 135). There they were warmly and ceremoniously received by Allard and Ventura at the head of the *Fauj-i-khas*.[31]

Allard and Ventura had left Persia in late 1821, and in March 1822 they reached Shadara, opposite Lahore on the Ravi river.[32] Native agents for the British noticed the arrival of two *feringhis*, Allard and Ventura, and one *ghora*, poor Csoma de Koros, who had joined the 'French' officers and their escort in Dakka,[33] in order to travel safely with them through the Khyber Pass. In Lahore, Allard and Ventura[34] were employed by Ranjit Singh to raise and train the *Fauj-i-khas*, or 'special' brigade,[35] which was immediately baptised 'Francisi Kampu' (French army) by the Punjabis and 'French Legion' by British intelligence. Trained along the same lines as the elite regiments of Napoleon's army, these units were immediately perceived as a potential threat by Calcutta, which appointed Claude Martine Wade, a brilliant young officer fluent in French, as Assistant Political Agent at Ludhiana to monitor activities in Punjab.[36] Wade remained politically in charge of the Sikh frontier until his appointment to Indore in 1842.

There are two interesting descriptions of the *Fauj-i-khas* in 1826–7: the first by a Dr Murray, who came to Lahore to attend the ill Maharaja (Chopra 1929, pp. 245–81); the second by Claude Martine Wade during his first visit to the Lahore Court, where he quickly observed that the French Legion 'appeared to be a remarkably fine body of men' and noticed 'the tri-colour Flag which the French officers I find have adopted as the distinguishing Ensign of their Corps' (Chopra 1929, pp. 283–329).[37] Wade then gives the following description of the brigade:

In proceeding to join the Raja on the morning of the 12 [June 1827] I observed the plain where the review were held occupied by the whole body of the troops under the command of Messrs. Allard and Ventura. They were formed in one line, the infantry on the right, the cavalry on the left, and had a very martial appearance. On approaching . . . I noticed a French officer . . . whom the Raja introduced to me as M. Allard, adding that he was the cleverest of all his officers. The cavalry commanded by M. Allard consists of two regiments of Dragoons and one of

Lancers. . . . The Dragoons are mostly Sikhs and wear the Sikh turban. The Lancers are chiefly Pathans from Hindustan. . . . There are however two troops of Sikhs in that corps. . . .

The Legion of infantry commanded by M. Ventura is composed of four Battalions of Sikhs and one of Gorkhas and Purbiahs. . . . M. Ventura put his Legion through several manoeuvres which the Corps executed with a steadiness and precision it would be difficult to excel. Their formation into close column, their march and deployment into line were performed with such a closeness and accuracy as to surprise the whole party. It was indeed impossible not to admire the high degree of perfection to which M. Ventura has brought his Legion. He was the only mounted officer in the field, and the facility with which he directed the movements of the whole corps evidently showed that he was an officer of skill and ability. The review concluded by the Legion marching past the Raja in open column of grand Division and, after expressing the pleasure I had derived from it, I retired to camp.

The infantry regiments of the *Fauj-i-khas* remained more or less the same until 1846, their numerical strength fluctuating between 4000 and 5000 men. The cavalry, about 3000 strong in 1823, was down to two light cavalry regiments of 2000 men by 1830, and was further reduced to one regiment by 1833. But when Allard returned from France in 1837, he raised two regiments of Cuirassiers (heavy cavalry) which were posted in Peshawar under the command of Colonel Mouton (Lafont 2002, pp. 192–8, appendix III, pp. 204–22). The regular artillery, which in 1823 comprised several *Deras*, ultimately came under the sole command of *Daroga* Ilahi Bakhsh who, as the commanding officer of the *Topkhana*, was placed right from the beginning (1822) under Allard and Ventura. There is no specific mention of the strength of the artillery of the *Fauj-i-khas* in the Khalsa Durbar Records, but we can more or less safely infer that the *Fauj-i-khas* – at its maximum capacity, infantry, cavalry and artillery included – was about 10,000 strong, although this strength fluctuated owing to the transfer of artillery units to other brigades and the reduction of the cavalry forces in the late 1820s and early 1830s.[38]

As we have seen, Oms came to Lahore in early 1826. His identity is not clear.[39] Was he a French officer of Napoleon's army who had been fighting in Russia (as he introduced himself to Dr Murray in Lahore), or was he a Spaniard (as Court clearly states in his *Mémoires* and Wade testified in one of his reports)? What is certain is that Allard, Ventura, Court and Avitabile did not want to have anything to do with him in Lahore. Ranjit Singh therefore gave Oms the command of a fully fledged brigade whose headquarters were in Shadara, and Oms took orders directly from the Maharaja. This brigade had five infantry regiments, probably 5000 men, and one very well trained cavalry unit when Oms died of cholera in 1828. We do not know anything about the fate of these regiments after his death.

Court and Avitabile also joined the Punjab army in 1826, a few weeks after Oms reached Lahore. They raised their own brigades, consisting of three battalions and one artillery unit under Court, and three battalions under Avitabile (Lafont 1992, pp. 139–40). Each of these regiments was about 900 strong: Court's brigade had approximately 3000 men, and Avitabile's 2700. These three 'French' brigades (or four if we include Oms's) of 13 to 15 regiments (or 18 to 20 if we include Oms's), plus their *Deras* of artillery, were the spearhead of the Punjab army, with General Allard being the acknowledged senior officer of these elite units.[40]

The purpose of creating such powerful 'modern' units in the Punjab army was dual: not only to fight against the external enemies of the state but also to contain and deter the various internal forces of internecine dissension and turmoil (Lafont 2002b, pp. 54–61). The whole Punjab army was nominally under the command of the Maharaja. But because of the feudal land system, and political and familial rivalries in the country and the Durbar, Ranjit Singh could not rely on the loyalty of most units of the army for the internal policy of the State. The *Fauj-i-khas* – and later the other 'French' brigades – were raised by the Maharaja as an instrument of might against any other military power which might rear its head against the *Sarkar* (government), as indeed happened after Ranjit Singh's death in June 1839. Besides the fact that Allard took orders directly from the Maharaja, and from no one else, the very locations of the military cantonments around Lahore clearly show the precautions Ranjit Singh took to prevent a coup d'état by his own troops. The French brigades were positioned in a strategic circle between the city and the other military forces: the *Fauj-i-khas* at Anarkali, Court's brigade at Naulakha, Avitabile's brigade at Buddha-ka-Ava (between the Lahore Fort and the Shalimar gardens) and Oms's brigade at Shadara, controlling the only boat-bridge, the ferry and the ford to the other side of the Ravi (Lafont 2002b, p. 135, map 4).

The other regular units of the Punjab army were a huge military component called the *Kampu-i-mualla* (Great Army) of some 25,000 strong under the command of Diwan Ganga Ram, whose headquarters were partly at Mian Mir[41] and partly at Nawankot, on the road to Multan.[42] When Ganga Ram died in 1826, Ranjit Singh offered the command to Ajudhya Prasad, then *Bakhshi* of the *Fauj-i-khas* and one of the best officers of the French brigades. That was the best way to unify all his regular forces under one single training and discipline. Ajudhya Prasad declined the offer, stating that he wanted to serve only in the *Fauj-i-khas*. Ranjit Singh then gave the command of the *Kampu* to General Tej Singh.[43] Moreover, in 1833 the Maharaja, highly satisfied with the discipline and the efficiency of the *Fauj-i-khas*, decided to transform the *Kampu-i-mualla* by modelling it on his French brigades. This was a huge task, considering the number of senior and low-ranking officers needed to discipline these soldiers who were already trained according to their own system of warfare. Ranjit Singh probably asked the *Fauj-i-khas* to part with a number of its own officers and men (the time coincides with the lowest ebb in Allard's cavalry) and most probably some of its *Dera* of artillery, but no assessment has yet been made of these transfers.

Another reference to some 'French' influence in the development of the Punjab army comes from the *Mémoires* of General Court. The French officers were part of an inner circle of friends within the Lahore Durbar and among the gentry of the country, and a strong friendship developed between Court and Raja Gulab Singh of Jammu, to such an extent that the latter entrusted the military education of his eldest son, Udham Singh, to the French general. Not a small vote of confidence from one who was later nicknamed the 'Fox' of Jammu! Court wrote in his *Mémoires* that he raised and organised for Raja Gulab Singh 'un régiment d'infanterie, deux batteries d'artillerie légère' (one infantry regiment and

Figure 136 Detail of Court's map of the Punjab: 'Carte pour l'intelligence des passages de l'Hydaspe et de l'Acésine par Alexandre le Grand'.

Figure 137 Drawing by Imam Bakhsh Lahori of the bronze naga raja/Shiva mask found by Court at Banamari. See also fig. 122.

two units of light artillery),[44] which may (or may not) have been the core of the troops which were later engaged in the conquest of Ladakh under the command of General Zorawar Singh. In 1830, when the explorer Victor Jacquemont (1801–32) was warmly received and entertained by Raja Gulab Singh in the area of Jhelum, Khewra and the Salt Range, the Raja noticed that his guest had a detailed map of Kashmir which had been drawn and given to him by Court (Lafont 2002b, p. 120, ill. 257). In the period 1826–35 Court also produced a comprehensive map of the Punjab, including the Jhelum region (fig. 136), part of which was published in the *Journal of the Asiatic Society of Bengal* (Court 1836a); and was declared the only accurate map available by Alexander Cunningham when he first visited the Peshawar Valley in 1848 (fig. 135; 1848, p. 130).

Court, as already noted, was a former cadet of the Special Military Academy of Saint-Cyr (class of 1813), a brilliant mathematician and an excellent engineer, besides his other academic achievements in history and archaeology which won him the reputation of being the *Aflatoun* (Plato) and the *Bocrates* (Socrates) of the Punjab (figs 122, 137, 178).[45] Apart from the command of his brigade, his main task was the renovation of the Punjab artillery, for which he had specifically been invited from Persia by the Maharaja on Allard's and Ventura's recommendation. Court, in his *Mémoires*, says that he translated into Persian the 'excellent book' on artillery by Théodore Durtubie (a brigadier-general in the artillery division of the French army), which became the standard manual of the Sikhs, who learnt from it how to produce shells, hollow cannon-balls and incendiary bombs. I have not yet found a single copy of this Persian translation, but the fifth edition (Durtubie 1795), a comprehensive treatise with illustrations, remained the standard handbook of the army and military academies in France until the 1850s. From Jacquemont, who was in Lahore in 1830, Court acquired not only valuable information concerning the iron deposits in Mandi but also new formulas for casting guns.

Court was mainly instrumental in creating modern artillery for the Punjab army, and we have numerous testimonies of his contribution to gun-casting: many of the guns captured by the English during the two Sikh wars bore his name or the names of his assistants. Soon after his arrival in 1827 he started making shells, for which he was awarded Rs 5000, jewels and other gifts by Ranjit Singh. He also worked with his Punjabi colleagues – one of them being

Lehna Singh Majithia – to develop the Idgah foundry near Lahore, which produced heavy, light and field guns, mounted on carriages of excellent quality. In 1831, three to four years after Court had taken over the modernisation of the artillery, Alexander Burnes witnessed a training session of the horse artillery in Lahore (Burnes 1834, vol. I, p. 16):

> We met his Highness at an appointed hour on the parade ground, with a train of fifty-one pieces of artillery which he had assembled on the occasion. They were brass 6-pounders, each drawn by six horses. The command was taken by a native officer, who put them through movements of horse artillery, and formed line and column in every direction. The evolutions were not rapidly performed, but the celerity was considerable; and no accident in overturning or firing occurred throughout the morning. There were no wagons in the field, and the horses and equipments were inferior. The guns however were well cast, and the carriages in good repair. They had been made at Lahore, and had cost him 1000 rupees each. . . . [The Maharaja added that he had] 100 pieces of field artillery, exclusive of battering guns and mortars.

This is a clear indication that Ranjit Singh did not wait for Lord William Bentinck's gift of four English guns in 1831 to start modernising his artillery. That this was in excellent condition in 1839 is attested by Lieutenant William Barr, himself an artillery man, who that year witnessed a firing exercise by Court's gunners in Peshawar. After giving a detailed description of the exercise and inspection of the guns, Barr concluded: 'When it is considered that all we saw was the work of the general's own knowledge, and we reflect on the difficulties he has had to surmount, it is a matter almost of wonder to behold the perfection to which he has brought his artillery' (1844, pp. 148–9).

The modernising drive of the whole Punjab army was followed by its reorganisation into major units called divisions and the creation – on 16 December 1836 – of eight generals (Lafont 1992, pp. 144–5). Allard was at that time in France where he had taken Bannu Pan Deï, his Indian (Hindu) wife, and their five children,[46] but Ventura, Court and Avitabile were all promoted generals. The *Umdat ut-Tawarikh* registered a protest from Ventura for being given the same grade as his other Punjabi colleagues since, as he said bluntly, he had been the instructor of them all. This was a protest which the Maharaja readily acknowledged, replying that Ventura would be soon given the rank of 'Great General' (Lafont 1992, p. 145). It does not seem that this title, the approximate equivalent of Army Chief of Staff, was ever created by Ranjit Singh. But the Maharaja paid Ventura an official visit at his headquarters in Anarkali the following day and offered him a *jagir* of Rs 5000 for his daughter Victorine. Five days later (21 December 1836), an official proclamation was read declaring Ventura 'faithful and devoted'. Three months later (March 1837) Allard, true to his salt, returned from France to Lahore. He was immediately promoted to the rank of general by the Maharaja and resumed the command of the *Fauj-i-khas*. Ventura left for Europe, and the matter subsided.

Allard had been appointed by King Louis-Philippe 'Agent de France' (ambassador) to the government of the Punjab.[47] Perhaps one of the secret messages Allard gave to King Louis-Philippe on behalf of Ranjit Singh was the need to send French officers to train his new units. Certainly, while he was in Paris, Allard received numerous letters from senior and junior military officers alike, offering to join him in Lahore (Lafont 1992, pp. 229–30). He always wrote back that he had no instructions from the Maharaja to recruit for the Punjab army. Nevertheless, English agents in Paris reported to London that he was on a recruiting drive; that young officers were submitting their resignation to the French government; and that they were secretly travelling to the Middle East in order to join him. All British stations between Marseilles and Bombay were put on alert to arrest any French traveller who might be an officer in disguise. And when the news of his diplomatic assignment leaked out in the Parisian press, the Court of Directors of the East India Company persuaded Palmerston to instruct Lord Granville, the ambassador to Paris, to get the appointment cancelled.[48]

The French government did not comply.[49] But it does not seem that they had any specific plan to send extensive military manpower to Ranjit Singh, although they were perhaps desirous of tying up British troops in India at a time (i.e. 1836) when the French in Algeria were advancing on Constantine.[50] In any event, when Allard returned to Lahore, he brought 205 enormous cases containing the necessary equipment for his cuirassier regiments (500 breast-plates, 2000 arms), a model of an artillery-park complete with cannon to scale (the latest French improvement in this field) and two million detonating caps, the latest replacement of flint for muskets and pistols. But no junior staff accompanied him to Lahore, and only a few officers like Colonels Mouton, Laroche, de Facyeu (and his son) and two Lafonts[51] managed to reach Lahore and enter the service of the Punjab by 1838. Some of them are depicted in the centre of August Schoefft's grand painting 'Der Hof von Lahor', otherwise known as the 'Court of Maharaja Ranjit Singh' (Lafont 2002b, pp. 42–3, ill. 24; Aijazuddin 1979, pp. 97–144).

There are several descriptions by British experts of the Punjab army after this last modernising drive. One of them is by Henry E. Fane, who came to Lahore in March 1837 with his uncle Lord Fane, Commander-in-Chief of the British army, to attend the wedding of Prince Nao Nihal Singh. An impressive review of the Punjab army took place. Fane wrote (1842, vol. I, pp. 84–5):

> We found them drawn up in line, extending two miles on the banks of the river, consisting of twenty-eight battalions of infantry and six of cavalry; altogether 18,000 men exceedingly well clothed and armed in the European fashion. . . . On the right of the line was General Ventura's brigade, consisting of eight regiments of infantry,[52] which he put to two movements, both of which they executed with equal steadiness and precision with our men. . . . [Their] discipline is really wonderful. . . .Generals Ventura and Allard have been now, for many years, in the Maha Raja's service. . . . To them, and to Monsieur Court in the artillery branch of his service, he owes principally the really advanced state of equipment and discipline to which his forces have been brought.

Another account comes from Lord Auckland, the Governor-General of British India, and his staff, when they met Ranjit Singh at Firozpur in December 1838 and at Amritsar and Lahore a few weeks later. This time, the French brigades with their French generals had been left in Peshawar to counter the imminent threat of an Afghan and Iranian invasion of the Punjab.[53] The 25,000 men (and 150 guns) that Auckland and Fane passed in review belonged to the *Kampu-i-mualla*. Although impressed by the modernisation of these forces and the precision of their manoeuvres, Auckland and Fane immediately noticed a weakness of these new units, i.e. not enough trained officers to command them, and therefore a defective chain of command in situations of real action.[54] Still, the mood of the Governor-General and his staff when they returned from the review was clearly expressed in a letter written to London by Emily Eden, dated 6 December 1838 (Eden 1866, vol. I, p. 209):

> All the Gentlemen went at day break yesterday to Ranjit's review, and came back rather discomfited. He had nearly as many troops out as Sir G. R.[55] had, they were quite as well disciplined, rather better dressed, repeated the same military movements and several others more complicated, and in short nobody knows what to say about it, so that they say nothing, except that they are sure the Sikhs would run away in a real fight. It is a sad blow to our vanities. You won't mention it to the troops in London. We say nothing about it to those here.

In 1839 British intelligence estimated the total strength of the Punjab army to be 150,000 men, of which 71,000 belonged to the *Fauj-i-ain* (the regular troops, French brigades and *Kampu-i-mualla* all included).

In order to have a more complete view of the military achievements of the French officers in the Punjab service from 1822 onwards, we must mention some of their activities in the field of military architecture, and some of the facilities they introduced in the country for the welfare of their soldiers. In 1822 Ranjit Singh gave Allard and Ventura the tomb and garden of Anarkali. There they built a house in classical style, with wings surrounded by a colonnade, a beautiful oval salon and rooms profusely decorated with paintings and gilded mirrors. Part of the building was their residence, part served as the headquarters of the *Fauj-i-khas*.[56] Outside Anarkali they developed a 'Champ de Mars' (parade ground) which they used for regular training of their regiments, including the artillery of the *Topkhana*. The Maharaja personally attended the manoeuvres whenever he could. All around the parade ground, cantonments were built with residences for the officers and barracks for the men. The banks of the Ravi were transformed into a long garden, the 'Jardin du Soldat',[57] and the road leading from the City gate to Anarkali quickly developed into a thriving 'modern' bazaar. These French cantonments were so comfortable and so well designed that in 1846 the British Resident, Henry Lawrence, settled into Allard and Ventura's house,[58] while the occupying British troops were garrisoned in the barracks of the *Fauj-i-khas*.

The regiments had specific uniforms of French/European design (Lafont 2002b, pp. 54–67, especially ill. 65, 78, 73, 74). Their flag was the French tricolour flag (blue, white, red) of the Revolution and Napoleon's empire, with the Sikh motto 'Wah Guruji-ki-Fateh' embroidered on it. Each unit also had imperial Eagles. Allard and Ranjit Singh created the military Order of Guru Govind Singh, whose cross and great cross were based on the design of the Légion d'Honneur (Lafont 2002b, p. 66 ill. 92). As Jacquemont observed, Allard alone granted promotions in his brigade, and all the words of command were given in French. Allard and Ventura translated into Persian for the infantry a French military handbook, a copy of which is preserved in the Maharaja Ranjit Singh Museum at Amritsar (Bajwa 1964, pp. 252–60; Lafont 2002b, p. 54, ill. 65; pp. 146–7, nos 65–9, ill. 69 and *passim*), and a French handbook for the cavalry, of which no copy seems to have survived. A mess was opened in 1825, and a medical service was created: Ranjit Singh, while attending a firing rehearsal of the *Topkhana* at Anarkali, expressed his surprise on seeing surgeons and physicians waiting in readiness as long as the firing exercise went on.

The French officers also helped to consolidate and modernise the fortifications of Lahore, Amritsar and other cities and forts of the kingdom. In Lahore, right from 1822, they worked with Fakir Nuruddin to complete the bastions protecting the twelve gates of the city. A model of Lahore shows the complexity of the defences of the capital of the Punjab as they stood before the British razed them to the ground in the 1850s.[59] Allard and Ventura repaired and modernised the fort of Phillaur, which became the headquarters of the *Fauj-i-khas* on the Anglo-Sikh border in 1825. They also helped to complete the Govindgarh Fort in Amritsar, and until the late 1960s the French inscription 'Ronde de l'Est' was still legible on one of the walls. Avitabile repaired and modernised the fort and the city of Wazirabad, on the Chenab river, when he was governor of that area. At Peshawar, Court and Avitabile rebuilt the Bala Hissar in 1834 and constructed the ramparts of the city over the next few years. In 1837 Allard, appointed military governor of the Peshawar province with Court as his assistant, was instructed by the Maharaja to survey and modernise all the forts on the north-west frontier, including Jamrud, and he took great care to clear the road from Peshawar to Jamrud to facilitate the quick movement of troops with drawn artillery.

General Allard died in Peshawar on 23 January 1839. For a while his death was concealed from Ranjit Singh, who was too weak to be informed, we are told, of the demise of his friend. Allard was buried in Lahore, and his tomb still survives, protected by the Department of Archaeology of the Government of Pakistan.[60] Ventura resigned in 1843, after first delivering a very thoughtful speech in the Durbar, a few weeks after the murders of Maharaja Sher Singh and Raja Dhyan Singh.[61] Avitabile and Court left a few months later. Only the French colonels stayed for a while, until the influential Pandit Jalla in his 'anti-foreigner' drive persuaded Raja Hira Singh, the young Prime Minister, to dismiss all the remaining French officers from the army in June 1844.[62] The *Panchayats* took over the command of the troops, including of the *Fauj-i-khas*. The officers were merely allowed to resume the training of their men in 1845, when imminent war between Lahore and Calcutta loomed. When the Punjab army began moving to the Sutlej in the last months of 1845, the soldiers of the *Fauj-i-khas*, under the very nominal command of Ajudhya Prasad, boasted that under their French generals they had not suffered a single reverse in twenty-three years of active service. But the French generals were no longer there. François-Henri Mouton, just returned from France, was the only French officer who served in the Punjab army during the first Anglo-Sikh war, but, being a mere colonel and a foreigner, he had, of course, no influence on the conduct of operations.[63]

The Punjab was annexed to British India after two bloody Anglo-Sikh wars (1845–6 and 1849), during which twice, at Ferozeshah and Chillianwalla, the cost of victory was such that the highest British authorities in India and at home took drastic action and made decisions as if they had lost the day. In the present-day Punjab (both in India and Pakistan), a memory survives of this close and fruitful connection between a handful of French officers in the service of the State, and the Punjabi people who received them.[64] Of course this memory is mainly centred on their contribution to the military might of the 'Sikh empire'.[65] But they are also remembered for other important reasons that have not been the focus here: their specific contribution to art and archaeological discoveries in the Punjab (figs 13, 122, 137, 177–8),[66] and their overall contribution to the peace and prosperity of the kingdom.[67]

Notes

1   On French policy towards the Indian states after the recall of Dupleix (1754) until Bonaparte's expedition to Egypt see Lafont 2001, pp. 14–20. Also my contribution (Lafont 2002, pp. 63–116) to the International Seminar on Tipu Sultan organised by the Asiatic Society of Calcutta, Calcutta, 2–3 October 1999, published with too many misprints in the French quotations. The revised and correct text of this seminar will form the introduction to the English translation (Lafont, forthcoming) of the 'Mémoire sur l'Inde' of Piveron de Morlat (see n. 2).

2   Piveron was Agent de France to Hyder Ali, then Tipu Sultan from 1778 to 1784. When he returned to France, he wrote a voluminous report, 'Mémoire sur l'Inde . . .' (1786, 4 vols, 450 pp.), for de Castries, Ministre de la Marine et des Colonies (Lafont, forthcoming). Selected by Bonaparte to be part of his staff in Egypt, Piveron did not sail with the fleet but took the overland route and was stranded in Corfu until the end of operations.

3   On this expedition see the appendix 'The British expedition from India to Egypt in 1801' (Malleson 1878, pp. 253–76). However the soldiers involved received a medal struck by the East India Company. Sheikh Basawan, one of the highest Indian officers commanding the *Fauj-i-khas* in the Punjab under the French, was observed wearing that medal by Captain Wade in Amritsar in 1827 (Lafont 1992, p. 95, n. 142).

4 An amazing quantity of documentation had been collected by the savants of the Expédition d'Egypte, who accompanied the army into every nook and cranny of the country. Long afterwards, the veterans of the expedition were still laughing about the ludicrous order shouted by officers whenever they were attacked by the Bedouins: 'Formez le carré! Les ânes et les savants au centre!' A condition imposed in 1801 by the English on the French when they surrendered was the delivery of all their archaeological discoveries to England. That is why the Rosetta Stone is in the British Museum today. But when Hutchinson also asked for all the scientific papers and notes, the French threatened to burn everything and reminded the British commanding officer of the Library in Alexandria. As a result, all papers were sent to France and the *Description de l'Egypte* was published.

5 Beauregard was purchased in 1802. See Desmond Young (1959, pp. 236–7) for the induction of Lord Wellesley on this point.

6 Young 1959, p. 238, says that the letter was last seen and read in 1914, but has since disappeared.

7 A copy in French, with the English translation, of the secret articles of the treaty concerning India were collected by British intelligence and sent to Calcutta and Ludhiana. I found the document in the Punjab Record Office, Lahore, vol. 99, no. 57 (French text and its English translation): see Lafont 1992, p. 107, n. 255.

8 Etienne de Jouy, who says he met Tipu Sultan personally, was given an audience by Napoleon after the première. The Emperor subjected him to a detailed analysis of Tipu's military mistakes against his enemies. What Napoleon could not foresee in 1813, however, was that he too was destined to meet the same British officer, Arthur Wellesley, by then the Duke of Wellington, two years later at Waterloo.

9 Pierre André de Suffren (1727–88) was a son of the Marquis of Saint Tropez, who entered the French navy and the Order of Malta in 1743. In 1775 the king appointed him Governor of the Citadel and Lieutenant du Roy of Saint-Tropez. From 1778, during the American War of Independence (1775–83), he formed part of the French squadron fighting the British off the coast of North America and in the West Indies. He was given the title Bailli (Bailiff) in the Order of Malta and, in 1781, became Vice-Admiral of France. As commander of the French fleet in the Indian ocean (1781–3), he is still remembered for his naval actions against the British at Praya Porto (Cape Verde islands, 1781) and along the coast of India south of Madras (1782–3), especially his capture of Trinkomalee and his meeting with Hyder Ali at Cuddalore in 1782.

10 As told to the author by the descendants of General Allard.

11 Denounced to the royalist authorities by fellow citizens, demoted because he had joined Napoleon during the 100 Days, and not being paid the over F 3000 due to him by the army, Allard was suspected by the Ministry of War, who asked General Baron de Damas, the military commander of his région militaire, to keep an eye on him: Lafont 1992, pp. 32–5; Allard's file in the Service Historique de l'Armée de Terre (SHAT), Château de Vincennes.

12 On this period of Allard's life see Lafont 1992, pp. 32–5. The letter, dated Tabriz, 15 February 1820, was duly received, but it was decided not to do anything about it. As a result of joining the service of a foreign army without permission from the French authorities, Allard lost his French nationality. He regained his citizenship in 1835 by decision of the French government.

13 On his father see Court MSS 1, vol. IV, p. 197. Court adds that his father last served in the 'famous' 32 demi-brigade in Italy. That is why he was educated at the Lycée de Casale in Italy.

14 Lafont 1992, pp. 35–6; Court's file in the Service Historique de l'Armée de Terre (SHAT), Château de Vincennes.

15 MSS 1, vol. I, p. 93. This is the first mention of Darmandy.

16 No information on this Dr Lafosse. We shall see later that another French officer, Hettier, was to join them on their journey to Lahore.

17 MSS 1, vol. I, pp. 177–80, where he mentions 'l'or anglais', which most probably refers to the 200,000 tomans promised annually in the treaty of 1809, and repeated in the treaty of 1814.

18 MSS 1, vol. I, pp. 229–35, with a map, pp. 230–1, of the positions taken by the two armies.

19 Avitabile was back in Italy, as I could ascertain from documents dated and signed in his own hand there: Lafont 1992, pp. 50–1 (Avitabile's archives in Italy).

20 MSS 1, vol. II, pp. 25–31: 'De l'artillerie et de l'infanterie organisées à l'européenne sous le Prince Mahmed Ali Mirza'.

21 As mentioned earlier, Allard, in his letter from Tabriz dated 1820, stated that Abbas Mirza offered him employment when he saw the Légion d'Honneur he was wearing on his uniform.

22 MSS 1, vol. II, p. 32: Bataillon de Korremabad 800; Songour et Khouliahis 600; Gourans de Cavaré 800; Gourans de Kherinte 400; Kermanshah et Arsin 800.

23 MSS 1, vol. II, p. 40. These were lancers, units which had long disappeared in the French army. But Napoleon reintroduced lancer regiments in the Great Army. General Allard was to create one regiment of lancers (Lansia) in the Punjab army.

24 MSS 1, vol. II, p. 40, translated as 'amusements européens' by Court.

25 I am not aware of any study done on the former officers and soldiers of the Grande Armée who took employment in the Russian service. They were not only French, but from all European units who served the French Empire, including Poles (hence the Lancers in Napoleon's army), etc.

26 He worked under Wade and then succeeded him as Political Agent to the Lahore Durbar during the first Anglo-Afghan War, from 1839 to 1843.

27 First Under-Secretary, then Secretary of the Board of Control, 1856–8: Buckland 1906, *s.v.* Clerk, Sir George Russell (1800–89).

28 Lafont 1992, p. 47. Court did not ask for any payment. On Wade's recommendation he was given Rs 5000 by the East India Company as a token of thanks. On Wade see below, n. 36.

29 Lafont 1992, p. 326 and notes. Grey, while preparing his book *European Adventurers of Northern India*, found the document in the Imperial Archives of India and made a typed copy which he translated – with slight mistakes – into English and published (1929, appendix III, pp. xxvii–xlviii). I found the typed copy in the Punjab Record Office, Lahore, and reproduced it in my thesis (1987, vol. III, no. 53, pp. 152–87).

30 Lafont 1992, pp. 158–61: on Syed Ahmed Barelvi and early contacts between Indian Islam and Wahabism.

31 On this *jihad* see Lafont 1992, pp. 161–6. On Court's journey from Peshawar to Lahore see his MSS 1, vol. IV, pp. 175–221. On the last leg of their journey from Peshawar to Attock and their reception by General Allard, MSS 1, vol. IV, pp. 182–4.

32 Dr Lafosse, as we have seen, did not join them on their journey to Lahore. A letter to Allard (then in France) from a Mr Hettier, dated Moscow, 20 September 1835, shows that he was also supposed to join them, but at the last moment he preferred to go to Russia. This letter gives interesting details on Allard and Ventura's departure: Lafont 1992, pp. 120–1.

33 A village on the north-west side of the entrance to the Khyber Pass. *Feringhi* is a noble word for distinguished foreigners. *Ghora* simply means a white man with no marks of distinction.

34 Csoma accompanied them as far as Lahore, visited the city and then left for the hills.

35 'Khas' means special, i.e. royal (as in the *Diwan-i-khas* of the Mughal imperial palaces). A 'khas' regiment commanded by Sheikh Basawan already existed in the Punjab army, and was the first unit placed under the French generals by Ranjit Singh. Sheikh Basawan, as we have seen, had been in British service and had campaigned in Egypt. He was the most trusted and efficient Indian officer of the *Fauj-i-khas*. In 1839 he took command of the 5000-strong 'Muslim' contingent of the Punjab army and he was also responsible for capturing the Khyber Pass. I am still trying to find out more about Sheikh Basawan.

36 His father was a close friend (and debtor) of Major-General Claude Martin of Lucknow fame (founder of the La Martinière schools in Lucknow, Calcutta and Lyons). Claude Martin accepted the role as godfather of Wade's little son, who was christened Claude Martine. The best study on Wade is by Kapadia 1938. See also Wade 1847.

37 From 1815 to 1830 the governments of Louis XVIII and Charles X had reclaimed the white (royalist) flag.

38 On all these points Lafont 1992, part II, ch. II, 'L'oeuvre militaire (1822–1839). Effectifs et organisation', pp. 117–49; ch. III, 'L'oeuvre militaire. Les missions', pp. 150–81; and ch. IV, 'L'oeuvre administrative', pp. 182–202.

39 There is only one file on a Mr Oms in the Military Archives (Vincennes), but it contains no mention of a career in India.

40 Except for Oms's brigade. Ranjit Singh was intrigued by the estrangement between his French officers and Oms, but none of them would let him know the reason for their attitude. The Maharaja, whose curiosity was piqued, even asked British intelligence (i.e. Captain Wade) about it, but they knew only that something had happened in Persia. The Maharaja drew the following distinctions between Allard, Ventura and Oms: 'M. Oms is well versed in the drill of a corps but he knows nothing else. Messrs. Allard and Ventura on the contrary are intelligent and conversant with all subjects, especially the art of diplomacy. I have entrusted them several times with the management of my affairs on the Attoc[k] and they have always proved very able in conciliating the good will and in securing the obedience of those with whom they had to treat' (Wade's report to C. T. Metcalfe dated 1 August 1827, para. 74: Chopra 1929, p. 323).

41 Transformed by the British into their own cantonments after the Annexation of Punjab in 1849.

42 On Ganga Ram, his 'son' Ajudhya Prasad and nephew Diwan Dina Nath see Lafont 1992, pp. 114–15 and *passim*; Lafont 2002b, pp. 52–3, 146, no. 63 and *passim*. Ganga Ram had served under the French officers in Sindhia's service, and he was the Diwan of Louis Bourquien in 1801–3. He is one of the ancestors of Pandit Jawaharlal Nehru's family.

43 Better remembered for his treacherous behaviour as commander-in-chief of the Punjab army during the first Anglo-Sikh war.

44 MSS 1, vol. V, p. 98. Court refers several time to the intimacy in which he was with the Dogra family, and more specifically with Raja Gulab Singh.

45 On Court's scholarly activities in Punjab see Lafont 1992, pp. 326–48 and *passim*; Lafont 2000b, pp. 106–20 and *passim*.

46 'An Indian Princess in Saint-Tropez', in Lafont 2000, pp. 215–49, ill. 48, 50, 53; Lafont 2000b, ill. 109, 208 and *passim*. General Court married Fezli Azam Joo, a Muslim from Kashmir: for a recently discovered oil painting of Fezli by August Schoefft, dated Lahore 1841, see Lafont 2002b, p. 106, ill. 209 and caption.

47 On this appointment, the reasons behind the French decision and the political situation in British India between the departure of Bentinck, the interim of Charles Metcalfe and the appointment of Auckland see Lafont 1992, part II, ch. V, 'Le projet politique (1835–1839)', pp. 203–55. For the reproduction of Louis-Philippe's letter to Ranjit Singh, see Lafont 2002b, p. 126, ill. 264.

48 Lafont 1992, pp. 231, 238–44, on Auckland's reaction in India to the appointment.

49 The French position was that both France and the Punjab were independent countries, so needed no approval from London before conducting diplomatic relations. When the French government was informed that Calcutta had not given free passage to General Allard's diplomatic mail, they replied by interrupting the British diplomatic bag between Marseilles and Calais for a while.

50 French conquest of Constantine in Algeria threatened Tunisia and, indirectly, Egypt. It is possible that the French government, remembering the expeditionary corps sent from Bombay to Egypt in 1801, thought to keep the British busy on their north-west frontier. But this is mere supposition.

51 Confirmed by Court, MSS 1, vol. V, p. 28: Achille and Auguste Lafont. One of them is evidently the same 'Colonel Lafont' whose collection of 145 coins was acquired by the British Museum in 1845 (British Museum 1845).

52 Certainly the *Fauj-i-khas* and probably some battalions from the two other French legions.

53 Although Auckland had specifically expressed to Ranjit Singh his desire to meet General Allard.

54 Lafont 1992, pp. 146–7, with quotations from the secret correspondence of Lord Auckland.

55 General Henry Fane, Commander-in-Chief of the British army in India.

56 Archer 1966, pp. 79–93; Lafont 1992, pp. 125–6. To be precise, not only was there the tomb of Anarkali in the garden of Anarkali, but there was also an old Mughal palace, as mentioned by Victor Jacquemont (visible in the drawing reproduced in Lafont 2002b, p. 62, ill. 96).

57 It was handed over to the care of the Horticultural Society after the British annexation of the Punjab in 1849: Lafont 1992, p. 472.

58 Hence the name 'The Residence' still applied today to what has become the office of the Secretary, Government of Punjab. Since it is a restricted area, I was never given permission to take a picture of the house. On how Henry Lawrence occupied and 'annexed' this property see Lafont 1992, pp. 466, 471.

59 They stood on the site of the present-day Circular Road. See the photograph of the 3D model (destroyed in 1949) in Lafont 1992, p. 125, pl. 6, or Lafont 2002b, p. 98, pl. 185.

60 Colour photograph in Lafont 1997, p. 86.

61 Court states that he was the first to get information on the coup d'état a few days before it took place (MSS 1, vol. V, pp. 126–7). He passed the information on to Ventura, who sent it to the Maharaja, but to no effect. After the murders everyone in Lahore went to the funeral of Raja Dhyan Singh, whose son Hira Singh was the new Prime Minister of Punjab. Nobody cared about the bodies of Maharaja Sher Singh and the young Prince Partab Singh, who was killed along with his father. They were both cremated by Ventura and Court, who took care that their ashes were sent to the Ganges river (MSS 1, vol. V, p. 140).

62 On this period see Lafont 1992, part II, ch. IX, 'La désintégration', pp. 406–39, and chapter X, 'La fin', pp. 440–75.

63 Mouton had one horse killed under him at Sobraon while leading a cavalry charge against the advancing British columns. When the rout began he was able to save most of his men by directing an orderly retreat under British gunfire. He was arrested by the East India Company and deported to France, where he published a short *Rapport sur les événements du Penjab* (Mouton 1846).

64 In Pakistan, as we have said, the Directorate of Archaeology took several steps to restore and protect the tomb of General Allard in Lahore (Old Anarkali, behind the 'Munshi building'). In April 2001 the Punjab government in India requested the author to organise the exhibition 'Life and Times of Maharaja Ranjit Singh' in the Rambagh Palace in Amritsar, for the bicentenary celebration of the Maharaja's coronation (13 November 2001). The book *Maharaja Ranjit Singh Lord of the Five Rivers* (Lafont 2002b) is an extended catalogue of the exhibition.

65 For people who are not very familiar with French, there are two other publications in English, albeit much shorter than Lafont 1992: Lafont 2000a, pp. 4–23 (with 31 colour illustrations) and Lafont 2002 (simultaneously published in English, Hindi and Punjabi).

66 See above pp. 8–9, and below pp. 183–6, 192–5, 211–13, 221–2. See also Lafont 1992, ch. VII, 'Vie familiale et activités personnelles', pp. 297–348; Lafont 2000, pp. 205–342 and 2000b, *passim*; Lafont and Schmitz 2002, pp. 74–99; La Fontaine 1989.

67 Lafont 1992, part II, ch. VI, 'Commerce et finances', pp. 256–96; ch. VIII, 'Le Penjab vers 1835', pp. 349–405.

6 Bushire and beyond: Some early archaeological discoveries in Iran

St John Simpson

Some of the greatest discoveries are made by chance rather than through design. Interesting discoveries are not the sole prerogative of scholars, and the history of archaeology is closely intertwined with the personal histories of amateurs, antiquarians and travellers. The latter, in particular, have played an important pioneering role in the discovery and advertisement of the monuments and antiquities of extinct cultures, sparking the enthusiasm necessary for the gradual evolution of academic disciplines focused on the specifics of where, why and how. This chapter highlights some significant yet little-known discoveries made in Iran during the opening and closing decades of the nineteenth century.

Sasanian remains on the Bushire peninsula

The first part relates to recurrent discoveries of Sasanian ossuaries at some eight sites on the Bushire peninsula. On 3 June 1826 one James Edward Alexander (1803–85) (fig. 138) landed at the Persian Gulf port and seat of the British Residency of Bushire (Alexander 1827, p. 92). Alexander had obtained a cadetship in Madras in 1820 and already served in the Burmese war of 1824 when he left the East India Company to join the 13th Light Dragoons as a cornet. This was to mark the beginning of a long and active army service in Persia, the Balkans, Portugal, South Africa, the Crimea, New Zealand and Canada, finally retiring with the rank of general.[1] Alexander also led exploratory expeditions in Africa and South America, but is most famous for his role in finally bringing 'Cleopatra's Needle' to London, some eighty years after it had been presented by Muhammad Ali (1769–1849) to King George IV on the occasion of his coronation (O'Donnell [1893], pp. 321–2, portrait facing 176; Lee 1901, pp. 31–2; Bierbrier 1995, 10).

In 1826 Alexander was a young man on temporary secondment to Colonel John Macdonald (Kinneir) (1782–1830), then British East India Company Envoy Extraordinary to the Shah. However, as his superior officer was delayed at Shiraz,[2] Alexander spent his time visiting sites in the vicinity of Bushire and Shiraz, including Naqsh-i Rustam and Bishapur. Alexander was also told tales of an ancient cemetery located some six miles south of Bushire, close to a spot called Sabzabad and a short distance east of the ruins at Rishahr (fig. 139). According to Alexander's host Colonel Ephraim Gerrish Stannus (1784–1850) (fig. 147), the official British Resident in the Persian Gulf (1824–6), 'urns [with] human bones, . . . are found in rows close to an ancient wall'. It is possible from this description that Stannus had conducted his own investigations at this site, but, if so, there is no published account of it.

However, the cemetery described to Alexander by Stannus was one of eight such sites on the Bushire peninsula. The first of these was discovered in March 1811 at a spot some

Figure 138 James Edward Alexander (1803–85).

one and three-quarter miles south of the town of Bushire when two or three asphalt-lined jars were unearthed by a pair of Arab workmen hired by the Acting Resident, Lieutenant William Bruce, on behalf of a diplomatic mission led by Sir Gore Ouseley (1770–1844). These jars were said to be found 'at about two feet from the surface of the ground', to contain bones and (Morier 1818, pp. 44–5)

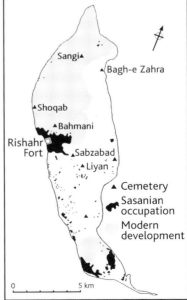

Figure 139 Map of Bushire.

were placed side by side, fronting east and west. They had a small cover at one extremity, and were terminated at the other by a handle. In length they were three feet and a half, and the diameter of the orifice eight inches. Our surgeon [Mr Sharpe] supposed that the bones were those of a woman and child; the enamel of the teeth was undecayed.

This discovery is also described by William Ouseley (1767–1842), Sir Gore Ouseley's older brother, who added that 'one old Arab assured me that he had himself dug up above a hundred' such vessels (Ouseley 1819, pp. 217–20, 404, pl. XXIII). William Ouseley kept a skull, the two covers and several sherds belonging to one of the jars as part of his embryonic collection of Iranian antiquities.[3]

Two years later, in February 1813, the construction of a temporary Residency by Bruce at the same spot resulted in the discovery of five further jars. Two of these were promptly shipped to Bombay by Captain Taylor, then in command of the Resident's guard of sepoys. This discovery was first reported by Sir John Malcolm (1769–1833), then resident in Tehran as Minister Plenipotentiary to the Shah, in his *History of Persia* (Malcolm 1815, vol. I, p. 198, n.*). They were later referred to in a slightly garbled description by Lt-Colonel John Johnson (1818, p. 19) who heard of the discovery when he passed through Bushire in 1817. Shortly afterwards they were the subject of a detailed paper presented to the shortlived Literary Society of Bombay by Mr William Erskine (1819) on the basis of correspondence with Bruce. They were found 'interred in a straight line lying east and west, the small end to the east'. Four of the jars were of a similar size, approximately three feet long, but the fifth was 'a small one for an infant I suppose'. Disarticulated unburnt human bones were found inside the jars, the restricted size of which led Erskine to conclude that they had been used for the burial of decomposed corpses that had been deliberately exposed (cf. also Malcolm 1815, vol. I, p. 198, n.*; Modi 1889; Casartelli 1890).[4]

This was not the only find-spot for such jar-burials. Bruce reported to Erskine (1819, pp. 191–2) that 'a few . . . were met with in a mound about twelve miles' from the first cemetery. Further jars appear to have been discovered at this spot on at least two subsequent occasions. Modi (1889, p. 3), quoting a letter from C. J. Malcolm dated 5 August 1888, described the site as being three miles south of Sabzabad,

> in the part of the country called Bakhtiar, [where] there is a small plain within two or three feet of the surface of which there were found, some forty-five years ago [i.e. c.1843], and may still be found, barrel-shaped coffins of baked earth, containing also human relics stowed away in the same fashion as these in the stone coffins, and the two sorts of repositories may be said to be of equal size and capacity, though far different in shape. The barrel-like coffins, which are termed jars, are of two equal parts, being divided in the middle breadthwise, and evidently joined together by metallic fasteners, which have, of course, rusted away, but the holes on the rims of each half, evidently intended as holds for the fasteners, bear evidence to this explanation.

A similar jar was presented to the British Museum in 1823 by Captain James Ashley Maude (Maude, p. 22, May 1823).[5] This was shipped from Bushire in 1817 and was

> found in a desert about three miles to the eastward of the walls of the town [of Rishahr] where at present, there are neither dwelling houses nor inhabitants. The vase is lined with bitumen, and a stone is generally found under the cover, placed upon the contents, which are human bones. These vases are found in groups of five or six, placed near each other in a horizontal

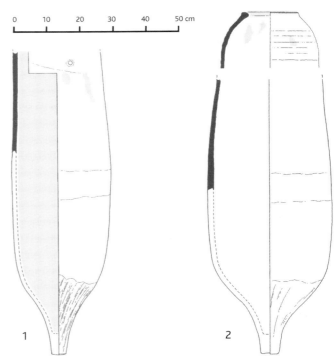

Figure 140 Reused torpedo jar ossuaries from Sabzabad: munsell pale yellow 5Y 8/2 surfaces with more heavily oxidised fabric; asphalt-lined.
1 Presented by Capt. J. A. Maude. Length as preserved 76 cm, maximum width 22 cm, circular hole, 1.5 cm across, drilled through the wall at height of 70 cm above the base.
2 Presented by Col. E. C. Ross. Length of lower portion 68 cm; interior rim diameter of second piece 11 cm.

position with the pointed end towards the east and about five or six feet under the surface of the earth. These groups of vases are supposed to contain the remains of families. Some of them are in the shape of a sarcophagus formed of talc.

These vessels have sandy fabrics, a cylindrical body thrown in sections with a paddled bottom, a pointed base and a rolled rim, and were lined with asphalt (fig. 140.1–2).[6] This type of so-called torpedo jar with a 'spitzfuss' base is possibly best known from Sasanian sites in central and southern Mesopotamia and south-west Iran (e.g. Adams 1981, p. 234), and indeed Captain Robert Mignan (1829, pp. 46–7) compared similar vases he found in southern Iraq in 1827 with 'some I have dug up near a village called Reschire, five miles to the south of Bushire in the Persian Gulph'. The form appears to have commenced in the Parthian period and continued to be made into the early 'Abbasid period. They were probably lined with asphalt so as to render them impervious, and were presumably the local equivalent of Roman transport amphorae which were used primarily to carry wine and oil but also other substances (Zemer 1977). The pointed bases – described by Morier as 'handles' – were probably designed to be set into supports, yet would have provided a suitable grip when carried slung over one shoulder.

The site of Sabzabad itself, close to an old fort at Rishahr, is known to have produced stone ossuaries as well as jar burials judging by Stannus' account to Alexander. The remains at Rishahr are marked on a number of early maps and gazetteers of the Persian Gulf owing to their use in navigation along this barren section of coastline. Niebuhr's map dated 1765 marks 'Rischahr *ruins*' (cf. Hansen 1964, p. 311), as does a later Memoir prepared for the Indian government in 1830 by Captain G. Barnes Brucks (reproduced by Bidwell 1985, p. 587, map facing p. 531); a later British naval intelligence report likewise comments that Rishahr 'is on the site of a medieval port, and has a ruined fort' (Mason 1945, p. 125). The date of this fort has not been firmly established although it is widely attributed to the Portuguese, who finally evacuated in 1622.[7] However, the site itself should be identified as the Sasanian port of Rev-Shapur.

According to later historical sources this town was founded by Ardashir I (c. AD 223/4–41), was a victim of Arab piracy culminating in bloody reprisals by Shapur II (AD 309–79)[8] and witnessed a major battle during the Arab conquest.[9] During the fifth century it was the seat of the Nestorian metropolitan of Fars. It is said to have been a source of (i.e. local market for) excellent pearls and clearly functioned as an important entrepot for the province of Fars and an early rival to Siraf within the context of Gulf trade (cf. Whitehouse 1971; Williamson 1972; Whitehouse and Williamson 1973). Early Sasanian Fine Orange Ware with Black Paint – probably imported from south-east Iran – Indian Red Polished Ware, Sasanian plain wares and so-called pedestal supports have been found here (Pézard 1914, pl. V.18; Williamson 1972, pp. 100, 104; Whitehouse and Williamson 1973, pp. 35–42, pl. II). In addition extensive remains of carnelian-working in the form of beads, gems, rings and waste flakes have been reported from the area of Rishahr (Whitehouse 1975; cf. Pézard 1914, p. 35). The date of these remains is unclear. Whitehouse implied that they may be Sasanian and states that there is a local source yet local informants told Ouseley (1819, pp. 200–1) that 'above seven hundred families [were] employed in cutting and polishing carnelians and other ornamental stones; which, it is affirmed, were not originally produced here; but brought in their rough state from Cambay in India'.

The importance of Rishahr was finally supplanted when Nadir Shah (1736–47) selected a fishing village situated at the northern tip of this narrow coral reef as the site of the principal Persian port and naval base of Bushire.[10] This was designed to make possible Persian control of the Persian Gulf, and soon afterwards the Persian navy indeed succeeded in seizing Bahrain and Muscat. In 1763 the British East India Company established a Residency at Bushire enabling exclusive trading rights in Persia and in the following year the Resident was upgraded to British Consul (Belgrave 1972a, pp. 19–20; Standish 1998, pp. 83–4). By 1820/1 Bushire was handling a quarter of all Persian exports although the population never exceeded 20,000 (Issawi 1971, pp. 27–8, 31, 130).

The town of Bushire was dominated by fine two-storey buildings with wind-catchers and an Armenian Church of St George built in 1819 (Greenway and St Vincent 1998, p. 305; Mason 1945, pp. 503, 583). The Residency itself was situated outside the south-east corner of the town walls but close to the seashore and was 'built in the Indian style, with big, high rooms and old-world sanitation, but comfortable and more dignified than the houses which are now being built in the Gulf' (Belgrave 1972b, p. 14). The plan consisted of a rectangular building with a defendable entrance and outer and inner courtyards surrounded by storerooms, offices, kitchens and living quarters (Belgrave 1972a, p. 85). This building remained in use as the Residency until the mid nineteenth century when Captain Felix Jones transferred it to

Figure 141 Friedrich Carl Andreas (1846–1930).

the former summer retreat at Sabzabad (Belgrave 1972a, p. 85; Wright 1977, p. 73).[11] The subsequent growth of Sabzabad must have been a factor for this being the find-spot of a number of further ossuaries in the second half of the nineteenth century.

Close to Sabzabad, and a short distance east of Rishahr, lie the remains of the important Neo-Elamite settlement of Liyan. Wilson (1928, p. 73) refers to 'numerous burial urns, bricks, and cuneiform inscriptions [being] discovered in the neighbourhood in 1873 and 1877'. A number of these bricks exist in the British Museum, one presented by A. S. Betts in 1873 but the majority being presented by Colonel Ross in 1875 (Walker 1981).[12] In c.1876 excavations were made at Liyan by the German philologist, Friedrich Carl Andreas (1846–1930) (fig. 141), during the course of his research into the languages of southern Iran (Kanus-Credé 1974; Budge 1920, vol. I, p. 331).[13] These investigations are unpublished: some 200 cases of Elamite and other antiquities were packed but 'owing to pecuniary difficulties he was unable to take them out of the country. Four cases belonging to this collection are on their way to the British Museum' (*Reports to the Trustees*, 19 May 1888).[14] The site was later re-investigated in 1913 by the French mission to Iran (Pézard 1914) but no further work has been undertaken there.[15]

In March 1888, as part of a more extensive trip to Mesopotamia and Egypt, Wallis Budge visited Bushire in order to investigate the possibility of new excavations. These were considered either at Bushire or on Bahrain where Captain E. L. Durand's discovery of a cuneiform inscription ten years before had attracted an (unclaimed) offer of a £100 grant from the Trustees of the British Museum towards further exploration on the island.[16] At Sabzabad, Budge 'called on Mr C. J. Malcolm, on whose property the antiquities had been found, and he welcomed us most kindly,

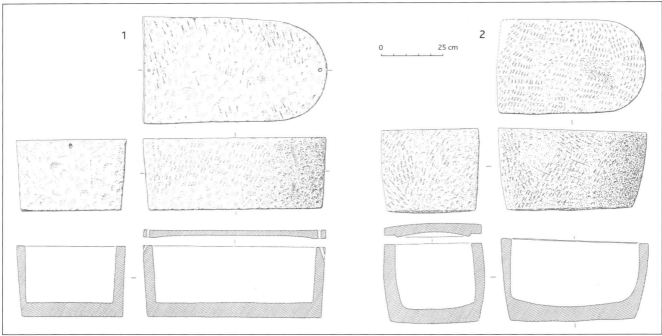

Figure 142 Limestone ossuaries:

1   From Sabzabad, presented by C. J. Malcolm. Length 59.7 cm, width 36.6 cm, height 24.5 cm. Lid length 59.5 cm, width 36 cm, thickness 3 cm.

2   Presented by Col. E. C. Ross. Length 48 cm, width 33 cm, height 27 cm. Lid length 48 cm, width 33 cm, thickness 2.5 cm.

and offered to afford every facility if the British Museum would excavate the whole site. He gave me for the Museum a small Parthian stone coffin, containing burnt human remains' (fig. 142.1; Budge 1920, vol. I, p. 331).[17]

This was not the only ossuary discovered by Joseph Malcolm [Malkomian], an Armenian employee of the Persian Telegraph company. In the same year he sent a second limestone ossuary and lid 'filled with human bones' – later reportedly identified as those of a sixty-year-old man – to the Anthropological Society of Bombay. This coffin was promptly published by Mr Jivangi Jamsedji Modi, a leading Parsi scholar in Bombay, who related the find to Avestan texts describing Zoroastrian burials in 'bone receptacles' or *astodans* (Modi 1889; cf. also Casartelli 1890). According to a letter to Modi from Malcolm, dated 5 August 1888 (Modi 1889, pp. 2–3), this ossuary

> was accidentally found in a vault about 5 or 6 feet below the surface . . . among others deposited there, and covered with the *débris* of parts of the vault that had fallen in from the effects of rain. The said vault is about 7 miles from the town of Bushire, and the ground surrounding it are covered with mounds, which are manifestly the ruins of what must once have been buildings. The particular vault itself was under a mound, and the removal of which for agricultural purposes led to the discovery of the said coffin.

The British Resident in Bushire at this time was Colonel Edward C. Ross, who had already presented the Museum with the inscribed bricks from Liyan mentioned above, a second and very similar limestone ossuary which was probably found at the same site (fig. 142.2) and a reused torpedo jar ossuary that was said to be from Sabzabad (fig. 140.2).[18] The stone ossuaries were later placed on display in a former Babylonian and Assyrian Room – now the Early Egypt gallery in Room 64 – in the British Museum, together with Parthian glazed 'slipper coffins' excavated at Warka by William Kennet Loftus (fig. 9; British Museum 1892, p. 135; British Museum 1908, p. 117; British Museum

1922, p. 80). The sizes and shapes of the two ossuaries in the British Museum compare favourably with that described by Modi: the three range from 48 to 60 cm in length, 33 to 36.6 cm in width and 24.5 to 27 cm in height. Each has one squared-off end and a rounded end and was covered with a flat lid carved from the same type of stone; two of the lids have single holes drilled through at either end. The shaping marks of an adze are very clear on both of the ossuaries and lids in the British Museum.

Curzon (1892, vol. II, p. 235) later described these discoveries as one of the characteristic features of Bushire, there being

> an immense collection of stone and earthenware vases of rude shape and fabrication, sealed up with earthenware lids or with coverings of talc, sometimes lined inside with a coating of bitumen, and containing human skulls and bones. A great number of these have been found between Bushire and Reshire, at a depth of about two feet below the surface, usually placed horizontally in a long line one after the other. The jars are about three feet in length and one foot in diameter. They are supposed to have contained the remains of Zoroastrians, after the body had perished by exposure.

Whitcomb (1987, p. 315) has ingeniously suggested that these reports may have referred to lines of ancient drain pipes, possibly water conduits leading from the Angali canal which appears to have supplied the peninsula with much of its water in antiquity. However, it is clear from the contemporary descriptions that bones were invariably found within both the asphalt-lined jars and the stone ossuaries. A further set of ossuaries were discovered in more recent years as a result of the construction of a national park at Shoqab next to the beach between Bushire and Rishahr. These finds included long narrow-mouthed jars measuring up to 87 cm in height, 14 cm across at the mouth, and containing human remains and plain stone ossuaries measuring 50 cm in length, 30 cm across and 25 cm in height (Mir Fattah 1374/1996; Curtis and Simpson 1997, p. 139; Yamauchi 1997, pp. 241–2).[19] These reports draw attention to similar finds being made in more recent years at Bahmani and Bagh-i Zahra, thus bringing the number of currently known burial sites to a total of eight, lying north, east and south of the Sasanian port of Rev-Shapur.

There has been much discussion over Sasanian funerary customs with a common assumption that these must be influenced by Zoroastrian belief as this was the official religion of the Empire (e.g. Trümpelmann 1984; Boucharlat 1991). However, the available archaeological evidence suggests a wide range of burial practices in different parts of the Empire which probably reflects more closely a diversity of religious belief and funerary tradition. In Mesopotamia primary Sasanian burials have been excavated at over forty sites, including Tell Mahuz (Negro Ponzi 1968/9) and Mohammed 'Arab (Roaf 1984, pp. 142–4, pl. XI). In other cases, particularly along the Euphrates, torpedo jars were likewise reused in a funerary context but employed in a different manner, namely placed in a row over the body, presumably in order to protect it from dogs and other animals (al-Haditti 1995).

Within Iran there is greater evidence for secondary burials although primary burials of this period have been excavated at some sites in western Iran, including Haftavan Tepe (Burney 1970, pp.169–71, pls VIIc–d, VIIIa–c). Across southern Iran individuals were interred inside cairns although the poor state of the surviving remains render it ambiguous as to whether these were disturbed primary burials or secondary interments (cf. Azarpay 1981). The practice of interring human remains inside torpedo jars is attested from Susa. Loftus (1856/7) remarked that this was the 'most common form of coffin' that he encountered at this site, especially on the huge Ville Royale mound (so-called 'Great Platform'), and speculated on how the bodies could have been placed inside such narrow-mouthed vessels (cf. also Loftus 1857, pp. 405–6). Similar jar burials have been reported from the Galalak district of Shushtar, suggesting that this was a funerary practice employed at a number of sites in this region (Mir Fattah 1374/1996). At other places in Fars there is evidence for burial in rock-cut ossuaries but the cemeteries found on the Bushire peninsula offer the first convincing archaeological evidence for stone and ceramic ossuaries within Iran at this date.

Early excavations at Persepolis and the discovery of a sphinx

Bushire was the traditional gateway to central Iran from the south. At a distance of some 200 km from Bushire lay the city of Shiraz. On arrival here the adventurous and the romantic usually rode out to the ruins of the Achaemenid royal citadel at Persepolis, a short distance away. These ruins were rediscovered by a European audience during the seventeenth century with the publication of travel accounts by Pietro della Valle and others. The standing remains were frequently illustrated by later travellers, some of whom made more extensive investigations. The story of these discoveries is still unfolding but this section illustrates another significant yet little-known episode.

On 29 June 1826 Alexander visited Persepolis where he found excavations by his superior officer to be in progress. After briefly describing the ruins, he added (1827, p. 140):

Figure 143 Royal sphinx.

Colonel Macdonald employed people in clearing away the earth from a staircase, and made the interesting discovery of a chimerical figure representing a lion or dragon winged, with a human head, resting one of its paws on a lotus-flower, supported by a stem like that of the date tree. No similar figure had ever previously been discovered at Persepolis.

This figure belongs to a category of Achaemenid male royal sphinxes (fig. 143). Facing pairs of these figures, each wearing a divine horned head-dress and with one paw raised in supplication, survive in the upper central panel on the processional staircases of four buildings at Persepolis, namely the Palace of Darius (fig. 32), the Palace of Xerxes, the Apadana and the so-called 'Central Building'. At the time of Macdonald's excavations, these façades were either still buried or in a highly fragmentary state (Ouseley 1821, pp. 255–6, n. 31, p. 532, pl. XLI [bound in out of sequence to follow p. 530]); indeed, a second fragment of sphinx relief from Persepolis was found reused at the site of Madar-i Sulaiman (Qasr-i Abu Nasr) where it was recorded by earlier travellers, including Sir William Ouseley in 1811 (Ouseley 1821, pp. 41, 534, pl. LV: 5).[20] However, the present example derives from a fifth location, probably the upper central portion of a façade belonging to Palace G, which was constructed next to the Palace of Darius by Artaxerxes III (359–338 BC) but which was physically transferred during or after his reign to replace the original north staircase of Palace H that had been constructed by Artaxerxes I (465–424 BC) (Shahbazi 1976, pp. 53, 55). The fact that it was not previously exposed to the elements helps explain its relatively crisp appearance.

The purpose of these sphinx figures was apotropaic and variations of the motif recur on a number of small objects of this period, including a gold appliqué in the Oxus Treasure (Dalton 1964, p. 14, pl. XII),[21] an ivory from Susa (de Mecquenem 1947, p. 88, fig. 56.2), gold appliqués from Sardis and elsewhere (Curtis 1925, 11, pl. I, no. 1; Bingöl 1999, 182, no. 203), Western Achaemenid stamp seals (Boardman 1970, pp. 34, 39, 42–3, pls 1, 5, nos 5, 116–25) and seal impressions from Daskyleion, Wadi Daliyeh and Ur (Leith 1997, pp. 191–2, pl. XV.1, cf. also pls XIX, XXI, XV; Collon 1996, p. 74, pls 20d–f, h–i).

Accompanying Alexander's description are three engravings taken from the author's drawings. These consist of the sphinx relief in question, a standard view of the site looking down from the mountain behind the Tomb of

Figure 144 View of Persepolis.

Artaxerxes III (fig. 144) and a detail of a processional scene showing servants ascending a staircase to the left (fig. 145). The processional scene may be identified with the bottom right flight of the eastern staircase of the Palace of Darius where these figures are missing yet closely paralleled by figures on the equivalent left side (Schmidt *et al*. 1953, pls 133, 135).[22]

The Persepolis sphinx was removed in 1828 by Sir John McNeill (1795–1883), a difficult process as he described in a letter to Macdonald.[23] The relief was generously presented to the British Museum in December 1937 by the National Art Collections Fund who had purchased it for the reduced price of £600 from the dealer Alfred Spero of 48 Duke Street, St James's (fig. 146; *Trustees Reports for 1936–38*, no. 17;[24] Smith 1938; Barnett 1957, pp. 62–3, pl. XXI: 4; Verdi 2003, p. 123,

cat. 53). Nothing was then known about its previous history although it was assumed that it had been in a private British collection since the nineteenth century.[25] Alexander's (1827) description and illustration are therefore particularly important as they establish, for the first time, a precise provenance for the British Museum relief. However, other details of Alexander's published drawing are incorrect: the

Figure 146 Royal sphinx from Persepolis, presented by the National Art Collections Fund. Length 75 cm, height 82 cm, preserved thickness 7.5 cm.

Figure 145 Processional scene.

tip of the winged disk symbol in front of the sphinx was mistaken for a rosette and the 14-line ruling to the left should correspond with the beginning of a row of plants. The vertical left side of this slab is original whereas the present thickness of 7.5 cm indicates that it has been thinned down as other slabs along this façade are uniformly 30 cm thick.

It is quite possible that Macdonald made other clearances at Persepolis as he appears to have been a regular visitor to the site, leaving graffiti within Xerxes' Gate of All Nations (the so-called 'Porch of Xerxes') dated 1808, 1810 and 1826, and the main north doorway of the Palace of Darius dated June 1820 (Curzon 1892, vol. II, pp. 157, 169). Indeed, the 1820 graffito lists the members of the delegation as 'Col. J. M. Macdonald Envoy, Cap. R. Campbell Asst., Sir Keith Jackson Bart., Cap. Jervis 3d Cav., Major Geo. Willock, Lt. McDonald, J. P. Riach Esq., Lt. Strong, Cornet Alexander, Geo. Malcolm', followed by the name of 'Mrs Macdonald Kinneir' (Simpson 2004). However, Macdonald's excavations were by no means the only such investigations conducted during this period, and the first quarter of the nineteenth century witnessed a minor flurry of activity at Persepolis. The early travellers' accounts provide a useful record of the state of the monuments and illustrate their progressive decay.[26] This was precisely the period when a number of sculptural fragments entered private European collections, notably belonging to Sir Gore Ouseley (Ambassador to Persia 1811–14) and the Fourth Earl of Aberdeen, many of which were later presented to the British Museum.[27] One of these little-known early excavators was Colonel Stannus, Alexander's host at Bushire in June 1826.

Stannus, the first plaster casts of Persepolis sculptures and the Weld expedition

'Stannus was a splendid-looking man with a tall soldier-like presence' (fig. 147; Vibart 1894, p. 107). He was from a wealthy Irish family who joined the service of the Indian army in 1800 and was posted to the Bombay European Regiment with which he served with distinction; he was promoted to Captain in 1811, rising to Colonel in 1829 (Vibart 1894, pp. 104–7; Crone 1937, p. 237; Burke's Peerage 1976, p. 1046). During his brief Residence at Bushire, Stannus produced an important report for the British government on the state of trade between Persia and India between 1817 and 1823 (quoted by Issawi 1971, pp. 89–91).

He retired to England from this post on health grounds in 1826 but was later appointed Lieutenant-Governor of the East India Company Military Seminary at Addiscombe, near Croydon, on 13 March 1834. This promotion followed the resignation of his predecessor over growing criticism of the discipline at Addiscombe, the breakdown of which was attributed to 'the pernicious habit of smoking cigars' and the availability of pocket money (Broadfoot 1893, p. 651). However, 'though just and kindly, he was no administrator, and was systematically irritated by the cadets into extraordinary explosions of wrath and violent language. During the latter years of his rule at Addiscombe the discipline seems to have got very slack' (Lee 1898, p. 86). 'Notwithstanding his quickness of temper and his use of strong language, Sir Ephraim Stannus was a favourite with the cadets' (Vibart 1894, p. 109).[28] In 1838 Stannus was promoted to the rank of Major-General and he remained in

Figure 147 Ephraim Gerrish Stannus (1784-1850).

post here until he died of a heart attack on 21 October 1850, aged 66. He had remained a close friend of McNeill's with whom he maintained regular correspondence 'in the most illegible of handwritings' ([MacAlister] 1910, p. 88). Stannus was buried in the churchyard of St John's in Croydon and a plaque was erected in his memory by 'a few of his oldest friends' in St James's Church, where the cadets used to attend and where many of the officers were buried (*Croydon Advertiser* 1882, p. 27).[29]

During his spell of residence in Bushire, Stannus made some limited yet previously unrecognised excavations at Persepolis. In 1825 he exposed 'a number of sculptured stones, capitals of columns etc.' but these were reburied a few days later by local villagers who blamed them for a sudden locust swarm (Alexander 1827, p. 137). Although not cited by Curzon (1892), Stannus's name recurs twice as a graffito on the interior of the main east doorway and a window on the south side of the Palace of Darius (Simpson 2004).

Despite his evidently mixed fortune in excavation, Stannus succeeded in making the first casts of Persepolis reliefs as an alternative record, through the expedient of making (Alexander 1827, pp. 97–8)

> several long shallow boxes of wood, in which he put quick lime, applied them to the sculptures, and allowed them to remain till thoroughly dry. The case was then taken off and sent to Bushire, containing the impression, from which the cast was again taken in lime. These, of course, are very valuable, as nothing can be more accurate. Processions were the subjects of these casts.

These casts were shipped to India following Stannus's departure from Bushire in 1826. The governor of Bombay during this period was Mountstuart Elphinstone (1779–1859) who was said to be 'immersed in classical literature' and had previously been responsible for 'the putting together of a valuable library in the handsome Residency' at Poona (Bellasis 1952, p. 211). In 1827, the year of Elphinstone's resignation, Edward Hawkins (1780–1867), numismatist and Keeper of the

Figure 148 Herbert Weld (1852–1935).

Department of Antiquities in the British Museum, reported to the Trustees that 'he has received 23 cases of casts of Persepolitan sculptures and inscriptions presented to the Museum by the Hon. Mountstuart Elphinstone, Governor of Bombay. They are at present placed upon shelves in the basement storage' (*Officers' Reports*, vol. X, May 1827).[30] These casts immediately appear to have been given a protective wash and sealed with oil (*Minutes of the Standing Committee of Trustees*, no. 3022, 12 May 1827); some were also mounted on stone slabs, a method that continued to be used in the nineteenth century to support fragile Assyrian reliefs and Parthian coffins within the Museum (*Sub-committee on Antiquities*, 14 June 1828, p. 13).[31] The casts were placed on display in the Central Saloon – later moved to the Assyrian Transept – of the British Museum, together with Persepolis sculptures presented by Sir Gore Ouseley in 1817 and Lord Aberdeen in 1825 (Jenkins 1992). However, these were not the only casts made by Stannus: he also made casts of the Parthian and Middle Persian inscriptions at Hajjiabad (Curzon 1892, vol. II, p. 116) which were displayed together with the Persepolis sculptures and casts.[32] However, since that date the existence and significance of these has been overlooked (Simpson 2000; 2003).

In 1844 a second group of Persepolis casts, totalling 27 reliefs and four inscriptions, was made by M. Pierre-Victorien Lottin (1810–1903) – also known as Lottin de Laval – using a different technique that was christened 'lottinoplastique'. These casts survive in the Musée de Berny and Musée du Louvre (Chevalier 1997, pp. 27, 33, 193, figs 11, 18, nos 8–9; Zapata-Aubé 1997).[33]

Almost fifty years later a third and even more extensive set of plaster casts was made through an expedition to Persepolis initiated by Cecil Harcourt Smith (1859–1944), a curator in the Department of Antiquities in the British

Museum. This followed an earlier reconnaissance trip to Persia for the purpose of 'examining some likely fields for archaeological research in Southern Persia' which Smith had made in May–August 1887; he was accompanied and assisted by Major-General Sir Robert Murdoch Smith (1835–1900), formerly a key player in Newton's expedition to Halicarnassus, later Director of the Persian Telegraph company and now Director of the Royal Scottish Museum (Dickson 1901, p. 311).[34] The ensuing expedition of 1892 was privately financed by Lord Savile and was directed by Mr Herbert Weld [Blundell] (1852–1935).

Herbert Joseph Weld was born in 1852 and was educated at Stonyhurst (fig. 148). He was the son of Thomas Weld-Blundell of Ince-Blundell but discontinued the name of Blundell in 1924 prior to inheriting the Weld seat at Lulworth. His career included further travels in Persia (1891), Libya (1894) and Cyrenaica (1895), hunting game and exploring the source of the Blue Nile in Somaliland, Abyssinia and Sudan (1898/9, 1905) and a spell as Boer War correspondent for *The Morning Post*. Weld was a notable philanthropist. In addition to his work at Persepolis, he presented a substantial collection of East African stuffed birds to the Natural History Museum and, in the winter of 1921/2, he travelled to Baghdad where he acquired an important collection of tablets. He presented this to the Ashmolean Museum, recommending Kish as the preferred site for a proposed joint expedition between Oxford University – largely funded by Weld himself – and the Field Museum in Chicago, and nominally directed by Stephen Langdon, then the Professor of Assyriology in the University (Field 1955, p. 53; Gibson 1972, pp. 70–1; Moorey 1978, pp. 13–14).

On 11 November 1925 Weld was elected an Honorary Fellow of Queen's College, Oxford, in recognition of his support for the Kish expedition, the citation in the minute-book referring to him as 'Hon. D.Litt., Fellow Commoner 1902'; at that time a Fellow Commoner was a person admitted to the college as a mature scholar, already a graduate of some standing, who was allowed to share the high table with the fellows as a mark of distinction. He would not be expected to read for any degree and would pay all expenses himself. Weld was a member of the Athenaeum and various learned societies (*Who Was Who 1929–1940*, pp. 1433–4) and in 1924 was elected a member of the Royal Yacht Squadron at Cowes, where his boat *Lulworth* 'won a good many races, including the King's Cup in 1925' although Weld's 'detachment from the excitement of the start was a general cause of astonishment' (Guest and Boulton 1903, pp. 179–80).[35] He had a house at 13 Arlington Street, London SW1 but in 1927 he inherited Lulworth Castle at East Lulworth in Dorset, 'a castle of a very special sort' that was constructed c.1608 in Gothic style (Pevsner 1972, pp. 45, 194–6). This was a tragic period in his life as his beautiful young wife died in 1929 and Lulworth Castle was gutted by fire in the same year. He died at Lulworth on 5 February 1935 after a brief illness, leaving the sum of £500 in his will to Queen's College, Oxford. He was buried in the Weld family chapel the following day. The members of the congregation included Langdon, who added a glowing appreciation to Weld's published obituary (*The Times*, 7 February 16b; funeral details on 9 February 15d, appreciation on 12 February 19c, details of the will on 27 August 13c and 22 June 9d).[36]

Figure 149 Lorenzo Giuntini (c.1844–1920) as a young man.

Figure 150 Lorenzo Giuntini in later years.

In November 1891 Herbert Weld had gone to Persia, arriving in Shiraz the following January. Plaster piece and papier maché moulds were made on site by the *formatore* Lorenzo Andrea Giuntini (c.1844–1920) and one of his four sons. Giuntini (figs 149–50) had previously worked for D. Brucciani who owned an important cast gallery at 40 Great Russell Street and had travelled to Meso-America with Alfred Maudslay to mould Mayan sculptures at Copán and Quirigua.[37] At Persepolis he moulded processional scenes along the north face of the Apadana and the western façade of the Palace of Darius, royal combat scenes inside doorways of the Palace of Darius and the Harem, an inscription of Artaxerxes III Ochus (359–338 BC) from the staircase on the western façade of the Palace of Darius, a column base excavated in the Treasury, a lion on the rock-cut tomb façade of Artaxerxes III and the winged figure in Gate R at Pasargadae (Smith [1931]). While at Persepolis, Weld and Giuntini made and presented duplicate papier maché moulds of the Artaxerxes inscription and a guardsman from the southern façade of the Palace of Darius to Truxton Beale, the United States Minister to Persia, during his otherwise unsuccessful visit to try and secure sculptures for what is now the Smithsonian Institution in Washington (Adler 1895).[38] After returning to England in the summer, Giuntini's moulds were used to make plaster casts and sold via Smith's London address of 3A The Avenue, Fulham Road (fig. 151).[39]

Extensive lime burning, erosion, removal of certain pieces and vandalism had already led to parts of the site – particularly the long-exposed north face of the Apadana – being damaged. The 1892 casts thus provide the best surviving record of these sculptures. Some casts were sold to defray costs, the buyers including the Musée du Louvre, the Vorderasiatische Museum in Berlin and the Metropolitan Museum in New York, but only two complete sets appear to have been made and the moulds were deliberately destroyed to ensure that these remained a limited edition (Budge 1925, p. 24; Smith [1931]).[40] One set was presented by Lord Savile to the Nottingham Museum and Art Gallery and the second was presented to the British Museum in July 1893 'with the

Figure 151 Interior of the Giuntini family studio, Fulham Road, London.

view of supplying adequate means of comparison of the
Persepolis sculptures with the Assyrian slabs exhibited in the
British Museum' (*Trustees Minutes*, 29 July 1893, no. 2798).[41]
However shortage of adequate space and the Trustees'
concern over showing casts rather than originals prevented
them from being placed on permanent display (a fate similar
to that of the Maudslay casts). Nevertheless, following the
popularity of an exhibition on Persian Art held at Burlington
House earlier in 1931 – at which some of the Nottingham casts
were exhibited – and the unexpected availability of a
temporary exhibition slot (normally hosting a temporary
display relating to Woolley's excavations at Ur), a display of
these casts was opened on 26 May 1931 in the former Assyrian
Basement of the British Museum (anon. 1931, p. 8; Smith
1932; cf. Royal Academy 1931, p. 6).[42]

During the course of his expedition Weld excavated a
number of trenches at Persepolis. These were in the Apadana
('The Great Hall of Xerxes'), the Central Building ('square
pylon at the south corner of the Hall of a Hundred Columns'),
the Hall of a Hundred Columns (fig. 34), Palace D ('tumulus
rising behind the Palace of Darius'), the Palace of Xerxes ('open
court below the Palace of Darius'), the Harem ('S. E. Edifice'),
the Treasury and the plain below the citadel; in addition, he
excavated some trenches in Palace P at Pasargadae.[43]

Most of the discoveries were architectural but they hinted
at the degree to which colour was an important factor in the
original decor of the palaces. Traces of 'a rich red' cement
pavement were found in the Treasury and Palace of Darius, a
fragmentary fluted pilaster 'with remains of the [yellow] paint
in the flutings … laid on a ground of white gesso' was
discovered in Palace D, and a blue and yellow glazed brick
found in or near the Apadana (Weld Blundell 1892, pp. 539,
541, 557); the discovery of this glazed brick is interesting as few
examples of this type of architectural decoration, better known
from Susa, had hitherto been reported from Persepolis. The
base of a relief in the Hall of a Hundred Columns was also
noted as being 'covered with a coating of blue paint, which
came away readily under the touch as fine blue powder. This
on examination is proved to be silicate of copper, or blue
fritte', confirming earlier suggestions that the sculptures were
originally coloured (Weld Blundell 1892, p. 557).[44]

Beneath the Apadana, Weld cleared out the series of
drains which had intrigued many of the earlier travellers to
the site and within the Treasury he found and moulded a
column base. The process of making moulds necessitated
some additional excavation, notably within the Palace of
Darius where he cleared the lower part of a doorway on the
southern side to reveal a royal combat scene, and along the
façade of the staircase on the western part of the Palace of
Xerxes (Smith [1931], p. 12, nos 10, 12).

Finds were few except in the north-east corner tower of
the Apadana where (Weld Blundell 1892, p. 546)

> buried in masses of charcoal, we found a quantity of red pottery
> vases, an iron axe-head, nails with round heads, and a copper pot
> full of pieces of bone and charcoal. Humble implements, but
> interesting as relics of an historical conflagration. They had been
> cracked by the fallen rafters and some blackened by the heat.

The nails and charcoal probably derive from the burnt
superstructure of one of the upper storeys whereas the
remainder of the finds perhaps reflect stored contents. A

Figure 152 Bronze bucket from the Apadana at Persepolis, presented by
H. Weld.

similar situation was noted by later excavators inside the
Treasury but unfortunately this evidence does not appear to
have been either recorded or retained by most excavators at
the site. Weld's 'copper pot' was presented to the Trustees of
the British Museum where it was recorded as a 'bronze vase'
(*British Museum Returns*, 16 August 1893, p. 54).

This particular vessel (figs 152–3) consists of a straight-
sided sheet-bronze bucket or pail standing 12.5 cm in height
with an original rim diameter of 28 cm, base diameter of
12 cm, height/width ratio of 1 : 2.2 and a capacity of 1.8 litres
(ME 1892.12.14.1/91163). It originally had a free-swinging
handle attached to two plain T-clamps, measuring 5 cm
across and 5.1 cm in height and each held in place below the
rim with three round-headed rivets; the handle was detached
and the bucket was badly crushed and distorted in antiquity.
Qualitative X-ray fluorescence analysis by J. R. Lang and
D. R. Hook (Department of Scientific Research) of the
corroded surfaces of the bucket indicate that it is a tin bronze
containing traces of lead whereas the suspension loop and
rivet analysed are copper with a trace of lead. Radiography
proves that the bucket had not been decorated in antiquity.[45]

Buckets such as this are frequently depicted in ninth- to
eighth-century BC Assyrian, Urartian and North Syrian art
although details such as the decoration and the shape of the
handle attachments vary (Madhloom 1970, pp. 109–16,
pl. LXXXV; Merhav 1976).[46] Several plain and one engraved
sheet-bronze buckets were excavated in ninth- to eighth-
century contexts in level IV at the site of Hasanlu in north-
west Iran (Burned Buildings I, II, IV, IV East) and an example
with Assyrian-style decoration was excavated at the eighth-
century cemetery of Chamahzi Mumah in western Luristan
(de Schauensee 1988, p. 49; Muscarella 1988, pp. 29–31,
no. 8; Haerinck and Overlaet 1998, pp. 27–9, fig. 43, pls
62–3). Further straight-sided buckets – some reportedly
found in Luristan – exist in other collections, some with
decoration added in recent times (Moorey 1971, pp. 268–9,
fig. 23, pl. 81, no. 513; Merhav 1976; Muscarella 1977, p. 184,
pl. XIV: top; Tanabe *et al.* 1982, pp. 68, 73, pl. III;
Mahboubian 1997, p. 242, no. 315).

Although it is conceivable that the bucket excavated by
Weld was an heirloom, it is more likely that this type had a
lengthier history than previously suspected. Indeed,
horizontally fluted metal buckets with swinging handles are

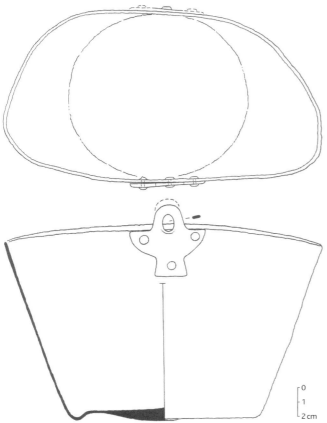

Figure 153 Bronze bucket from the Apadana at Persepolis. Height 12.5 cm, rim diameter 28 cm, base diameter 12 cm.

shown being carried by royal attendants on sculptures in the Palace of Darius (521–486 BC) and the Hall of a Hundred Columns (Schmidt *et al.* 1953, pls 183–4; Tilia 1972, pl. XCVII). Horizontal fluting was widely used as a surface technique by Achaemenid metalworkers and recurs on bowls, beakers and animal-head vessels as well as contemporary Attic pottery copies and column bases, both at East Greek sites and Palace P at Persepolis (Miller 1993; Stronach 1978, pp. 84–5, pls 73–6). However, this bucket suggests that plain versions of this type were also manufactured. Their function is unclear. In Assyrian art, buckets are shown being used by apotropaic figures in purifying ceremonies whereas the Persepolis reliefs show them being carried by attendants next to the king. The excavated finds from Hasanlu and Chamahzi Mumah suggest that they may have had other practical functions, supported by the excavated context of the Persepolis bucket.

Herbert Weld's work at Persepolis is a classic example of nineteenth-century problem-orientated research building on earlier discoveries and observations of Political Residents, Envoys and travellers such as Ephraim Stannus, John Macdonald (Kinneir) and James Alexander, highlighted above. This was the beginning of archaeological research in Iran, yet the full story has yet to be told and further episodes are certain to unfold with continued research in libraries, archives and other collections.[47]

Notes

1 His long absence abroad between 1831 and 1854 occasioned a minor incident at the Oriental Club in London, to which he had been elected in 1829, when he was refused re-entry by the hall porter (Forrest 1968, p. 28).

2 This episode is briefly mentioned by Wright (1977, p. 18); see also Simpson (2004).

3 This collection included seals, coins and other small objects acquired in Bushire bazaar, two fragments of Persepolis sculptures and three inscribed bricks collected from 'Babylon' by one Mr Martin, then staying in Bushire (Ouseley 1819, pp. 209, 213, 219, 417, pl. XXI). The reliability of the Babylon provenance might be questioned as the correct location of the site had been firmly established only in 1818 by the East India Company's Resident in Baghdad, Claudius James Rich (1786–1821), and it is more likely that these bricks derive from the Kassite capital of Aqar Quf, the spectacularly eroded ziggurat which was frequently mistaken for the Tower of Babel.

4 This may be the report to which Keppel (1827, p. 107) refers in his comments on the use of clay rather than wooden coffins in Mesopotamia.

5 British Museum archives: Department of Greek and Roman Antiquities, *Letters on Antiquities*, no. 75.

6 A photograph of one of these vessels was published by Bilkadi (1996, p. 103).

7 There is some evidence to suggest that the Portuguese may have remodelled an earlier fort dating to the thirteenth century or before (Whitehouse and Williamson 1973, p. 40); a similar pattern of reuse is evident at the so-called Portuguese Fort on Bahrain (Vine 1993, pp. 99–103).

8 Bandar Abbas and other Persian ports were the subject of similar raids during a period of weakened central authority following the death of Nadir Shah in 1747.

9 The Arab sources are ambiguous as a second Rishahr existed near the head of the Persian Gulf in the district of Arrajan (Le Strange 1905, p. 271) but most modern writers accept that this is the site of Rishahr near Bushire (Hinds 1984, pp. 51–2, n. 87).

10 In March 1811 the wreck of Nadir Shah's man-of-war, constructed at great effort with wood brought from Mazanderan, was still visible in Bushire harbour (Morier 1818, pp. 38–9). Further information on the history and topography of the town is given by Curzon (ed. 1892, vol. II, pp. 229–36), Wilson (1928), Mason (1945, pp. 125, 502–4, pls 270–1), Bidwell (1985, pp. 584–6) and de Planhol (1990); Wright (1998, pp. 167–8) lists funerary monuments of British individuals interred in the church of St George and at Rishahr Cemetery. Useful detailed maps of the island can be found in Pézard (1914, pl. IX), [Moberly] (1987, endpapers: 'to illustrate operations at Bushire 1915'), Whitehouse and Williamson (1973, p. 36) and Whitcomb (1987, p. 312).

11 The Sabzabad Residency was used until 1946 when the Political Residency was transferred to Bahrain and the old buildings handed over to the Persian government for use as a sanatorium; the British consulate closed in 1951 following the nationalisation of the Anglo-Iranian Oil Company (Belgrave 1972a, p. 85).

12 These are registered as ME 1873.7.26.1; 1875.7.24.1–2 (part); 1875.7.25.1–37; 1895.5.14.2–7. An inscribed brick of Shilhak-Inshushinak I passed through the London salerooms in recent years; according to the attached nineteenth-century paper label, this was one of a group of seven (Bonhams 5 July 1994, pp. 62–3, lot 268 = Bonhams 7 April 1998, p. 47, lot 237 = Bonhams 22 September 1998, p. 43, lot 140).

13 Andreas is better known for his philological contributions and co-operation with F. Stolze in the publication of the first photographic album of the standing ruins at Persepolis (Andreas and Stolze 1882). The bulk of his papers are held by the University Library in Göttingen (Lentz 1987).

14 British Museum archives: Department of the Middle East. The bricks are registered as ME 1875.7.25.1–26 (cf. Walker 1981, pp. 149–50).

15 This site is briefly described by Mostafavi (1978, p. 92).

16 Budge decided against working on Bahrain but Mr and Mrs Bent excavated a large tumulus there the following year. Their finds were later presented to the British Museum (Reade and Burleigh 1978).

17 This acquisition is listed in reports by Mr Renouf (then Keeper of the Department of Egyptian and Assyrian Antiquities) to the British Museum Trustees (*Reports to the Trustees*, 19 May 1888, 28 June 1888). Publication of a new anthropological study of these remains is under way.

18 The stone ossuary was reported in later gallery guides as being from Susa but this is not supported by documentation at the time of its registration.

19 These discoveries are mentioned in a recent guide. 'Excavations along the same road [between Bushire and Rishahr] have revealed a more or less continuous line of buried earthenware vases, believed to contain the remains of Zoroastrians after the vultures had done their work' (Greenway and St Vincent 1998, p. 307).

20 This fragment has since been restored to its original position (Carbone 1968, p. 36, fig. 5). In 1933 the American excavators of Qasr-i Abu Nasr found traces of the nineteenth-century excavations (Whitcomb 1985, pp. 16, 32).

21 Pfrommer (1993, pp. 17–18, 238, nn. 122, 127, 148) has suggested a post-Achaemenid date for this appliqué (ME 1897.12.31.26/23927).

22 Compare the scene at the bottom right flight of the staircase on the western side which was moulded by the Weld expedition (Smith 1932, no. 3, pl. 8).

23 We are very grateful to Mrs F. S. Farmanfarmaian for kindly drawing our attention to this description (Scottish Record Office, Edinburgh: McNeill Papers, GD371/-). McNeill first visited Persia as an Assistant-Surgeon to Major Henry Willock's mission in January 1821. After his first marriage he was re-appointed at Willock's request as medical officer to the East India Company legation in Tehran in 1824, later becoming assistant to Macdonald and eventually promoted to Minister Plenipotentiary to Tehran from 1836 to 1842 (Lee 1893, pp. 249–51; [MacAlister] 1910; Wright 1977, pp. 21–2). McNeill finally retired to Edinburgh in 1842 where his house at 53 Queen Street was 'fitted up entirely in Persian materials' ([MacAlister] 1910, p. 271). It is likely from this description that the sphinx relief featured prominently among these furnishings.

24 British Museum archives: Department of the Middle East, S. Smith, *Report of Donations*, 29 December 1937.

25 Sidney Smith (Keeper of the Department of Egyptian and Assyrian Antiquities) suggested in a letter to Sir Robert Witt (Chairman of the National Art Collections Fund) that the sphinx might have belonged to Lord Amherst of Hackney but this is clearly mistaken (British Museum archives: Department of the Middle East, *Correspondence*, 30 October 1937). I am also grateful to Mrs M. Yule of the National Art Collections Fund for her assistance.

26 Not all travellers were so thorough. For instance John Hyde, a businessman from Manchester, visited Persepolis on 4 and 6 October 1821 – the days immediately before and after the premature death of Claudius James Rich in Shiraz – but his (unpublished) journal makes no further reference to his activities there (British Library Add. MS 42106).

27 Barnett (1957); Mitchell (2000); Roaf (1987) and Curtis (1998) list additional pieces in other collections; cf. also Christie's (2003, pp. 132–33, lot 244).

28 See also his obituary in *The Gentleman's Magazine*, December 1850, p. 659.

29 I am grateful to Mr S. Griffiths of Croydon Local Studies Library for this information. The Seminary was finally closed in 1861 with the merging of the Indian and British armies after the Indian Mutiny when the War Office decided that the existing training facilities at Sandhurst and Woolwich were sufficient. Addiscombe House, which was built by Hawksmoor, and the surrounding buildings were later demolished for housing (Farrington 1976; Pevsner 1971, p. 51).

30 British Museum archives: Central Archives. A second group of eighteen casts, listed by Stannus in a paper sent to Edward Hawkins (*Letters on Antiquities*, no. 100), were offered by Stannus to the Royal Dublin Society but not delivered owing to 'some mistake of his agent'.

31 I am very grateful to Dr Ian Jenkins (Department of Greek and Roman Antiquities) for first drawing my attention to these archives and to Christopher Date (Central Archives) for his kind assistance.

32 *A Guide to the Exhibition Galleries of the British Museum, Bloomsbury* (London 1884), p. 80. Two of these casts were transferred in 1880 from the India Museum (ME 1880.1.30.9). It might be noted that the original colour of the objects – visible on the backs of the casts – and the method of mounting of the Stannus casts from Persepolis and Hajjiabad are identical yet contrast greatly with that of the later Weld series. I am very grateful to Ken Uprichard (Head of Inorganic Conservation) for his insightful comments on these and the possible original displayed appearance of other sculptures.

33 Lottin de Laval also made casts of Assyrian reliefs at Khorsabad (Fontan 1994). His own *Manuel complet de Lottinoplastique*,

published in 1857, has been re-issued electronically at http://www.bmlisieux.com/normandie/lottinop.htm.

34 British Museum archives: Department of Greek and Roman Antiquities, *Reports to the Trustees 1887–8*, pp. 119–31. Harcourt Smith was later appointed Director of the South Kensington Museum (later Victoria & Albert Museum) on the basis of experience 'learned on the job at the British Museum' (Burton 1999, p. 171) and it was on behalf of that museum that Murdoch Smith built up a rich Islamic collection from Iran, partly acquired from M. Richard, 'a French gentleman long resident in Persia' (Murdoch Smith 1876, preface). The activities of M. Richard at Ray had been detailed by Cecil Smith to the Trustees of the British Museum some years before as he noted that 'M. Richard of Teheran has made some tentative excavations here, the most interesting result of which was the acquisition of fragments proving the existence here in very early times of the manufacturing of *reflêt* pottery' (*Reports to the Trustees* 1887–8, p. 131).

35 My thanks to Mrs Diana Harding (Royal Yacht Squadron Archivist) for kindly referring me to this source.

36 I am very grateful to Mr J. M. Kaye (Keeper of the Archives at Queen's College) for information relating to Weld's Oxford connection, to the late Dr Roger Moorey for suggesting other leads, to Mr D. Greenhalf (Custodian of Lulworth Castle) for kindly sending further information and to Lady Agnes Grey for giving her permission to publish fig. 149.

37 Maudslay described Giuntini as 'a very good fellow and good companion – does not grumble' (Graham 2002, p. 111). There are some interesting similarities between the Maudslay and Weld expeditions. Both were directed by modest men of private means whose objective was, in Maudslay's words, 'to enable scholars to carry on their work of examination and comparison, and to solve some of the many problems of Maya civilisation, whilst comfortably seated in their studies at home' (quoted by Drew 1999, p. 89). Maudslay learnt the technique of making paper squeezes at Yaxchilán in 1881 from the French explorer Desiré Charnay; his subsequent expeditions relied heavily on making squeezes of low-relief sculptures and inscriptions using 'a special tissue like orange wrappers that travelled out from England in large bales' or making plaster piece-moulds of stelae and sculptures in the round. 'The logistical problems were formidable. Besides photographic and survey equipment, and supplies for many weeks in the field, he had to arrange for the shipment of the plaster [bought for 50 shillings a ton in Carlisle but reckoned by Maudslay to cost £50 by the time it reached Copán], the bales of paper, wrapping materials for the moulds and specially designed boxes to transport them. . . . At Copán, Maudslay and Giuntini used four tons of plaster and produced some 1400 separate piece moulds' (Drew 1999, p. 93; cf. also Graham 2002). I am very grateful to Susan Gill for drawing my attention to Drew's account.

38 My thanks to Dr Ann C. Gunter for kindly telling me about these casts.

39 I am very grateful to Mrs Valerie Emmons for kindly sending me further information about Lorenzo Giuntini and his family. He had two brothers (Frederico Eugene and Angelo Robert), four sons (Lawrence Mark Angelo, Joseph Albert Victor, Lelio and Renaldo) and four daughters (Flora Kate, Cecilia Alice, Ada Maud and Mabel Adela); the brothers and sons all worked in the family studio and together were partly responsible for making a number of well-known monumental bronze sculptures erected in public spaces across London.

40 The Musée du Louvre holdings include cast sections of the north façade of the Apadana and the west staircase of the Palace of Darius, recently exhibited in two temporary exhibitions (anon. 1997 = Smith 1932, no. 2 [part]; Fontan 1998, pp. 228–9, nos 93–4 = Smith 1932, no. 4 [part of sections I and IV]). I am indebted to Dr A. Caubet for kindly supplying this information. Nine plaster casts of Achaemenid sculptures were registered by the Vorderasiatische Museum and transferred to the University of Hamburg in 1993; for this information I am grateful to Dr R.-B. Wartke. The reassembled cast of the enthroned Xerxes which was made for the Metropolitan Museum is illustrated by Rogers (1929, figs 18, 26–7).

41 These two sets have now been reunited following the acquisition by the British Museum of the Nottingham casts in November 1997: many were placed on temporary display as part of the 'Forgotten Empire' exhibition at the British Museum (September

2005–January 2006). They have since been installed on permanent display in the redesigned Ancient Iran gallery and adjacent east staircase.

42 The exhibition was open for a year before being dismantled in May 1932 (*Reports to the Trustees*: S. Smith, p. 8 June 1931, no. 137, 6 May 1932, no. 69). In a letter to George Hill, then Director of the British Museum, Smith wrote that a 'rough calculation shows that the approximate length of exhibition space required would be over 100 feet, and the only safe way of exhibiting them temporarily would be to have two sets of planking about 30 feet long run down the centre of the room; at least that is the only way that suggests itself to me at present as feasible, without interfering with the public view of the Assyrian sculptures', and continued by referring to his desire that they be displayed in a permanent gallery once 'the temporary Persian exhibition in the Print Room is dismantled' (*Reports to the Trustees*, 7 March 1931, no. 228). In preparation for this temporary exhibition, the casts were fitted together, cleaned and coloured by the Cast Department of the Victoria & Albert Museum (*Officer's Reports* 1931). The Assyrian Basement was later restricted to its present size and height with the construction of galleries above.

43 Surprisingly, Weld's pioneering excavations at Palace P are not mentioned by Stronach (1978) although they must have informed Herzfeld's later trenches.

44 Traces of black, red, green, blue and yellow or golden pigment have been noted on reliefs in the Apadana, Central Building and the Hall of a Hundred Columns (Tilia 1978, pp. 31–69; Lerner 1971, 1973; Roaf 1983, p. 8). Lumps of pigment or pigment-encrusted sherds have also been found at the south-west corner of the Terrace wall, in and near the tripylon and on the northern side of the Apadana (Tilia 1972, pp. 245–6; Tilia 1978, pp. 68–9). Analyses indicate the black to be asphalt, the red to be a vitreous material, the blue to be 'Egyptian Blue' and the red floor in the Treasury to be lime plaster coloured with red ochre (Tilia 1978; Lerner 1973; Matson 1953, p. 287). More recent analyses of samples obtained by Shahrokh Razmjou (Iran National Museum) suggest that cinnabar, obtained from mercury oxide which occurs in two major sources in northern and western Iran, was also employed to create a red pigment (Razmjou, personal communication, November 2001). Comments on these and other traces of pigment have been published by Ambers and Simpson (2005).

45 Department of Scientific Research file: Project rad7066 dated 20 January 1999.

46 See Goldman (1961) for the development of bucket clamps.

47 I am very grateful to John Curtis and the late Roger Moorey for their helpful comments on this chapter. The drawings are by Ann Searight.

7 The British and archaeology in nineteenth-century Persia

Vesta Sarkhosh Curtis

Until the beginning of the nineteenth century British interests in Persia were primarily of a commercial nature. The East India Company in Bombay regulated and controlled the import of goods (mainly wool) and the trade of Asian goods via the Persian Gulf. The main headquarters in Persia was first at Bandar-i Abbas; then, after 1763, Bushire became the centre for British trade, as well as acting as the principal port for Shiraz and Isfahan. But with growing French influence in Europe under Napoleon and the invasion of Egypt in 1798, British India began to fear a French invasion of India via Persia and Afghanistan. The sense of anxiety grew when Napoleon made peace with the Russian Tsar Alexander I in Tilsit in 1807 and suggested to him a possible joint French–Russian alliance and advance into India. British India became more and more concerned about India's western frontier and a possible invasion of India via Persia (Hopkirk 1990, p. 3). In addition India's north-western frontier was causing problems, and French support for the rebellious Afghanistan was a distinct possibility. All these factors gave rise to the necessity – as some British officials saw it – of turning Persia into a buffer state between the hostile forces of France and Russia on the one hand and British India on the other. A joint Franco-Russian invasion was no longer on the cards by the end of the first decade of the nineteenth century, after Napoleon's attempted invasion of Russia had failed. However, Russia continued its advance into the north-western and north-eastern khanates and moved geographically closer to British India.

British politicians in India wished to halt what was perceived as growing Russian influence in territories close to the subcontinent, and it was for this specific reason that politicians and army officers appointed in British India flocked into Persia. The aim of these missions was to negotiate on a political level with Persian officials, as well as to collect information about the country, its people, culture, geography and routes. The missions, headed by political appointees, also included members who either were scholars in the field of oriental studies or were interested in ancient and exotic cultures. They had a good knowledge of the Old Testament as well as Classical sources.

By this time some ancient languages and scripts such as Avestan and Pahlavi had already been deciphered. The Iranian epic, the *Shahnameh*, had already been translated into French by Jules Mohl by 1771, when Anquetil du Peron translated the holy book of the Zoroastrians, the *Avesta*, again into French (V. S. Curtis 1993, p. 10). Also available were Greek and Latin sources, as well as the travelogues of earlier explorers. A certain amount of information was therefore accessible, but the archaeology and monuments of Persia were, on the whole, poorly recorded.

One of the earliest European descriptions of Persepolis goes back to the early fourteenth century, when the Franciscan monk Odoric of Pordenone, on his way to China, wrote a short account of the site, which he called Comum (Wieshöfer 2002, p. 271; Curtis 2005, p. 253). Giosofat Barbaro, a Venetian ambassador, visited Persepolis, Naqsh-i Rustam and Pasargadae in 1472. Travellers in the seventeenth century included the Augustinian friar Antoine de Gouvea, who, in 1602, regarded Takht-i Jamshid as old Shiraz. John Cartwright went to Persia to obtain trade permission for English merchants in 1611. Don Garcia de Silva Figueroa arrived there in 1617 and correctly identified Takht-i Jamshid as Persepolis (fig. 154). Pietro della Valle travelled there in 1621, saw the the ruins of Persepolis and produced the first copies of Old Persian cuneiform inscriptions. Heinrich von Poser and Sir Thomas Herbert visited the site in 1624 and 1626 respectively. J. A. de Mandelslo was sent to Persia with the mission of Adam Oeleschlager (Olearius) and he saw the ruins of Persepolis in 1638. A careful examination of the site with detailed drawings was prepared by André Daulier des Landes, a French artist who accompanied Jean-Baptiste Tavernier to Persia between 1664 and 1668 (Wiesehöfer 2002, pp. 272–3). During his last visit to Persepolis, des Landes saw Jean Chardin and his artist Joseph Grelot at Takht-i Jamshid. In the same year Samuel Flower, an agent of the East India Company, copied some of the Persepolis inscriptions. Engelbert Kaempfer saw the ruins in 1686 and Cornelis De Bruin visited the site in 1704 and made copies of some of the reliefs (Budge 1920, pp. 12–22; Wiesehöfer 2001, pp. 229–30). In the spring of 1765 Carsten Niebuhr spent three weeks at Persepolis, making plans of buildings and copying various inscriptions. These copies were later used by the German scholar Georg Friedrich Grotefend to decipher Old Persian cuneiform in 1802 (Hinz 1975, pp. 15–18).

The present discussion concentrates on a selection of nineteenth-century British travellers who either contributed to the collections of the British Museum, like Rich, Loftus and Rawlinson, or were also interested in coins, like Ker Porter. Others made significant discoveries and all of them greatly advanced our knowledge of the monuments of ancient Persia. It is fascinating that many contemporary explorers knew each other and often referred to each other's work (e.g. Rich, Bellino and Ker Porter, Layard, Loftus and Rawlinson). It is also important to emphasise that the term archaeology cannot be used for many of these early expeditions, which were often little more than treasure hunts. It was only Layard, in particular, and to an extent also Loftus, who recorded the exact find-spots of objects and made detailed notes of their excavations.

On 5 March 1811 an important mission headed by Sir Gore Ouseley, 'Ambassador Extraordinary and Minister

Figure 154 View of Persepolis.

Plenipotentiary', landed at Bushire on the Persian Gulf. The mission had the specific task of negotiating a new treaty with the Persian authorities. This was to replace the Preliminary Treaty of 1809, whereby Persia would not allow any European force to pass through its territories on its way to India, and, if Persia were invaded by a foreign force, Britain would supply military help. The mission included, as First Secretary, James Morier, who had earlier visited Persia for the first time as a member of Sir Harford Jones's mission in 1809; Robert Gordon, brother of the fourth Earl of Aberdeen (Curtis 1998, p. 45); and Ouseley's own brother William, a distinguished Orientalist who had studied in Paris and Leiden (Wright 1977, p. 151).

On their way from Bushire to Tehran they stopped at Shiraz for several months and Lady Ouseley gave birth to a baby girl. It was here that Sir Gore sent members of his mission on fact-finding expeditions in the surrounding area, with the intention of collecting as much information as possible about ancient monuments, including the well-known sites of Persepolis and Naqsh-i Rustam, north of Shiraz.

We have detailed descriptions of these early expeditions by William Ouseley, James Morier and Robert Gordon (Curtis 1998, pp. 45–51). When William Ouseley visited Persepolis for the first time from 4 to 6 May 1811, he found that James Morier had already engaged some workmen to dig for sculptures, and he also noticed how some pieces had fallen from their original positions. The 'digging' lasted only two days, before work on the site was prohibited by the local governor (Curtis 1998, p. 48).

Morier visited Persepolis once again between 11 and 13 July, this time together with Sir Gore and Lady Ouseley. By this time Robert Gordon and a team of local workmen had dug up some sculptures from the east wing of the northern stairway of the Apadana palace, which were immediately shipped to Britain via Bombay. Accounts of this treasure hunt by members of Ouseley's mission at Persepolis are preserved in letters written at the site by Robert Gordon to his brother, the Earl of Aberdeen. In a letter dated 16 July 1811, he lists the

sculpture that was shipped to England. In another, written in Isfahan on 21 August 1811, he says how much he looks forward to seeing the Persepolis sculptures in the hall of the Argyll House, the home of Lord Aberdeen, which 'is about to become the admiration of London' (Curtis 1998, p. 49). Lists and drawings of the sculptures were prepared at the site by Morier. Some of these pieces remained in the possession of the Earl of Aberdeen; many were apparently on display in Sir Gore Ouseley's house in Bruton Street, London; and others were given to the British Museum in 1817. Two pieces – originally part of a horse and chariot relief at Persepolis but then subsequently separated – are once again reunited through a temporary loan to the British Museum (fig. 155; Curtis 1998, pp. 49–50, pls IV–Va; 2000, p. 51, fig. 52).

Some of the same individuals also made important discoveries during their travels in the province of Fars. William Ouseley correctly identified the relief at Darabgird as that of the Sasanian king Shapur I, but came to the wrong conclusion about the ruins of Fasa, south of Shiraz, which he believed to be ancient Pasargadae, the capital of Cyrus the Great (Wright 1977, p. 152). During his first journey to Persia with Harford Jones in 1809, James Morier visited the Sasanian city of Bishapur (built by Shapur I in AD 262) and the nearby rock reliefs of the Sasanian kings. At Pasargadae he made a sketch of the monument traditionally known as the tomb of the Mother of Solomon, and described it as an

Figure 155 Persepolis relief reunited from fragments in the British Museum and the Miho Museum, Japan.

Figure 156 Gate of All Nations, Persepolis.

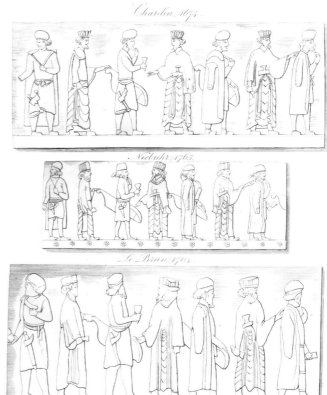

Figure 157 Drawings of Persepolis reliefs by Chardin, Niebuhr and Le Brun.

illustrious building, which he was tempted to identify (correctly) as the tomb of Cyrus (fig. 29; Wright 1977, p. 152). A few years later, in 1821, a well-known scholar stood before the same monument and wrote (J. Curtis 2000, p. 41):

> The very venerable appearance of this ruin instantly awed me. I sat nearly for an hour on the steps, contemplating it until the moon rose on it; and I began to think that this in reality must be the tomb of the best, the most illustrious, and the most interesting of Oriental Sovereigns.

These were the words of Claudius James Rich, who at the age of twenty-two was appointed Resident at the Court of the Pasha of Baghdad by the Directors of the East India Company. The Residency under Rich was open to many travellers, including Sir Robert Ker Porter (see below), who stayed there for almost a month and drew some of the objects in Rich's collection (Ker Porter 1822, p. 425, pl. 80.3). During this time a close friendship developed between the two men, Rich writing his last letter to Ker Porter on 8 December 1820, some months before his untimely death (Ker Porter 1822, pp. 809–12).

Rich travelled for the first time to Iran in the summer of 1820, accompanied by his wife Mary, her female entourage and his German secretary, Carl Bellino. They left the unbearable heat of Baghdad for the mountains of Kurdistan, crossed the Zagros mountains – called Shahoo by the Kurds – and arrived at 'Sinna, a colloquial abbreviation' for Sanandaj, in late August (Rich 1836, vol. I, pp. 139–241, especially pp. 199–222).

In June 1821 Rich left Baghdad for a new post in Bombay, but interrupted his voyage at Bushire. So unbearable was the heat there that he and his two companions, Dr Todd and Mr Sturney, decided to travel northwards. This gave them an opportunity to visit Shiraz and the nearby ancient sites, which had been a childhood dream of Rich. They travelled by night and arrived in Shiraz after some ten days, seeing snow-capped mountains on their way (Alexander 1928, pp. 303–4). In a letter dated 11 August 1821 Rich expressed his liking for the climate and air of Shiraz, which he preferred 'much beyond that of Koordistan' (1836, vol. II, p. 215). Rich's diary entries are full of excitement about the ruins of Persepolis and describe how, as a child, he had been inspired by the

seventeenth-century Frenchman Jean Chardin. He was anxiously waiting to see the ruins, in later times remembering his beloved late friend and secretary Carl Bellino, and often referring to his friend Robert Ker Porter's 'admirable drawings' (Rich 1836, vol. II, pp. 216–17, 221, 223). It took the party two days to reach Persepolis from Shiraz (Alexander 1928, p. 307):

> My sensation on approaching Persepolis can hardly be described. Gradually the pointed summit of the mountain, under which the ruins of Persepolis stand, began to detach itself from the range. . . . At that moment the moon rose with uncommon beauty. . . . Ages seemed at one to present themselves to my fancy.

Despite his exhilaration at seeing the ruins, Rich continued his journey to Pasargadae ('Mughaub') before returning to explore Persepolis more fully. En route he stopped for half an hour at nearby Naqsh-i Rajab and its Sasanian rock reliefs and also visited the ruins of Istakhr. At Pasargadae he copied the Old Persian inscription over the winged genie (fig. 162; Rich 1836, vol. II, pp. 219–20):

> Near it are some pilasters with cuneiform inscriptions, and a curious figure, beautifully executed and most correctly copied by Sir R. K. Porter, to the unrivalled fidelity and character of whose delineations I can in every instance bear testimony.

On the way back from Pasargadae they spent five days at Persepolis, where Rich left his name and the date of his visit on the stone *lamassu* adorning the Gate of All Nations (fig. 156). He 'copied all the inscriptions but one, . . . found much to corroborate Georg Friedrich Grotefend's system' and believed that his hard work would help the German scholar. At Naqsh-i Rustam (Rich 1836, vol. II, p. 223), he described the tombs of

> the four kings of the first dynasty; and the more recent Sasanian sculptures beneath them. . . . These latter are but coarse

Figure 158 Prince Abbas Mirza (1789–1833) by Ker Porter.

Figure 159 Fath 'Ali Shah (1797–1834) by Ker Porter.

performances, and clearly indicate a more barbarous age than the Persepolitan. . . . There was something affecting, at the first view of it, to see the majesty of Rome, even the Rome of Valerian, prostrate before a barbarian.

News of the death of Claudius James Rich from cholera on 5 October 1821 in Shiraz was received with sadness amongst travellers of the time, for he was recognised as

> a man whose luminous mind and benevolence enlightened and smoothed the way of all travellers who came within his sphere of influence. His mastery of science, and the depth of his erudition in every subject connected with antiquity, are well known to all who sought those pursuits in the East.

The eulogy to this great scholar was written by Robert Ker Porter (1822, p. 809), whose own contribution to the recording and interpretation of the monuments of ancient Iran was tremendous. As noted above (pp. 3–4), Ker Porter was commissioned to record the monuments of Persia by A. Olinen, the President of the Russian Academy of Fine Arts in 1817 (Ker Porter 1821, p. viii), who gave strict instructions to

> Correct nothing; and preserve, in your copies, the true character of the originals. Do not give to Persian figures a French tournure, like Chardin; nor a Dutch like Van Bruyn, nor a German, or rather Danish, like Niebuhr; nor an English grace, like some of your countrymen.

It is interesting that Olinen refers here to the drawings of earlier travellers, which were known to him, but did not meet his approval (fig. 157; Ker Porter 1821, p. v):

> Here, you may observe the same figure of the same Persepolitan bas-relief, transmitted to us in three perfectly different forms of outline; and the same personages which le Brun represents in the year 1704, with their noses, mouths, and beards mutilated, re-

appear, quite whole in every feature, in the drawings of Niebuhr from Persia, in the year 1765. You will confess that without some miracle, both these accounts cannot be true; and Chardin shews [*sic*] the like inaccuracy to so great an extent, that I know not to wish to yield any belief.

In Tabriz, Ker Porter was invited by the Qajar crown prince Abbas Mirza (fig. 158) to accompany him to Tehran, where they arrived a few days before the Iranian New Year celebrations of Nowruz on the Spring Equinox on 21 March 1818. Ker Porter describes Abbas Mirza as a learned and knowledgeable man interested in the ancient past of his country (1821, p. 248), and a close friendship seems to have developed between the two men (Luft 2001, p. 40, n. 30). With the help of interpreters (Major Lindesay-Bethune of the horse artillery and Hart of the Persian infantry), the artist was able to question the heir apparent about the visible remains of ancient sites between Qazvin and Tehran.

> I enquired of Abbas Mirza what he thought of the origin of those heaps of earth. He had no doubt of their having been raised by man; but by whom, and for what purpose, he said, he knew of no written nor traditionary [*sic*] account. But he supposed that they were the work of the fire-worshippers of former ages, who usually erected their altars on high places; and there being none, naturally, so many farsangs from the hills, these idolaters had constructed mounds to supply the deficiency.

At the imperial court in Tehran, Ker Porter caught his first glance of His Majesty Fath 'Ali Shah during the Nowruz celebrations (1821, pp. 327–8):

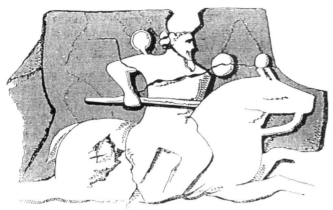

Figure 160 Drawing of the lost Sasanian relief of Shapur II (?) at Sorsoreh, Ray, by William Ouseley (1811).

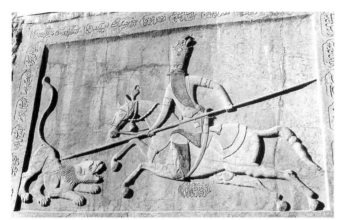

Figure 161 Hunting relief of Fath 'Ali Shah at Sorsoreh, Ray, destroyed in the 1960s.

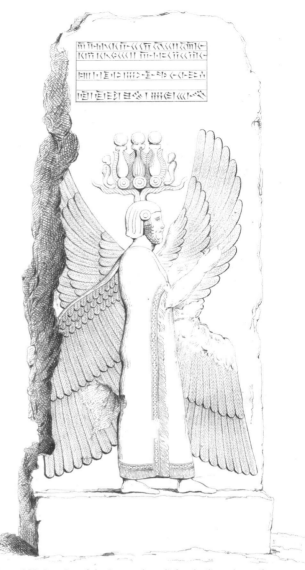

Figure 162 Drawing of the Pasargadae relief and trilingual cuneiform inscriptions in Old Persian, Elamite and Babylonian by Ker Porter.

His face seemed exceedingly pale, of a polished marble hue; with the finest contour of features; and eyes dark, brilliant, and piercing; a beard black as jet, and of a length which fell below his chest. The extraordinary amplitude of beards appears to have been a badge of royalty, from the earliest times; for we find it attached to the heads of the sovereigns, in all the ancient sculptures remains throughout the empire.

When he returned to Tehran in 1819, Ker Porter presented the Qajar ruler with the finished drawing of his royal portrait (fig. 159). He and Fath 'Ali Shah discussed, amongst other things, the ancient past of Persia (Ker Porter 1821, p. 523; Luft 2001, p. 42).

In the spring of 1818 Ker Porter visited the sites surrounding Tehran, and it was during one of these excursions to Sorsoreh, Ray, that he saw a colossal ancient relief, about six feet in height, already recorded by William Ouseley in 1811. It showed a horseman in full charge with a long spear. Ker Porter described this relief, 'by order of some of the Sasanian monarchs', as crude and uncompleted, and concluded that it probably represented the founder of the dynasty, Ardashir I (1821, p. 363). This ancient relief – probably in fact depicting the Sasanian king Shapur II in a jousting scene (fig. 160) – was destroyed by Fath 'Ali Shah and replaced by a rock relief showing the Qajar ruler on horseback and hunting a lion (fig. 161). Unfortunately this Qajar relief of Sorsoreh, Ray, was in turn destroyed when the rock was used by a nearby cement factory in the late 1960s.

On 13 May 1818 Ker Porter left Tehran, heading southwards. Arriving at Isfahan on 25 May, he prepared a detailed description of the monuments of the city. From there

he travelled southwards, reaching Pasagadae on 13 June. On seeing the site, he wrote correctly that 'the ruins scattered over the vale of Mourg-aub, are those of Pasargadae' (Ker Porter 1821, p. 501). He made detailed sketches of the monuments and regularly quoted classical sources such as Strabo, Arrian and Plutarch, as well as earlier travellers and scholars. He copied the famous winged genie on the stone relief of Gate R, both in a sketch and in watercolour. He also recorded the trilingual inscription[1] in Old Persian, Elamite and Babylonian above the figure and referred to the pioneering work of Grotefend (fig. 162; 1821, pp. 493, 505, pl. 13):

> From the amazing progress that Professor Grottefund [sic] has made in decyphering [sic] this perhaps most ancient form of writing, he has been able to translate the present interesting and often repeated inscriptions: . . . 'Cyrus, Lord King, Ruler of the world!'

In fact the correct reading is 'I, Cyrus the King, an Achaemenian' (Hinz 1973, pls III–V). Ker Porter also compared this inscription with a passage from Strabo, the Greek historian of the first century AD, who recorded the epitaph on Cyrus' tomb (1821, p. 506):

> O man! I am Cyrus son of Cambyses, founder of the Persian empire, and sovereign of Asia, therefore grudge me not this sepulchre.

Figure 163 Composite drawing by Ker Porter of an Achaemenid tomb relief at Naqsh-i Rustam showing the worshipping figures of the Achaemenid king and a soldier.

Ker Porter's next stop was Naqsh-i Rustam, where he recorded the Achaemenid tombs (fig. 163), and even ascended by a rope to see the inside of one of the chambers. He sketched the Sasanian rock reliefs, the Kaba-i Zardusht, and all the Greek, Parthian and Pahlavi/Middle Persian inscriptions. His drawings are accurate and full of life, leaving those of us who have compared these copies with the actual monuments overwhelmed with admiration for his artistic skill and precise depiction of detail. His descriptions are lively and usually, but not always, correct. His knowledge of Classical history and the religion of ancient Persia was immense. He often compared the figures carved on the Sasanian reliefs with portraits of the kings on Sasanian coins, sometimes drawing the right conclusion, but at other times giving a wrong identification (Ker Porter 1821, pp. 533, 542).

He correctly compared the Kaba-i Zardusht at Naqsh-i Rustam (fig. 64) with the stone building called the Zindan-i Sulaiman at Pasargadae. He also recorded the two stone monuments on top of the mound, which are now believed to be not fire altars but *astudan* troughs, i.e. containers for human bones (Ker Porter 1821, p. 566; Huff 1998, pp. 78–81, pl. Xa).

When discussing the Middle Persian inscriptions, he often refers to the decipherment of the Naqsh-i Rustam trilingual inscriptions in 1787 by the eminent French scholar Baron Antoine Sylvestre de Sacy, who had used copies made by Carsten Niebuhr in 1765 (Ker Porter 1821, p. 572; Wiesehöfer 2001, pp. 233–4). Ker Porter's quotations of classical sources make his descriptions amusing and informative. For example, when examining the tomb of Darius, he recounts the story of Ctesias about the tomb. It was inspected by members of Darius' family, who attached themselves to ropes and were then pulled to the top of the cliff. When suddenly snakes were spotted on the rocks, the terrified helpers dropped the

rope and Darius' father, Vishtaspa, plunged down from a terrific height and met his death (Ker Porter 1821, pp. 520–1; Ctesias, *Persica* § 15, cf. Briant 2002, p. 171). Ker Porter could also be influenced by some of the traditional interpretations

Figure 164 Drawings by Ker Porter of two reliefs at Naqsh-i Rajab showing
1 Shapur I and Ahuramazda on horseback;
2 Ardashir I and his family in the presence of Ahuramazda.

Figure 165 Drawing by Ker Porter of the relief of Ardashir I and his son Shapur I at Salmas, near lake Urmia, north-west Iran.

of the monuments. For example he wrongly believed that the tombs at Naqsh-i Rustam and Persepolis dated to the pre-Achaemenid period, to the so-called Pishdadian dynasty and their famous king Jamshid, who according to Persian folklore built Takht-i Jamshid (the throne of Jamshid), now better known as Persepolis (Ker Porter 1821, p. 527).

After having seen and recorded the reliefs at Naqsh-i Rajab (figs 103; 164) and the ruins of Istakhr, Ker Porter arrived at Persepolis on 21 June 1818. He stayed there until 1 July, recording the architecture, reliefs and inscriptions (1821, p. 576):

> On the morning of the 23rd, under a sun which made a fire-altar on the rock, I began my investigations. Certainly, a positive knowledge of the original names of ancient cities is a great satisfaction to both historian and antiquary; but since these magnificent remains are sufficiently recognised, to identify their having made part of the splendid capital of the East, so long celebrated by authors under the name of Persepolis, it seems to me a subject of no material consequence, that we do not know whether it were primevally called Elamais, Istaker, or Tackt-i-Jamsheed. After the establishment of the empire by Cyrus, it is well known that he and his immediate descendants divided their residence chiefly between Babylon, Susa and Ecbatana.

Ker Porter clearly associated the ruins of Persepolis with 'Cyrus and his successors', and again used Classical sources as well as the Old Testament. At the same time he was critical of the incorrect information given in some of the earlier travellers' accounts (1821, pp. 577–8).

Ker Porter was also the first traveller and artist to record the Achaemenid rock relief of Darius at Bisitun (fig. 22; 1822, pl. 60) and would have liked to copy the inscriptions on the rock, but regarded it as a 'great personal risk' to be hoisted up by a rope, so left it to some future traveller to 'accomplish so desirable a purpose' (1822, p. 158). He further recognised the eroded relief of a row of standing figures at the site as Parthian, datable to the reign of Mithradates II (c.123–91 BC) and he produced a copy of its ancient Greek inscription (1822, p. 151). He left Bisitun on 23 September and continued to Kirmanshah.

At Taq-i Bustan he produced magnificent sketches of all the Sasanian reliefs in the grottoes, and also copied the Middle Persian inscriptions of Shapur II and III, identifying these two kings correctly (1822, pls 62–5). His discoveries of Sasanian remains included the site of Takht-i Sulaiman near Saqqiz. He then travelled to Lake Urmiah in north-western Iran, where at Salmas he copied the relief of Ardashir I and his son Shapur I (fig. 165; 1822, pl. 82), which he dated to the reign of the latter king (1822, pp. 597–9).

Ker Porter was a keen collector of coins, proudly describing his collection as 'numerous, though rare' (1821, p. x) and while at Hamadan he was able to add some Sasanian and Parthian coins, as well as 'a large silver coin of Alexander the Great' to his collection (1822, p. 124). He illustrated some of his Sasanian coins and discussed them in great detail, identifying some correctly and others not (fig. 24; 1821, pl. 58; 1822, pp. 124–32). The same applies to his readings of the coin legends.

Travelling through Qasr-i Shirin and Sar-i Pul-i Zuhab (4–5 October), Ker Porter crossed the border into Ottoman territory. Some ten days later he arrived at the gate of the British Resident's mansion in Baghdad and was warmly received by Claudius James Rich. Ker Porter was much impressed with this young man and a close friendship developed between them. Ker Porter also got to know Rich's personal secretary, Carl Bellino, who wrote on 7 November 1818 that (Barnett 1974, p. 16)

> Sir Robert arrived here three weeks ago with a good number of drawings of Persian antiquities, some of which have never before been drawn previously by him, or if so, only in an incomplete way, as for example Tak-i Bustan and Bisutun. . . . Apart from the fact that they frequently differ from those of early travellers, even Niebuhr, we have here no doubt Sir Robert has made truthfulness in his drawings his main objective, for most he has drawn here . . . are uncommonly accurate.

Ker Porter, Rich and Bellino shared a common interest in antiquities and ancient cuneiform scripts. Bellino, who was in touch with German scholars working in this field, passed on their information to Ker Porter and the two men often discussed cuneiform scripts (Ker Porter 1822, p. 420; Barnett 1974, p. 14). It was during his stay at the residency in Baghdad that Ker Porter first found out about Grotefend's achievements and the deciphering of the Old Persian script. In a letter to Ker Porter dated 14 February 1819, Bellino writes (Barnett 1974, p. 17):

> If you should have got the copy of the great inscription on the high and single standing stone [at Persepolis], I will send you the reading and translation of it which Mr Grotefend made after the very bad copy which Le Brun has given of that inscription.

Ker Porter finally left Baghdad on 2 December 1818, and returned via Kurdistan to north-western Iran, before leaving Iran for good through Erzerum. It is interesting to note that he never visited Susa. His description of this ancient site, 'Susa, or Shushan, . . . the capital of that part of ancient Elam' was based on the research and accounts of Major Monteith and Macdonald Kinnier, which they gave him during their meeting in Tabriz on his arrival in Persia (1822, pp. 411–18). He returned to St Petersburg after an absence of three years. A subsequent new diplomatic career in South America ended his contact with Persia for good (Barnett 1972, p. 24).

Ker Porter was one the few eighteenth-century European travellers in Persia who described the country and its people in a positive light and who seems to have had an understanding of not just the antiquities but also the country he had visited (cf. Luft 2001, p. 40). Perhaps his professionalism as an artist allowed him to understand the people and the country as accurately as the objects he recorded (1821, p. 493):

> I considered it a duty to the history of the art, to copy the forms before me, exactly as I saw; without allowing my pencil to add, or diminish, or to alter a line. May I be excused in repeating here, that such undeviating accuracy to the utmost of my power, is the principle to which I bound myself in the execution of all the drawings I made in the East.

The next visitor of note was a scholar of outstanding talent in ancient languages, who produced paper squeezes of the late sixth-century BC rock-carving and trilingual inscriptions of Darius the Great at Bisitun near Kirmanshah (fig. 23; pp. 5–7 above). This was Henry Creswicke Rawlinson (figs 7–8), who was a young officer of twenty-two when he first went to Persia as part of a British military mission from India to organise the army of the Qajar ruler Muhammad Shah. He arrived at Bushire in 1834, but did not reach Kirmanshah until almost a year later. Here he saw, for the first time, the monumental and impressive rock relief and cuneiform inscriptions of Darius I, carved in 519 BC some 3807 feet (c.1000 m) above the ground, now overlooking the main Baghdad to Kirmanshah highway (fig. 22).

While stationed at Kirmanshah he took every opportunity to ride to Bisitun to study the trilingual inscriptions in Old Persian, Elamite and Babylonian and make paper casts. Rawlinson copied major parts of the Old Persian version between 1835 and 1837, and completed his copies between 1844 and 1847, when he was appointed Resident in Baghdad. In 1846/7 he published the Old Persian inscription of Bisitun, followed in 1851 by the Babylonian version (Wiesehöfer 1996, p. 240). He also produced copies of the Ganj-nameh inscriptions of Darius and Xerxes at Mount Alvand, Hamadan. However, his greatest achievement was the decipherment for the first time of the Babylonian cuneiform script on the basis of the Bisitun inscriptions. Rawlinson himself gives a vivid description of how he copied the inscriptions (1852, pp. 73–6; see also p. 17 above):[2]

> The small paper Casts which are lying on the table are impressions of the epigraphs that are attached to the line of captive figures sculptured on the great triumphal Tablet of Behistun. The rock of Behistun doubtless preserved its holy character in the age of Darius, and it was on this account chosen by the monarch as a fit spot for the commemoration of his warlike achievements. The name itself, Bhagistan, signifies 'the place of the god'. I certainly do not consider it a great feat in climbing to ascend to the spot where the inscriptions occur. When I was living at Kermanshah fifteen years ago, and was somewhat more active than I am at present, I used frequently to scale the rock three or four times a day without the aid of a proper ladder: without any assistance, in fact, whatever. During my late visits I have found it more convenient to ascend and descend by the help of ropes. The Babylonian transcript at Behistun is still more difficult to reach. The writing can be copied by the aid of good telescope from below, but I long despaired of obtaining a cast of the inscription; for I found it quite beyond my powers of climbing to reach the spot where it was engraved, and the craigsmen of the place, who were accustomed to track the mountain goats over the entire face of the mountain, declared the particular block inscribed with the Babylonian legend to be unapproachable. At length, however, a wild Kurdish boy, who had come from a distance, volunteered to make the attempt, and I promised him a considerable reward if he succeeded. The method of forming these paper casts is exceedingly simple, nothing more required than to take a number of sheets of paper without size, spread them on the rock, moisten them, and then beat them into the crevices with a stout brush, adding as many layers of paper as it may be wished to give consistency to the cast. The paper is left there to dry, and on being taken off it exhibits a perfect reversed impression of the writing.

It was during his Resident years at Baghdad that Rawlinson met another distinguished scholar who had travelled through Persia and was soon to achieve fame as the excavator of the two major Assyrian capitals, Nimrud and Nineveh: Austen Henry Layard. A solicitor by training, Layard left England in 1939 to travel overland to Sri Lanka. Since childhood he had been interested in Persia, its language and culture and had even taught himself some Persian and Arabic. He had read Claudius James Rich's *Babylon and Assyria* and James Morier's *Adventures of Hajji Baba of Ispahan*, and had also listened to the advice of Sir John McNeil, former Resident at Baghdad (Layard 1887, vol. I, pp. 8–9). Accompanied by his friend Edward Mitford, Layard reached Baghdad via Istanbul, Syria and the Holy Land.

Despite frequent warnings from friends of the dangers in Persia and the 'fanaticism' of the Shia sect, they set off from Baghdad at the end of June 1840, a time when diplomatic relations between England and Persia had reached a low (Layard 1887, vol. I, p. 229). Layard carried very little luggage apart from 'a copy of Major Rawlinson's highly interesting memoir, . . . which served . . . as a text book', travelling by night and resting during the day (1887, vol. I, p. 12). Immediately after leaving the Baghdad Residency, Layard decided to dress in the Persian manner, in order to attract less attention (1887, vol. I, pp. 201–3):

> I accordingly threw aside my Turkish dress . . . and replaced it by the long flowing robes, confined at the waist by a shawl, shalwars or loose trousers, and the tall, black lambskin cap, or 'kulâh', then universally worn by the Persians. In addition I wore when riding a pair of baggy trousers of cloth, tied at the ankles, into which the

ends of the long outer garment were thrust. . . . I shaved the crown of my head, leaving a ringlet on each side, and dyed my hair and beard a deep shining black with henna and 'rang'. I could thus pass very well, so long as my mouth was closed, for an orthodox Persian.

Their caravan entered Persia via Qasr-i Shirin and Sar-i Pul-i Zohab, where Layard visited the nearby post-Achaemenid rock tomb of Dukan-i Davud, and compared the dress of the standing priest/king with that of a Zoroastrian *mubad*/priest (1887, vol. I, pp. 215–16). He also visited the rock carvings at Taq-i Bustan, 'made some sketches of them and copied the inscriptions in the ancient Persian or Pehlevi character' (1887, vol. I, p. 226). It was here that he met two French travellers, the painter Eugene Flandin and the architect Pascal Coste, who were recording the monuments (Layard 1887, vol. I, pp. 225–6). At nearby Kirmanshah they spent 'some hours examining the celebrated bas-reliefs and cuneiform inscription carved on the scarped rock by King Darius' at Bisitun, but the great height made it impossible for Layard to copy the 'inscription in three columns and three languages', which Rawlinson had already published (Layard 1887, vol. I, p. 242, n. 6). Layard wrongly identified the Elamite version as Median.

Layard then visited the ruined Sasanian temple at Kangavar, 'where the Assyrian queen [Semiramis] is said to have erected a temple to Anaïtis, or Artemis, and to have established an erotic cult' (1887, vol. I, p. 246). He records also seeing a copy of a stone inscription in Greek letters from a nearby mosque. At Hamadan, 'Ecbatana, the ancient capital of the Medes', he looked for ruins of the ancient site and found only 'the shafts of some marble columns, and the figure of a lion rudely sculptured in stone' (Layard 1887, vol. I, p. 270). The stone lion, known nowadays as *sang-i shir*, probably dates from the Hellenistic period and is a popular monument in modern Hamadan. He visited the tomb of Esther and Mordechai, but was unable to locate the tomb of the famous physician and philosopher Ibn Sina (Avicenna).

Layard and Mitford waited a whole month to obtain permission from the Shah, who was camping at Kangavar and Kirmanshah, to continue their journey through Persia. When they finally received his *firman* on 8 August, the two friends separated. Mitford continued through northern Persia to Qandahar, and Layard went south-east towards Isfahan, where he met Manuchihr Khan Gurji, Mu'tamid al-Daulah the ruthless governor of the province. From here, he set off on a journey through the Bakhtiari region. During this period of hostility between the Qajar government and the Bakhtiari tribes, Layard was accepted with open arms by Mohammad Taqi Khan, the head of the Chahar Lang tribe of the Bakhtiaris. He wrote in detail about the wild life of Khuzistan; how the killing of a lion in single combat was considered a great feat amongst the Bakhtiaris; and how stone lions were placed over the graves of their warriors. At Kala Tul near Fahlian, he actually spotted some lions and, on the banks of the Karun river, buffaloes, while on a ride to Pul-i Negin and Tang-i Butan, he came across wild boars (1887, vol. I, pp. 443–5; vol. II, p. 257). He travelled extensively in this area, visiting the sites of Susa, Shushtar, Ahvaz, Ram Hormuz, Bushire and Bihbihan. On his way to Susa he came across Baron de Bode, first Secretary of the Russian Embassy and discoverer of the early third-century AD Elymaian reliefs at Tang-i Sarvak, whom he had already met once before in Hamadan (Layard 1887, vol. I, p. 485).

Layard was the first European explorer to discover the series of rock reliefs around Izeh: the carvings and inscriptions at Shikaft-i Salman and Kul-i Farah, near Mal-i Amir (Malamir), which he correctly dated to the eighth to seventh century BC, and the Elymaian reliefs of Tang-i Butan near Shimbar, which he wrongly identified as Sasanian (1887, vol. I, pp. 405-6; vol. II, p. 260). He also visited the ancient ruins of Masjid-i Sulaiman, which he found disappointing, as 'there was little to justify the exaggerated accounts which Major Rawlinson had received from his informants' (1887, vol. II, pp. 266–7).

Layard's contribution to the discovery of the archaeological monuments of Iran is immense beyond doubt. His journeys were difficult, for he was robbed and arrested several times. But he shows a clear dislike, or perhaps lack of understanding, of the mentality of ordinary Persians of the time, holding negative views about the Shias and 'fanatical Persians' (Layard 1887, vol. I, p. 334). His judgement of the local people, their customs and religious beliefs, is often subjective and arrogant (1887, vol. I, pp. 307–8):

> During my journey from Hamadan I had made careful notes of the country, taking bearings with my Kater's compass of the mountain ranges and peaks, fixing by the same means, as well as I could, the course of streams and rivers, and the position of the towns and villages through which I passed or which I saw in the distance. I found great difficulty in obtaining the correct names of places. Whether from that inveterate habit of lying which appears to be innate in every Persian, . . . the people whom I met on my way, and of whom I asked the name of a village, almost invariably gave me a wrong one – generally that of another in an entirely different direction.

It is quite likely that the mid-nineteenth-century Persian peasants gave Layard the wrong information simply because they did not understand his Persian pronunciation. It is still the case in Iran that different villages have their own local pronunciation of one and the same name. Although Layard believed he spoke 'the language with some fluency, although, of course, incorrectly' (Layard 1887, vol. I, p. 395), it does not follow that he was as fluent as he supposed or that the villagers necessarily understood his questions. Furthermore, it is possible that the sight of a foreigner in local dress wandering around the landscape with a compass may have unsettled them. After all, while inspecting ancient sites in the Bakhtiari region, he was warned that his 'watch and compass . . . were likely to excite the cupidity of the people' (1887, vol. I, p. 401).

In contrast, Layard had a close relationship with the nomadic Bakhtiari Lurs, who were in serious dispute with the central authority and the Qajar ruler. He was looked after by, and travelled with, these tribes throughout the Bakhtiari region. Their nomadic lifestyle appealed to him and he was hoping to open trade connections between the Bakhtiaris, British India and Europe (Layard 1887, vol. II, p. 471):

> I had been able to collect much political, geographical, and commercial information which I believed might prove useful. . . . I was still not without hope that I might persuade some English merchants at Baghdad, who were seeking to find . . . new outlets for British trade, to enter into commercial relations with the Bakhtiari and Arab tribes in Khuzistan, and that in this case the little influence I had acquired among them might prove of advantage.

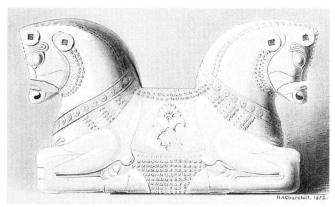

Figure 166 Double-bull column capital from the Palace of Darius at Susa, found during the excavations of W. K. Loftus in 1850–2, by H. A. Churchill.

The first and only systematic nineteenth-century British excavations in Persia were undertaken by William Kennet Loftus (fig. 9). He was originally appointed as a geologist to the Boundary Commission set up to define the border between Persia and the Ottoman empire. However, he was encouraged by the head of the Commission, Lieutenant-Colonel W. F. Williams, to pursue his archaeological interests, first at Warka in southern Mesopotamia, and then at Susa (Shush) in southern Iran (J. Curtis 1993, pp. 1–55).

His archaeological activities began in May 1850 at Susa (fig. 10), where, despite a series of initial problems such as hostility from the local people and heavy spring rains, he was able to work for a month (Loftus 1857, p. 334):

> The great mound was, I thought, more imposing than on my previous visit, but the old tomb [the tomb of Daniel] looked the picture of desolation and misery, the trees around had lost their green leaves, and the white spire stood out prominent and cold against the dark rain-bearing clouds.

During the summer Loftus and other members of the team travelled north to escape the immense heat and it was at this time that they visited Persepolis and Bisitun. Loftus carved his name in the palace of Darius at Persepolis and also, during a visit to Taq-i Bustan, near Kirmanshah, on the seventh-century rock relief of Khusrau II. Back in Susa in January 1851, permission to excavate was finally obtained from the Qajar king of Persia, Nasir al-Din Shah. It was during this season that some column bases were found belonging to the Apadana palace built by the Achaemenid king Darius (522–486 BC) and completed by Artaxerxes II (404–359 BC). The column bases, capitals and other objects from Susa, were carefully drawn by the artist Henry Churchill (fig. 166; Loftus 1857, pp. 364–80). Loftus could clearly see the close similarity between the buildings of Persepolis and Susa and noted 'Even if not erected by the same architect, they were the works of the same dynasty' (Loftus 1857, p. 377). When describing the architecture of 'the Great Hall of Columns' of the Apadana, Loftus 'refers the reader to the admirable works of Chardin, Le Brun, Niebuhr, Texier, Ker Porter, Flandin and Coste' at Persepolis (1857, p. 367, n.). The 'capital and base of column at Susa' he describes as follows (figs 33; 166; 1857, p. 369, n.):

> The total height of this compound capital was 28 feet. The horns and ears of the two bulls were not found; these were let in with lead, but had disappeared. The beams represented in the woodcut are, of course, imaginary. There was no means of ascertaining the height of the fluted column, because no portion

Figure 167 Glazed brick panel from Susa showing an Elamite guard.

Figure 168 Qajar coins:
1–4 Fath 'Ali Shah (1797–1834);
5–6 Nasir al-Din Shah (1848–96).

remained *in situ*. The total height of the tallest column at Persepolis is from the floor to the architrave, 67 feet 4 inches.

Loftus continued his excavations in 1852 with a grant from the Treasury secured with the help of Sir Henry Rawlinson. From the area in Trench D of the Donjon came 21 copper coins. These are mostly bronze tetradrachms of the local Elymaian kings of the second century AD. Rawlinson hoped that Loftus would lay 'the great mound at Susa completely bare'. He employed 350 local workmen at a cost of a *qaran* (*c*.2 pence) a day. But despite the discovery of a fair number of objects (fig. 167), coins and architectural remains with cuneiform inscriptions, the Trustees of the British Museum, in particular Rawlinson, felt that Loftus had not found enough to justify continuing the excavations.

Larsen (1996, p. 282) describes Loftus as 'apparently a deeply traditional man without much imagination, and a man who found it extremely difficult to discover anything positive to say about the inhabitants of the country where he worked'. Indeed, when reading about his arrival in Persia, one cannot help agreeing, for Loftus is hardly complimentary about any Persian, 'who usually overacts the part he desires to perform'. He describes the people as deceitful, untrustworthy, with fanatical expressions, the places as dirty and filthy, and even the food 'the chilaw and pilaw, and lamb stuffed with rice, almond and raisins . . . is impossible to enumerate' (Loftus 1857, pp. 295–305, 324).

As an archaeologist Loftus proved that Susa was indeed the Biblical Shushan mentioned in the Old Testament, the Books of Daniel and Esther (1857, pp. 317, 335–65), but it was left to the French Archaeological Mission to Persia to reveal the true splendour of this site. In 1895, during the reign of Nasir al-Din Shah, a monopoly on the excavation of all the archaeological sites in Persia was sold for a sum of FF 50,000 to the French. The result was the formation in 1897 of an official French archaeological organisation, the Délégation scientifique française en Perse, under Jacques de Morgan. In

1900 the treaty was renewed under Muzaffar al-Din Shah, giving the French access to many important sites in in Iran until 1979 (Chevalier 1997a, pp. 10–15).

After Susa, Loftus turned his attention to Warka in southern Mesopotamia, where he had undertaken a short season of excavations before working in Persia. And it was to Mesopotamia that British archaeologists turned their attention for the rest of the nineteenth century, conducting excavations at the Assyrian capitals of Nineveh and Nimrud.

An article by Chahryar Adle (2000, pp. 7–11, 29) has shed new light on the Persian reaction to Loftus's excavations at Susa and the coverage it received in the Iranian press in the middle of the nineteenth century. The Iranian representative of the Boundary Commission determining the border between Persia and the Ottoman empire was Mirza Seyyed Ja'far Khan Mushir-

Figure 169 Tile decoration from the Takiyeh of Muavenulmulk in Kirmanshah (early twentieth century), showing Varhran V (AD 420–38), the Sasanian king, fighting two lions to save his crown.

Figure 170 Qajar stamps of 1914 showing reliefs and ruins at Persepolis.

al Daulah. He had studied engineering in England from 1815 to 1818 and for six years was the representative in Baghdad of the Qajar government in connection with the boundary issues. Upon his return to Tehran in 1854–5 he submitted a report about the British excavations at Susa, the discovery of architectural remains (such as the 36 columns from the Apadana) and the coins from the site. He rightly concluded that the columns must have belonged to a building which was used for 'salâm [audience] ceremonies' (Adle 2000, p. 8).

It is interesting to note that at the time of Loftus's excavations at Susa, the young Qajar ruler, Nasir al-Din Shah (1848–96) (fig. 168.5–6), commissioned his own royal photographer, Jules Richard, to record the ruins of Persepolis. Unfortunately, financial problems prevented Richard from even starting. Five years later, in 1858, a complete album of photographs of Persepolis was presented to Nasir al-Din Shah by an Italian-born officer, Luigi Pesce, who served in the Qajar government (Adle 2000, pp. 9–10). This enterprising act was largely a result of the personal interest taken by the Qajar ruler in photography and ancient ruins in general. Excavations of archaeological sites, including Persepolis, were also undertaken by the Persians at this time (Curtis 2005, p. 255). Hence a number of ancient sites, including the Hellenistic/Parthian ruins of Khurreh were recorded and photographed during Nasir al-Din Shah's reign (Adle 2000, pp. 13–16, 19, n. 29, pp. 20–8). But the interest in the past and a revival of ancient traditions under the Qajars can be traced back to the time of Fath 'Ali Shah. This ruler, who referred to himself on coins as *khusrau* ('king') in the Sasanian fashion (fig. 168.1–4), followed the tradition of Partho-Sasanian rock reliefs showing enthronement and hunting scenes (fig. 161). He was also an enthusiastic supporter of an archaic literary movement, the *bāzgasht* (return), which saw Firdowsi's epic of the *Shahnameh* (Book of Kings) as its source of inspiration (Luft 2001, pp. 43–5).

The arrival of European travellers to Persia from the eighteenth century onwards and their interest in Persepolis and Persian antiquities must have contributed to a corresponding awakening and revival of interest in Persia's

rich cultural heritage amongst the Qajar elite. It is during this time that the Persians themselves began to record the ancient monuments. In AH 1314/AD 1896 Mirza Fursat Shirazi's *Asar-i 'Ajam* was published in Bombay and contained plans of Persepolis and drawings of reliefs from a number of the sites. The ruins of Persepolis were equated in general with the ancient Persian kings, but the early history of Iran was seen within the framework of the *Shahnameh* and the legendary king Jamshid (Curtis 2005, p. 256). It was also at this time that they began to copy coin motifs and ancient relief images on to tiles (fig. 169). At the beginning of the twentieth century, postage stamps carried images of the ruins of Persepolis (fig. 170).

The end of the nineteenth century produced one more outstanding English explorer who became an expert *par excellence* on Persia and the Persian Question. George Nathaniel Curzon, correspondent for *The Times*, Member of Parliament for Southport and later Viceroy of India, arrived in Persia in 1889 via Baku, Ashkabad and Mashad and spent several months travelling around the country observing and recording the Persian way of life and the monuments. He came to the conclusion that 'If Persia had no other claim to respect, at least a continuous national history of 2,500 years is a distinction which few countries can exhibit' (Curzon 1892, vol. I, p. 7).

Curzon was a staunch believer in the British Empire and in the importance of Persia in providing an extensive and profitable market for British and Anglo-Indian trade (1892, vol. I, p. 2). He saw Persia as a piece on a chessboard to be moved about in the power struggle for British domination (Curzon 1892, vol. I, pp. 3–4) and felt very strongly about keeping it as a buffer state between Tsarist Russia and British India and denying the Russians access to the Persian Gulf (Gilmour 1994, p. 90). Like most of his contemporaries, he was intrigued by the lineage of the Persians, their 'Aryan' background, 'the first Indo-European family to embrace a purely monotheistic faith', the appearance of the prophet Zarathushtra, the holy books, the *Avesta*, and even the fate of the Parsis in Bombay (Curzon 1892, vol. I, p. 6). It was within the framework of a strict political agenda coupled with his admiration for the glorious Persian past that Curzon wrote his two volumes of *Persia and the Persian Question* in 1892. This masterpiece has been rightly described by E. G. Browne (1893, p. 2) as an 'encyclopaedic work on Persia' which 'will for some time to come prevent any similar attempt on the part of anyone else who is not either remarkably rash or exceedingly well-informed'. Indeed Curzon gives detailed information on every aspect of Persia, including its antiquities and monuments (Curzon 1892, vol. I, p. ix):

> in the domain of Archaeology I have not forgotten that, while Persia is primarily the battle-ground of diplomatists and the market of tradesmen, it also contains antiquarian remains in great number that have employed the pen, and still engage the intellects, of famous scholars.

Painstakingly detailed lists of earlier travellers and complete bibliographical references are provided for each site he visited and a comprehensive chart records the names of all these explorers from 1300 to 1891 (Curzon 1892, vol. I, pp. 16–18; vol. II, p. 131):

> The earliest mention of the Persepolitan ruins, of which I am aware by a European writer, is that of Friar Odoricus, who in about 1325 A.D. journeyed from Iest (Yezd) to Huz (Khuzistan). . . . It is amusing enough, in the light of ascertained knowledge, to look back upon the conjectural labours of others who have toiled in darkness. That, however, should not diminish our gratitude to those who like Chardin, Kaempfer and Le Brun, at the end of the seventeenth century and the beginning of the eighteenth centuries, first essayed on a considerable scale the work on transcription and illustration of the Achaemenian monuments; to Niebuhr, whose scholarly industry dignified the middle of the latter century; or to those like Rich, Ouseley, and Ker Porter, early in the nineteenth century, brought back to Europe more careful drawings.

Curzon is often critical of the works of earlier travellers and sometimes draws the wrong conclusions. When writing about the Tomb of Cyrus at Pasargadae, he does not accept that Morier was the first to identify the tomb correctly in 1809, on the grounds that he had said 'nothing about the identity' of the monument during his second visit in 1811 (Curzon 1892, vol. II, p. 78, n. 1), even though Ouseley, after visiting the site with Morier in 1811 concurred with his earlier conclusion (p. 167 above). However, ignoring this, Curzon states that 'Ker Porter was, I believe the first Englishman to adopt the identification; but I fancy that its original author was Professor Grotefend' (Curzon 1892, vol. II, p. 78).

When Curzon visited Pasargadae, the trilingual inscription above the winged genie relief had been removed and so he refers to Ker Porter's drawing which records the original inscription (fig. 162, Curzon 1892, vol. II, p. 74, n. 2; fig. p. 75). For the Sasanian reliefs and their inscriptions he regularly refers to Sylvestre de Sacy's readings through secondary sources (Curzon 1892, vol. II, p. 126, n. 2; p. 128, n. 1). Curzon did not make any drawings of the monuments. Instead, he described them in detail and produced black and white photographs (figs 34, 72), which were taken by himself, students at the Royal College in Tehran and friends such as Herbert Weld Blundell (Curzon 1892, vol. I, p. xiii).

Curzon's fascination with ancient Persia and its culture was partly political and partly a result of his admiration of the Aryan race, to which Iranians, as Indo-Europeans, belong (Curzon 1892, vol. I, p. 5):

> It ought not to be difficult to interest Englishmen in the Persian people. They have the same lineage as ourselves. Three thousand years ago their forefathers left the uplands of that mysterious Aryan home from which our ancestral stock had already gone forth.

His views were not uncommon in late nineteenth-century Europe and, unfortunately, this ideology led to the racist views adopted by the Nazis in 1930s Germany. The original meaning of the word 'Aryan' is nothing more than Iranian, as can be seen from its use by the Achaemenid king Darius the Great (522–486 BC) in his tomb inscription at Naqsh-i Rustam, where he described himself as 'a Persian, son of a Persian, an Aryan [Iranian], having Aryan lineage' (DNa.II; Kent 1953, pp. 137–8).

But despite his eulogy on ancient Persia and its monuments, Curzon, like Rich, Layard and Loftus, had little understanding and sympathy for the Persians, their beliefs and their way of life. The typical Persian village is described as 'a cluster of filthy mud huts', the panorama is 'an enchantment and a fraud' and the people are regarded as 'despicable and noble' (Curzon 1892, vol. I, pp. 14–15). One cannot help but agree with an interpretation of such views as 'deep-rooted prejudices', which were 'based on highly personal judgements born of the ideological thinking of nineteenth-century Europe amongst many travellers and politicians of the time' (Luft 2001, p. 39). It is certainly beyond the scope of the present chapter to discuss in detail the attitudes of nineteenth-century scholars towards the inhabitants of Qajar Persia, but it must be emphasised that the accounts of Robert Ker Porter are noticeably different (see above); for he seems to have had a more positive approach to Persia and its people (Luft 2001, p. 40). Perhaps this was partly because of his professionalism. He was sent to Persia as an artist to record ancient monuments, which he did in the most careful manner. He was also a cosmopolitan man, who was married to a Russian princess and lived in Russia. In addition, one would like to think of Ker Porter as a product of the Age of Enlightenment. But this did not necessarily guarantee an unprejudiced mind. James Morier, for example, who travelled to Persia in 1809 and 1811 (p. 167), was highly critical of the Persians in *The Adventures of Hajji Baba of Ispahan*, first published in 1824. Claudius James Rich's attitude towards the local inhabitants of Persia was also unsympathetic and derogatory.

By the middle of the nineteenth century when Layard and Loftus appeared on the archaeological scene, the British Empire was already at its height and British India was a centre of world politics, trade and colonialism. It is therefore not surprising to find a colonial attitude in the works of mid-nineteenth-century scholars. By now politics was the driving force behind the quest for the unknown and the discovery of the ancient sites of Persia and elsewhere in the Middle East.

Notes

1 The last time the inscription was seen *in situ* was by John Ussher in 1861. In 1874, when the photographer Friedrich Stolzer visited the site, it was no longer there: see Stronach 1978, p. 48.
2 I am grateful to Julian Reade for drawing my attention to this article published by the Society of Antiquaries, London.

8 Rediscovering the Kushans

Joe Cribb

The Kushan kings played an important part in the ancient history of India and Central Asia, worthy contemporaries of the three great world powers of the early centuries of the first millennium AD, the Roman Empire, the Han Empire of China and the Parthian and Sasanian Empires of Iran. During the first four centuries of the millennium they controlled a vital space between these empires, acting the role of entrepreneurs in international trade and restoring unified rule to northern India. Their patronage of Buddhism enabled it to spread through Central Asia into China. However, in spite of their importance, very little information of their activities has survived into the modern period.

A few cryptic references to the Kushans, some hidden by misspellings, are all that survived in the western historical record. A few equally difficult references also survived in the historical sources relating to ancient Iran and its satellite states. The name Kushan was not preserved in Indian historical tradition, but the names of three Kushan rulers were preserved in an Indian chronicle from Kashmir, and one of them, Kanishka, is also mentioned in a Khotanese chronicle, preserved in a Tibetan text (Petech 1968). It is in China that the only direct references to the Kushan Empire are to be found. In the official histories of the Han dynasty and of its successors there are records of armed conflict with the Kushans in Central Asia and brief descriptions of their kingdom. The only detailed account of a Kushan king comes from Buddhist records from China and Tibet, which document the patronage of Buddhism by the Kushan king Kanishka (Zürcher 1968).

The relative obscurity of these sources kept the existence of the Kushans hidden from western historians for more than a thousand years. The first substantial records of their extensive empire began to emerge in the early nineteenth century in the form of coins. Their discovery across northern India and in Central Asia, particularly the regions now called Afghanistan and Pakistan, was at first misunderstood and it took several decades before their true identity was revealed and the relationships between the coins and the sources understood. This chapter sets out to document these discoveries and the process they set in train which led to the rediscovery of the Kushan Empire as an important force in the history of India and Central Asia.

A step in the dark

The first appearance of the Kushans in a European historical publication was in 1756, when the French priest Abbé Joseph de Guignes published his extensive survey of the nomad peoples of Central Asia (de Guignes 1756). In a section based on the Chinese historical text the Book of the Han (*Han Shu*), he named the Kushan as the 'Kuei-choam' (Guishuang) in a

list of the tribes of the Da Yuezhi, whom he calls the Ta-yue-chi (vol. I, part 2, pp. lxxxviii–lxxxix). Elsewhere he identified the Da Yuezhi as occupiers of Bactria (p. xciii). He placed these references in the context of the Greek and Roman references to Scythian tribes in Central Asia, but made no attempt to equate the Chinese names with Greek equivalents.

Twelve years later, also in France, the first Kushan relic was brought to the attention of western scholarship, a gold coin published by the French numismatist Joseph Pellerin (1684–1782) (Pellerin 1767, title page, p. iii). The coin was a regular issue of the Kushan king Huvishka, a gold stater with a portrait bust of the king on the obverse and the Kushan goddess Ardochsho standing on the reverse (cf. Göbl 1984, type 286). Although Pellerin was able to recognise the object as a coin, he was unable to identify when, where and by whom it was issued. In order to avoid the problems of classifying it, he published his drawing of it on the title page of the third of his supplements to his six-volume catalogue of ancient coins. In his preface he explained what he had deduced about the coin:

> I have inserted into this ornament the singular gold coin which is represented there, because I do not know into which series I should otherwise place it. The portrait to be seen on it is unknown to me, just as its inscriptions are unintelligible to me. This head should be of some king, or some great pope, as can be judged by the magnificence of his dress and the richness of his mitre. The form of his mitre ending in a point seems to me extraordinary; I have never seen anything like it on a coin before. As to the inscriptions, I recognise that the letters with which it has been written have the shape of ancient Greek letters, but without being able to draw any meaning for the words which are written there. I think that maybe some barbarian peoples have used these Greek letters to write something in their own language. This is the case of some Arab books which have been found written in Syriac script. For the rest it is up to scholars of ancient languages to examine and interpret this coin and several others in various unknown scripts which I present to them in this new supplement.

It would be almost two centuries before an answer to Pellerin's questions could be given.

The search for Alexander and India's past

The key period for the discovery of the Kushans is between 1825 and 1845. Three driving forces combined to bring enough evidence to light to enable scholars to produce a satisfactory explanation of that evidence. The first force was the search for evidence of Alexander the Great's exploits in the east, the focus of British and French adventurers in Afghanistan and the Punjab. The second was a growing interest in Indian antiquities, led by British scholars based in India, particularly those in Calcutta, but also shared by scholars in Europe. The third was an increased awareness of oriental coins as a source of history, a development from the

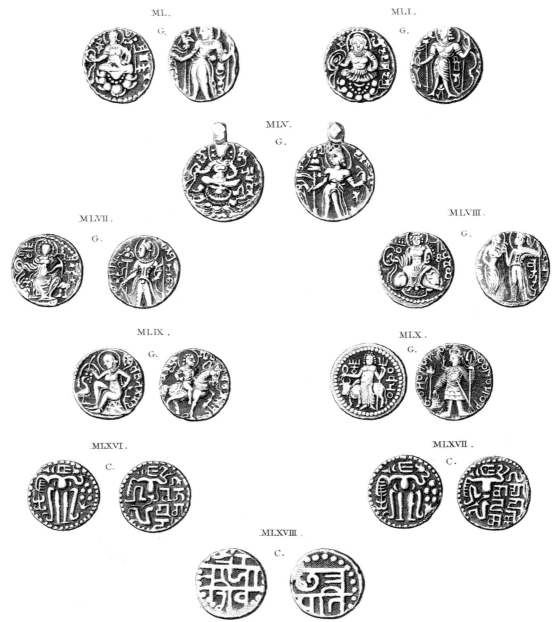

Figure 171 Marsden's plate of Indian coins, including a facsimile of a Kushan gold coin of Vasudeva I (no. MLX).

eighteenth-century numismatics of Pellerin and his contemporaries. William Marsden was a pioneer in making oriental coins known to an English-speaking audience, publishing the substantial catalogue of his collection of oriental coins in 1823–5 (fig. 171). At the same moment British collectors in India were beginning to put material from their own collections into print.

These three forces arose at a time when the political circumstances allowed them to flourish. The Sikh and Afghan wars and the role of the Bukharan Emirate in Anglo-Russian relations brought, for the first time, European adventurers into the regions which had been visited by Alexander the Great. The most widely available remains providing evidence of a Greek presence in the area were coins. The growing confidence of British control over India enabled officers of the East India Company to indulge their interests in local history. The establishment of a sense of local history was acknowledged to be a vital tool in demonstrating Britain's right to rule in the subcontinent. As mint officials, two of the most active investigators, Horace Wilson and James Prinsep, had

unrivalled access to India's numismatic past. The three forces (the search for Alexander, antiquities and coins as a source for history) flourished because there were collectors and scholars ready and able to produce dramatic results from the evidence they brought to light. They also flourished because they coincided with the political aims of the employers of many of those involved, i.e. the British East India Company and the British government. Chakrabarti has pointed to the stated aims of Alexander Cunningham one of the most active and successful collector/scholars involved. As a serving military officer of the Company, then of the British Imperial army, Cunningham saw his discoveries as vital tools in the establishment of both British rule and Christianity, a key agent of British rule, in India (Chakrabarti 1988, pp. 43–4).

The combined forces which led to the rediscovery of the Kushans also created for them a broad historical context. The same collectors and scholars who worked on the identification of the Kushans were also working on the coins, inscriptions and archaeological remains of the dynasties which ruled India and Central Asia before and after the

Kushans. This wider research was instrumental in deciphering the ancient scripts of India and creating a broad chronological framework. The decipherment of these scripts eventually enabled inscriptions of the Kushan period to be read and an overall picture of their empire to emerge. By the mid 1820s these processes had begun.

Marsden's first certain step

Marsden was responsible for presenting the first image of a Kushan coin in a British publication. In 1825, in the second volume of his catalogue, he presented an engraving of a facsimile of a gold stater of the Kushan king Vasudeva I (fig. 171.MLX; Marsden 1823/5, vol. II, pl. XLVII, no. MLX, now in the British Museum; cf. Göbl 1984, type 509; p. 130, no. F509/X). His commentary on it (1823–5, p. 730) explained that it was a facsimile made under the direction of a collector, Peter Speke (1745–1811), a prominent member of the Supreme Council in Calcutta (1789–1801) and subsequently Acting President of the Board of Trade and President of the Marine Board until his death. The facsimile was brought back to England from Bengal in 1806 by Sir John Anstruther, Chief Justice of the Supreme Court of Indicature, Calcutta, and President of the Asiatic Society (1799–1807), and given to Marsden before Anstruther died in 1811. The source of the facsimile, and the other Indian coins he had in his collection (including six Gupta coins), gave Marsden some advantage over Pellerin in understanding the original from which the copy was made. He was able to see the relationship of the coin to the Gupta pieces in his collection, which he dated to the fourth to sixth century, and was secure in his knowledge that the Vasudeva I model for the facsimile was an Indian coin.

Tod's coins

The first significant publication of Kushan coins, however, was made in the same year by the British East India Company military officer James Tod. On 18 June 1825 he submitted to the Royal Asiatic Society in London an account of his coin collection (Tod 1825). Tod claimed to have collected about 20,000 coins 'as an auxiliary to history' during his time 'amongst the Rajputs and Mahrattas'. The nature of his interest in Indian history seems curious as he considered that there were, out of these 20,000 coins, 'not above one hundred calculated to excite interest, and perhaps not above one-third of that number to be considered of value'. Fortunately among the pieces he thought of interest are several which can now be recognised as Kushan issues.

Tod's main focus was on two Indo-Greek coins of Menander and Apollodotus found at Mathura and another site on the Yamuna River. He related these finds to the mention of these kings in the *Periplus of the Erythraean Sea*, a Greek text of the first century AD describing trading conditions in the Indian Ocean, with which he was familiar from the recently published translation by William Vincent (1807). He identified these two coins as part of a group (Series 1, coins 1–2) relating to Greek rule in Bactria, in spite of the coins being found over a thousand kilometres from Bactria.

His second group (Series 2, coins 3–9) he also identified with Greek rule because he was able to read the Greek title 'Great King' on some of them. Four of the illustrated

examples (no. 4 and three unnumbered examples, referred to here for convenience as nos 4a, 4b and 4c) can be identified as anonymous 'Soter Megas' issues of the second Kushan king Wima I Tak[to] (no. 4 is a quarter unit of the general series of Soter Megas type, nos 4a and 4c are full units of the same series, no. 4b is an example of the local Soter Megas coinage from Mathura). The fifth example (no. 3) is an Alexandrian coin of the Roman empress Severina (wife of Aurelian, AD 270–5). The other two coins are not illustrated, but Tod implies that they are also like the other Wima I coins.

He compared the coins of this group with a silver coin of Eucratides, Greek king of Bactria, as published by Bayer (1738) in the first serious study of the Greek kingdom of Bactria, and pointed to their common use of the Greek title 'Great King'. He, however, also observed the non-Greek appearance of the mounted figure on them and drew parallels with Parthian designs. On the basis of these relationships he suggested that they were issues made by Mithradates the Parthian overlord of Eucratides, or 'his successors, or a minor dynasty in India'. He also suggested an association with the Scythian peoples who overthrew the Greeks in Bactria at the same period as Mithradates. Because of their role in India, he termed these Scythians as Indo-Scythic kings.

He also read the title 'Great King' in Greek on at least one example (no. 10) of his next group (Series 3, nos 10–14, and one unnumbered example, referred to here as no. 11a). These are all Kushan copper issues of Wima II Kadphises (no. 10), Kanishka I (nos 11, reverse: Miiro, 13, reverse: Oado, and 14, reverse: Nana) and Huvishka (nos 11a, seated figure, reverse: Miiro, and 12, elephant rider, reverse: Oesho). He attributed this group to 'a race of this description', i.e. the Parthians, or to the Indo-Scythic tribes, the same attribution as his previous group. He also thought that they represented issues 'all evidently of the same family'. Although he illustrated only a few examples, he stated that he had 'collected some thousands; but only these few have escaped the corroding tooth of time'.

His fourth group (Series 4, four unnumbered examples) consisted of Gupta gold coins, and his fifth (Series 5, three unnumbered examples) of silver coins of the Western Satraps and Guptas. He identified them as 'Hindu, of a very remote period'.

Tod's sources

Tod's approach to these coins was systematic, but he lacked the resources to identify them apart from the Greek issues of Menander and Apollodotus. He applied his limited knowledge of the successors of the Greeks to reach towards an understanding of the Kushan coins of his second and third groups. His starting points were the discovery of these coins in India and the use of Greek writing on them. He deduced from the absence of Greek names in their inscriptions and the non-Greek elements in their designs that they were probably issued by the rulers who succeeded the Greeks in Bactria and northern India. His only information about the successors of the Greeks was derived from Classical sources, Strabo's *Geography*, Justin's summary of Pompeius Trogus' *History* and the anonymous *Periplus of the Erythraean Sea*.

From these sources, often at second hand, he dated the end of Greek rule to 134 BC and attributed it to both the

Scythians and Mithradates I of Parthia. The identification of the Scythian successors of the Greeks in Bactria was derived from Strabo (XI.viii.2):

> Now the greatest part of the Scythians, beginning at the Caspian Sea, are called the Däae, but those who are situated more to the East than these are named Massagetae and Sacae, whereas all the rest are given the general name of the Scythians, though each people is given a separate name of its own. They are all for the most part nomads. But the best known of the nomads are those who took away Bactriana from the Greeks, I mean the Asii, Pasiani, Tochari and Sacarauli, who originally came from the country on the other side of the Jaxartes River that adjoins that of the Sacae and the Sogdiani and was occupied by the Sacae.

The role of the Parthians seems to have been derived from Justin (XLI.vi.1–5):

> Almost at the same time that Mithradates ascended the throne among the Parthians, Eucratides began to reign among the Bactrians; both of them being great men. But the fortune of the Parthians being the more successful, raised them under this prince, to the highest degree of power; while the Bactrians, harassed with various wars, lost not only their dominions, but their liberty; for having suffered from contentions with the Sogdians, the Drangians, and the Indians, they were at last overcome, as if exhausted, by the weaker Parthians.

Tod also found evidence of the presence of both Parthians and Scythians in western India in the *Periplus* (*Periplus* 38; cf. Casson 1989):

> inland is the metropolis of Skythia itself, Minnagar. The throne is in the hands of Parthians, who are constantly chasing each other off it.

Tod (1825, p. 339) also linked this event with the account of Central Asian barbarians already constructed from Chinese and Classical sources by the French priest Abbé Joseph de Guignes (1756). According to Tod, Mithradates, the king of Parthia (c.171–138 BC), made himself overlord of Eucratides and then 'established himself in all the power the Greeks ever had in India. He conquered the whole of the countries from the Indus to the Ganges, including the domain of Porus; and such was his moderation and clemency that many nations voluntarily submitted to him'. As the coins of his second and third groups seemed to Tod to have enough Greek features to be issued close in time to the Greek period and at the same time had features which he associated with the Parthians, he had no hesitation in suggesting that they were issued by Mithradates or one of his successors or subordinates. On the Wima I Tak[to] coins Tod saw titles and design features which suggested to him a close association with Eucratides, i.e. probably issues of his successor Mithradates. On the coin of Wima II Kadphises he saw the king as 'adorned with the high cap of the Magi' and 'feeding the flame on a low altar' and on its back he saw in the Kharoshthi inscription an 'epigraphe . . . in the Sassanian character', all features suggesting to him an Iranian issuer.

Although his evidence and therefore his results were limited, Tod had established the antiquity of coinage in India and identified issues of coins in northern India showing strong connections with the Greeks and their successors in Bactria. Tangible evidence, separate from the testimony of ancient authors, now existed to show the reality of Greek, Parthian and Scythian rule in ancient India. Tod was fully justified in his conclusion that he had initiated the process by which an understanding of India's past could be achieved:

> I trust I have provided matter for others to expiate one, who may by these aids throw new light on Indian history. The field is ample, and much yet remains to reward patience and industry; nor is there a more fertile and less explored domain for the antiquary.

Tod had made the first attempt at a systematic publication of Kushan coins, but he had done so unwittingly and produced for them an identification as 'Indo-Scythic' which was at first misleading and which subsequently continued to confuse long after its significance had been undermined.

It can also be observed that Tod's interest in his huge coin collection was largely related to the evidence of European (Greek) influence on India. Tod, like many of his contemporaries, had a contempt for Indian culture, particularly as a manifestation of the commonly held view that the India of his day was the consequence of a long period of intellectual degeneration, and that only western sources were of use in understanding India's past. 'The Hindus, with the decrease in their intellectual power . . . lost the relish for the beauty of truth, and adopted the monstrous in their writings . . . in the moral decrepitude of ancient Asia. . . . Plain historical truths have long ceased to interest this artificially-fed people' (Tod 1829).

Schlegel on Tod's coins

Within three years Tod's publication (1825, pp. 313–42) had provoked a detailed response from a German scholar, August Wilhelm von Schlegel, published in France in the *Journal Asiatique*, November 1828. Schlegel's account (1828, pp. 321–49) of the illustrated coins was more detailed and analytical than Tod's, but also primarily focused on the Greek issues. Of the non-Greek pieces he commented that they were issues of a period 'cloaked in shadows even thicker than those' obscuring the Greek kings. Nevertheless he was able to reject Tod's Parthian attribution of any of the non-Greek coins on the basis that they showed no resemblance to known Parthian coins. He also questioned Tod's date for the end of Greek rule in Bactria and referred to Chinese sources (quoting de Guignes 1756) suggesting a date c.125 BC.

Schlegel identified the coins of Wima I Tak[to] as issues from the period following the end of the reign of Eucratides and before the Scythian conquest of Bactria. He misread the inscription of one example as 'King of the Bactrians' and of another as 'Saviour . . . King' (Tod 1825, nos 4, 4a). The similarities to Greek issues prompt him to identify their issuer as a local Bactrian or Sogdian ruler taking over the throne of Bactria after the Greeks were defeated by the Parthians, but before the Scythian conquest of Bactria. He identified the Alexandrian coin (Tod 1825, no. 3) as a local issue by a Greek colony in Bactria.

A brief encounter with Edobirgis

The remaining Kushan coins illustrated by Tod as his third group were identified by Schlegel as Indo-Scythic, adopting Tod's terminology. The first coin (Tod 1825, no. 10), an issue of Wima II Kadphises, he attributed to a king called Edobirgis (his misreading of Tod's badly drawn 'Kadphises'). On the back of the coin he recognised the Hindu deity Shiva, surrounded by what he thought was a Bactrian or Pahlavi inscription ('légende circulaire en caractères bactriens ou pehlvis').

Schlegel compared Edobirgis with Attila, as another, but previously forgotten, great barbarian conqueror. He used the term 'Tartar', meaning Central Asian barbarian, rather than 'Scythian', because of the uncertainty of the exact tribal affiliation of this ruler. He however showed that the term 'Shaka', widely used by ancient Indian sources, was recognised by ancient Greek authors as an alternative to 'Scythian'. He marvelled at the integration of the Scythian conquerors into the cultures of the people they had conquered as exhibited in this coin (Schlegel 1828, p. 341):

> Here we have this numismatic record of the Indo-Scythic Empire, of which we have so few remains. What a strange combination! A Tartar khan, converted to the Brahmanic cult, ruling the provinces of India and ancient Persia, and having Greeks at his court who give him the title 'King of Kings'.

Schlegel also attributed the coins of Kanishka I (Tod 1825, nos 11, 13–14) and Huvishka (Tod 1825, nos 11a, 12) illustrated by Tod to the Indo-Scythic Empire, perhaps to the same king Edobirgis as he had identified as the issuer of coin no. 10, because he could see the same monogram on them as on no. 10. He recognised that the inscriptions were in Greek script, but could not decipher them as they were 'sparse and mixed with non-Greek letters'. He compared the obverse designs of the Kanishka coins with that of coin no. 10 (king standing throwing incense on small altar). He thought the seated king on no. 11a was a kneeling archer. The other designs he saw as mythological subjects: the reverses of nos 11 and 11a (both Miiro) representing the sun god; the four armed god (Oesho) on no. 12 as the Hindu god Shiva and the elephant rider (Huvishka) on the other side of the same coin as the Hindu god Indra.

Schlegel's analysis of the Kushan coins illustrated by Tod made more detailed use of the designs and inscriptions on the coins, and drew on a wider repertoire of historical sources. He was able to dismiss Tod's suggestion that the coins were issued by Parthians (by comparing them with known Parthian coins), but the limitations of the material and the sources prevented him from attributing the coins. His introduction of the name Edobirgis was not justified by Tod's drawing. He failed to make full use of the provenance of the coins, still focusing on the ancient sources relating to Bactria, while their Indian origin was not given sufficient weight. The dating of the coins, like that hinted at by Tod, still relied on this Bactrian connection, and therefore placed the coins in the second century BC. From Indian sources, particularly the use of the name Shaka for the Indian era of AD 78 and the legend of a defeat of the Shakas by an Indian king related to the Vikrama era of 57 BC, he was, however, able to consider a later role for the Indo-Scythic kings in India. On the basis of the *Periplus*, he also discussed the role of Minnagara as their capital in India. His introduction of evidence from Chinese sources was another step forward, but it was limited to his discussion of the dating of the Scythian conquest of Bactria.

Ventura's discoveries in the Punjab

In 1830 an important development took place in the study of ancient India with the excavation by Ventura, an Italian officer employed by the Sikhs, of a site containing Kushan and later coins. News of the excavation and impressions of three of the coins were sent by Ventura to the Asiatic Society

of Bengal, Calcutta, and were also forwarded to Paris. Ventura explained, in his letter to Calcutta, that he had found coins with Greek inscriptions while excavating a large dome-shaped monument in the Punjab, at a site called Manikyala (1832, pp. 600–3; pp. 211–12, fig. 177 below). He was certain that he had located the site of the city of Bucephala founded by Alexander the Great and that the monument had been erected there by a king and recorded the passing of Alexander through the region. In March 1832 the French scholar Reinaud published an account of the excavation based on Ventura's report in the *Journal Asiatique* (1832, pp. 276–9). Like Ventura he simply listed the number, metal and location of the coins found during the excavation, but he concluded that the coins bore Greek or Sanskrit inscriptions and, therefore, were likely to be issues of the local rulers of the region following its invasion by Alexander.

To Reinaud's report was appended a commentary by Saint-Martin (1832, pp. 280–1) on the coins found by Ventura. From the three coin impressions he was able to remark on their similarity to the pieces published by Tod and commented on by Schlegel. He observed that there were some differences in the new coins, but felt that better specimens were needed before a full explanation was possible. However he was able to draw some observations from the gold coin of the Kushan king Huvishka (Göbl 1984, type 151.1). He transcribed the inscriptions in Greek letters, but was unable to interpret them. He also compared the dress of the king depicted on it to modern Persian dress. On the back he found the Kushan symbol which he linked with the symbol appearing on all the 'gréco-indiennes' (i.e. Kushan) coins published by Tod. He identified the god on the back as a moon god from its crescent-shaped halo. On the basis of the *Periplus*, he dated these coins to the second century AD, attributing them to Greek kings after Alexander or to their oriental successors, about whom nothing was now known.

Wilson's catalogue

Later in the same year Horace Wilson of the Asiatic Society of Bengal published the same coin (fig. 172.1; Wilson 1832, no. 1), with two other coins found by Ventura, together with details of 124 other coins, either in the Society's collection or recorded by the Society. The other two Manikyala coins were a copper coin of Kanishka I (fig. 173.35; drachm-size, reverse Mao: Wilson 1832, no. 35) and a post-Kushan Kashmir issue (fig. 173.44–5; base gold Kushan-style issue of the Hindu kingdom of Kashmir, in name of Yashovarman: Wilson 1832, no. 43; Cunningham 1894, pl. III.11). From the Society's collection and records Wilson was able to add 21 more Kushan coins to the two examples from Manikyala (table 6).

Wilson included these coins in the class he thought to be issues 'either of early Hindu Princes or of foreign Sovereigns ruling over territories in *Hindustan*'. He referred to the recent publication of similar coins in the articles by Tod and Schlegel and suggested that their publication had 'thrown light upon the history of the people, by whom the *Bactrian* kingdom was overthrown'. In the collection of the Asiatic Society he had found pieces identical to those published by Tod and, although he thought that they added no further information on their origin and date, he published them as a

Figure 172 Coins published by Wilson in *Asiatick Researches*.

contribution 'to a branch of enquiry hitherto almost unattempted' and as a prompt to further investigation. He provided drawings, many by James Prinsep, and descriptions of these coins (figs 172–3; Wilson 1832, pls I–II).

Wilson on Ventura's discoveries

His discussion of the gold coin found by Ventura added little to the comments by Saint-Martin, but was able to draw direct parallels between it and other Kushan coins. He compared it specifically with the gold coins of Kanishka I (fig. 172.2) and of Vasudeva I (fig. 172.3–4) and the copper coins of Wima I Tak[to] (fig. 173.25), Wima II Kadphises (fig. 173.26–8, 30) and Huvishka (fig. 173.31, 34). He also pointed to the common use of the Kushan emblem in various forms on many of these coins. On the basis of these comparisons he also included in the same category the Gupta and Kashmir coins illustrated on his plates.

His discussion of the context of the Manikyala coins did, however, lead him to suggest a later date for the monument. He observed that the coins found in it were 'of evidently different periods' and therefore that the monument was likely to be 'a structure of the 3rd or 4th century of the Christian era, if not earlier'. He also compared the Huvishka

coin with Greek, Parthian and Sasanian coins and judged it to be 'utterly distinct' from them.

In an appendix to his paper Wilson presented the reports from Ventura on his excavations at Manikyala (1832, p. 600; pp. 211–12, fig. 177 below), sent to the Asiatic Society in Calcutta in late 1830, repeating the information already passed to Reinaud. To them have, however, been added a brief note on the excavations by Lieutenant Alexander Burnes, a British officer, who had passed through the Punjab and visited the site at Manikyala in March 1832. In the vicinity of the site Burnes was able to acquire two coins like those found in the excavations. Wilson published one of them as his no. 25, i.e. a small 'Soter Megas' general issue of Wima I Tak[to] (1832, pl. II.25: fig. 173.25), but the other one was illegible. Burnes was also shown the Manikyala excavation coins by Allard, one of Ventura's colleagues. Burnes was able to inform Wilson that most of the Manikyala coins were like the Wima II Kadphises large copper coins he had published (fig. 173.26–8, 30). Burnes also told Wilson that he had found a similar coin (like fig. 173.26) at Balkh in northern Afghanistan. The location of this discovery passed without remark, but proves to be the first find of a Kushan coin in Bactria itself.

Table 6
Kushan coins recorded by Horace Wilson in 1832

Wima I Tak[to]	general issue copper unit	nos 23, 24
	general issue copper quarter	no. 25
Wima II Kadphises	large copper unit	nos 26, 27, 28, 30
Kanishka I	gold stater (Nana)	no. 2
	large copper unit (Oado)	no. 36
	small copper quarter (Mao)	no. 35 (Manikyala find)
Huvishka	gold stater (Manaobago)	no. 1 (Manikyala find)
	large copper unit (elephant rider, Miiro)	no. 31
	large copper unit (elephant rider, illegible)	nos 32, 33, 34
	large copper unit (cross-legged, illegible)	no. 40
	reduced copper unit (cross-legged, illegible)	nos 39, 42
Vasudeva I	modern copies of gold stater (the same as illustrated by Marsden)	nos 3, 4
	copper	no. 29
Vasudeva imitation	copper (Oesho and bull)	no. 41
Vasishka	gold stater (Göbl 1984, type 558)	no. 6

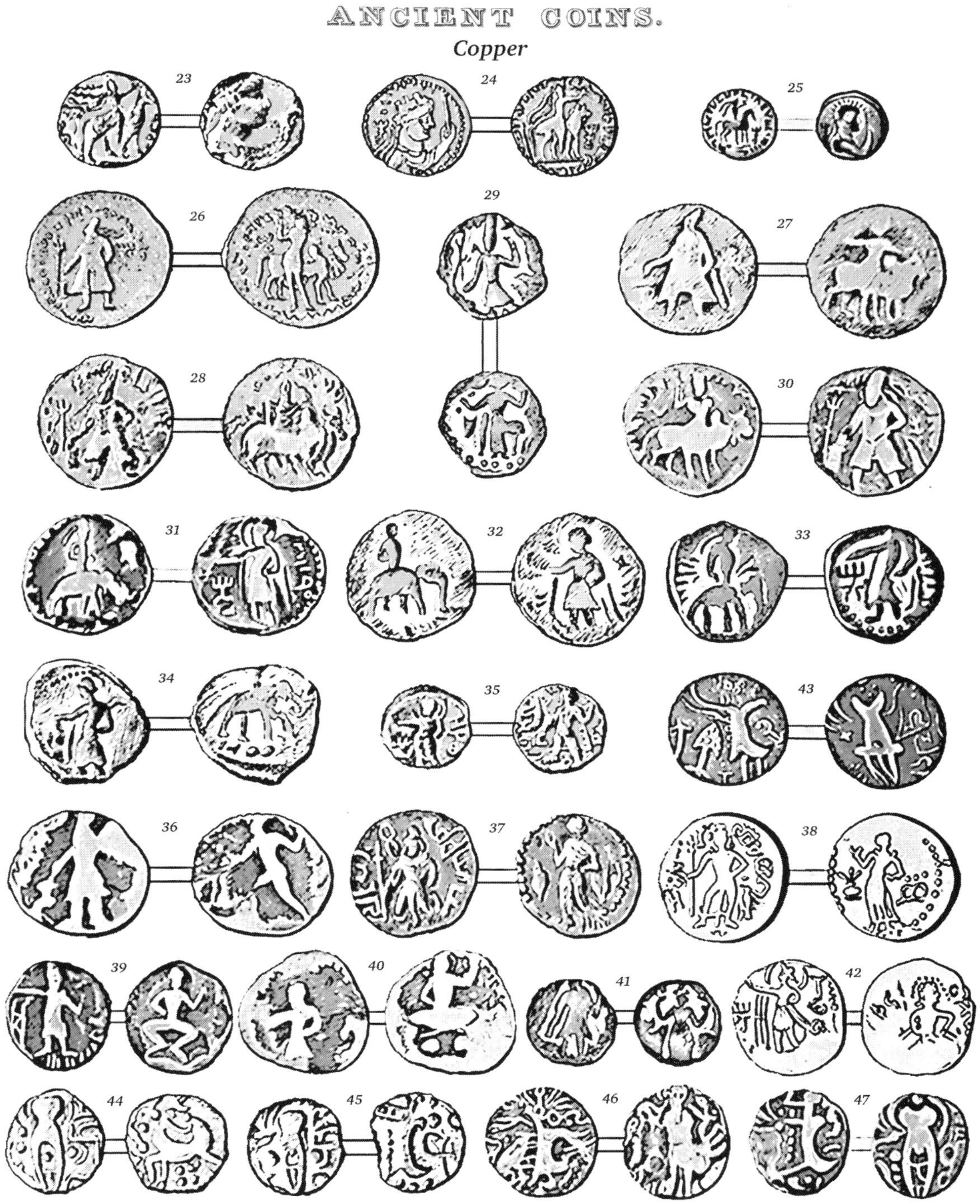

ANCIENT COINS.

Copper

Figure 173 Kushan coins published by Wilson in *Asiatick Researches*.

Wilson's answers

On the basis of his observations Wilson attributed the gold coin of Huvishka to 'the *Indo-Scythic* princes of Western India, about the commencement of the Christian era', but he also speculated 'from the decidedly Hindu character of the reverse' that this coin 'is no doubt the Coin either of an Indian prince or of a prince ruling over a Hindu people probably in the *Panjab*, or on the north-western frontier, about the commencement of the Christian era'. The presence of Sasanian-style coins and Kashmir Hindu coins in the Manikyala monument were obviously influential in suggesting to Wilson a date in the third or fourth centuries. The first- to second-century dates are presumably based on Saint-Martin's association of the 'Indo-Scythic' coins with the *Periplus*.

Alongside the Huvishka gold coin from Manikyala Wilson was able to present a gold coin of Kanishka (1832, pl. I.2:

fig. 172.2), which had been found at the opposite end of northern India, at Comilla (now in eastern Bangladesh). Wilson pointed to its similarities to the Huvishka coin and was able to suggest that it was probably 'the Coin of a different prince, although of the same dynasty'. He also pointed to the relationship of both the Huvishka and Kanishka I coins with the Society's facsimiles of a Vasudeva I gold coin (fig. 172.3–4, examples of the facsimile made by Speke and published by Marsden (fig. 171.MLX, which had been made before 1806) and a gold coin of Vasishka found in the Hooghly District, Bengal (fig. 172.6).

Wilson illustrates three examples of the 'Soter Megas' general issue series of Wima I Tak[to], one found by Prinsep at Benares (fig. 173.23), the second from a drawing of an example in a private collection (fig. 173.24) and the third found near the Manikyala monument by Lieutenant

Alexander Burnes (fig. 173.25). He repeats Tod's and Schlegel's opinions, adding his view that 'there can be little doubt that they are Bactrian coins, and it is only a question of to what reign or period they belong'. Like his predecessors he seems to maintain reliance on an explanation based on Classical authors, rather than recognising the evidence of where the coins are being found, i.e. in the Punjab and northern India.

He was, however, able to recognise the Indian origin of the four coins of Wima II Kadphises he published (fig. 173.26–8, 30). One of them (fig. 173.27) was found by Prinsep at Chunar, near Benares, others (fig. 173.28, 30) seem to be the pieces collected by Tytler at Allahadad (Wilson 1841, p. 353). He pointed to the parallels between the design of the standing king at an altar on these coins and on the other Kushan coins of Kanishka I and Vasudeva I, but had nothing to add to the 'Parthian or Indo-Scythic' attributions of Tod and Schlegel.

Wilson compared the small copper of Kanishka (fig. 173.35), found by Ventura at Manikyala, with the large Kanishka copper illustrated by Tod (1825, no. 10) and the other Kushan coins in his own plates. He considered it to be an 'Indo-Scythic' issue on the basis of its find-spot. He identified the Society's large Kanishka copper (Wilson 1832, no. 36) as identical to one illustrated by Tod (1825, no. 13).

Wilson also attributed the coins of Huvishka he illustrated (fig. 173.31–4, 39–40, 42) to the 'Indo-Scythic kingdom' following Tod and Schlegel's attribution of an elephant-rider type of this king (Tod 1825, no. 12). He disputed Schlegel's identification of Shiva on Tod's coin, because his examples mostly seemed to represent a two-armed figure. From Prinsep's information he was able to state that the elephant-rider types were 'very common in Upper India, particularly around *Benares*, *Mirzapore* and *Allahabad*'. Two of the cross-legged king types (fig. 173.39–40) were also acquired at Allahabad.

The Vasudeva copper types illustrated by Wilson (1832, pl. II. 29, 41; fig. 173.29, 41) were both found by Colonel Mackenzie at Dipaldinna, an ancient site near Amaravati in South India. Wilson noted their similarity to both the smaller Huvishka coins (fig. 173.39, 40) and the large coppers of Wima II Kadphises (fig. 173.26–8, 30).

Wilson's conclusions expressed his dissatisfaction with the progress of his investigation into the 'history of *Hindu* Numismatics', and he admitted that classification was his only real achievement. Like Tod he separated the coins of Wima I Tak[to] into one class and the remainder of the Kushan coins he had recorded into a second, and, like Tod, he attributed the first group to 'Bactrian princes of Greek or Parthian descent' and connected them, by their common use of the Kushan symbol, with the second class which he attributed to 'Scythian or Parthian . . . princes, whilst they occupied the western provinces of *Hindustan*'. Although he had assembled more material and been more rigorous in breaking them down into classes and sub-classes by their designs, Wilson offers no opinions beyond those already proffered by Tod and Schlegel. The growing body of evidence was, however, now showing a much wider distribution of Kushan coinage than their attributions suggested. Many of the coins he described and most of those shown by Tod had not been found in Bactria, or even close to it, in north-western India. Only Ventura's discoveries indicated any kind of geographical connection between these coins and the region being suggested for their origin (fig. 176). Wilson offered no comments on this mismatch between his evidence and conclusions.

Prinsep's first steps

The year 1832 also saw James Prinsep's first published approach to Kushan coinage. A short aside in an article on Roman coins found in India, published in the September 1832 volume of the *Journal of the Asiatic Society of Bengal*, shows the beginnings of his interest in Kushan coinage. His comments were derived from Tod's and Wilson's pioneering publications (Thomas 1858, vol. I, p. 4):

> The Indian coins . . . described by Wilson in the *Asiatic Researches*, and the Indo-Grecian coins of Major Tod, are evidently *descendants* from the Bactrian coinage, from the types of which they gradually progress into purely Hindu models.

Prinsep's first descriptions of Kushan coins followed a few months later in the January 1833 volume of the same journal, where he discussed two of the casts of coins found at Manikyala (sent to Calcutta by Ventura), together with two similar coins. As noted above, these had already been published by Wilson in 1832, but Prinsep illustrated them 'to shew the general appearance of these curious coins' (Thomas 1858, vol. I, p. 16, pl. 1.17–20, respectively Wilson 1832, pls II.35; I.1; II.25, 23). He mistakenly identified a copper drachm of Kanishka from Manikyala (no. 17: fig. 173.35), as a gold coin, otherwise describing it in much the same way as Wilson, but with more attention to interpretation, recognising that the king is shown 'presenting an offering on an altar', a detail missed by Wilson. His mistake in thinking it was gold can be explained by the fact that the coin was only represented by the impression of it sent by Ventura, rather than the original. He also followed Wilson in his description of the gold Huvishka coin (no. 18: fig. 172.1) found in the Manikyala monument, but added the observation that the king had a 'Persian head-dress'. He was also aware of the French responses to the Manikyala coins and repeated their transcription of the inscription on this gold coin.

The other two coins he illustrated were both general issue 'Soter Megas' pieces of Wima I Tak[to] (Thomas 1858, vol. I, p. 16, pl. 1.19–20). Wilson (1832) had reported one as found by Burnes near Manikyala (no. 19: fig. 173.25), but according to Prinsep it was 'sent to me in a letter by Dr. Gerard, from the neighbourhood of Manikyala'. Prinsep compared it with the other coin (no. 20: fig. 173.23) of the same type 'procured by myself at Benares'.

He also noted Burnes's comments that 'the greatest proportion of the coins found at Manikyala . . . have figures of a Raja, dressed in a tunic, sacrificing on an altar, on the obverse; and a figure standing by a bull, on the reverse', i.e. issues of Wima II Kadphises (Thomas 1858, vol. I, p. 17).

Burnes's coins

In 1834 Burnes published an account of his travels in the Punjab, Afghanistan and Bukhara. He reported that altogether he was able to acquire about 70 coins near Manikyala (Burnes 1834, vol. I, pp. 66–8). Of these coins he

Table 7
Kushan coins collected by Alexander Burnes in 1832–3

Wima I Tak[to]	general issue copper unit	no. 19
Wima II Kadphises	large copper unit	no. 21 (from Balkh)
	large copper unit	no. 23
Kanishka I	large copper unit (Mao)	no. 20 (from Balkh)
	large copper unit (reverse not illustrated)	no. 22
	middle copper half (Nanaia)	no. 18
	small copper quarter (Miiro)	nos 27, 30
	small copper quarter (Nana)	no. 26
Huvishka	large copper unit (elephant rider, Oesho)	no. 25
Vasudeva I	copper unit (Oesho and bull)	no. 24

observed: 'the value of the latter is much heightened by their corresponding with those found in the interior of the tope [i.e. the stupa, a Buddhist monument] by M. Ventura'. He sent some of the coins to the Asiatic Society of Bengal, and James Prinsep was able to study them. According to his own account Burnes was also able to acquire several copper coins like those from Manikyala at Balkh (1834, p. 241). He also procured a few coins at a smaller tope, at Belur near Rawalpindi, which were like those found at Manikyala.

Burnes's opinion of Manikyala followed the views of Tod and Schlegel, as repeated by Wilson (1832), that the coins found within showed the monument to be 'either the sepulchres of the Bactrian kings or their Indo-Scythic successors, mentioned in the Periplus. . . . The rudeness of the coins would point to the latter age, or the second century of the Christian era' (Burnes 1834, p. 73).

In relation to the coins he acquired in Balkh, however, he was more swayed by what he saw as the Persian nature of the cap worn by the king represented on them, but thought it of interest that they were also to be found in India. The Persian connection led him to ponder whether the ancient Persian contacts with India were related to the history of the coins: 'It is well known that India formed one of the satrapies of Darius; and we read of a connexion between it and Persia in ancient times, which will perhaps clear up the history of these coins' (Burnes 1834, p. 241).

The plates of Burnes's account of his travels (Burnes 1834, following p. 454) illustrate eleven Kushan coins. They also feature a tetradrachm of the Bactrian Greek king Diodotus (no. 8), six Bukharan imitations of silver tetradrachms of Euthydemus I, another Bactrian Greek king (nos 1–6), a square copper coin of the Indo-Greek king Apollodotus I (no. 7), a gold stater of the Sasanian emperor Shapur II (no. 10), two local Sogdian coins (nos 9 and 11), two copper coins of the Indo-Scythian king Azes (nos 28 and 29), and a copper coin of the Hindu Shahis (no. 31). The Kushan coins are all copper (table 7).

Prinsep and Wilson on Burnes's coins

As an appendix to the 1834 account of his travels Burnes added two appendices on the coins ('Professor Wilson's notes', pp. 457–62, and 'Mr. James Prinsep's notes', pp. 463–73). Prinsep's notes were based on those he had written for the *Journal of the Asiatic Society of Bengal* in June 1833 (Thomas 1858, vol. I, pp. 23–44, pl. II). Prinsep's observations were used by Wilson in writing his notes in May the following year.

In 1833 Prinsep recognised the importance of these coins, observing that in difficult circumstances Burnes had been 'very successful in the store of coins he has brought back from the Panjab and the valley of the Oxus' (Thomas 1858, vol. I, p. 23). He reported that Burnes had given ten examples to the Bombay Literary Society and a similar number to the Asiatic Society of Bengal. Among the coins sent to Calcutta was 'one coin of the dynasty which supplanted the Macedonian princes of Bactria, calculated to excite much curiosity among antiquarians'. The coin in question provided Prinsep with the first real clue towards establishing the identity of the Kushans as a historical entity.

Among the coins collected by Burnes in the vicinity of Manikyala was a copper didrachm of Kanishka with a Greek inscription. Prinsep was able to decipher the Greek inscription and recognised the king's name (Thomas 1858, vol. I, pp. 37–41, pl. II.10). He described the coin as follows:

> OBVERSE. – A king or warrior holding a spear in the left hand; and with the right hand sacrificing on a small altar (?). Epigraphe *ΒΑΣΙΛΕΥΣ ΒΑΣ . . . ΚΑΝΗΡΚΟΥ*.
> REVERSE. – A priest or sage standing, and holding a flower in his right hand; a glory encircles his head; on the left, the letters *ΝΑΝΑΙΑ* – on the right, the usual Bactrian monogram with four prongs.

He also recognised the importance of being able to read the king's name (Thomas 1858, vol. I, p. 37):

> This coin is of very great value, from its circumstance of being the only one, out of the many discovered in the same neighbourhood, upon which the characters are sufficiently legible to afford a clue of the prince's name.

He realised that, in spite of the Greek title king of kings (*ΒΑΣΙΛΕΥΣ ΒΑΣ* [*ΛΕΩΝ*]), the name was not one previously recorded for the Greek kings of Bactria. He was confident of the reading, except for the fifth letter in the name, which he thought could also be the Greek letters *Θ* or *Σ* (i.e. *ΚΑΝΗΘΚΟΥ* or *ΚΑΝΗΣΚΟΥ*) From this uncertainty he was misled into a reading which nevertheless enabled him to identify the issuer: 'I suppose it to be a coin of Kanishka, a Tartar or Scythic conqueror of Bactria' (Thomas 1858, vol. I, p. 38). He recognised the importance of this identification: 'the discovery of this coin will be hailed as of the greatest value by all who are engaged in the newly-developed study of Bactrian antiquity'. He was so overcome by his discovery that he returned the coin to Burnes, so that he could take it back to England 'for the personal satisfaction of numismatologists in Europe'.

He was able to recognise the name because of his familiarity with recent scholarship. From the work of the

Hungarian scholar Alexander Csoma de Körös (Sandor Csoma Körösi 1957), he had learned of Tibetan Buddhist texts which named a king called Kanishka as a patron of Buddhism, ruling in northern India four hundred years after the Buddha. From the work of his colleague Horace Wilson, he had also encountered Kanishka (Canishca), named as king of Kashmir in Wilson's translation of the *Rājataraṅgiṇī*, a chronicle of Kashmir (Wilson 1825, p. 23), along with two other kings Hushca and Jushca, all of the Turushca race, who had introduced Buddhism into Kashmir, 150 years after the death of the Buddha.

Prinsep preferred the date provided by the Tibetan source and therefore dated Kanishka in the late second century BC, i.e. about four hundred years after the death of the Buddha, which he concluded was about 520 BC. From Schlegel and the Classical authors he had consulted, he had also found that the Scythians had overthrown the Greeks in Bactria in about 134 BC or 125 BC. Prinsep presumed that the coin he had found was of a Scythian prince, who had either overthrown the Greeks or was the immediate successor of those who had done so. He also drew the conclusion that the coin demonstrated that the *Rājataraṅgiṇī* was a 'historical work' and that therefore the date of *c*.520 BC for the death of the Buddha was no longer in doubt (Thomas 1858, vol. I, p. 40).

There were further conclusions to be drawn from Prinsep's attribution. He re-examined the other 'Indo-Scythic' coins and concluded that these coins 'tend to confirm the supposition of a Buddhist succession to the Greek princes' (Thomas 1858, vol. I, p. 40). He saw the reverse designs of Kanishka's coins as representing 'a sacred person' related to Buddhism. He also connected the inscriptions on late Kushan coins with Buddhism, because he thought that 'we find the same kind of character which appears upon the Dihli and Allahabad pillars . . . belonging to the Buddhist religion' (Thomas 1858, vol. I, pp. 40–1), i.e. late Kushan to Gupta period Brahmi. The Manikyala monument was also thereby confirmed as a Buddhist monument, as had been suggested by Wilson (1832). This analysis also led Prinsep to suggest, on the basis of his interpretation of the Wima Kadphises and Vasudeva I coins showing a 'Brahmani bull, accompanied by a priest in the common Indian dhoti', that the Buddhist issues were soon followed by those of a 'Brahmanical dynasty, which in its turn overcame the Buddhist line' (Thomas 1858, vol. I, p. 41).

In spite of the misconceptions he derived from his discovery, Prinsep's fortuitous misreading of the inscription on the coin found by Burnes had enabled him to link together three vital pieces of evidence in the discovery of the identity of the Kushans: the coins, the Kashmir chronicle and Buddhist traditions all bore testimony to the existence and importance of a king called Kanishka, his close relationship with Buddhism and the extent of his domain, across northern India and into Bactria and Kashmir. Prinsep was able to conclude that:

> My task increases upon me daily, but I shall be amply rewarded if my humble notice of the discoveries of others shall, by connecting them with ancient history, eventually turn these most interesting reliques to the true end of numismatic study.

The notes added to Burnes's account of his travels repeated Prinsep's 1833 paper, but added a short description of the Kanishka, Wima Tak[to], Wima Kadphises, Huvishka and Vasudeva I coins found by Burnes (1834, pp. 472–3). His description of these focuses on the relationships between the imagery of the Wima Tak[to] coins and those of Eucratides and the other Greek kings of Bactria, and on the Brahmanical elements in the designs of Wima Kadphises (Burnes 1834, nos 21, 23), Vasudeva I (no. 24) and Huvishka (no. 25) coins. Prinsep identified two of Burnes's coins as finds from Balkh, a tetradrachm of Wima Kadphises (Burnes 1834, no. 21) and another of Kanishka I (no. 20).

Wilson related Burnes's finds to the coins published by Tod and himself, and identified the Kushan pieces as examples of the Indo-Scythian division. He observed that there were some new varieties and that no. 18 was the clearest example of the series that he had so far seen, and therefore 'of singular interest and value' (Burnes 1834, p. 461). Of the Kushan coins found by Burnes, Wilson described the Kanishka coin (Burnes 1834, no. 18) which was the focus of Prinsep's commentary, a standard issue coin of Wima Tak[to] (no. 19), the coins of Kanishka I and Wima Kadphises found at Balkh (nos 20–1), but summarised the remainder as coins which 'belong to the same series as the foregoing' (nos 22–30).

Wilson referred to what had been 'conjectured by Mr Prinsep' about the legible Kanishka coin. He observed that the 'name, date, and locality are therefore in favour of the verification, and it must be admitted, until, at least, something more satisfactory can be proposed' (Burnes 1834, p. 461). His tone suggested that he was sceptical about Prinsep's proposal. His further comments drew attention to the parallels between Burnes's coin and those of similar design published by Tod (1824) and himself (Wilson 1832).

Further finds from India

In his next articles – August 1833 and May 1834 – in the *Journal of the Asiatic Society of Bengal* (Thomas 1858, vol. I, pp. 45–62, 82–5), Prinsep paid attention to two further collections of coins. The first was a random assemblage of early coins which had been made by Dr Swiney, while the latter was the product of excavations being carried out by a military engineer, Captain P. T. Cautley (January and April 1834).

Among Swiney's coins Prinsep found two Wima Tak[to] coins, units of the standard Soter Megas type (Thomas 1858, vol. I, p. 52, nos 9–10, pl. III.9–10). He compared them to the other published examples of the same type and observed that these coins all had the title of the king in the nominative, unlike their Greek prototypes which used the genitive.

Prinsep also discovered in Swiney's collection a gold coin of the late Kushan period (Thomas 1858, vol. I, p. 52, no. 13, pl. III.13), an issue of Vasudeva II (cf. Göbl 1984, type 577). He confused it with the Hindu gold (i.e. Gupta) series, which coins of the late Kushan closely resemble (as they are the prototypes used by the Gupta moneyers). Prinsep noted that a similar coin had been published by Wilson (1832, no. 6; a gold coin of Vasishka, cf. Göbl 1984, type 558), recognising that they both had a trident on the front, where the Gupta coin had garuda (eagle mount of Vishnu). Prinsep also turned to the detail of these coins to draw attention to the continuity of detail from the Bactrian (Greek) through the Indo-Scythian (Kushan) to the Hindu (Gupta) coinage. He remarked on the continuation of the use of Greek inscriptions into the Indo-Scythian period, 'where, otherwise, they would have been little expected' (Thomas 1858, vol. I, p. 55). He also noted that a 'further direct and incontestable proof of their connection is derived from the similarity of the monograms or symbols visible on most of them'. On the associated plate (pl. 3) he drew the Greek monograms and Kushan tamghas he had recorded, and pointed to the evidence they provided for the Greek origins of Indian coinage. He concluded: 'The medley of types once collected and preserved, however, may eventually afford the means of a proper classification, although it cannot be attempted in the present state of our scanty knowledge' (Thomas 1858, vol. I, p. 61).

He also added to his description of coins from Dr Swiney's collection two more Kushan coins found at Manikyala by Burnes (Thomas 1858, vol. I, p. 52, nos 16, 18, pl. III.16, 18). Both were copper drachms of Kanishka I (no. 16, with Nana reverse; no. 18, a rare seated king type, with Oesho reverse). Prinsep recognised no. 16 as belonging 'to the Kanishka group' and compared the seated figure on no. 18 with that on the reverse of the Huvishka/Manaobago gold coin found by Ventura at Manikyala.

While excavating a canal near Behat (near Saharanpur, Uttar Pradesh, north of Delhi), Captain Cautley had uncovered ancient remains, yielding many ancient Indian coins, including coins of the 'Kanerkos series' (i.e. Kanishka I coins) and two later Kushan coppers (Thomas 1858, vol. I, p. 84, nos 9–10, pl. IV.9–10). Some of Cautley's coins are now in the British Museum. Cautley's coins (170 in total) included 26 'Indo-Scythic' coins, but only one which Prinsep recognised was an issue of Vasudeva I (Göbl 1984, type 1002), which he assigned to the 'Christian era' (Thomas 1858, vol. I, p. 74, pl. IV.9). Prinsep also illustrated a Kushan copper, in degenerate style of the seated Ardochsho type issued by Kanishka II and Vasishka (Göbl 1984, type 1017; Thomas 1858, vol. I, pl. IV.10). Prinsep illustrated these coins 'to shew that what has been called the Indo-Scythic series occurs plentifully among the exhumed relics of Behat' (Thomas 1858, vol. I, p. 84). Regarding the attribution and significance of the Kushan coins found at Behat, he considered them to be the latest coins of the site and thought that their relatively large number suggested they had been in circulation when the ancient city was destroyed in 'the first centuries of the Christian era'. In discussing these 'Indo-Scythic' coins Prinsep called on new evidence which had just arrived in Calcutta. Although he was able to link some coins with Kanishka because of his own research, he could now also attribute some of the coins (including the illustrated Vasudeva I coin) to 'the Kadphises series, in compliance with the successful researches of Mr. Masson'.

The successful researches of Mr Masson

Prinsep was referring to Charles Masson's account of his coin finds sent from Kabul on 28 November 1833 with Dr Gerard, who had just arrived in Calcutta. Gerard – a British physician who had accompanied Burnes to Bukhara – had also brought coins from Burnes. Masson sent drawings and a commentary which were destined to transform the understanding of the place of the Kushans in Bactrian and Indian history. Masson's contribution was remarkable in three ways: firstly, the

number of coins he had discovered was far more than had been previously seen; secondly, his collecting was methodical and, by restricting his source of coins primarily to one site, Begram,[1] he was able to give some meaning to the coins he was acquiring; finally, his research was rigorous, producing more accurate descriptions than was previously possible, while at the same time creating a classification which enabled a preliminary sequence of the coins to be established. He collected coins of all types from Begram and was therefore able to understand the relationship between the Greek and non-Greek coins of the ancient period (figs 27, 53, 55, 174). The insight that encouraged him to collect and study coins in this way was very deliberate. It was a remarkable achievement for a numismatist of the early nineteenth century (Masson 1834, p. 154):

> I confined my attentions to the more distant and ample one of Begram . . . as my object was not merely the amassing of coins, but the application of them to useful purposes, I hailed with satisfaction the prospect of obtaining a collection from a known spot, with which they would have, of necessity, a definite connection, enabling me to speculate with confidence on the points they involved.

By the time he dispatched his report to Calcutta for publication in the April 1834 edition of the *Journal of the Asiatic Society of Bengal*, Masson had been able to collect 962 Kushan coins, of which he classed 357 as Grecian (i.e. Kushan issues with Greek inscriptions) and 605 as Indo-Scythic (i.e. Kushan issues with Bactrian inscriptions). For clarity they are listed according to modern classification, rather than Masson's arrangement (table 8).

With such a large sample of coins Masson's classification was more refined than any achieved so far. Although there was much still to accomplish, he was able to distinguish the coins of the main Kushan rulers. He could not name them, but was able to group them together under the same headings. The early Kushan coins of the first two Kushan kings, Kujula Kadphises and Wima Tak[to] were listed under the heading 'Grecian, series no. 4, coins of the Nysaean Dynasty', while the following Kushan kings were listed as 'Indo-Scythic' (following Tod's attribution), in three series:

1 Kanishka
2 Kadphises and Vasudeva I (and later coins of the same type)
3 Huvishka and Kanishka II (and later coins of the same type)

With the issues of first two Kushan kings he also included coins made by the Yuezhi before Kujula Kadphises became their leader (Hermaeus imitations, fig. 55), together with the coins of Kujula's Indo-Parthian contemporary Gondophares (Masson 1834, pl. X.34–6) and the imitation Indo-Scythian coins in the name of Azes of the same period (Masson 1834, pl. X.31, 33). He thought that the Nysaean dynasty (a kingdom he invented to explain the coins he was finding, whose capital Nysa he located in the Jalalabad area) had 'sprung up on the subversion of that of Bactria' (i.e. after the fall of the Greek kingdom of Bactria) and 'flourished for a long subsequent period' (Masson 1834, p. 160).

He asserted that he had identified the tombs of some of these kings because their coins had been found in his and other excavations of Buddhist stupas which he mistakenly

Table 8
Kushan coins collected by Charles Masson at Begram 1833–4

Yuezhi	Hermaeus imitation copper unit (Bopearachchi type 7)	pl. IX.20 [34 examples, units and quarters]
	Hermaeus imitation copper quarter (Bopearachchi type 7)	pl. IX.21
Kujula Kadphises	Hermaeus imitation unit (Bopearachchi type 8)	pl. IX.22–3 [10 examples]
	Hermaeus imitation, Heracles reverse (Bopearachchi type 10)	pl. X.24 [136 examples, including Kujula Heracles type]
	Heracles type in own name	pl. X.25
Wima I Tak[to]	general issue copper unit	pl. X.26–8 [55 examples]
	helmeted bust unit	pl. X.29 [1 example]
	bilingual unit	pl. X.30 [1 example]
	bilingual quarter	pl. X.32 [1 example]
	Heliocles imitation, horse reverse, unit	pl. XI.48 [1 example collected at Jalalabad]
	Heliocles imitation, horse reverse, quarter	pl. X.37 [6 examples]
Wima II Kadphises	large copper unit	pl. XII.8 [37 examples, units and quarters]
	small copper quarter	pl. XII.9
	gold stater (bust left/Oesho)	pl. XIII.24 [1 example, bought in Kabul bazaar]
Kanishka I	middle copper half (Nanaia)	pl. XII.1 [24 examples, including Helios type]
	middle copper half (Helios)	pl. XII.2
	large copper unit (Oesho)	pl. XII.3 [22 examples, including Miiro type]
	large copper unit (Miiro)	pl. XII.4
	large copper unit (Oado)	pl. XII.5 [6 examples]
	small copper quarter (Nana)	pl. XII.6 [16 examples, including Mao type]
	small copper quarter (Mao)	pl. XII.7
Huvishka	large copper unit (early elephant rider, Athsho)	pl. XIII.13 [56 examples, including all elephant rider types]
	large copper unit (late elephant rider, Mao)	pl. XIII.14
	large copper unit (middle elephant rider, Oesho)	pl. XIII.15–16
	large copper unit (elephant rider, reverse not shown)	pl. XIII.17–18
	large copper unit (throne, Mao)	pl. XIII.19–21 [56 examples]
	large copper unit (cross-legged, Mioro)	pl. XIII.22 [9 examples]
Vasudeva I/imitations	copper unit (Oesho)	pl. XII.10–12 [254 examples]
Kanishka II/Vasishka	copper unit (Ardochsho)	pl. XIII.23 [113 examples]

thought were royal burial mounds (Masson 1834, pp. 168–9). In this way he located the issuer of Kujula's Hermaeus imitations, whom he identified as 'Hermaeus III' as ruling near Jalalabad, as his coins were found by Dr Martin Honigberger (a physician from Transylvania, i.e. Romania, working for the Sikh court; see pp. 213–16, figs 179–82) in 'the tope called Janni Tope [Bimaran stupa 5] in its [i.e. Jalalabad's] neighbourhood'. Likewise the coins of Wima Tak[to], named 'Sotereagas' by Masson, also found in another mound near Bimaran (stupa 3) by Honigberger, located this ruler in the same area (fig. 180).

Although Masson misunderstood the meaning of coins found in the stupa mounds, his recognition of the significance of find-spots as numismatic evidence for understanding political history was evident: 'The princes whose coins are found on any known spots or sites, may fairly be held to have reigned there' (Masson 1834, p. 161). He could also understand the implications of the distribution of find-spots, e.g. he noted that Wima Tak[to] coins had been reported from various parts of the subcontinent, and concluded from this that 'When we learn that this monarch's coins are found generally over the Punjab and north-western provinces of India, even to Benares, we form high notions of his extended empire' (Masson 1834, p. 169).

After the series containing the first two Kushan kings Masson placed the third king of the dynasty, Wima Kadphises (fig. 174.1–6). He was able to read only the second part of his name, but recognised the link between his copper coins and a gold coin found 'at Jalalabad' (actually in the relic deposit of Shevaki stupa 1 near Kabul) by Honigberger (fig. 181; Masson 1834, p. 173), on which a more legible inscription was transcribed but not read. He also recognised the relationship between these coins and those of the ruler he placed next, Kanishka I (fig. 174.9–20). He had been able to collect 24 of the Greek inscription coppers of Kanishka I and was therefore able to confirm Prinsep's reading. Curiously, in spite of suggesting the correct order for these coins, he designated Kanishka I's coins 'Series 1' and Wima Kadphises 'Series 2'. He did not attempt to explain the sequence he suggested – 'I incline to place the series of ΚΑΔΦΙΣΕΣ before that of ΚΑΝΗΡΚΟΣ in a chronological point of view' – whereas in his discussion of the absolute chronology on the basis of a mistaken reading of the name Ooe[mo] as a date, year 800 in the Buddhist era (according to his calculation c. AD 200), he suggested that the order ought to be reversed if Prinsep's identification of Kanishka was correct (Masson 1834, pp. 160, 173–4).

He added Vasudeva I (and imitation) coins to Series 2 (apparently on the basis of their Oesho and bull reverses). He

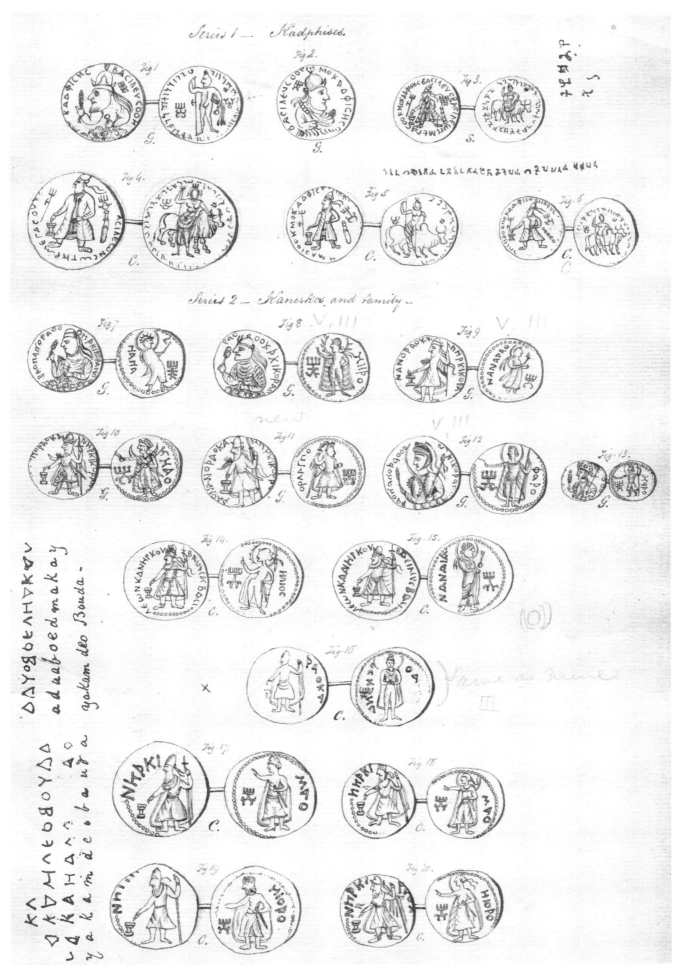

Figure 174 Kushan coins of Wima Kadphises, Kanishka I and Huvishka recorded by Masson in 1833–5.

questioned Tod's and Schlegel's identification of the reverse deity as Shiva on the basis that 'the figure is certainly feminine'. On the basis of their variation in types and quality – 'from tolerable to wretched' – he also suggested that these coins might represent several rulers and commented that they represented the most numerous series he had encountered in Begram (Masson 1834, p. 174).

In spite of their varied designs he was able to recognise that Huvishka's coppers formed a single group, which he designated 'Indo-Scythic, Series no. 3'. He recognised them as 'Indo-Scythic' because of their use of the Kushan tamgha, but distinguished them from his first two groups (i.e. Series no. 1 Kanishka I, and Series no. 2 Wima Kadphises) because of the absence of the fire-altar design. Accordingly he thought the Huvishka coins should be 'safely placed in succession to the two former' series (fig. 174.7–8; Masson 1834, p. 160).

Masson's great achievements in collecting, classification, attribution and in recognising the value of provenance were somewhat undermined by his speculative interpretations of some of the data he had collected. In spite of the distances from Kabul to the British centres of scholarship in India and Europe, his research was able to take into account the recent scholarly discussions of the coins collected by Tod and Wilson, the finds of Ventura and Burnes and the articles published by Schlegel and Prinsep, but at the same time some of his interpretations of the designs were naive or simply mistaken.

His thirst for chronological information encouraged him to see dates wherever he could not understand the Greek inscriptions, such as his attempt to read the first part of the name of Wima Kadphises as year 800, a date in the Buddhist era. Likewise on the imitation Hermaeus coins of Kujula Kadphises he read as dates the letters ΣY (74?) or ΣE (75) which he found at the end of the legend in miswritten Greek (fig. 55).

His isolation in Kabul prevented him from the closer contact with other scholars that would have dealt with such problems arising from the new discoveries he was making. The large number of Kanishka coins at his disposal prompted him, for example, into a discussion of Prinsep's inspired attribution of them to the king Kanishka named in the Kashmir chronicle and in Tibetan Buddhist texts. But his discussion was very distorted by his confusion of the sources used by Prinsep. He mistook Csoma de Körös's references to Kapilavatsu, as the capital of the Shakya ancestors of the Buddha, with the capital of Kanishka I, arguing that the place name must be a wrong transcription of the name of Kabul, where Kanishka I clearly ruled as his coins were so numerous there. His proposition was that, if Kapilavatsu was Kabul, then he would admit that Prinsep's identification of Kanishka as the issuer of the coins was correct, but if the two could not be equated then Prinsep would be wrong. His discussions about chronology are equally confused, mixing his clear understanding of the coins with an assemblage of inappropriate or misunderstood evidence. A dialogue with other scholars would have quickly remedied Masson's problems. In spite of this, his dating of Kanishka I 'considerably later than 130 BC', i.e. about '155 AD' (Masson 1834, pp. 160, 174), is a great improvement on Prinsep's date in the late second century BC.

Further progress on Manikyala in Calcutta

By 1834 James Prinsep in Calcutta had become a conduit for the study of the coins being found in Afghanistan and the Punjab. Through the *Journal of the Asiatic Society of Bengal*, he was able to publish the coins as they were being found and to contribute articles discussing them. After Masson's contribution of April 1834, Prinsep began, through a series of articles (July 1834 – December 1835; Thomas 1858, vol. I, pp. 90–231), to present an updated view of the coins and antiquities found by Ventura at Manikyala, using the objects themselves, delivered to him from Ventura by Captain C. M. Wade. His analysis was made in the light of the discoveries of Tod, Wilson, Burnes, Masson and Honigberger. He also had available new numismatic resources in the form of the coins shown to him by Gerard and Karamat 'Ali (both collecting in the Pakistan and Afghanistan region; Karamat 'Ali was a news-writer for the British in Qandahar and then Kabul) and by British military officers Colonels Stacy and Smith (collecting in northern India). In addition he had the good fortune of examining the rest of Ventura's coin collection as it was in transit to Paris (via Calcutta) in the hands of Ventura's colleague Allard.

He began by republishing Ventura's account of the Manikyala stupa finds, with detailed drawings of some of the coins (Thomas 1858, vol. I, pp. 90–117): two gold coins of Huvishka (a gold stater with Manaobago reverse and a quarter stater with Miiro[2] reverse: Göbl 1984, types 151 and 311; Thomas 1858, vol. I, pls V.2 and VI.24 respectively); two copper units of Kanishka I (Oado reverse and Mao reverse: Göbl 1984, types 783 and 774; Thomas 1858, vol. I, pl. VI.30–1 respectively); and three copper units of Huvishka (elephant rider/Athsho reverse, king on throne/Mioro reverse, king on mountain/Athsho reverse: Göbl 1984, types 832, 824, 834; Thomas 1858, vol. I, pl. VI.28–9, 32 respectively).

His examination of the remainder of the 80 copper coins from the stupa suggested that there were, in total, 70 legible specimens: 2 copper units of Wima Kadphises, 20 copper units and 17 copper quarters of Kanishka I; and 15 elephant rider, 12 king on throne and 4 king on mountain copper units of Huvishka.

In order to understand fully the context of the finds Prinsep re-examined in detail all the examples of 'Indo-Scythic' (i.e. Kushan) coins available to him. Using over 300 specimens, drawn from other collections, he was able to do an accurate drawing of the inscriptions on Wima Kadphises, Kanishka and Huvishka coins. He transcribed the Greek inscriptions of both gold and copper Wima Kadphises coins. He retained the nomenclature Kadphises for them, but on the basis of Masson's analysis of the inscription, and comparison with the gold coinage, accepted that the Greek *OOHMO* was probably 'a part or an adjunct of the name of the prince' (Thomas 1858, vol. I, pp. 127–8).

He continued to call the coins of Kanishka the 'Kanerkes' group, and by comparing the Greek Bactrian inscription examples deduced that the titles *ÞAO* and *ÞAONANOÞAO* were equivalents of the Greek titles signifying 'king' and 'king of kings', and compared the term *PAO* with the Indian regional royal title *rao*, derived from *raja* (Thomas 1858, vol. I, pp. 127, 130). To illustrate this reading he showed drawings of Greek inscription coins from the collections of Karamat 'Ali

(Nanaia, pl. VII.7) and Gerard (Helios, pl. VII.8) alongside two Bactrian script examples from his own collection (unit Mioro, half unit Sakamano Boudo, Thomas 1858, vol. I, pl. VII.10–11). He attempted, on the basis of a very limited knowledge of the languages he thought might be represented by the Bactrian inscription, to understand its significance. He correctly understood it to represent a translation of the Greek, but found along with it the word KOÞANO (Koshano) which he tried to render into a Greek, Iranian or Sanskrit term, deciding that he preferred the Iranian version and translated it as 'shining' or 'splendid' (Thomas 1858, vol. I, pp. 130–1).

His recognition of the titles ÞAO and ÞAONANOÞAO on the coins of Kanishka led him also to see the close link between them and the coins of Huvishka on which he also found these titles. He had difficulty with the rest of the legend, but once again compared them with the gold coins found in the Manikyala stupa and realised that the fragmentary legends he could see on the coppers were closely related to the gold coins. This recognition that they were issued by the same ruler did not yet reveal the name, but led him to suggest two possible readings OOHÞKI and KENOÞANO (a mistaken version of [OOHÞ]KE KOÞANO). He remained uncertain at this point about the name, but suggested that the version OOHÞKI might be a form of the name Kanerkes (Thomas 1858, vol. I, p. 128).

The reading ÞAONANOÞAO also enabled Prinsep to include in the Indo-Scythic group the gold stater of Vasudeva I illustrated by Wilson (1832, no. 3: actually a facsimile, like the one illustrated by Marsden 1823/5), and two coins that had been shown him by Karamat 'Ali (Thomas 1858, vol. I, p. 129). One is illustrated and is clearly a gold stater issued by the Kushano-Sasanians in imitation of the coins of Vasudeva I (Thomas 1858, vol. I, pl. VIII.10: Göbl 1984, type 698). The second is only partly shown (Thomas 1858, vol. I, pl. VIII.11, depicting the head of the king and the inscription), but can still be recognised as a Kidarite copy of a Kushano-Sasanian gold dinar (Göbl 1984, type 736). In the plate associated with these gold coins Prinsep illustrated – but did not discuss – two copper coins of Vasudeva I (Thomas 1858, vol. I, pl. VIII.6–7). He also illustrated drawings of their fragmentary legends in a way that suggests he recognised a degenerating version of the inscription ÞAONANOÞAO and therefore linked them with the Kanishka I and Huvishka issues.

By examining the details of their inscriptions Prinsep had reinforced the coherence of the group designated by Tod as Indo-Scythic. His observations also suggested a sequence placing Wima Kadphises types first because of their use of Kharoshthi, linking them to earlier coins, followed by Kanishka I because of his continuation of the use of Greek, with Huvishka retaining the Bactrian title introduced by Kanishka and Vasudeva I showing a degenerating version of the same title.

Although the results of understanding the Bactrian inscriptions were limited by the brevity of the coin inscriptions, Prinsep had achieved an understanding of their meaning, if not of their linguistic function. An amusing contrast to the sobriety of his approach and analysis can be found in a later edition of his journal where the coin collector Swiney launched himself into a fantasy translation of the Bactrian inscriptions by imagining that they represented a language close to Celtic; by chance, however, this enabled Swiney to identify the NANO ending of ÞAONANO as a genitive plural (Swiney 1837).

Mithraic coins

Prinsep also turned his interest to the reverse designs of Kanishka I and Huvishka coins (Thomas 1858, vol. I, pp. 131–6). He recognised that the Kushan coins followed Greek tradition by placing divine images on their reverses, but that these images were distinguished from their Greek prototypes by their non-Greek dress. Looking first at the Greek inscription coins of Kanishka I, he sought to associate Nanaia and Helios with their Iranian counterparts Anahita and Mithra. He reinforced this connection by showing that Kanishka I's non-Greek coins largely featured coins with an inscription which he thought was a reference to Mithra, 'typifying the power of the sun' (Thomas 1858, vol. I, p. 133). On some he correctly read the god's name as MIOPO, but on others he mistakenly thought this should be read as MIΘPO. He also suggested that the inscriptions MAO and AΘPO could be seen as corruptions of the name of Mithra, or they could be interpreted, through a process which he admitted was 'more or less strained and unnatural', as 'epithets or mythological attributes of the sun, or as we may conjecture, through that resplendent image, of Zoroaster, the son and manifest effulgence of the deity' (Thomas 1858, vol. I, p. 135). By the same process of adaptation he grouped the Manaobago and Buddha coins with the issues naming Nanaia.

Prinsep summed up his achievement (Thomas 1858, vol. I, p. 136):

> Under the risk of being tedious, I have now gone through the whole series of corrupted Greek coins connected with the Manikyala tope, and I trust that the result of my investigation will throw some light on the subject. I have ventured to give the appellation of 'Mithraic' to the numerous coins which have been proved to bear the effigy of the sun, for they afford the strongest evidence of the extension of the religion of Zoroaster in some parts of Bactria and the Panjab at the time of its reassumption of consequence in Persia.

Unfortunately in the process of this achievement he felt inclined to disassociate the Kanishka coins he was publishing from his earlier suggestion that they were issued by the king Kanishka named in the Kashmir Chronicle and Buddhist sources. He did so because the Manikyala stupa contained Sasanian-style coins which he recognised as later than the date suggested for Kanishka by these sources (Thomas 1858, vol. I, p. 131):

> I have not alluded to the hypothesis advanced in my former note, that Kanerkos might be the Kanishka of Kashmirian history, because the discovery of Sasanian coins, and the consequent modern date of the present monument, at once overthrow that supposition.

More news from Manikyala

During 1834 another discovery at Manikyala, also by a French officer, Claude-Auguste Court, placed further evidence in the hands of scholars. In November 1834 Prinsep published an account by Court of his discovery in the *Journal of the Asiatic Society of Bengal*, and his own commentary on it (pp. 212–13, fig. 178 below). Court excavated some of the smaller monuments in the neighbourhood of the Great Stupa opened by

Table 9

Coins from the relic deposit of the Mera-ka-Dheri stupa at Manikyala

Kujula Kadphises	Hermaeus imitation, Heracles reverse (Bopearachchi 1991, type 10)	pl. XXXIV.12 [from its size no. 13 might also be this type]
Wima II Kadphises	large copper unit	pl. XXXIV.1, 9
Kanishka I	gold quarter stater (bust/Oesho)	pl. XXXIV.16–17
	gold quarter stater (standing king/Mao)	pl. XXXIV.17
	gold quarter stater (standing king/Athsho)	pl. XXXIV.18
	large copper unit (Oesho)	pl. XXXIV.3–4
	large copper unit (Oado)	pl. XXXIV.2, 10
	large copper unit (Mao)	pl. XXXIV.10
	large copper unit (reverse illegible)	pl. XXXIV.14–15
Roman	silver denarius, Q. Minucius Thermus, Rome 103 BC (Crawford type 319.1)	pl. XXXIV.22
	silver denarius, Lucius Julius Bursio, Rome 85 BC (Crawford type 352.1)	pl. XXXIV.24
	silver denarius, Publius Forius Crassipes, Rome 84 BC (Crawford type 356.1)	pl. XXXIV.25
	silver denarius, Mn. Cordius Rufus, Rome 46 BC (Crawford type 463.1)	pl. XXXIV.21
	silver denarius, Lucius Aemelianus Buca for Julius Caesar, Rome 44 BC (Crawford type 480.6)	pl. XXXIV.20
	silver denarius, P. Accoleius Lariscolus, Rome 43 BC (Crawford type 486.1)	pl. XXXIV.23
	silver denarius, Marcus Antonius, military mint, 42 BC (Crawford type 496.2)	pl. XXXIV.19

Ventura. Court, like Ventura and Masson, was convinced that the monuments were burial monuments 'nothing more than a tomb of some ancient king of the country, or it may be the work of some conqueror from Persia or Bactria, who may have raised it in memory of some battle fought on the spot, intended to cover the remains of the warriors who fell in the combat'. In one at Mera-ka-Pind he found reliquaries, coins and an inscription, which he thought 'particularly calculated to throw light upon these curious monuments of antiquity', because it contained Roman and Kushan coins and an inscription 'in an unknown character' (Thomas 1858, vol. I, p. 139).

Court was unable to identify the Roman coins, not knowing if they were Greek or Roman, or from the period of Alexander or 'Augustus or Justinian', but thought that they might have been 'brought into the country through the ordinary channels of commerce by the Red Sea' (Thomas 1858, vol. I, p. 140). The Kushan coins, on which he saw emblems that 'may be observed in Persia with some slight difference', were not recognised by Court, who classed them as 'Graeco-Scythic or Graeco-Indian' (Thomas 1858, vol. I, p. 141). Soon after receiving Court's report and drawings Prinsep was shown the actual coins and reliquaries by Court's compatriot Allard (fig. 126), who was en route to Paris via Calcutta. He got permission to reproduce the drawings in his journal and was able to identify the coins as copper issues of Kadphises (distinguishing issues of Wima and Kujula by their types) and gold and copper issues of Kanerkes. Among the Kanishka coins he found both gold and copper examples with the reverse type showing a four-armed god (Oesho-Shiva), which he read as *OKRO*, and sought to identify as the Indian sun god, Surya (named Arka on the coins), a 'substitution of the Hindu form of the solar deity for the Persian effigy of Mithra' (Thomas 1858, vol. I, p. 142). The Roman coins (Thomas 1858, vol. I, pp. 148–9) he identified as late Republican issues of the first century BC, except one of Q. Minucius Thermus (no. 22) which he incorrectly attributed to Constantine the Great (AD 307–27). All the Roman coins in fact range between 103 BC and 42 BC in date (table 9).

Prinsep's misattribution of the coin of Q. Minucius Thermus as a fourth-century AD issue encouraged him to date the Mera-ka-Pind site to the same period as the Manikyala Great Stupa, which contained coins of Sasanian type. Prinsep was unable to recognise that that the Sasanian type coins in the Great Stupa were in fact Islamic and Turkish copies of late Sasanian coins issued in the seventh century, so on the basis of the erroneous attribution by Ker Porter of the coins of Khusrau II (AD 591–628), which they copied, to Shapur II (AD 309–79), he dated the stupa to the fourth century (Thomas 1858, vol. I, pp. 120–1).

The combination of these errors of both information and judgement encouraged Prinsep to date the 'Indo-Scythic Rao Kanerki' to the fourth century 'as established from these two concurring evidences, and it may serve as a fixed point whence to track back the line of strange names of other equally unknown and obscure monarchs, whose names are now daily coming to light through the medium of these coins' (Thomas 1858, vol. I, p. 150). Having made this first stab at the thorny problem of Kushan chronology, Prinsep almost immediately discovered that his faith in Ker Porter's attribution of Sasanian coins was shattered by a fresh reading of Marsden's *Numismata Orientalia Illustrata* (Marsden 1823/5), where he had found coins attributed to Khusrau II closely matching the Arab copy of a Sasanian coin from Ventura's Stupa. His attention had also been called to recent research in Russia which had discovered Arab copies like Ventura's coin. He was therefore quickly convinced that Ventura's stupa could not have been constructed in the seventh century. He was now puzzled by the inclusion of first-century BC coins in a monument of such a late date, and expressed his frustration and optimism. 'The more we endeavour to examine the subject, the more difficulties and perplexities seem to arise around us; but it is only by bringing every circumstance forward that we can hope to arrive at last at any satisfactory conclusion' (Thomas 1858, vol. I, p. 152).

Before the end of the year Prinsep's mistaken identification of the Roman coins had been rectified by a new adventurer in the study of Kushan coins, his young friend Alexander Cunningham, who had recently arrived in Bengal. Cunningham, making his first step into print in the *Journal of the Asiatic Society of Bengal*, was able to point out that the coin attributed by Prinsep to the reign of Constantine the Great was, like the other coins in the deposit, a first-century BC Roman Republican coin (Cunningham 1834). Prinsep's editorial note on Cunningham's article referred again to the comparison with the seventh-century coins in Ventura's stupa, which contained 'Rao Nano Rao' coins like Court's monument. In Prinsep's view the Roman coins must have been antiquities at the time of deposit and 'the inference is stronger than ever, of their having been antiques at the time, and of the party buried there having been an antiquary in his day' (Cunningham 1834, p. 637).

Apart from the coins in Court's Manikyala stupa, Prinsep recognised that the most important find was the inscription on a large stone slab enclosing the reliquaries (fig. 178). 'This is doubtless the most valuable and important of his discoveries; for it will inform us of the precise nature and object of the monument in question' (Thomas 1858, vol. I, p. 143). He was certainly correct in this judgement as the inscription gave the name of Kanishka I and of the Kushans and a date – year 18 – in Kanishka's reign, as well as revealing that the monument was a Buddhist stupa. As yet, however, it could not be read, but Prinsep was able to recognise that it was written in the same script as used on many of the coins which had been found in the region, and he was already trying to crack the code of this script. He recognised a word in the second line of the inscription which appeared on many coins, and he knew what it meant – king – but his attempt at transcribing it '*malikao*' was not yet accurate, except for the first syllable. Six months later he was to publish his first attempt at decipherment of the script and this single word was the first hint at progress.

Breaking the code

Prinsep's interest in deciphering Kharoshthi script, which he called 'Pehlvi' or 'Bactrian-Pehlvi', seems to have been stimulated by a letter sent to him by Masson via Gerard before March 1835 (the original is preserved in Prinsep's notebooks in the Ashmolean Museum, Oxford). Masson showed him how elements of the Greek and Kharoshthi inscriptions on several Indo-Greek coins could be equated with each other (p. 23, fig. 27; Thomas 1858, vol. I, p. 179). From this Prinsep was able to draw up a table of correspondence between the representations of particular sounds in Greek and Kharoshthi. Although he made several mistakes, he was able to correctly transcribe about eight of the basic units of the Kharoshthi syllabary. His misconception, shared with most other scholars, that Kharoshthi was a form of 'Pehlvi' (i.e. Pahlavi, the Iranian script of the Sasanian period) was responsible for some of his mistakes, making him try to match some Kharoshthi shapes to Iranian letter forms. Although he was wrong in looking for an Iranian parallel, he correctly diagnosed that the script was written in the same right to left direction as Pahlavi.

He published his findings in the June 1835 edition of the *Journal of the Asiatic Society*, along with six plates illustrating the new coins he had seen in Gerard's, Karamat 'Ali's and

Ventura's collections (Thomas 1858, vol. I, pp. 176–94). Most of these were Indo-Greek coins, but he included three more Heliocles imitation coins of Wima Tak[to] (Thomas 1858, vol. I, pl. XV.12–14), two from Ventura and one from Masson (1834, no. 34). Prinsep referred to them as '*sui generis*', i.e. in a class of their own, distinct from Greek and Indo-Scythic coins. He also illustrated – but identified as issues of Azes – three bull/camel coins of Kujula Kadphises (Thomas 1858, vol. I, pl. XVI.6–8).

Once again, among the coins he examined, he found Soter Megas issues of Wima Tak[to], distinguishing two types: the bilingual issue – on which he recognised the correspondence between the first two words of the Greek and 'Pehlvi' inscriptions – and the standard rayed-bust type (Thomas 1858, vol. I, pl. XVII.23, 26 respectively). He also recalled Tod's publication of this type as the first coin with a Greek inscription to be 'found in India on which Greek characters were discovered or noticed' (Thomas 1858, vol. I, p. 192). The illustrated piece was an example from Stacy's collection, found in Malwa, but he observed that 'This is by far the commonest coin discovered in the Punjab and Afghanistan'. In spite of this, these coins could not yet be attributed: 'Bags-full have been sent down in excellent preservation, and yet nothing can be elicited from them'. He positioned them among what he termed 'Azos' coins, his group covering the horseman-type issues of Azes, the Indo-Scythian king, and Indo-Parthian coins with similar designs.

He also illustrated several of the imitation Hermaeus coinages previously reported by Masson (Zeus type, Thomas 1858, vol. I, pl. XVIII.2–4; Heracles type of Kujula Kadphises, pl. XVIII.9–13), but now recognised the name Kadphises in Greek on one of them (Thomas 1858, vol. I, p. 193, no. 11) and compared part of the Kharoshthi inscription on them with that on Wima Kadphises copper coins. He concluded that he should place the type 'at the lowest station of the present series, as a link with the series, already fully described, of the Indo-Scythic sovereign' and that he should place the Wima Kadphises coins next as the 'first coinage of the series' of Indo-Scythic coins because of their continued use of Kharoshthi. To this emerging picture of the early stages of the Kushan coinage he was also able to add a new coin-type of Kujula Kadphises, the Roman head type, from several specimens, one from Burnes, six from Ventura and three from Karamat 'Ali, on which he read Kadaphes in Greek and matched the reverse inscription to that of the Hermaeus imitation coins (Thomas 1858, vol. I, p. 194, pl. XVIII.14–16).

Mithraics again

In December 1835 Prinsep continued his reassessment of the coins from the Punjab and further west by focusing on the Indo-Scythic coins without 'Pehlvi' inscriptions. Again using the coins made known to him by Masson, Karamat 'Ali, Gerard, Stacy and Smith, he continued his analysis of the different types. Following the results of his previous analysis, he divided the 'Indo-Scythic' coins into 'two principal families of this type, the Kadphises and the Kanerkos group' and presented what he now understood to be the 'principal varieties of the Kanerkos Mithraics subsequent to the adoption of the vernacular titles of *rao* and *rao nano rao*' (1835a; Thomas 1858, vol. I, pp. 224–5). He now suggested

Table 10
Kushan coins classified by James Prinsep in 1835

Wima II Kadphises	gold stater, chariot/Oesho (Göbl type 1)	pl. XXII.1 (Smith collection from Benares)
	gold stater, bust/Oesho and bull (Göbl type 5)	pl. XXII.2 (Smith collection from Benares; second example seen by Prinsep in Karamat 'Ali's collection)
	gold stater, bust/Oesho (Göbl type 14)	pl. XXII.3 (Smith collection from Benares; duplicate in Honigberger's collection 'extracted from the Jalalabad tope')
Kanishka I	gold stater, Oesho (Göbl type 62)	pl. XXI.1 (Karamat 'Ali collection)
	gold quarter stater, bust/Athsho (Göbl type 41)	pl. XXI.2 (Karamat 'Ali collection)
	copper unit, Nana	pl. XXI.3- 4
	copper unit, Mioro	pl. XXI.5
	copper unit, Athsho	pl. XXI.6
	copper unit, Oesho	pl. XXI.7
	copper unit, Oado	pl. XXI.8
Huvishka	gold stater, Mao (Göbl 148)	pl. XXII.10 (Ventura collection)
	gold stater, Ardochsho (Göbl type 286)	pl. XXII.9 (Ventura collection)
	gold quarter stater, Oesho-Nana (Göbl type 167)	pl. XXII.7 (Ventura collection)
	gold quarter stater, Miro (Göbl type 371)	pl. XXII.8
	copper unit, throne/Mao	pl. XXI.9 (Ventura collection)
	copper unit, elephant-rider/Miuro	pl. XXI.10
	copper units, king on mountain (obverses only)	pl. XXI.14 (Smith collection) pl. XXI.11–13 (Stacy collection)
Vasudeva I	gold stater (Göbl type 509)	pl. XXII.5 (Ventura collection)
Vasishka	gold stater (Göbl type 622)	pl. XXII.4 (Ventura collection)
Kanishka III	gold staters (Göbl type 563)	pl. XXII.11–12 (Ventura collection)
Kipunadha	gold stater (Göbl type 596)	pl. XXII.14 (Ventura collection)
Kidarites, Kidara	gold stater (Göbl type 613)	pl. XXII.13 (Stacy collection)
Kushano-Sasanian	gold stater 'Peroz' (Göbl type 705)	pl. XXII.6

the coin sequence: Kujula Kadphises, Wima Kadphises, Kanishka I, Huvishka, although he had not yet identified them as individual kings, 'it would perhaps be better to place Kadphises as the last of the Pehlvi group, immediately *before* Kanerkos, and he will thus follow conveniently the *Kadaphes choranos* described in my last paper', i.e. Kujula Kadphises issues (Thomas 1858, vol. I, pp. 227–8).

The term 'Mithraic' was a reference to his previous analysis of the reverse designs of Kanishka and Huvishka coins. The varieties he described were *NANO* and *NANA* (identified as Anahita in his article of September 1834: Thomas 1858, vol. I, pp. 131–6), *MAO* and *NANAO* (which he had previously thought represented misspellings of Mithra and Nana, but now identified as a male moon deity, because of the crescent moon on the shoulders of one example), *MIΘPA*, *MITPO*, *MIOPO* and *MIPA* (already identified by him as Mithra), *AΘPO* (described as 'the igneous essence of the Sun': Thomas 1858, vol. I, p. 225), *OKPO* (equated with the Hindu sun god) and *OAΔO* (unexplained). He observed that 'the same devices in every respect are continued upon the several succeeding coins of the *rao nano rao* series' (Thomas 1858, vol. I, p. 226), i.e. the 'couch-lounger' (king on throne, with raised leg type) and 'elephant-rider' of Huvishka. On the coins of Huvishka, both in gold and in copper, he had found the name *OOHPKI*, but he could not be sure of the name on the copper coins as he also found *KOPANO* i.e. Kushan and *KENOPANO* which he did not recognise. To illustrate his analysis he showed drawings of the coins listed in table 10.

In a footnote Prinsep was also able to allude to the first recorded hoard of Kushan coins found in India. His friend

Alexander Cunningham was becoming a keen coin collector and had obtained a treasure of 163 Kushan coppers found in a village near Benares. It contained, according to Cunningham's identification, based on Prinsep's classification: Wima Kadphises (Kadphises and bull) 12; Kanishka I (Kanerki) 60; Huvishka elephant-rider 48, couch-lounger 13, cross-legged 5, squatting figure 8; Oado types of Kanishka I or Huvishka (running or dancing figure on reverse) 13; and illegible 4. He also illustrated a Kushan artefact from Ventura's collection, a bronze buckle depicting Huvishka riding an elephant, of a type which is now well known (Göbl 1987, p. 176, no. 20.1).

Prinsep's discussion does not indicate how he understood the relationship between the post-Huvishka coins and their predecessors, but he identified them as part of his '*rao nano rao*' series, with designs resembling those used by Kadphises and Kanerkos (Thomas 1858, vol. I, pp. 230–1). He also saw them, particularly the coins of Vasishka and Kanishka III, as prototypes for the coins of the Guptas, which he called the Kanauj series: 'hence we have the Indo-Scythic paternity of the Kanauj coinage proved by the best evidence' (Thomas 1858, vol. I, pl. XXII.4, 11–12).

The association Prinsep recognised between the Kushan and Gupta series, through this 'ocular demonstration of the intimate relation' (1835b; Thomas 1858, vol. I, p. 282) prompted him to speculate again about the identity of Kanishka. In Tod's *Annals and Antiquities of Rajast'han* (1829) Prinsep had looked for north-western Indo-Scythic origins for the Rajput dynasties and found a reference to a ruler Kenek-sen, founder of the Balhara dynasty, who 'according to the

Table 11
Masson's 1836 published list of Kushan coins

Kujula Kadphises	Heracles type in name of Hermaeus	Uncat. MSS 2, pl. 4, figs 33–5; 1836, pl. III.22–4
	Heracles type in name of Kujula	Uncat. MSS 2, pl. 4, figs 36–40; 1836, pl. III.25–9
	helmeted bust/soldier type	Uncat. MSS 2, pl. 3, fig 30; 1836, pl. III.19
Wima Kadphises	gold stater, bust/Oesho (Göbl type 14)	Uncat. MSS 2, pl. 5, fig. 1; 1836, pl. III.1; one of six similar staters from stupa at Guldara, near Kabul, also containing two Huvishka staters, see below
Kanishka I	gold stater, Nanashao (Göbl type 54)	Uncat. MSS 2, pl. 5, fig. 4; 1836, pl. III.4; acquired near Kabul
Huvishka	gold stater, Nana (Göbl type 300)	Uncat. MSS 2, pl. 5, fig. 2; 1836, pl. III.2; from Guldara stupa
	gold stater (Göbl type 138, Miiro)	Uncat. MSS 2, pl. 5, fig. 3; 1836, pl. III.3; from Guldara stupa
	gold stater, Pharro (Göbl type 206)	Uncat. MSS 2, pl. 5, fig. 5; 1836, pl. III.5; acquired near Kabul
	copper unit, king on mountain/Nana	Uncat. MSS 2, pl. 5, fig. 8
	copper unit, king on mountain/Mao or Miiro	Uncat. MSS 2, pl. 5, fig. 9
Kushano-Sasanian	Vasudeva imitation gold stater (Göbl type 691)	Uncat. MSS 2, pl. 5, fig. 6; acquired near Kabul
	Vasudeva imitation gold stater (Göbl types 666–85)	Uncat. MSS 2, pl. 5, fig. 7; acquired near Kabul

concurrent testimony of all the chronicles consulted by Tod, emigrated to Saurashtra about the year 144 A.D. "from the most northern province of India, Lokhot or Lahor" [Tod 1829, vol. I, p. 215]' and, according to Prinsep 'in date and locality this origin would well agree with Kanerki; nor would it even set aside the former supposition of the same prince being the Tartar Kanishka of Kashmir history' (1835b; Thomas 1858, vol. I, p. 284).

Although Prinsep left this suggestion hanging, in this and his preceding articles he had created a more real understanding of the 'Indo-Scythic' coinages by achieving a classification of the main Kushan types and by setting them in a context between the coins of the Azes and Kanauj series (except the coins of Wima Tak[to], which he included among the Azes series). He had also established the range of designs most commonly used. In spite of his earlier identification of Kanerkos as Kanishka, he still hesitated to accept his own insight and made only limited progress in understanding the precise historical meaning of the Kushan series beyond that outlined by Tod a decade before. Through the range of places from which their coins were being collected and their position in the coinage series he could now show that their issuers had a major role in the history of the northern part of the Subcontinent from Bactria to Bengal. He had also identified the 'Azos' group as a series of coins which also seemed to be 'Indo-Scythic', but which separated the main Indo-Scythic group, i.e. the Kushan coins of Wima Kadphises and his successors from the period of Greek rule. His work on Kharoshthi had not yet yielded significant results for understanding the Kushans. He had been able to read the royal titles on a few early Kushan coins, but had not progressed beyond that.

Although Prinsep continued to question his own discovery of the name of the Kashmir king Kanishka on a coin, now known to be an issue of Kanishka I, his suggestion was given credence by others, and in 1836 in an article in Prinsep's journal George Turnour included a reference to the important evidence of the 'coin of Kanishka' in the context of his discussion of Buddhist chronology (Turnour 1836).

More reports from Kabul

In January 1836 Prinsep published in his journal a second report from Charles Masson in Kabul on the coins he had collected in 1834, with an extensive account of his discoveries (Masson 1836). Prinsep published Masson's report in full except for the five sheets of illustrations, from which he reproduced only a selection of the pieces he thought were new (the original illustrations survive in the British Library, as part of Masson Uncat. MSS 2).

One of Masson's main preoccupations was trying to understand the role of the site of Begram in the Greek period, but he drew a conclusion about the end of Greek rule which questioned the authority of the Classical sources. He suggested that the large number of Greek coins he was finding in Begram indicated that 'a Greek authority must have existed to a much later period in the countries west of the Indus, which would appear to have been finally subverted by the Sakyan princes, who had established themselves in the regions east of the Indus' (Masson 1836, p. 19). By 'Sakyan princes' Masson appears to have been referring to the Kushans, confusing 'Sakyan' in the Buddhist sense with the Sacae, i.e. Scythians (see Masson 1834, p. 159).

Included in his new coin finds were many examples – classed by him as 'coins of the Nysaean Kings' – excavated from Buddhist stupas (which he thought were royal burial mounds) in the Jalalabad region (p. 221 below). By 'Nysaean kings', Masson meant the rulers who had their capital at the Greek city of Nysa, which he thought was located near Jalalabad. He identified two main groups of stupas by their association either with coins of Kujula Kadphises (whom he still named 'Hermaeus', from their obverse inscriptions) or of horseman type, including the Soter Megas coins of Wima Tak[to] (Masson 1836, p. 20). In other stupas at Kabul, Chaharbagh and Jalalabad, he also found coins of Wima Kadphises, Kanishka and Huvishka. As well as his own discoveries he was also well informed about the coins found by Martin Honigberger.

Along with the coins of Kujula Kadphises and Wima Tak[to], Masson reported finds at Begram of the horse-type

Heliocles imitation coins, now attributable to Wima Tak[to], but without having any suggestion as to how to identify them (1836, p. 20). The illustrated listing he sent to Prinsep provided details of the Kushan coins (table 11).

In May 1836 Masson dispatched a third memoir to Prinsep (Masson 1836a). He had drafted the main part of it by 31 December 1835 (according to the date on the manuscript) and attached to it a letter dated 12 February 1836. Prinsep published the introductory text of the memoir, together with Masson's summary list of his finds in 1833, 1834 and 1835, in the *Journal of the Asiatic Society of Bengal*, September 1836, but decided that the illustrations and associated list and commentary provided so little that was new that he did not publish them with the introduction but included a few of the coins in his own next article. Fortunately the manuscript and illustrations survive in the British Library (figs 27, 53, 55, 174; Masson Uncat. MSS 2) and from them it is clear that Masson was attempting to make an illustrated account of the whole coinage.

Masson listed all the types of Kushan coins he had so far seen, but, because the latest Prinsep article available to him was the one published in June 1835, the order did not reflect Prinsep's most recent results but was based on Masson's earlier analysis, with the issues of Kujula Kadphises and Wima Tak[to] listed under unknown Greek rulers. Masson's views were often highly imaginative, such as his belief that the Buddhist stupas were royal tombs and that the coins in them indicated the identity of the ruler for whom they were erected, with the number of coins indicating the age of the ruler at death. He did, however, have some insights which pushed forward the understanding of the coinage.

For the Heliocles imitation coinage he was able to deduce that the blundered legend at the base of the design was probably a corruption of the Greek ΔΙΚΑΙΟΥ (Uncat. MSS 2, f. 8). He noted that Kujula Kadphises coins had been found with Gondophares coins in a stupa excavated by Honigberger ('Janni tope', i.e. Bimaran stupa no. 5). He therefore dated them to the first century AD, on the basis of Prinsep's suggestion that the Gondophares coins from Masson's first memoir might be issues of the mid-first-century AD Parthian king of Taxila mentioned in the life of Apollonius of Tyana (1835; Thomas 1858, vol. I, p. 193). In his discussion of this idea (Uncat. MSS 2, ff. 11, 20), Masson pointed out the interrelationship between the coins of Kujula Kadphises, Wima Tak[to] and Wima Kadphises, on the basis of the shared style and content of their inscriptions. He suggested a context for these kings between AD 50 and AD 200, when he thought Kanishka reigned.

For the main Kushan series of coins Masson adopted Prinsep's 'Indo-Scythic or Mithraic' terminology and broke them down into seven series by type:
1   'Kadphises' (Wima Kadphises)
2   'Kanerkos and family' (Kanishka I and gold coins only of Huvishka)
3   Huvishka, king seated on mountain coppers
4   Huvishka, king on throne coppers
5   Huvishka, elephant rider coppers
6   Vasudeva and later Oesho and bull gold and coppers
7   Kanishka II and later seated Ardochsho coppers.

He remarked in classifying them that 'their connection with, and descent into, each other becomes evident' (Uncat. MSS 2, f. 22). His arrangement followed – with the exception of the gold coins of Huvishka – the chronological sequence being advocated by Prinsep, and comes close in most details to the sequence agreed by present-day scholars. As well as his classification of the coins, Masson also provided a commentary on Prinsep's published discussions. Masson was inclined, for example, to agree with Prinsep's attribution of the coins listed as 'Kanerkos' or 'Kanerki' to the king Kanishka named in the Kashmir Chronicle, even though Prinsep himself seemed to abandon it.

As well as providing clear examples of known provenance, often from excavated contexts, Masson also gave accurate drawings of the coin inscriptions in his memoir. Although there were few new types in his third memoir, Masson's three reports, when placed together, gave a detailed and accurate account of the Kushan coinage, based on an extensive examination drawn from a remarkably broad range of examples, of which the illustrated coins were a tiny sample. The summary list prepared by Masson, and included by Prinsep in his journal, showed that in three years Masson had seen at least 3270 Kushan coins (totals for Wima Kadphises onwards omit the total for the middle year 1834):

Kujula Kadphises	593
Wima Tak[to]	590
Wima Kadphises	99+
Kanishka I	139+
Huvishka	390+
Vasudeva I and successors	746+
Kanishka II and successors	274+
Kushano-Sasanian	439+

Masson's unpublished catalogue

The coins in table 12 were illustrated and listed in Masson's third memoir (1836a; Uncat. MSS 2). The seven examples later illustrated by Prinsep (1836) are indicated by the reference to Thomas (1858, vol. I).

In spite of Prinsep's decision not to make Masson's illustrations and descriptions available to the public, he kept them before him and referred to them in articles during September and October 1836. In the September 1836 article (Thomas 1858, vol. I, pp. 352–9, pl. XXVIII) he looked at new 'Greek' coins, including Kushan coins of Kujula Kadphises and Wima Tak[to]. He illustrated from Masson's manuscript examples of Kujula Kadphises' Heracles reverse Hermaeus imitations, with the name of Hermaeus and Kujula's own name, providing 'more perfect' specimens and offering corroboration of his own earlier readings, particularly ΚΟΖΟΥΛΟ ΚΑΔΦΙΣΕΣ ΧΟΡΑΝΟΥ (Thomas 1858, vol. I, pp. 357–8, pl. XXVIII.10, 12). Alongside he illustrated two examples of a rare type of Kujula Kadphises showing a Roman emperor's head on the obverse and a seated king on the reverse. One of these had been collected in Bengal (in the Mofussil) by an Indian civil servant, Mr Neave, the other came from Court's collection (Thomas 1858, vol. I, pl. XXVIII.14, 13), and together they provided the full name of the king ΚΟΖΟΛΑ ΚΑΔΑΦΕΣ ΧΟΡΑΝΟΥ matching the legend on Masson's Heracles type.

The same article also provided, from Court's collection, a clear example of the larger denomination Heliocles imitation with Zeus reverse from the early Kushan period, probably an issue of Wima Tak[to] (Thomas 1858, vol. I, pl. XXVIII.4). Prinsep compared it with the small example of the same type illustrated in Masson's manuscript, and passes on without due acknowledgement Masson's suggestion that the inscription may be a corrupt form of the Greek ΔΙΚΑΙΟΥ.

Prinsep's October 1836 article (1836a; Thomas 1858, vol. I, pp. 360–96) focused on the new Indo-Scythic or 'Mithraic' coins, with particular emphasis on his investigation of the transition from the Kushan to the Gupta series. His main interest in the main Kushan series seems to have been to highlight new examples, as he considered most of the classification work done, 'from the variety of Mithraic reverses already made known, it might have been imagined that the series was nearly exhausted', but his work continued as 'every year, however, adds a few new types', so he had to 'limit the admission even of golden novelties to those of one size, weight and value!' (Thomas 1858, vol. I, p. 360). From Masson he published two new gold staters of Kanishka and three of Huvishka, together with one more Kanishka (Thomas 1858, vol. I, pl. XXIX.9: Göbl type 77, Ardochsho) and two more Huvishkas from Court's collection (Thomas 1858, vol. I, pl.XXIX.6–7: no. 6, Göbl type 230, Athsho; no. 7 Göbl type 333, Oron). These all provided new reverses for the usual obverse types. Prinsep's explanations of the designs followed in the general line of his earlier articles, attempting to explain everything in terms of the Mithraic, and to identify the gods with solar entities. A real novelty, however, was a gold stater of Kanishka III from Cunningham's collection (Thomas 1858, vol. I, pl. XXIX.10, Göbl type 559). This late Kushan coin was recognised by Prinsep as a prototype for the early Gupta coinage, 'the very link of connection' (Thomas 1858, vol. I, p. 364), as in his article of December 1835 he had already recognised the link from a coin of Vasishka and two other Kanishka III coins (1835a; Thomas 1858, vol. I, pp. 195–200, 224–31).

Prinsep was also able to show how the coinage of Kashmir was derived from the 'Indo-Scythic'. Kashmir coins were included in the finds from Ventura's stupa at Manikyala and were therefore of importance to understanding the chronology of this monument. Although he managed, with the help of Cunningham, to assemble twenty coins of this series, he was unable to determine where they came from or begin the process of identifying them.

Alongside the Gupta and Kashmir series Prinsep sought to range a third group of derivatives of the coins of Vasishka and Kanishka III, which he suggested had 'a better claim to be considered the genuine descendant of the "Ardokro" [Ardochsho] coin in situ' (1836a; Thomas 1858, vol. I, p. 394). The coins in question were, in reality, the copper coins issued by the rulers Vasishka and Kanishka III, their immediate predecessor Kanishka II and their successor Vasudeva II. Prinsep illustrated three examples of Kanishka II or Vasishka's Ardochsho reverse coppers (Thomas 1858, vol. I, pl. XXXI.15–17), without indicating the collection from which they came, and reported Masson's comments on the series, viz. that they were 'very extensively found in Western Afghanistan' and that it was possible to distinguish between the early coins of Kanishka II and Vasishka 'generally found at Begram' and the later issues of Kanishka III 'prevalent on

the banks of the Indus and in the Panjab' (Thomas 1858, vol. I, p. 394). Prinsep also reported the discovery of coins of the same general type at Behat. Later in the month Prinsep corrected his misconception about these coins (1836b; Thomas 1858, vol. I, pp. 397–401). He was now able to identify them accurately as copper coins issued by the same rulers as the late Indo-Scythic gold coins – 'direct descendants of the Mithraic series in the Kanerkan line' – because he had found the inscription Ardochsho on a copper coins of Kanishka II in the Stacy collection (Thomas 1858, vol. I, p. 400, pl. XXII.14). In the same article of October 1836, Prinsep also published two new Huvishka coins collected by Stacy in the Punjab, both coppers of the elephant rider type, with Athsho and Ardochsho reverses (Thomas 1858, vol. I, pl. XXXII.12–13).

A final word from Prinsep

Prinsep continued to work on problems relating to Indian coins and inscriptions until he became too ill to work in October 1838. He then returned to England in hope of improvement of his health, but died without recovering in April 1840. He published only one more article mentioning Kushan coins in July 1838 (Thomas 1858, vol. II, pp. 125–44). The article was devoted primarily to his continuing work on deciphering Kharoshthi from coins. In addition to the resources already available he had been able to see a second collection of coins assembled by Ventura, as well as a few new coins belonging to Court and Allard. The coins collected by Burnes in Kabul were also shown to him. Ventura's collection included some gold Indo-Scythic coins, but these were stolen before Prinsep had a chance to record them other than to observe that there were no new types.

Prinsep did not illustrate any Kushan coins in the article, but from his revisions showed that he was now able to read with increasing accuracy the Kharoshthi inscriptions on the coins of Kujula Kadphises, Wima Tak[to] and Wima Kadphises. On coins of Kujula Kadphises he read the Kharoshthi version of his name Kujula Kasa . . . Kadaphasa, which he was able to match with the names written on the same coins in Greek letters 'Kosoula (also written Kozulo and Kozola), and Kadphizes (also written Kadaphes and Kadphises)'. From the Kharoshthi inscription he was also able to confirm that the Heracles-type coins retaining the name of Hermaeus were also Kujula Kadphises' issues. Although he struggled with the Kharoshthi inscriptions on Wima Kadphises copper coins, he was able to confirm from a gold example that the Kharoshthi 'vavahima Kadphisasa' supported his reading of the Greek version of this king's name as 'OOHMO KAΔΦΙΣΗΣ'. He hoped to extend this new success to the inscriptions found in association with Kushan coins, 'It remains only to apply my theory of the Bactrian alphabet to the inscriptions on the cylinders and stone slabs extracted from the topes at Manikyala, etc. but this is a task of much more serious difficulty, and one not to be done off-hand, as all the above has been! I must, therefore, postpone the attempt until I am better prepared with my lesson' (Thomas 1858, vol. II, p. 135).

Tragically his hope was not fulfilled, as ill-health overtook him. While completing the process of breaking the code of Kharoshthi, he started to suffer from the headaches and nausea which eventually led to his death.

Table 12
Coins listed in Masson's unpublished 1835–6 third memoir

Kujula Kadphises	Heracles type in name of Hermaeus	Uncat. MSS 2, pl. 5, figs 112–14, 122, 126, 128 (Figs 112–14 = 1858, pl. XXVIII.10: the reverses are united into a single image)
	Heracles type in name of Kujula	Uncat. MSS 2, pl. 5, figs 115–21, 123–5, 127, 129, 130, 131. Fig 116 = 1858, pl. XXVIII.12
	Su-Hermaeus/Zeus type	Uncat. MSS 2, pl. 3, figs 62–5
	helmeted bust/soldier type	Uncat. MSS 2, pl. 7, figs 144–6
	Heraus type silver obol	Uncat. MSS 2, pl. 7, fig. 147
Wima Tak[to]	Heliocles imitation/horse unit	Uncat. MSS 2, pl. 4, fig. 67
	Heliocles imitation/horse quarter	Uncat. MSS 2, pl. 4, figs 68–74
	Heliocles imitation/Zeus quarter	Uncat. MSS 2, pl. 4, fig. 75
	helmeted bust type	Uncat. MSS 2, pl. 5, fig. 99
	bilingual unit	Uncat. MSS 2, pl. 5, fig. 104
	bilingual quarter	Uncat. MSS 2, pl. 5, figs 107, 109
	uninscribed Oesho/Ardochsho	Uncat. MSS 2, pl. 5, fig. 110
	standard issue unit	Uncat. MSS 2, pl. 5, figs 100–1, 103
	standard issue quarter	Uncat. MSS 2, pl. 5, fig. 102
Wima Kadphises	gold stater (Gobl type 19)	Uncat. MSS 2, pl. 8, fig. 1
	gold stater (Göbl type 14)	Uncat. MSS 2, pl. 8, fig. 2; same coin as listed in Masson 1836
	silver pattern (Göbl type 4)	Uncat. MSS 2, pl. 8, fig. 3
	copper unit	Uncat. MSS 2, pl. 8, fig. 4
	copper half	Uncat. MSS 2, pl. 8, fig. 5
	copper quarter	Uncat. MSS 2, pl. 8, fig. 6
Kanishka I	gold stater, Nanashao (Göbl type 54)	Uncat. MSS 2, pl. 8, fig. 9; same coin as listed in Masson 1836 = 1858, pl. XXIX.4
	gold stater, Mao (Göbl type 76)	Uncat. MSS 2, pl. 8, fig. 10
	gold stater, Orlagno (Göbl type 63)	Uncat. MSS 2, pl. 8, fig. 11 = 1858, pl. XXIX.1
	large copper unit (Mao)	Uncat. MSS 2, pl. 8, fig. 17
	large copper unit (Mioro)	Uncat. MSS 2, pl. 8, fig. 19
	large copper unit (Athsho)	Uncat. MSS 2, pl. 9, fig. 21
	large copper unit (Oado)	Uncat. MSS 2, pl. 9, fig. 23
	large copper unit (Oesho)	Uncat. MSS 2, pl. 9, fig. 25
	large copper unit (Nana)	Uncat. MSS 2, pl. 9, fig. 27
	middle copper half (Helios)	Uncat. MSS 2, pl. 8, fig. 14
	middle copper half (Nanaia)	Uncat. MSS 2, pl. 8, fig. 15
	middle copper half (Sakamano Boudo)	Uncat. MSS 2, pl. 8, fig. 16
	middle copper half (Mao)	Uncat. MSS 2, pl. 8, fig. 18
	middle copper unit (Mioro)	Uncat. MSS 2, pl. 8, fig. 20
	middle copper unit (Athsho)	Uncat. MSS 2, pl. 9, fig. 22
	middle copper unit (Oado)	Uncat. MSS 2, pl. 9, fig. 24
	middle copper unit (Oesho)	Uncat. MSS 2, pl. 9, fig. 26
	small copper quarter (Miiro)	Uncat. MSS 2, pl. 9, fig. 29
	small copper quarter (Oesho)	Uncat. MSS 2, pl. 9, fig. 30
	small copper quarter (Nana)	Uncat. MSS 2, pl. 9, figs 28, 31
Huvishka	gold stater, Nana (Göbl type 300)	Uncat. MSS 2, pl. 8, fig. 7; same coin as listed in Masson 1836 = 1858, pl. XXIX.5
	gold stater, Miiro (Göbl type 138)	Uncat. MSS 2, pl. 8, fig. 8; same coin as listed in Masson 1836 = 1858, pl. XXIX.3
	gold stater, Pharro (Göbl type 206)	Uncat. MSS 2, pl. 8, fig. 12; same coin as listed in Masson 1836 = 1858, pl. XXIX.2
	copper unit (elephant rider/Miiro)	Uncat. MSS 2, pl. 10, figs 45, 50
	copper unit (elephant rider/Athsho)	Uncat. MSS 2, pl. 10, fig. 47
	copper unit (elephant rider/Oesho, with four arms)	Uncat. MSS 2, pl. 10, fig. 46
	copper unit (elephant rider/Oesho, with two arms)	Uncat. MSS 2, pl. 10, figs 48–9
	copper unit (king on throne/Miiro)	Uncat. MSS 2, pl. 9, fig. 41
	copper unit (king on throne/Mao)	Uncat. MSS 2, pl. 9, fig. 39
	copper unit (king on throne/Athsho)	Uncat. MSS 2, pl. 9, fig. 40

	copper unit (king on mountain/Miiro)	Uncat. MSS 2, pl. 9, figs 33, 37
	copper unit (king on mountain/Mao)	Uncat. MSS 2, pl. 9, figs 34–5, 38
	copper unit (king on mountain/Nana)	Uncat. MSS 2, pl. 9, fig. 32; same coin as listed in second memoir
Vasudeva I	gold stater (Göbl type 509)	Uncat. MSS 2, pl. 10, figs 51–2
	copper unit	Uncat. MSS 2, pl. 10, figs 54–8
Kanishka II	copper unit	Uncat. MSS 2, pl. 10, figs 61–3
Kanishka III	copper unit	Uncat. MSS 2, pl. 10, figs 64–5, 67
Late Kushan	Oesho and bull type	Uncat. MSS 2, pl. 10, figs 59–60
	Ardochsho type	Uncat. MSS 2, pl. 10, fig. 66
Kushano-Sasanian	Vasudeva imitation gold stater (Göbl types 680–1)	Uncat. MSS 2, pl. 5, figs 6–7
	copper unit, Pirozo Shaho (Göbl type 1123)	Uncat MSS 2, pl. 11, figs 8–11
	copper unit, Kabod lion crown (Göbl type 1124)	Uncat. MSS 2, pl. 11, figs 1–7
	copper unit, Meze bull-horn crown (Göbl type 1127)	Uncat. MSS 2, pl. 11, figs 15–16
	copper unit, Shapur II (Göbl type 1121)	Uncat. MSS 2, pl. 11, figs 12–13
	copper unit, Shapur II (Göbl type 1120)	Uncat. MSS 2, pl. 11, fig. 14

Henry Thoby Prinsep later found among his brother James's papers an attempt at the Kharoshthi inscription from Court's Manikyala stupa, based on his revisions of the decipherment published in 1838, which showed that he had already deciphered the ruler's name in the inscription as Maharaja Kanishka (fig. 178; Prinsep 1844, p. 124). At the point when ill-health forcibly stopped his research, just short of adding the dynastic identity Kushan to Kanishka's name, James Prinsep was about to crown his achievements of an almost complete classification of the main Kushan coin types with the confirmation of his original identification of Kanishka I as the Buddhist patron who had ruled in Kashmir.

Meanwhile in Europe

As Prinsep – with help from Masson and others – made his amazing progress with the classification and attribution of Kushan coins, together with an understanding of their archaeological and geographical context, the material they were investigating became more widely known in Europe and became the subject of study and debate among scholars in France, Germany and Britain.

The French scholar Raoul Rochette, in the *Journal des Savants*, reviewed Schlegel's discussion of Tod's coins in August 1834, comparing them with Ventura's finds from Manikyala, and reported the discovery of a gold double stater of Wima Kadphises (Rochette 1834, fig. VII) near Delhi by the French military commander General Peyron (Perron) (Göbl 1984, type 11). He compared the new coin with Tod's copper coins of Wima Kadphises, reading *Mokypsises* and linked it with Schlegel's *Edobirgis* reading. A better reading had already been made by Prinsep, so his efforts were wasted, but he did see a connection between the coins being found and the gold coin of Huvishka published by Pellerin (he reproduced the original engraving, Rochette 1834, fig. X), which he particularly compared with Ventura's gold coin of the same king. His most original observation was to remark on their relationship with Roman coins, suggesting that Pellerin's coin 'must be a coin struck in this Indo-Scythic state in imitation of the Roman coins of the final period of the Republic or the commencement of the Empire, which trade had brought into Bactria and India' (Rochette 1834, p. 27). He was also able to make a correction to Prinsep's view on the

identity of the god on the back of the new Wima Kadphises coin, identifying it with the Hindu god Shiva, by recognising his usual trident attribute, as opposed to the identification as the Hindu sun god Surya proposed by Prinsep.

Alongside Burnes's publication of his coins (see above), 1834 also saw reports of Honigberger's coins appearing in the press in Russia, Germany and France, as he made his way home and showed his coins to all comers. They soon began to provoke serious scholarly interest, and in November 1835 Rochette began to discuss Honigberger's newly arrived coins and illustrated a few Kushan examples: another gold stater of Wima Kadphises (Rochette 1835, pl. II, fig. 22, Göbl type 19) and copper coins of Wima Tak[to] (figs 17–18, regular type unit and quarter; fig. 19, helmeted bust type), Wima Kadphises (fig. 23, unit) and Kanishka I (fig. 24, middle size with Nanaia reverse).

The gold coin of Wima Kadphises had first been brought to Rochette's attention in a letter from C. L. Grotefend in Hanover, Germany, and in a newspaper article from St Petersburg, Russia. It enabled him to improve on his previous reading of the king's name, but still left him insisting on omitting its initial syllable, Mokadphises (1835, pp. 2, 28).

Grotefend was also putting into print an account of the new discoveries. His first article in the *Blätter für Münzkunde* (Hanover) appeared in September 1834 and reported Rochette's findings of the previous month. His next appeared in October (Grotefend 1834a) and pre-empted Rochette's revised reading of the gold coin of Wima Kadphises together with an account of the new discoveries in India based on Prinsep's reports in the *Journal of the Asiatic Society*. A third article by Grotefend appeared in April the following year (1835a). A more extended account of the same information appeared in November 1835 in another German learned journal, the *Göttingische Gelehrte Anzeigen*, from the pen of K. O. Müller, whose account was based on Prinsep's articles of July, September and November 1834. Müller reported the discoveries of Prinsep, Tod, Ventura, Court, Honigberger, Gerard, Karamat 'Ali and Masson, as well as debating the opinions presented by Rochette and Grotefend. On the basis of his knowledge of the separate cults of Nana and Anahita among the ancient Armenians he argued against Prinsep's identification of Nana on Kushan coins as a representation of

Anahita (1835, pp. 1777–8). Müller's comment on Nana and Anahita were reported in a short note in the *Journal of the Asiatic Society of Bengal* (Avdall 1836).

Little to add

Rochette (1834, p. 24; 1835, p. 25) attempted to re-evaluate the evidence assembled by Prinsep, but his observations on the Wima Tak[to] coins pointing to the similarity of the royal symbol on them to that on the coins of Wima Kadphises and Kanishka I, 'the trident and cross on ring symbol, which is reproduced on all the Indo-Scythic coins already known to us, shows that these coins are truly of the same family', contributed little, as he was simply echoing the same point made two years before by both Saint-Martin (1832) and Wilson (1832). He agreed with Prinsep that the issuer or issuers were among the first Indo-Scythic rulers to conquer the Greeks, and suggested that the coins might be issues of the king Azes whose name had been found on several related coins (1835, p. 24). Honigberger's helmeted bust type Soter Megas coin was previously unknown to Rochette and he attributed it to Bactria on the basis of its similarity to the helmeted bust coins of the Greek king Eucratides (1835, pp. 26–7).

Rochette also identified the issuers of the Wima Kadphises and Kanishka I coins which he illustrated as early Indo-Scythic rulers reigning soon after the defeat of the Greeks in Bactria. He pointed to Schlegel's misreading of Wima Kadphises' name as Edobirgis, but from the copper continued to confirm his reading of the gold coin as naming Mokadphises. He discussed Prinsep's attribution of the coins of Kanishka I to the Kanishka named in the Kashmir chronicle, dismissing it as a conjecture (Rochette 1835, p. 32). His own conclusion returned to the hypothesis of Tod that the Indo-Scythic kings succeeded to Greek rule from the late second century BC (1835, p. 34).

In June 1836 Rochette expanded on his previous analysis on the basis of new material arriving in France in the form of Ventura's collection, brought by his colleague Allard. He was also able to take account of the material collected by Honigberger and Masson, of which he had had time to take further account. Most of his discussion related the Greek coins from Afghanistan, but he paid close attention also to the issues of Kujula Kadphises with the name of Hermaeus and of Wima Tak[to] on the basis of Masson's and Ventura's finds. His analysis adds little to an understanding of the issuers of these coins, but consists of questioning Masson's and Prinsep's theories and proposing his own. The various coins in the name of Hermaeus were, in his opinion, unlikely to have been issued by more than one king (Masson proposed three), but he agreed that their issuer ruled in the city of Nysa, near Jalalabad (Rochette 1836, p. 37).

He agreed with Masson in placing the Soter Megas coins of Wima Tak[to] close in time to the Hermaeus type coins of Kujula Kadphises, but thought that they could not be the issues of a single king. He therefore suggested that they were the issues of a group of allied, but independent, neighbouring states, who had made an agreement to issue anonymous coins (Rochette 1836, p. 38). He compared the Soter Megas coins with the issues of Azes which he placed between the Greeks and Wima Kadphises, but observed again that the

Soter Megas was unlike the Azes coins in that it shared the symbol with the coins of Wima Kadphises and his successors (1836, p. 48). Grotefend had also corresponded with him on the same point.

Rochette's three articles have little to contribute to the classification or identification of Kushan coins, apart from his recognition of the Roman connections of Kushan gold coins, and often his comments seem to have stem from his hostility to his fellow scholars: 'I won't occupy myself with discussing the conjectures furnished by the English scholars Wilson and Prinsep. . . . It wouldn't occur to me to get mixed up in a discussion beyond the context of my studies' (Rochette 1835, p. 32). Unwilling to discuss issues of significance, his aim seems to be to protect and promote his own academic standing. His self-regard is clear when he once again returned forcefully to the reading of the name on the coins of Wima Kadphises, clinging desperately to the version Mokadphises and rejecting outright Prinsep's correct suggestion Ooemo Kadphises (Rochette 1836, p. 56):

> The reading $ΚΑΔΦΙΣΕΣ$, adopted by all the English travellers and scholars, for want of a sufficient examination of the detail of this inscription, can no longer be sustained in the light of so many of these coins having simultaneously appeared in various parts of India. The effort, which has been made by Mr Prinsep to take account of the letters $OOKMO$ or $OOHMO$, has been completely wasted; and his conjecture, that this pretend word ookmo or oohemos is an appendage of the name of the prince, finds itself completely undone. The manner in which the letters OOK, which follow the word $ΒΑΣΙΛΕΥΣ$, are separated from the letters MO which are joined to $ΚΑΔΦΙΣΕΣ$ on both the gold coins I have published . . . would have undone this error of the Calcutta scholar, if he had known or studied these two coins himself; and I am surprised that an antiquary as skilled as Mr K. O. Müller, who is familiar with at least the first of these coins, should have fallen into the same error.

His rigid approach to the subject also found him agreeing with Prinsep and Müller in misinterpreting the inscriptions on the gold coins of Huvishka as a reference to Kanishka (Rochette 1836, p. 57). Even when he presents new examples of Wima Kadphises and Huvishka gold coins from the collections of Honigberger and Ventura in support of his arguments he fails to illustrate them.

Rochette's colleague Jacquet had little to add to the information already available in his articles on the collections of Ventura (delivered to Paris by Allard, and often referred to as Allard's collection) and of Honigberger (Jacquet 1836–9). His posthumously published essay on Indo-Scythic coins (Jacquet 1840) is 48 pages of rhetoric which does not address a single point of interest to this study.

The German scholars Müller and Grotefend continued to contribute to the developing debate. Müller (1838–9) published an extended series of articles presenting and reviewing the new discoveries of Prinsep and the discussion by Rochette. Müller was able to refine Prinsep's 'Mithraic' attribution of gods on Kanishka I and Huvishka's coins, by pointing to the similarity of the pantheon on their coins and the divine entities of the Zoroastrian religion (1838, vols 22–3, p. 233). Grotefend's attempt at deciphering the Kharoshthi inscriptions on Indo-Greek and Kushan coins appeared in May 1836 and had some advantages over that proposed by Prinsep in his article of June 1835. In 1839 he published a longer study, re-examining all the coins being discovered in Afghanistan and north-western India. It was largely focused on the Greek issues, cataloguing them on the basis of the coins published by Prinsep, Masson and others. His listing places Kujula Kadphises' Heracles types in the name of Hermaeus and Wima Tak[to]'s Heliocles imitations among the Indo-Greek coins ('*Reges Transcaucasiorum et Indorum Graeci*'). Grotefend (1839, p. 746) picked up Rochette's suggestion that the Heliocles imitation types were copied from the silver issues of the Bactrian king Heliocles. Kujula Kadphises' Heracles types in his own name and Wima Tak[to]'s Soter Megas issues were included with the coins of Azes in a category entitled: '*Reges Transcaucasiorum et Indorum barbari*' (Barbarian kings of the peoples of the Transcaucasus and India). The coins of the Kushans from Wima Kadphises were listed under the heading '*Reges Indoscythae*', i.e Indo-Scythic Kings, in the following order: Cadphises II (Wima Kadphises), Canercu (Kanishka I), Ooerki (Huvishka), Incerti (unidentified, including issues of Vasudeva I, Kanishka II and Vasishka, but also illegible coins of Kanishka I and Huvishka). Only a handful of these coins were illustrated, but full references were made to his sources.

His listing was not a profoundly original piece of work, because he was able to take advantage of a very similar list compiled by the French numismatist Mionnet, adding only cross-references to Prinsep's and Masson's publications. As part of his attempt to create a catalogue of all known Greek and Roman coin types, Mionnet had included in his eighth supplementary volume (1837, pp. 460–506) a listing of the Greek and Indo-Scythic coins: Pellerin's gold coin of Huvishka had been listed under uncertain in volume six (Mionnet 1813, p. 715), based on the collections of Honigberger and Ventura (Allard), and the publications of Rochette and Jacquet, but without any commentary. Following Rochette's erroneous understanding he lists the coins of Wima Kadphises under the heading 'Mokadphises' and both Kanishka I and Huvishka coins under 'Kanerkes'.

Grotefend's discussions were largely related to the presentation and analysis of the Greek coinages, but he reviewed the Kharoshthi inscriptions of Kujula, Wima Tak[to] and Wima Kadphises (1839, pp. 90–1), on the basis of the latest findings of another German scholar, Christian Lassen (1838). The latest articles by Müller also reviewed Lassen's new research.

Lassen's progress
Lassen's research was published in book form in 1838 and represented a carefully structured review of the decipherment of Kharoshthi, advancing from the views of Prinsep and Grotefend, published in 1835 and 1836 respectively, together with a detailed study of the linguistic and historical evidence of Greek and Indo-Scythic coins. His results closely paralleled the revised decipherment published by Prinsep in July of the same year (Thomas 1858, vol. II, pp. 125–44, pp. 271–6). Lassen had not yet seen Prinsep's new decipherment when preparing his book, and Prinsep seems to have been unaware of the work by Grotefend and Lassen, but he reached similar conclusions, except he corrected his misunderstanding, as an '*o*', of the value of the Kharoshthi letter '*sa*', whereas Lassen retained Prinsep's original mistake. His ill-health did not allow him to extend his discovery in the

way that Lassen was able to in his new book. After Prinsep had left Calcutta, a letter arrived from Lassen congratulating him on the excellence of his new decipherment article, acknowledging that Prinsep had solved several problems of transcription which had defied Lassen. Prinsep's brother published it as footnote in the translated version of Lassen's book (Lassen 1840, p. 44).

Like Prinsep (Thomas 1858, vol. II, pp. 134–5), Lassen attempted to decipher the legends on the coins of Kujula Kadphises and Wima Kadphises (1840, pp. 53–60). Both found evidence of Kujula's name in the Kharoshthi legends on his coins, but the name Wima Kadphises still posed a problem. Lassen suggested reading it *dima kaphisa*, while Prinsep found two different versions *dhi makadphishasa* and *vavahima kadphisasa*. Their main concern seemed to be to establish the correct Greek name Mokadphises or Ooemo Kadphises, but nothing conclusive emerged. Lassen speculated on the etymology of the words Korano(u) (i.e. Koshanou) and Zathou (i.e. Zaoou) on the coins of Kujula, but to no avail, except to recognise that they were neither Greek nor Indian.

Lassen recognises Huvishka and the Kushans' Iranian links
Lassen also re-examined the regal inscriptions on Kanishka I and Huvishka's coins (1840, pp. 63–6) in light of his knowledge of Indian languages. His observations were misplaced because he was mistaken about the language in which they were written, but he was able on the basis of his analysis to come to a useful observation on the identity of Huvishka. He re-examined Prinsep's identification of Kanishka I with the king named Kanishka in the *Rājataraṅgiṇī*, the Kashmir Chronicle, and in Buddhist texts. He found no problem in believing that the Kanerki on the coins represented the Sanskrit Kanishka and went on the re-examine Huvishka's coin inscription in the same light, 'I would not scruple at the *r*, as supplied by the *sh*, and if the comparison of them was well founded, I would even proceed a step further, and find in OHPKI the same *Hushka*, who is mentioned with *Kanishka*' (1840, p. 65). He hesitated to accept the insight he had gained and, apart from the chronological problems involved in this attribution, cited their coin designs as contrary evidence: 'another reason from the coins themselves is opposed to our recognising *Hushka* and *Kanishka* in OHPKI and KANHPKI. Both of them are described as Buddhist; upon the coins of these latter, however, a worship, evidently deviating from that of the Buddhists, is distinctly obvious'.

In the light of the identification by Müller (1838) of Zoroastrian elements in Kushan coin design, Lassen re-examined the reverse inscriptions. Once again he focused on his knowledge of Indian languages and saw many parallels with Sanskrit in the divine names on the coins, but was also able to identify some which had Iranian rather than Indian origins. In his opinion these exceptional names 'point out a dialect' (Lassen 1840, p. 70) and he saw Iranian affinities in both this 'dialect' and the worship exhibited on the coins.

Lassen's and Prinsep's identification of Kanishka
Although Prinsep had recognised Kanishka from his acquaintance with Buddhist references to him as a patron of

Buddhism, there was little other evidence available to him of the Buddhist traditions relating to Kanishka. Lassen was able to take advantage of the recent translation and commentary by Rémusat (1836) on the accounts left by Buddhist monks who travelled from China to India in the fourth to seventh centuries. Rémusat provided the accounts of the Chinese monks who travelled through the area where Kushan coins are found and reported seeing the Great Stupa of Kanishka at Peshawar. Lassen remarked on the existence of a large stupa seen at Peshawar, 'but this can hardly be the tower of the king Kanishka' (Lassen 1840, p. 97). He does not discuss this evidence in the context of the coins attributed by Prinsep to Kanishka.

The connections with Buddhism were still, however, difficult to recognise and, although Kanishka and Huvishka's coins were known to be associated with stupas, there was still lacking a general appreciation that these mounds were Buddhist: 'lastly, the opinion, that the Kanerkis were Buddhists, or in other words, that we have to recognise Kanishka in Kanerki, must continue to be improbable, until Kanerki be also discovered on Buddhistic monuments' (Lassen 1840, pp. 125–6). This comment is surprising as Wilson (1832) in his first article, publishing Kushan coins from the Manikyala stupa, was able to report that the Manikyala stupa had already been recognised as a Buddhist 'Dagope' (i.e. stupa) by a Mr Erskine in Bombay on the basis of the description of it made by Elphinstone following his mission to Kabul in 1808. Wilson (1834) had himself also been sceptical about Prinsep's identification of Kanerki as Kanishka.

Lassen and the ancient sources

The identity of the various rulers who issued 'Indo-Scythic' coins was Lassen's next topic. In analysing the Classical accounts of the end of Greek rule in Bactria, he sought to distinguish the Parthian and Scythian role in conquering Bactria. He interpreted the sources as indicating that the Parthians overthrew the Greek rule in 139 BC and the Scythians then captured Bactria about 126 BC. He then examined the Chinese sources, as reported by de Guignes (1756), and sought to equate the Tocharians and Shakas of the Greek and Roman sources with the Yuetchis (Da Yuezhi) and Sai in the Chinese sources. From de Guignes's account, he traced the movement of the Yuetchis into Bactria (Lassen 1840, pp. 164–6) and their unification under Khieou-tsiouhi (i.e. Kujula) and their capture of Kaofu (Kabul), followed by their defeat of the Parthians and the Sai and their conquest of India under Khieou-tsiouhi's son Yenkaotching (Wima Tak[to]). He also observed that in AD 98 the Yuetchis were fighting the Chinese in Khotan. Lassen reported the various dates proposed for the accession of Khieou-tsiouhi proposed by de Guigne and Rémusat, ranging from 26 BC into the first century AD (1840, pp. 167–9). In spite of being able to reconstruct this sequence of events from the historical sources, Lassen was unsure how it fitted the numismatic evidence: 'it is uncertain, whether we still have the coins belonging to the Yuetchis, whose dominion was only in the north. We could only be inclined to assign to them those having on the reverse a horse, and not Cabulian legends', i.e. Wima Tak[to]'s imitation Heliocles coins (Lassen 1840, p. 170). He was, however, willing to suggest that the 'coins

with elephants' might have 'belonged to the earlier period of the Yuetchis', but it is unclear whether he was referring to coins of Azes or of Huvishka.

Lassen recognises, but fails to name the Kushans

In his conclusions Lassen made some bold connections between the coins and the history he outlined. The picture he created is remarkably close to our understanding today. He identified 'Kadphises or the nameless Soter-Megas . . . as the great conqueror under the Yuetchis' and realised that 'the monogram of the nameless king . . . recurs as well on the coins of Kadphises as on those described above; it occurs last on those of the Kanerkis . . . it seems therefore to be the monogram of the Yuetchis' (1840, pp. 179–80). He also recognised that the Kushans are mentioned in the *Periplus*: 'the author of the Periplus mentions . . . an independent kingdom of the very warlike Bactrians; the Yuetchis alone can be understood by this'. His chronology for the Kushan kings Kanishka I and Huvishka – the 'Kanerkis' – is equally close to today's views, placing them at 'the commencement of the the second century', but he suggested that they were a distinct group separated in time from the earlier 'Kadphises' rulers.

In spite of these achievements Lassen closed his discussion with an expression of regret and hesitation. From the Chinese Buddhist sources he had evidence that the Da Yuezhi were Buddhists, but he failed to see the connection between this and the coins he now attributed to them found by Ventura, Court, Masson and Honigberger in Buddhist monuments. He still hoped for the clinching evidence of such coins being found in a Buddhist context (Lassen 1840, p. 183):

> hence rises the question, whether there still exist with the Yuetchis monuments of this religion. . . . There is accordingly no want of Buddhist monuments, but it is the question whether we want to attribute them to the Yuetchis . . . of Azes, Kadphises, the Kanerkis, no really Buddhist coin has been discovered.

His conclusions were followed by a chronological table which confirms his confusion about what he had achieved, dating Kadaphes (Kujula Kadphises) about 120 BC; Khieou-tsiouhi (also Kujula Kadphises) in 40 BC and his son Yenkaotching in 20 BC; Kadphises (Wima Kadphises) followed by the Kanerkis (Kanishka I and Huvishka) about AD 100 (1840, p. 185).

Wilson returns

In 1841 Horace Wilson, whose publication of 1832 was the first to illustrate a broad range of Kushan coins, produced a new study, *Ariana Antiqua*, of the antiquities of ancient Afghanistan, based on the discoveries of Charles Masson. The 1833–6 Masson collections had by that date been placed in the East India Company's Museum in London and Wilson offered his services to present them to a wider audience.

Since 1832 Wilson had added his comments to those of Prinsep on the coins collected by Burnes (1834, see above) and had published a brief note on coins in the Royal Asiatic Society, featuring a standard issue Soter Megas coin of Wima Tak[to] (1836). He also gave a paper at a meeting of London's new Numismatic Society on 1 December 1837, an account of which was published in its new journal (Wilson 1837). The paper was a review of the research which had been published by Prinsep, Masson and Rochette. In the following year's

Proceedings of the Numismatic Society a detailed account of the paper was also published (Wilson 1838), with attached tables outlining in summary form the chronology proposed by Wilson, dating Wima Kadphises and Kanishka I in the first century AD.

The new study – *Ariana Antiqua* – was a far more substantial one and gave Wilson the opportunity to work through all the results of recent scholarship and at the same time examine what was certainly the most extensive collection of coins from Afghanistan. He was also, for the first time, able to apply to his presentation the further work on deciphering Kharoshthi, because neither Prinsep, through ill-health, nor Lassen, through his general lack of interest in the minutiae of coin designs, had given detailed coin descriptions incorporating their discoveries.

In examining the post-Greek coinages of the region, Wilson followed the path already trodden by Lassen and integrated the Classical and the Chinese sources in his analysis of the arrival of the Yuchi (Da Yuezhi) in Bactria and subsequently the Kabul region (Wilson 1841, pp. 300–7). His only original contribution was to raise the possibility that the various forms of the name of Kujula on his Heracles types might represent 'the monarch of the Yu-chi [Da Yuezhi] whose name the Chinese endeavoured to express, at least as it come to us through the French translation, by Kiu-tsiu-kio' (1841, p. 308). However, because Lassen's analysis had placed the Shakas in the Kabul region before the Da Yuezhi, Wilson hesitated to believe his own insight and was willing to attribute the Heracles-type coins to the Shakas, and so contemplated the possibility that 'the conjecture that these coins bear the name of the Yu-Chi prince, Kiu-tsiu-kio, would fall to the ground' (1841, p. 309). The same view of the sequence of events in the Kabul region prompted him to attribute the Heliocles imitation horse-type coins of Wima Tak[to] to the Shakas.

The remaining coins of Wima Tak[to] were labelled by Wilson as 'coins of the Great King of Kings, the Preserved' (1841, pp. 332–40) and listed among the coins of the Indo-Scythian kings Azes and Azilises. Wilson summarised the information which had accumulated over the previous decade and a half. He dismissed Rochette's suggestion that they were the issues of a confederacy. He also rejected Lassen's identification of them with the Indo-Scythic (i.e. Kushan) kings, as they were found 'extensively in India' and he thought the Scythians had not advanced so far. He thought the design showed Indian features, 'and there is especially one decoration which is decidedly Indian, the use of large ear-rings', so he preferred to see them as issues of an Indian prince: 'the features of the face are also Indian' (Wilson 1841, p. 334). He dated them between Azes and Kadphises (i.e. Wima Kadphises), 'in the first century of the Christian era' (1841, p. 335). He referred to the three-pronged symbol as a prominent feature of the coinage, but made no allusion to the repeated observation of other scholars that this symbol linked the Soter Megas coins with those of Wima Kadphises and his successors.

Wilson on Wima Kadphises, Kanishka I and Huvishka

Wilson's discussion of the main Kushan coin types is prefaced by the observation that they 'may be thought to indicate a material change in the political state of the country, the re-establishment of a season of tranquillity, and an advance in national wealth' (1841, p. 347), because he had realised that the gold–copper coinage of the Kushans represented a substantial shift from the silver based coinage of the Greeks and the debased-silver coinage of the Azes rulers. It also represented a much wider geographical distribution than the earlier coinages: 'the copper coins of Kadphises and Kanerkes are found in considerable quantity in the hands of money-changers of most of the large towns of Hindustan' (Wilson 1841, p. 349).

Identifying Wima Kadphises as the first of the kings of this new regime, dating him to the late first century AD, Wilson described him as of 'Turkish' appearance, and 'his costume is precisely that which prevails to the north of the Hindu Kush to the present day, and to a great extent amongst the Afghans' (1841, pp. 353, 349). He correctly identified the image on the reverse as showing the common attributes of the Hindu god Shiva, and observed that the king is represented in an act of worship involving the same god. In his listing of the coins he hesitated between the various interpretations of the first part of the king's name, although he implied agreement with Prinsep by not using the name Mokadphises as advocated by Rochette. He also included among the coins of Wima Kadphises both the issues of Vasudeva I and his successors using king sacrificing/Oesho with bull designs, and those of Kujula Kadphises which feature his name in Greek.

The place of Kanishka I as the successor of Wima Kadphises was confirmed, for Wilson, by the circulation of their coins together, as well as by their common design features, and he dated him to the first half of the second century (1841, p. 364).

Wilson outlined the findings of Prinsep and Müller concerning deities depicted in the reverse designs of Kanishka I, together with Lassen's observations on the linguistic features of their names. He conceded that Prinsep's identification of the Shiva-like image, labelled Oesho, as a version of Surya the Hindu solar deity, was contradicted by the Shiva attributes of the depiction, but also questioned Müller's interpretation of the inscription as a version of Ugra, one of the Sanskrit names of Shiva. Wilson, referring to Lassen, argued that an Iranian origin should be sought for the name Oesho, in line with the Iranian origins of the names of the other deities appearing on Kanishka I's coins (Wilson 1841, pp. 359–62). Following Lassen he accepted the Zoroastrian nature of the majority of the deities featured on Kanishka I's coins.

Among the coins he listed Wilson also included and recognised three coins of Kanishka I with Buddhist images, from Masson's collection, but failed to notice their significance. He saw them and the coins depicting Oesho with the attributes of Shiva as evidence that the Zoroastrian religion had not taken complete hold of the Kushan authorities, 'at any rate it [the Zoroastrian religion] soon gave way to that faith [Hinduism] . . . and Siva and his bull speedily resumed their place upon the Indo-Scythic coins. Even in the reign of Kanerki the new system did not monopolise the favour of the ruling authorities, and they struck some, although not many, coins in which types of Buddhism appear to be stamped upon the currency' (Wilson

1841, p. 363). He made no observations, however, on the test of connection between Kanishka I and Buddhism, demanded by Lassen for accepting Prinsep's conjectured link between the coins and the textual references to Kanishka in Buddhist literature and the Kashmir Chronicle. He did, however, observe the remarkable similarity between the Buddha images on the Kanishka I's coins and those on the Bimaran casket (figs 113.7–9; 186; Wilson 1841, p. 370).

Although he listed the copper coins of Huvishka under the heading 'Kenorano' and his gold under 'Ooerki', Wilson had the wisdom to observe that the two inscriptions represented the same name and that the copper and gold coins were issues of the same king, the successor of Kanishka I.

At the end of the Indo-Scythic coins Wilson grouped gold and copper issues of Vasudeva I and his successors, illustrating two new examples of post-Vasudeva I gold, of Kanishka II collected by Colonel Miles and Kanishka III from Wilson's own collection, found at Hoogly in Bengal (1841, pl. XIV.19–20, Göbl types 541, 558 respectively). He observed that some of these coins (i.e. the Kushano-Sasanian gold) had Sasanian features and therefore attributed them to local princes in Afghanistan under Sasanian rule, or 'original coins of a late period of the Indo-Scythian' (Wilson 1841, p. 381).

On the whole Wilson's presentation is derivative, drawing principally from the collecting of Masson and others and from the scholarship of Prinsep, Rochette, Müller, Grotefend and particularly Lassen. His insights were few and largely defused by his attempt at a balanced view. With hesitation he had established a link between the Chinese textual account of the Da Yuezhi and the early Kushan coins, but he did not exploit this discovery. Nevertheless he placed all the new discoveries of the previous fifteen years in an accessible form and his book remains a valuable reference work for Masson's finds in Afghanistan.

A tribute to Prinsep

In 1844 James Prinsep's brother Henry Thoby decided to reassert the importance of his brother's contribution to the study of the history of ancient Afghanistan, by publishing a summary of recent research with commentary based on his brother's coin collection and research notes (Prinsep 1844). The resulting volume focused largely on the Greek period and contributes little to the process of understanding the coinages and history of the Kushan period. But it shows clearly how far James Prinsep's classification and sequencing of the Kushan coins had advanced, leaving Lassen and Wilson little to add. Henry Thoby was also able to demonstrate from his brother's notebook that he was close to deciphering Court's Manikyala inscription, and had already read on it the name and title of Kanishka I (Prinsep 1844, p. 124).

Henry Thoby's regret that the loss of his brother had deprived the subject of its pioneer was tempered by the uses Lassen and Wilson were making of it and by the hope that James's young friend Alexander Cunningham would follow in his footsteps (Prinsep 1844, p. 10). Cunningham did not disappoint that expectation.

Cunningham discovers the Kushans

The scholarly community in Calcutta were unequipped to 'kindle into light an life the dust and ashes dug out of these interesting ruins' following Prinsep's death (Prinsep 1844, p. 10), until his baton was taken up by Alexander Cunningham. There were others interested in the subject when Prinsep died (Swiney 1837; Torrens 1840 and 1851), but only Cunningham shared his passion and intellectual powers.

Cunningham's first papers were brief and dealt with forgeries and other minor issues, but from 1840 he started to look carefully at coins and quickly achieve some important insights, correcting Prinsep and Lassen's decipherment of Kharoshthi and more carefully re-examining the Heracles coins of Kujula Kadphises and ordering the coins of Azes and the Indo-Parthians. It was not until 1843 that he began to tackle questions relating to the Kushans. In a long article on the coinage of Kashmir presented to the Numismatic Society in London, he returned to Prinsep's suggestion that the coins read as Kanerki were issues of the Buddhist king Kanishka who ruled Kashmir, and those reading Ooerki were issues of another king of the same dynasty Hushka (already suggested by Lassen): 'the earliest coins which I can attribute with certainty to the kings of Kashmir, belong to the first Indo-Scythian princes OHPKI, Hoerki or Hushka; and *KANHPKI*, Kanerki or Kanishka' (Cunningham 1843–4, p. 5). His confidence was based on the evidence he had already assembled and had at press in an article to be published in 1845. In confirmation of Prinsep's conjecture, he also showed how closely the later coins of Kashmir followed Kushan designs.

The article Cunningham had at press was an investigation of some new Kushan coins. Among them were two Kanishka coins with Buddha images. One showed a seated image of Maitreya (1845, pl. II.6; Cribb 1999/2000, p. 180, no. 100), the other a standing image of the historical Buddha (1845, pl. II.7; Cribb 1999/2000, p. 170, no. 32). The condition of the coins prevented a clear reading of the inscriptions, but he detected the word Buddha in both of them. He made the connection that Wilson had failed to make from Masson's Buddha image coins, 'the happy conjecture made by Mr. James Prinsep in 1833, that the KANERKI of the coins was the great Buddhist Prince KANISHKA of Kashmir, has been amply confirmed by the Bauddha figures, emblems and legends of the coins which I have just described'. The tradition dating of Kanishka in the Kashmir Chronicle placed Kanishka too early, but Cunningham had reassessed the evidence and now believed that Kanishka 'flourished at the beginning of the Christian era'. He used the evidence of Court's Manikyala stupa, containing Roman coins from the mid first century BC, together with coins of Kujula Kadphises and Wima Kadphises to place 'the death of Kanishka in about AD 25' (1845, p. 441).

Cunningham's solution was not as well executed as he believed, since part of the evidence he presented for recognising Buddhism in Kushan coins was an issue of Huvishka with an image of Mithra on the reverse (1845, pl. II.3; Göbl type 321) and the curious blundered inscription *OYBOΔ*, which Cunningham read as a reference to the Buddha (the coin is part of a series full of blundered inscriptions). He also thought the club being held by the king on the obverse of this and another coin (1845, pl. II.2; Göbl type 242), both from his own collection, was a Buddhist prayer wheel.

He was also mistaken in trying to identify a new Kushan king Balano, from his misreading of a new gold coin of

Vasudeva I from Dr Lord's collection (pl. 2.4; Göbl type 525 obverse, with type 500 reverse), but correctly observed that it showed a three-headed, multi-armed Shiva image (under the guise of Oesho) on its reverse.

In spite of these errors Cunningham had another major contribution to make towards identifying the Kushans in this short article. He had been examining Kharoshthi inscriptions in the light of Prinsep's and Lassen's decipherment and had found a letter form on both Ventura's disk and casket from the great Manikyala stupa which they had not decoded. By decoding it Cunningham was able to re-examine the Kharoshthi inscription on the coins of Kujula Kadphises and read the word '*Kushanga*',which he identified with the 'Kuei-shang [Guishuang]' named as a tribe of the 'Great Yu-chi [Da Yuezhi]' in the Chinese sources. As with his comments on the Buddha images, he accompanied this important insight with erroneous speculation, that OOHMO on the coins of Wima Kadphises was a reference to the Hieu-mi (Xiumi), another Da Yuezhi tribe.

In 1854 Cunningham was able to extend the association between the coins and the Kushans, by his reading of Court's Manikyala slab inscription. In it he read 'in the reign of Kanishka, Maharaja of the Gushang (tribe)' (1854a, p. 703). Unfortunately he misread the date (year 18) as year 446 and attempted to equate it with a Buddhist era, equal to 31 BC. He also illustrated two new Kharoshthi inscriptions recently found at Panjtar and Und, but also misread their dates (p. 25 above; Cunningham 1854a, p. 705, pl. XXVI.4–5; Konow 1929: Panjtar inscription no. XXVI, pp. 67–70; Und inscription no. LXXXVII, pp. 170–1). The Panjtar inscription provided him with another instance of the word Kushan '*mahodayasa [maharajasa] Gushangasa raja*' and he was able to state that 'the *Gushang* of the inscriptions I identify with the *Khushang* and *Kushang* of the coins, and with the Kieu-shang . . . of the Chinese. And, as we find that Kanishka of the Raja Tarangini become Kanerki on the coins, so do I believe that the Kushang or Gushang are represented by the Greek KORANO of the coins' (Cunningham 1854a, p. 705).

His examination of the Kharoshthi inscriptions and his identification of the Buddhist king Kanishka also prompted him to re-examine the role of the stupa mounds and to confirm their Buddhist role in spite of the widespread use of deposit in them of coins with non-Buddhist designs. He also extended his ability to read the inscription on the coins of Kujula Kadphises to suggest that he was also a Buddhist, because he found the phrase 'sachadharma', meaning the true law, in his titles. Cunningham's reading was correct, but it is now recognised to be a reference to the worship of Oesho-Shiva, rather than to the Buddhist Dharma.

Cunningham had, nevertheless, established a firm basis for matching the 'Indo-Scythic' coins with the Chinese and Kashmiri historical accounts and with the Chinese and Tibetan Buddhist legends, confirming their issuers identity as Kushans. From this certainty historical research could progress.

It took Cunningham some more time to discover that the inscription KOϷANO on Kushan coins identified them as Kushan. At first he thought the Greek *rho* represented a sound change from the *sh* sound used in the Chinese sources and the Kharoshthi inscriptions (Cunningham 1872, p. 300),

but by 1890 he had realised, by finding the same phenomenon on the coins of the Indo-Scythian king Spalarises, that the *rho* (ρ) was in fact being used in an adapted form, with a projection from its top ($\not{p}$) to represent the *sh* sound (1890, pp. 6–7). Cunningham makes no reference to it, but he may have been helped in making this deduction by reading a brief note by Marc Aurel Stein reaching the same conclusion a few years earlier (Stein 1887a).[3] Finally the coins of the Kushans could be recognised because their name was written on them.

Conclusions

The two decades spanning 1825–45 were a remarkable period for the study of the history of India and Afghanistan. The discovery of coins – and their relationship with scattered and brief historical texts – gradually unfolded one of the most important periods of the history of the region; one moreover which had been completely obscured for more than a millennium. Although western scholarship had first named the Kushans in 1756, almost two centuries were to pass before their true identity and role became apparent. Emerging from the steppes of Inner Asia, they conquered Greeks, Scythians, Parthians and Indians to establish an empire stretching from Uzbekistan to Bengal which lasted for three centuries. The classification and the distribution of their coins, followed by the discovery of inscriptions naming their kings, gradually revealed the geographical and chronological extent of their dominion. The coins and inscriptions confirmed the legends of their patronage of Buddhism, and led to an understanding of the role they played in disseminating the religion throughout Central Asia and into China.

Once this foundation had been laid, archaeologists and collectors began to reveal the astonishing flowering of sculptural art which took place as a result of the unity and peace they brought to their empire. Archaeology has also discovered their religious sanctuaries, confirming the evidence of their coins, that they were adherents to a religion closely associated with Zoroastrianism. Excavation of the sanctuaries has also uncovered the portrait sculptures of their kings, unfortunately damaged by their successors and the ravages of time.

The study of the Kushans continues, particularly in terms of understanding their chronological context. Numismatics and inscriptions continue to play a key role and it is only a decade since the resources became available to reveal the identity and relationships of the second Kushan king Wima Tak[to] (Sims-Williams and Cribb 1995/6). The dating of this king and his father, son and grandson continues to provoke debate, but seems to be moving towards a resolution with the discovery of a textual description of a Kushan era in use in India in the third century AD (Falk 2001), providing a date for the first year of the reign of the fourth Kushan king Kanishka I in AD 127, a date remarkably close to that proposed by Wilson (1832, 1841), Masson (1834) and Lassen (1838).

Modern research on the Kushans continues to progress, but still remains firmly embedded in the research done during those two vital decades. As today, the greatest progress is made when collectors, excavators and scholars work together, or are even embodied in the same individuals, sharing their evidence and their ideas. As well as finding and researching new discoveries, perhaps the most important work was that done by Masson and Prinsep in creating a systematic classification of the coins, which enabled the evidence of the coins to be used. Having the right ideas, like Prinsep's recognition of Kanishka and Cunningham's proving he was correct, had to be built on a solid basis. Of all the individuals involved, I would pick out Masson as the greatest contributor. His wisdom in choosing to assemble a firm statistical base for coin circulation in Begram, together with his studious and detailed recording of excavated material from a large number of sites, provided such a foundation. Both these research techniques were self-taught and remain to the present day fundamental for sound numismatic research. Being in Kabul in the 1830s was a remarkable opportunity for historical research, but it took a remarkable man to take advantage of it.

In Cunningham's (and Pope's) words, these discoveries (1845, p. 441)

> we owe chiefly to the science of Numismatology; and the numismatist may proudly point to it as one of the many useful rays which the beacon of his favourite study has thrown over the treacherous quicksands of history. So true are the words of the poet,
>
> The medal, faithful to its charge of fame,
> Through climes and ages bears each Prince's name.

Chronological bibliographic chart of discoveries

1756
J. de Guignes, *Histoire générale des Huns, des Turcs, de Mogols, et des autres tartares occidentaux*, Paris.

1759
J. de Guignes, 'Sur quelques événements qui concernent l'histoire des rois grecs de la Bactriane et particulièrement la destruction de leur royaume par les Scythes, etc.', *Mémoires de l'académie des inscriptions et belle-lettres* XXV.Ii, pp. 17–33.

1767
J. Pellerin, *Troisième supplément aux six volumes de recueils des médailles des rois, de villes, &c., publiés en 1762, 1763 & 1765*, Paris.

1807
W. Vincent, *The Commerce and Navigation of the Ancients in the Indian Ocean*, vol. II, *The Periplus of the Erythraean Sea*, London.

1813
T. E. Mionnet, *Descriptions de médailles antiques, grecques et romaines avec leur degré de rareté et leur estimation*, vol. VI, Paris.

1823–5
W. Marsden, *Numismata Orientalia Illustrata. The Oriental Coins, Ancient and Modern, of his Collection, Described and Historically Illustrated*, London, vol. I: 1823; vol. II: 1825.

1825
J. Tod, 'An account of Greek, Parthian, and Hindu medals, found in India', *Transaction of the Royal Asiatic Society of Great Britain and Ireland* I.1, London, pp. 313–42 (paper read to the Society 18 June).
H. H. Wilson, 'An essay on the Hindu history of Cashmir', *Asiatic Researches* XV, Serampore, pp. 1–119.

1828
November
A. W. von Schlegel, 'Observations sur quelques médailles bactriennes et indo-scythiques nouvellement découvertes', *Journal Asiatique* 2ème sér. VII, pp. 321–49.

1829
J. Tod, *The Annals and Antiquities of Rajast'han*, London.

1830
April–June
Jean-Baptiste Ventura opens the Manikyala Great Stupa, 30 April – 3 June.

1832
H. H. Wilson, 'Description of select coins, from originals or drawings in the possession of the Asiatic Society', *Asiatic Researches* XVII, pp. 559–600, pls I–V.
J. B. Ventura, 'Account of the excavations of the tope Manikyala', appendix to H. H. Wilson, *Asiatic Researches* XVII, pp. 600–3.
March
R. Reinaud, 'Lettre au rédacteur du Journal Asiatique', *Journal Asiatique* 2ème sér. IX, pp. 276–9.
J. Saint-Martin, 'Note sur les médailles gréco-indiennes mentionées dans la lettre précédente', *Journal Asiatique* 2ème sér. IX, pp. 280–1.
Alexander Burnes's visit to Manikyala (6 March, with Ventura) and journey to Bukhara (March–June).
September
J. Prinsep, 'On the ancient Roman coins in the cabinet of the Asiatic Society', *JASB* I, pp. 392–408: Thomas 1858, vol. I, pp. 1–6.

1833
January
J. Prinsep, 'On the Greek coins in the cabinet of the Asiatic Society', *JASB* II, pp. 27–41: Thomas 1858, vol. I, pp. 7–22.
May
Burnes exhibited collection of coins from Manikyala, Afghanistan and Bukhara at Asiatic Society, Calcutta, 29 May: Proceedings of the Asiatic Society 17, *JASB* II, p. 263.
June
J. Prinsep, 'Note on Lieutenant Burnes' collection of ancient coins', *JASB* II, pp. 310–18: Thomas 1858, vol. I, pp. 23–44 (paper read at Asiatic Society, Calcutta, 29 May; repr. as 'Mr. James Prinsep's notes', appendix to A. Burnes, *Travels into Bokhara*, 1834, vol. II, pp. 463–73).
August
J. Prinsep, 'Bactrian and Indo-Scythic coins – continued', *JASB* II, pp. 405–16: Thomas 1858, vol. I, pp. 45–62.

1834
A. Burnes, *Travels into Bokhara, being the Account of a Journey from India to Cabool, Tartary and Russia*, 3 vols, London (with appendix, vol. II, pp. 457–73: 'Observations on Lieutenant Burnes' collection of Bactrian and other coins').
January
P. T. Cautley, 'Discovery of an ancient town near Behat, in the doab of the Jamna and Ganges', *JASB* III, pp. 43–4: Thomas 1858, vol. I, pp. 73–5 (extract of a letter read at Asiatic Society meeting 30 January).
April
C. Masson, 'Memoir on the ancient coins found at Beghram, in the Kohistán of Kábul', *JASB* III, pp. 153–75, pls VIII–XIII (paper read at Asiatic Society, Calcutta, by Dr J. G. Gerard, who proposed that the Society should fund Masson's research in Afghanistan: Proceedings of the Asiatic Society 28, p. 195).
P. T. Cautley, 'Further account of the remains of an ancient town, discovered at Behat, near Saharanpur', *JASB* III, pp. 221–7: Thomas 1858, vol. I, pp. 76–80 (extract of a letter read at Asiatic Society meeting 30 April).
May
J. Prinsep, 'Note on the coins found by Captain Cautley in Behat', *JASB* III, pp. 227–8: Thomas 1858, vol. I, pp. 82–5.
H. H. Wilson, 'Professor Wilson's notes', appendix to A. Burnes, *Travels into Bokhara*, 1834, vol. II, pp. 457–62.
July
J. Prinsep, 'On the coins and relics discovered by M. le chevalier Ventura, general in the service of Mahá Rájá Ranjit Singh, in the tope of Manikyála', *JASB* III, pp. 313–20: Thomas 1858, vol. I, pp. 90–117.
August
R. Rochette, 'Notice sur quelques médailles grecques inédites appartenant à des rois inconnus de la Bactriane et de l'Inde', *Journal des Savants*, pp. 2–28.
September
J. Prinsep, 'Continuation of observations on the coins and relics discovered by General Ventura, in the tope of Manikyála', *JASB* III, pp. 436–55: Thomas 1858, vol. I, pp. 118–37.
C. L. Grotefend, 'Münzen baktrischer könige', *Blätter für Münzkunde – Hannoversche Numismatische Zeitschrift* II, pp. 23–4.

October

C. L. Grotefend, 'Münzen baktrischer könige (Zweiter Artikel)', *Blätter für Münzkunde – Hannoversche Numismatische Zeitschrift* 13, pp. 1–2.

November

A. Court, 'Further information on the topes of Mánikyála, being the translation of an extract from a manuscript memoir on ancient Taxila', *JASB* III, pp. 556–62, pls XXXIII–XXXIV: Thomas 1858, vol. I, pp. 138–41.

J. Prinsep, 'Note on the coins discovered by M. Court', *JASB* III, pp. 562–73: Thomas 1858, vol. I, pp. 141–53.

December

A. Cunningham, 'Correction of a mistake regarding some of the Roman coins found in the Tope at Manikyala opened by M. Court', *JASB* III, pp. 635–7.

1835

C. L. Grotefend, 'Die unbekannte Schrift der baktrischen Münzen', *Zeitschrift für die Alterumswissenschaft* 104.

April

C. L. Grotefend, 'Über baktrische und indische Münzen', *Blätter für Münzkunde – Hannoversche Numismatische Zeitschrift* 25, pp. 3–5.

June

J. Prinsep, 'Further notes and drawings of Bactrian and Indo-Scythic coins', *JASB* IV, pp. 327–48: Thomas 1858, vol. I, pp. 176–94.

November

R. Rochette, 'Supplément à la notice sur quelques médailles grecques inédites de rois inconnus de la Bactriane et de l'Inde', *Journal des Savants*, pp. 1–35.

K. O. Müller, *Göttingische Gelehrte Anzeigen* 177, 9 November, Calcutta, pp. 1761–8.

K. O. Müller, *Göttingische Gelehrte Anzeigen* 178–9, 12 November, Calcutta, pp. 1769–83.

December

J. Prinsep, 'On the connection of various ancient Hindu coins with the Grecian or Indo-Scythic series', *JASB* IV, pp. 621–43: Thomas 1858, vol. I, pp. 195–200, 224–31, 277–88.

J. Prinsep, 'Notice of ancient Hindu coins, continued from page 643', *JASB* IV, pp. 668–90: Thomas 1858, vol. I, pp. 289–319.

1836

A. Rémusat, *Foe koue ki, ou relations des royaumes bouddhiques, voyage dans la Tartarie, dans l'Afghanistan et dans l'Inde, exécuté, à la fin du IVe siècle*, Paris.

January

C. Masson, 'Second memoir on the ancient coins found at Beghrám, in the Kohistán of Kábul', *JASB* V, pp. 1–28, pls II–IV.

A. Cunningham, Letter identifying 'ΑΡΔΟΧΡΟ' on one of Ventura's coins, Proceedings Asiatic Society, 6 January, *JASB* V, p. 58.

February

E. Jacquet, 'Notice de la collection de médailles bactriennes et indo-scythiques rapportées par M. le général Allard', *Journal Asiatique* 3ème sér. II, pp. 122–90.

May

C. L. Grotefend, 'Die unbekannte Schrift der baktrischen Münzen', *Blätter für Münzkunde – Hannoversche Numismatische Zeitschrift* 26, pp. 1–2.

June

J. Avdall, 'Note on some of the Indo-Scythian coins found by C. Masson at Beghrám, in the Kohistán of Kábul', *JASB* V, pp. 266–8.

R. Rochette, 'Deuxième supplément à la notice sur quelques médailles grecques inédites de rois inconnus de la Bactriane et de l'Inde', *Journal des Savants*, pp. 1–61.

A. Court's 'Memoir on geography of Peucelaotis' and drawings of all coins and relics discovered by himself made available to Asiatic Society, Calcutta, Proceedings of the Asiatic Society, 1 June, *JASB* V, p. 303.

September

C. Masson, 'Third memoir on the ancient coins discovered at a site called Beghrám in the Kohistán of Kábul', *JASB* V, pp. 537–48, pls VIII–XIII.

J. Prinsep, 'New varieties of Bactrian coins engraved as pl. XXXV, from Masson's drawings and other sources', *JASB* V, pp. 548–54: Thomas 1858, vol. I, pp. 352–9, pl. XXVIII.

G. Turnour, 'Examination of some points of Buddhist chronology', *JASB* V, pp. 521–36.

E. Jacquet, 'Notice sur les découvertes archéologiques faites par Mr. Honigberger dans l'Afghanistan', *Journal Asiatique* 3ème sér. II, pp. 234–77, pls I–VIII.

October

J. Prinsep, 'New varieties of the Mithraic or Indo-Scythic series of coins, and their imitations', *JASB* V, pp. 639–57: Thomas 1858, vol. I, pp. 360–96.

November

J. Prinsep, 'New types of Bactrian and Indo-Scythic coins engraved as pl. XLIX', *JASB* V, pp. 720–4: Thomas 1858, vol. I, pp. 397–401, pl. XXXII.

December

H. H. Wilson, 'Observations on some ancient Indian coins in the cabinet of the Royal Asiatic Society', *JRAS* III, article XVIII, pp. 381–6.

1837

T. E. Mionnet, *Descriptions de médailles antiques, grecques et romaines avec leur degré de rareté et leur estimation*, supplement, vol. VIII, Paris.

H. H. Wilson, 'Graeco-Bactrian coins', *The Numismatic Journal* (later renamed *Numismatic Chronicle*) II, pp. 144–81.

January

J. Swiney, 'On the explanation of the Indo-Scythic legends of the Bactrian coins through the medium of Celtic', *JASB* VI, pp. 98–100.

March

J. R. von Arneth, 'Numi Graeci regni Bactriani et Indici', *Wiener Jahrbüchern* 77, January–March, pp. 211–45.

June

J. Lee, 'Presidential Address, 15 June 1837', *Proceedings of the Numismatic Society of London 1836–37*, London, pp. 50–1, 70–1 (Announcement of Wilson's paper to be given in December).

November

E. Jacquet, 'Notice sur les découvertes archéologiques faites par Mr. Honigberger dans l'Afghanistan', *Journal Asiatique* 3ème sér. IV, pp. 401–40.

December

Ventura 'submitted for inspection some Bactrian coins and Hindu antiques from the Panjâb', Proceedings of the Asiatic Society, 6 December, *JASB* VI, pp. 986–7.

1838

C. Lassen, *Einleitung zur Geschichte des Griechischen und Indoskythischen Könige in Bactrien, Kabul und Indien, durch Entzifferung der Alt-kabulischen Legenden auf ihren Münzen*, Bonn (translated by T. H. E. Röer, with commentary by H. Torrens, as *Greek and Indo-Scythian Kings and their Coins*, Calcutta 1840).

H. H. Wilson, 'A memoir on the recently discovered Graeco-Bactrian coins', *Proceedings of the Numismatic Society of London 1837–38*, London, pp. 107–32.

February

K. O. Müller, 'Über Indo-Griechische Münzen', *Göttingische Gelehrte Anzeigen* 21, 5 February, Calcutta and Paris, pp. 201–8.

K. O. Müller, *Göttingische Gelehrte Anzeigen* 22–3, 8 February, Calcutta and Paris, pp. 209–24.

K. O. Müller, *Göttingische Gelehrte Anzeigen* 24, 10 February, Calcutta and Paris, pp. 225–40.

K. O. Müller, *Göttingische Gelehrte Anzeigen* 25, 12 February, Calcutta and Paris, pp. 241–8.

K. O. Müller, 'Über Indo-Griechische Münzen', *Göttingische Gelehrte Anzeigen* 26–7, 15 February, Calcutta and Paris, pp. 249–52.

E. Jacquet, 'Notice sur les découvertes archéologiques faites par Mr. Honigberger dans l'Afghanistan', *Journal Asiatique* 3ème sér. V, pp. 163–97.

July

J. Lee, 'Presidential Address, 19 July 1838', *Proceedings of the Numismatic Society of London 1837–38*, London, pp. 18–23,

41–2 (including a table of Prinsep's decipherment of the Kharoshthi alphabet, 'furnished by Professor Wilson').

J. Prinsep, 'Additions to Bactrian numismatics, and the discovery of the Bactrian alphabet', *JASB* VII, pp. 636–55: Thomas 1858, vol. II, pp. 125–44.

1839

C. L. Grotefend, *Die Münzen der griechischen, parthischen und indoskythischen Könige von Baktrien und den Ländern am Indus*, Hanover.

A. de Longpérier, 'Rapport de M. Adr. De Longpérier sur la collection numismatique du Général Court', *Revue Numismatique*, pp. 81–8.

February

K. O. Müller, *Göttingische Gelehrte Anzeigen* 29, 18 February, Bonn, Berlin, Calcutta, pp. 281–8.

K. O. Müller, *Göttingische Gelehrte Anzeigen* 30–1, 21 February, Bonn, Berlin, Calcutta, pp. 289–304.

K. O. Müller, *Göttingische Gelehrte Anzeigen* 32, 23 February, Bonn, Berlin, Calcutta, pp. 305–20.

K. O. Müller, *Göttingische Gelehrte Anzeigen* 33, 25 February, Bonn, Berlin, Calcutta, pp. 321–5.

May

E. Jacquet, 'Notice sur les découvertes archéologiques faites par Mr. Honigberger dans l'Afghanistan', *Journal Asiatique* 3ème sér. VII, pp. 385–404.

July

J. Lee, 'Presidential Address, 18 July 1839', *Proceedings of the Numismatic Society of London 1838–39*, London 1840, pp. 10–15.

1840

C. Lassen, *Greek and Indo-Scythian Kings and their Coins*, trans. T. H. E. Röer, with commentary by H. Torrens, Calcutta (first published as C. Lassen, 'Points in the history of the Greek and Indo-Scythian kings in Bactria, Cabul and India, as illustrated by deciphering the ancient legends on their coins', *JASB* IX, pp. 251–76, 339–78, 449–88, 627–76, 733–65).

A. Cunningham, 'Notice of some counterfeit Bactrian coins', *JASB* IX, pp. 393–6.

A. Cunningham, 'Notes on Captain Hay's Bactrian coins', *JASB* IX, pp. 531–42.

A. Cunningham, 'Appendix to the notice of forged Bactrian coins', *JASB* IX, pp. 543–4.

A. Cunningham, 'Description of, and deductions from a consideration of, some new Bactrian coins', *JASB* IX, pp. 867–89, 1008.

A. Cunningham, 'A second notice of some forged coins of the Bactrians and Indo-Scythians', *JASB* IX, pp. 1217–30.

January

E. Jacquet, 'Mémoire sur la série des médailles indiennes connues sous le denomination d'indo-scythique', *Journal Asiatique* 3ème sér. VIII, pp. 54–66.

April

W. Hay, 'Account of coins found at Bameean' (dated 7 April), *JASB* IX, pp. 68–9.

H. Torrens, 'Note on the Bameean coins', *JASB* IX, pp. 70–5.

September

E. Jacquet, 'Mémoire sur la série des médailles indiennes connues sous le denomination d'indo-scythique [continued]', *Journal Asiatique*, pp. 202–36.

1841

H. H. Wilson, *Ariana Antiqua. A Descriptive Account of the Antiquities and Coins of Afghanistan with a Memoir on the Buildings called Topes by C. Masson Esq.*, London.

1842

A. Cunningham, 'Second notice of some new Bactrian coins', *JASB* XI, pp. 130–7.

1843

A. Cunningham, 'The ancient coinage of Kashmir', *NC* 6, April 1843 – January 1844, pp. 1–38 (paper read to Royal Numismatic Society 26 January).

1844

H. T. Prinsep, *Historical Results from Bactrian Coins, discovered in Afghanistan*, London.

1845

A. Cunningham, 'Notice of some unpublished coins of the Indo-Scythians', *JASB* XIV, pp. 430–41.

1851

H. Torrens, 'Coins of the Indo-Scythian princes of Cabul: translation of some uncertain Greek legends', *JASB* XX, pp. 137–53.

1854

A. Cunningham, *The Bhilsa Topes*, London.

A. Cunningham, 'Coins of the Indian Buddhist Satraps, with Greek inscriptions', *JASB* XXIII, pp. 679–714.

1863

A. Cunningham, 'Remarks on the Bactro-Pali inscription from Taxila', *JASB* XXXII, pp. 139–52.

1864

A. Cunningham, 'Note on the Bactro-Pali inscription from Taxila', *JASB* XXXIII, pp. 35–8.

1868

A. Cunningham, 'Coins of Alexander's successors in the East', *NC* II.8, pp. 93–136, 181–213, 257–83.

1869

A. Cunningham, 'Coins of Alexander's successors in the East', *NC* II.9, pp. 28–46, 121–53, 217–46, 293–318.

1870

A. Cunningham, 'Coins of Alexander's successors in the East', *NC* II.10, pp. 65–90, 205–36.

1872

A. Cunningham, 'Coins of Alexander's successors in the East', *NC* II.12, pp. 157–85.

1873

A. Cunningham, 'Coins of Alexander's successors in the East', *NC* II.13, pp. 187–219.

1884

A. Cunningham, *Coins of Alexander's Successors in the East*, London.

1887

M. A. Stein, 'The Greek *sanpi* on Indo-Scythian coins', *The Academy*, 10 September, no. 801.

1888

A. Cunningham, 'Coins of the Indo-Scythian king Miaüs or Heraüs', *NC* III.8, pp. 47–58.

A. Cunningham, 'Coins of the Indo-Scythians', *NC* III.8, pp. 199–248.

1889

A. Cunningham, 'Coins of the Tochari, Kushâns, or Yue-ti', *NC* III.9, pp. 268–311.

1890

A. Cunningham, 'Coins of the Sakas', *NC* III.10, pp. 103–72.

1892

A. Cunningham, 'Coins of the Kushâns, or Great Yue-ti', *NC* III.12, pp. 40–82, 98–159.

A. Cunningham, *Coins of the Indo-Scythians*, London (repr. articles *NC* III.8–12, 1888–92).

1893

A. Cunningham, 'Coins of the Later Indo-Scythians, Introduction and Later Kushâns, *NC* III.13, pp. 93–128.

A. Cunningham, 'Coins of the Later Indo-Scythians – Scytho-Sassanians', *NC* III.13, pp. 166–77.

A. Cunningham, 'Coins of the Later Indo-Scythians – Little Kushâns', *NC* III.13, pp. 184–202.

1894

A. Cunningham, 'Coins of the Later Indo-Scythians – Ephthalites, or White Huns', *NC* III.14, pp. 243–93.

1895

A. Cunningham, *Later Indo-Scythians. Ephthalites, or White Huns*, London (repr. articles *NC* III.13–14, 1893–4).

1904

V. A. Smith, *The Early History of India from 600 B.C. to the Muhammadan Conquest*, Oxford.

Notes

1   Apart from excavated coins from Buddhist monuments and documented purchases in Kabul and a few other locations.

2   There are a variety of spellings of this name on Kushan coins, the most common being Miiro and Mioro.

3   I would like to thank David Bivar for drawing my attention to this fact.

9 Exploring Gandhara

Elizabeth Errington

In the early nineteenth century European travellers began to report the existence of extensive mounds and ruined monuments in the Punjab and regions to the north-west, particularly along the main route leading from Peshawar through the Khyber Pass to Kabul in Afghanistan. The story of the discovery of the Buddhist sites of Gandhara (fig. 176) begins in 1808, when a British diplomatic mission under Mountstuart Elphinstone (1779–1859) was sent to Peshawar. On their way back through the region south of Rawalpindi towards the Jhelum river, they attempted to find the site of the capital of Taxiles, the ally of Alexander the Great. In this they were unsuccessful, which is hardly surprising, since Taxila is in fact located to the north-west of Rawalpindi. But instead, they discovered 'a remarkable building, which seemed at first to be a cupola, but when approached, was found to be a solid structure on a low artificial mound. . . . The natives called it the Tope of Maunicyaula, and said it was built by the gods' (fig. 175; Elphinstone 1815, pp. 213–14, pl. I).

Exploring the archaeological remains of this region began in earnest in the 1830s. By this time there was a core of European officers in the Punjab who were employed by the Sikh Maharaja Ranjit Singh to train his troops in the art of contemporary French warfare. Chief amongst them were Claude-Auguste Court, another Frenchman, Jean-François Allard (1785–1839), and two Italians, Paolo Crescenzo Avitabile (1791–1850) and Rubino Ventura (1794–1858) (pp. 141–6, figs 11–12; 124–6; Lafont 1992; 2000, pp. 205–382). The first three men had served in the armies of Napoleon I, and had quit Europe after his defeat to seek their fortunes in the east. Ventura, a Jew from the ghetto of Finale near Modena, although an ardent Bonapartist, had not seen active service. In fact, contrary to his later claims to having been with Napoleon in Russia (Lafont 1982, pp. 37–8), he had only just enrolled in the Dragoni della Regina regiment when the Treaty of Paris (12 June 1814) ended French rule in Italy and his dreams of military glory in Europe (Balboni 1993, pp. 4–9, 14, 21–6). In 1820, while he and Allard were employed by the Persian prince Abbas Mirza in Tabriz, he changed his name from Rubino to Jean-Baptiste and began passing himself off as French (Balboni 1993, p. 56). In 1821–2 the British successfully negotiated with Fath 'Ali Shah (1797–1834) to dismiss all French officers in service in Persia (Lafont 1992, pp. 118–20). Together, Allard and Ventura travelled in disguise via Afghanistan to the Punjab, where they were the first two officers to be employed by Ranjit Singh in 1822 (above pp. 142, 146).

For Ventura the link between Alexander the Great and India was the reason he 'felt compelled' to excavate at Manikyala in April 1830 (Ventura 1832, pp. 600–3). Imitating the methods used by Belzoni, his compatriot in Egypt, whose

Figure 175 The Great Stupa at Manikyala.

spectacular finds he claims were his source of inspiration (Prinsep 1833, p. 28), he dug a shaft through the centre of the stupa mound, from top to bottom. In the process he unearthed a series of twelve relic deposits regularly placed within the core (fig. 177; Cunningham 1875, pls XXI–XXIV). Most of the deposits were coins, of which no details survive, but he did carefully record the depth of each find and also the details of the principal deposits. His belief that he had discovered the site of Bucephala, the city Alexander founded in memory of his horse, was immediately refuted because Manikyala lies about 40 miles from the banks of the Jhelum (Wilson 1832, pp. 601, 605; p. 36 above). This river had already been identified from Classical sources as the ancient Hydaspes, beside which Alexander's city is said to have been sited (Arrian V.19.4; Strabo XV.1.29).

Ventura was moreover unaware that Manikyala had already been correctly identified in 1823 as a Buddhist 'tope' (from Sanskrit *stūpa*) of the same type as the 'dahgopas' (*dagapas*) still worshipped in Sri Lanka (Erskine 1823, p. 519). 'Dahgopa' was slightly misinterpreted at the time as 'body what preserves', but this was close enough to the actual meaning of *dagapa* (from Sanskrit *dhatu* 'relics' and *garbha* 'womb' or 'chamber') to provide a basic understanding of the cult function of these structures.

The finds from Ventura's excavation (fig. 177) attest that the Manikyala Great Stupa dates at least from the second century AD, for the reliquary deposit ('D') at the base of the dome contained coins of the Kushan kings Kanishka I (*c.* AD 127–50) and Huvishka (*c.* AD 150–90) (Prinsep 1834a, pls XXI–XXII; Errington 1987, pp. 532–3, fig. 2.2). It is possible that the seven copper coins found below this point may have been earlier in date, but no details of their issues were recorded. At the time of excavation only the Sasanian coins of Khusrau II (AD 590/1–628), found at a depth of 64 ft/19.5 m from the top of the stupa, could be positively identified ('Deposit C'; Prinsep 1834a, p. 318), but these provided the first

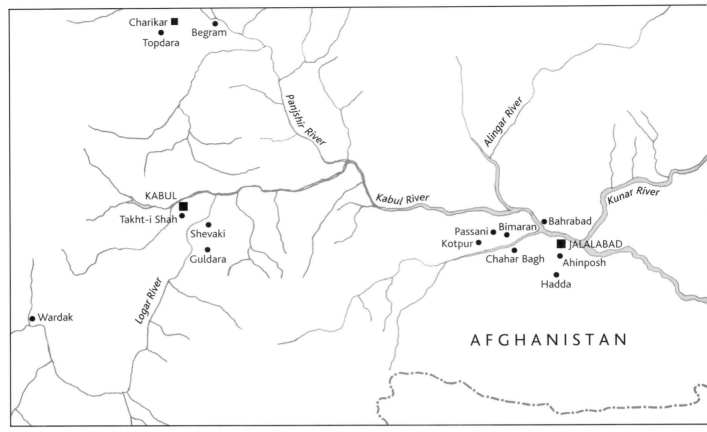

Figure 176 Buddhist sites of south-east Afghanistan and Gandhara.

definite indication of when the stupa could have been in cult. The final deposit ('A') contained coins of the seventh/eighth century, mixed with finds of apparent Kushan date: a gold reliquary containing a gold coin of Huvishka in excellent preservation and a ring inscribed with five Bactrian letters (the fifth indistinct). Nicholas Sims-Williams has read the first four as *Zono*, 'the expected Bactrian spelling of the god Zun, who was worshipped in Zabulistan [the Ghazna region]' (Zwalf 1996, p. 351). The coins included a silver drachm of 'Abdallah b. Khazim, the governor of Khurasan, minted at Merv in AH 66: AD 685 and late seventh-century issues of Tigin (Göbl 1967, type 208), a ruler in the Kabul region, and Yashovarman of Kashmir. In addition there were small silver Raja Vigraha issues which, from their association with the other coins of this deposit, can be similarly dated to the late seventh or early eighth century. The coin evidence overall shows that there were at least two or more phases of building: one in the Kushan period; perhaps an enlargement in the late Sasanian period; and another at the beginning of the eighth century. The presence of the ring with its Bactrian inscription and the coins from Khurasan and Kabul in the last deposit make it moreover tempting to link this last phase of rebuilding with a possible Buddhist migration southwards from Afghanistan in the face of the advance of Islam into these regions from the seventh century onwards (Errington and Cribb 1992, p. 185).

One aspect of this stupa which has been completely ignored since its excavation was the presence of a further seven coin deposits interspersed at regular intervals throughout the centre core of the dome. The first six copper coins were placed at a depth of 75 ft/22.85 m at the junction between the stupa platform and the base of the dome (fig. 177). Five single copper coins were found at a depth of

72 ft/21.94 m, 54 ft/15.65 m, 36 ft/10.97 m, 22 ft/6.69 m and 3 ft/0.91 m respectively from the top of the dome, and a larger deposit of one silver and six copper coins occurred at 33 ft/10.05 m. Although the individual coin types were not recorded, these subsidiary deposits can probably be identified as items donated during consecration rituals when the stupa was constructed and each time it was subsequently enlarged or repaired. By the time of Song Yun's visit to Gandhara in AD 519–20 moreover, the idea existed that such deposits were intended for funding any restoration of the monument that might be necessary in the future (Chavannes 1903, pp. 425–6, cf. Scherrer-Schaub forthcoming).

Following Ventura's success, Court investigated the remains of fifteen other sites at Manikyala, and remarked, 'If these monuments are the remains of temples, there can be no doubt that Manikyala must have been the principal seat of the religion of the country' (Court 1834, p. 560). His most significant find was in the ruins of a stupa near Mera-ka-Dheri. This contained a Kharoshthi inscription dated in the year 18 of Kanishka I (fig. 178; Konow 1929, pp. 145–50, pl. XXVII.1), coins of the Kushan kings Kujula Kadphises, Wima Kadphises and Kanishka I (including four gold quarter staters of the last king, now in the Cabinet des Médailles, Bibliothèque Nationale, Paris), and seven worn Roman silver denarii of the Republican period. The condition of the Roman coins indicated that they must have been in circulation for a considerable time prior to burial. They ranged in date from *c*.96 BC to 41 BC, and included coins of Julius Caesar (*c*.44 BC) and Mark Antony (*c*.42 BC) (Court 1834, pls XXXIII–XXXIV; Errington 1999/2000, pp. 212, 216). Used Roman silver coins appear to have been exported to India as bullion in increasing quantities in the

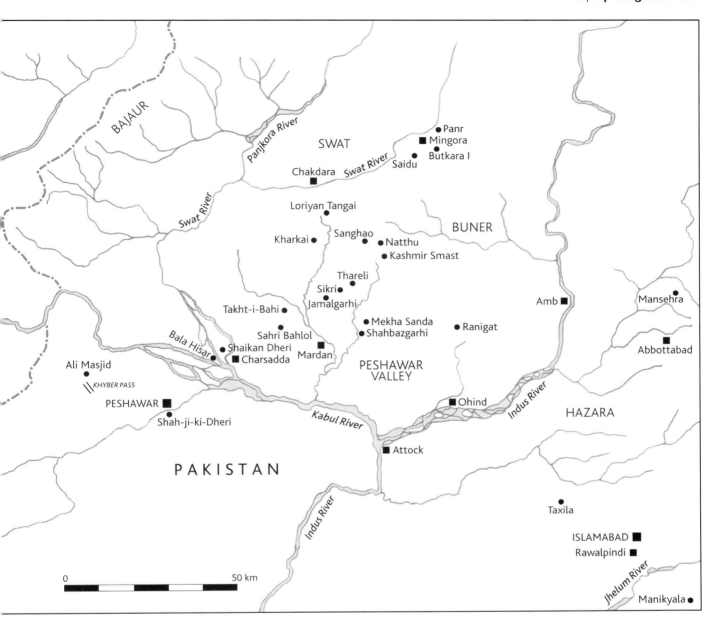

first centuries AD to pay for luxury goods from the east (Casson 1989, pp. 30–1; Ray 1991, p. 139). Their presence in the deposit provided, for the first time, an approximate date, not only for the stupa but also for the early Kushan kings, of the first to second century AD.

As Ventura had been inspired by Belzoni, so did his discoveries inspire others, most notably in Afghanistan. Some of the extensive Buddhist remains at Ishpola in the Khyber Pass and Chahar Bagh near Jalalabad were first seen in 1824 by the East India Company's veterinary surgeon and Superintendent of the Stud, William Moorcroft (c.1767–1825), and his assistant, George Trebeck (d. 1825), while en route to Bukhara in search of better breeding stock for the Company's cavalry horses (Moorcroft and Trebeck 1841, pp. 349–50, 362–5). When Court passed this way in 1826 he also noted the Buddhist site of Hadda, south of Jalalabad, and the remains of the sixteenth-century fort at Adinapur, near Balabagh (Lafont 1992, p. 328, nn. 271–2; Beveridge 1970, p. 209; Ball and Gardin 1982, no. 10). But it was only in 1833 that Charles Masson, together with Martin Honigberger (fig. 179), began to explore the sites in the neighbourhood of Jalalabad and Kabul (Masson 1842, vol. III, pp. 171–2).

Johann Martin Honigberger (1795–1869) was a doctor from Kronstadt in Transylvania, Hungary. He practised his own unique brand of homeopathic medicine throughout his extensive travels in the Near and Middle East and claimed to have effected some remarkable cures despite his unorthodox methods (Honigberger 1852). From c.1828 to 1832, and again from 1836 onwards, he was employed by Ranjit Singh as a physician to the Sikh court and, concurrently, as superintendent of the Lahore gunpowder mill and gun factory. Additional duties included the invention and distillation of an extremely potent 'brandy' for the Maharaja. When describing her visit to the Sikh court in 1838, Emily Eden refers to this concoction of raw spirit, crushed pearls, musk, opium, gravy and spices as 'a sort of liquid fire, that none of our strongest spirits approach, and in general Europeans cannot swallow more than a drop of it' (Eden 1866, vol. I, p. 282; Keay 1977, p. 72). Ranjit Singh, however, downed the 'horrible spirit . . . like water' with little obvious effect (Eden 1866, vol. I, p. 297), although Honigberger does cite the Maharaja's 'extreme devotedness to sensuality, spirits and opium' as the cause of his death in 1839 (Honigberger 1852, pp. 95–6).

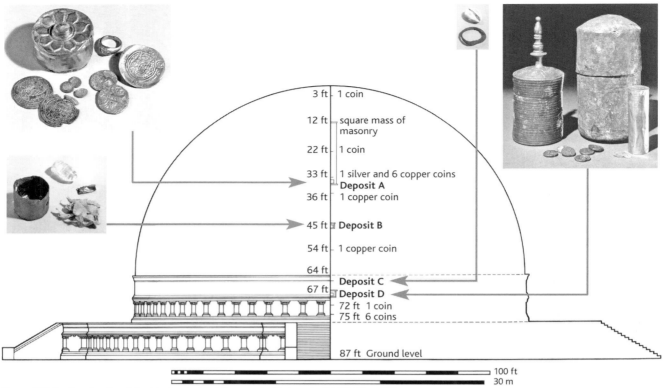

Figure 177 Section drawing of the Manikyala Great Stupa and relic deposits 'A', 'B', 'C' and 'D'.

In 1832 Honigberger was 'affected with nostalgy' and applied for permission to return home, 'which was after many applications ultimately granted' (Honigberger 1852, p. 56). He travelled overland to Europe via Afghanistan, north-westwards through Balkh, Bukhara, Orenburg and Russia (Honigberger 1835). En route he spent four months in 1833 in Kabul. He claims to have opened twenty stupas in the neighbourhood of the city and in the Darunta district west of Jalalabad, but describes only the seven in which he found relic deposits (figs 180–1; Jacquet 1836a; 1837; 1838). It appears that all his finds were uncovered more by luck than by any systematic excavation technique, for many of the stupas in which he found nothing later produced deposits when excavated by Masson. Whether he personally excavated many sites seems unlikely. According to a contemporary witness, Dr James Gerard (1795–1835), who spent some time in Kabul on his way back from an exploratory mission with Alexander Burnes to Bukhara for the East India Company, Honigberger sent a servant to the Khyber Pass, 'habited as a faqir or mendicant, his best or only passport among people who live by pillage. He tempted the Khyberis to dig [the Ishpola stupa] by the prospect of treasure, but they would do nothing without pay, and the object was thus (fortunately) abandoned' (Gerard 1834, p. 327).

When Honigberger subsequently tried to sell his finds to the British Museum in 1835, he did not endear himself to the Trustees by saying that 'it would be utterly impossible for me to fix any particular value on objects of such great and invaluable importance', and then suggesting £1200 as an adequate renumeration 'for the expenses I incurred of making the overland journey from Lahor [*sic*] to London and to the dangers to which I was exposed, the precautions I adopted, the fatigue I underwent, and the difficulties I had to overcome for the sole purpose of seeing these treasures safely lodged in England' (Honigberger 1835). As Edward Hawkins

(1835a) remarked at the time, 'we might plead that if he had discovered objects of ten times more value than the amount of his expenses he would not have thought of making those expenses the standard of their value, neither should he now'. Nevertheless he recommended paying 'an extravagant sum' rather than lose the coins and gems. 'What to say about the boxes [reliquaries] I do not know, . . . we know so absolutely nothing about Bactrian workmanship, that we are unable to form a reasonable judgement. . . . With some scepticism founded upon the apparent humbug of the German I am in favour of their antiquity and would buy; . . . for the objects are extremely interesting, and rare; indeed, where at present can anything like them be found?' A few days later, he urged (Hawkins 1835b)

> Do not on any account omit securing some part of the abominable German's treasures: first, one of the Gold coins and a cast of the other [both coins of Wima Kadphises, *c*. AD 113–27]; next, one at least of each of the varieties of his copper coins in good preservation, I should say two, when the whole inscription cannot be ascertained from one. By no means let the square coins escape, especially one which has upon it a head covered with a cap [Macedonian helmet]. . . . You *must* also secure two stone cups, one with *turned* ornament and one with carved ornament. I should like the gold box and the silver one with the philosopher's stone, but I suppose I must be content without them.

The 'stone cups' referred to by Hawkins were steatite reliquaries respectively from Shevaki stupa 3, south-east of Kabul, and the stupas of Bimaran 5 and Bahrabad, west of Jalalabad (Jacquet 1836a, pls IV, VII–VIII; Errington 1987, figs 2.4, 2.8–9). The gold reliquary was in the form of a miniature stupa and was found in the foundation deposit of Bimaran 3 (fig. 180; Jacquet 1836a, pl. XI.12; 1838, pp. 174–7; Errington 1987, p. 424, fig. 2.7). One of the Wima Kadphises gold staters and the silver reliquary with the 'philosopher's stone' came from another of the Kabul group of stupas known

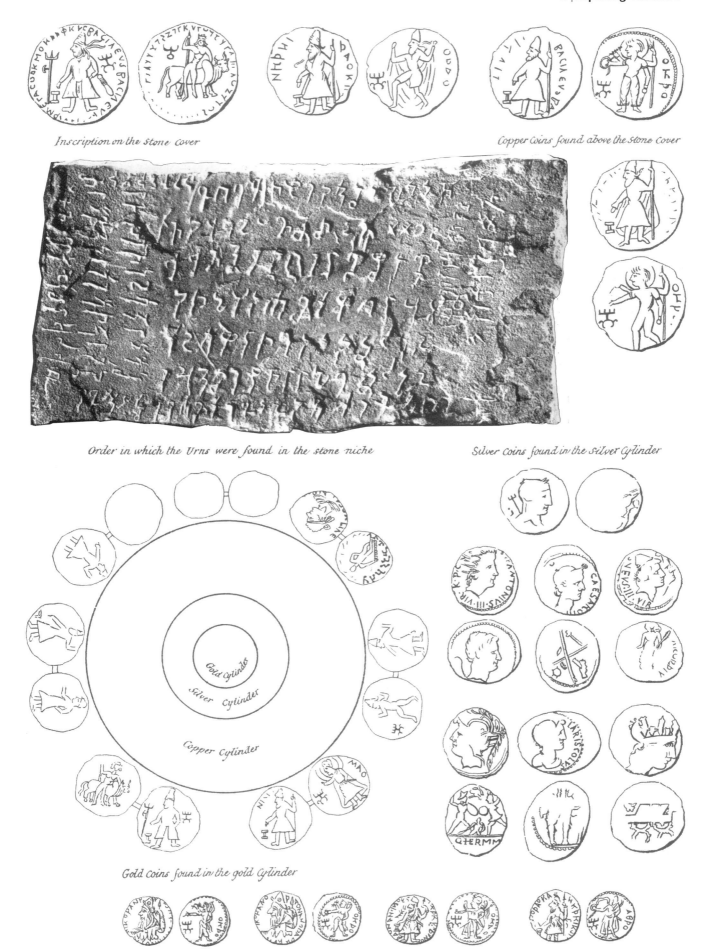

Inscription on the Stone Cover

Copper Coins found above the Stone Cover

Order in which the Urns were found in the stone niche

Silver Coins found in the Silver Cylinder

Gold Cylinder

Silver Cylinder

Copper Cylinder

Gold Coins found in the gold Cylinder

Figure 178 Kharoshthi inscription dated year 18 of Kanishka and coins from the relic deposit of the Mera-ka-Dheri stupa near Manikyala excavated by Court.

Figure 179 Johann Martin Honigberger (1795–1869).

Figure 180 Finds from the relic deposit of Bimaran stupa 3, Darunta District.

as Kamari or Shevaki 1 (figs 181, 183.1; Jacquet 1836a, pl. XIII Wilson 1841, p. 114; Mizuno 1970, p. 125, pl. 45). Honigberger discovered this relic deposit in a stone cell placed in the centre of the stupa at base level. Traces of fine material, probably silk – as at Manikyala Great Stupa (Zwalf 1985, p. 30) – were found covering the remains of a bronze bowl, 8–12 in. in diameter (202 mm: Jacquet 1836a, pp. 265–6; 305 mm: Honigberger 1835, no. 2). This was half-filled with a resinous substance, earth, fragments of wood and gold, the coin of Wima Kadphises and a domed silver reliquary containing a 'petrification . . . as large as a well sized egg' which, when first uncovered, was thought by local Afghans to be the philosopher's stone.

Despite Hawkins's belief (1835) that 'the Museum must, yes must buy them even if it pawns something to raise the money', the Trustees authorised the purchase only of gems and 24 copper coins, to the value of £50 (British Museum 1835a). The single item in Hawkins's list which was acquired is a square bronze coin depicting the Greco-Bactrian king Eucratides I (c.174–145 BC) in a Macedonian helmet (fig. 182.1).[1] Honigberger contrived to sell more coins from his collection elsewhere in Europe (Errington 1987, pp. 45–6), but not the relic deposits. These were placed in the care of Geymüller, a Viennese banker, who went bankrupt shortly afterwards. Honigberger's collection was amongst assets confiscated and eventually sold at auction 'for about three pounds as belonging to the creditors of Geymüller, with the pretext that the real proprietor no longer existed' in June 1850 (Honigberger 1852, pp. 59–60). Honigberger failed to trace their whereabouts and they have not resurfaced subsequently: the only records of these finds are the drawings published by Jacquet (1836a, pls I–VIII).

A far more systematic investigation of the ancient remains in the region of Kabul and Jalalabad was begun by Masson in 1833. From early 1834 he received a small annual grant from the Bombay Government of the British East India Company for archaeological and antiquarian research, a stipulation being that all finds should be sent to the Company (Whitteridge 1986, p. 76). This provided sufficient funds in the next three years for Masson to excavate a number of stupas, principally at Hadda, Chahar Bagh and the Darunta district west of Jalalabad, and to a lesser extent in the neighbourhood of Kabul. In the early years he supervised the excavations himself and meticulously recorded his discoveries, so that, even when his interpretations are incorrect, it is still possible to ascertain in the majority of instances what he actually found. However, his appointment in 1835 as news-writer for the British in Kabul drastically curtailed his freedom of movement and the subsequent excavations undertaken for him at Wardak, south-west of Kabul (fig. 114), are not documented in the same detail. Nevertheless, his manuscripts and the published accounts of his finds provide a unique and important record of the Buddhist remains in the Kabul–Jalalabad region, many of which have since been destroyed (figs 17–18; 183; 185; Wilson 1841, pp. 55–119; Masson MSS Eur.; Uncat. MSS; 1842, vol. II, pp. 223, 234–5; III, pp. 92–7, 125, 134–6, 145, 165–6, 254, 273–8).

Inevitably, as an archaeological pioneer in this region, he misinterpreted the evidence in a number of instances. A principal misconception is his use of the terms 'tope' and 'tumulus' to delineate what he saw as two different categories of stupa (fig. 8; Wilson 1841, topes pl. IV). 'Tope' is applied to the more prominent structures, 'comprising two essential parts, a basement and perpendicular body' or cylindrical dome ornamented with a band of mouldings, usually of arches and pilasters (figs 109–10; Wilson 1841, p. 57). Above this on some of the Kabul stupas – like Topdara and Shevaki 1 – he noted an

Figure 181 Finds from the relic deposit of Kamari (Shevaki stupa 1) near Kabul.

Figure 182 Coins collected by Honigberger, Masson and Court respectively:
1 Greco-Bactrian coin of Eucratides I (c.174–138 BC).
2 Posthumous imitation of Azes coin (c. mid first century AD), from Bimaran stupa 2 relic deposit.
3 Kharahostes (c. early first century AD). Obv. horseman; rev. lion.

additional large east-facing niche for a cult statue (fig. 183.1–2; Wilson 1841, topes pl. IX). A 'tumulus', he considered, had a low, undecorated dome (fig. 183.7). However, as the artist William Simpson (1823–99) commented, following his own survey of the Jalalabad Valley from 20 December 1878 to 12 April 1879 (1879–80, p. 45, pls III–V):

> Masson counted the topes in the Jellalabad valley, and gives the result as a definite number. Here I think he makes a great mistake. He only included those on which he found fragments of their structure remaining, for he made an imaginary distinction between topes and tumuli. . . . This is the reason that there are yet in the Jellalabad valley the remains of topes in the condition of mounds, which escaped the operations of his industrious activity. The Ahin Posh Tope which I explored might be described as a second class one as to size, and being apparently only a heap of earth he never touched it. On the site of ancient Nagarahara [Masson's 'Beghram' below] is another one of the largest size [fig. 183.6: Nagara Gundi, the largest stupa of Masson's Tapa Khwaja Lahoree, with a basement c.120 ft/36.6 m square], but it presents only the appearance of a mass of water-worn stones, and thus it escaped his attention. Had he excavated for the architecture he would not have attempted an enumeration of the topes. . . . I believe there are monuments of this kind of every size, some being only a few feet in diameter; and such has been their quantity that, even when they were perfect above ground, it would have been a long piece of work to have determined the exact number, and now it is impossible.

It is true that Masson's distinctions relied solely on how much of the surviving structure was visible: a 'tope' was generally well preserved with obvious architectural features (fig. 183.1–5), while the more dilapidated form of a 'tumulus' was obscured by a mound of debris (figs 18; 183.6–7). However, although he never excavated Ahinposh, he was perfectly aware of its existence, even to the extent of drawing

a plan of the site (Masson MSS Eur. E 164, f. 109). He also noted 'Tupper Lahore' (Tapa Khwaja Lahoree: fig. 183.6; Mizuno 1970, pl. 39), but the published version of his description is confused, owing to bad editing by Wilson (1841, p. 99, topes pl. VII). In contrast Masson's unpublished original account is clear and easy to understand (MSS Eur. E 164, f. 133):

> This is a remarkable artificial mound of about — feet in height and — in circumference [1800 ft/329.38 m, according to Wilson 1841, p. 99; 760 yds/694.96 m, according to MSS Eur. F 63, no. 657, f. 49(77)]. It has been found either entirely or partially [constructed] with masonry, the stones inserted after the chequered manner [diaper masonry]. On the summit at the western extremity is a tumulus. Coins, fragments of iron, silver and gold are occasionally found on the mound – and funeral jars are also sometimes exposed. The tumulus was situated amid a huge square enclosure, the remains of which are clearly discernible in the huge mounds encompassing it. Without this enclosure are seven remarkable tumuli and vast heaps of stones. The adjacent site is called Beghram and the natives have a tradition that the city of Lahore once stood here. The fact is that Tupper Lahore is a sepulchral erection, as are the various tumuli and heaps of stones in the vicinity. . . . Beghram was the name more recently conferred upon capital cities, and being a general one, was common to many large cities.

Masson subdivided 'tumuli' further into two classes: 'superior' or large 'detached and independent structures' and 'inferior' smaller versions (votive stupas) that 'invariably accompany topes' (Wilson 1841, p. 91). As Simpson also noted (1879–80, p. 45):

> Every monastery, in addition to its larger tope, has numerous small ones of various sizes. We subscribed a few rupees and had a small exploration carried on at Hada [sic]. This was close to one of the larger topes which had an extensive chasm in its side – most probably made by Masson; our operations did not extend over a great space, still we cleared out part of what had been a tope 29 feet [8.84 m] in diameter, and it was surrounded by a series of smaller topes, about 4 or 5 feet [1.22–1.52 m] in diameter. Here we found some interesting fragments of sculpture; the quantity of plaster figures embedded in the earth, and close to the surface, was a matter of surprise to us all.

It is not clear from this account which of the sites Simpson excavated. But his sketch of Hadda (1881, pl. II) shows the village and Tope Kelan in the distance and a series of stupas on a ridge in the foreground, one of which has a large excavated hole on one side. Several sketches by Masson identify the location of these ruins as Gundi Kabul (MSS Eur. E 164, ff. 126–7, 129; Tarzi 1990, p. 707, fig. 1). This suggests that Simpson's excavations most probably took place in this

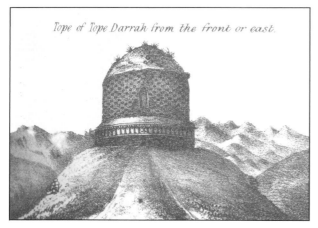

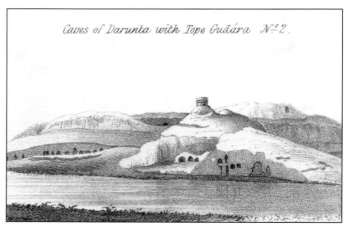

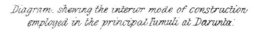

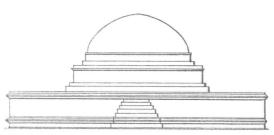

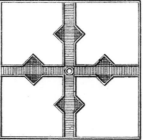

Figure 183 Drawings by Masson:
1 Shevaki stupa 1;
2 Topdara stupa;
3 Gundi Kabul, Hadda;
4 Bimaran stupa 2;
5 Gudara stupa and Fil Khana caves;
6 Tapa Khwaja Lahoree/Nagarahara;
7–8 Section and plan of a 'tumulus'.

vicinity, or perhaps near Tope Momand on the southern slopes of the ridge (Wilson 1841, pp. 110–11),[2] where Masson records in 1835 that the villagers uncovered the remains of a stupa decorated with stone reliefs and twelve seated Buddha statues, their hair coated with gold leaf (Wilson 1841, p. 111;

Errington 2006). Simpson's excavation revealed a series of small votive stupas (1879–80, p. 39, pl. I, fig. 2), similar to those found in the chapels of the Tope Kelan stupa courtyard (fig. 184; Tarzi 1990, p. 14, figs 9, 11, chapels 5 and 1 respectively).

Figure 184 View of Tope Kelan, Hadda (1978–9), showing the hole in the stupa from Masson's excavation and one of the excavated stupas of chapel 5 in the foreground.

Simpson's and the later twentieth-century excavations also reveal that an extensive part of the sites lay buried beneath the surface. Masson mentions being puzzled by the 'large oblong areas enclosed within huge mounds of earth' which he found beside all the stupas at Hadda and Chahar Bagh, but which were absent at Darunta (Wilson 1841, p. 57). These are recognisable as monasteries. At Darunta the numerous caves of the Siah Koh ridge and Fil-Khana probably served the same function (fig. 183.4; Mizuno 1967, pp. 68–77, pls 25–54; 1970, fig. 24).

When Masson describes stupas as being divided internally into four quarters by filled 'passages', and speaks also of finding tunnels within the body of the mounds at Gudara and elsewhere, he is clearly referring to the system of ribs commonly used to strengthen the core of the structure (fig. 183.8; Wilson 1841, pp. 87–8, 92–3, topes pls IV–VI). The Japanese survey of Gudara found a core of mud and boulders reinforced by eight stone walls radiating from the centre (Mizuno 1967, pp. 46–8, plan 11b). Simpson describes a similar form of construction quite clearly at Nagara Gundi, the largest stupa of Tapa Khwaja Lahoree: the mound 'had a number of lines radiating from the centre of the Tope; none of them seem to extend exactly to the centre, and they disappear again among the boulders towards the circumference. They are formed of Buddhist masonry, with a face formed only on one side. . . . The conclusion is that these spines or diaphragms were constructed all through the Tope, to give stability to the mass' (Simpson 1879–80, p. 53).

In 1879, during a lull in the Second Afghan War, Colonel Jenkins of the Corps of Guides began excavating Nagara Gundi. His tunnel reached only 28 ft 7 in./9 m into the basement area (c.120 ft/393.7 m square) of the mound but it unearthed a bronze 'coin of Apollodorus [*sic*], with the tripod of Delphi on it' (Simpson 1879–80, p. 57). Whether this was a coin of Apollodotus I (c.180–160 BC) or Apollodotus II (c.65–50 BC) is not known (figs 54.9; 113.1), but in either case it remains the earliest coin to have been found in any of the Afghanistan stupas. However, as a stray find, it indicates only that the stupa must have been erected at some unspecified time after the mid second or mid first century BC. The substantial coin evidence from Masson and Honigberger's excavations, to be discussed below, suggests a much later date of the first century AD for the building of Buddhist monuments in this region.

Masson often speaks of finding the relic deposit 'at foundation level', but, since he left the debris surrounding the stupas largely untouched, he often had little idea of the actual ground level, or of the architecture of the obscured lower part of the structures. Such was the case at Tope Kelan, Hadda, where the square podium with its flight of steps and stucco decoration remained totally hidden from view until excavated in 1978–9 (Tarzi 1990, figs 5–9). Tarzi's excavation showed further that the relic deposit was located about 2 m above the basement within the centre of the stupa dome (fig. 184; 1990, pp. 722–3, fig. 15).

Simpson's excavation of the Ahinposh stupa however confirms that the relic deposit was in some instances located where Masson placed it in his section drawings: in the centre of the platform structure, not within the dome (fig. 185.1–2, 4–8; 1879–80, pp. 48–9, pls II–III.1). Simpson's description of Ahinposh moreover suggests that the relic deposit was contemporary with the outer structure of the stupa:

> I began a tunnel . . . so as to penetrate to the centre of the Tope. . . . [The interior structure was] all water-worn boulders, the largest being a couple of feet in size; embedded in mud, the whole formed a compact mass so firm that no supports were necessary while making the tunnel. The boulders were to a certain extent built in layers. . . . I determined on . . . making the original surface of the ground the floor of my tunnel. This turned out to be a fortunate plan, for it led me direct on the central cell, which had been constructed on this level. . . . There was no variety in the manner of building, and when at last it was reported that some slabs were visible I knew it was the cell which had been come upon . . . the stones were removed on each side and beyond the slates; and it was only after the space was cleared out, and the part containing the cell could be seen all round, that I began to open it. It formed an oblong heap, quite rude externally, about 4 feet [1.21 m] long and about 3 feet [0.91 m] wide. On the top was a large slate extending nearly to these dimensions, and about 1 inch [2.5 cm] thick . . . embedded in mud, with another slate slightly larger in size under it. On raising this last the cell was disclosed; it was a cube of 16 inches [40.6 cm], formed of small slates about 6 inches [15.2 cm] long and half an inch [1.2 cm] thick, and their edge, which formed the surface of the cell, were smoothly trimmed, but not polished. . . . The bottom was formed of another large slab. . . . [The cell contained] about two handfuls of dark brown dust, which I presume were the ashes . . . a golden reliquary [and] gold coins.

Although Simpson states that his tunnel was at ground level, in a footnote and in his section drawing he gives a precise measurement for floor of the tunnel and the relic cell as '12 feet 2 inches [3.71 m] above the ground floor of the Tope'. This can hardly be classified as ground or foundation level, and evokes the suspicion that an earlier structure could have been buried below this point within the mass of the stupa.

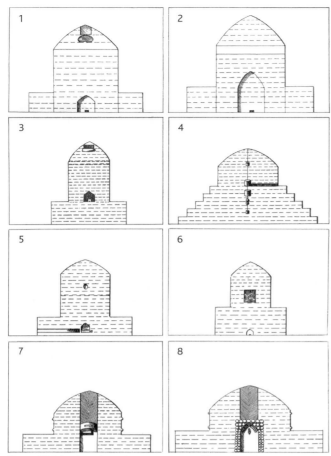

Figure 185 Sections through stupas excavated by Masson showing the locations of relic deposits:
1–2 Kotpur stupas 1 and 2;
3   Nandara stupa 1;
4   Gudara;
5–6 Chahar Bagh stupas 4 and 1;
7–8 Passani tumuli 7 and 5.

Figure 186 Bimaran 2 relic deposit: inscribed steatite reliquary 'gift of Shivaraksita . . . presented for Lord's relics, in honour of all Buddhas'; repoussée gold reliquary inset with garnets; four posthumous Azes coins; beads, semi-precious stones and gold ornaments.

From the evidence uncovered by Masson and Honigberger it is clear that the position of the relic deposit varied according to the type of stupa. In the centre of the monument near Begram and the stupas Seh Top 2, Kotpur 1 and 2, Bimaran 1 and 3, Chahar Bagh 1 and 4, Nandara 1, Sultanpur and Passani tumulus 5 (fig. 185.3, 5–6, 8) were 'internal topes, or structures of the same form as the outer mass, only wanting the platform. . . . They are covered with cement, and their separation from the mass of the monuments is often marked by a line of unburnt bricks, sometimes by stones of a description different to that employed in the mass' (Wilson 1841, pp. 60, 117; Jacquet 1836a, p. 275). These are identifiable as earlier, much smaller stupas, encased within the later enlarged monuments. Good examples have subsequently been excavated at Ranigat in the Peshawar Valley, Kunala at Taxila and Butkara I in Swat (fig. 112; Nishikawa 1994, pl. 8; Marshall 1951, vol. I, p. 350; III, pl. 87). The 'cement' covering evidently refers to a stucco coating, which in the case of Passani tumulus 5 was decorated with painted flowers (fig. 185.8; Wilson 1841, p. 95, topes pl. V). At Hadda, in one of the stupas on Gundi Kabul excavated by Masson, Simpson also found the matrix of a core stupa about 9 ft/2.74 m in diameter, and 'of a different shape from the later topes' (1879–80, p. 56, pl. VII.1).

The relic deposits were often placed in specially constructed square cells (as at Ahinposh), in the centre of the

original core stupa, or in the body of the later enlargement, or both (figs 177; 185). In some stupas there was no evidence of any enlargement, only a relic chamber, while in others the deposit was simply buried within the solid mass of the mound. A number of stupas are said to have held no deposit, but may in fact have contained ashes and bones, as recorded at several other sites. Most of the reliquaries contained ashes, which were often mixed with small precious objects.

At Sultanpur the ashes were housed in a miniature stupa (Wilson 1841, antiquities pl. III.1). Most of the other reliquaries discovered by Masson were turned steatite caskets of various shapes and sizes; some with carved decoration; some subdivided internally (e.g. Passani tumulus 2); others inscribed (Bimaran 2). Many of these stone caskets contained smaller reliquaries of gold, silver, bark or ivory, as well as gems, semi-precious stones, pearls, beads, coins and small items or scraps of precious metal. His most spectacular find was the gold repoussée casket decorated with standing images of the Buddha and other divinities, which was found inside the inscribed steatite casket at Bimaran 2 (fig. 186). The four base metal coins from the deposit – variously identified by Masson as 'horseman-Ceres type' or 'of the Azes dynasty' (MSS Eur. 161/VII, f. 2; Wilson 1841, p. 71) – are in the name of the Indo-Scythian king Azes (c.46–1 BC), but were issued posthumously c. AD 60 (fig. 182.2). They provide the earliest evidence for dating the fully developed iconography of the standing Buddha image, as exhibited on the gold casket.

Dating the gold reliquary however is complicated by the fact that it was included in the relic deposit together with other miscellaneous damaged objects that could have all been deposited at a much later date than the numismatic evidence suggests. Not only were its lid and several garnets already missing when first excavated, but it contained a broken bronze ring and gold ornament fragments, while the outer steatite casket – chipped and also missing its upper lid – has had its original five internal compartments chiselled out to house the gold reliquary. The intact steatite casket of the same type from the nearby site of Passani tumulus 2, contained coins of Wima Tak[to] (c. AD 90–113) (figs 61.14–15; 181), which extends the possible date of the

Bimaran 2 deposit into the second century (Errington 1999, pp. 212–13, 221, 231–2, pls 10–11.1–2, 7–8, 12; Zwalf 1996, no. 652, p. 346). In fact detailed analysis of the Buddha images on the gold casket and those on Kushan coins produced late in the reign of Kanishka I (*c*. AD 127–50; fig. 113.7–8) shows they are comparable in date, thereby suggesting that the reliquary was produced at least a century later than the coins found with it initially seem to indicate (Cribb 1999/2000; 2005a).

Coins were found in twenty-six of the stupas excavated by Masson, Honigberger and Simpson in the Kabul–Jalalabad region. Bearing in mind that coins provide only a *terminus post quem*, this limited numismatic evidence indicates that the earliest Buddhist monuments in Afghanistan were founded in the Darunta district west of Jalalabad from *c*. AD 50 onwards. A coin of the same posthumous 'Azes' type as the Bimaran 2 deposit was found near the summit of Passani tumulus 5 (fig. 182.2; MSS Eur. E 161/VII, ff. 2, 6, Uncat. MSS 1, f. 5), while the stupas Bimaran 5 and Hadda 3 had two of the same 'Azes' coins and a tetradrachm of the Indo-Parthian king Gondophares (*c*. AD 32–60) (fig. 59.2), mixed with larger numbers of Hermaeus imitations of the first Kushan king, Kujula Kadphises (*c*. AD 40–90; fig. 61.5). The original core stupa deposit of Kotpur 2 uniquely contained a broken silver Heraus obol coated on the back with gold leaf (As. 1880–3735; type fig. 61.2),[3] together with bronze Hermaeus imitations of Kujula Kadphises. Coins of the last type alone are recorded in the relic cell of Deh Rahman 1 (Wilson 1841, pp. 66, 79, coins pl. V.8).

Masson also found six small coins, one 'a novel type, but apparently of the Azes family', in Passani tumulus 2 (MSS Eur. E 161/VII, ff. 10, 18; Wilson 1841, p. 94). Wilson (1841, p. 51) identifies these all as 'Soter Megas' hemidrachms, now recognised as issues of the second Kushan king, Wima Tak[to] (*c*. AD 90–113) (fig. 61.14–15; Sims-Wiliams and Cribb 1995/6, pp. 111–23, figs 11–15). That Masson considered the issuer of the Soter Megas ('Great Saviour') coins a member of the Azes dynasty is clear from his discussion of them (Wilson 1841, pp. 72–3). He gives more detailed information on the 'Azus [*sic*] dynasty' in his illustrated manuscript sent to James Prinsep in early 1836 (Uncat. MSS 2, ff. 11–12, 41, pl. 5, figs 99–111), but this section was omitted from the severely edited version which appeared in the *Journal of the Asiatic Society of Bengal* later that year (Masson 1836a). However, the unpublished illustrations include three rarer hemidrachm issues of Wima Tak[to] (fig. 61.8; Uncat. MSS 2, f. 41, pl. 5, figs 107, 109–110; Mitchiner 1978, p. 399, nos 2919–22) and it is most probable that the 'novel type' from Passani tumulus 2 was one of these and not, as previously suggested, the square horseman/lion issue of Kharahostes (fig. 182.3; Errington 1999/2000, pp. 195–6, fig. 35). The reasons for this are threefold. The Kharahostes coin is not small or round; it is a rare type not recorded at all by Masson; and, although one example was uncovered by Lieutenant Pigou in the Darunta stupa of Tope-i-Kutchera, it was found with contemporary, mid-first-century AD coins of Kujula Kadphises, not with issues of his successor (Pigou 1841, pl. facing p. 381). It is perhaps also worth noting that coins of Wima Tak[to] occur only on their own in the relic deposits. In contrast, coins of Kujula are often found with coins of other contemporary

rulers, while the coins of subsequent Kushan kings – from Wima Kadphises (*c*. AD 113–27) onwards – are also frequently mixed together in stupa deposits.

Generally in the Darunta region the largest number of new stupas, or enlargements of earlier structures (e.g. Bimaran stupa 3), date from the late first or early second century, during the reign of Wima Tak[to] (Errington 1999/ 2000, pp. 214–15). There are no coins later than the time of Wima Kadphises in any of the core stupa deposits. The monasteries on the Jalalabad plain and in the neighbourhood of Kabul and Wardak generally appear to be later in date than the Darunta monuments, with the largest number dating from the time of Huvishka (*c*. AD 150–90). These deposits usually included a mix of earlier coins. Both Guldara (fig. 109) and Hadda 4 contained coins of Wima Kadphises and Huvishka, while the bronze vase from Wardak 1, inscribed in the reign of Huvishka, in the year 51 (*c*. AD 178) of the Kushan era founded by Kanishka I (*c*. AD 127–50), contained a mix of bronze coins of Wima Kadphises, Kanishka and Huvishka (fig. 114). At Ahinposh gold staters of the same three rulers (including one of Kanishka depicting the standing Buddha) were deposited with three Roman gold aurei of Domitian (AD 81–96), Trajan (AD 98–117) and Sabina, wife of Hadrian (*c*. AD 128–36) (figs 113.7; 115; Cunningham 1879, pls II–III; Hoernle 1879, 1879a; Simpson 1879). With the exception of the single coin of Huvishka, all the coins in the deposit were very worn, which suggests they had been in circulation for some time prior to burial.

Finally Masson's excavation of Tope Kelan, the principal stupa at Hadda, shows that Buddhism continued to flourish even after the Hun invasions of the early fifth century. Over 200 coins were found in this relic deposit (figs 82–3; pp. 93–5). Only fourteen silver coins depicting the distinctive elongated heads of the Alchon Huns were included, which suggests that these particular issues come late in the coin sequence (Masson Uncat. MSS 2, ff. 49–50, figs 1–27). There was a larger number of Hun imitations of Sasanian coins bearing the tamgha associated with the Alchon, but the majority were issues of the late fourth- to fifth-century Sasanian kings Varhran IV (AD 388–99), Yazdagird II (AD 438–57) and Peroz (AD 457/9–84) (Errington 1999, pp. 215–16, 234–7). These, together with five local imitations of gold solidi of the fifth-century Roman emperors Theodosius II (AD 409–50), Marcianus (AD 450–7) and Leo (AD 457–4), provided a chronological context of the mid or late fifth century not only for the stupa but also for the undated Hun coins in the deposit.

As a result of the wealth of material gathered in Afghanistan and at Manikyala in these early years of discovery, a basic understanding of the raison d'être for these Buddhist monuments had already been reached by the mid 1830s. The situation was neatly summed up at this time by Horace Wilson. He gives the probable time-span that they remained in cult as the first or second century to the eighth century AD and says (1841, p. 45):

> all are agreed that the topes are monuments peculiar to the faith of the Buddha; there is some difference, not very material, as to their especial appropriation. Lieutenant Burnes, Mr Masson and M. Court, adopting the notions that prevail amongst the people of the country, are inclined to regard them as regal sepultures;

Figure 187 General view of the site of Jamalgarhi, with a section drawing and plan of the main stupa courtyard by Lieutenant Maisten.

Figure 188 Mound D, Sahri Bahlol, showing the destroyed base of stupa I reused as a platform on which broken sculptures had been placed for worship.

but I am disposed with Mr. Erskine and Mr Hodgson . . . to regard them as dahgopas on a large scale, that is, as shrines enclosing and protecting some sacred relic, attributed . . . to Sakya Sinha or Gautama, or to some inferior representative of him, some Bodhisatwa [*sic*], some high-priest or Lama of local sanctity. Mr Prinsep has manifested a disposition to effect a kind of compromise between these opinions, and suggests . . . that the two objects of a memorial to the dead, and a shrine to the divinity, may have been combined in a meritorious erection of these curious monuments.

This initial period of intense research was brought abruptly to a halt by the First Anglo-Afghan War (1838–42). Afterwards, of the people who had been interested in the subject from the beginning, Prinsep, Jacquet and Gerard were dead, while Masson, Ventura and Court returned to Europe. After the death of Ranjit Singh in 1839, the break-up of the Sikh Empire resulted in the British annexation of the Punjab in 1849. Honigberger stayed on in Lahore in charge of the jail and lunatic asylum long enough to receive a British pension, but, perhaps scarred by the experience of trying to sell his collection, took no further interest in antiquities. Only Cunningham remained to refine the details and carry on the process of discovery within British India. Apart from the brief flurry of excavation by William Simpson and others during the Second Afghan War (1878–9), Afghanistan remained effectively barred to European (especially British) archaeological exploration until well into the twentieth century.

Annexation of the Sikh territories in 1849, however, gave the British access for the first time to the Punjab and the North-West Frontier region, including the area comprising the heartland of ancient Gandhara: the plain bounded by the Swat, Kabul and Indus rivers north-east of Peshawar, which was known in the British period as the Yusufzai District, and now forms part of the Peshawar Valley. One of the first to explore the area was Alexander Cunningham (1848, pp. 89–132), who went in search of sites associated with Alexander the Great, but instead saw the Shahbazgarhi rock edict of the Mauryan emperor Ashoka (*c*.269–232 BC) and the Buddhist monasteries of Jamalgarhi and Ranigat, although the latter, he was convinced, was the fortress of Aornus mentioned by the Greek historians (p. 36; fig. 37; Cunningham 1848, p. 131). He also mistook the relief image of a female guard which he collected at the site as a depiction of Athena (Errington 1990, pp. 19–30).

In 1851 the new British administration of the Punjab introduced the first official system for gaining information

and preserving ancient monuments. The inspiration for this was partly political, for the directive from the Governor-General, Dalhousie (Punjab Board of Administration 1851), states 'it is obviously impossible to go to much expense on such works, but a great deal may be done at small expense by a little care and interest, and all will tend to gratify the inhabitants over which British rule has been established'. The system included compulsory annual lists of antiquarian remains and reports of any discoveries. In response officers resident in the district began recording and excavating sites and set up a small museum at Peshawar to house the finds. Jamalgarhi was the first site to be excavated, by Harry Lumsden, commander of the newly formed Guides Corps stationed at Mardan, in the centre of the Peshawar Valley (fig. 187; Bayley 1852, pp. 606–21). In the early 1860s the Reverend Isidore Loewenthal (1861; 1863), a missionary of the American Presbyterian Mission stationed at Peshawar, reported more noteworthy finds from Jamrud and Tahkal, to the west of Peshawar, and in the vicinity of Naogram and Ranigat on the Buner frontier.[4] But the most comprehensive account of the remains of the Peshawar Valley in their unexcavated state was made by Dr Henry Bellew (1864, pp. 109–51). Resident at Mardan throughout the 1860s, he investigated the urban site of Sahri Bahlol and the major monasteries, including Takht-i-Bahi, Jamalgarhi and Ranigat. Much of this evidence was subsequently destroyed or not noted by later excavators at the sites. In the lower courtyard at Takht-i-Bahi (fig. 111), for example, he found stucco fragments of 'a hand, a foot, and portion of the head . . . fully four times the natural size' that he deduced must have belonged to statues at least 16 feet high (Bellew 1864, pp. 131–2). This detail confirms that the shrines of this courtyard contained colossal stucco figures similar to the six examples found during the 1907 excavation in front of the wall to the west of the main complex (Spooner 1911, pp. 132–48, pl. XXI). Bellew also excavated the stupa at Dhamami, south-east of Sahri Bahlol, where he discovered the first evidence of the reuse of cult statues: a small broken Bodhisattva was buried with human, animal and bird bones and ashes in the relic chamber of the stupa, while the schist image of Maitreya, minus its feet, was found placed on a granite pedestal, with an oil lamp on either side (Bellew 1864, pp. 140–3; Tissot 1985, pp. 575–6, figs 2–3). This situation was mirrored at other Sahri Bahlol sites (fig. 188; Stein 1912). More recent evidence for the reuse of earlier schist sculpture also occurs elsewhere, for example at Butkara I and Panr in Swat (fig. 189; Faccenna 1980, vol. I,

Figure 189 Reused schist relief *in situ* on the Butkara I main stupa.

p. 113; III, pl. C; Faccenna *et al*. 1993, pp. 51–2, 129–31, pls 70–3), or as late as the twentieth century, at Rajar (Errington 1999/2000, p. 204, fig. 7).

From 1867 onwards officers were exhorted to 'use their best endeavours to obtain contributions' for the newly founded Lahore Central Museum. As a result all the sculptures from the local Peshawar Museum were transferred to Lahore (Errington 1987, pp. 100–2, 192). An active policy to collect more sculpture was also implemented by the Punjab government. This resulted in the first official excavations, which were carried out annually by the Sappers and Miners for the Public Works Department between 1871 and 1882, at Takht-i-Bahi, Jamalgarhi, Kharkai, Thareli, Shah-ji-ki-Dheri, Tahkal, Charsadda and several monasteries on the eastern slopes of Mount Karamar (Errington 1987, pp. 125–55, 434–50; Crompton 1875; Errington 1987a; Martin 1882; Maxwell 1882).

How did the Archaeological Survey fit into this programme? In 1861 Alexander Cunningham was appointed Director of Archaeology, with the brief 'to make an accurate description of such remains as most deserve notice, with the history of them as far as it is traceable, and a record of the traditions that are retained regarding them' (Abu Imam 1966, pp. 54–6; Marshall 1904, pp. 3–4). The Archaeological Survey was initially conceived in the same spirit as the Great Trignometrical Geographical Survey: as a project that would be completed within a few years. This idea of a limited existence and equally limited funding persisted despite the Resolution of 1871 (*Punjab Government Gazette* 1871, pp. 237–8) which elevated Cunningham to the position of Director-General of a newly created Archaeological Survey of India, and required him to make 'a complete search over the whole country and a systematic record and description of all architectural and other remains that are remarkable alike for their antiquity, or their beauty, or their historical interest'. The principal objectives were that Cunningham should produce 'a brief summary of the labours of former enquirers, and of the results which have already been obtained' and, secondly, 'a general scheme of systematic enquiry' as a guideline for research. It was desired that people native to the subcontinent should be trained to do 'the work of photographing, measuring, and surveying buildings, directing excavations, and the like'. It was also recognised that they were better qualified to decipher inscriptions 'than any European'. The importance of photography was already realised and, in fact, the earliest comprehensive photographic records of finds from Gandharan sites are of the material excavated at Jamalgarhi in 1873 (Errington 1987, pp. 311–24, 484–9; ASI Photographs, nos 973–1020). This practice subsequently became standard, and the Archaeological Survey photographic record is now a primary source for identifying the site provenance of sculptures from nineteenth- and early twentieth-century collections.

In reality Cunningham was in charge of northern India only, while, from 1874, James Burgess had responsibility for the survey of the Madras and Bombay Presidencies. All the work of the survey was done by Cunningham himself and a few assistants. In this light it is easy to understand why the annual tours of exploration by Cunningham, and, more especially, his less experienced assistants, were often so superficial and undertaken at such speed. The task was only possible during the short winter months. In one three-month season as many as thirty sites would be visited and vast distances covered, by any available means of transport, including elephant, camel, horse, bullock-cart, or on foot. Garrick, for example, records that in the 1881–2 season he covered 2700 miles by rail and walked the remaining 750 miles (1885, p. 1; Abu Imam 1966, pp. 174, 181). In a letter to Tremlett, recently discovered by Michael Willis in the Ashmolean Museum archives, Cunningham mentions in another year that his trip to the Punjab was cancelled 'for want of camels'. There were no provisions for excavation, other than the most cursory explorations to ascertain the nature of the remains. The job of the surveyors was to recommend promising sites to the Public Works Department. Any decision to dig was taken by the provincial governments – in the case of the Gandharan sites, this meant the Punjab government – who then provided funding and requisitioned a company of Sappers and Miners to excavate the site. Cunningham followed his brief to the letter. Large sections of his reports simply summarise or repeat verbatim the information gleaned from investigations or excavations carried out by others – Ventura and Court at Manikyala, Bellew and the Sappers and Miners in the Yusufzai (Cunningham 1871; 1875) – to which he added observations derived from his own, often superficial, excavations.

With regard to the Punjab (which at this time included the British territories of the North-West Frontier and Peshawar region) he considered that (1871a, p. 1)

> the most interesting subject of enquiry is the identification of those famous peoples and cities, whose names have become familiar to the whole world through the expedition of Alexander the Great. To find the descendants of those peoples and the sites

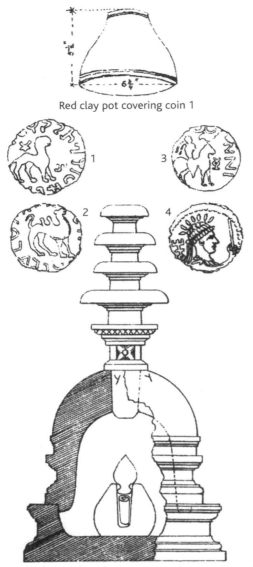

Red clay pot covering coin 1

Figure 190 Relic deposit of Sonala Pind: terracotta pot, steatite model stupa, crystal reliquary, rolled gold foil with inscription (now lost), (1–2) coins of Kujula Kadphises and Zeionises, with (3–4) coins of Sasan and Wima Tak[to] found in the surface debris.

Figure 191 Excavated Buddhist sculptures from the lower monastery at Natthu, 1884.

of those ancient cities amongst the scattered inhabitants and ruined mounds of the present day, I propose, like Pliny, to follow the track of Alexander himself. This plan has a double advantage, for as the Chinese pilgrims, as well as the Macedonian invaders, entered India from the West, the routes of the conquerors and the pilgrims will mutually illustrate each other.

However, no evidence of any Greek presence in these regions, apart from Indo-Greek coins and apparent Classical influences in Gandharan sculpture, was uncovered during his lifetime. So it was perhaps just as well that his principal historical source, other than the Greek writers, was the newly translated account of the seventh-century Chinese pilgrim Xuan Zang (Julien 1857). Use of this text enabled him to identify several major sites, including Taxila (Cunningham 1871, p. 116) and also Shah-ji-ki-Dheri, the renowned stupa said to have been founded by Kanishka I at Peshawar (Cunningham 1874, pp. 420–1), although the latter identification was not verified until 1908 (fig. 115; Spooner 1912).

Cunningham's work at Manikyala provides a good example of his methods (fig. 117; Cunningham 1871, pp. 152–72, pls LXII–LXV; 1875, pp. 75–9, pls XXI–XXIV; 1882, pp. 3–5, pls II–III). His account begins with the identification of the site

in the records of the Chinese pilgrims. This is followed by a report on the discoveries made in the neighbourhood by Ventura, Court and local people, while his maps incorporate information derived from Court's survey of the sites (Court 1836, pl. XXVI), as well as from his own survey 'of the few ruins about Mânikyâla which escaped the researches of General Court' (Cunningham 1871, p. 166, pl. LXII; 1882, pl. II). Limited excavations were undertaken largely to ascertain the nature of the ruins or, in the case of stupas, to find relic deposits. Following up a local's discovery of two small bronzes (a Buddha's head and 'a grotesque-looking face') in the 'remains of a large square building on the lower Sonâla lands', for example, he 'set twenty diggers to work' and after about an hour, 'had roughly traced the positions of several rooms of a considerable building'. In this way, five complete rooms were cleared (Cunningham 1871, p. 171, no. 22).

It is evident that Cunningham employed the same roughshod excavation techniques of his contemporaries, with the notable exception that he was also a numismatist and almost always identified the coins he unearthed. So it is possible to gain some idea of the approximate date of site no. 22, because he records finding two bronze Kushan coins of Wima Kadphises (c. AD 113–27) and Vasudeva I (c. AD 190–227) respectively. The major find from the site (which Cunningham identified as a monastery) was a bronze statue of the Buddha (BM 1958.7.14.1; height 41.3 cm), stylistically dated c. fifth to seventh century (Errington and Cribb 1992, pp. 222–3).

The coin evidence of another excavation by Cunningham at the Sonala Pind stupa (no. 15) further revealed (as in Afghanistan) a mid-first-century AD date for the establishment of the first Buddhist monasteries in the neighbourhood of Manikyala (figs 21; 190; Cunningham 1871, pp. 166–8, pls LXIV–LXV): a red clay pot in the centre of the mound covered a bronze coin of the Indo-Scythian satrap Zeionises (c. AD 30–50) and another of the first Kushan king Kujula Kadphises (c. AD 40–90). Below this was the relic deposit: a steatite reliquary which contained a small crystal

Figure 192 Excavated sculptures from Loriyan Tangai, Swat, 1895–6.

reliquary and an inscribed gold scroll (since lost). The steatite reliquary replicates the form of the stupa in Gandhara in this period: a square or round base platform, and a dome, which is crowned by a railing or harmika and a series of umbrellas (figs 109–10).

The first attempt at organised conservation for British India was made in 1881, when Major Henry Cole of the Royal Engineers was appointed as Curator of Ancient Monuments for three years, in order to prepare 'classified lists of the monuments in each Province and assess the costs of repair and maintenance in each case' (Marshall 1904, p. 4). This appointment and task was completely separate from the work of the Archaeological Survey. Instead Cole was attached to the Public Works Department, 'fortified' by a Committee of Taste, which decided difficult questions of repair and restoration. After his survey of the Yusufzai district (i.e. Peshawar Valley), Cole published an account of the sites of Sanghao, Rhode and Natthu, together with a comprehensive photographic record of the sculptures he collected (fig. 191; Cole 1883; 1884–5). However, at the end of his term of office, responsibility for the preservation of ancient monuments reverted to the local authorities – in the case of Gandhara, this meant the Punjab Public Works Department – while the task of recording new finds rested with the District and Assistant Commissioners (NWFP 1884–91). The discovery of Sikri in 1888, for example, was reported by Harold Deane, the Assistant Commissioner at Mardan, and, following an

inspection by the Archaeological Survey, was excavated by him the following year for the Punjab government (NWFP 1884–91, nos 1–2).

Following the retirement of Cunningham in 1885 and his successor, Burgess, in 1889, there was further retrenchment, due to what were considered the unduly high costs of the Archaeological Survey (Marshall 1904, p. 6). Official belief was that the Survey should be completed by 1895 and that the limited funds available should be spent on 'conserving the known rather than searching for the unknown' (Marshall 1904, p. 7). Although by 1895 public opinion had convinced the government of India not to disband the Archaeological Survey, no Director-General was appointed until 1902.

In the meantime military campaigns beyond the frontiers of British India in 1895–6 opened the way for archaeological research in the independent tribal territories of Buner, Ranizai (south of the Malakand Pass) and Swat (ancient Udyana). Freed from the constraints of the Preservation of Ancient Monuments laws of British India, a number of sites were ransacked before Harold Deane, as Political Agent, put a stop to the amateur diggings by confiscating the sculptures (Mainwaring *et al.* 1903, p. 94; Errington 1990a, pp. 775–9). There were also official Archaeological Survey excavations for the Bengal government, most notably at Loriyan Tangai (fig. 192), while the French scholar Alfred Foucher and the Hungarian Aurel Stein carried out extensive surveys of the extant remains of the Swat Valley (Waddell 1896; Foucher 1901; Stein 1929, 1930).

John Marshall's appointment as Director-General in 1902 was part of a comprehensive reform of the Archaeological Survey of India, in which its role was expanded to include not only surveys but also excavations, conservation, research and epigraphy. In line with this policy Marshall prepared a comprehensive Antiquities Law for India, promoted the extensive conservation and restoration of existing structures and authorised the excavation of the major Gandharan sites in the Peshawar Valley (Takht-i-Bahi, Sahri Bahlol, Shah-ji-ki-Dheri, Tahkal and Jamalgarhi) as well as conducting his own extensive archaeological explorations at Charsadda and Taxila (1913–34). As a gesture to contemporary Buddhists in Sri Lanka, the relic deposit from his excavation of the votive stupa S8 at Dharmarajika was presented by the Indian government in 1917 to the Temple of the Tooth at Kandy (Marshall 1951, pp. 241–2), thus laying the foundation for great potential confusion among any archaeologists or art historians who might chance upon it in the future.

Notes

1 For another coin from Honigberger see fig. 54.6 (Hermaeus imitation, CM BMC 34, Honigberger no. 2).
2 Incorrectly numbered 'Hadda no. 12' in the text; actually Hadda no. 8 as marked on Masson's map (Wilson 1841, topes pl. I: for discussion see Errington 2006).
3 Identified as a Bactrian issue of Kujula: see p. 67, fig. 61.2 and Cribb 1993.
4 Loewenthal translated the New Testament into Pushtu. He was shot by his chokidar (watchman) on 27 April 1864. A note by the officiating minister, David Bellamy, recording his death in the Peshawar Burial Register, states 'Well done! thou true and faithful servant' (Farrington 1988, pp. 33, 110).

10 Sir Aurel Stein: the next generation

Helen Wang

Sir Aurel Stein is renowned as 'the most prodigious combination of scholar, explorer, archaeologist and geographer of his generation' (Lattimore 1973, p. 276), and for 'the most daring and adventuresome raid upon the ancient world that any archaeologist has attempted' (Woolley 1958, p. 122).[1] Fêted and reviled around the world, even his own government would come to call him 'a white elephant in the shape of an educational officer who had turned out to be a very distinguished archaeologist' (Mirsky 1977, p. 336). Proof of these characterisations can be found in Stein's three important reports, *Ancient Khotan* (1907), *Serindia* (1921) and *Innermost Asia* (1928), the results of his three arduous expeditions into Chinese Central Asia in 1900–1, 1906–8 and 1913–16, respectively, and in the vast Stein collections now housed in various institutions in Britain and India (Wang 1999).[2] To this day Stein's reports remain the 'bibles' for information about sites in Chinese Central Asia, and whilst his activities might not always be acceptable in the modern world, his methods and procedures should be seen in the context of his own times.

Marc Aurel Stein was born in Budapest on 26 November 1862. At the age of seventeen he went to the University of Vienna to study Sanskrit and comparative philology, then to the University of Leipzig, and finally to Tübingen, where he studied Indology and Old Persian. In 1884 he came to Britain, and, apart from returning to Budapest in 1884–5 for military service, he made Britain – in the largest sense – his national base. He spent much of 1886 studying the coin collections at the British Museum and the Ashmolean Museum in Oxford and produced his first article, 'Zoroastrian deities on Indo-Scythian coins', which was published in the *Oriental and Babylonian Record* of 1887. Stein was clearly familiar with how the European explorers had collected coins in Afghanistan and India in the earlier half of the nineteenth century; how close examination of these coins had revealed the extent of Greek culture in the region; and how this had helped in the decipherment of various scripts and in the determination of chronologies (Wang 1997; Errington and Cribb 1992). In his first publication Stein wrote (1887, p. 1):

> The philological enquiry into the types and legends of the Indo-Scythic coinage has made but comparatively slow progress since the days of Prinsep and Lassen; but, perhaps, it may now be resumed with some chance of success, since Von Sallet's exhaustive monograph, based on true historical criticism, and more recently Prof. Percy Gardner's excellent catalogue of the rich collection under his care [Gardner 1886], have placed us in full possession of the numismatic facts. At the same time the great advance made in our knowledge of Zoroastrianism, through the more extensive study of its sacred literatures, enables us to utilise, with a clearer view of the issue, the fresh evidence of the coins.

He ends his first publication by saying (1887, p. 12):

> The testimony of the types and legends examined above is, however, in itself sufficient to establish the important fact, that Iranian language and traditions as well as Zoroastrian religion were introduced into India by its Indo-Scythian conquerors. The eloquent and most authentic evidence of the Turushka coinage thus furnishes a safe starting point for all future enquiries into that fascinating epoch in the history of the Aryan nations, which witnessed the interchange of Buddhism and Magian influences between India and Iran.

Stein's first paper was published when he was twenty-five, when he was looking for a safe starting point for his future career. He did not have to wait long. The following year, 1888, proved to be a turning point in his life. Henry Rawlinson (1810–95), a Member of the Council of India, had met Stein after a lecture at the Royal Asiatic Society in 1887, and had recommended him as a suitable candidate for the post of Registrar of the Punjab University and Principal of the newly opened Oriental College at Lahore (Mirsky 1997, p. 31). The Punjab University was one of five institutions in India created since the 1850s to train well-born Indians to become civil servants for the empire (Walker 1995, p. 29). Stein went to India to begin the next stage in his life.

The most significant breakthrough came in the summer vacation of 1888. Stein headed for Kashmir to search for Sanksrit manuscripts, in particular the *Rājataraṅgiṇī*, or Chronicle of the Kings of Kashmir, by Kalhana, the twelfth-century scholar-poet. He took with him letters of recommendation from the Secretary of State for the Punjab, the Vice-Chancellor of the University and the British Resident in Kashmir, and on arriving there went straight to see the Governor, Dr Bal. By the end of his first vacation in Kashmir, Stein had been commissioned to compile a catalogue of the contents of the Library of the Raghunatha Temple in Jammu, documents which European scholars were longing to see, and had arranged for the learned Pandit Govind Kaul to work with him in Lahore on a number of scholarly projects (Walker 1995, pp. 31–3). In his first summer, then, Stein had located the prized documents, had found a learned colleague with local knowledge and had made formal arrangements for his discoveries to be brought to a wider audience.

Stein worked efficiently: thoroughly and at speed. In 1889 he secured the *codex archetypus* of all extant manuscripts of the *Rājataraṅgiṇī*, and three years later (1892) published his critical edition of the text. In the preface he expressed his intention of preparing a commentary on the *Rājataraṅgiṇī*, which he wished to publish as a second volume. Yet, as Stein explains (1900, p. vii),

> heavy official labours and another literary duty did not allow me to approach this portion of my task until the summer of 1895, when an arrangement between the Kashmir Darbar and the Punjab University, adopted on the recommendation of the Tenth International Congress of Orientalists, secured to me the

necessary facilities. Availing myself of the two months' periods of 'special duty' granted to me in extension of the summer vacations of 1895, 1896, and 1898, I was able to expand the plan of my labours and ultimately to complete the annotated translation of the Chronicle which, together with its Introduction and various Appendices, is now offered in place of the commentary originally contemplated.

The *Rājataraṅgiṇī* was important 'for the study of ancient Kashmir and for Indian historical research generally'. Stein wrote, 'this importance and the exceptional interest which attaches to Kalhana's "River of Kings" as practically the sole extant product of Sanskrit literature possessing the character of a true Chronicle, account for the efforts which have been directed towards the elucidation of the work ever since European scholarship became aware of its existence'. Stein reviewed earlier European accounts of the *Chronicle of the Kings of Kashmir*, beginning with Bernier in 1664, and expressing the greatest appreciation of the work of George Bühler (indeed, Stein dedicated this publication to him). Stein pointed out the difficulties due to the insufficiency of materials available to European scholars, particularly those 'required for the proper comprehension of all those points in Kalhana's narrative which are connected with the history, topography, economic conditions and other local features of Kashmir'. He praised the work of the 'Indologist of the first rank' Sir Alexander Cunningham (1814–93), soon after the Kashmir Valley became fully accessible to Europeans (Stein 1900, pp. x–xi):

> General (then Captain) A. Cunningham, whom political duty had brought to Kashmir after the first Sikh war and the establishment of Dogra rule in the Valley, was able to elucidate with remarkable success a series of important questions bearing on the chronological system of the Rajatarangini and on the numismatic history of the country. With the help of the information obtained through local inquiries he correctly ascertained the era employed in Kalhana's chronological reckoning, and thus succeeded in fixing with fair accuracy the dates for almost all the kings from the advent of the Karkota dynasty onwards. In the same paper, published in the *Numismatic Chronicle* for 1846, he communicated the results of his search for ancient Kashmirian coins, and proved by their analysis the great value of numismatic evidence for the critical control of Kalhana's records. Equally useful for the study of Kashmirian antiquities was his rapid survey of the most conspicuous architectural remains of the Hindu period still extant in the Valley. It threw light on the history of interesting temple-buildings mentioned in the Chronicle, and also enabled General Cunningham to identify a number of localities which are important for the ancient topography of the country.

Whilst it may seem long-winded to quote so extensively from Stein's own words, he was in modern phraseology 'a man with a mission'. He spoke for himself (Stein 1900, p. xviii):

> The detailed study of the historical geography of Kashmir and the neighbouring hill-regions was from the first recognised by me as a condition of primary importance for my task, and as these researches had also otherwise a special attraction for me I have spared no effect to make my survey of the sites and tracts which form the scene of Kalhana's narrative, as thorough and accurate as possible.

Stein was thirty-four when his *Chronicle of the Kings of Kashmir* was published in 1900. By then, Cunningham and Rawlinson had died, in 1893 and 1895 respectively. India had changed since the days of the earlier European explorers. The Indian Mutiny of 1857 had led to the transference of the government of India from the East India Company to the Crown in 1858, and, when Cunningham complained to Lord Canning, the first viceroy in 1861, about the apathy of the government towards the antiquities of India, Canning immediately appointed him as Archaeological Surveyor (1861). Despite the brief that only objects considered attractive, unusual, or architecturally significant to western taste were deemed to be worthy of measurement or recording – excavation, conservation and reconstruction were dismissed as unnecessary and expensive – Cunningham's reports were so impressive that in 1871 a new government department was created, known as the Archaeological Survey, with Cunningham as the Director-General. After Cunningham and his successor, James Burgess, retired (in 1885 and 1889 respectively), the post of Director-General lapsed and the Archaeological Survey was in the process of being retrenched, just at the time Stein arrived in India (p. 225 above).

The second breakthrough in Stein's career came ten years later, in 1898, when he was offered the post of Principal of the Calcutta Madrasa, as successor to Rudolph Hoernle (1841–1918). On 27 December 1898 he wrote to his sister-in-law, Hetty, of his intention to accept the offer (Mirsky 1977, pp. 84–5):

> I received a letter written by the Lt. Governor of Bengal to Dr. Hoernle offering me a job at Calcutta. Its conditions are as follows: I will be taken into the Indian Educational Service as principal of the Calcutta Madresa with a salary of 800 rupees per month. . . . Further advancement up to 1500 per month will depend on vacancies in the department. In addition I will have free quarters in the Principal's house – this represents an additional 250 rupees; also a part of the servants, garden and lighting are free. The main fact is that the job has a pension and is a more satisfactory type of work – no teaching, only administration. Dr. H. has been on 'deputation' several times for scholarly work and thus has established precedents for me. Also it has almost a four-month vacation as against two and a half at Lahore. . . . Dr. H. thinks I can get along on half my salary.

In 1898 a new viceroy was appointed, Lord Curzon, who introduced reforms throughout the administration, and revived archaeology in India. Curzon reported (Mirsky 1977, p. 90):

> I cannot conceive any obligation more strictly appertaining to a Supreme Government than the conservation of the most beautiful and perfect collection of monuments in the world, or more likely to be scamped and ignored by a delegation of all authority to provincial administrations. . . . The continuance of this state of affairs seems to me a little short of a scandal. Were Germany the ruling power in India, I do not hesitate to say that she would be spending many lakhs [hundred thousands] a year on a task to which we have hitherto rather plumed ourselves on our generosity in devoting Rs. 61,000, raised only a little more than a year ago to 88,000. . . . When I reflect on the sums of money that are gaily dispensed on the construction of impossible forts in impossible places, which are to sustain an impossible siege against an impossible foe, I do venture to hope that so mean a standard may not again be pleaded, at any rate in my time.

On the strength of these words Stein too ventured to hope. In 1893 and 1897 articles by Rudolph Hoernle had appeared in the *Journal of the Asiatic Society of Bengal*. Stein had been corresponding with Hoernle since at least 1891, when he hoped the Society, of which Hoernle was then Secretary, would publish his *Rājataraṅgiṇī*. In the 1897 article Hoernle wrote of his study of the manuscript fragments found near Khotan in Chinese Central Asia, and the intriguing problem they posed: the script was Indian Brahmi, but the language was an unknown Indian language (Hoernle 1897, p. 245).

In September 1898 Stein submitted a proposal to make a 'tour of archaeological exploration. . . . The object of the tour will be to explore the ancient sites at and around Khotan from an archaeological point of view, to search for such data as will throw light on their history, and to make collections of ancient remains on which full reliance can be placed' (Mirsky 1977, pp. 78–9). Stein heard on New Year's Eve that the Home and Finance Department had sanctioned the tour.

By 17 January 1900 Stein was in Peshawar buying 'interesting coins from the Greek and Indo-Scythian periods very cheaply' (Mirsky 1977, pp. 103–4).[3] In his letter to his brother Ernst of that date, he says 'I went in quick marches to the Indus where I tracked down a Kharoshthi inscription, from the start of the Christian era, and last night actually took possession of the large stone which now, under guard, awaits my return'. With Stein's typical efficiency, a week later the same Kharoshthi inscription, weighing over 200 pounds, was on its way to Lahore (Mirsky 1977, p. 104).[4] In his subsequent report (1900, p. 146) Stein says that on his march to Nilab, an old crossing place on the south bank of the Indus river, about ten miles south-south-west of Attock,

> I succeeded in tracing and acquiring an important Kharoṣṭhī inscription of the Kushana period, which had been found a short time ago near an ancient well and subsequently carried away by villagers. My search for the stone was attended with a good deal of trouble and a series of incidents which gave it quite the character of an exciting chase. All the greater was my satisfaction when I ultimately obtained this interesting epigraphical relic which mentions a date and the name of a hitherto unknown Indo-Scythian prince.

This is known – from its find-spot – as the Ara inscription, which is dated in year 41 of Kanishka, the son of Vasishka, i.e Kanishka III (c. AD 267–80) and year [1]41 of the Kushan era of Kanishka I (Konow 1929, pp. 162–5, no. LXXXV, pl. XXXII.1; see table 1 and p. 84 above).

In the spring of 1900 Stein received his passport for Chinese Central Asia. Issued by the Chinese Foreign Office, the document called 'upon local authorities upon the line of the route to examine Dr. Stein's passport at once whenever he presents it for inspection, to afford him due protection according to a Treaty, and not to place any difficulties or obstacles in his way'. It was issued in response to H. B. M. Minister, Sir Claude Macdonald's letter requesting a passport so that Stein might 'travel with some servants from India to the New Dominion and the Khotan neighbourhood'. The British minister in Peking, who had secured the passport at Lord Curzon's request, forwarded the passport with a covering letter: 'It was thought not advisable to ask for the special facilities asked for by Dr Stein. He will probably find no difficulty in executing the surveys he mentions: as to the excavations and purchase of antiquities, it is considered that any reference to them would hinder rather than assist his objects' (Mirsky 1977, p. 105).

In May 1900 Stein set out upon the first of his major expeditions. It was a huge success. Almost immediately upon his return to England in 1901, he published his 'Preliminary report of a journey of archaeological and topographical exploration in Chinese Turkestan'. Two years later his travelogue, *Sand-buried Ruins of Khotan: Personal Narratives*

of a Journey, appeared, and four years after that, his detailed scientific report *Ancient Khotan* (1907). On the strength of this phenomenal success Stein would make another three expeditions to Chinese Central Asia and a series of expeditions in Iran. He became something of a celebrity: one of the 'Great Explorers of the Moment', according to *The Illustrated London News* of 30 January 1909 (fig. 193). The journal presented him on three occasions as one of their 'Personalities of the Week: people in the public eye', initially for receiving the Royal Asiatic Society gold medal (25 May 1932); then the Society of Antiquaries gold medal (27 April 1935); and finally in reporting his death (6 November 1943).

All Stein's expeditions were meticulously well-planned and enviably well-financed. With his proven track record he offered a good investment with no risk. An example of this came in December 1929, when Paul Sachs and Langdon Warner of the Fogg Art Museum, Harvard, arranged for Stein to give a series of lectures about his adventures on the Silk Road, first at the Lowell Institute, then at the Boston Museum of Fine Arts and the Freer Art Gallery in Washington (Wilson 1995, p. 274).[5] The aim was to raise funds for a fourth expedition to Chinese Central Asia. It was a sell-out, and Stein left Boston confident that 'the whole of the money for my future explorations, whether in China, Persia or elsewhere in Asia has been secured: £20,000. One half is to be contributed by a big endowment left to Harvard recently for researches bearing on China. . . . All my conditions are agreed to' (Mirsky 1977, p. 466). The British Museum supplied $5000 and 'naturally hoped to receive a characteristic and representative selection' of his finds (Brysac 1997, p. 56).

Stein's fourth expedition (1930–1) was a disaster. Although 'thirty years had scarcely seen any change in the condition of the ruins' at his favourite Niya site (Mirsky 1977, p. 469), China had changed enormously since Stein's third expedition. But he blundered in with the conviction that his old proven methods and demands would still win. The Chinese press alleged that, when, at a meeting of the Board of Trustees of the Harvard-Yenching Institute, Massachusetts, in 1930, several American professors favoured co-operation with Chinese cultural organisations in archaeological research, pointing out that China had changed, Stein had responded with the statement:[6]

> I only know Old China and do not pay the least attention to the slogans and catch-words of Young China. The Kuomintang is most disreputable and should not be heeded by foreigners. There have been several cases where foreign scientific organisations co-operated with similar bodies in China, but invariably the result has been negative. Moreover, Sinkiang is not Chinese territory, and there is no central government in China. Sinkiang is not fully civilised. I think I can do with Sinkiang officials today what I used to do with those of the old regime. If you can give me some additional money with which to bribe them, I can have everything my own way in Sinkiang.

These were the remarks that were relayed to the Chinese press by indignant Chinese representatives who had attended the Board of Trustees meeting. The exaggerated arrogance and aggression permeating Stein's alleged statement had the desired effect; the Chinese academic world and the Chinese press eventually persuaded the Chinese Ministry of Foreign Affairs to cancel Stein's passport and to expel him from

THE ILLUSTRATED LONDON NEWS, JAN. 30, 1909. — 170

LURED BY THE UNKNOWN: MEN WHO FILL IN THE BLANKS.

THE GREAT EXPLORERS OF THE MOMENT

1. DR. M. A. STEIN, WHO HAS JUST RETURNED FROM EXPLORING CENTRAL ASIA.

2. CAPTAIN EJNAR MIKKELSEN, WHO HAS RETURNED FROM AN ATTEMPT TO REACH THE GREAT ARCTIC CONTINENT, AND IS TO EXPLORE DUTCH NEW GUINEA.

3. DR. T. LONGSTAFF, WHO IS TO EXPLORE THE NORTH-WEST HIMALAYAS.

4. CAPTAIN D'OLLONE, LEADER OF AN EXPEDITION AT WORK ON THE CHINO-TIBETAN FRONTIER.

5. LIEUTENANT SHACKLETON, AT PRESENT EXPLORING IN THE ANTARCTIC.

6. COMMANDER PEARY, AT PRESENT IN SEARCH OF THE NORTH POLE.

7. DR. W. H WORKMAN, WHO HAS BEEN EXPLORING THE HIMALAYAS.

8. MRS. BULLOCK WORKMAN, WHO HAS BEEN EXPLORING THE HIMALAYAS.

9. MR. HANNS VISCHER, WHO HAS JOURNEYED ACROSS THE EASTERN SAHARA FROM TRIPOLI TO LAKE TCHAD.

10. MR. P. E. L. GETHIN, WHO IS TO ACCOMPANY MR. G. W. BURY DURING HIS EXPLORATION OF ARABIA.

11. DR. CHARCOT, LEADER OF AN EXPEDITION TO THE ANTARCTIC.

12. LIEUTENANT BOYD ALEXANDER, LEADER OF AN EXPEDITION TO THE CAMEROON MOUNTAINS AND THE ISLAND OF SAO THOMÉ.

13. CAPTAIN ROALD AMUNDSEN, WHO IS TO ATTEMPT TO REACH THE NORTH POLE.

14. MR. A. H. HARRISON, WHO WISHES TO CROSS THE NORTH POLAR OCEAN.

15. DR. SVEN HEDIN, WHO HAS BEEN EXPLORING TIBET, AND HAS FILLED MANY BLANKS IN THE MAPS.

The unknown is as great a lure as ever. It has been said that the day of the pioneer explorer is past, and that the explorer of the moment must be one who re-covers old ground, but has a greater knowledge than his predecessors. This, as the "Times" points out, is not altogether a fact, and there are many tracts of land, still blank on the maps, awaiting the tread of the explorer.

PHOTOGRAPHS BY ELLIOTT AND FRY, FLORMAN, BANG, LAFAYETTE, THOMSON, MAULL AND FOX, TOPICAL, AND ARNOLD.

China. Whatever his actual words might have been Stein was wrong to disregard the genuine concerns of the Chinese academic world, and his own description of events reveals just how out of touch he was with public sentiment in China (Mirksy 1977, pp. 466–7):

In addition to the grievance of not having a full share in such [recovered] material, there was also felt a supposed slight in Western-educated Chinese savants not being associated with famous discoveries. All this had resulted in a self-constituted 'National Council of Cultural Societies' at Peking, endeavouring to lay down by decree that no foreign scientific expeditions were to be permitted except with a Chinese co-leader and a staff of Chinese savants: that all objects collected were to remain in China, etc., . . . I had to make it clear from the start with all those who would help at Peking, Simla, Kashgar, the Foreign Office, Harvard, etc., that it would not be possible to take up work if such conditions were imposed. To drag a party of Chinese savants about with me in a waterless desert and inhospitable mountains, to have to settle my plans with a Chinese co-leader necessarily ignorant of local climatic conditions, could only imply a waste of time, energy and money.

How vividly these comments contrast with Stein's proposal five years earlier to the Indian Archaeological Survey for a two-and-a-half-year expedition to Chinese Central Asia! He had written in the 1925 proposal:[7]

The need of scientifically conducted exploration of such and other remains hitherto safely hidden in the ground is all the more urgent because in spite of traditional Chinese interest in all relics of the past, the systematic recovery and study of these by means of methodical excavation and other archaeological field work has so far remained practically unknown in China. There is, however, every reason to believe that Chinese scholars of the necessary literary attainments could under competent European guidance be readily trained to apply modern Western methods of archaeological research. The employment of one or two carefully selected young *literati* in connection with the proposed explorations is a measure which practical considerations based upon my previous experience would in any case make highly desirable. But it might in addition serve a very useful purpose by training suitable men for employment on archaeological survey work under Chinese authority, whenever conditions may permit of this being organised.

The 1925 proposal had shown a marked change of attitude towards the Chinese, and Stein's estimated expenses allocated £1600 for two Chinese assistants, to be paid £320 per annum for two and a half years. It is somewhat ironic that he suggested the expedition could be paid for by the Boxer

Figure 193 *The Illustrated London News*, 30 January 1909, 'Man of the moment'

Lured by the unknown: Men who fill in the blanks
The Great Explorers of the Moment

1 *Dr M. A. Stein, who has just returned from exploring Central Asia.*
*Sir Marc Aurel Stein (1862–1943), Hungarian, later British. Archaeological explorer (A. Walker, *Aurel Stein, Pioneer of the Silk Road*, London 1995).

2 *Captain Ejnar Mikkelsen, who has returned from an attempt to reach the Great Arctic Continent, and is to explore Dutch New Guinea.*
Ejnar Mikkelson (1880–1971), Danish. Member of the Danish Expedition to East Greenland, 1900 (D. Laursen, 'Ejnar Mikkelsen [1880–1971]', *Artic* 24.3, Sept 1971, p. 240).

3 *Dr T. Longstaff, who is to explore the North-West Himalayas.*
*Tom George Longstaff (1875–1964), British. Mountaineer (T. G. Longstaff, *This my Voyage*, London 1950).

4 *Captain D'Ollone, leader of an expedition at work on the Chino-Tibetan Frontier.*
Henri Marie Gustave d'Ollone (1868–1943), French. Officer of the French army; carried out the d'Ollone Mission in China and Tibet, 1906–9 (Author of *In Forbidden China – the d'Ollone Misson. China–Tibet–d'Ollone*. Translated from the French by Bernard Miall, London 1912).

5 *Lieutenant Shackleton, at present exploring in the Antarctic.*
*Sir Ernest Henry Shackleton (1874–1922), British. Antarctic explorer (Author of *The Heart of the Antarctic*, 2 vols, London 1909).

6 *Commander Peary, at present in search of the North Pole.*
Robert Erwin Peary (1856–1920), American. Leader of expedition to the North Pole, 1909 (Author of *Northward over the 'Great Ice', a narrative of life and work along the shores and up on the interior ice-cap of the little tribe of Smith-sound Eskimos, the most northerly human beings in the world, and an account of the discovery and bringing home of 'Saviksue', or Great Cape-York meteorites . . .* , London 1898).

7 *Dr W. H. Workman, who has been exploring the Himalayas.*
William Hunter Workman (1847–1937), American. Husband of Mrs Bullock Workman; carried out mapmaking and detailed scientific observations in the Himalayas and Karakorum (M. Plint, 'The Workmans: Travellers extraordinary', *Alpine Journal* 97 [341], pp. 230–7).

8 *Mrs Bullock Workman, who has been exploring the Himalayas.*
The token woman: Fanny Bullock Workman (1859–1925), American. Wife of Dr W. H. Workman. Mountaineer; carried out mapmaking and detailed scientific observations in the Himalayas and Karakorum; campaigner for women's rights (S. A. Tingley, 'From jungle to mountain peak: voice and place in Fanny Bullock and William Hunter Workman's

collaborative travel writing', http://english.cla.umn.edu//abstracts/Tingley.html).

9 *Mr Hanns Vischer, who has journeyed across the Eastern Sahara from Tripoli to Lake Tchad.*
*Sir Hanns Vischer (1876–1945), Swiss, later British. Educationalist.

10 *Mr P. E. L. Gethin, who is to accompany Mr G. W. Bury during his exploration of Arabia.*
(E. Macro, 'The Austrian Imperial Academy's expeditions to South Arabia 1897–1900 – C. de Landberg, D. H. Mueller and G. W. Bury', *New Arabian Studies* 1, 1994).

11 *Dr Charcot, leader of an expedition to the Antarctic.*
Jean-Baptiste Étienne Auguste Charcot (1867–1936), French. Explorer and oceanographer (Author of *Autour du pole sud: 1. Expédition du 'Français', 1903–1905; 2. Expédition du 'Pourquoi pas?', 1908–1910*, Paris 1910).

12 *Lieutenant Boyd Alexander, leader of an expedition to the Cameroon Mountains and the island of Sao Thome.*
*Boyd Alexander (1873–1910), British. Traveller and ornithologist (Author of *From the Niger to the Nile*, 2 vols, London 1907).

13 *Captain Roald Amundsen, who is to attempt to reach the North Pole.*
Roald Engelbregt Gravning Amundsen (1872–1928), Norwegian. Polar explorer (Author of *The South Pole: an Account of the Norwegian Antarctic Expedition in the Fram, 1910–1912*, London 1912).

14 *Mr A. H. Harrison, who wishes to cross the North Polar Ocean.*
Alfred H. Harrison, author of *In search of a polar continent, 1905–1907* (London 1908).

15 *Dr Sven Hedin, who has been exploring Tibet, and has filled many blanks in the maps.*
Sven Hedin (1865–1952), Swedish. Explorer and collector (The Sven Hedin Foundation, National Museum of Ethnography, Stockholm).

The unknown is as great a lure as ever. It has been said that the day of the pioneer explorer is past, and that the explorer of the moment must be one who re-covers old ground, but has a greater knowledge than his predecessors. This, as the 'Times' points out, is not altogether a fact, and there are many tracts of land, still blank on the maps, awaiting the tread of the explorer. Photographs by Elliott and Fry, Florman, Bang, Lafayette, Thomson, Maull and Fox, Topicae, and Arnold.
* Listed in the *Dictionary of National Biography*, www.oxforddnb.com.

Indemnity Fund, which he had probably heard was then financing the Geological Survey of China.[8] The application fell through.

The 1925 proposal, in particular, reflected Stein's awareness of the need to keep abreast of changes. However, his earlier major successes had been made possible with the support of diplomats and personal contacts in officialdom. With political change and the passing of time came new personnel with new priorities.[9] New approaches were necessary; negotiation was perhaps more appropriate than dogged determination.[10] Yet, with the growing nationalism in China, fuelled by the Guomindang's anti-foreign campaigns, even negotiation was fraught, as Sven Hedin experienced in the preparations for the Sino-Swedish Expedition. Why didn't Stein learn from Hedin?

The Sino-Swedish Expedition had three proposed phases. Phase (1) was to found an airline between Berlin and Peking–Shanghai. Deutsche Lufthansa would finance this phase of the expedition, which would comprise German air-experts, Swedish and Chinese scientists. Phase (2) would be financed chiefly by the Swedish state, and would concentrate on mainly scientific tasks, with a crew of mainly Swedish personnel. Phase (3) would be a motor car expedition, to investigate the possibility of laying two car roads between China proper and Xinjiang, and to make proposals for the same (Hedin et al. 1943–5).

The negotiations for the expedition were fraught. The first part of the expedition proposed an international team of Swedish, Danish, German and Chinese personnel. The Chinese complained it was insulting to use the term 'expedition' and insisted it should be replaced by 'mission', offering the equally racist explanation that 'expeditions' were 'carried out only among blacks and savages, and not in a country with such an ancient culture as China'. Although Deutsche Lufthansa had agreed to fund much of the first part, Chinese opposition demanded that the 'mission' should be regarded as a purely Chinese initiative in which a number of Europeans had been granted permission to participate. Frustration drove Hedin to write in the draft contract 'No archaeological excavation is to be undertaken by the mission except on such a small scale as will not in a serious way hinder the movements of the mission, and the material thus collected requires no special equipment for transportation'. Professor J. G. Andersson, representative of the Swedish China Committee, urged him to do what he could for archaeology, and Hedin agreed to add a sentence allowing for 'large scale excavations so long as they do not hinder the movements of a mission'. Eventually, it was agreed that there were to be two Field Directors, one Chinese and one Swede, and all the archaeological collections were to be taken to Peking, though, after further negotiation, it was agreed that duplicates should be given to the Swedes as a goodwill gesture. Whilst Hedin admits to remarking coldly during the negotiations 'This is a Peace of Versailles that you want to impose on me', he none the less writes later in the report of the expedition that 'As far as I myself am concerned, I never had occasion to regret my acceptance of the conditions laid down by the Chinese' (Hedin et al. 1943–5, ch. 2).

One of the Chinese specialists on Hedin's mission was a young man, Huang Wenbi (1893–1958), trained in Chinese philosophy at the prestigious Peking University. He had been kept on to teach at the University, where he was a member of the University's Archaeological Association, more important than it might at first appear, since there was no formal archaeological training in China at that time.[11] The Sino-Swedish Expedition to north-west China in 1927 marked the formal beginnings of Huang's archaeological fieldwork. He would go on to lead a further three, Chinese-only, expeditions to Xinjiang, in 1933, 1945 and 1958, and his name would become synonymous with archaeology in the region.[12] To help train future Chinese archaeologists had been one of Stein's stated aims in his 1925 proposal.

In short the world order was changing, and not only in China. When the First World War broke out in 1914, Stein was engaged on his third expedition to Chinese Central Asia (1913–16). During the course of the war India added millions to its debt: the Indian government sent overseas about a million Indian troops, over £80,000,000 worth of military stores and equipment to the various fronts, and nearly five million tons of wheat to Britain. The Indian government paid for all its troops overseas, and before the end of the war the Viceroy presented a gift of £1,000,000 to the British government (Encyclopaedia Britannica 1994, vol. 21, p. 104). In 1920 Gandhi proclaimed in a letter to the Viceroy his adoption of non-cooperation as a remedy against a government for which he retained 'neither respect nor affection' on account of its 'unscrupulous, immoral and unjust' actions and its failure to punish adequately the officials responsible for 'the wanton cruelty and inhumanity' with which disorders in the Punjab had been suppressed. The Viceroy, Lord Chelmsford, resigned and India headed for self-government (Encyclopaedia Britannica 1937, vol. 12, p. 201).

Stein made numerous visits to the Middle East between 1924 and 1939, and there too, major political changes were taking place. The Shah of Iran had fled to Europe in 1923, and Reza Khan Pahlavi had appointed himself prime minister, soon to become the new, progressive Shah. After the First World War Iraq was formed out of the former Ottoman vilayets of Mosul, Baghdad and Basra, and by 1932 had been admitted to the League of Nations.

In 1935–6 Stein made a fifteen-month tour of Iran accompanied by Bahman Karimi, Inspector of Antiquities. Karimi produced two reports of this tour: a fuller version in Persian and an abridged version in French, both published in 1950. His reports are unique eye-witness accounts of how Stein worked in the field:

> Dans tout le parcours de ce voyage, Sir Aurel Stein fit des essais pour pratiquer les fouilles. À mon avis Sir Aurel Stein ne veut pas faire des fouilles, mais il cherche à connaître la situation géographique des terrains, l'importance du lieu, la hauteur et la profondeur des couches, et puis il fait faire dessiner des sites fouillés et de leurs alentours, en resulta la communication de civilisation.[13]

It was not an easy journey, and the concise French version is scattered with Karimi's personal comments on the dangers and discomforts seldom mentioned by the hardy seventy-three-year-old Stein:

> En terminant ce rapport, j'ajoute que ce voyage à dos de cheval et pendant l'hiver en se reposant la nuit sous des tentes dans le

désert et chaque jour dans un lieu plus ou moins sûr devient en le continuant de plus en plus difficile et il faudrait des jeunes gens en fer pour pouvoir supporter toutes ces difficultés dans un air humide et froid.[14]

Avant de terminer ce rapport, je dois porter à votre connaissance ce qui suit: on ne peut pas donner le nom de promenade à notre voyage. On doit le nommer voyage de difficulté, de peine, d'amertume, de danger et de maladis. On doit subir les rigueurs de l'hiver dans les cols des montagnes neigneuses et sur les kaleks dangereux des rivières.[15]

One of Stein's comments, repeated by Karimi, was that many of the sites had been seen and described previously, but before the existence of cameras.[16] Stein liked to keep abreast with changes in technology, and this was particularly true for photography. He had written of the importance of illustrations in his *Rājataraṅgiṇī* in 1900, and had learnt how to photograph well. On his expeditions in India, China, Iran, Iraq and Jordan between the 1890s and 1938 Stein took over 14,000 photographs and lantern slides.[17] In 1919 Stein signalled an interest in aerial photography (Stein 1919, p. 200), and made contact with Antoine Poidebard (1878–1955) who had been photographing sites from the air in Syria.[18] In 1938–9, with the help of the Royal Air Force, the seventy-six-year-old Stein made his own aerial surveys of the Roman *limes* in Iraq and Jordan, first in a Vickers Vincent general-purpose biplane and then in a Wellesley, a newly introduced monoplane bomber (Gregory and Kennedy 1985).[19]

Stein's achievements were great, indeed so great that they caused problems. In 1909, when Stein was transferred from the Education Department to the Archaeological Survey, a civil servant wrote: 'The Government find themselves required to provide for a white elephant in the shape of an educational officer who had turned out to be a very distinguished Archaeologist.' In China to this day Stein remains the scapegoat for all foreign archaeologists who removed antiquities from Chinese soil: the verb *qie* ('to use illegal and unreasonable means to acquire') is regularly used to describe his activities. Even in Britain, which funded much of his work and which houses many of his acquisitions, it is hard to find a mention of Sir Aurel Stein in a general dictionary of archaeology. And this for a man who, in just two of his expeditions, covered over 25,000 miles doing what he did best: archaeological reconnaissance.

Stein died in 1943. Having spent his life following the tracks of Alexander the Great, the Chinese monk Xuan Zang, and Marco Polo, and making far flung regions of the world accessible to armchair travellers as well as to academics, he left provision for a trust fund to enable future generations to continue working in those distant regions. This is the Stein–Arnold Fund, administered by the British Academy. True to his character, he desired that these funds should be used 'for the encouragement of research on the antiquities or historical geography or early history or arts of those parts of Asia which come within the sphere of the ancient civilisations of India, China and Iran, including Central Asia' and without any consideration of the age of the applicants, only that they be Hungarian or British.

Notes

1 Compare this with Renfrew and Bahn's account (1991, pp. 27–8) of the competition between Paul Emile Botta (1802–70) and Austen Henry Layard (1817–94) for the 'largest number of works of art with the least possible outlay of time and money'. Some of the practices carried out by earlier archaeologists would not be considered acceptable today, and some would no doubt be horrified to read the subsequent criticisms of their work which they conducted with a clear conscience.

2 The best-known parts of the Stein collections are undoubtedly the paintings and manuscripts from Cave 17 at the Caves of the Thousand Buddhas, Dunhuang (Stein 1921; Whitfield 1982–3, Whitfield and Farrer 1990; see also http://www.thebritishmuseum.net/thesilkroad and http://idp.bl.uk/). However, his collections covered a vast range of archaeological finds; see Wang 1999, 2002, 2004; Falconer *et al.* 2002; and Falconer *et al.* 2007.

3 Stein's personal coin collection is now in the Heberden Coin Room of the Ashmolean Museum, Oxford.

4 In his letter to Ernst on 24 January, he writes by mistake that the inscription 'is on its way to London', instead of 'Lahore', its actual destination.

5 The lectures were later published as *On Ancient Central Asian Tracks*.

6 British Museum Central Archives: Document dated 27 December 1930, being Enclosure no. 2 in despatch to Foreign Office no. 94 of 13 January 1931.

7 Stein to Indian Archaeological Survey, dated London, 16 March 1926, Royal Geographical Society Archives, Correspondence Block 1921–30, no. 6.

8 Royal Geographical Society Archives, Correspondence Block 1921–30, no. 6. His estimated expenses came to a total of £12,000, of which £2000 was reserved to provide for presents, £1600 to pay for two Chinese assistants, £400 to pay for two Indian NCOs, £7000 for the cost of transport, excavations, guides, technical equipment, and £1000 actual travel expenses of personnel. Hedin *et al.* 1943–5, p. 15, mentions the funding for the Geological Survey of China.

9 Wilson (1995, pp. 45–7) has questioned Stein's motives and rightly states that 'his enterprises have to be situated against a background of colonial collecting and appropriating in which world history was to a greater or lesser degree made subject to the narrative of European civilization'.

10 This is mirrored in correspondence relating to Stein in the Royal Geographical Society Archives. 'There are certain penalties attached to friendship with this great man, and I am sure you will pay them cheerfully' (RGS to Foster, 29 May 1919, RGS Correspondence Block 1911–20). 'You need not hope that Stein has been born again. His characteristics of a beggar are even more pronounced than ever. I shall be heartily glad when the [first Asia] lecture is over' (Secretary, RGS, to Hogarth, 31 October 1924, RGS Correspondence Block 1921–30).

11 For a history of archaeology in China see Falkenhausen (1993), and Wang Tao (1997).

12 The material collected on these expeditions is in the National Museum of Chinese History, Beijing.

13 Karimi 1950a, 7th Report, p. 19. 'Throughout this journey, Sir Aurel Stein has made trials for excavation. It is my opinion that Sir Aurel Stein does not wish to excavate but seeks to establish the geography of the land, the importance of the location, and the height and depth of the strata. He then has plans of the excavated sites drawn up, to show the communication of civilisation.'

14 Karimi 1950a, 1st Report, p. 4. 'In closing this report I should add that this journey on horseback and during winter, spending the nights in tents in the desert, and the days in not entirely safe locations, becomes more and more difficult as we proceed. One would need to be a young man of steel to be able to endure all these difficulties in this cold, damp air.'

15 Karimi 1950a, 4th Report, p. 11. 'Before finishing this report I must inform you of the following: one cannot call this tour a promenade. It should be called a journey of difficulty, of pain, of bitterness, of danger and illness. One must accept the rigours of winter on snowy mountain passes and the hazards of rafts on the rivers.'

16 Karimi 1950a, 3rd Report, p. 8: 'Sir Aurel Stein dit que De Bode, Ranking et Layard ont vu ces bas reliefs, mais ils n'avaient pas des appareils pour en faire photographier.'

17 Of these about 11,000 are in the British Library, Oriental and India Office Collections, Prints, Drawings and Photographs, with details available on a database compiled by John Falconer. About 4500 photographs in the Stein Collection at the Library of the Hungarian Academy of Sciences, Budapest, have been catalogued (John Falconer *et al*. 2002). Another batch of photographs was subsequently located in the LHAS and has been catalogued (John Falconer *et al*. 2007).

18 Poidebard 1934 (being the publication of his work between 1925 and 1932). Stein's correspondence with Poidebard (1929–42) is in the Bodleian Library, Oxford.

19 In May 1998 Kennedy undertook the first aerial archaeological survey of Jordan since Stein.

Abbreviations

A²H	Artaxerxes II Hamadan inscription	Göbl	Göbl 1967 (Huns) or 1986 (Kushans), type no.
A²S	Artaxerxes II Susa inscription	IOC	India Office Collection (British Museum
A³P	Artaxerxes III Persepolis inscription		Department of Coins and Medals)
As.	British Museum Department of Asia	IOLC	British Library India Office Loan Collection
BMC	British Museum Catalogue (Department of Coins		(British Museum Department of Coins and
	and Medals)		Medals)
CM	British Museum Department of Coins and Medals	Ismeo	Istituto Italiano per il Medio ed Estremo Oriente
CNRS	Centre National de la Recherche Scientifique	*JASB*	*Journal of the Asiatic Society of Bengal*
CRAI	*Comptes Rendus de l'Académie des Inscriptions et*	*JRAS*	*Journal of the Royal Asiatic Society*
	Belles-Lettres	ME	British Museum Department of Middle East
DB	Darius Bisitun inscription	Mit.	Mitchiner 1976, type no.
DN	Darius Naqsh-i Rustam inscription	*NC*	*Numismatic Chronicle*
DP	Darius Persepolis inscription	n. s.	new series
DS	Darius Susa inscription	OIOC	British Library, Oriental and India Office
ed.	editor/edited by		Collections
edn	edition	PD	British Museum Department of Prints and
eds	editors		Drawings
EIC	East India Company	rev.	revised
Exc. de Leg.	*Excerpta de Legationibus Iussu Imp. Constantini*	ser.	series
	Porphyrogeniti Confecta	ŠKZ	Shapur Kaba-i Zardusht inscription
Exc. de Leg. Gent.	*Excerpta de Legationibus Gentium*	tr.	translator/translated by
Exc. de Leg. Rom.	*Excerpta de Legationibus Romanorum*	transcr.	transcribed by
frags	fragments	XP	Xerxes Persepolis inscription

References

Abbott, J. (1847) 'Sculpture from the site of the Indo-Greek city of Bucephalia', *JASB* XVI, pp. 664–6.

Abbott, J. (1852) 'On the sites of Nikaia and Boukephalon, with an appendix on Taxila', *JASB* XXI, pp. 214–63.

Abbott, J. (1854) 'Gradus ad Aornon', *JASB* XXIII, pp. 309–63.

Abgarians, M. T. and Sellwood, D. G. (1971) 'A hoard of early Parthian drachms', *NC* 31, pp. 103–19.

Abu Imam (1966) *Sir Alexander Cunningham and the Beginnings of Indian Archaeology*, Dacca.

Acquisitions (1857) Coins 13 August: 118 coins purchased from Major Cunningham. British Museum Department of Coins and Medals Archives.

Acquisitions (1882) Coins IOC: India Office Collection presented by the Rt Hon. the Secretary of State for India in Council. British Museum Department of Coins and Medals Archives.

Acquisitions (1838) Medal Room 10 February: 118 Bactrian and Indo-Scythic coins presented by the Hon. East India Company. British Museum Department of Coins and Medals Archives.

Adams, R. McC. (1981) *Heartland of Cities. Surveys of Ancient Settlement and Land Use on the Central Floodplain of the Euphrates*, Chicago.

Adle, C. (1379/2000) 'Khorheh. The dawn of Iranian scientific archaeological excavation', *Tavoos* 3/4, pp. 3–43 (in Persian and English).

Adler, C. (1895) 'Two Persepolitan casts in the U.S. National Museum', *Report of the U.S. National Museum for 1893*, Washington, pp. 751–3.

Aelian, *Varia Historia*, tr. D. O. Johnson, *An English Translation of Claudius Aelianus' Varia Historia*, Studies in Classics II, Lampeter 1997.

Ahn, G. (1992) *Religiöse Herrscherlegitimation im Achämenidischen Iran*, Acta Iranica 31, Leiden.

Aijazuddin, F. S. (1979) *Sikh Portraits by European Artists*, London.

Alexander, C. M. (1928) *Baghdad in Bygone Days*, London.

Alexander, J. E. (1827) *Travels from India to England: Comprehending a Visit to the Burman Empire, and a Journey through Persia, Asia Minor, European Turkey, &c. in the Years 1825–26*, London.

Allan, J. (1936) *A Catalogue of the Indian Coins in the British Museum. Catalogue of the Coins of Ancient India*, London (repr. 1967).

Allchin, F. R. and Norman, K. R. (1985) 'Guide to the Aśokan inscriptions', *South Asian Studies* I, pp. 43–50.

Allen, C. (2002) *The Buddha and the Sahibs. The Men Who Discovered India's Lost Religion*, London.

Alram, M. (1986) *Iranisches Personennamenbuch. Nomina Propria Iranica in Nummis. Materialgrundlagen zu den iranischen Personennamen auf antiken Münzen*, Vienna.

Alram, M. (1999) 'Indo-Parthian and early Kushan chronology: the numismatic evidence', in M. Alram and D. Klimburg-Salter (eds), *Coins, Art and Chronology. Essays on the pre-Islamic History of the Indo-Iranian Borderlands*, Vienna, pp. 19–48.

Alram, M. (1999/2000) 'A hoard of copper drachms from the Kāpiśa–Kabul region', *Silk Road Art and Archaeology* 6, *Papers in Honour of Francine Tissot*, pp. 129–50.

Alram, M. (2002) 'A rare Hunnish coin type', *Silk Road Art and Archaeology* 8, pp. 149–53.

Alram, M. (2006) 'Ardashir's eastern campaign and the numismatic evidence', in G. Herrmann and J. Cribb (eds), *After Alexander: Central Asia before Islam. Themes in the History and Archaeology of Western Central Asia* (Papers from the British Academy Conference 23–5 June 2004), London (in press).

Alram, M. and Gyselen, R. (2003) *Sylloge Nummorum Sasanidarum Paris – Berlin – Wien*, vol. I, *Ardashir I. – Shapur I.*, Veröffentlichungen der Numismatischen Kommission 41, Vienna.

Aman ur Rahman, Grenet, F. and Sims-Williams, N. (2006) 'A Hunnish Kushan-shah', *Journal of Inner Asian Art and Archaeology* 1, pp. 125–31.

Ambers, J. and Simpson, St J. (2005) 'Some pigment identifications for objects from Persepolis', http://www.achemenet.com/ressources/enligne/arta/arta.htm.

Amini, I. (1999) *Napoleon and Persia*, London.

References

Ammianus Marcellinus, *History*, tr. J. C. Rolfe, 3 vols, Loeb Classical Library, London–Cambridge, Mass. 1937.

Andreas, F. C. and Stolze, F. (1882) *Persepolis, die Achämenidischen und Sasanidischen Denkmäler und Inschriften von Persepolis, Istakhr, Pasargadae, Shahpur*, 2 vols, Berlin.

Anon. (1931) 'Persian casts at the British Museum: reliefs from Persepolis', *The Times* 7 May, p. 8.

Anon. (1976) *Tarikh-e Sistān*, tr. M. Gold, Rome.

Anon. (1997) *Redécouverte d'une civilisation ancienne: la Mésopotamie*, La Maison des Arts brochure, Antony.

Anon. *Periplus of the Erythraean Sea* (see Casson 1989).

Archer, W. (1966) *Paintings of the Sikhs*, London.

Arneth, J. R. von (1837) 'Numi Graeci regni Bactriani et Indici', *Wiener Jahrbüchern* 77, January–March, pp. 211–45.

Arrian, *History of Alexander and Indica*, tr. P. A. Blunt, 2 vols: I. *Anabasis of Alexander*, books I–IV; II. *Indica*, books V–VII, ed. J. Henderson, Loeb Classical Library, London–Cambridge, Mass. 1976–83 (I repr. 1989; II repr. 2000).

Assar, G. F. (2006). 'A revised Parthian chronology of the period 165–91 BC', *Electrum* 11, pp. 87–158.

ASI Photographs (British Library, India Office Collection, Archaeological Survey of India photographs and negatives) *A List of the Photographic Negatives of Indian Antiquities in the Collection of the Indian Museum, with which is Incorporated the List of Similar Negatives in the Possession of the India Office*, Calcutta 1909.

Avdall, J. (1836) 'Note on some of the Indo-Scythian coins found by C. Masson at Beghrám, in the Kohistán of Kábul', *JASB* V, pp. 266–8.

Azarpay, G. (1981) 'Cairns, *kurums* and *dambs*: a note on pre-Islamic surface burials in eastern Iran and central Asia', *Acta Iranica* 21 [= 2nd ser. VIII], pp. 12–21.

Bailey, H. W. (1932) 'Iranian Studies', *Bulletin of the School of Oriental Studies*, pp. 945–55.

Bailey, H. W. (1942) 'Kaṇaiska', *JRAS*, pp. 14–28.

Bajwa, F. S. (1964) *Military System of the Sikhs*, Delhi.

Balboni, M. P. (1993) *Ventura: dal ghetto del Finale alla corte di Lahore*, Modena.

Ball, W. and Gardin, J. C. (1982) *Archaeological Gazetteer of Afghanistan*, 2 vols, Paris.

Banerji, R. D. (1909–10) 'New Brahmi inscriptions of the Scythian period', *Epigraphia Indica* X, pp. 106–8.

Barnett, R. D. (1957) 'Persepolis', *Iraq* 19, pp. 55–77.

Barnett, R. D. (1972) 'Sir Robert Ker Porter – Regency artist and traveller', *Iran* 10, pp. 19–24.

Barnett, R. D. (1974) 'Charles Bellino and the beginning of Assyriology', *Iraq* 36, pp. 5–28.

Barr, W. (1844) *Journal of a March from Delhi to Peshawar, and from Thence to Cabul with the Mission of Lieut-Colonel Sir C. M. Wade*, London (repr. Patiala 1970).

Barthold, W. and Sourdel, D. (1960) 'al-Baramika', *Encyclopaedia of Islam*, vol. I, Leiden–London (2nd edn), pp. 1033–6.

Basham, A. L. ed. (1968), *Papers on the Date of Kaniṣka, submitted to the Conference on the Date of Kaniṣka, London, 20–22 April, 1960*, Leiden.

Bayer, T. S. (1738) *Historia Regni Graecorum Bactriani, in qua simul Graecorum in India, Coloniarum Vetus Memoria Explicatur*, St Petersburg.

Bayley, E. C. (1852) 'Notes on some sculptures found in the district of Peshâwar', *JASB* XXI, pp. 606–21.

Beal, S. (1964) *Travels of Fah-Hian and Sung-Yun, Buddhist Pilgrims from China to India (400 A.D. and 518 A.D.). Translated from the Chinese*, London 1869 (2nd edn).

Bechert, H. ed. (1995) *When Did the Buddha Live? The Controversy on the Dating of the Historical Buddha*, Delhi.

Belgrave, Sir Charles (1972a) *The Pirate Coast*, Beirut.

Belgrave, Sir Charles (1972b) *Personal Column*, Beirut.

Bellasis, M. (1952) *Honourable Company*, London.

Bellew, H. W. (1864) *A General Report on the Yusufzais*, Lahore (repr. 1977).

Bengal Secret Consultations (1833) vol. 372, 19 March: 'Abstract of intelligence from Cabul [*sic*] from 3rd to 25th December 1832'. British Library India Office Collections.

Bénisti, M. (1960) 'Étude sur le stūpa dans l'Inde ancienne', *Bulletin de l'École Française d'Extrême-Orient* L, pp. 37–146.

Bénisti, M. (2003) *Stylistics of Buddhist Art in India*, 2 vols, New Delhi.

Benveniste, E. (1929) *The Persian Religion*, Paris.

Bernard, P. (1967) 'Deuxième campagne de fouilles d'Aï Khanoum en Bactriane', *CRAI*, pp. 306–21.

Bernard, P. (1969) 'Quatrième campagne de fouilles à Aï Khanoum (Bactriane)', *CRAI*, pp. 313–55.

Bernard, P. (1971) 'La campagne de fouilles de 1970 à Aï Khanoum (Afghanistan)', *CRAI*, pp. 385–452.

Bernard, P. (1972) 'Campagne de fouilles à Aï Khanoum (Afghanistan)', *CRAI*, pp. 605–32.

Bernard, P. (1973) *Fouilles d'Aï Khanoum. I (campagnes 1965, 1966, 1967, 1968). Rapport préliminaire*, 2 vols, Mémoires de la Délégation Archéologique française en Afghanistan XXI, Paris.

Bernard, P. (1974) 'Fouilles de Aï Khanoum (Afghanistan), campagnes de 1972 et 1973', *CRAI*, pp. 280–308.

Bernard, P. (1976) 'Campagne de fouilles 1975 à Aï Khanoum (Afghanistan)', *CRAI*, pp. 287–322.

Bernard, P. (1982) 'Alexandrie du Caucase ou Alexandrie de l'Oxus', *Journal des Savants*, juillet–décembre, pp. 217–42.

Bernard, P. (1985) *Fouilles d'Aï Khanoum. IV. Les monnaies hors trésors. Questions d'histoire gréco-bactrienne*, Mémoires de la Délégation Archéologique française en Afghanistan XXVIII, Paris.

Bernard, P. (1994) 'The Greek kingdoms of Central Asia', in J. Harmatta (ed.), *History of the Civilizations of Central Asia*, vol. II, *The Development of Sedentary and Nomadic Civilizations: 700 BC to AD 250*, Paris, pp. 99–129.

Beveridge, A. S. tr. (1970) *Bābur-nāma (Memoirs of Bābur)*, London 1922 (repr. New Delhi).

Bhandare, S. (2006) 'Numismatics and history: the Maurya-Gupta interlude in the Gangetic plain', in P. Olivelle (ed.), *Between the Empires: Society in India 300 BCE to 400 CE*, OUP Oxford–New York, pp. 67–112.

Bhandare S. (2007) 'Not just a pretty face: interpretations of Alexander's numismatic imagery in the Hellenic East', in H. P. Ray and D. Potts (eds.), *Memory as History: The Legacy of Alexander in Asia*, New Delhi, pp. 208–56.

Bhandarkar, D. R. (1981) *Inscriptions of the Early Gupta Kings*, Corpus Inscriptionum Indicarum III, ed. B. Chhabra and G. S. Gai, New Delhi (rev. edn).

Bidwell, R. ed. (1985) *Arabian Gulf Intelligence* [= *Selections from the Records of the Bombay Government, New Series, No. XXIV, 1856 concerning Arabia, Bahrain, Kuwait, Muscat and Oman, Qatar, United Arab Emirates and the Islands of the Gulf*], London.

Bierbrier, M. (1995) *Who Was Who in Egyptology*, London (3rd edn).

Bilkadi, Z. (1996) *Babylon to Baku*, Windsor.

Bingöl, F. R. I. (1999) *Museum of Ancient Civilizations: Ancient Jewellery*, Ankara.

al-Biruni, Abu Rayhan Muhammad, *al-Āthār al-bāqiyah 'an al-qurūn al-khāliyah*, Persian tr. A. Danaseresht, Tehran 1363/1984.

Bivar, A. D. H. (1963) 'The Kaniṣka dating from Surkh Kotal', *Bulletin of the School of Oriental Studies* 26, pp. 498–502.

Bivar, A. D. H. (1970) 'Hārītī and the chronology of the Kuṣāṇas', *Bulletin of the School of Oriental Studies* 33, pp. 10–21.

Bivar, A. D. H. (1979) 'The absolute chronology of the Kushano-Sasanian governors of Central Asia', in J. Harmatta (ed.) *Prolegomena to the Sources on the History of Pre-Islamic Central Asia*, Budapest, pp. 317–32.

Bivar, A. D. H. (1981) 'The Azes era and the Indravarma casket', in H. Härtel (ed.), *South Asian Archaeology 1979*, Berlin, pp. 369–6.

Bivar, A. D. H. (1982) 'Bent bars and straight bars: an appendix to the Mir Zakah hoard', *Studia Iranica* 11, pp. 49–60.

Bivar, A. D. H. (1983) 'The political history of Iran under the Arsacids' and 'The history of eastern Iran', in E. Yarshater (ed.) *The Cambridge History of Iran*, vol. III.1, *The Seleucid, Parthian and Sasanian Periods*, Cambridge–London–New York, pp. 21–99, 181–231.

Bivar, A. D. H. (1998) 'A coinage for Asoka', in A. K. Jha and S. Garg (eds), *Ex Moneta. Essays on Numismatics in Honour of Dr. David W. MacDowall*, vol. I, New Delhi, pp. 55–65.

Bivar, A. D. H. (1999) *The Personalities of Mithra in Archaeology and Literature*, New York.

Bivar, A. D. H. (2005) 'The jewel of Khingila: a memento of the great Buddha of Bamiyan', in O. Bopearachchi and M.-F. Boussac (eds), *Afghanistan, ancient carrefour entre l'est et l'ouest*, Turnhout, pp. 319–29.

Bivar, A. D. H. (2006) 'Hephthalites', *Encyclopaedia Iranica Online*, http://www.iranica.com/articlenavigation/index.html.

Bivar, A. D. H. (2007) 'Gondophares and the Indo-Parthians', in V. S. Curtis and S. Stewart (eds), *The Age of the Parthians*, London–New York, pp. 24–34.

Blockley, R. (1981, 1983) *The Fragmentary Classicising Historians of the Later Roman Empire: Eunapius, Olympiodorus, Priscus and Malchus*, 2 vols, Liverpool.

Blurton, T. R. (1981) 'Excavations at the stūpa and vihāra of old Kandahar (summary)', in H. Härtel (ed.), *South Asian Archaeology 1979*, Berlin, p. 439.

Boardman, J. (1970) 'Pyramidal stamp seals in the Persian Empire', *Iran* VIII, pp. 19–45.

Bombay Dispatches (1834) Bombay Political Department, Political Consultations 1230/183, 16 April, no.6, pp. 781–90. British Library India Office Collections E/4/1057.

Bonhams (1994) *Fine Antiquities*, London Knightsbridge, auction Tuesday 5 July, 2 pm.

Bonhams (1998a) *Antiquities*, London Knightsbridge, auction Tuesday 7 April, 11 am and 2 pm.

Bonhams (1998b) *Antiquities*, London Knightsbridge, auction Tuesday 22 September, 11 am and 2.30 pm.

Bopearachchi, O. (1991) *Monnaies gréco-bactriennes et indo-grecques. Catalogue raisonné*, Paris.

Bopearachchi, O. (1997) 'The posthumous coinage of Hermaios and the conquest of Gandhara by the Kushans', in R. and B. Allchin, N. Kreitman and E. Errington (eds), *Gandharan Art in Context*, Cambridge, pp. 189–213.

Bopearachchi, O. (1999) 'Recent coin hoard evidence on pre-Kushana chronology', in M. Alram and D. Klimburg-Salter (eds), *Coins, Art, and Chronology. Essays on the Pre-Islamic History of the Indo-Iranian Borderlands*, Vienna, pp. 99–144.

Bopearachchi, O. (2001) 'Les données numismatiques et la datation du bazaar de Begram', *Τοποι* 11/1, pp. 411–35.

Bopearachchi, O. and Aman ur Rahman (1995) *Pre-Kushana Coins in Pakistan*, Karachi.

Bopearachchi, O. and Flandin, P. (2005) *Le portrait d'Alexandre le grand. Histoire d'un découverte pour l'humanité*, Paris.

Bopearachchi, O. and Fröhlich, C. (2001) 'An Indo-Greek and Indo-Scythian coin hoard from Bara (Pakistan)', unpublished mss.

Borger, R. (1975) 'Grotefends erste "Praevia"', in R. Borger *et al.*, *Die Welt des Alten Orients. Keilschrift – Grabungen – Gelehrte. Handbuch und Katalog zur Ausstellung zum 200. Geburtstag Georg Friedrich Grotefends*, Göttingen, pp. 157–84.

Bosworth, C. E. tr. (1999) *The History of al-Ṭabarī. The Sāsānids, the Byzantines, the Lakmids, and Yemen*, vol. V, New York.

Boucharlat, R. (1991) 'Pratiques funéraires à l'époque sassanide dans le sud de l'Iran', in P. Bernard and F. Grenet (eds) *Histoire et cultes de l'Asie Centrale préislamique*, pp. 71–8, Paris.

Boussac, M.-F. and Alam, M. S. (2001) 'A hoard of silver punchmarked coins', in M. S. Alam and J.-F. Salles (eds), *France–Bangladesh Joint Venture Excavations at Mahasthangarh. First Interim Report*, Dhaka, pp. 237–59

Boyce, M. (1984) *Textual Sources for the Study of Zoroastrianism*, Manchester.

Boyce, M. (2001) *Zoroastrians. Their Religious Beliefs and Practices*, London–New York 1979 (rev. repr.).

Boyce, M. and Grenet, F. (1991) *A History of Zoroastrianism*, vol. III, Leiden–New York–Copenhagen–Cologne.

Boyer, A.-M. (1904) 'Deux inscriptions en Kharoṣṭhī du Musée de Lahore', *Bulletin de l'École Française d'Extrême Orient* IV, pp. 680–6.

Briant, P. (1987) 'Alexander the Great', in E. Yarshater (ed.), *Encyclopaedia Iranica* II, London–New York, pp. 827–30.

Briant, P. (2002) *From Cyrus to Alexander. A History of the Persian Empire*, Winona Lake, Indiana.

Briant, P. (2005) 'History of the Persian empire (550–350 BC)', in J. Curtis and N. Tallis (eds), *Forgotten Empire. The World of Ancient Persia*, London, pp. 12–17.

British Museum (1835) Trustees Minutes, Standing Committee Papers 4 September, nos 4069–70: Honigberger collection.

British Museum (1835a) Register of Department of Coins and Medals, September: 'Copper coins, purchased of Dr. Hönigberger', reg. nos Honigberger 1–24.

British Museum (1845) Register of Department of Coins and Medals, vol. III, pp. 11–14: Coins 'purchased of Col. Lafont, 13 June', reg. nos Col. Lafont 1–145.

British Museum (1845a) Register of Department of Coins and Medals, vol. III, pp. 14–15: 'Sasanian coins presented by the Hon. East India Company, 14 June', reg. nos EIC 1–59.

British Museum (1847) Trustees Minutes, Standing Committee, 10 July, no. 7288; 24 July, nos 2301–2, Central Archives.

British Museum (1887) Book of Presents, no. 893, Central Archives CE 30/25.

British Museum (1892) *A Guide to the Babylonian and Assyrian Antiquities*, London.

British Museum (1908) *A Guide to the Babylonian and Assyrian Antiquities*, London (2nd edn revised and enlarged).

British Museum (1922) *A Guide to the Babylonian and Assyrian Antiquities*, London (3rd edn revised and enlarged).

Broadfoot, W. (1893) 'Addiscombe: the East India Company's military college', *Blackwood's Magazine* CVIII, May, pp. 647–57.

Browne, E. G. (1893) *A Year Amongst the Persians*, London.

Brysac, S. B. (1997) 'Last of the "Foreign Devils": Sir Aurel Stein's fourth foray into China was a humiliating failure. Who conspired to undermine the expedition and why?' *Archaeology* November–December, pp. 53–9.

Brysac, S. B. (2004) 'Sir Aurel Stein's fourth "American" Expedition', in H. Wang (ed.), *Sir Aurel Stein, Proceedings of the British Museum Study Day, 23 March 2002*, pp. 17–22. London.

Buckland, C. E. (1906) *Dictionary of Indian Biography*, London (repr. Lahore 1985).

Budge, E. A. W. (1920) *By Nile and Tigris. A narrative of journeys in Egypt and Mesopotamia on behalf of the British Museum between the years 1886 and 1913*, 2 vols, London.

Budge, E. A. W. (1925) *The Rise and Progress of Assyriology*, London.

Bühler, G. (1892) 'The new inscription of Toramana Shaha', *Epigraphia Indica* I, pp. 238–9.

Bühler, G. (1894) 'Further Jaina inscriptions from Mathurā', *Epigraphia Indica* II, pp. 195–212.

Burke's Peerage (1976) *Burke's Irish Family Records*, London.

Burnes, A. (1834) *Travels into Bokhara, being the Account of a Journey from India to Cabool, Tartary and Russia*, 3 vols, London (repr. Karachi 1973).

Burney, C. (1970) 'Excavations at Haftavan Tepe 1968: first preliminary report', *Iran* VIII, pp. 157–71.

Burton, A. (1999) *Vision & Accident: The Story of the Victoria & Albert Museum*, London.

Callieri, P. (2002) 'The Bactrian seal of Khiṅgila', *Silk Road Art and Archaeology* 8, pp. 121–41.

Carbone, C. (1968) 'Comment on à commencé les restaurations a Persepolis', in G. Zander (ed.), *Travaux de restauration de monuments historiques en Iran*, Rome, pp. 31–58.

Carl, J. (1940) 'Le monastère bouddhique de Fondukistān', *Journal of the Greater India Society* VII, pp. 1–14, 85–91.

Carradice, I. (1987) 'The "regal" coinage of the Persian empire', in I. Carradice (ed.), *Coinage and Administration in the Athenian and Persian Empires. The Ninth Oxford Symposium on Coinage and Monetary History*, BAR International Series 343, Oxford, pp. 73–108.

Carter, M. L. (1968) 'Dionysiac aspects of Kushan art', *Arts Orientalis* VII, pp. 121–46.

Casartelli, I. C. (1890) 'Astodans, and Avestic funeral prescriptions', *The Babylonian and Oriental Record* IV/VII, June, pp. 145–52.

Casson, L. (1989) *The Periplus Maris Erythraei. Text, with Introduction, Translation and Commentary*, Princeton.

Cautley, P. T. (1834) 'Discovery of an ancient town near Behat, in the doab of the Jamna and Ganges', *JASB* III, pp. 43–4 (repr. Thomas 1858, vol. I, pp. 73–5).

Cautley, P. T. (1834a) 'Further account of the remains of an ancient town, discovered at Behat, near Saharanpur', *JASB* III, pp. 221–7 (repr. Thomas 1858, vol. I, pp. 76–80).

Chakrabarti D. K. (1988) *A History of Indian Archaeology from the Beginning to 1947*, New Delhi.

Chakrabarti, D. K. (1997) *Colonial Indology. Sociopolitics of the Ancient India Past*, New Delhi.

Chavannes, É. (1903) 'Voyage de Song Yun dans l'Udyāna et Gandhāra 518–522 AD', *Bulletin de l'École Française d'Extrême-Orient* 3, pp. 379–441.

Chavannes, É. (1903a) *Documents sur les Tou-Kiue (Turcs) occidentaux: recueilles et commentés, suivi de notes additionnelles*, St Petersburg (repr. Paris 1941).

Chavannes, É. tr. (1897) *Les mémoires historiques de Se-ma Ts'ien*, Paris.

Chevalier, N. (1997) 'La découvert de la Perse antique par les voyageurs français au début du XIXe siecle', in N. Chevalier (ed.), *Une mission en Perse 1897–1912*, Paris, pp. 24–35.

Chevalier, N. (1997a) 'Les débuts de la recherche archéologique en Iran', *Dossiers d'archéologie, Iran. La Perse de Cyrus à Alexandre* no. 227, pp.10–15.

Chopra, G. L. (1929) *The Punjab as a Sovereign State*, Lahore.

Christie's (2003) *Antiquities, Including an English Private Collection of Ancient Gems*, Part II, London South Kensington, auction Wednesday 29 October 2003, 10.30 am and 2.30 pm.

Cole, H. H. (1883) *Memorandum on Ancient Monuments in Eusofzai*, Simla.

Cole H. H. (1884–5) *Preservation of National Monuments, India: Graeco-Buddhist Sculptures from Yusufzai*, Paris.

Colebrooke, H. T. (1801) 'Translation of one of the inscriptions on the pillar at Dehlee, called the Lāt of Feerōz Shah', *Asiatick Researches* VII, pp. 175–82.

Colebrooke, H. T. (1807) 'On ancient monuments containing Sanskrit inscriptions', *Asiatick Researches* IX, pp. 398–444.

References

Collon, D. (1996) 'A hoard of sealings from Ur', in M.-F. Boussac and A. Invernizzi (eds), *Archives et sceaux du monde hellénistique*, Torino, pp. 65–84.

Cosmas Indicopleustes, *Christian Topography*, tr./ed. J. W. McCrindle, *The Christian Topography of Cosmas, an Egyptian Monk*, London 1897. Online edn transcr. by R. Pearse, 2003: http://www.tertullian.org/fathers/cosmas.

Court, A. (1827) 'Itinerary of a journey from Persia to Kabul made in the year 1826', in C. Grey, (1929) *European Adventurers of Northern India, 1785 to 1849*, ed. H. L. O. Garrett, Lahore, appendix II, pp. xxvii–xlviii.

Court, A. (1834) 'Further information on the topes of Mánikyála, being the translation of an extract from a manuscript memoir on ancient Taxila', *JASB* III, pp. 556–62 (repr. Thomas 1858, vol. I, pp. 138–41).

Court, A. (1836) 'Conjectures on the march of Alexander', *JASB* V, pp. 387–95.

Court, A. (1836a) 'Extracts translated from a memoir on a map of Pesháwar and the countries comprised between the Indus and the Hydaspes, the Peucelaotis and Taxila of ancient geography', *JASB* V, pp. 468–80.

Court, A. (1839) 'Collection of facts which may be useful for the comprehension of Alexander the Great's exploits on the western banks of the Indus', *JASB* VIII, pp. 304–13.

Court, C.-A. (MSS 1) *Mémoires manuscrits du général Claude-Auguste Court*, 5 vols, Musée des Arts asiatiques Guimet, Paris, BG 64836.

Court, C.-A. (MSS) 'La collection numismatique du Général Court', 3 vols, British Museum Department of Coins and Medals Archives.

Crawford, M. (1974) *Roman Republican Coinage*, Cambridge.

Cribb, J. (1981) 'Gandharan hoards of Kushano-Sasanian and Late Kushan coppers', *Coin Hoards* IV, pp. 84–108.

Cribb, J. (1985) 'Dating India's earliest coins', in J. Schotsmans and M. Taddei (eds), *South Asian Archaeology 1983*, Naples, vol. II, pp. 535–54.

Cribb, J. (1985a) 'Some further hoards of Kushano-Sasanian and Late Kushan coppers', *Coin Hoards* VII, pp. 308–19.

Cribb, J. (1990) 'Numismatic evidence for Kushano-Sasanian chronology', *Studia Iranica* 19, pp. 151–93.

Cribb, J. (1991) 'The Greek contacts of the Mauryan kings and their relevance to the date of the Buddha' (unpublished).

Cribb, J. (1993) 'The "Heraus" coins: their attribution to the Kushan king Kujula Kadphises, *c.* AD 30–80', in M. Price, A. Burnett and R. Bland (eds), *Essays in Honour of Robert Carson and Kenneth Jenkins*, London, pp. 107–34.

Cribb, J. (1997) 'Shiva images on Kushan and Kushano-Sasanian coins', in K. Tanabe, J. Cribb and H. Wang (eds), *Studies in Silk Road Coins and Culture. Silk Road Art and Archaeology Special Volume*, pp. 11–66.

Cribb, J. (1998) 'The end of Greek coinage in Bactria and India and its evidence for the Kushan coinage system', in R. Ashton and S. Hurter, *Studies in Greek Numismatics in Memory of Martin Jessop Price*, London, pp. 83–98.

Cribb, J. (1999) 'The early Kushan kings: new evidence for chronology', in M. Alram and D. Klimburg-Salter (eds), *Coins, Art and Chronology. Essays on the pre-Islamic History of the Indo-Iranian Borderlands*, Vienna, pp. 177–205.

Cribb, J. (1999/2000) 'Kanishka's Buddha image coins revisited', *Silk Road Art and Archaeology* 6 (*Papers in Honour of Francine Tissot*), pp. 151–89.

Cribb, J. (2000) 'Early Indian history' in M. Willis, *Buddhist Reliquaries from Ancient India*, London, pp. 39–54.

Cribb, J. (2004) 'The Greeks in Bactria (northern Afghanistan) and their successors', *Newsletter of the London Numismatic Club* VIII/7, pp. 58–69.

Cribb, J. (2005) 'The Greek kingdom of Bactria, its coinage and its collapse', in O. Bopearachchi and M.-F. Boussac (eds), *Afghanistan, ancient carrefour entre l'est et l'ouest*, Turnhout, pp. 207–26.

Cribb, J. (2005a) 'Dating the Bīmarān casket and the development of Gandhāran Buddha images', Paper of the XIVth Conference of the International Association of Buddhist Studies, London 29 August – 3 September, London (unpublished).

Cribb, J. (2005b) *The Indian Coinage Tradition. Origins, Continuity and Change*, Nashik.

Cribb, J. (2006) 'Money as a marker of cultural continuity and change in Central Asia', in G. Herrmann and J. Cribb (eds), *After Alexander: Central Asia before Islam. Themes in the History and Archaeology of Western Central Asia* (Papers from the British Academy Conference 23–5 June 2004), London (in press).

Crompton, A. (1875) 'Report on the explorations at Shāhji-ka-Dheri, near Peshawar, by a detachment of the Sappers and Miners', *Punjab Government Gazette*, Supplement 18 November, pp. 717–18.

Crone, J. S. (1937) *A Concise Dictionary of Irish Biography*, Dublin.

Croydon Advertiser (1882) *Croydon in the Past*, Croydon.

Csoma Körösi, S. (1957) *The Life and Teachings of Buddha*, Calcutta (repr.).

Ctesias, *Persica* in F. Jacoby (1958) *Die Fragmente der Griechischen Historiker,* part 3, Leiden.

Cunningham, A. (1834) 'Correction of a mistake regarding some of the Roman coins found in the Tope at Manikyala opened by M. Court', *JASB* III, pp. 635–7.

Cunningham, A. (1836) Letter identifying 'ΑΡΔΟΧΡΟ' on one of Ventura's coins, Proceedings Asiatic Society, 6 January, *JASB* V, p. 58.

Cunningham, A. (1840) 'Notice of some counterfeit Bactrian coins', *JASB* IX, pp. 393–6.

Cunningham, A. (1840a) 'Notes on Captain Hay's Bactrian coins', *JASB* IX, pp. 531–42.

Cunningham, A. (1840b) 'Appendix to the notice of forged Bactrian coins', *JASB* IX, pp. 543–4.

Cunningham, A. (1840c) 'Description of, and deductions from a consideration of, some new Bactrian coins', *JASB* IX, pp. 867–89, 1008.

Cunningham, A. (1840d) 'A second notice of some forged coins of the Bactrians and Indo-Scythians', *JASB* IX, pp. 1217–30.

Cunningham, A. (1841) 'Abstract journal of the route of Lieutenant A. Cunningham, Bengal Engineers, to the sources of the Punjab rivers', *JASB* X.1, pp. 105–15.

Cunningham, A. (1842) 'Second notice of some new Bactrian coins', *JASB* XI, pp. 130–7.

Cunningham, A. (1843) 'An account of the discovery of the ruins of the Buddhist city of Samkassa' (Letter from Cunningham to Colonel Sykes, dated Aligarh, 15 September 1842), *JRAS* VII, pp. 241–9.

Cunningham, A. (1843–4) 'The ancient coinage of Kashmir, with chronological and historical notes, from the commencement of the Christian era to the conquest of the country by the Moguls', *NC* VI, pp. 1–38.

Cunningham, A. (1845) 'Notice of some unpublished coins of the Indo-Scythians', *JASB* XIV, pp. 430–41.

Cunningham, A. (1848) 'Correspondence of the commissioners deputed to the Tibetan frontier', *JASB* XVII, pp. 89–132.

Cunningham, A. (1854) *The Bhilsa Topes*, London.

Cunningham, A. (1854a) 'Coins of the Indian Buddhist Satraps, with Greek inscriptions', *JASB* XXIII, pp. 679–714.

Cunningham, A. (1863) 'Remarks on the Bactro-Pali inscription from Taxila', *JASB* XXXII, pp. 139–52.

Cunningham, A. (1864) 'Note on the Bactro-Pali inscription from Taxila', *JASB* XXXIII, pp. 35–8.

Cunningham, A. (1868) 'Coins of Alexander's successors in the East', *NC* II.8, pp. 93–136, 181–213, 257–83.

Cunningham, A. (1869) 'Coins of Alexander's successors in the East', *NC* II.9, pp. 28–46, 121–53, 217–46, 293–318.

Cunningham, A. (1870) 'Coins of Alexander's successors in the East', *NC* II.10, pp. 65–90, 205–36.

Cunningham, A. (1871) *Report of 1863–64*, Archaeological Survey of India Report II, in *Four Reports made during the Years 1862–63–64–65*, 2 vols, Simla.

Cunningham, A. (1871a) *The Ancient Geography of India*, London.

Cunningham, A. (1872) 'Coins of Alexander's successors in the East', *NC* II.12, pp. 157–85.

Cunningham, A. (1873) 'Coins of Alexander's successors in the East', *NC* II.13, pp. 187–219.

Cunningham, A. (1874) Director-General, Archaeological Survey of India, to Secretary to Government, Public Works Department, no. 130, 18–9–1874, 'Exploration for archaeological remains in the Peshawar District', *Punjab Home Department Proceedings*, October, no. 8A, pp. 420–2.

Cunningham, A. (1875) *Report for the Year 1872–73*, Archaeological Survey of India V, Calcutta.

Cunningham, A. (1875a) Letter to Secretary, Government of India Home Department, dated 12 August, Lahore Civil Secretariat Archives, Home General Department, October, no. 37.

Cunningham, A. (1879) 'Notes on the gold coins found in the Ahin Posh Tope', August Proceedings of the Asiatic Society of Bengal, *JASB* XLVIII, pp. 205–10.

Cunningham, A. (1881) Letter to A. W. Franks, dated 1 May, British Museum Department of Prehistory and Europe Archives.

Cunningham, A. (1881a) 'Relics from ancient Persia in gold, silver and copper', *JASB* L, pp. 151–86.

Cunningham, A. (1882) *Report for the Year 1878–79*, Archaeological Survey of India XIV, Calcutta.

Cunningham, A. (1883) 'Relics from ancient Persia in gold, silver and copper (second notice)', *JASB* LII, pp. 64–7; '(third notice)', pp. 258–60.

Cunningham, A. (1884) *Coins of Alexander's Successors in the East*, London.

Cunningham, A. (1888) 'Coins of the Indo-Scythian king Miaüs or Heraüs', *NC* III.8, pp. 47–58.

Cunningham, A. (1888–93) Letters to E. J. Rapson, British Museum Department of Coins and Medals Archives.

Cunningham, A. (1888a) 'Coins of the Indo-Scythians', *NC* III.8, pp. 199–248.

Cunningham, A. (1889) 'Coins of the Tochari, Kushāns, or Yue-ti', *NC* III.9, pp. 268–311.

Cunningham, A. (1890) 'Coins of the Sakas', *NC* III.10, pp. 103–72.

Cunningham, A. (1891) *Coins of Ancient India from the Earliest Times down to the Seventh Century A.D.*, London.

Cunningham, A. (1892) 'Coins of the Kushāns, or Great Yue-ti', *NC* III.12, pp. 40–82, 98–159.

Cunningham, A. (1892a) *Coins of the Indo-Scythians*, London (repr. articles *NC* III.8–12, 1888–92).

Cunningham, A. (1892b) *Mahābodhi or the Great Buddhist Temple under the Bodhi Tree at Buddha-Gaya*, London.

Cunningham, A. (1893) 'Coins of the Later Indo-Scythians, Introduction and Later Kushāns', *NC* III.13, pp. 93–128.

Cunningham, A. (1893a) 'Coins of the Later Indo-Scythians – Scytho-Sassanians', *NC* III.13, pp. 166–77.

Cunningham, A. (1893b) 'Coins of the Later Indo-Scythians – Little Kushâns', *NC* III.13, pp. 184–202.

Cunningham, A. (1894) 'Coins of the Later Indo-Scythians – Ephthalites, or White Huns', *NC* III.14, pp. 243–93.

Cunningham, A. (1895) *Later Indo-Scythians. Ephthalites, or White Huns*, London (repr. articles *NC* III.13–14, 1893–4).

Curiel, R. and Fussman, G. (1965) *Le trésor monétaire de Qunduz*, Mémoires de la Délégation archéologique française en Afghanistan XX, Paris.

Curiel, R. and Schlumberger, D. (1953) *Trésors monétaires d'Afghanistan*, Mémoires de la Délégation Archéologique française en Afghanistan XIV, Paris.

Curtis, C. D. (1925) *Sardis XIII. Jewelry and Gold Work, Part I 1910–1914*, Rome.

Curtis, J. (1984) *Nush-i Jan III. The Small Finds*, London.

Curtis, J. (1993) 'William Kennett Loftus and his excavations at Susa', *Iranica Antiqua* 28, pp.1–55.

Curtis, J. (1997) 'Franks and the Oxus Treasure', in M. Caygill and J. Cherry (eds), *A. W. Franks. Nineteenth-century Collecting and the British Museum*, London, pp. 231–49.

Curtis, J. (1998) 'A chariot scene from Persepolis', *Iran* XXXVI, pp. 45–51.

Curtis, J. (2000) *Ancient Persia*, London (2nd rev. edn).

Curtis J. and Tallis N. eds, (2005) *Forgotten Empire. The World of Ancient Persia*, London.

Curtis, V. S. (1988) 'The Parthian costume: origin and distribution', Ph.D thesis, London University, University College.

Curtis, V. S. (1993) *Persian Myths*, London.

Curtis, V. S. (1996) 'Parthian and Sasanian furniture', in G. Herrmann (ed.), *The Furniture of Western Asia. Ancient and Traditional*, Mainz, pp. 233–44.

Curtis, V. S. (1999) 'Some observations on coins of Peroz and Kavad I', in M. Alram and D. Klimburg-Salter (eds), *Coins, Art and Chronology. Essays on the pre-Islamic History of the Indo-Iranian Borderlands*, Vienna, pp. 303–9.

Curtis, V. S. (2000) 'Parthian culture and costume', in J. Curtis (ed.), *Mesopotamia and Iran in the Parthian and Sasanian Periods. Rejection and Revival c.238 BC–AD 642*, Proceedings of a seminar in memory of Vladimir G. Lukonin, London.

Curtis, V. S. (2004) 'Investiture. ii. Parthian', *Encyclopaedia Iranica Online*, http://www.iranica.com/articlenavigation/index.html.

Curtis V. S. (2005) 'The legacy of ancient Persia' in J. Curtis and N. Tallis (eds), *Forgotten Empire. The World of Ancient Persia*, London, pp. 250–7.

Curtis, V. S. (2007) 'The Iranian revival in the Parthian period', in V. S. Curtis and S. Stewart (eds), *The Age of the Parthians*, pp. 1–25, London.

Curtis, V. S. and Pazooki, N. (2004) 'Aurel Stein and Bahman Karimi on Old Routes of Western Iran', in H. Wang (ed.), *Sir Aurel Stein, Proceedings of the British Museum Study Day, 23 March 2002*, pp. 23–8, London.

Curtis, V. S. and Simpson, St J. (1997) 'Archaeological news from Iran', *Iran* XXXV, pp. 137–44.

Curzon, G. N. (1892) *Persia and the Persian Question*, 2 vols, London.

Dahmen, K. (2007) *The Legend of Alexander the Great on Greek and Roman Coins*, London.

Dalton, O. M. (1964) *The Treasure of the Oxus with Other Examples of Early Oriental Metal-work*, London.

Dani, A. H. (1965–6) 'Shaikhan Dheri excavation (1963 and 1964 seasons)', *Ancient Pakistan* II, pp. 17–113.

Darmesteter, J. (1975) *The Zend-Avesta*, Delhi–Patna–Varanasi (4th edn).

Daryaee, T. (2002) *Šahrestānīhā ī Ērānšahr*, Costa Mesa, California.

Davary, G. D. (1982) *Baktrish. Ein Wörterbuch auf Grund der Inschriften, Handschriften, Münzen und Siegelsteine*, Heidelberg.

De Jong, A. (2003) 'Vexillologica sacra: searching the cultic banner', in C. G. Cereti, M. Maggi and E. Provasi (eds), *Religious Themes and Texts of pre-Islamic Iran and Central Asia. Studies in honour of Professor Gherardo Gnoli on the occasion of his 65th birthday on 6 December 2002*, Wiesbaden, pp. 191–202.

De Mecquenem, R. (1947) 'Contribution à l'étude du palais achéménide de Suse', in R. de Mecquenem, R. le Breton and M. Rutten, *Archéologie Susienne*, Mémoires de la Mission Archéologique en Iran XXX, Paris, pp. 1–119.

De Planhol, X. (1990) 'Bušehr', in E. Yarshater (ed.), *Encyclopaedia Iranica* IV, London–New York, pp. 569–72.

De Schauensee, M. (1988) 'Northwest Iran as a bronzeworking centre: the view from Hasanlu', in J. Curtis (ed.) *Bronzeworking Centres of Western Asia c. 1000–539 B.C.*, London–New York, pp. 45–62.

Deane, H. A. (1896) 'Note on Udyāna and Gandhāra', *JRAS*, pp. 655–75.

Desmond, R. (1982) *The India Museum 1801–1879*, London.

Diamond, E. and Rogers, T. D. (1983) 'Catalogue of the papers of Sir (Marc) Aurel Stein (1862–1943)', Bodleian Library, Oxford (unpublished).

Dickson, W. K. (1901) *The life of Major-General Sir Robert Murdoch Smith K. C. M. G., Royal Engineers*, Edinburgh–London.

Dietz, S. (1995) 'The dating of the historical Buddha in the history of western scholarship up to 1980', in H. Bechert (ed.), *When Did the Buddha Live? The Controversy on the Dating of the Historical Buddha*, Delhi.

Dörner, F. K. and Goell, T. (1963) *Arsaemia am Nymphaios. Die Ausgrabungen im Hierothesion des Mithradates,* Berlin.

Drew, D. (1999) *The Lost Chronicles of the Maya Kings*, London.

Duchesne-Guillemin, J. (1983) 'Zoroastrian religion', in E. Yarshater (ed.), *The Cambridge History of Iran*, vol. III.1, *The Seleucid, Parthian and Sasanian Periods*, Cambridge–London–New York, pp. 866–908.

Durtubie, T. (1795) *Manuel de l'artilleur contenant tous les objets dont la connoissance est nécessaire aux officiers et sous-officiers de l'artillerie suivant l'approbation de Gribeauval*, Paris (repr. 2003).

Eden, E. (1866) *'Up the Country'. Letters written to her Sister from the Upper Provinces of India*, 2 vols, London (repr. 1930).

Edmonds, C. J. (1934) 'A tomb in Kurdistan', *Iraq* 1, pp. 183–92.

Eggermont, P. H. L. (1992), 'New notes on Aśoka and his successors', in H. Bechert, *The Dating of the Historical Buddha. Die Datierung des historischen Buddha (Symposien zur Buddhismusforschung, IV.2)*, 2 vols, Göttingen, part 2, pp. 501–24.

Elišē, *Vasn Vardanay ew Hayoc Paterazmin*, ed. E. Ter-Minasean, Erivan 1957.

Elphinstone, M. (1815) *An Account of the Kingdom of Caubul*, 2 vols, London (repr. 1972).

Encyclopaedia Britannica (1974–98) *The New Encyclopaedia Britannica*, 29 vols, Chicago (15th edn).

Enoki, K. (1969) 'On the date of the Kidarites (1)', *Memoirs of the Research Department of the Tokyo Bunko* 27, Tokyo, pp. 1–26.

Enoki, K. (1970) 'On the date of the Kidarites (2)', *Memoirs of the Research Department of the Tokyo Bunko* 28, Tokyo, pp. 13–38.

Errington, E. (1987) 'The western discovery of the art of Gandhāra and the finds of Jamālgarhī', Ph.D. thesis, London University, School of Oriental and African Studies.

Errington, E. (1987a) 'Tahkāl: the nineteenth-century record of two lost Gandhāra sites', *Bulletin of the School of Oriental and African Studies* L.2, pp. 301–24.

Errington, E. (1990) 'Documents relating to the so-called Athena of the Lahore Museum', *Lahore Museum Bulletin* III.1, pp. 19–30.

Errington, E. (1990a) 'Towards clearer attributions of site provenance for some 19th-century collections of Gandhāra sculpture', in M. Taddei (ed.), *South Asian Archaeology 1987*, vol. II, Rome, pp. 765–81.

Errington, E. (1993) 'In search of *Pa-lu-sha*, a city of the central Gandhāra plain', *Bulletin of the Asia Institute* 7, *Iranian Studies in Honor of A. D. H. Bivar*, pp. 55–66.

Errington, E. (1995) 'Rediscovering the coin collection of General Claude-Auguste Court. A preliminary report', *Τόποι* 5.2, pp. 409–24.

Errington, E. (1999) 'Rediscovering the collections of Charles Masson', in M. Alram and D. Klimburg-Salter (eds), *Coins, Art, and Chronology. Essays on the Pre-Islamic History of the Indo-Iranian Borderlands*, Vienna, pp. 207–37.

Errington, E. (1999/2000) 'Numismatic evidence for dating the Buddhist remains of Gandhāra', *Silk Road Art and Archaeology* 6, *Papers in Honour of Francine Tissot*, pp. 191–216.

Errington, E. (2001 [2003]) 'Charles Masson and Begram', *Τόποι Orient-Occident* 11.1, pp. 357–409.

Errington, E. (2002) 'Numismatic evidence for dating the "Kanishka" reliquary', *Silk Road Art and Archaeology* 8, pp. 101–20.

References

Errington, E. (2003) 'A survey of late hoards of Indian punch-marked coins', *NC* 163, pp. 69–121.

Errington, E. (2004) 'Masson, Charles', *Encyclopedia Iranica Online*, http://www.iranica.com/articlenavigation/index.html.

Errington, E. (2006) 'Boots, female idols and disembodied heads', *Journal of Inner Asian Art and Archaeology* 1, pp. 89–96.

Errington, E. and Cribb, J. eds (1992) *The Crossroads of Asia. Transformation in Image and Symbol*, Cambridge.

Erskine, W. (1819) 'Observations on two sepulchral urns found at Bushire in Persia', *Transactions of the Literary Society of Bombay* I, pp. 191–7.

Erskine, W. (1823) 'Observations on the remains of the Bouddhists [*sic*] in Ceylon', *Transactions of the Literary Society of Bombay* III, pp. 494–537.

Esin, E. (1977) 'Tarkhan Nīzak or Tarkhan Tirek?', *Journal of the American Oriental Society* 98, pp. 323–32.

Euripides, *The Bacchae*, http://www.mala.bc.ca/~johnstoi/euripides/euripides.html.

Faccenna, D. (1980) *Butkara I (Swāt, Pakistan) 1956–1962*, 5 vols, IsMEO Reports and Memoirs II, Rome.

Faccenna, D., Khan, A. N. and Nadiem, I. H. (1993) *Pānr I (Swat, Pakistan)*, IsMEO Reports and Memoirs XXVI, Rome.

Falconer, J., Kartészi, Á., Kelecsényi, Á. and Russell-Smith, L. (ed. by É. Apor and H. Wang) (2002) *Catalogue of the Collections of Sir Aurel Stein in the Library of the Hungarian Academy of Sciences*. Budapest: British Museum and Library of the Hungarian Academy of Sciences.

Falconer, J. et al. (2007) *Supplement to the Catalogue of Sir Aurel Stein in the Library of the Hungarian Academy of Sciences*, Budapest: Library of the Hungarian Academy of Sciences.

Falk, H. (2001) 'The *yuga* of Sphujiddhava and the era of the Kuṣāṇas', *Silk Road Art and Archaeology* 7, pp. 121–36.

Falk, H. (2002) 'Appendix: the inscription on the so-called Kaniṣka casket' in E. Errington, 'Numismatic evidence for dating the "Kaniṣka" reliquary', *Silk Road Art and Archaeology* 8, pp. 111–13.

Falk, H. (2002/3) 'Some inscribed images from Mathurā revisited', *Indo-Asiatische Zeitschrift* 6.7, pp. 31–47.

Falk, H. (2005) 'The introduction of stūpa-worship in Bajaur', in O. Bopearachchi and M.-F. Boussac (eds), *Afghanistan, ancien carrefour entre l'est et l'ouest*, Turnhout, pp. 347–58.

Falkenhausen, L von (1992) 'Serials on Chinese archaeology published in the People's Republic of China: a bibliographical survey', *Ancient China* XXVII, pp. 247–95.

Falkenhausen, L von (1993) 'On the historical orientation of Chinese archaeology', *Antiquity* 647, pp. 839–49.

Fane, H. E. (1842) *Five Years in India . . .* , 2 vols, London (repr. Patiala 1970).

Farrington, A. (1976) *The Records of the East India College Haileybury, and Other Institutions*, London.

Farrington, S. M. (1988) *Peshawar Cemetery, North West Frontier Province, Pakistan*, London.

Faxian, *Fo guo ji* (Account of the Buddhist kingdoms), *Taisho shinshu Daizokyo* (Japanese translation of *Taisho Tripiṭaka*, vol. 51, no. 2085).

Field, H. (1955) *The Track of Man. Adventures of an Anthropologist*, London.

Finkel, I. L. (2005) 'The decipherment of Achaemenid cuneiform', in J. Curtis and N. Tallis (eds), *Forgotten Empire. The World of Ancient Persia*, London, pp. 25–9.

Fischer-Bosser, W. (2006) Review of O. Bopearachchi and P. Flandin, *Le portrait d'Alexandre le grand. Histoire d'un découverte pour l'humanité*, in *American Numismatic Society Magazine* 5.2, pp.62–5.

Fleet, J. F. (1888) *Inscriptions of the Early Gupta Kings and their Successors*, Corpus Inscriptionum Indicarum III, Calcutta, repr. Varanasi 1963.

Flood, F. B. (1989) 'Herakles and the "perpetual acolyte" of the Buddha: some observations on the iconography of Vajrapani in Gandharan art', *South Asian Studies* 5, pp. 17–27.

Fontan, E. (1994) 'Lottin de Laval (1810–1903): l'inventeur de la "lottinoplastique" qui se voulait orientaliste', in E. Fontan and N. Chevalier (eds) *De Khorsabad à Paris. La découverte des Assyriens*, Paris, pp. 176–83.

Fontan, E. (1998) 'Lottin de Laval et la lottinoplastique', *Regards sur la . . . Perse antique*, Argentomagus, pp. 228–9.

Forrest, D. (1968) *The Oriental. Life Story of a West End Club*, London.

Foucher, A. (1901) *Sur la frontière indo-afghane*, Paris.

Foucher, A. (1942/7) *La vielle route de l'Inde de Bactres à Taxila*, Mémoires de la Délégation Archéologique française en Afghanistan II, Paris.

Francfort, H.-P. (1984) *Fouilles d'Aï Khanoum. III. Le sanctuaire du temple à niches indentées. 2. Les trouvailles*, Mémoires de la Délégation Archéologique française en Afghanistan XXVII, Paris.

Frye, R. N. (1960) 'Balkh', *Encyclopaedia of Islam*, vol. II, Leiden–London (2nd edn), pp. 1000–2.

Frye, R. N. (1983) 'The political history of Iran under the Sasanians', in E. Yarshater (ed.), *The Cambridge History of Iran*, vol. III.1, *The Seleucid, Parthian and Sasanian Periods*, Cambridge–London–New York, pp. 116–77.

Frye, R. N. (1987) 'Andragoras', in E. Yarshater (ed.), *Encyclopaedia Iranica* II, London–New York, p. 26.

Fussman, G. (1974) 'Documents épigraphiques kouchans', *Bulletin de l'École Française d'Extrême-Orient* 61, pp. 1–76.

Fussman, G. (1987) 'Numismatic and epigraphic evidence for the chronology of early Gandharan art', in M. Yaldiz (ed.), *Investigating Indian Art*, Berlin, pp. 67–88.

Fussman, G. (1989) 'The Māṭ *devakula*: a new approach to its understanding', in D. M. Srinivasan (ed.) *Mathurā. The Cultural Heritage*, New Delhi, pp. 193–9.

Fussman, G. (1991) 'Villes indiennes, prolégomènes', *Annuaire du Collège de France 1990–1991, résumés des cours et travaux*, Paris, pp. 659–68.

Fussman, G. (1993) 'L'indo-grec Ménandre ou Paul Demiéville revisité' *Journal Asiatique* 281, pp. 61–138.

Fussman, G. (1998) 'L'inscription de Rabatak et l'origine de l'ère śaka', *Journal Asiatique* 286, pp. 333–400.

Gardanne, A. (1809) *Voyage dans la Turquie et la Perse 1807–1808*, Paris–Marseilles.

Gardner, P. (1877) *Numismata Orientalia. The Parthian Coinage*, London.

Gardner, P. (1886) *The Coins of the Greek and Scythic Kings of Bactria and India in the British Museum*, London.

Garrick, H. B. W. (1885) *Tour through Behar, Central India, Peshawar and Yusufzai, 1881-82*, Archaeological Survey of India Report XIX, Calcutta.

Garsoïan, N. (1983) 'Byzantium and the Sasanians', in E. Yarshater (ed.), *The Cambridge History of Iran*, vol. III.1, *The Seleucid, Parthian and Sasanian Periods*, Cambridge–London–New York, pp. 568–92.

Garsoïan, N. G. tr. (1989) *The Epic Histories attributed to P'awstos Buzand (Buzandaran Patmut'wnk')*, Cambridge Mass.

Gerard, J. G. (1834) 'Memoir on the topes and antiquities of Afghanistan', *JASB* III, pp. 321–9.

Gershevitch, I. (1957) 'Sissoo at Susa', *Bulletin of the School of Oriental and African Studies* XIX.2, pp. 317–20.

Gershevitch, I. (1958) 'Ad Sissoo at Susa', *Bulletin of the School of Oriental and African Studies* XXI.1–3, p. 174.

Ghirshman, R. (1946) *Begram, recherches archéologiques et historiques sur les kouchans*, Institut français d'Archéologie orientale, Cairo.

Ghirshman, R. (1962) *Iran. Parthes et Sassanides*, Paris.

Ghirshman, R. (1971) *Bîchâpour I et II*, Paris.

Ghirshman, R. (1974) 'Un tetradrachm d'Andragoras de la collection de M. Foroughi', in D. K. Kouymjian (ed.), *Near Eastern Numismatics, Iconography, Epigraphy and History. Studies in Honor of George C. Miles*, Beirut, pp. 1–8.

Gibson, McG. (1972) *The City and Area of Kish*, Miami.

Gilmour, D. (1994) *Curzon*, London.

Gnoli, G. (1999) 'Farr(ah)', in E. Yarshater (ed.), *Encyclopaedia Iranica* IX, London–New York, pp. 312–19.

Göbl, R. (1967) *Dokumente zur Geschichte der Iranischen Hunnen in Baktrien und Indien*, 4 vols, Wiesbaden.

Göbl, R. (1971) *Sasanian Numismatics*, Würzburg.

Göbl, R. (1976) *A Catalogue of Coins from Butkara I (Swāt, Pakistan)*, Ismeo Reports and Memoirs IV, Rome.

Göbl, R. (1984) *System und Chronologie der Münzprägung des Kušānreiches*, Vienna.

Göbl, R. (1987) 'Die kušānischen Bronze-Appliken mit Königsdarstellungen', *Litterae Numismaticae Vindobonenses* 3, pp. 193–202.

Göbl, R. (1999) 'The Rabatak inscription and the date of Kanishka', in M. Alram and D. Klimburg-Salter (eds), *Coins, Art and Chronology. Essays on the pre-Islamic History of the Indo-Iranian Borderlands*, Vienna, pp. 151–75.

Golding, W. (1991) *To the Ends of the Earth. A Sea Trilogy*, London.

Goldman, B. (1961) 'An oriental solar motif and its western extension', *Journal of Near Eastern Studies* 20, pp. 239–47.

Gombrich, R. (1992) 'Dating the Buddha: a red herring revealed', in H. Bechert, *The Dating of the Historical Buddha. Die Datierung des historischen Buddha (Symposien zur Buddhismusforschung IV.2)*, 2 vols, Göttingen, part 2, pp. 237–59.

Graham, I. (2002) *Alfred Maudslay and the Maya: A Biography*, London.

Grant C. (1838) *Public Characters*, Calcutta.

Greenway, P. and St Vincent, D. (1998) *Lonely Planet Iran*, Victoria.

Gregory, S. and Kennedy, D. eds (1985) *Sir Aurel Stein's Limes Reports*, BAR International Series 272.i–ii, Oxford.

Grenet, F. (2002) 'Regional interaction in Central Asia and Northwest India in the Kidarite and Hephthalite periods', in N. Sims-Williams (ed.), *Indo-Iranian Languages and Peoples*, Proceedings of the British Academy 116, pp. 203–24.

Grenet, F. (2005) 'An archaeologist's approach to Avestan geography', in V.S. Curtis and S. Stewart (eds), *The Birth of the Persian Empire*, London, pp. 29–51.

Grey, C. (1929) *European Adventurers of Northern India, 1785 to 1849*, ed. H. L. O. Garrett, Lahore.

Grotefend, C. L. (1834) 'Münzen baktrischer Könige', *Blätter für Münzkunde – Hannoverische Numismatische Zeitschrift* 11, pp. 23–4.

Grotefend, C. L. (1834a) 'Münzen baktrischer Könige (Zweiter Artikel)', *Blätter für Münzkunde – Hannoverische Numismatische Zeitschrift* 13, pp. 1–2.

Grotefend, C. L. (1835) 'Die unbekannte Schrift der baktrischen Münzen', *Zeitschrift für die Altertumswissenschaft*, no. 104.

Grotefend, C. L. (1835a) 'Über baktrische und indische Münzen', *Blätter für Münzkunde – Hannoverische Numismatische Zeitschrift* 25, pp. 3–5.

Grotefend, C. L. (1836) 'Die unbekannte Schrift der baktrischen Münzen', *Blätter für Münzkunde – Hannoverische Numismatische Zeitschrift* 26, pp. 1–2.

Grotefend, C. L. (1839) *Die Münzen der griechischen, parthischen und indoskythischen Könige von Baktrien und den Ländern am Indus*, Hannover.

Guest, M. and Boulton, W. B. (1903) *Memorials of the Royal Yacht Squadron*, London.

Guignes, J. de (1756) *Histoire générale des Huns, des Turcs, des Mogols, et des autres tartares occidentaux*, Paris.

Guignes, J. de (1759) 'Sur quelques événements qui concernent l'histoire des rois grecs de la Bactriane et particulièrement la destruction de leur royaume par les Scythes, etc.', *Mémoires de l'Académie des Inscriptions et Belle-lettres* XXV.Ii, pp. 17–33.

Guillaume, O. (1983) *Fouilles d'Aï Khanoum. II. Les propylées de la rue principale*, Mémoires de la Délégation Archéologique française en Afghanistan XXVI, Paris.

Guillaume, O. ed. (1991) *Greco-Bactrian and Indian Coins from Afghanistan*, tr. O. Bopearachchi, London–New York.

Guillaume, O. and Rougeulle, A. (1987) *Fouilles d'Aï Khanoum, VII. Les petits objets*, Mémoires de la Délégation Archéologique française en Afghanistan XXXI, Paris.

Gupta P. L. (1963) *The Amaravati Hoard of Silver Punch-marked Coins*, Hyderabad.

Gupta P. L. and Hardaker, T. R. (1985) *Ancient Indian Punchmarked Coins of the Magadha – Maurya Kārshāpana Series*, Nasik.

Gupta, P. L. (1989) 'Early coins of Mathurā region', in D. M. Srinivasan (ed.), *Mathurā. The Cultural Heritage*, New Delhi, pp. 124–39.

Güterbock, H.G. (2005), 'Cuneiform', *Microsoft Encarta Online Encyclopedia*, http://encarta.msn.com/encyclopedia_761563112/Cuneiform.html.

Hackin, J. and Carl, J. (1933) *Nouvelles recherches archéologiques à Bamiyan*, Mémoirs de la Délégation Archéologique française en Afghanistan III, Paris.

Hackin, J. and Hackin, J.-R. (1939) *Recherches archéologiques à Begram*, 2 vols, Mémoirs de la Délégation Archéologique française en Afghanistan IX, Paris.

Hackin, J., Carl, J. and Hamelin, P. (1954) *Nouvelles recherches archéologiques à Begram, ancienne Kâpicî (1939–1940)*, 2 vols, Mémoirs de la Délégation Archéologique française en Afghanistan XI, Paris.

Hackin, J., Carl, J. and Meunié, J. (1959) *Diverses recherches archéologiques en Afghanistan (1933–1940)*, Mémoires de la Délégation Archéologique française en Afghanistan VIII, Paris.

Haditti, A.-M. M. A. R. al- (1995) 'Umm Kheshm – summary report', *Mesopotamia* XXX, pp. 217–39.

Haerinck, E. and Overlaet, B. (1998) *Chamahzi Mumah. An Iron Age III Graveyard*, Luristan Excavation Documents vol. II, Acta Iranica 3ème sér., Textes et Mémoires XIX, Louvain.

Hamzah al-Isfahani, *Tārikh-i payāmbarān va shāhān*, tr. J. Shu'ar, Tehran 1367/1988.

Hansen, T. (1964) *Arabia Felix. The Danish Expedition of 1761–1767*, London.

Han Shu [History of the (former) Han] compiled by Pan Ku and Pan Chao (Zürcher 1968, pp. 359, 363–6).

Hardaker, T. R. (1992) 'Punch-marked coinage of Kośala – towards a classification', in D. W. MacDowall, S. Sharma and S. Garg (eds), *Indian Numismatics, History, Art, and Culture. Essays in Honour of Dr. P. L. Gupta*, vol. I, Delhi, pp. 3–27.

Hargreaves, H. (1914) 'Excavations at Takht-i-Bāhī', *Archaeological Survey of India Annual Report 1910–11*, Calcutta, pp. 33–9.

Hargreaves, H. (1921) 'Excavations at Jamālgarhī', *Archaeological Survey of India Frontier Circle Annual Report 1920–21*, Peshawar, pp. 2–7, Appendix V, pp. 20–8.

Harmatta, J. (1996) *History of Civilizations of Central Asia*, vol. II, *The Development of Sedentary and Nomadic Civilizations: 700 B.C. to A.D. 250*, Paris (2nd edn).

Hawkins, E. (1835) Letter to Reverend J. Forshall, dated 20 August, British Museum Original Papers 21–8–1835: Honigberger collection.

Hawkins, E. (1835a) Letter to Reverend J. Forshall, dated 26 August, British Museum Original Papers 21–8–1835: Honigberger collection.

Hawkins, E. (1835b) Letter to Reverend J. Forshall, dated 31 August, British Museum Original Papers 21–8–1835: Honigberger collection.

Hay, W. (1840) 'Account of coins found at Bameean' (dated 7 April), *JASB* IX, pp. 68–9.

Head, B. V. (1894) Reports, Department of Coins and Medals, British Museum, 1 May, pp. 91–6.

Hedin, S. A. *et al.* (1943–5) *History of the Expedition in Asia, 1927–1935*, 4 parts, Reports from the Scientific Expedition to the North-Western Provinces of China under the Leadership of Dr Sven Hedin. Sino-Swedish Expedition Publications 23–6, Stockholm.

Helms, S. (1997), *Excavations at Old Kandahar in Afghanistan 1976–1978. Stratigraphy, Pottery and Other Finds*, Society for South Asian Studies Monograph no. 2, BAR International Series 686, Oxford.

Henning, W. B. (1948) 'The date of the Sogdian ancient letters', *Bulletin of the School of Oriental and African Studies* 12, pp. 601–15.

Herrmann, G. (1977) *Naqsh-i Rustam 5. Sasanian Reliefs attributed to Hormizd II and Narseh*, Iranische Denkmäler 8/2, Iranische Felsreliefs D, Berlin.

Herrmann, G., Kurbansakhatov, K. *et al.* (1995) 'The international Merv project. Preliminary report on the third season (1994)', *Iran* XXXIII, pp. 31–60.

Herodotus, *Histories*, tr. A. D. Godley, vols I–II, ed. G. P. Goold, Loeb Classical Library, 4 vols, London–Cambridge Mass. 1981 (7th repr.).

Hill, G. F. (1922) *Catalogue of the Greek Coins of Arabia, Mesopotamia and Persia in the British Museum*, London.

Hinds, M. (1984) 'The first Arab conquests in Fars', *Iran* XXII, pp. 39–53.

Hinz, W. (1973) *Neue Wege im Altpersischen*, Göttinger Orientforschungen III.1, Wiesbaden.

Hinz, W. (1975) 'Grotefends genialer Entzifferungsversuch', in R. Borger *et al.*, *Die Welt des Alten Orients. Keilschrift – Grabungen – Gelehrte. Handbuch und Katalog zur Ausstellung zum 200.Geburtstag Georg Friedrich Grotefends*, Göttingen, pp. 15–18.

Hodgson, B. H. (1834) 'Ancient inscriptions in the characters of the Allahabad column', *JASB* III, pp. 481–3.

Hoernle, A. F. R. (1879) 'Gold coins from Jalalabad', April Proceedings of the Asiatic Society of Bengal, *JASB* XLVIII, pp. 123–38.

Hoernle, A. F. R. (1879a) 'Remarks on General Cunningham's notes', August Proceedings of the Asiatic Society of Bengal, *JASB* XLVIII, pp. 210–12.

Hoernle, A. F. R. (1893) 'Another collection of ancient manuscripts from Central Asia', *JASB* LXII, pp. 1–40.

Hoernle, A. F. R. (1897) 'Three further collections of ancient manuscripts from Central Asia', *JASB* LXVI.1, pp. 213–59.

Holt, F. (1995) *Alexander the Great and Bactria*, Leiden–New York–Cologne.

Holt, F. (1999) *Thundering Zeus. The Making of Hellenistic Bactria*, Berkeley–Los Angeles–London.

Homer, *The Iliad*, tr. A. T. Murray, vol. II, ed. E. H. Warmington, Loeb Classical Library 2 vols, London–Cambridge Mass. 1967 (8th repr.).

Honigberger, J. M. (1834) 'Journal of a route from Dêra Ghazi Khan, through the Veziri country to Kabul', *JASB* III, pp. 175–8.

Honigberger, J. M. (1835) Letter to Reverend J. Forshall, dated 21 August, British Museum Original Papers 21–8–1835: Honigberger collection.

Honigberger, J. M. (1852) *Thirty-five Years in the East. Adventures, Discoveries, Experiments, and Historical Sketches, relating to the Punjab and Cashmere*, 2 vols, London.

Hopkirk, P. (1980) *Foreign Devils on the Silk Road*, London (6th repr. Oxford 1991).

Hopkirk, P. (1990) *The Great Game. On Secret Service in High Asia*, Oxford.

Houghton, A. and Lorber, C. (2002) *Seleucid Coins. A Comprehensive Catalogue*, part I, *Seleucus I through Antiochus III*, 2 vols, New York–London.

Hou Han Shu [History of the Later Han], compiled by Fan Yeh (Zürcher 1968, pp. 367–71).

Huff, D. (1998) ' "Fire altars" and *astodans*', in V. S. Curtis, R. Hillenbrand and J. M. Rogers (eds), *The Art and Archaeology of Ancient Persia*, London–New York, pp. 74–3, pls. VIII–IX.

Humann, K. and Puchstein O. (1890) *Reise in Kleinasien und Nord-Syrien*, Berlin.

Humbach, H. (1966) *Baktrische Sprachdenkmäler*, vol. 1, Wiesbaden.

Humbach, H. (1975) 'Vayu, Śiva und der Spiritus Vivens im Ostiranischen Syncretismus', *Acta Iranica. Monumentum H. S. Nyberg I*, Leiden, pp. 397–408.

Humbach, H. (1994) 'The Tochi inscriptions', *Studia Iranica* 19, pp. 137–56.

References

Huyse, P. (1999) *Die dreisprachige Inschrift Šābuhrs I. an der Ka'ba-i Zardušt (ŠKZ)*, 2 vols, Corpus Inscriptionum Iranicarum III/1, London.

Ibn al-Faqih (1885) *Kitāb al-buldān*, ed. M. J. de Goeje, *Compendium libri Kitâb al-boldan*, Leiden.

Ibn al-Nadim, *Kitāb al-Fihrist*, tr. B. Dodge, *The Fihrist of al-Nadīm*, 2 vols, London–New York 1970.

Ingholt, H. and Lyons, I. (1957) *Gandhāra Art in Pakistan*, New York.

IOR/B/233 India Office Records, British Library.

al-Isfahani, Hamzah ibn al-Hasan, *Tarikh sini muluk al-ardh wa'l-anbiya'*, Beirut 1961.

Isidore of Charax, *Parthian Stations. An Account of the Overland Trade Route between the Levant and India in the First Century* BC, tr. W. H. Schoff, Chicago 1989.

Issawi, C. ed. (1971) *The Economic History of Iran 1800–1914*, Chicago–London.

Jacoby, F. (1958) 'Karmania and Khorezmia', *Die Fragmente der Grieschischen Historiker*, Leiden.

Jacquet, E. (1836) 'Notice de la collection de médailles bactriennes et indo-scythiques rapportées par M. le général Allard', *Journal Asiatique* 3ème sér. II, pp. 122–90.

Jacquet, E. (1836a) 'Notice sur les découvertes archéologiques faites par Mr. Honigberger dans l'Afghanistan', *Journal Asiatique* 3ème sér. II, pp. 234–77.

Jacquet, E. (1837) 'Notice sur les découvertes archéologiques faites par Mr. Honigberger dans l'Afghanistan', *Journal Asiatique* 3ème sér. IV, pp. 401–40.

Jacquet, E. (1838) 'Notice sur les découvertes archéologiques faites par Mr. Honigberger dans l'Afghanistan', *Journal Asiatique* 3ème sér. V, pp. 163–97.

Jacquet, E. (1839) 'Notice sur les découvertes archéologiques faites par Mr. Honigberger dans l'Afghanistan', *Journal Asiatique* 3ème sér. VII, pp. 385–404.

Jacquet, E. (1840) 'Mémoire sur la série des médailles indiennes connues sous le denomination d'indo-scythique', *Journal Asiatique* 3ème sér. VIII, pp. 54–66, 202–36.

James, M. R. tr. (1985) *The Acts of Thomas*, in *The Apocryphal New Testament: being the Apocryphal Gospels, Acts, Epistles, and Apocalypses with other Narratives and Fragments*, Oxford 1924 (repr.).

Jayaswal, K. (1928) 'The historical data of the *Gārgī Saṃhitā* and the Brahmin empire', *Journal of the Bihar and Orissa Research Society* 14, pp. 397–421.

Jenkins, I. (1992) *Archaeologists and Aesthetes in the Sculpture Galleries of the British Museum 1800–1939*, London.

Jenkins, K. (1957) 'Azes and Taxila', *Congrés internationale de numismatique*, Paris, vol. II, pp. 123–30.

Jha, A. and Rajgor, D. (1994), *Studies in the Coinage of the Western Ksatrapas*, Nasik.

Johnson, J. (1818) *A Journey from India to England, through Persia, Georgia, Russia, Poland, and Prussia, in the Year 1817*, London.

Jomard, E. F. ed. (1809–28) *Description de l'Egypte: ou, recueil des observations et des recherches qui ont été faites en Egypte pendant l'expédition de l'armée française, publié par les ordres de Sa Majesté l'empereur Napoléon le Grand*, 23 vols, Paris.

Jones, J. M. (1986) *A Dictionary of Ancient Greek Coins*, London.

Joshua the Stylite, *Chronicle*, tr. F. R. Trombley and J. W. Watt, *The Chronicle of Pseudo-Joshua the Stylite*, Translated Texts for Historians 32, Liverpool 2000.

Julien, S. (1857) *Mémoires sur les contrées occidentales, traduits du sanskrit en chinois, en l'an 648, par Hiouen thsang, et du chinois en français . . .*, Paris.

Justin [Summary of Pompeius Trogus' *History*], in *Justin, Cornelius Nepos and Eutropius*, tr. J. S. Watson, London 1853.

Justin [Justinus, Marcus Junianus], *Epitome of the Philippic History of Pompeius Trogus*, tr. J. C. Yardley, intro. R. Develin, Philological Association Classical Resources 3, Atlanta 1994.

Kalhana, *Rājataraṅgiṇī*, tr. M. A. Stein, London 1900.

Kalidasa, *Mālavikāgnimitra*, ed./tr. R. D. Karmarkar, Poona 1950 (4th rev. edn).

Kanus-Credé, H. ed. (1974) 'Aus dem Nachlass von F. C. Andreas', *Iranistische Mitteilungen* 8, pp. 42–75.

Kapadia, E. R. (1938) 'The diplomatic career of Sir Claude Martine Wade', M.A. thesis, London University, School of Oriental and African Studies, Av. 109.

Karimi, B. (1950) *Rahha-yi bastani va paytakhtha-yi qadami-yi gharb-i*, Tehran.

Karimi, B. (1950a) *Rapport résumé de quinze mois de voyage de Dr. Brahmen Karimi: les anciennes routes de l'Iran*, [Tehran].

Keay, J. (1977) *When Men and Mountains Meet*, London.

Keay, J. (1981) *India Discovered. The Recovery of a Lost Civilization*, London.

Keay, J. (2000) *India: a History*, London.

Kejariwal, O. P. (1988) *The Asiatic Society and the Discovery of India's Past*, Delhi.

Kennedy, D. (2000) 'Relocating the past: missing inscriptions from Qasr Al-Hallabat and the air photographs of Sir Aurel Stein for Transjordan', *The Palestine Exploration Quarterly*, January–June.

Kennedy, D. and Riley, D. (1990) *Rome's Desert Frontier from the Air*, London.

Kent, R. G. (1953) *Old Persian. Grammar, Texts, Lexicon*, New Haven (2nd rev. edn).

Keppel, G. (1827) *Personal Narrative of a Journey from India to England . . . in the Year 1824*, London.

Ker Porter, R. (1821/2) *Travels in Georgia, Persia, Armenia, Ancient Babylonia . . . 1817–1820*, 2 vols, London (I: 1821; II: 1822).

Kielhorn, F. (1962–5) *The Vyakarhāna-Mahābhāsya of Patañjali*, rev. K. V. Abhyankar, 3 vols, Poona (3rd edn).

King, L. W. and Thompson, R. C. (1907) *The Sculptures and Inscription of Darius the Great on the Rock of Behistûn in Persia*, London.

Kinneir, J. M. (1813) *A Geographical Memoir of the Persian Empire*, London.

Kirby, P. (2001) *Online Text for Tertullian*, http://www.earlychristianwritings.com/tertullian.html.

Klimburg-Salter, D. (1989) *The Kingdom of Bāmiyān. Buddhist Art of the Hindu Kush*, Naples–Rome.

Konow, S. (1929) *Kharoshṭhī Inscriptions with the Exception of those of Aśoka*, Corpus Inscriptionum Indicarum II/1, Calcutta.

Kovalenko, S. (1995/6) 'The coinage of Diodotus I and Diodotus II, Greek kings of Bactria', *Silk Road Art and Archaeology* IV, pp. 17–74.

Kraay, C. M. (1976) *Archaic and Classical Greek Coins*, London.

Kruglikova, I. (2004) 'Dilberdjin [Dal'verzin; Dil'berdzn]', *The Grove Dictionary of Art Online*, http://www.groveart.com.

Kuwayama, S. (1997) *The Main Stūpa of Shāh-jī-kī-Dherī*, Kyoto.

Kuwayama, S. (1999) 'Historical notes on Kāpiśī and Kābul in the sixth–eighth centuries', *Zinbun: Annals of the Institute for Research in Humanities, Kyoto University* 34, pp. 25–77.

Kuwayama, S. (2002) 'The Hephthalites in Tokharistan and Gandhara', *Across the Hindukush of the First Millennium. A Collection of the Papers*, Kyoto (pp. 107–39: repr. 'The Hephthalites in Tokharistan and northwest India', *Zinbun: Annals of the Institute for Research in Humanities, Kyoto University* 24, 1991, pp. 89–134; pp. 208–21: repr. 'Not Hephthalite but Kapiśan Khingal: identity of the Napki coins', in A. K. Jha and S. Garg, *Ex Moneta: Essays in Numismatics, History and Archaeology in Honour of Dr David W. MacDowall*, New Delhi 1998, pp. 331–49; pp. 249–59: repr. 'The inscription of Ganeśa from Gardez and a chronology of the Turki Shahis', *Journal Asiatique* 279/3–4, 1992, pp. 267–87).

La Fontaine, J. de (1989) *Le songe d'un habitant du Mogol et autres fables illustrées par Imam Bakhsh Lahori*, Paris (repr. 1994).

Lafont, J.-M. (1982) 'Military activities of French officers of Maharaja Ranjit Singh', *Journal of Sikh Studies* IX.1, pp. 29–73.

Lafont, J.-M. (1983) 'Private business and cultural activities of the French officers of Maharaja Ranjit Singh', *Journal of Sikh Studies* X.1, pp. 74–104.

Lafont, J.-M. (1987) 'La présence française dans le royaume sikh du Penjab, 1822–1849', thèse d'Etat 1 June, Université de Paris III–Sorbonne Nouvelle.

Lafont, J.-M. (1992) *La présence française dans le royaume sikh du Penjab, 1822–1849*, Paris.

Lafont, J.-M. (1994) 'Les indo-grecs. Recherches archéologiques françaises dans le royaume sikh du Penjab, 1822–1843', *Τόποι* 4.1, pp. 9–68.

Lafont, J.-M. ed. (1997) *Reminiscences. The French in India*, Delhi.

Lafont, J.-M. (2000) *Indika. Essays in Indo-French Relations, 1630–1976*, New Delhi.

Lafont, J.-M. (2000a) 'Vive le Punjab! The French role in the building of Maharaja Ranjit Singh's army', *Nishaan* IV, Delhi, pp. 4–23.

Lafont, J.-M. (2001) *Chitra. Cities and Monuments of Eighteenth Century India from French Archives*, Delhi.

Lafont, J.-M. (2002) *Fauj-i-khas. Maharaja Ranjit Singh and his French Officers*, Amritsar.

Lafont, J.-M. (2002a) 'French military intervention in India compared to the French intervention in North America, 1776–1785', in A. Ray (ed.), *Tipu Sultan and His Age. A Collection of Seminar Papers* (Papers from Asiatic Society International Seminar 2–3 October 1999), Calcutta.

Lafont, J.-M. (2002b) *Maharaja Ranjit Singh Lord of the Five Rivers*, Delhi.

Lafont, J.-M. and Schmitz, B. (2002) 'The painter Imam Bakhsh of Lahore', in B. Schmitz (ed.), *After the Great Mughals. Paintings in Delhi and the Regional Courts in the 18th and 19th Centuries*, Bombay, pp. 74–99.

Lafont, J.-M. and R. tr./eds (forthcoming) *Piveron de Morlat's 'Mémoire sur l'Inde'*.

Lamotte, É. (1988) *History of Indian Buddhism from the Origins to the Śaka Era*, tr. S. Webb-Boin, Louvain-la-Neuve.

Larsen, M. T. (1994) *The Conquest of Assyria. Excavations in an Antique Land 1840–1860*, London–New York.

Lassen, C. (1838) *Einleitung zur Geschichte des Griechischen und Indoskythischen Könige in Bactrien, Kabul und Indien, durch Entzifferung der Alt-kabulischen Legenden auf ihren Münzen*, Bonn (English tr.: Lassen 1840).

Lassen, C. (1840) *Greek and Indo-Scythian Kings and their Coins*, tr. T. H. E. Röer, with commentary by H. Torrens, Calcutta (repr. C. Lassen, 'Points in the history of the Greek and Indo-Scythian kings in Bactria, Cabul and India, as illustrated by deciphering the ancient legends on their coins', *JASB* IX, 1840, pp. 251–76, 339–78, 449–88, 627–76, 733–65).

Lassen, C. (1844) Letter to H. T. Prinsep, dated Bonn 11 March, Prinsep MSS, vol. III, Ashmolean Museum, Oxford, Hebenden Coin Room Archives, Arch. Ash. fol. 18.

Lassen, C. (1874) *Geschichte von Buddha bis zu dem Ende der älteren Gupta-Dynastie. Nebst Umriß der Kulturgeschichte dieses Zeitraums* (vol. II of *Indische Althertumskunde*, 4 vols, Leipzig 1847–61) Leipzig (2nd edn.).

Lattimore, O. and E. (1973) *Silks, Spices and Empires – Asia as Seen through the Eyes of its Discoverers*, London.

Layard, A. H. (1887) *Early Adventures in Persia, Susiana, and Babylonia*, 2 vols, London.

Lazar of P'arp, *Patmut'iun Hayoc*, ed. Ter-Mkrtzean, Tiflis 1904.

Lee, J. (1837) 'Presidential Address, 15 June 1837', *Proceedings of the Numismatic Society of London 1836–37*, London, pp. 50–1, 70–1.

Lee, J. (1838) 'Presidential Address, 19 July 1838', *Proceedings of the Numismatic Society of London 1837–38*, London, pp. 18–23, 41–2.

Lee, J. (1840) 'Presidential Address, 18 July 1839', *Proceedings of the Numismatic Society of London 1838–39*, London, pp. 10–15.

Lee, J. and Sims-Williams, N. (2003) 'The antiquities and inscription of Tang-i Safedak', *Silk Road Art and Archaeology* IX, pp. 159–84.

Lee, S. ed. (1893) *Dictionary of National Biography*, vol. XXXV, London.

Lee, S. ed. (1898) *Dictionary of National Biography*, vol. LIV, London.

Lee, S. ed. (1901) *Dictionary of National Biography*, supplement vol. I, London.

Leith, M. J. W. (1997) *Wadi Daliyeh I. The Wadi Daliyeh Seal Impressions*, Discoveries in the Judaean Desert XXIV, Oxford.

Lemaire, A. (1989) 'Remarques à propos du monnayage cilician d'epoque perse et de ses legendes araméenes', *Revue des Études anciennes* 91, pp. 141–56.

Lenski, N. (1997) 'Valens (364–378 AD)', *De Imperatoribus Romanis. An Online Encyclopaedia of Roman Emperors*, http://www.roman-emperors.org/valens.htm.

Lentz, W. (1987) 'Andreas', in E. Yarshater (ed.), *Encyclopaedia Iranica* II, London–New York, p. 27.

Leriche, P. (1986) *Fouilles d'Aï Khanoum. V. Les remparts d'Aï Khanoum et monuments associés*, Mémoires de la Délégation Archéologique française en Afghanistan XXIX, Paris.

Le Rider, G. (2001) *La naissance de la monnaie*, Paris.

Lerner, J. (1971) 'The Achaemenid relief of Ahura Mazda in the Fogg Art Museum', *Bulletin of the Asia Institute* 2, Shiraz, pp. 19–35.

Lerner, J. (1973) 'A painted relief from Persepolis', *Archaeology* 26, pp. 116–22, 305.

Leschhorn, W. (1993) *Antike Ären. Zeitrechnung, Politik und Geschichte im Schwarzmeerraum und im Kleinasien Nördlich des Tauros*, Stuttgart.

Leslie, D. D. and Gardiner, K. H. J. (1996) *The Roman Empire in Chinese Sources*, Rome.

Le Strange, G. (1905) *The Lands of the Eastern Caliphate. Mesopotamia, Persia, and Central Asia from the Moslem Conquest to the Time of Timur*, Cambridge.

Lieu, S. (1997) 'Manichaean art and texts from the Silk Road', in K. Tanabe, J. Cribb and H. Wang (eds), *Studies in Silk Road Coins and Culture. Silk Road Art and Archaeology Special Volume*, pp. 261–312.

Litvinsky, B. A. and Pichikyan, I. R. (1981) 'Découvertes dans un sanctuaire du dieu Oxus de la Bactriane septentrionale', *Revue Archéologique* II, pp. 195–216.

Loewenthal, I. (1861) 'Account of some of the sculptures in the Peshawar Museum', Proceedings of the Asiatic Society, *JASB* XXX, pp. 411–13.

Loewenthal, I. (1863) 'On the antiquities of the Peshawur [*sic*] District', *JASB* XXXII, pp. 1–18.

Loftus, W. K. (1856/7) 'On the excavations undertaken at the ruins of Susa in 1851–2', *Transactions of the Royal Society of Literature* V, pp. 422–53.

Loftus, W. K. (1857) *Travels and Researches in Chaldaea and Susiana*, London.

Longpérier, A. de (1839) 'Rapport de M. Adr. De Longpérier sur la collection numismatique du Général Court', *Revue Numismatique*, pp. 81–8.

Longpérier, A. de (MSS) 'Rapport sur la collection numismatique du Général Court', Bibliothèque Nationale archives.

Lüders, H. (1940) 'Zu und aus den Kharoṣṭhī-Urkunden', *Acta Orientalia* 18, pp. 15–49.

Lüders, H. (1961) *Mathurā Inscriptions*, ed. K. L. Janert, Göttingen.

Ludlow, J. M. (1847) Letter to H. B. Ker, dated 20 June, British Museum Original Papers, Central Archives.

Luft, J. P. (2001) 'Qajar rock-reliefs', *Iranian Studies* 34.1–4, ed. L. Diba, pp. 31–49.

[MacAlister, F.] (1910) *Memoir of the Right Hon. Sir John McNeill, G. C. B. and of his Second Wife Elizabeth Wilson*, London.

McCrindle, J. W. tr./ed. (1897) *The Christian Topography of Cosmas, an Egyptian Monk*, London.

McCrindle, J. W. (1901) *Ancient India as described in Classical Literature*, London.

MacKenzie, D. N. (1989) 'Kerdir's inscription: synoptic text in transliteration, transcription and commentary', in G. Herrmann, *The Sasanian Rock Reliefs at Naqsh-i Rustam. Naqsh-i Rustam 6*, Iranische Denkmäler, Lieferung 13, Reihe II, Iranische Felsreliefs I, Berlin, pp. 35–72.

Madhloom, T. A. (1970) *The Chronology of Neo-Assyrian Art*, London.

Maheshwari, K. K. (1977) 'Some interesting coins from Andhra Pradesh', *Numismatic Digest* I.1, pp. 1–13.

Mahboubian, H. (1997) *Art of Ancient Iran. Copper and Bronze*, London.

Mainwaring, F. G. L., Burgess, J., Colley March, H. and Okakura, K. (1903) 'The Gandhara sculptures. A symposium', *Proceedings, Dorset Natural History and Antiquarian Field Club* XXIV, pp. 93–102.

Maisey, F. C. (1892) *Sanchi and its Remains*, London.

Majumdar, N. G. (1937–8) 'The Bajaur casket of the reign of Menander', *Epigraphia Indica* XXIV, pp. 1–8.

Majumdar, R. C. ed. (1980) *The History and Culture of the Indian People*, vol. II, *The Age of Imperial Unity*, Bombay 1951, 5th repr.

Majumdar, R. C. ed. (1988) *The History and Culture of the Indian People*, vol. I, *The Vedic Age*, Bombay 1951 (5th repr.).

Majumdar, R. C. ed. (1988a) *The History and Culture of the Indian People*, vol. III, *The Classical Age*, Bombay 1951 (4th repr.).

Malcolm, Sir John (1815) *The History of Persia*, 2 vols, London.

Malleson, G. B. (1878) *Final French Struggles in India and in the Indian Sea*, London (repr. Delhi 1977).

Manikant Shah (2004) 'Indian astronomy through ages', http://www.infinityfoundation.com.

Mankad, D. R. (1947) 'A critically edited text of the *Yugapurāna*', *Journal of the Uttar Pradesh Historical Society*, pp. 32–64.

Marquart, J. (1901) *Ērānšahr nach der Geographie des Ps. Moses Xorenac'i*, Berlin.

Marsden, W. (1823/5) *Numismata Orientalia Illustrata. The Oriental Coins, Ancient and Modern, of his Collection, Described and Historically Illustrated*, 2 vols, London (I: 1823; II: 1825).

Marshall, J. H. (1904) 'Introduction', *Archaeological Survey of India Annual Report 1902–03*, Calcutta, pp. 1–13.

Marshall, J. (1951) *Taxila*, 3 vols, Cambridge.

Martin, M. (1882) 'Exploration of Buddhist ruins at Charsada, Peshawar Valley', *Punjab Public Works Department Proceedings*, Civil Works, Miscellaneous Public Improvements, March, Part A, p. 19, no. 1, Appendix A.

Martin, M. F. C. (1937) 'Coins of Kidāra and the Little Kushāns', *Journal of the Royal Asiatic Society of Bengal Numismatic Supplement* XLVII, pp. 23–50.

Mason, K. (1945) *Persia*, Naval Intelligence Division Geographical Handbook Series B.R. 525 (September), London.

Masson, C. (1834) 'Memoir on the ancient coins found at Beghram, in the Kohistán of Kábul', *JASB* III, pp. 153–75.

Masson, C. (1836) 'Second memoir on the ancient coins found at Beghrám, in the Kohistán of Kábul', *JASB* V, pp. 1–28.

Masson, C. (1836a) 'Third memoir on the ancient coins discovered at a site called Beghrám in the Kohistán of Kábul', *JASB* V, pp. 537–48.

Masson, C. (1837) Letter to Col. H. Pottinger, dated 7 November, *Bombay Political Proceedings* 23 October – 13 November 1839, no. 4870: Bombay Castle 13 November, Political Consultations no. 31. British Library India Office Collections P/389/18.

Masson, C. (1837a) 'Suggestions on the sites of Sangala and the altars of Alexander, being an extract from notes of a journey from Lahore to Karychee, made in 1830', *JASB* VI, pp. 57–61.

Masson, C. (1842) *Narrative of Various Journeys in Balochistan, Afghanistan and the Panjab*, 3 vols, London (repr. Karachi 1974).

References

Masson, C. (1843) *Narrative of Various Journeys in Balochistan, Afghanistan and the Panjab*, vol. IV: *Narrative of a Journey to Kalat. Including an Account of the Insurrection at that Place in 1840, and a Memoir on Eastern Balochistan*, London.

Masson, C. (1846) 'Narrative of an excursion from Peshawar to Shah-Baz Garhi', *JRAS* VIII, pp. 292–302.

Masson, C. (1848) *Legends of the Afghan Countries. In Verse, with Various Pieces, Original and Translated*, London.

Masson, C. (MSS Eur.) British Library India Office Collections, Masson Manuscripts: listed in E. H. Kaye and E. H. Johnston, *Catalogue of Manuscripts in European Languages*, vol. II, part II, Minor collections and miscellaneous manuscripts, section II; M. Archer, *British Drawings in the India Office Library*, London 1969, pp. 248–53:
    (MSS Eur. E 161) Correspondence I, copies of letters to Masson; Correspondence VII, copies of letters from Masson.
    (MSS Eur. E 162) Letters to the Press.
    (MSS Eur. E 164) Journals and Narratives III.
    (MSS Eur. F 63) Sketches and Drawings I, ff. 1–73.
    (MSS Eur. G 42) 'Caves of Bamian', ff. 30–42.

Masson, C. (Uncat. MSS) Uncatalogued Manuscripts, British Library India Office Collections. Two separate bundles boxed together in 1961 as 'Masson Papers', the one 'found in a box with other miscellaneous papers in 1958'; the other 'discovered in the Newspaper Room in 1958 by Mrs M. C. Poulter (archivist)'. Bundle 1:
    (Uncat. MSS 1) 'Coins. Bactrian . . . Tope Hidda . . . Jannu Tope' (List of coins acquired 1833–4, sketches of relic deposits).
    (Uncat. MSS 2) 'Enumeration of coins collected from Beghram during the years 1833, 1834 & 1835', dated Kabul 31 December 1835.
    (Uncat. MSS 3) 'Silver coins from Kabul' (List of acquisitions from Kabul and Begram 1834–8).
    (Uncat. MSS 4) 'List of coins. A [and] B' (Two inventories of coins in Masson's possession post publication of Wilson 1841).

Mathews, E. G. (2003) Review of I. Ramelli, *Il Chronicon di Arbela: Presentazione, traduzione e note essenziali*, Madrid 2002, *Bryn Mawr Classical Review* 2003.11.01, http://ccat.sas.upenn.edu/bmcr/2003/2003–11-01.html.

Matson, F. R. (1953) 'A study of wall plaster, flooring, and bitumen', in E. F. Schmidt *et al.*, *Persepolis I: Structures, Reliefs, Inscriptions*, Chicago, pp. 285–8.

Maxwell, C. (1882) *Report on Buddhist Explorations in the Peshawar District by the 10th Company Sappers and Miners, April 1882*, Lahore.

Mehta, N. C. (1928) 'Jaina record on Toramana', *Journal of the Bihar and Orissa Research Society* XIV, pp. 28–38.

Melikian-Chirvani, A. S. (1974) 'Le bouddhisme dans l'Iran musulman', *Le Monde Iranien et l'Islam* II, pp. 1–72.

Melzer, G. (forthcoming) 'A copper scroll inscription from the time of the Alchon Huns' (in collaboration with L. Sander), in J. Braarvig, P. Harrison, J.-U. Hartmann, K. Matsuda, L. Sander (eds), *Manuscripts in the Schøyen Collection, Buddhist Manuscripts*, vol. 3, Oslo.

Merhav, R. (1976) 'Ceremonial and everyday use of the bucket in Mesopotamia and neighbouring lands', *The Israel Museum News* 11, pp. 67–82.

Meshorer, Y. and Qedar, S. (1999) *Samarian Coinage*, Jerusalem.

Meyer, K. and Brysac, S. (2001) *Tournament of Shadows. The Great Game and the Race for Empire in Asia*, London.

Mignan, R. (1829) *Travels in Chaldaea, including a Journey from Bussorah to Bagdad, Hillah and Babylon, Performed on Foot in 1827. With Observations on the Sites and Remains of Babel, Seleucia, and Ctesiphon*, London.

Mildenberg, L. (1993) 'Über das Münzwesen im Reich der Achämeniden', *Archäologische Mitteilungen aus Iran* 26, pp. 55–79.

Miller, M. C. (1993) 'Adoption and adaptation of Achaemenid metalware forms in Attic Black-gloss Ware of the fifth century', *Archäologische Mitteilungen aus Iran* 26, pp. 109–46.

Mionnet, T. E. (1813) *Descriptions de médailles antiques, grecques et romaines avec leur degré de rareté et leaur estimation*, vol. VI, Paris.

Mionnet, T. E. (1837) *Descriptions de médailles antiques, grecques et romaines avec leur degré de rareté et leur estimation*, supplement, vol. VIII, Paris.

Mir Fattah, Seyyed Ali Asghar (1374/1996) 'Gurastan-i Shuqab 'arzeh dashtan dar havay-i azad va dafn beh shiveh-yi ustukhandan [The necropolis of Shuqab: practices of exposure with ossuaries]', *Athar* 25, pp. 41–61.

Mirsky, J. (1977) *Sir Aurel Stein – Archaeological Explorer*, Chicago.

Mitchell, T. C. (2000) 'The Persepolis sculptures in the British Museum', *Iran* XXXVIII, pp. 49–56.

Mitchiner, M. (1975) 'Some late Kushano-Sassanian and early Hephthalite silver coins', *East and West* n. s. 25.1–2, pp. 157–65.

Mitchiner, M. (1976) *Indo-Greek and Indo-Scythian Coins*, 9 vols, London.

Mitchiner, M. (1978) *Oriental Coins and their Values. The Ancient and Classical World, 600 BC–AD 650*, London.

Mizuno, S. ed. (1967) *Hazar-sum and Fil-khana. Cave-sites in Afghanistan Surveyed in 1962*, Kyoto.

Mizuno, S. ed. (1970) *Basawal and Jelalabad–Kabul. Buddhist Cave-temples and Topes in South-east Afghanistan Surveyed Mainly in 1965*, Kyoto.

[Moberly, F. J.] (1987) *Operations in Persia 1914–1919*, London (facsimile edn, intro. by G. M. Bayliss).

Mochiri, M. I. (1996) 'Petite liste de quelques ateliers sassanides inédits', *Iran* XXXIV, pp. 61–78.

Modi, J. J. (1889) *Astodan*, Bombay.

Mohan Lal (1846) *Travels in the Panjab, Afghanistan, and Turkistan, to Balk [sic] Bokhara, and Herat; and a Visit to Great Britain and Germany*, London (repr. New Delhi 1986).

Moorcroft, W. and Trebeck, G. (1841) *Travels in the Himalayan Provinces of Hindustan and the Panjab from 1819 to 1825*, vol. II, ed. H. H. Wilson, London (repr. Karachi 1979).

Moorey, P. R. S. (1971) *Catalogue of the Ancient Persian Bronzes in the Ashmolean Museum*, Oxford.

Moorey, P. R. S. (1978) *Kish Excavations 1923–1933*, Oxford.

Morier, J. (1818) *A Second Journey through Persia, Armenia, and Asia Minor, to Constantinople, between the Years 1810 and 1816*, London.

Morier, J. (1824) *The Adventures of Hajji Baba of Ispahan*, London.

Mørkholm, O. (1991) *Early Hellenistic Coinage from the Accession of Alexander to the Peace of Apamea*, Cambridge–New York *et al.*

Mosig-Walburg, K. (1990) 'Šāpūr I. "Faktum oder Irrtum"', *Schweizerische Numismatische Rundschau* 69, pp. 103–26.

Mostafavi, S. M. T. (1978) *The Land of Pars (The Historical Monuments and Archaeological Sites of the Province of Fars)*, Chippenham.

Mouton, F.-H. (1846) *Rapport sur les événements du Penjab*, Paris.

Müller, C. (1868) *Fragmenta Historicorum Graecorum*, vol. V, Paris.

Müller, K. O. (1835) *Göttingische Gelehrte Anzeigen* 177, 9 November, Calcutta, pp. 1761–8.

Müller, K. O. (1835a) *Göttingische Gelehrte Anzeigen* 178–9, 12 November, Calcutta, pp. 1769–83.

Müller, K. O. (1838) 'Über Indo-Griechische Münzen', *Göttingische Gelehrte Anzeigen* 21, 5 February, Calcutta–Paris, pp. 201–8.

Müller, K. O. (1838a) *Göttingische Gelehrte Anzeigen* 22–3, 8 February, Calcutta–Paris, pp. 209–24.

Müller, K. O. (1838b) *Göttingische Gelehrte Anzeigen* 24, 10 February, Calcutta–Paris, pp. 225–40.

Müller, K. O. (1838c) *Göttingische Gelehrte Anzeigen* 25, 12 February, Calcutta–Paris, pp. 241–8.

Müller, K. O. (1838d) 'Über Indo-Griechische Münzen', *Göttingische Gelehrte Anzeigen* 26–7, 15 February, Calcutta and Paris, pp. 249–52.

Müller, K. O. (1839) *Göttingische Gelehrte Anzeigen* 29, 18 February, Bonn–Berlin–Calcutta, pp. 281–8.

Müller, K. O. (1839a) *Göttingische Gelehrte Anzeigen* 30–1, 21 February, Bonn–Berlin–Calcutta, pp. 289–304.

Müller, K. O. (1839b) *Göttingische Gelehrte Anzeigen* 32, 23 February, Bonn–Berlin–Calcutta, pp. 305–20.

Müller, K. O. (1839c) *Göttingische Gelehrte Anzeigen* 33, 25 February, Bonn–Berlin–Calcutta, pp. 321–5.

Murdoch-Smith, R. (1876) *Persian Art*, London.

Murgotten, F. C. tr. (1924) Ahmad b. Yahya al-Baladhuri, *Kitāb Futūh al-Buldān (The Origins of the Islamic State)*, 2 vols, New York.

Muscarella, O. W. (1977) 'Unexcavated objects and ancient Near Eastern art', in L. D. Levine and T. Cuyler Young (eds), *Mountains and Lowlands: Essays in the Archaeology of Greater Mesopotamia*, Bibliotheca Mesopotamica VII, pp. 153–207, Malibu.

Muscarella, O. W. (1988) *Bronze and Iron. Ancient Near Eastern Artifacts in the Metropolitan Museum of Art*, New York.

Narain, A. K. (1957) *The Indo-Greeks*, Oxford.

Nasim Khan, M. (1998–9) 'A proto-Śāradā inscription from Hund, Pakistan', *Indo-Kōkko-Kenkyū* 20, pp. 77–83.

Nasim Khan, M. (2001) 'Re-interpretation of the copper plate inscription and the discovery of more epigraphic specimens from Kashmir Smast', *Ancient Pakistan* XIV, pp. 1–8.

Nasim Khan, M. (2001a) 'Exploration and excavation of the earliest Śivaite [sic] monastic establishment at Kashmir Smast (a preliminary report)', *Ancient Pakistan* XIV, pp. 218–309.

Nasim Khan, M. (2007) *Kashmir Smast. Cross Route of Civilization. A Study Based on Numismatic Evidence* (forthcoming).

Negro Ponzi, M. M. (1968/9) 'Sasanian Glassware from Tell Mahuz (north Mesopotamia)', *Mesopotamia* III/IV, pp. 293–384, figs 153–61, appendices A–G.

Nehru, L. (1989) *Origins of the Gandhâran Style. A Study of Contributory Influences*, Delhi–Bombay–Calcutta–Madras.

Newell, E. T. (1918) *The Seleucid Mint of Antioch*, American Journal of Numismatics LI, 1917, New York.

Niebuhr, C. (1774/8) *Reisebeschreibungen nach Arabien und anderen umliegenden Ländern*, 2 vols, Copenhagen.

Nietzsche, F. (1885–7) *Nachgelassene Fragmente*, vol. 12, *Nachlass, Sämtliche Werke, Kritische Studienausgabe*, 15 vols, ed. G. Colli and M. Montinari, Munich–New York 1980.

Nishikawa, K. ed. (1994) *Ranigat. A Buddhist Site in Gandhara, Pakistan, Surveyed 1983–1992*, 2 vols, Kyoto.

Nöldeke, T. (1973) *Geschichte der Perser und Arabere zur Zeit der Sasaniden aus der Arabischen Chronik des Tabari*, Leiden 1879, repr.

Norris, E. (1846) 'On the Kapur-di-Giri rock inscription', *JRAS* VIII, pp. 303–14.

NWFP (1884–91) North-West Frontier Province Central Record Office, Peshawar, Deputy Commissioner's Office, Peshawar, serial no. 123, bundle no. 3, file no. 41/XXIIIb, 'Preservation of buildings of architectural and historical interest':
> (1) Deputy Commissioner, Peshawar, letter no. 200, 21 April 1888, to Commissioner and Superintendent, Peshawar Division, forwarding 'Report regarding the Buddhist remains beyond Sawaldher and Jamalgarhi', by H. A. Deane.
> (2) Deputy Commissioner, Peshawar, letter no. 254, 14 May 1889, to the Commissioner and Superintendent, Peshawar Division.

NWFP (1888) North-West Frontier Province Central Record Office, Peshawar, Record of the Commissioner's Office, Peshawar, 1852–1901, serial no. 1845, bundle no. 59, file no. 331, head XLIII, sub-head A, 1871–88, 'Impressions of the inscribed rock at Shahbaz Garhi and rules as to the discovery of objects of archaeological interest'.

O'Donnell, H. ed. [1893] *Historical Records of the 14th Regiment, now the Prince of Wales's Own (West Yorkshire Regiment) from its Formation, in 1685, to 1892*, Devonport.

Osborne, W. G. (1840) *The Court and Camp of Runjeet Singh*, London (rev. edn Karachi 1973).

Ouseley, Sir William (1819–23) *Travels in Various Countries of the East; more particularly Persia*, 3 vols, London (I: 1819; II: 1821; III: 1823).

Palmer, M., Mak Hin Chung, Kwok Man Ho and Smith, A. eds/tr. (1986) *T'ung Shu: The Ancient Chinese Almanac*, London.

Patanjali, *Mahābhāṣya*, tr./ed. S. D. Joshi and J. A. F. Roodbergen, *Patañjali's Vyakarhāna-Mahābhāṣya*, Bhandarkar Oriental Research Institute no. 11, Poona 1990.

P'awstos Buzand, *Buzandaran Patmut'wnk'*, tr. N. G. Garsoïan, *The Epic Histories attributed to P'awstos Buzand*, Cambridge Mass. 1989.

Pearse, R. (2003) 'Cosmas Indicopleustes', *Christian Topography*, tr./ed. J. W. McCrindle, *The Christian Topography of Cosmas, an Egyptian Monk*, London 1897, online edn http://www.tertullian.org/fathers/cosmas.

Pellerin, J. (1767) *Troisième supplément aux six volumes de recueils des médailles des rois, de villes, &c., publiés en 1762, 1763 & 1765*, Paris.

Petech, L. (1968) 'Kashmiri and Tibetan materials on the date of Kaniṣka', in A. L. Basham (ed.), *Papers on the Date of Kaniṣka*, Leiden, pp. 244–6.

Pevsner, N. (1971) *The Buildings of England: Surrey*, Harmondsworth (2nd edn rev. B. Cherry).

Pevsner, N. (1972) *The Buildings of England: Dorset*, Harmondsworth.

Pézard, M. (1914) *Mission à Bender-Bouchir: documents archéologiques et épigraphiques*, Mémoires de la Délégation Archéologique en Perse XV, Paris.

Pfrommer, M. (1993) *Metalwork from the Hellenized East*, Malibu.

Philostratus, *Life of Apollonius of Tyana*, books I–VIII, tr./ed. C. P. Jones, Loeb Classical Library 2 vols, London–Cambridge Mass. 2005.

Pigou, R. (1841) 'On the topes of Darounta and the caves of Bahrabad', *JASB* X, pp. 381–6.

Plutarch, *Crassus*, tr. B. Perrin, *Plutarch's Lives* III, ed. E. H. Warmington, Loeb Classical Library 11 vols, London–Cambridge Mass. 1967 (5th repr.).

Plutarch, *Alexander*, tr. B. Perrin, *Plutarch's Lives* VII, ed. E. H. Warmington, Loeb Classical Library 11 vols, London–Cambridge Mass. 1971 (5th repr.).

Plutarch, *Artaxerxes*, tr. B. Perrin, *Plutarch's Lives* XI, ed. G. P. Goold, Loeb Classical Library 11 vols, London–Cambridge Mass. 1975 (5th repr.).

Plutarch, *Moralia*, tr. H. N. Fowler, part X: 771E–854D, *Plutarch's Moralia*, 16 vols tr. F. C. Babbitt *et al.*, Loeb Classical Library, London–Cambridge Mass. 1969 (2nd repr.).

Poidebard, A. (1934) *La trace de Rome dans le désert de Syrie*, 2 vols, Paris.

Polybius, *The Histories*, tr. W. R. Paton, vol. IV, Loeb Classical Library 6 vols, Cambridge Mass. 1976 (5th repr.).

Poole, R. S. (1888) Reports, Department of Coins and Medals, British Museum, 11 April, 1 October, 19 November, pp. 35–9, 123, 145.

Possehl, G. (1990) 'An archaeological adventurer in Afghanistan: Charles Masson', *South Asian Studies* 6, pp. 111–24.

Pottinger, H. (1833) Letter to Charles Norris, Chief Secretary to Government, Bombay, 27 November, no. 456 of 1833, British Library India Office Collections MSS Eur. E 161/I, f. 3(9).

Potts, D. T. (2005) 'Cyrus the Great and the Kingdom of Anshan', in V. S. Curtis and S. Stewart (eds), *The Birth of the Persian Empire*, London pp. 1–26.

Prasad, D. (1937–8) 'Observations on different types of silver punch-marked coins, their periods and locale', *Journal of the Royal Asiatic Society of Bengal Numismatic Supplement* XLVII, pp. 51–92.

Price, M. J. (1991) *The Coinage in the Name of Alexander the Great and Philip Arrhidaeus. A British Museum Catalogue*, 2 vols, Zurich–London.

Priestman, S. M. N. (2004) 'Leave no stone unturned: Stein and Williamson's surveys compared', in H. Wang (ed.), *Sir Aurel Stein, Proceedings of the British Museum Study Day, 23 March 2002*, pp. 29–35. London.

Prinsep, H. T. (1844) *Historical Results from Bactrian Coins, discovered in Afghanistan*, London.

Prinsep, H. T. (1858) 'Memoir of the author', in E. Thomas (ed.) *Essays on Indian Antiquities, Historic, Numismatic, and Palaeographic, of the late James Prinsep, F. R. S., Secretary to the Asiatic Society of Bengal*, vol. I, London, pp. i–xvi.

Prinsep, J. (1831–4) *Benares Illustrated, in a Series of Drawings*, 3 vols, London.

Prinsep, J. (1832) 'On the ancient Roman coins in the cabinet of the Asiatic Society', *JASB* I, pp. 392–408 (repr. Thomas 1858, vol. I, pp. 1–6).

Prinsep, J. (1833) 'On the Greek coins in the cabinet of the Asiatic Society', *JASB* II, pp. 27–41 (repr. Thomas 1858, vol. I, pp. 7–22).

Prinsep, J. (1833a) 'Note on Lieutenant Burnes' collection of ancient coins', *JASB* II, pp. 310–18 (repr. Thomas 1858, vol. I, pp. 23–44, and as 'Mr. James Prinsep's notes', appendix to A. Burnes, *Travels into Bokhara*, 1834, vol. II, pp. 463–73).

Prinsep, J. (1833b) 'Bactrian and Indo-Scythic coins – continued', *JASB* II, pp. 405–16 (repr. Thomas 1858, vol. I, pp. 45–62).

Prinsep, J. (1834) 'Note on the coins found by Captain Cautley in Behat', *JASB* III, pp. 227–8 (repr. Thomas 1858, vol. I, pp. 82–5).

Prinsep, J. (1834a) 'On the coins and relics discovered by M. le chevalier Ventura, general in the service of Mahá Rájá Ranjit Singh, in the tope of Manikyála', *JASB* III, pp. 313–20 (repr. Thomas 1858, vol. I, pp. 90–117).

Prinsep, J. (1834b) 'Continuation of observations on the coins and relics discovered by General Ventura, in the tope of Manikyála', *JASB* III, pp. 436–55, pl. XXVI (repr. Thomas 1858, vol. I, pp. 118–37).

Prinsep, J. (1834c) 'Note on the brown liquid contained in the cylinders from Manikyála', *JASB* III, pp. 567–9.

Prinsep, J. (1834d) 'Remarks on the nature and origin of the topes of Manikyála', *JASB* III, pp. 569–73.

Prinsep, J. (1834e) 'Note on the coins discovered by M. Court', *JASB* III, pp. 562–7 (repr. Thomas 1858, vol. I, pp. 141–53).

Prinsep, J. (1834f) 'Notes on inscription no. 1 of the Allahabad column', *JASB* III, pp. 114–18.

Prinsep, J. (1834g) 'Note on the Mathiah Lāth inscription', *JASB* III, pp. 483–7.

Prinsep, J. (1835) 'Further notes and drawings of Bactrian and Indo-Scythic coins', *JASB* IV, pp. 327–48 (repr. Thomas 1858, vol. I, pp. 176–94).

Prinsep, J. (1835a) 'On the connection of various ancient Hindu coins with the Grecian or Indo-Scythic series', *JASB* IV, pp. 621–43 (repr. Thomas 1858, vol. I, pp. 195–200, 224–31, 277–88).

Prinsep, J. (1835b) 'Notice of ancient Hindu coins, continued from page 643', *JASB* IV, pp. 668–90 (repr. Thomas 1858, vol. I, pp. 289–319).

Prinsep, J. (1836) 'New varieties of Bactrian coins engraved as pl. XXXV, from Masson's drawings and other sources', *JASB* V, pp. 548–54 (repr. Thomas 1858, vol. I, pp. 352–9, pl. XXVIII).

Prinsep, J. (1836a) 'New varieties of the Mithraic or Indo-Scythic series of coins, and their imitations', *JASB* V, pp. 639–57 (repr. Thomas 1858, vol. I, pp. 360–96).

Prinsep, J. (1836b) 'New types of Bactrian and Indo-Scythic coins engraved as pl. XLIX', *JASB* V, pp. 720–4 (repr. Thomas 1858, vol. I, pp. 397–401, pl. XXXII).

Prinsep, J. (1837) 'Note on the facsimiles of inscriptions from Sanchí near Bhilsa, taken for the Society by Captain Ed. Smith, Engineers', *JASB* VI, pp. 451–77.

Prinsep, J. (1838) 'Additions to Bactrian numismatics, and the discovery of the Bactrian alphabet', *JASB* VII, pp. 636–55 (repr. Thomas 1858, vol. II, pp. 125–44).

Prinsep, J. (1838a) 'Completion of the alphabet', *JASB* VII, pp. 271–6.

Prinsep, J. (1858) 'Useful tables illustrative of the coins, weights and measures of British India; together with chronological tables and genealogical lists having reference to India and other kingdoms of Asia', in E. Thomas (ed.), *Essays on Indian Antiquities, Historic, Numismatic, and Palaeographic, of the late James Prinsep, F.R.S., Secretary to the Asiatic Society of Bengal*, vol. II, London.

Prinsep, J. (1871) 'Extracts of letters to A. Cunningham, 11.5.1837–28.9.1838, in A. Cunningham, *Four Reports made during the Years 1862–63–64–65*, 2 vols, Simla, pp. ix–xvi.

Prinsep, J. (MSS) 'James Prinsep Oriental Coins', 3 vols, Ashmolean Museum, Oxford, Heberden Coin Room Archives, Arch. Ash. fol. 18.

Priscus, *History*, 8 vols: fragments preserved in *Excerpta de Legationibus Iussu Imp. Constantini Porphyrogeniti Confecta*, ed. V. P. Boissevain, Berlin 1906, tr. Blockley 1983.

Proc. ASB (1838) 'V. Coins and relics from Bactria', Proceedings Asiatic Society of Bengal, December, *JASB* VII, pp. 1047–8.

Proc. ASB (1839) 'Literary and antiquities', Proceedings Asiatic Society of Bengal, December, *JASB* VIII, p. 341.

Proc. ASB (1845) 'Report on Shahbazgarhi inscription from Royal Asiatic Society, London', Proceedings Asiatic Society of Bengal, May no. IX, *JASB* XIV.i, pp. xxxix–liv.

Procopius, *History of the Wars*, books I–II, tr. H. B. Dewing, vol. I, Loeb Classical Library, 7 vols, London–Cambridge Mass. 1914 (3rd repr. 1961).

Pugachenkova, G. A. (1996) 'Khalchayan', *The Grove Dictionary of Art Online*, http://www.groveart.com.

Pulleybank, E. G. (1962) 'The consonantal system of Old Chinese, part II', *Asia Major* 9, pp. 206–65.

Pulleybank, E. G. (1968) 'Chinese evidence for the date of Kaniṣka', in A. L. Basham (ed.), *Papers on the Date of Kaniṣka*, Leiden, pp. 247–58.

Punjab Board of Administration (1851) Lahore Civil Secretariat, Press List XII, serial no. 772, Punjab Proceedings, Board of Administration General Department, week ending 24–5–1851, nos 32–4: 'Preservation of historical monuments'.

Quintus Curtius, Rufus, *The History of Alexander*, tr. J. Yardley, with commentary by W. Heckel, Harmondsworth 1984.

Rahman, Abdur (1968/9) 'Excavation at Damkot', *Ancient Pakistan* IV, pp. 103–250.

Rahman, Abdur (1993) 'Shnaisha Gumbat: first preliminary excavation report', *Ancient Pakistan* VIII, pp. 38–222.

Rahman, Abdur (2002) 'New light on the Khingal, Turk and the Hindu Sāhis', *Ancient Pakistan* XV, pp. 37–42.

Rapin, C. (1992) *Fouilles d'Aï Khanoum, VIII. Les trésories du palais hellénistique d'Aï Khanoum*, Mémoires de la Délégation Archéologique française en Afghanistan XXXIII, Paris.

Rawlinson, H. C. (1840) 'Memoir on the site of the Atropatenian Ecbatana', *Journal of the Royal Geographical Society* X, pp. 65–158

Rawlinson, H. C. (1846/7) *The Persian Cuneiform Inscription at Behistun, Deciphered and Translated, with a Memoir on Persian Cuneiform Inscriptions*, Journal of the Royal Asiatic Society X (whole number).

Rawlinson, H. C. (1852) 'Notes on some paper casts of cuneiform inscriptions upon the sculptured rock at Behistun . . . ,' *Archaeologia or Miscellaneous Tracts relating to Antiquity, published by the Society of Antiquaries of London* 34, pp. 73–6.

Ray, S. C. (1991) 'A revised study into the numismatic evidence of the Indo-Roman trade', in A. K. Jha (ed.), *Coinage, Trade and Economy. 3rd International Colloquium*, Nasik, pp. 138–44.

Raychaudhuri, H. (1996) *Political History of Ancient India. From the Accession of Parikshit to the Extinction of the Gupta Dynasty, with a commentary by B. N. Mukherjee*, Calcutta 1923 (rev. ed. New Delhi).

Razmjou, S. (2005) 'Religion and burial customs', in J. Curtis and N. Tallis (eds), *Forgotten Empire. The World of Ancient Persia*, London, pp. 150–6.

Reade, J. E. and Burleigh, R. (1978) 'The 'Ali cemetery: old excavations, ivory and radiocarbon dating', *Journal of Oman Studies* 4, pp. 75–83.

Reinaud, R. (1832) 'Lettre au rédacteur du Journal Asiatique', *Journal Asiatique* 2ème sér. IX, pp. 276–9.

Rémusat, A. (1836) *Foe koue ki, ou relations des royaumes bouddhiques, voyage dans la Tartarie, dans l'Afghanistan et dans l'Inde, exécuté, à la fin du IVe siècle*, Paris.

Renfrew, C. and Bahn, P. (1991) *Archaeology: Theories, Method and Practice*, London.

Rhys Davids, T. W. tr. (1890–4) *The Questions of King Milinda [Milindapañha]*, The Sacred Books of the East, ed. F. M. Müller, vols 35–6, London–Oxford 1879–1900.

Rich, C. J. (1836) *Narrative of a Residence in Koordistan by the late Claudius James Rich Esquire, Edited by his Widow*, 2 vols, London.

Roaf, M. D. (1983) 'Sculptures and sculptors at Persepolis', *Iran* XXI (whole number).

Roaf, M. D. (1984) 'Excavations at Tell Mohammed 'Arab in the Eski Mosul Dam Salvage Project', *Iraq* XLVI, pp. 141–56.

Roaf, M. D. (1987) 'Checklist of Persepolis reliefs not at the site', *Iran* XXV, pp. 155–8.

Rochette, R. (1834) 'Notice sur quelques médailles grecques inédites appartenant à des rois inconnus de la Bactriane et de l'Inde', *Journal des Savants*, pp. 2–28.

Rochette, R. (1835) 'Supplément à la notice sur quelques médailles grecques inédites de rois inconnus de la Bactriane et de l'Inde', *Journal des Savants*, pp. 1–35.

Rochette, R. (1836) 'Deuxième supplément à la notice sur quelques médailles grecques inédites de rois inconnus de la Bactriane et de l'Inde', *Journal des Savants*, pp. 1–61.

Rogers, R. W. (1929) *A History of Ancient Persia from its Earliest Beginnings to the Death of Alexander the Great*, Chicago.

Root, M. C. (1988) 'Evidence from Persepolis for the dating of Persian and archaic Greek coinage', *NC* 148, pp. 1–12.

Root, M. C. (1989) 'The Persian archer at Persepolis: aspects of chronology, style and symbolism', in R. Descat (ed.), *Revue des études anciennes. L'or perse et l'histoire grecque. Table ronde*, CNRS, Bordeaux.

Rosenfield, J. M. (1967) *The Dynastic Arts of the Kushans*, Berkeley–Los Angeles.

Royal Academy (1931), *Catalogue of the International Exhibition of Persian Art, 7 January – 28 February 1931*, London (2nd edn).

Sachau, E. C. (1888) *Alberuni's India*, 2 vols, London.

Sadakata, A. (1996) 'Quelques inscriptions kharoṣṭhī provenant du marché aux antiquites de Peshawar couvertes', *Journal Asiatique* 284, pp. 301–24.

Safadi, Y. and Reade, J. (1986–7) *Claudius James Rich. Diplomat, Archaeologist, Collector*, British Library exhibition notes, London.

Safar, F. and Mustafa, M. A. (1974) *Hatra. The City of the Sun God*, Baghdad.

Saint-Martin, J. (1832) 'Note sur les médailles gréco-indiennes mentionées dans la lettre précédente', *Journal Asiatique* 2ème sér. IX, pp. 280–1.

Salomon, R. (1995) 'A Kharoṣṭhī reliquary inscription of the time of the Apraca prince Viṣṇuvarman', *South Asian Studies* 11, pp. 27–32.

Salomon, R. (1996) 'An inscribed silver Buddhist reliquary of the time of king Kharaosta and prince Indravarman', *Journal of the American Oriental Society* 116, pp. 418–52.

Salomon, R. (1997) 'The re-dedication of Buddhist reliquaries: a clue to the interpretation of problematic Kharoṣṭhī inscriptions', *South Asian Archaeology 1995*, vol. I, Cambridge–New Delhi, pp. 365–76.

Salomon, R. (1998) *Indian Epigraphy. A Guide to the Study of Inscriptions in Sanskrit, Prakrit, and the other Indo-Aryan Languages*, New York.

Salomon, R. (1999) *Ancient Buddhist Scrolls from Gandhāra. The British Library Kharoṣṭhī Fragments*, London.

Salomon, R. (2002) 'Gāndhārā and the other Indo-Aryan languages in the light of newly-discovered Kharoṣṭhī manuscripts', in N. Sims-Williams (ed.), *Indo-Iranian Languages and Peoples*, Proceedings of the British Academy 116, pp. 119–34.

Salomon, R. (2005) 'The Indo-Greek era of 186/5 B.C. in a Buddhist reliquary inscription', in O. Bopearachchi and M.-F. Boussac (eds), *Afghanistan, ancient carrefour entre l'est et l'ouest*, Turnhout, pp. 359–402.

Salomon, R. and Schopen, G. (1984) 'The Indravarman (Avaca) casket inscription reconsidered: further evidence for canonical passages in Buddhist inscriptions', *Journal of the International Association of Buddhist Studies* 7, pp. 107–23.

Sami, A. (n.d.) *Pasargad: qadimitarin paytakht-i keshvar-i shahanshahi Iran*, Shiraz.

Sarianidi, V. (1985) *Bactrian Gold from the Excavations of the Tillya-Tepe Necropolis in Northern Afghanistan*, Leningrad.

Scherrer-Schaub, C. (forthcoming) *The Bodhimaṇḍālaṃkāra-nama-dhāraṇi-upacāra*, Arbeitskreis für tibetische und buddhistische Studien Universität Wien, Wiener Studien zur Tibetologie und Buddhismuskunde, Vienna.

Schindel, N. (2004) *Sylloge Nummorum Sasanidarum Paris – Berlin – Wien*, vol. III/2, *Shapur II. – Kawad I./2. Regierung. Katalog*, Veröffentlichungen der Numismatischen Kommission 42, Vienna.

Schippmann, K. (1980) *Grundzüge der parthischen Geschichte*, Darmstadt.

Schippmann, K. (1990) *Grundzüge der Geschichte des sasanidischen Reiches*, Darmstadt.

Schlegel, A. W. von (1828) 'Observations sur quelques médailles bactriennes et indo-scythiques nouvellement découvertes', *Journal Asiatique* 2ème sér. VII, pp. 321–49.

Schlumberger, D., Le Berre, M. and Fussman, G. (1983) *Surkh Kotal en Bactriane, I. Les temples, architecture, sculpture, inscriptions*, 2 vols, Mémoires de la Délégation Archéologique française en Afghanistan XXV, Paris.

Schmidt, E. (1970) *Persepolis, III. The Royal Tombs and Other Monuments*, University of Chicago Oriental Institute Publications IXX, Chicago.

Schmidt, E. F. *et al.* (1953) *Persepolis I: Structures, Reliefs, Inscriptions*, Chicago.

Schmitt, R. (1990) 'Der Name Hyspasines (samt Varianten)', *Bulletin of the Asia Institute* 4, pp. 245–9.

Schmitt, R. (1998) 'Parthische Sprach- und Namenüberlieferung aus arsakidischer Zeit', in J. Wiesehöfer (ed.), *Das Partherreich und seine Zeugnisse*, Stuttgart, pp. 163–204.

Schneider, R. M. (1998) 'Die Faszination des Feindes. Bilder der Parther und des Orients in Rom', in J. Wiesehöfer (ed.), *Das Partherreich und seine Zeugnisse*, Stuttgart, pp. 95–127.

Schneider, R. M. (2007) 'Friend *and* foe : the Orient in Rome', in V. S. Curtis and S. Stewart (eds) *The Age of the Parthians*, pp. 50–86, London.

Schwartzberg, J. E. ed. (1992) *A Historical Atlas of South Asia*, New York–Oxford (2nd edn).

Sellwood, D. (1980) *An Introduction to the Coinage of Parthia*, London.

Sellwood, D. (1983) 'Parthian coins', in E. Yarshater (ed.) *The Cambridge History of Iran*, vol. III.1, *The Seleucid, Parthian and Sasanian Periods*, Cambridge–London–New York, pp. 279–98.

Senior, R. (2000) *A Catalogue of Indo-Scythian Coins. An Analysis of the Coinage*, 3 vols, Glastonbury.

Shahbazi, A. S. (1976) *Persepolis Illustrated*, Tehran.

Shahbazi, A. S. (1983) 'Studies in Sasanian prosopography', *Archäologische Mitteilungen aus Iran* n. s. 16, pp. 255–68.

Shahbazi, A. S. (1987) 'Apamā', in E. Yarshater (ed.), *Encyclopaedia Iranica* II, London–New York, p. 150.

Shahbazi, A. S. (1994) 'Persepolis and the Avesta', *Archäologische Mitteilungen aus Iran* n. s. 27, pp. 85-97.

Shahbazi, A. S. (1379/2000–1) *Rahnamay-i jam'eh Takht-e Jamshid* [Persepolis Complete Guide], Tehran.

Shahbazi, A. S. (2002) 'Recent speculations on the "traditional date of Zoroaster"', *Studia Iranica* 31.1, pp. 7–45.

Shahbazi, A. S. (2003) 'Yazdegerd I', *Encyclopaedia Iranica Online*, http://www.iranica.com/articles/supp4/Yazdegerd.html.

Shahbazi, A. S. (2004) *The Authoritive Guide to Persepolis*, Tehran.

Shahnameh of Firdowsi, Jules Mohl edn, 5 vols, Tehran 1354/1975.

Sharma, R. C. (1989) 'New inscriptions from Mathurā', in D. Meth Srinivasan (ed.), *Mathurā. The Cultural Heritage*, New Delhi, pp. 308–15.

Sharma, R. C. (1995) *Buddhist Art. Mathura School*, New Delhi.

Shayegan, R. (forthcoming) *The Antecedents of Early Sasanian Political Ideology*.

Shih-Chi [Historical Records] compiled by Ssu-ma T'an and Ssu-ma Ch'ien (Zürcher 1968, pp. 358–63).

Shrimali, K. M. (1983) *History of Pañcāla to AD 550*, 2 vols, New Delhi.

Silvestre de Sacy, A. I. (1793) *Mémoires sur diverses antiquités de la Perse et sur les médailles des rois de la dynastie des sassanides, suivis de l'histoire de cette dynastie, traduite du Persan de Mirkhond*, Paris.

Simpson, St J. (2000) 'Rediscovering past splendours from Iran: 19th-century plaster casts of sculptures from Persepolis', *British Museum Magazine* 36 (spring), pp. 28–9.

Simpson, St J. (2003) 'From Persepolis to Babylon and Nineveh: the rediscovery of the ancient Near East', in K. Sloan (ed.), *Enlightenment. Discovering the World in the Eighteenth Century*, pp. 192–201, 293–4, London.

Simpson, St J. (2004) 'Making their mark. Foreign travellers at Persepolis', http://www.achemenet.com/ressources/enligne/arta/arta.htm.

Simpson, W. (1879) Letter to Colonel Colley, regarding 'Coins from the Ahin Posh Tope near Jelálabád', March Proceedings of the Asiatic Society of Bengal, *JASB* XLVIII, pp. 77–9.

Simpson, W. (1879–80) 'Buddhist architecture in the Jellalabad valley', *Transactions of the Royal Institute of British Architects*, pp. 37–58.

Simpson, W. (1881) 'On the identification of Nagarahara, with reference to the travels of Hiouen-thsang', *JRAS* n. s. XIII, pp. 183–207.

Sims-Williams, N. (1997) *New Light on Ancient Afghanistan. The Decipherment of Bactrian*, London.

Sims-Williams, N. (1999) 'From the Kushan-shahs to the Arabs. New Bactrian documents dated in the era of the Tochi inscriptions', in M. Alram and D. Klimburg-Salter (eds), *Coins, Art and Chronology. Essays on the pre-Islamic History of the Indo-Iranian Borderlands*, Vienna, pp. 245–54.

Sims-Williams, N. (2000) *Bactrian Documents from Northern Afghanistan. I: Legal and Economic Documents*, Studies in the Khalili Collection III/Corpus Inscriptionum Iranicarum VI, Oxford.

Sims-Williams, N. (2002) 'Ancient Afghanistan and its invaders: linguistic evidence from the Bactrian documents and inscriptions', in

N. Sims-Williams (ed.), *Indo-Iranian Languages and Peoples*, Proceedings of the British Academy 116, pp. 225–42.

Sims-Williams, N. (2002a) 'The Bactrian inscription on the seal of Khiṅgila', *Silk Road Art and Archaeology* 8, pp. 143–8.

Sims-Williams, N. and Cribb, J. (1995/6) 'A new Bactrian inscription of Kanishka the Great', *Silk Road Art and Archaeology* 4, pp. 75–142.

Sinor, D. (1990) *The Cambridge History of Early Inner Asia*, Cambridge.

Sircar, D. C. (1963) 'Three early mediaeval inscriptions: (1) Kabul inscription of Shāhi Khingāla', *Epigraphia Indica* 35.1, pp. 44–6.

Sircar, D. C. (1965) *Select Inscriptions Bearing on Indian History and Civilization*, vol. I, *From the Sixth Century B.C. to the Sixth Century A.D.*, Calcutta.

Sircar, D. C. (1965a) *Indian Epigraphy*, Delhi.

Sircar, D. C. (1966) *Indian Epigraphical Glossary*, Delhi.

Skaff, J. K. (1998) 'Sasanian and Arab-Sasanian silver coins from Turfan: their relationship to international trade and the local economy', *Asia Major* 3rd ser. XI.2, pp. 67–109.

Skjaervø, O. P. (2005) 'The Achaemenids and the *Avesta*', in V. S. Curtis and S. Stewart (eds), *The Birth of the Persian Empire*, London, pp. 52–84.

Sloan, K. (2003) '"Aimed at universality and belonging to the nation": the Enlightenment and the British Museum', in K. Sloan and A. Burnett (eds), *Enlightenment: Discovering the World in the Eighteenth Century*, London, pp. 12–25.

Smirnova, N. (1999) 'Nakhodki ellinisticheskikh monet na gorodishche Gyaur-kala (Turkmenistan)' [Finds of Seleucid and Graeco-Bactrian coins at the city-site of Giaour-kala (Turkmenistan)], *Numismatika i Epigraphika* XVI, pp. 242–64.

Smith, C. H. [1931] *Catalogue of Casts of Sculptures from Persepolis and the Neighbourhood, with List of Prices, Illustrating the Art of the Old Persian Empire, from 550–340 BC*, London.

Smith, C. H. (1932) *Photographs of Casts of Persian Sculptures of the Achaemenid Period Mostly from Persepolis*, London.

Smith, D. S. (2000) 'Early Central Asian imitations I: the coinage of Eukratides I', *The Celator* 14.7, July, pp. 6–20.

Smith, D. S. (2001) 'Early Central Asian imitations III: coinage of Heliokles I and the Kushan connection', *The Celator* 15.11, November, pp. 6–16.

Smith, R. R. R. (1988) *Hellenistic Royal Portraits*, Oxford Monographs on Classical Archaeology ed. M. Robertson, J. Boardman, J. Coulton and D. Kurtz, Oxford.

Smith, S. (1938) 'An Achaemenean relief from Persepolis', *British Museum Quarterly* 12, p. 35, pl. XI.

Smith, V. A. (1904) *The Early History of India from 600 B.C. to the Muhammadan Conquest*, Oxford.

Sotheby, Wilkinson & Hodge (1887) *Catalogue of . . . a Most Extensive Series of Indo-Scythic, Hindu & Indian Coins, Sold on Behalf of the Government of India*, 6 August, London, pp. 54–64.

Splendeur des Sassanides. L'empire perse entre Rome et la Chine, Musées royaux d'Art et d'Histoire exhibition 12 February – 25 April 1993, Brussels.

Spooner, D. B. (1911) 'Excavations at Takht-i-Bahi', *Archaeological Survey of India Annual Report 1907–08*, Calcutta, pp. 132–48.

Spooner, D. B. (1912) 'Excavations at Shāh-jī-kī-Dherī', *Archaeological Survey of India Annual Report 1908-09*, Calcutta 1912, pp. 38–59.

Spooner, D. B. (1914) 'Excavations at Sahri Bahlol', *Archaeological Survey of India Annual Report 1909–10*, Calcutta, pp. 46–62.

Srinivasan, D. (1997/8) 'Skanda/Kārttikeya in the early art of the Northwest', *Silk Road and Archaeology* V, pp. 233–68

Standish, J. F. (1998) *Persia and the Persian Gulf. Retrospect and Prospect*, Richmond.

Stark, F. [1966] *Rome on the Euphrates: The Story of a Frontier*, London (n. d.).

Staviskij, B. J. (1986) *La Bactriane sous les Kushans. Problèmes d'histoire et de culture*, Édition revue et augmentée, tr. P. Bernard, M. Burda, F. Grenet and P. Leriche, Paris.

Stein, M. A. (1887) 'Zoroastrian deities on Indo-Scythian coins', *Oriental and Babylonian Record*, London.

Stein, M. A. (1887a) 'The Greek *sanpi* on Indo-Scythian coins', *The Academy*, 10 September, no. 801.

Stein, M. A. tr. (1892) *Kalhaṇa's Rājataraṅgiṇī. A Chronicle of the Kings of Kaśmīr, with introduction, commentary and appendices*, 2 vols, Bombay (repr. London 1900).

Stein, M. A. (1896) 'The district of Cuksha', *Indian Antiquary* XXV, pp. 174–5.

Stein, M. A. (1900) 'Preliminary note on an archaeological tour of the Indus', *Indian Antiquary* XXIX, pp. 145–6.

Stein, M. A. (1901) *Preliminary Report of a Journey of Archaeological and Topographical Exploration in Chinese Turkestan*, London.

Stein, M. A. (1905) 'The alleged site of Aornos', *Report of the Archaeological Survey Work in the North-West Frontier Province and Baluchistan, January 1904 – March 1905*, Peshawar, part II, section vi, pp. 28–31.

Stein, M. A. (1907) *Ancient Khotan. Detailed Report of Archaeological Explorations in Chinese Turkestan*, 2 vols, Oxford (repr. New York 1975).

Stein, M. A. (1912) 'Excavations at Sahri-Bahlol', *Archaeological Survey of India Frontier Circle Annual Report 1911–12*, part II.v, Peshawar, pp. 9–16.

Stein, M. A. (1915) 'Excavations at Sahri Bahlōl', *Archaeological Survey of India Annual Report 1911–12*, Calcutta, pp. 95–119.

Stein, M. A. (1919) 'Air photography of ancient sites', *Geographical Journal* LIV, p. 200.

Stein, M. A. (1921) *Serindia. Detailed Report of Explorations in Central Asia and Westernmost China*, 5 vols, Oxford (repr. Delhi 1980, 4 vols).

Stein, M. A. (1928) *Innermost Asia: Detailed Report of Exploration in Central Asia, Kansu and Eastern Iran*, 4 vols, Oxford (repr. New Delhi 1981).

Stein, M. A. (1929) *On Alexander's Track to the Indus*, London.

Stein, M. A. (1930) 'An archaeological tour in upper Swat and adjacent hill tracts', *Memoirs of the Archaeological Survey of India* 42, Calcutta, pp. 1–104.

Stein, M. A. (1933) *On Ancient Central Asian Tracks*, London.

Stolper, M. W. (2005) 'Achaemenid languages and inscriptions', in J. Curtis and N. Tallis (eds), *Forgotten Empire. The World of Ancient Persia*, London, pp. 18–24.

Strabo, *Geography*, book II, tr. H. L. Jones, *The Geography of Strabo* I, ed. G. P. Gould, Loeb Classical Library 8 vols, London–Cambridge Mass. 1969 (5th repr.).

Strabo, *Geography*, book XI, tr. H. L. Jones, *The Geography of Strabo* V, ed. G. P. Gould, Loeb Classical Library 8 vols, London–Cambridge Mass. 1968 (5th repr.).

Strabo, *Geography*, book XV, tr. H. L. Jones, *The Geography of Strabo* VII, ed. G. P. Gould, Loeb Classical Library 8 vols, London–Cambridge Mass. 1983 (5th repr.).

Stronach, D. (1978) *Pasargadae. A Report on the Excavations Conducted by the British Institute of Persian Studies from 1961 to 1963*, Oxford.

Sundermann, W. (1990) 'Shapur's coronation: the evidence of the Cologne Mani Codex reconsidered and compared with other texts', *Bulletin of the Asia Institute* 4, pp. 295–9.

Swiney, J. (1837) 'On the explanation of the Indo-Scythic legends of the Bactrian coins through the medium of Celtic', *JASB* VI, pp. 98–100.

Ṭabari, Abā Ja'far Muḥammad b. Jarir, *Ta'rīkh al-rusul wa'l-mulūk*, ed. Abī Ja'far Moḥammad Abūl Faḍl Ibrahim, 11 vols, Cairo.

Tabari, Abu Ja'far Muhammad b. Jarir, *Ta'rīkh al-rusul wa'l-mulūk* (see Bosworth 1999).

Tacitus, *Annals*, tr. A. J. Church and W. J. Brodribb. London–New York 1888.

Taddei, M. (1968) 'Tapa Sardār: first preliminary report', *East and West* XVIII, pp. 109–24.

Taddei, M. (1973) 'The Mahisamardini image from Tapa Sardar', in N. Hammond (ed.), *South Asian Archaeology 1971*, Cambridge, pp. 203–13.

Taddei, M. (1985) 'A new early Śiva image from Gandhāra', in J. Schotsmans and M. Taddei (eds), *South Asian Archaeology 1983*, vol. II, Naples, pp. 203–13.

Taddei, M. and Verardi, G. (1978) 'Tapa Sardār: second preliminary report', *East and West* XXVIII, pp. 33–157.

Takakusu, J. tr. (1998) *A Record of the Buddhist Religion as Practised in India and the Malaya Archipelago (AD 671–695) by I-Tsing*, London 1896, repr. New Delhi.

Tanabe, K. *et al.* (1982) 'Studies in the Urartian bronze objects from Japanese Collections (1)', *Bulletin of the Ancient Orient Museum* IV, Tokyo.

Tarn, W. W. (1938) *The Greeks in Bactria and India*, Cambridge.

Tarzi, Z. (1976) 'Hadda à la lumière des trios dernières campagnes de fouilles de Tapa-é-Shotor (1974–1976)', *CRAI*, pp. 381–410.

Tarzi, Z. (1977) *L'architecture et le décor rupestre des grottes de Bāmiyān*, 2 vols, Paris.

Tarzi, Z. (1990) 'Tapa-e-Top-e-Kalān (TTK) of Hadda', in M. Taddei (ed.), *South Asian Archaeology 1987*, vol. II, Naples, pp. 707–26.

Tertullian, *Against Praxeas*, in P. Kirby (2001) *Online Text for Tertullian*, http://www.earlychristianwritings.com/tertullian.html.

Thapar, R. (1997) *Aśoka and the Decline of the Mauryas*, Calcutta–Chennai–Mumbai (rev. edn).

Thapar, R. (2000) *Cultural Pasts. Essays in Early Indian History*, New Delhi.

Thaplyal, K. K. (1985) *Inscriptions of the Maukharīs, Later Guptas, Puṣpabhūtis and Yaśovarman of Kanauj*, Delhi.

Thierry, F. (1993) 'Sur les monnaies sassanides trouvées en Chine', *Circulation des monnaies, des marchandises et des biens*, Res Orientalis V, Bures-sur Yvette, pp. 89–139.

Thomas, E. ed. (1858) *Essays on Indian Antiquities, Historic, Numismatic, and Palaeographic, of the late James Prinsep, F.R.S., Secretary to the Asiatic Society of Bengal*, 2 vols, London.

Thomas, F. W. (1912) Letter to S. C. Cockerell, Director of the Fitzwilliam Museum, dated 15 November. Cambridge, Fitzwilliam Museum Library Archives.

Tilia, A. B. (1972/8) *Studies and Restorations at Persepolis and Other Sites of Fars*, 2 vols, IsMEO Reports and Memoirs 18, Rome (I: 1972; II: 1978).

Tissot, F. (1985) 'The site of Sahrī-Bāhlol in Gandhāra', in J. Schotsmans and M. Taddei (eds), *South Asian Archaeology 1983*, vol. II, Naples, pp. 567–614.

Tissot, F. (1990) 'The site of Sahrī-Bāhlol (Part III)', in M. Taddei (ed.), *South Asian Archaeology 1987*, vol. II, Naples, pp. 737–64.

Tod, J. (1825) 'An account of Greek, Parthian, and Hindu medals, found in India', *Transaction of the Royal Asiatic Society of Great Britain and Ireland* I.1, London, pp. 313–42 (paper read to the Society 18 June).

Tod, J. (1829) *The Annals and Antiquities of Rajast'han or the Central and Western Rajpoot States of India*, London.

Torrens, H. (1840) 'Note on the Bameean coins', *JASB* IX, pp. 70–5.

Torrens, H. (1851) 'Coins of the Indo-Scythian princes of Cabul: translation of some uncertain Greek legends', *JASB* XX, pp. 137–53.

Trümpelmann, L. (1971) 'Šāpur mit der Adlerkopfkappe. Zur Investitur bei den Sasaniden', *Archäologische Mitteilungen aus Iran* n.s. 4, pp. 173–85.

Trümpelmann, L. (1984), 'Sasanian graves and burial customs', in R. Boucharlat and J.-F. Salles (eds), *Arabie orientale, Mésopotamie et Iran méridional de l'age du fer au début de la période islamique*, pp. 317–29, Paris.

Tsuchiya, H. (1999/2000) 'An iconographic study of the Buddhist art of Shotorak, Paitava and Kham Zargar', *Silk Road Art and Archaeology* 6, *Papers in Honour of Francine Tissot*, pp. 97–114.

Tulard, J. (1988) *Napoléon*, Paris (5th edn).

Turnour, G. (1836) 'Examination of some points of Buddhist chronology', *JASB* V, pp. 521–36.

Turnour, G. (1837) *The Maháwanso in Roman Characters, with the Translations Subjoined; and an Introductory Essay on Páli Buddhist Literature*, 2 vols, Ceylon [Colombo].

Turnour, G. (1837–8) 'An examination of the Páli Buddhistical annals', *JASB* VI, pp. 501–28, 713–37; VIII, pp. 686–701, 789–817, 919–33.

Twitchett, D. and Loewe, M. eds (1986) *The Cambridge History of China*, vol. 1, *The Ch'in and Han Empires, 221 B.C.–A.D. 220*, Cambridge–New York–Melbourne.

Ulansey, D. (2005) 'Mithraism. The Cosmic Mysteries of Mithras', http://www.well.com///.html.

Van der Spek, R. (1998) 'Cuneiform documents on Parthian history: the Rahimesu archive', in J. Wiesehöfer (ed.), *Das Partherreich und seine Zeugnisse*, Stuttgart, pp. 205–58.

Ventura, J. B. (1832) 'Account of the excavations of the tope Manikyala', appendix to H. H. Wilson, 'Description of select coins, from originals or drawings in the possession of the Asiatic Society', *Asiatic[k] Researches* XVII, pp. 600–3.

Verardi, G. (1996) 'Religions, rituals, and the heaviness of Indian history', *Annali dell'Istituto Orientale di Napoli* LVI.2, pp. 216–53.

Verdi, R. ed. (2003) *Saved! 100 Years of the National Art Collections Fund*, London.

Veuve, S. (1987) *Fouilles d'Aï Khanoum, VI. Le gymnase. Architecture, céramique, trouvailles*, Mémoires de la Délégation Archéologique française en Afghanistan XXX, Paris.

Vibart, H. M. (1894) *Addiscombe. Its Heroes and Men of Note*, London.

Vincent, W. (1807) *The Commerce and Navigation of the Ancients in the Indian Ocean*, vol. II, *The Periplus of the Erythraean Sea*, London.

Vine, P. (1993) *Bahrain National Museum*, Manama.

Vogelsang, W. (2005) 'Gandhara', *Encyclopaedia Iranica Online*, http://www.iranica.com.

Waddell, L. A. (1896) 'Graeco-Buddhist sculptures in Swat', *Imperial and Asiatic Quarterly Revue* 3rd ser. I, pp. 192–4.

Wade, C. M. (1834) Letter to W. H. Macnaghten, 9 April, British Library India Office Collections, Bengal Secret Consultations 19 June, vol. 380.

Wade, C. M. [1847] *A Narrative of the Services, Military, and Political, by Lt. Colonel Sir C. M. Wade*, Isle of Wight, n. d.

Waldmann, H. (1973) *Die Kommagenischen Kultreformen des Königs Mithradates I Kallinikos und seinem Sohne Antiochos I*, Leiden.

Walker, A. (1995) *Aurel Stein, Pioneer of the Silk Road*, London.

Walker, C. B. F. (1981) *Cuneiform Brick Inscriptions in the British Museum, the Ashmolean Museum, Oxford, the City of Birmingham Museums and Art Gallery, the City of Bristol Museum and Art Gallery*, London.

Walsh, E. H. C. (1939) *Punch-marked Coins from Taxila*, Memoirs of the Archaeological Survey of India 59, Calcutta.

Wang, H. (1997) 'The Stein collection of coins from Chinese Central Asia', in K. Tanabe, J. Cribb and H. Wang (eds), *Studies in Silk Road Coins and Culture: Papers in Honour of Professor Ikuo Hiryama on his 65th Birthday*, Kamakura, pp. 187–99.

Wang, H. (1998) 'Stein's recording angel – Miss F. M. G. Lorimer', *JRAS* ser. 3, VIII, pp. 207–28.

Wang, H. ed. (1999) *Handbook to the Stein Collections in the UK*, British Museum Occasional Paper 129, London.

Wang, H. ed. (2002) *Sir Aurel Stein in The Times*, London.

Wang, H. (2004) 'Catalogue of the Sir Aurel Stein papers in the British Museum Central Archives', in H. Wang (ed.) *Sir Aurel Stein. Proceedings of the British Museum Study Day, 23 March 2002*, pp. 37–62, London.

Wang, H. (2005) *Money on the Silk Road. The Evidence from Eastern Central Asia to c. AD 800, including a Catalogue of the Coins collected by Sir Aurel Stein*, London.

Wang Tao (1997) 'Establishing the Chinese archaeological school: Su Bingqi and contemporary Chinese archaeology', *Antiquity* LXXI, pp. 31–9.

Watters, T. (1904) *On Yuan-Chwang's Travels in India 629–645 A.D.*, 2 vols, ed. T. W. Rhys Davids and S. W. Bushell, London (repr. 1975).

Weld Blundell, H. (1892) 'Persepolis', in E. Delmar Morgan (ed.), *Transactions of the Ninth International Congress of Orientalists (London, 5th–12th September 1892)*, vol. II, pp. 537–59, London.

West, E. W. (2005) 'Pahlavi literature', in W. Geiger and E. Kuhn, *Grundriss der iranischen Philologie*, vol. II, Strassburg, 1896–1904, http://www.farvardyn.com/pahlavi5.php.

Whitcomb, D. S. (1985) *Before the Roses and Nightingales. Excavations at Qasr-i Abu Nasr, Old Shiraz*, New York.

Whitcomb, D. S. (1987) 'Bushire and the Angali Canal', *Mesopotamia* XXII, pp. 311–36.

Whitehead, R. B. (1913), 'A find of Ephthalite or White Hun coins', *JASB Numismatic Supplement* XXI (repr. *JASB* n.s. IX), pp. 481–3.

Whitehead, R. B. (1950) 'Notes on the Indo-Greeks. Part III', *NC* 6th ser. 10, pp. 205–32.

Whitehouse, D. (1971) 'Siraf: a Sasanian port', *Antiquity* XLV, no. 180, December, pp. 262–5.

Whitehouse, D. (1975) 'Carnelian in the Persian Gulf', *Antiquity* XLIX, no. 194, June, pp. 129–30.

Whitehouse, D. and Williamson, A. (1973) 'Sasanian maritime trade', *Iran* XI, pp. 29–49.

Whitfield, R. (1982–3) *The Art of Central Asia. The Stein Collection in the British Museum*, 3 vols. Tokyo: Kodansha International in co-operation with the Trustees of the British Museum.

Whitfield, R. and Farrer, A. (1990) *Caves of the Thousand Buddhas*. New York.

Whitfield, S. (2004) *Aurel Stein on the Silk Road*, London.

Whitteridge, G. (1986) *Charles Masson of Afghanistan. Explorer, Archaeologist, Numismatist and Intelligence Agent*, Warminster.

Who Was Who 1929–1940 (1941) London.

Wiesehöfer, J. (2001) *Ancient Persia*, London (2nd rev. ed.).

Wiesehöfer, J. (2002) '"Sie waren für ihn das Juwel von allem, was er gesehen". Niebuhr und die Ruinenstätten des alten Iran', in J. Wiesehöfer and S. Conermann (eds), *Carsten Niebuhr (1733–1815) und seine Zeit*, Stuttgart, pp. 267–99.

Wilhelm, F. (1968) 'Kanika and Kaniṣka – Aśvaghoṣa and Mātṛceṭa (with regard to Tibetan sources)', in A. L. Basham (ed.), *Papers on the Date of Kaniṣka*, Leiden, pp. 337–45.

Wilkins, C. (1788) 'A royal grant of land, engraved on a copper plate, bearing date twenty-three years before Christ; and discovered among the ruins at Monqueer. Translated from the original Sanskrit in the year 1781', *Asiatick Researches* I, pp. 123–30.

Wilkins, C. (1788a) 'An inscription on a pillar near Buddal', *Asiatick Researches* I, pp. 131–41

Wilkins, C. (1788b) Letter of 17 March 1785 [Translation of Nagarjuni hill cave inscription], *Asiatick Researches* I, pp. 279–83.

Will, É. (1979–80) *Histoire politique du monde hellénistique (323–30 av. J.C.)*, 2 vols, Nancy (2nd edn).

Williamson, A. (1972) 'Persian Gulf commerce in the Sassanian period and the first two centuries of Islam', *Bastan Chenassi va Honar-e Iran* 9/10 (December), pp. 97–109 (foreign section), pp. 142–51 (Persian section).

Willis, M. (2005) 'Later Gupta history: inscriptions, coins and historical ideology', *JRAS* 3rd ser. 15.2, pp. 131–50.

Wilson, A. T. (1928) *The Persian Gulf. An Historical Sketch from the Earliest Times to the Beginning of the Twentieth Century*, London.

Wilson, H. H. (1825) 'An essay on the Hindu history of Cashmir', *Asiatic[k] Researches* XV, Serampore, pp. 1–119.

Wilson, H. H. (1832) 'Description of select coins, from originals or drawings in the possession of the Asiatic Society', *Asiatic[k] Researches* XVII, pp. 559–600.

Wilson, H. H. (1834) 'Professor Wilson's notes', appendix to A. Burnes, *Travels into Bokhara*, vol. II, London, pp. 457–62.

Wilson, H. H. (1836) 'Observations on some ancient Indian coins in the cabinet of the Royal Asiatic Society', *JRAS* III, article XVIII, pp. 381–6.

Wilson, H. H. (1837) 'Graeco-Bactrian coins', *The Numismatic Journal* (later renamed *Numismatic Chronicle*) II, pp. 144–81.

Wilson, H. H. (1838) 'A memoir on the recently discovered Graeco-Bactrian coins', *Proceedings of the Numismatic Society of London 1837–38*, London, pp. 107–32.

Wilson, H. H. (1841) *Ariana Antiqua. A Descriptive Account of the Antiquities and Coins of Afghanistan: with a Memoir on the Buildings called Topes, by C. Masson, Esq.*, London (repr. Delhi 1971).

Wilson, H. H. (1850) 'On the rock inscriptions of Kapur di Giri, Dhauli and Girnar', *JRAS* XII, pp.153–251.

Wilson, V. (1995) 'Early textiles from Central Asia: approaches to study with reference to the Stein loan collection in the Victoria and Albert Museum, London', *Textile History* XXVI/I, pp. 23–52.

Woolley, L. (1958) *History Unearthed: A Survey of Eighteen Archaeological Sites throughout the World*, London.

Wright, D. (1977) *The English amongst the Persians during the Qajar Period 1787–1921*, London.

Wright, D. (1998) 'Burials and memorials of the British in Persia', *Iran* XXXVI, pp. 165–73.

Wright, W. tr. (1882) *The Chronicle of Joshua the Stylite*, Cambridge.

Wroth, W. (1903), *A Catalogue of the Greek Coins in the British Museum. Catalogue of the Coins of Parthia*, London.

Xuan Zang, *Da-Tang xi yu ji quan yi*, tr. Li Rongxi, *The Great Tang Dynasty Record of the Western Regions* (Taisho, vol. 51, no. 2087), BDK English Tripiṭaka 79, Berkeley 1996.

Yamauchi, K. (1997) 'New discoveries of Iranian archaeology (2)', *Bulletin of the Ancient Orient Museum* XVIII, pp. 233–57.

Yapp, M. E. (1980) *Stategies of British India. Britain, Iran and Afghanistan 1798–1850*, Oxford.

Yapp, M. E. (2001) 'The legend of the Great Game', *Proceedings of the British Academy* 111, pp. 179–98.

Ya'qubi, Ahmad b. Abi Ya'qub (1937) *Kitāb al-buldān*, tr. G. Wiet, *Textes et traductions d'auteurs orientaux*, vol. I, Publications de l'Institut français d'Archéologie orientale, ed. M. P. Jouguet, Cairo.

Ya'qubi, Ahmad b. Abi Ya'qub, *Tarikh al-Ya'qubi*, ed. Muhammad Ibrahim Ayati, Tehran 1977.

Yaqut al-Rumi, *Mu'jam al-buldān*, ed. F. Würstenfeld, *Jacut's geographisches Wörterbuch*, 6 vols, Leipzig 1866–72.

Young, D. (1959) *Fountain of the Elephants*, London.

Yule, H. and Burnell, A. C. (1903) *Hobson Jobson. A Glossary of Colloquial Anglo-Indian Words and Phrases, and of Kindred Terms, Etymological, Historical, Geographical and Discursive*, ed. W. Crook, London.

Zaehner R. C. (1961) *The Dawn and Twilight of Zoroastrianism*, London.

Zaehner R. C. (2005) 'Zurvânism', http://www.cais-soas.com/CAIS/Religions/iranian/zurvanism.htm.

Zapata-Aubé, N. (1997) *Lottin de Laval. Archéologue et Peintre Orientaliste 1810-1903*, Bernay.

Zeimal, E. V. (1996) 'The Kidarite Kingdom in Central Asia', in B. A. Litvinsky (ed.), *History of Civilizations of Central Asia*, vol. III, *The Crossroads of Civilizations: A.D. 250 to 750*, Unesco, pp. 119–33.

Zemer, A. (1977) *Storage Jars in Ancient Sea Trade*, Haifa.

Zeymal, E. V. (1997) 'Coins from the excavations at Takht-i Sangin (1976–1991)', in K. Tanabe, J. Cribb and H. Wang (eds), *Silk Road Art and Archaeology. Studies in Silk Road Coins and Culture. Papers in Honour of Professor Ikuo Hirayama on his 65th Birthday*, Kamakura, pp. 89–110.

Zürcher, E. (1968) 'The Yüeh-chih and Kaniṣka in the Chinese sources', in A. L. Basham (ed.), *Papers on the Date of Kaniṣka*, Leiden, pp. 346–90.

Zwalf, W. ed. (1985) *Buddhism: Art and Faith*, London.

Zwalf, W. (1996) *A Catalogue of the Gandhara Sculpture in the British Museum*, 2 vols, London.

Websites

http://www.biography.ms/Constantine_I_%28emperor%29.html
http://en.wikipedia.org/wiki/Seleucid
http://www.nestorian.org/nestorian_theology.html
http://www.roman-emperors.org

Glossary of Chinese names

Wang Tao

Pinyin	Other systems	Chinese	Translation
Andi	An-ti	安帝	Later Han emperor, reg. AD 107–25
Anxi	An-hsi	安息	Parthia
Ban Biao	Pan Piao	班彪	(AD 3–54) Compiler of the *Han Shu*
Ban Chao	Pan Ch'ao	班超	(c. AD 32–102) Governor-general, Western Regions (Xinjiang), AD 84–102
Ban Gu	Pan Ku	班固	(AD 32-92) Compiler of the *Han Shu*
Ban Yong	Pan Yung	班勇	General, Western Regions, c. AD 123–5
Ban Zhao	Pan Chao	班昭	(c. AD 48–116) Compiler of the *Han Shu*
Bei Shi		北史	History of the Northern and Southern Dynasties (AD 386–589)
Bei Tianzhu		北天竺	'Northern' India, i.e. Kabul–Jalalabad region
Bosi	Po-sseu	波斯	Persia
Caoguo		曹國	Kapishi in Sui period (AD 518–618)
Chile / Chiqin	Tch'e-le / Tch'e ch'in	敕勒/敕懃	Vassal state of Yanda in AD 519–20[1]
Chiqin	*tch'e-k'in*	敕勤	Prince/*tegin*
Da Shan		大山	Great mountains
Daxia	Ta-hsia	大夏	Bactria
Da Yuezhi	Ta Yüeh-chih	大月支	Great Yuezhi
Dieluo	Tie-lo	牒羅	Unidentified region in Hindu Kush
Dong Wan		董琬	Chinese envoy to the west c. AD 437
Dumi	Tu-mi	都密	Yuezhi tribe
Fan Ye	Fan Yeh	范曄	(AD 398–445) Compiler of *Hou Han Shu*
Gaofu	Kao-fu	高附	Parapamisidae
Guishui	Kuei-shui	嬀水	Oxus river
Guishuang	Kuei-shuang / Juchang	貴霜	Kushan
Jianwu	Ch'ien-wu	建武	Later Han reign period (AD 25–7)
Jibin	Chi-pin	罽賓	Kashmir
Jiduoluo	Cheduoluo	寄多羅	Kidara / Kidarites
Lanshi	Lan-shih	藍氏/藍市	Tashkurgan
Li Yanshou		李延壽	(d. 628) Compiler of *Bei Shi*
Luoyang	Loyang	洛陽	Later Han capital
Puda	P'u-ta	濮達	Pushkalavati
Qiujiuque	Ch'iu-chiu-ch'üeh	丘就卻	Kujula Kadphises
Saiwang	Sai-wang	塞王	Shaka king
Shiji	*Shih-Chi*	史記	*Historical Records*, compiled c.110–90 BC
Shuangmi	Shuang-mi	雙靡	Yuezhi tribe
Sima Qian	Ssu-ma Ch'ien	司馬遷	(b. 145 BC) Compiler of *Shiji*

Pinyin	Other systems	Chinese	Translation
Sima Tan	Ssu-ma T'an	司馬談	(c.190–110 BC) Sima Qian's father; compiler of *Shiji*
Tianzhu	T'ien-chu	天竺	India
Wei Shu		魏書	History of the Northern Wei (AD 386–534)
Xiao Yuezhi		小月支	Lesser Yuezhi
Xidun	Hsi-tun	胗頓	Yuezhi tribe
xihou	*hsi-hou*	翕侯	*yabgu*
Xiongnu	Hsiung-nu	匈奴	Hun
Xiumi	Hsiu-mi	休密	Yuezhi tribe
Yangaozhen	Yen-kao-chen	閻膏珍	Wima Tak[to]
Yanda	Yen-ta	厭達	Hephthalite
Yuezhi	Yüeh-chih	月支	Yuezhi
Yutian	Yu-t'ien	于闐	Khotan
Zhang Qian	Chang Ch'ien	張騫	(d. 114 BC) Chinese envoy to Yuezhi c.130 BC

1   Chavannes 1903, p. 404, n. 5.

Rulers and dynasties
c.560 BC–AD 652

Europe/Western Asia

Lydia
Croesus (c.560–547/6 BC)

Macedonia
Alexander the Great (336–323 BC)
Ptolemy Ceraunus (281–279 BC)
Antigonus Gonatus (276–239 BC)

Cyrene
Magas (c.277–250 BC)

Epirus
Alexander (272–255 BC)

Pontus
Mithradates VI (c.112–63 BC)

Commagene
Mithradates I Kallinikos (c.100–70 BC)
Antiochus I Theos (c.70–36 BC)

Seleucids (312–64 BC)
Seleucus I (312–281 BC)
Antiochus I Soter (281–261 BC)
Antiochus II (261–246 BC)
Seleucus II (246–226 BC)
Antiochus III (223–187 BC)
Andragoras (c.246–239 BC)
Demetrius I (162–150 BC)
Demetrius II (145–139/8 BC)
Antiochus VII Sidetes (139/8–129 BC)
Alexander II (128–123 BC)

Armenia
Tigranes I (c.97–56 BC)
Tiridates III (AD 238–314)

Romans and Byzantines
Augustus (31 BC–AD 14)
Trajan (AD 98–117)
Gordian III (AD 238–44)
Philippus (AD 244–9)
Valerian (AD 253–60)
Diocletian (AD 284–305)
Galerius (AD 305–11)
Constantine I (AD 306–37)
Constantius II (AD 337–61)
Julian the Apostate (AD 360–3)
Arcadius (AD 395–408)
Theodosius II (AD 408–50)
Leo I (AD 457–74)
Zeno (AD 474–91)
Justinian (AD 527–65)
Justin II (AD 565–78)
Maurice (AD 582–602)
Phocas (AD 602–10)
Heraclius (AD 610–41)

Iran

Achaemenids (550–330 BC)
Cyrus the Great (550–530 BC)
Cambyses (530–522 BC)
Darius I (522–486 BC)
Xerxes (486–465 BC)
Artaxerxes I (465–424 BC)
Artaxerxes II (404–359 BC)
Artaxerxes III (359–338 BC)
Arses (Artaxerxes IV) 338 BC
Darius III (338–331 BC)

Achaemenid satraps
Tissaphernes (c.420–395 BC)
Tiribazos (c.387–380 BC)
Tarkamuwa/Datames) (c.378–372 BC)

Parthians (c.238 BC–AD 223/4)
Arsaces (c.238–211 BC)
Mithradates I (c.171–138 BC)
Phraates II (c.138–127 BC)
Artabanus I (c.127–124 BC)
Mithradates II (c.123–91 BC)
Gotarzes I (c.91–87 BC)
Orodes I (c.90–80 BC)
Mithradates III (c.57–54 BC)
Orodes II (c.57–38 BC)
Phraates IV (c.38–2 BC)
Phraataces/Phraates V (c.2 BC–AD 4)
Tiridates (c.29–27 BC)
Vonones I (c. AD 8–12)
Artabanus II (c. AD 10–38)
Vardanes (c. AD 39–45)
Gotarzes II (c. AD 40–51)
Vonones II (c. AD 51)
Vologases I (c. AD 51–78)
Artabanus III (c. AD 80–90)
Pacorus II (c. AD 78–105)
Vologases III (c. AD 105–47)
Osroes I (c. AD 109–29)
Parthamaspates (c. AD 116)
Mithradates IV (c. AD 140)
Vologases IV (c. AD 147–91)
Vologases V (c. AD 191–208)
Vologases VI (c. AD 208–28)
Artabanus IV (c. AD 216–23/4)

Sasanians (AD 223/4–652)
Ardashir I (AD 223/4–41)
Shapur I (c. AD 240–72/3)
Hormizd I (AD 272/3)
Varhran I (AD 273–6)
Varhran II (AD 276–93)
Varhran III (AD 293)
Narseh (AD 293–303)
Hormizd II (AD 303–9)
Shapur II (AD 309–79)
Ardashir II (AD 379–83)
Shapur III (AD 383–8)
Varhran IV (AD 388–99)
Yazdagird I (AD 399–420)
Varhran V (AD 420–38)
Yazdagird II (AD 439–57)
Hormizd III (AD 457–9)
Peroz (AD 457/9–84)
Valkash (AD 484–8)
Kavad I (AD 484, 488–96, 499–531)
Jamasp (AD 497–9)
Khusrau I (AD 531–79)
Hormizd IV (AD 579–90)
Varhran VI (AD 590–1)
Vistham (AD 591/2–97)
Hormizd V (c. AD 593)
Khusrau II (AD 590, 591–628)
Kavad II (AD 628)
Ardashir III (AD 628–30)
Khusrau III (AD 629)
Boran (AD 630–1)
Azarmidukht (AD 631)
Hormizd VI (?) (AD 631/2)
Yazdagird III (AD 632–51)

Afghanistan – Gandhara

Mauryans (*c.*321–187 BC)
Chandragupta (*c.*321–297 BC)
Ashoka (*c.*269–232 BC)
Sophagasenus (*c.*206 BC)

**Greco–Bactrians and Indo–Greeks
(*c.*250 BC–AD 10)**
Diodotus (*c.*250–230 BC)
Euthydemus I (*c.*230–200 BC)
Demetrius I (*c.*200–190 BC)
Euthydemus II (*c.*190–185 BC)
Pantaleon (*c.*190–185 BC)
Agathocles (*c.*190–180 BC)
Antimachus I (*c.*180–170 BC)
Apollodotus I (*c.*180–160 BC)
Eucratides I (*c.*174–145 BC)
Plato (*c.*145–140 BC)
Antimachus II (*c.*160–155 BC)
Menander I (*c.*155–130 BC)
Heliocles I (*c.*120–90 BC)
Strato I (*c.*125–110 BC)
Lysias (*c.*120–110 BC)
Antialcidas (*c.*115–95 BC)
Philoxenus (*c.*100–95 BC)
Hermaeus I (*c.*90–70 BC)
Philoxenus (*c.*100–95 BC),
Diomedes (*c.*95–90 BC)
Amyntas (*c.*95–90 BC)
Archebius (*c.*90–80 BC)
Artemidorus (*c.*85 BC)
Apollodotus II (*c.*65–50 BC)
Telephus (*c.*60–55 BC)
Hippostratus (*c.*50–45 BC)
Strato II (*c.*25 BC–AD 10)

Indo–Scythians (*c.*75 BC–AD 64)
Maues (*c.*75–65 BC)
Vonones (*c.*65–50 BC)
Spalyrises (*c.*50–40 BC)
Azes I (*c.*46–1 BC)
Azilises (*c.*1 BC–AD 16)
Azes II (*c.* AD 16–30)
Kharahostes (*c.* early first century AD)
Zeionises (*c.* AD 30–50)

Apracas
Vijayamitra (*c.* AD 1–32)
Indravasu (*c.* AD 32–3)
Aspavarma (*c.* AD 33–64)

Indo–Parthians
Gandhara (*c.* AD 32–70):
Gondophares (*c.* AD 32–60)
Orthagnes/Gadana (*c.* AD 52–64)
Abdagases (*c.* AD 52–64)
Sasan (*c.* AD 64–70)
Seistan: Sanabares (*c.* AD 135–60)

Kushans (*c.* AD 40–360)
Kujula Kadphises (*c.* AD 40–90)
Wima Tak[to] (*c.* AD 90–113)
Wima Kadphises (*c.* AD 113–27)
Kanishka I (*c.* AD 127–50)
Huvishka (*c.* AD 150–90)
Vasudeva I (*c.* AD 190–227)
Kanishka II (*c.* AD 227–46)
Vasishka (*c.* AD 246–67)
Kanishka III (*c.* AD 267–80)
Vasudeva II (*c.* AD 280–320)
Shaka (*c.* AD 320–60)

Kushano–Sasanians (*c.* AD 233–370)
Ardashir 'I'–'II' (*c.* AD 233–46)
Peroz 'I' (*c.* AD 246–85)
Hormizd 'I' (*c.* AD 285–300)
Hormizd 'II' (*c.* AD 300–9)
Peroz 'II' (*c.* AD 309–35)
Varhran (*c.* AD 335–70)

Huns (*c.* AD 350–657)
Kidarites (*c.* AD 360–468) in Bactria
Kidarites (*c.* AD 360–477) in Gandhara
'Varhran' (*c.* AD 370–95)
Kirada (*c.* AD 380)
'Varhran'/'Peroz' (*c.* AD 395–425)
Kidara (*c.* AD 425–57)
Son of Kidara (*c.* AD 457–77)
Chionites (*c.* AD 359–420)
Grumbates (AD 359/60)
Gurambad, ruler of Rob *c.* AD 420
Alxan (*c.* AD 360–580)
Khingila I *mahāṣāhi* (*c.* AD 440–90)
Mehama *mahāṣāhi* (*c.* AD 480–90)
Javukha *mahārāja* (*c.* AD 480–90)
Toramana *devarāja* (*c.* AD 485–515)
Mihirakula (*c.* AD 515–40)
Narana/Narendra (*c.* AD 540–80)
Nezak
Napki Malka (*c.* AD 460–560)
Shri Shahi (*c.* AD 560–620)
Helphthalites (*c.* AD 420–651/2)

Turks conquer Kapishi *c.* AD 612–30
Tang protectorate established in Afghanistan
AD 657/8–705
Khingila II (at Gardez) *c.* sixth–seventh century
Khinjil/Khinkhil Kabulshah (*c.* AD 775–85)

India

Shungas
Pushyamitra (*c.*187–151 BC)

Mathura Satraps
Rajavula (*c.* first half of first century AD)
Sodasa (*c.* mid first century AD)

Western Satraps/Kshatrapas
Nahapana (*c.* AD 54–78)
Chastana (AD 78–130)

Kashmir
Shailanaviraya (*c.* late fifth century)

Guptas
Chandragupta I (*c.* AD 319/20–35)
Samudragupta (*c.* AD 335–80)
Chandragupta II (*c.* AD 380–414)
Kumaragupta I (*c.* AD 414–55)
Skandagupta (*c.* AD 455–67/8)
Narasimhagupta Baladitya (*c.* AD 468–73)
Kumaragupta II (*c.* AD 473–6)
Budhagupta (*c.* AD 476–90)

List of British Museum numbers

Figure	Registration number
1	PD 1851.9.1.1164
3	ME —
6	ME —
7	ME —
9	ME —
10	ME —
13	CM Court MSS 2
14	PD —
15	CM 1853.1.5.2
21	As. 1887.7.17.34
21	As. 1887.7.17.35
21	As. 1887.7.17.36
21	As. 1887.7.17.37
21	As. 1887.7.17.38
21	As. 1887.7.17.39
25	ME 29455
26.1	CM 1888.12.8.114
26.2	CM 1888.12.8.124
26.3	CM 1894.5.6.13
26.4	CM 1889.7.12.1
26.5	CM 1894.5.6.170, Court 3
26.6	CM 1896.5.6.1877
26.7	CM 1889.1.5.120
26.8	CM 1888.12.8.122
26.9	CM 1888.12.8.223
30	ME 89132
35.1	CM 1852.10.27.3
35.2	CM 1845.12.17.227
35.3	CM 1845.12.7.179
35.4	CM BMC–Persia 83
35.5	CM 1888.12.8.3
35.6	CM BMC–Ionia 325.13
35.7	CM BMC–Mallus 28
35.8	CM 1985.11.14.4
35.9	CM BMC–Lycia 111
35.10	CM BMC–Lycia 102
35.11	CM1888.12.8.6
35.12	CM 1919.11.20.114
35.13	CM 1971.5.10.1
35.14	CM 1995.10.15.1
35.15	CM 1989.9.4.3987
35.16	CM BMC 9.Cat.1
36.1	CM 1872.7.13.12
36.2	CM 1929.8.11.106
36.3	CM 1897.3.5.16
36.4	CM 1874.11.1.1
36.5	CM 1866.12.1.3839
36.6	CM 1911.7.6.6
36.7	CM 1872.11.2.7
36.8	CM TC.P.128.N.43
36.9	CM IOLC Greek 2
40.1	As. 1892.11.3.14
40.2	CM 1894.5.7.657
40.3	CM 1894.5.7.659
40.4	CM 1894.5.7.669
40.5	CM OR 0541
41.1	CM 1989.9.4.3747
41.2	CM 1922.2.24.4452
41.3	CM BMC 2.Cat.2.VIIc, Prinsep
41.4	CM BMC 7.Cat.2.Vc
41.5	CM 1894.5.7.588
41.6	CM IOLC
41.7	CM 1850.3.5.413
41.8	CM 1890.1.2.4
41.9	CM IOC 1050.
41.10	CM 1923.3.17.4
41.11	CM BMC–Mathura 44
41.12	CM 1922.4.24.4547
41.13	CM 2001.10.5.4
43.1	CM BMC–Seleucus I.1
43.2	CM BMC–Antiochus I.2
43.3	CM IOLC Greek 4
43.4	CM 1924.10.18.19
43.5	CM 1858.5.7.5
43.6	CM BMC–Antiochus VII.13
45.1	CM 1879.4.1.2
45.2	CM 1969.12.10.2
45.3	CM BMC–Parthia 9
45.4	CM 1903.5.5.20
45.5	CM BMC–Mithradates I.15
45.6	CM BMC–Mithradates I.5
45.7	CM 1894.5.6.339
45.8	CM 1894.5.6.2292
45.9	CM 1926.3.2.1
45.10	CM 1848.8.3.9
45.11	CM 1900.4.5.7
45.12	CM 1894.5.6.349
45.13	CM 1906.4.6.1
45.14	CM 1891.6.3.4
46.1	CM 1850.4.12.125
46.2	CM BMC–Characene, p. 307, 25
46.3	CM BMC–Characene, p. 308, 36
46.4	CM BMC–Characene, p. 304, 1
46.5	CM 1936.7.7.3
46.6	CM BMC–Kamanskires II and Anzaze.1
46.7	CM 1848.8.3.95
46.8	CM 1856.9.23.2
46.9	CM 1911.1.6.1
48.1	CM 1878.3.1.403
48.2	CM 1924.5.9.4
48.3	CM 1894.5.6.429
48.4	CM 1894.5.6.453
48.5	CM 1918.5.1.14
48.6	CM 1958.2.6.3
48.7	CM 1949.1.8.37
48.8	CM 1900.4.2.6
48.9	CM 1894.5.6.2052
48.10	CM G 1046
48.11	CM 1892.7.4.32
48.12	CM 1894.5.6.2101
48.13	CM 1894.4.12.53
48.14	CM 1894.5.6.2106
49.1	CM BMC–Augustus 10
49.2	CM BMC–Augustus 671
49.3	CM BMC–Augustus 681
50.1	CM 1850.4.12.53
50.2	CM 1894.5.6.2156
50.3	CM 1876.7.8.4
50.4	CM 1894.5.6.2162
50.5	CM 1866.4.1.21
50.6	CM 1894.5.6.220
50.7	CM 1894.5.6.2216
50.8	CM 1900.4.5.59
50.9	CM 1900.7.6.97
50.10	CM 1894.5.6.2222
50.11	CM 1894.5.6.2233
50.12	CM 1894.5.6.2267
50.13	CM 1894.5.6.2274
50.14	CM 1860.12.31.3
52.1	CM 1995.5.5.1
52.2	CM 1901.2.3.1
52.3	CM 1888.12.8.66
52.4	CM OR 0277, Burnes 6
52.5	CM 1847.12.1.25, Burnes 7
52.6	CM 1870.7.1.1
52.7	CM 1872.7.9.356
52.8	CM 1888.12.8.111
52.9	CM IOC 33
52.10	CM 1888.12.8.159
52.11	CM 1872.5.9.1
52.12	CM 1869.1.2.2
52.13	CM 1894.5.6.1007, Court 40
52.14	CM IOC 30
52.15	CM BMC–Antimachus II.1,.Lafont 70
52.16	CM EIC 10
52.17	CM EIC 54
52.18	CM IOC 98
54.1	CM 1888.12.8.204
54.2	CM 1888.12.8.178
54.3	CM 1888.12.8.361
54.4	CM 1894.5.6.868, Court 319
54.5	CM 1888.12.8.388
54.6	CM BMC–Hermaeus 34, Honigberger 2
54.7	CM 1894.5.6.1712
54.8	CM 1922.4.24.2919
54.9	CM 1922.4.24.4711
56.1	CM IOC 155
56.2	CM 1894.5.6.515, Court 382
56.3	CM 1894.5.6.414
56.4	CM IOC 222
56.5	CM 1894.5.6.701
56.6	CM 1888.12.8.498
56.7	CM 1847.12.1.85
56.8	CM 1888.12.8.500
56.9	CM 1888.12.8.428
56.10	CM IOC 197
56.11	CM 1888.12.8.467
56.12	CM IOC 215
56.13	CM 1847.12.1.57
56.14	CM 1894.5.6.584, Court 208
56.15	CM 1894.5.6.604
56.16	CM IOC 200
56.17	CM IOLC
56.18	CM IOLC
56.19	CM 1894.5.6.1721. Court 362
57	As. 1889.3.14.1
58.1	CM 1857.8.13.179
58.2	CM 1894.5.6.179
58.3	CM 1907.1.2.1
58.4	CM 1894.5.6.323
58.5	CM 1889.12.3.22
58.6	CM 1894.5.6.670
58.7	CM 1903.11.6.2
58.8	CM 1894.5.6.1719, Court 48
58.9	CM 1894.5.6.1808
59.1	CM 1894.5.6.1550, Court 244
59.2	CM EIC 113
59.3	CM 1889.8.8.67
59.4	CM 1857.8.13.514
59.5	CM 1888.12.8.514
59.6	CM 1894.5.6.1599
59.7	CM 1894.5.6.2144
59.8	CM 1894.5.6.237
59.9	CM 1938.4.13.8

59.10	CM BMC–Sanabares 1		71.8	CM 1949.8.3.192		80.8	CM 1894.5.6.289
61.1	CM 1890.4.4.1		74.1	CM 1890.11.4.3		80.9	CM IOC 2368
61.2	CM 1890.4.4.8		74.2	CM IOC 563		80.10	CM 1922.4.24.3737
61.3	CM 1894.5.6.1724		74.3	CM 1894.5.6.162, Court 6		80.11	CM 1894.5.6.258
61.4	CM 1894.5.6.1818		74.4	CM 1894.5.6.168		80.12	CM 1894.5.6.209
61.5	CM 1894.5.6.1677		74.5	CM 1986.6.42.1		80.13	CM 1894.5.6.210
61.6	CM IOC 264		74.6	CM 1922.1.16.25		80.14	CM 1894.5.6.1174
61.7	CM 1894.5.6.797, Court 249		74.7	CM 1860.12.20.220		80.15	CM 1894.5.6.206
61.8	CM 1894.5.6.826		74.8	CM 1892.2.2.3		80.16	CM 1894.5.6.1287
61.9	CM 1998.12.2.18		74.9	CM 1894.5.6.171, Court 4		80.17	CM 1983.5.25.1
61.10	CM 1922.4.23.27		74.10	CM 1995.5.7.7		81.1	CM 1857.8.13.95
61.11	CM 1894.5.6.815		74.11	CM 1922.4.24.4501		81.2	CM IOLC
61.12	CM 1890.4.4.24		74.12	CM 1982.11.7.1		81.3	CM IOLC
61.13	CM 1894.5.6.762		74.13	CM 1894.5.6.124, Court 183		81.4	CM 1874.10.3.1
61.14	CM 1894.5.6.771		74.14	CM 1922.4.24.3949		81.5	CM 1894.5.6.979
61.15	CM 1894.5.6.789, Court 260		74.15	CM 1986.8.12.1		81.6	CM 1922.4.24.3733
61.16	CM IOC 272		74.16	CM IOLC		81.7	CM IOC 2372
61.17	CM 1847.12.1.153		74.17	CM 1982.6.26.2		81.8	CM 1894.5.6.217
61.18	CM 1894.5.6.28, Court 18		74.18	CM OR 0376, Prinsep		81.9	CM 1894.5.6.228
61.19	CM IOC 299		74.19	CM 1922.4.24.3947		81.10	CM 1885.4.3.343
61.20	CM 1888.12.8.555		74.20	CM 1894.5.6.173		81.11	CM 1894.5.6.246
61.21	CM 1893.5.6.22		74.21	CM 1906.11.3.5323		81.12	CM 1894.5.6.265
61.22	CM IOC 358		74.22	CM 1894.5.6.1288, Court 316		81.13	CM 1894.5.6.283
61.23	CM 1894.5.6.1531		74.23	CM 1894.5.6.1289, Court 187		81.14	CM 1894.5.6.271
61.24	CM 1921.3.6.12		74.24	CM 1894.5.6.125		81.15	CM 1894.5.6.1192, Court 173
61.25	CM 1893.5.6.31		76	As. 1890.11.16.1		82.1	CM IOC 1223
61.26	CM 1893.5.6.41		77	CM 1850.4.12.107		82.1	CM IOC 1225
61.27	CM 1894.5.6.110		77	CM 1848.8.3.262		82.2	CM IOC 1224
61.28	CM 1894.5.6.111		77	CM IOC 438		82.3	CM IOC 1226
66.1	CM 1894.5.6.122		77	CM 1939.3.9.3		82.3	CM IOC 1227
66.2	CM 1935.2.19.2		77	CM 1984.7.19.27		82.6	CM IOC 445
66.3	CM 1848.8.3.219		77	CM 1848.8.3.276		82.7	CM IOC 444
66.4	CM 1855.5.12.76		77.1	CM 1985.7.50.1		82.7	CM IOC 447
66.5	CM 1866.7.21.2		77.2	CM 1894.5.6.1296		82.9	CM IOC 570
66.6	CM 1887.12.1.27		77.3	CM cast: Martin 1937, pl. 4.51		82.10	CM 1894.5.6.1402
66.7	CM 1918.5.1.43		77.4	CM 1917.4.1.5		82.11	CM 1894.5.6.197
66.8	CM 1848.8.3.242		77.5	CM 1894.5.6.173 (detail)		83.2	CM 1894.5.6.1293
66.9	CM 1848.8.3.246		77.5	CM 1860.12.20.218 (detail)		83.2	CM 1894.5.6.1291
66.10	CM 1894.5.6.1309		77.6	CM 1893.2.4.4 (detail)		83.3	CM 1894.5.6.1167
66.11	CM 1894.5.6.1307		77.6	CM 1906.11.3.5316 (detail)		83.4	CM 1894.5.6.201
66.12	CM 1912.12.10.2		77.6	CM 1894.5.6.174 (detail)		83.5	CM 1894.5.6.1164
66.13	CM 1894.5.6.1313		77.7	CM 1989.6.25.2 (detail)		83.5	CM OR 0476
66.14	CM 1894.5.7.1292		77.8	CM 1894.5.6.1336		83.6	CM 1894.5.6.215
66.15	CM OR 0033		77.9	CM 1922.4.24.3820		84.1	CM 1894.5.6.1242
66.16	CM 1957.7.8.1		77.10	CM 1923.3.3.2		84.2	CM 1922.4.24.3678
66.17	CM Baron de Bode 1845.2		77.11	CM 1894.5.6.139		84.3	CM 1922.1.16.36
66.18	CM 1947.4.6.553		77.12	CM 1894.5.6.134		84.4	CM 1894.5.6.302
66.19	CM IOC 433		77.14	CM cast: Martin 1937, pl.4.49		84.5	CM 1894.5.6.1196
66.20	CM 1862.10.4.34		77.15	CM cast: Martin 1937, pl.4.47		84.6	CM 1894.5.6.1356
66.21	CM 1984.9.10.1		77.16	CM 1894.5.6.126 (detail)		84.7	CM 1997.7.6.80
66.22	CM 1982.11.41.3		77.17	CM 1860.12.20.29		84.8	CM 1894.5.6.1381, Court 166
69.1	CM OR 0043		77.18	CM 1985.2.23.29		84.9	CM IOC 542
69.2	CM IOC 434		77.19	CM cast: Martin 1937, pl. 1.18		84.10	CM IOC 2357
69.3	CM 1894.5.6.1333		77.22	As. 1963.12.10.1 (detail)		86	As. 1973.6.18.1
69.4	CM 1894.5.7.1294		77.23	CM 1982.11.10.1		87	ME 1900.2.9.2
69.5	CM 1850.4.12.108		77.24	CM 1894.5.6.188		88.1	CM 1888.12.8.110
69.6	CM 1894.5.7.2082		77.25	CM 1948.4.7.1		88.2	CM 1888.12.8.71
69.7	CM 1938.6.3.14		78.1	CM 1982.6.26.5		88.3	CM 1888.12.8.96
69.8	CM 1869.12.3.1		78.2	CM 1894.5.6.126		88.4	CM 1922.4.24.2886
69.9	CM IOC 439		78.3	CM 1894.5.6.131		88.5	CM 1888.12.8.354
69.10	CM 1841.12.21.92		78.4	CM 1847.12.1.265		88.6	CM 1969.5.25.1
69.11	CM 1894.5.6.1352		78.6	CM 1991.6.40.17		88.7	CM 1859.3.1.41
69.12	CM 1920.7.8.2		78.7	CM 2000.5.8.4		88.8	CM 1888.12.8.98
69.13	CM 1894.5.6.1353		78.8	CM 1893.5.6.48		88.9	CM 1888.12.8.539
69.14	CM 1848.8.3.252		78.9	CM IOC 570		88.10	CM 1894.5.6.12
69.15	CM 1862.10.3.19		78.10	CM 1893.5.6.46		88.11	CM 1894.5.6.537
69.16	CM 1862.10.4.130		78.11	CM 1845.6.13.119, Lafont		88.12	CM 1894.5.6.16
69.17	CM 1848.8.3.288		79	As. 1963.12.10.1		88.13	CM 1888.12.8.538
69.18	CM 1923.11.5.57		80.1	CM 1848.8.3.232		88.14	CM 1860.12.20.209
69.19	CM 1862.30.3.22		80.2	CM 1983.7.9.11		88.15	CM IOC 343
69.20	CM 1895.10.6.11		80.2	CM Vaux 1910		89	As. 1951.5.8.1
71.1	CM 1923.11.5.58		80.2	CM 1922.6.22.21		90	As. 1950.7.26.2
71.2	CM 1935.3.3.1		80.2	CM 1983.5.17.1		91	As. photographic archive
71.3	CM 1949.8.3.174		80.3	CM 1894.5.6.1292		94	As. 1970.7.18.1
71.4	CM 1937.2.6.18		80.4	CM 1894.5.6.254		95	As. 1880–4073
71.5	CM 1894.5.6.1371		80.5	CM 1922.4.24.3747		96	ME 123901
71.6	CM 1934.2.16.1		80.6	CM 1922.4.24.3748		96	ME 123902
71.7	CM 1956.4.9.38		80.7	CM 1847.4.21.33		97.1	CM 1929.8.11.3

97.2	CM 1872.12.2.3	113.10	CM IOC 158	168.1	CM BMC–Fath 'Ali Shah 484
97.3	CM 1929.8.11.4	113.11	CM 1888.12.8.482	168.2	CM 1853.12.16.11
97.4	CM 1872.7.9.353	113.12	CM 1888.12.8.557	168.3	CM BMC–Fath 'Ali Shah 476
97. 5	CM 1850.3.18.2	113.13	CM 1860.12.20.123	168.4	CM 1968.9.4.1
97.6	CM 1850.4.12.86	113.14	CM 1867.12.18.11	168.5	CM 1885.8.5.92
97.7	CM 1888.12.8.54	114	As. 1880–93	168. 6	CM 1885.8.5.116
97.8	CM BMC–Darius II.9	114	CM 1979.2.15.21–40	171	CM OR 2690
97.9	CM 1915.1.8.18	115	As. photographic archive	177	As. 1848.6.2.1–6
97.10	CM 1866.4.1.44	116	As. 1880–29	177	CM 1847.12.1.214
97.11	CM 1888.12.8.410	116	CM BMC–Hadrian 938	177	CM 1847.12.1.237
97.12	CM 1894.5.6.490	116	CM IOC 270	177	CM 1847.12.1.258
97.13	CM 1888.12.8.542	116	CM IOC 271	177	CM 1847.12.1.259
97.14	CM 1865.8.3.17	116	CM IOC 282	177	CM 1847.12.1. 450
97.15	CM IOC 329	116	CM IOC 291	177	CM 1894.5.6.1271
97.16	CM 1893.5.6.17	116	CM IOC 333	177	CM OR 0526, Prinsep
97.17	CM IOC 303	116	CM 1896.5.6.16	177	CM OR 5202, Prinsep
105	GR 1825.6.13.1	119	As. Marshall photographic archive	177	CM BMC–'Abdallah b. Khazim 171, Prinsep
107	As. 1899.7.15.9	140.1	ME 1823.6.14.1/91952	182.1	CM BMC–Eucratides I.50, Honigberger 1
108	As. 1880–68	140.2	ME 1875.7.24.41/91954	182.2	CM IOC 202
113.1	CM 1888.12.8.226	142.1	ME 1888.7.14.1/91333/134691	182.3	CM 1894.5.6.1722, Court 361
113.2	CM 1894.5.6.1949	142.2	ME 1875.7.24.42	186	As. 1880–27
113.3	CM 1894.5.7.39	146	ME 1938.1.10.1/129381	186	As. 1900.2.9.1
113.4	CM IOC 104	152	ME 1892.12.14.1/91163	186	CM IOC 201
113.5	CM 1888.12.8.328	153	ME 1892.12.14.1/91163	186	CM IOC 202
113.6	CM 1888.12.8.327	155	ME 118843	186	CM IOC 203
113.7	CM IOC 289	163	ME —	186	CM IOC 204
113.8	CM IOLC	166	ME —		
113.9	CM 1894.5.6.1457	167	ME 132525		

Concordance of British Museum numbers

Registration number	Figure				
As. 1848.6.2.1–6	177	CM 1847.12.1.450	177	CM 1866.4.1.44	97.10
As. 1880–27	186	CM 1848.8.3.9	45.10	CM 1866.7.21.2	66.5
As. 1880–29	116	CM 1848.8.3.95	46.7	CM 1867.12.18.11	113.14
As. 1880–68	108	CM 1848.8.3.219	66.3	CM 1869.1.2.2	52.12
As. 1880–93	114	CM 1848.8.3.232	80.1	CM 1869.12.3.1	69.8
As. 1880–4073	95	CM 1848.8.3.242	66.8	CM 1870.7.1.1	52.6
As. 1887.7.17.34	21	CM 1848.8.3.246	66.9	CM 1872.5.9.1	52.11
As. 1887.7.17.35	21	CM 1848.8.3.252	69.14	CM 1872.7.9.353	97.4
As. 1887.7.17.36	21	CM 1848.8.3.262	77	CM 1872.7.9.356	52.7
As. 1887.7.17.37	21	CM 1848.8.3.276	77	CM 1872.7.13.12	36.1
As. 1887.7.17.38	21	CM 1848.8.3.288	69.17	CM 1872.11.2.7	36.7
As. 1887.7.17.39	21	CM 1850.3.5.413	41.7	CM 1872.12.2.3	97.2
As. 1889.3.14.1	57	CM 1850.3.18.2	97. 5	CM 1874.10.3.1	81.4
As. 1890.11.16.1	76	CM 1850.4.12.53	50.1	CM 1874.11.1.1	36.4
As. 1892.11.3.14	40.1	CM 1850.4.12.86	97.6	CM 1876.7.8.4	50.3
As. 1899.7.15.9	107	CM 1850.4.12.107	77	CM 1878.3.1.403	48.1
As. 1900.2.9.1	186	CM 1850.4.12.108	69.5	CM 1879.4.1.2	45.1
As. 1950.7.26.2	90	CM 1850.4.12.125	46.1	CM 1885.4.3.343	81.10
As. 1951.5.8.1	89	CM 1852.10.27.3	35.1	CM 1885.8.5.92	168.5
As. 1963.12.10.1 (details)	77.22	CM 1853.1.5.2	15	CM 1885.8.5.116	168. 6
As. 1963.12.10.1	79	CM 1853.12.16.11	168.2	CM 1887.12.1.27	66.6
As. 1970.7.18.1	94	CM 1855.5.12.76	66.4	CM 1888.12.8.3	35.5
As. 1973.6.18.1	86	CM 1856.9.23.2	46.8	CM 1888.12.8.54	97.7
As. photographic archive	91	CM 1857.8.13.95	81.1	CM 1888.12.8.110	88.1
As. photographic archive	115	CM 1857.8.13.179	58.1	CM 1888.12.8.111	52.8
As. Marshall photographic archive	119	CM 1857.8.13.514	59.4	CM 1888.12.8.114	26.1
CM 1841.12.21.92	69.10	CM 1858.5.7.5	43.5	CM 1888.12.8.122	26.8
CM 1845.12.7.179	35.3	CM 1859.3.1.41	88.7	CM 1888.12.8.124	26.2
CM 1845.12.17.227	35.2	CM 1860.12.20.29	77.17	CM 1888.12.8.159	52.10
CM 1845.6.13.119, Lafont	78.11	CM 1860.12.20.123	113.13	CM 1888.12.8.178	54.2
CM 1847.4.21.33	80.7	CM 1860.12.20.209	88.14	CM 1888.12.8.204	54.1
CM 1847.12.1.25, Burnes 7	52.5	CM 1860.12.20.218 (detail)	77.5	CM 1888.12.8.223	26.9
CM 1847.12.1.57	56.13	CM 1860.12.20.220	74.7	CM 1888.12.8.226	113.1
CM 1847.12.1.85	56.7	CM 1860.12.31.3	50.14	CM 1888.12.8.327	113.6
CM 1847.12.1.153	61.17	CM 1862.10.3.19	69.15	CM 1888.12.8.328	113.5
CM 1847.12.1.214	177	CM 1862.10.4.34	66.20	CM 1888.12.8.354	88.5
CM 1847.12.1.237	177	CM 1862.10.4.130	69.16	CM 1888.12.8.361	54.3
CM 1847.12.1.258	177	CM 1862.30.3.22	69.19	CM 1888.12.8.388	54.5
CM 1847.12.1.259	177	CM 1865.8.3.17	97.14	CM 1888.12.8.410	97.11
CM 1847.12.1.265	78.4	CM 1866.12.1.3839	36.5	CM 1888.12.8.428	56.9
		CM 1866.4.1.21	50.5	CM 1888.12.8.467	56.11

CM 1888.12.8.482	113.11	CM 1894.5.6.414	56.3	CM 1896.5.6.16	116
CM 1888.12.8.498	56.6	CM 1894.5.6.429	48.3	CM 1896.5.6.1877	26.6
CM 1888.12.8.500	56.8	CM 1894.5.6.453	48.4	CM 1897.3.5.16	36.3
CM 1888.12.8.514	59.5	CM 1894.5.6.490	97.12	CM 1900.4.2.6	48.8
CM 1888.12.8.538	88.13	CM 1894.5.6.515, Court 382	56.2	CM 1900.4.5.7	45.11
CM 1888.12.8.539	88.9	CM 1894.5.6.537	88.11	CM 1900.4.5.59	50.8
CM 1888.12.8.542	97.13	CM 1894.5.6.584, Court 208	56.14	CM 1900.7.6.97	50.9
CM 1888.12.8.555	61.20	CM 1894.5.6.604	56.15	CM 1901.2.3.1	52.2
CM 1888.12.8.557	113.12	CM 1894.5.6.670	58.6	CM 1903.5.5.20	45.4
CM1888.12.8.6	35.11	CM 1894.5.6.701	56.5	CM 1903.11.6.2	58.7
CM 1888.12.8.66	52.3	CM 1894.5.6.762	61.13	CM 1906.4.6.1	45.13
CM 1888.12.8.71	88.2	CM 1894.5.6.771	61.14	CM 1906.11.3.5316 (detail)	77.6
CM 1888.12.8.96	88.3	CM 1894.5.6.789, Court 260	61.15	CM 1906.11.3.5323	74.21
CM 1888.12.8.98	88.8	CM 1894.5.6.797, Court 249	61.7	CM 1907.1.2.1	58.3
CM 1889.1.5.120	26.7	CM 1894.5.6.815	61.11	CM 1911.1.6.1	46.9
CM 1889.12.3.22	58.5	CM 1894.5.6.826	61.8	CM 1911.7.6.6	36.6
CM 1889.7.12.1	26.4	CM 1894.5.6.868, Court 319	54.4	CM 1912.12.10.2	66.12
CM 1889.8.8.67	59.3	CM 1894.5.6.979	81.5	CM 1915.1.8.18	97.9
CM 1890.1.2.4	41.8	CM 1894.5.6.1007, Court 40	52.13	CM 1917.4.1.5	77.4
CM 1890.11.4.3	74.1	CM 1894.5.6.1164	83.5	CM 1918.5.1.14	48.5
CM 1890.4.4.1	61.1	CM 1894.5.6.1167	83.3	CM 1918.5.1.43	66.7
CM 1890.4.4.24	61.12	CM 1894.5.6.1174	80.14	CM 1919.11.20.114	35.12
CM 1890.4.4.8	61.2	CM 1894.5.6.1192, Court 173	81.15	CM 1920.7.8.2	69.12
CM 1891.6.3.4	45.14	CM 1894.5.6.1196	84.5	CM 1921.3.6.12	61.24
CM 1892.2.2.3	74.8	CM 1894.5.6.1242	84.1	CM 1922.1.16.25	74.6
CM 1892.7.4.32	48.11	CM 1894.5.6.1271	177	CM 1922.1.16.36	84.3
CM 1893.2.4.4 (detail)	77.6	CM 1894.5.6.1287	80.16	CM 1922.2.24.4452	41.2
CM 1893.5.6.17	97.16	CM 1894.5.6.1288, Court 316	74.22	CM 1922.4.23.27	61.10
CM 1893.5.6.22	61.21	CM 1894.5.6.1289, Court 187	74.23	CM 1922.4.24.2886	88.4
CM 1893.5.6.31	61.25	CM 1894.5.6.1291	83.2	CM 1922.4.24.2919	54.8
CM 1893.5.6.41	61.26	CM 1894.5.6.1292	80.3	CM 1922.4.24.3678	84.2
CM 1893.5.6.46	78.10	CM 1894.5.6. 1293	83.2	CM 1922.4.24.3733	81.6
CM 1893.5.6.48	78.8	CM 1894.5.6.1296	77.2	CM 1922.4.24.3737	80.10
CM 1894.4.12.53	48.13	CM 1894.5.6.1307	66.11	CM 1922.4.24.3747	80.5
CM 1894.5.6.16	88.12	CM 1894.5.6.1309	66.10	CM 1922.4.24.3748	80.6
CM 1894.5.6.12	88.10	CM 1894.5.6.1313	66.13	CM 1922.4.24.3820	77.9
CM 1894.5.6.13	26.3	CM 1894.5.6.1333	69.3	CM 1922.4.24.3947	74.19
CM 1894.5.6.28, Court no.18	61.18	CM 1894.5.6.1336	77.8	CM 1922.4.24.3949	74.14
CM 1894.5.6.110	61.27	CM 1894.5.6.1352	69.11	CM 1922.4.24.4501	74.11
CM 1894.5.6.111	61.28	CM 1894.5.6.1353	69.13	CM 1922.4.24.4547	41.12
CM 1894.5.6.122	66.1	CM 1894.5.6.1356	84.6	CM 1922.4.24.4711	54.9
CM 1894.5.6.124, Court 183	74.13	CM 1894.5.6.1371	71.5	CM 1922.6.22.21	80.2
CM 1894.5.6.125	74.24	CM 1894.5.6.1381, Court 166	84.8	CM 1923.11.5.57	69.18
CM 1894.5.6.126 (detail)	77.16	CM 1894.5.6.1402	82.10	CM 1923.11.5.58	71.1
CM 1894.5.6.126	78.2	CM 1894.5.6.1457	113.9	CM 1923.3.17.4	41.10
CM 1894.5.6.131	78.3	CM 1894.5.6.1531	61.23	CM 1923.3.3.2	77.10
CM 1894.5.6.134	77.12	CM 1894.5.6.1550, Court 244	59.1	CM 1924.10.18.19	43.4
CM 1894.5.6.139	77.11	CM 1894.5.6.1599	59.6	CM 1924.5.9.4	48.2
CM 1894.5.6.162, Court 6	74.3	CM 1894.5.6.1677	61.5	CM 1926.3.2.1	45.9
CM 1894.5.6.168	74.4	CM 1894.5.6.1712	54.7	CM 1929.8.11.3	97.1
CM 1894.5.6.170, Court 3	26.5	CM 1894.5.6.1719, Court 48	58.8	CM 1929.8.11.4	97.3
CM 1894.5.6.171, Court 4	74.9	CM 1894.5.6.1721. Court 362	56.19	CM 1929.8.11.106	36.2
CM 1894.5.6.173	74.20	CM 1894.5.6.1722, Court 361	182.3	CM 1934.2.16.1	71.6
CM 1894.5.6.173 (detail)	77.5	CM 1894.5.6.1724	61.3	CM 1935.2.19.2	66.2
CM 1894.5.6.174 (detail)	77.6	CM 1894.5.6.1808	58.9	CM 1935.3.3.1	71.2
CM1894.5.6.179	58.2	CM 1894.5.6.1818	61.4	CM 1936.7.7.3	46.5
CM 1894.5.6.188	77.24	CM 1894.5.6.1949	113.2	CM 1937.2.6.18	71.4
CM 1894.5.6.197	82.11	CM 1894.5.6.2052	48.9	CM 1938.4.13.8	59.9
CM 1894.5.6.201	83.4	CM 1894.5.6.2101	48.12	CM 1938.6.3.14	69.7
CM 1894.5.6.206	80.15	CM 1894.5.6.2106	48.14	CM 1939.3.9.3	77
CM 1894.5.6.209	80.12	CM 1894.5.6.2144	59.7	CM 1947.4.6.553	66.18
CM 1894.5.6.210	80.13	CM 1894.5.6.2156	50.2	CM 1948.4.7.1	77.25
CM 1894.5.6.215	83.6	CM 1894.5.6.2162	50.4	CM 1949.1.8.37	48.7
CM 1894.5.6.217	81.8	CM 1894.5.6.2216	50.7	CM 1949.8.3.174	71.3
CM 1894.5.6.220	50.6	CM 1894.5.6.2222	50.10	CM 1949.8.3.192	71.8
CM 1894.5.6.228	81.9	CM 1894.5.6.2233	50.11	CM 1956.4.9.38	71.7
CM 1894.5.6.237	59.8	CM 1894.5.6.2267	50.12	CM 1957.7.8.1	66.16
CM 1894.5.6.246	81.11	CM 1894.5.6.2274	50.13	CM 1958.2.6.3	48.6
CM 1894.5.6.254	80.4	CM 1894.5.6.2292	45.8	CM 1968.9.4.1	168.4
CM 1894.5.6.258	80.11	CM 1894.5.7.39	113.3	CM 1969.12.10.2	45.2
CM 1894.5.6.265	81.12	CM 1894.5.7.588	41.5	CM 1969.5.25.1	88.6
CM 1894.5.6.271	81.14	CM 1894.5.7.657	40.2	CM 1971.5.10.1	35.13
CM 1894.5.6.283	81.13	CM 1894.5.7.659	40.3	CM 1979.2.15.21–40	114
CM 1894.5.6.289	80.8	CM 1894.5.7.669	40.4	CM 1982.6.26.2	74.17
CM 1894.5.6.302	84.4	CM 1894.5.7.1292	66.14	CM 1982.6.26.5	78.1
CM 1894.5.6.323	58.4	CM 1894.5.7.1294	69.4	CM 1982.11.10.1	77.23
CM 1894.5.6.339	45.7	CM 1894.5.7.2082	69.6	CM 1982.11.41.3	66.22
CM 1894.5.6.349	45.12	CM 1895.10.6.11	69.20	CM 1982.11.7.1	74.12

Concordance of British Museum numbers

CM 1983.5.17.1	80.2
CM 1983.5.25.1	80.17
CM 1983.7.9.11	80.2
CM 1984.7.19.27	77
CM 1984.9.10.1	66.21
CM 1985.2.23.29	77.18
CM 1985.7.50.1	77.1
CM 1985.11.14.4	35.8
CM 1986.6.42.1	74.5
CM 1986.8.12.1	74.15
CM 1989.6.25.2 (detail)	77.7
CM 1989.9.4.3747	41.1
CM 1989.9.4.3987	35.15
CM 1991.6.40.17	78.6
CM 1995.5.5.1	52.1
CM 1995.5.7.7	74.10
CM 1995.10.15.1	35.14
CM 1997.7.6.80	84.7
CM 1998.12.2.18	61.9
CM 2000.5.8.4	78.7
CM 2001.10.5.4	41.13
CM Baron de Bode 1845.2	66.17
CM BMC 2.Cat.2.VIIc, Prinsep	41.3
CM BMC 7.Cat.2.Vc	41.4
CM BMC 9.Cat.1	35.16
CM BMC–'Abd. b. Khazim 171, Prinsep	177
CM BMC–Antimachus II.1	52.15
CM BMC–Antiochus I.2	43.2
CM BMC–Antiochus VII.13	43.6
CM BMC–Augustus 10	49.1
CM BMC–Augustus 671	49.2
CM BMC–Augustus 681	49.3
CM BMC–Characene, p. 304, 1	46.4
CM BMC–Characene, p. 307, 25	46.2
CM BMC–Characene, p. 308, 36	46.3
CM BMC–Darius II.9	97.8
CM BMC–Eucratides I.50, Honigberger 1	182.1
CM BMC–Fath 'Ali Shah 476	168.3
CM BMC–Fath 'Ali Shah 484	168.1
CM BMC–Hadrian 938	116
CM BMC–Hermaeus 34, Honigberger 2	54.6
CM BMC–Ionia 325.13	35.6
CM BMC–Kamanskires II and Anzaze.1	46.6
CM BMC–Lycia 102	35.10
CM BMC–Lycia 111	35.9
CM BMC–Mallus 28	35.7
CM BMC–Mathura 44	41.11
CM BMC–Mithradates I.15	45.5
CM BMC–Mithradates I.5	45.6
CM BMC–Parthia 9	45.3
CM BMC–Persia 83	35.4

CM BMC–Sanabares 1	59.10
CM BMC–Seleucus I.1	43.1
CM cast: Martin 1937, pl. 1.18	77.19
CM cast: Martin 1937, pl. 4.51	77.3
CM cast: Martin 1937, pl.4.47	77.15
CM cast: Martin 1937, pl.4.49	77.14
CM Court MSS 2	13
CM EIC 10	52.16
CM EIC 54	52.17
CM EIC 113	59.2
CM G 1046	48.10
CM IOC 30	52.14
CM IOC 33	52.9
CM IOC 98	52.18
CM IOC 104	113.4
CM IOC 155	56.1
CM IOC 158	113.10
CM IOC 197	56.10
CM IOC 200	56.16
CM IOC 201	186
CM IOC 202	182.2
CM IOC 202	186
CM IOC 203	186
CM IOC 204	186
CM IOC 215	56.12
CM IOC 222	56.4
CM IOC 264	61.6
CM IOC 270	61.16
CM IOC 271	116
CM IOC 272	113.7
CM IOC 282	116
CM IOC 289	61.19
CM IOC 291	97.17
CM IOC 299	97.15
CM IOC 303	116
CM IOC 329	88.15
CM IOC 333	61.22
CM IOC 343	66.19
CM IOC 358	69. 2
CM IOC 433	77
CM IOC 434	69.9
CM IOC 438	82.7
CM IOC 439	82.6
CM IOC 444	82.7
CM IOC 445	84.9
CM IOC 447	74.2
CM IOC 542	78.9
CM IOC 563	82.9
CM IOC 570	41.9
CM IOC 570	82.1
CM IOC 1050	
CM IOC 1223	

CM IOC 1224	82.2
CM IOC 1225	82.1
CM IOC 1226	82.3
CM IOC 1227	82.3
CM IOC 2357	84.10
CM IOC 2368	80.9
CM IOC 2372	81.7
CM IOLC	81.2
CM IOLC	81.3
CM IOLC	113.8
CM IOLC	41.6
CM IOLC	56.17
CM IOLC	56.18
CM IOLC	74.16
CM IOLC Greek 2	36.9
CM IOLC Greek 4	43.3
CM OR 0033	66.15
CM OR 0043	69.1
CM OR 027, Burnes 6	52.4
CM OR 0376, Prinsep	74.18
CM OR 0476	83.5
CM OR 0526, Prinsep	177
CM OR 0541	40.5
CM OR 2690	171
CM OR 5202, Prinsep	177
CM TC.P.128.N.43	36.8
CM Vaux 1910	80.2
GR 1825.6.13.1	105
ME —	3
ME —	6
ME —	7
ME —	9
ME —	10
ME —	163
ME —	166
ME 29455	25
ME 89132	30
ME 118843	155
ME 123901	96
ME 123902	96
ME 132525	167
ME 1823.6.14.1	140.1
ME 1875.7.24.41	140.2
ME 1875.7.24.42	142.2
ME 1888.7.14.1/134691	142.1
ME 1892.12.14.1/91163	152
ME 1892.12.14.1/91163	153
ME 1900.2.9.2	87
ME 1938.1.10.1/129381	146
PD —	14
PD 1851.9.1.1164	1

Principal collections

Prinsep
As. 1848.6.2.1–6
CM 1847.12.1.1–2642

Masson
As. 1880–27
As. 1880–29
As. 1880–68
As. 1880–93
As. 1880–4073
CM EIC
CM IOC
CM IOLC

Cunningham
As. 1887.7.17.1–406
As. 1892.11.3.1–196
CM 1857.8.13.1–118
CM 1888.3.2.1
CM 1888.12.7.1–844
CM 1890.4.4.1–31
CM 1893.5.6.1–49
CM 1893.10.9.1
CM 1894.5.6.1–2465
CM 1894.5.7.1–2142
ME 1897.12.31.1–177

Index

References such as '178–9' indicate continuous discussion of a topic across a range of pages, whereas '142f122' indicates a reference to Figure 122 on page 142 (and where figures are themselves subdivided, a reference such as 142f123.5 refers to Item 5 in Figure 123). Similarly, a reference in the form '142t5' indicates that the topic is referred to in Table 5 on page 142. In rare instances *passim* immediately following a page range (e.g. '181–208 *passim*') is used to indicate that the topic is discussed extensively but discontinuously on the pages in question. Wherever possible, topics with many references have either been divided into sub-topics or the most significant discussions of the topic are indicated by page numbers in bold. For Chinese names, the reader should also consult the Glossary on pages 250–51, which has not been repeated in the Index. The notes have not been indexed.